D0630043

WITHDRAWN

REDWOOD

LIBRARY
NEWPORT
R.I.

Anonymous Gift

Also by Brooke Kroeger
Nellie Bly

Fannie

GERHARD SISTERS
ST LOUIS
1914

Fannie

The Talent for Success of
Writer Fannie Hurst

Brooke Kroeger

TIMES 𝕿 BOOKS

RANDOM HOUSE

Copyright © 1999 by Brooke Kroeger

All rights reserved under International and Pan-American Copyright Conventions.
Published in the United States by Times Books, a division of Random House, Inc., New
York, and simultaneously in Canada by Random House of Canada Limited, Toronto.

Page 479 constitutes an extension of this copyright page.

Library of Congress Cataloging-in-Publication Data
Kroeger, Brooke.
    Fannie: the talent for success of writer Fannie Hurst / Brooke Kroeger.
        p.   cm.
    ISBN 0-8129-2497-5 (acid-free paper)
    1. Hurst, Fannie, 1885–1968.   2. Women and literature—United States—
History—20th century.   3. Women authors, American—20th century—Biography.   I.
Title.
PS3515.U785Z75   1999
813'.52—dc21
[B]   98-52900

Frontispiece: Fannie Hurst, 1914, photographed by Gerhard Sisters (courtesy of Temple
University Libraries Urban Archives)

Printed in the United States of America on acid-free paper
Random House website address: www.atrandom.com
98765432
First Edition
Book design by Janice Olson

PS
3515
.U785
Z75
1999

SEP 27 1999

114539

Contents

PART 1

PART 2

PART 3

PART 4

PART 5

Introduction

Fannie Hurst had achieved just about everything that mattered to her by the age of thirty-seven. "Just fancy," she mused in a letter she wrote that fall of 1923. "Write a book which is the literary sensation of the year and *then* losing 29 pounds. O it's a glorious old world."

By the time her second novel, *Lummox,* created its gratifying splash, Fannie Hurst had been the quintessence of the American success story for more than a decade. Since 1912, a magazine's inclusion of one of her short stories could almost guarantee the issue would sell out. But these tales of boarders and German-Russian-Jewish immigrants and twelve-dollar-a-week shopgirls had even more significant reach. Of the sixty-odd Fannie Hurst short stories published during her rise to renown (there would be well over a hundred before she was through, not to mention the scores of short fiction columns she wrote for newspaper syndicates), nearly half earned honored status in Edward J. O'Brien's prestigious annual *Best Short Stories* anthologies. It was O'Brien who predicted that inquiring literary historians in the centuries ahead would single out Fannie's tales of life among New York's working and immigrant classes as the most essential literary documents of their time. Even as early as 1915, when Fannie's oeuvre consisted of no more than a couple of dozen stories published in popular magazines, the esteemed editor of *Harper's Monthly,* William Dean Howells, placed her in the first rank of writers of "Hebrew comedy." Fannie's deep understanding of the common and superficial reality she sought to describe in these stories impressed Howells, along with her immense gift for "penetrating to the heart of life." Her shopgirl and boardinghouse tales had like appeal. It soon became commonplace for academic arbiters to select her stories as masterworks for high school and college textbooks. It was clear testament to Fannie's power as a storyteller that she managed to garner this level of affirmation despite a writing style that even her most forgiving critics found labored and overwrought. Harper & Brothers, her longtime publisher, thought enough of her work to bring out five collections of her short stories before she wrote *Lummox.* Three more story compilations would follow in the next fourteen years.

By 1923 Fannie had branched into other creative arenas. Three of her plays had appeared on Broadway, and the fledgling movie industry had turned eight of her titles into motion pictures. Twenty-four more would follow, including a remake of the 1920 box-office sensation *Humoresque,* three versions of *Back Street,* three of *Imitation of Life,* including one in Spanish, and two of *Back Pay. Four Daughters,* from Fannie's story "Sister Act," generated not only a remake but three sequels if you include *Daughters Courageous,* which used Fannie's four-sister idea without crediting her.

Almost from the start, celebrity pay accompanied the celebrity status. Her first novel, *Star-Dust,* netted her fifty thousand dollars, including book, film, and magazine serial rights—big money in 1920. No wonder the tag line "world's highest paid short-story writer" attached itself to her name. With fees that reached four thousand dollars per short story in the late 1920s, and held steady at that price throughout the Great Depression, it was nearly even true.

In 1923 *Lummox* represented Fannie's highest personal attainment, salving an old wound in the process. Many years after its publication Fannie, despite her ever-growing success and recognition, seethed at the recollection of a snipe her memory attributed to an erudite college classmate: "I would rather be a classic failure than a popular success like Fannie Hurst." *Lummox* delivered that classic success. As Fannie explained, her epic account of drudgery and pain in the life of a domestic servant provided "*artistic* acclaim that is as great as any popular acclaim has been. That's what I wanted—being a pig for success," she wrote after her first notices came in. "Now I have *both* crowds and I'm the happiest person on earth." (Oddly, two years earlier she had remembered the college incident differently. In that telling Fannie was the purported speaker, belittling the accomplishment of another classmate: "I would rather be a popular success than a classical failure." As would become plain in the course of researching this book, imagination and a good story line often overwhelmed both Fannie's ability and her inclination to recall events accurately.)

Not only did Fannie write in the rhythms and dialect and vernacular of her age, dissecting the emotional core of rich and poor alike, but she lent her prominence and pen to the day's significant socialist, liberal, humanitarian, and feminist causes. Soon she would become a forceful advocate for the rights of black Americans; she was an early literary supporter of both Zora Neale Hurston and Dorothy West. Politically, she broke her policy of nonaffiliation for Franklin Roosevelt and became a darling of his administrations, in both Albany and Washington. She liked to joke that she had slept in every bedroom at the White House—the Lincoln was a special favorite—except the president's and first lady's. There seems to have been no one of importance—in science, the arts, Hollywood, industry, academia, government, or politics, from Albert Einstein to Eleanor Roosevelt—on whose banquet dais Fannie did not have an honored place. There seems to have been no aspect of early-twentieth-century American popular culture—dieting figures heavily here—in which she was not involved.

Least heralded of all her accomplishments was her unique and prescient place as a vociferous and incisive commentator on the progress of women's advancement after the granting of the vote in 1920. Fannie had the forthrightness never to hesitate to fault women themselves for the opportunities they squandered, especially after each of the twentieth century's two world wars. Her ideas and attitudes help clarify why, when "the New American Woman" was already old news by the end of the 1890s, another women's revolution would be necessary seventy years later, as if the idea were being thought of for the first time.

Fannie's name and face were constant newspaper fodder, and lecture agents clamored for her to tour. Her alabaster skin, jet-black hair, red lips, exotic jewelry and clothes helped create her striking persona, but these were only part of what gave her Aura with a capital A. In every way, especially given her ordinary origins, her life epitomized what was exciting, important, and forward-thinking about her times. Fannie Hurst was a human nexus of creativity, success, and powerful access to everyone who mattered. She was usually at the forefront on matters of vital national, local, or humanitarian concern; her delayed response to Hitler's brutality toward the Jews is the one unfortunate exception. To lead a stranger through the first half of the twentieth century in gritty and glamorous New York, there is no better hand than Fannie's, even with its flashy uncut faux emerald ring as big as the egg of a pullet.

Fannie's fame didn't just recede after her funeral and the tributes occasioned by her death; it evaporated. Her major works were out of print; she had outlived the majority of her loyal fans and important friends. Childless, she had no surviving close family members to perpetuate her memory. *The New York Times* index provides a chilling indication of how fleeting fame can be. From the time Fannie moved to New York in 1911 until her death in 1968, her name appears in the newspaper some 250 times. Yet after the probating of her will, there is not another mention for six years and only then because someone finally bought her fabulous Gothic-style triplex in the Hotel des Artistes.

Nonetheless, in the years since 1974, small, select audiences have continued to show interest in Fannie's work. Susan Koppelman's efforts on behalf of the short story in general and Fannie in particular have contributed mightily, as have the many scholars who use the film version of *Imitation of Life* in their study and teaching of race and gender. In the broader culture there is evidence of a modest Fannie Hurst revival, thanks in part to the repeated showing of the film versions of her stories on late-night cable television. Again, the evidence is in the listings. After two decades of near-invisibility, the computerized newspaper indexes now record a couple of hundred references to Fannie's name. It appears in profiles of Zora Neale Hurston, in discussions of race in America; in obituaries of Lana Turner, Claudette Colbert, and the film director Pandro Berman; in stories about the restoration of the Over-the-Rhine district in Cincinnati, the opening setting of *Back Street*. Phrases such as "a Fannie Hurst tearjerker" or "a Fannie Hurst marriage" appear repeatedly, and the Parisians, it turns out, still refer to the mistress of an important man as "*une Back Street.*"

Ann Douglas, in her 1995 book, *Terrible Honesty: Mongrel Manhattan in the 1920s,* cites Fannie's work as "a rich and neglected source on the emergence of modern feminine sexuality." The New York *Daily News* in 1995 reported survey results that place *Imitation of Life* among the ten most popular movies ever made.

As if all this were not sign enough, Fannie's fabulous triplex, the "house within an apartment house," the "most famous studio in the most famous studio building in New York City," came back on the market in 1993, just as research for this biography began. Five years later, at the work's completion, the apartment was still for sale, prospective buyers likely put off by a very high charge for its monthly maintenance. Advertisements in glossy brochures make much of its history as the studio and lair of this intriguing celebrity author. It may be the hype of agentry, but it is also fact. Fannie was by no means a has-been in the thirty years she lived in that grand but quirky indoor mansion, until her death at age eighty-two. Just before she moved in, Irving Thalberg of MGM paid her the highest price ever offered by 1936 for the screen rights to an unpublished novel. In 1954 Edward R. Murrow anointed Fannie with a coveted celebrity slot on that most prestigious of all live television interview programs, *Person-to-Person.* And fourteen years later her obituary across two columns of the front page of *The New York Times* left no possible doubt: As an American cultural icon, Fannie's status was unassailable.

That said, it is the thirty years of Fannie's life *before* the move to the Hotel des Artistes that make her story worth telling. Her phenomenal rise to prominence and success began where this book begins, in 1905, in the fall of her freshman year at Washington University. Within days of her arrival on campus, she established herself as a talented, attention-grabbing coed with the clear promise of greatness.

PART *1*

Preceding page: photograph from the Collections of the St. Louis Mercantile Library Association

Chapter 1

"What I lack is rhythm"

The first known published work of Fannie Hurst appeared in her high school newspaper at Christmastime 1904, the month before she graduated. "An Episode," a nine-paragraph story, sketches a few moments in the life of a wealthy, powerful, but godless man alone with his conscience in a cathedral. Overcome by the haunting majesty of his surroundings, he watched his misdeeds pass before him. Pain and remorse engulfed him. He sat crouched alone on a pew until the last echoes of "Ave Maria" died away.

> Then he rose, and went out, and as he went he said, "I have knowledge, I have power—what I lack is rhythm."
> Then he threw back his head and laughed, long and loud and bitterly, and went off into the dusk.

Fannie Hurst, the daughter of now quite comfortable, assimilated German Jews with deadening middle-class aspirations, wanted to be a writer. She liked to claim that the *Saturday Evening Post* mailed back her manuscripts as if by boomerang from the time she was fourteen. This did not deter her. Nor did her mother's dire prediction that she would end up "an old-maid schoolteacher like Tillie Strauss," the sad and lonely spinster daughter of one of her mother's friends. Fannie defied this well-meant but suffocating opposition and compromised only enough to go to college in St. Louis, her hometown. She entered Washington University in the fall of 1905, a month before she turned twenty.

Fannie and her classmates watched much ground break. The handsome new Gothic-style "Quad" had been a site for the most defining seven months of the century for St. Louis, the "Universal Exposition," more commonly known as the 1904 World's Fair. The trees that lined the campus drives were only saplings in those days, reminding Fannie of "the knees of newborn calves." By her sophomore year the first girls' dormitory opened, and every city girl who could afford to do so took a room in McMillan Hall to get a better feel for college life. This did not stop the trips back to Mama, however. The sight of coeds toting overnight bags out the door of the new red-brick building was so common that some of the professors took to calling the campus Suitcase U. Although McMillan had space for 125 girls, only 16 moved in that first year, and together they became a tight little band. Every evening they joined in a kind of family party. Fannie usually provided the entertainment, amusing the group with parodies, anecdotes, and character sketches. She could concoct a spooky mystery yarn with no more inspiration than the sight of the same car parked at the edge of campus day after day. Fannie laid claim to the most exotic suite of rooms, in a little tower at the dormitory's very top. She dubbed it "the test tube," a name that stuck. So did Fannie's penchant for snaring the best and most unusual living spaces.

Her vitality was legendary on campus; she never seemed to sleep. From the Quad, friends often saw the lights in the test-tube windows burn till daylight, the sole indication that she was making time to study. For Fannie, classwork always came a distant second to acting, writing, editing, sports, and, as McMillan's first president, even dorm life.

Nevertheless she took pains to project the air of a serious scholar and desperately wanted the approval of the university's intellectual elite. With pretentious displays of verbiage, she dazzled friends and classmates, but her academic average was no better than a straight B-minus. Her A's in subjects that mattered to her, like composition and literature, did not quite balance out the C's. "More conspicuous than distinguished" was the way she later described her academic performance. Thinking back on those days years later, a dormmate remembered Fannie not as brilliant but as robust and vigorous, someone who "enjoyed living in every fiber of her being." Fannie showed no inclination for social activism in those years; that came later. Nor did she engage in any experimentation with the opposite sex.

Nothing seems to have sated Fannie's need for attention—not her stage performances, not her student compositions, not the admiration of her friends or even a coveted nod from a professor who might occasionally acknowledge a flash of talent. She found herself "slashing around in all directions at once"— silently tormented, violently ambitious, jealous of the achievements of others.

This anguish, which she deftly concealed, seemed to center on her inability to get any of her writing published professionally. As yearnings go this one was not so far-fetched. Fannie was among a number of students in this St. Louis litter to show precocious promise. Among the young women in her age-group, a few already had distinguished themselves in the greater St. Louis community. Zoë Akins, poet and future playwright, spent a term on the Washington University campus in Fannie's sophomore year. By that time Akins's work was appearing regularly in the *Mirror,* a local magazine of national literary repute owned and edited by the legendary William Marion Reedy. Sara Teasdale, another poet about Fannie's age, had her first book of verse published in 1907, when Fannie was a junior. Reedy had been publishing Teasdale's poems in the *Mirror* for a year. Especially irksome to Fannie was the publication in book form of *Completion of Coleridge's Christabel* by her classmate Edna Wahlert. Years later Fannie oddly remembered this work as her own unpublished effort as a child of sixteen in one telling, and eleven in another. Yet of all this local achievement, Cornelia Catlin Coulter stirred the most envy. Brilliant, austere, and scholarly, Coulter had little time for Fannie in their days at Washington U. After graduation she went straight to Bryn Mawr and earned a doctorate on the strength of a dissertation titled "Retraction in the Ambrosian and Palatine Recensions of Plautus; a Study of the *Persa, Poenulus, Pseudolus, Stichus,* and *Trinummus.*" Next to Coulter, Fannie always felt diminished, "transparent . . . a cheap and garish thing."

∞

Fannie may not have been the most outstanding student on campus, but she did stand out. Of the 109 students in the freshman class in September 1905, she was one of only twenty girls and, by her own reckoning, the best-known girl on campus. When a famous mind reader performed at the local vaudeville theater, a classmate in the audience yelled out, "Will Fannie Hurst become famous?" Years afterward another classmate remembered the wonderment Fannie always managed to provoke in those who knew her: "Even away [sic] back then we knew Fate had picked you for some high spot."

The campus newspaper, *Student Life,* leaves little doubt of Fannie's ubiquity among the university's more than three hundred students. In the first term she joined the dramatics club and hoped to be invited into the Potters, an elite literary society founded by Sara Teasdale and seven other young intellectuals on and off campus who "came together as a matter of temperament—that elusive type of mind which holds only the inner spirit of importance." They welcomed Edna Wahlert and even Zoë Akins, but they blackballed Fannie, likely with the disdain for her prose that would dog her for years to come. (College sororities, new on campus in these years, also ignored Fannie, but for an entirely different reason. When she understood why she felt scorn rather than hurt. What could be more ridiculous than a club that would exclude a girl as popular and assimilated as Fannie because she also happened to be a Jew?)

On the stage there were no such barriers, and Fannie appeared in most of the student productions. She had the panache to bring off a part as sophisticated as Mrs. Cheveley in Oscar Wilde's *Ideal Husband.* By the time she was a senior, her appearance onstage was enough to set off spontaneous applause before she uttered her first line. Next to Fannie Hurst, one student reviewer remarked, "the others appeared amateurish."

Fannie wrote a play, too, a two-act comic operetta for the senior class in which she gave herself the lead. She based the story on the struggles the college was having finding chaperones for school dances. The girls in McMillan crowded around the piano in the Pi Phi sorority rooms night after night while Fannie labored to fit words to tunes for the show. It even caused what passed in 1909 for a major student-faculty confrontation. The cast demanded the right to appear onstage in ballet costumes, but their parents, scandalized, objected, and in the end the young women wore gauzy stiffened skirts of tarlatan cotton that reached to four inches from the floor.

The *St. Louis Post-Dispatch* gave *The Official Chaperone* a splashy write-up, proclaiming it "a triumph of realism." A newspaper illustrator drew caricatures of the student stars—there was a busty, sexy line drawing of Fannie—and as the author her photograph also ran, set off by an oval frame. In this picture she is full-faced and pretty, posed with her chin exultantly lifted under the enormous saucer of a heavily plumed hat. "Marguerite Martyn Discovers Real College Playwright in Fannie Hurst," read the words in bold type, and under that the observation that Fannie had "dominated the hearts, if not, indeed the heads of her associates in college life, just as she did in the leading role of her clever play."

One of the most striking aspects of Fannie's college experience was the extent of her personal impact on everyone around her. Decades after classmates had relegated scrapbooks to the attic, they recalled with precision the most specific details of their encounters with Fannie. An underclasswoman named Meta Gruner was assigned to do a takeoff on Fannie during graduation festivities. For days she followed Fannie around, trying to get the rhythm of her walk and the intricacies of her hair knot, which Meta replicated with a hair switch. This worked well, because Fannie fashioned her own knot with a switch cut from her abundant black hair, which she twisted into a bun and pinned low at the back of her head. At night in the dorm she hid the switch in the sleeve of her kimono to keep the other girls from hiding it for a prank. Meta completed her Fannie ensemble by stuffing a pillow in the bodice of a princess-style dress she borrowed from her mother for the occasion.

Olna Hudler, "a beautiful, gifted, careless creature," was Fannie's closest college friend. Forty years later, with no contact in between, she could still catalog Fannie's college wardrobe. She remembered the sailor suits of fine woolen serge, faultless princess dresses, and well-tailored suits in handsome broadcloths. "How all the girls envied you!" she wrote. Other friends, however, were more indelibly struck by Fannie's willingness to try out any style or fad, no matter how extreme, unbecoming, or downright ugly.

Olna could still remember Fannie describing the interior of her dream apartment in New York: It would be dark and mysterious in the way of a medieval castle, with black walls and high windows draped in heavy curtains. "What an imagination!" Olna sighed in recollection. "How we listened spellbound when you set off on your magic carpet!"

∞

Rarely had there been a student more devoted to college life or more reluctant to leave it behind. For two days after commencement Fannie hung around campus, as if unable to imagine a future outside it. For years to come her legend on campus grew. Forty years after Fannie's graduation a college dean could recite the litany of anecdotes that successive waves of freshmen liked to tell:

Fannie Hurst wore her hair in a Psyche knot. Fannie Hurst owned a fabulous
dress with a Roman-striped sash. Professors read aloud the compositions Fannie Hurst dashed off on the way to class. One of Fannie Hurst's professors predicted she could become famous in any of three fields.

Olna remembered the night Terry Allen kissed Fannie and how exciting
that had been. If anyone Fannie knew was practicing "premarital irregularities," it passed her right by. "There were those who 'spooned' or let the boys
touch or 'fool' around with them," she once wrote. "I knew what I knew, and it
was plenty, from the unbridled hours of reading and piecing together scraps of
sotto voce information from Mama's conversation with the ladies of the *kaffeeklatsches*. Not infrequently I sat on the stairs eavesdropping."

Sixty years later Meta Gruner remarked to Fannie on how chaste their feminine culture had been in those early years of the century, when the automobile was still too much of a novelty to have released inhibitions, "sexual and
otherwise."

Though Fannie had two "incombustible" college beaux, neither made romantic overtures and Fannie remained a naïf. Her outspoken mother looked
on both of these men with disgust. They were not *"Unserer Leute"*—our people—she scoffed in German. One was "a gentile," the other "a kike," a Jew of
Eastern European descent—even less desirable, in her world, than a non-Jew.
Worse yet, neither was rich. The ugly words and thoughts rubbed Fannie "like
sandpaper," much as did the notion of a restricted club. Throughout university
both men wrote jointly composed long, unamorous letters to Fannie, analyzing
her as "aloof, cold, tantalizing, terribly poetic, terribly hurt somewhere inside,
needing to be awakened," afraid to live the emotions she wrote about, afraid to
let herself go. Bemused, Fannie loved the idea of being "terribly hurt somewhere inside—whatever that meant." Lacking a nimble retort, she recalled, "I
threw a wide cordon of aloofness about me."

Aloofness was a guise she assumed often over the course of her life, but it
was only a guise. Olna, who knew her so well in those years, had much more
vivid recollections of Fannie's "ringing, mirthful laughter," her "cheerful,
happy, unselfish disposition," her "sense of humor," and her "clean mind." She
too had remembered the semester Zoë Akins spent on campus in 1906, especially the day Akins's "pearls broke bounds and scattered over the floor in [Pro-
fessor] Smith's history class." It was surely Akins whom Fannie disguised as
Neal Patterson in her autobiography, identifying this early nemesis as a Missouri senator's daughter whose arrival had the campus all abuzz. Fannie's father was a shoe manufacturer, financially comfortable in those days but
without wide or important social reach. "We did not know anybody who was
anybody," Fannie said, wishing her parents were more cultured and intellectual, "out of the rut, instead of keeping me down in one with them." Her jealousy of Akins was palpable; she recalled hating her "for the things she was and
I was not." In English class, where Fannie most often was chosen to read her
work aloud, she suddenly felt "rigid and speechless before the worldliness of,

the flair, the professional status of Neal." There was also the day they walked along together downtown, "Neal" regaling Fannie with her long list of ardent admirers. Fannie suspected even Reedy, although a generation older than Akins, had more than a professional interest in her. "What did men see in her?" Fannie wondered. "She too was on the bulky side." Nonetheless, Fannie did get the idea she was missing out on something. Sometimes she blamed her weight, sometimes her parents, and sometimes even herself, "for holding back when I wanted to rush in."

Olna could still picture Fannie in the "tall plush hat of the drum major" and remembered the day they both "went among the gypsies to learn our fortunes, you suppressing laughter, carrying your diamond rings under your tongue for safety." There was also the time Fannie seemed to fall apart at the prospect of making a presentation in Dean Swift's psychology class and convinced her friends that she had gotten her turn postponed by making a date to meet them in the library. Her performance was a ruse to get Olna and Irma to miss class, so that Fannie could give her paper without either of them present. "How you laughed at us afterwards!" Olna chided. "How we all three laughed!" Fannie never liked anyone close to her to be in a room when she gave a speech.

⌘

Fannie had the ability to forge relationships with solid enough foundations to last a lifetime. Yet none of the deepest friendships she formed in college continued afterward in any significant way. Decades later, when these old friends resumed contact, moved to write by word of some new success of Fannie's that reminded them of times past, they expressed warmth, regard, and endearment. It was Fannie who always threw up the cordon. As she herself admitted, it was easier for her to be "more intimate with the anonymous public than with my closest friend." During school and later there were too many aspects of her life she preferred to keep to herself.

As one of the editors of *Student Life,* Fannie deluged the paper with her writings, starting in November of her sophomore year with a silly poem, "The Blasé Junior Soliloquizes." ("This world's a hollow bubble, / Don't you know; / Built of flunks, exams and trouble, / Don't you know.") She recalled long hours spent hunched on the white stone steps as she struggled to "capture the winged words that seemed to fly through my mind in flocks. . . . It did not matter that once on paper they lost much of their iridescence—there was always the next clean page of the composition book."

She wrote prose sketches, short-short stories, and poetry. She explored the themes of God, faith, love, career, death, and the meaning of life in the manner of a bright college girl who thought she could write. She was already good at titles: "A Mood," "The Girl and the Woman" ("She was alone with the last night of her girlhood . . ."), "Her Decision," "Druscilla's Proposal," "The GodHead." The work was distinctive enough to warrant a parody in *Student Life* her senior year: "Slush . . . With Apologies to Fannie Hurst" ("Near the center of a long alley, a little boy was sitting crying . . ."). Nothing, however, was good enough for the *Mirror,* though Fannie stuffed stories into envelopes addressed to Reedy week after week. Not even the manuscripts came back.

As a graduation present there was not just a trip to New York but a revelation: "No foreigner arriving to our shores for the first time could have thrilled more eloquently than I," she wrote years later. She experienced "a challenge . . . an invitation to the dance."

And then, two weeks before graduation in 1909, a victory. Olna came running across the quad to Fannie, waving a copy of the *Mirror*'s May 27 issue. On page 4 was a story under Fannie's name that *Student Life* published the same week. Fannie originally wrote it as a theme for English class, the last assignment of the year, a tale of a poor couple's simple delights in an otherwise dismal existence. Her professor had pointed out "*for* her" her facility with "the mass class—the shop people and their kin" and convinced her to stop writing "the hectic stuff" she had been turning in all term.

Reedy paid Fannie three dollars for "The Joy of Living," and with it she bought herself a morocco-bound notebook, which she inscribed:

Notes and Jottings
Fannie Hurst—Author.

Chapter 2

"The Dominant Force"

Fannie never liked anyone to think that her rise to fame had been too facile. Whenever her personal story appeared in print, and this was often, she favored her portrait in anguish and struggle, rebuff and triumph over bruising odds. An artist's tale. Typical passages had Sisyphean dimensions. Readers learned of "the heartaches, the bitter resentments, the almost invincible opposition of love, which landed me somewhat unsteadily out in the open road that led so zigzaggedly, so crazily, so up-and-downly toward the horizon." She told of how she worked to "straight-jacket myself into a rigidity of purpose which made the sore and lonely hours the more sore and lonely because they were voluntarily filched from a girlhood singularly free of responsibilities." She moaned of "long hours outside editorial doors; of solitary day-long tramps through streets that poured a hot lava of impersonal humanity; of writing, rewriting; of rejections and rejections."

All the same Fannie's full adult tenure in obscurity and rejection lasted about three years. Her life, from college graduation in June 1909 until her first avalanche of positive national attention midway through 1912, evokes only the most worn-out ways to say instant ascent. The biggest hurdle was not her rejection by editors, though she had that, but the battle to convince her parents to let her move to New York, unmarried, alone, to pursue the writer's life.

At first the opposition was adamant. Reluctantly, for more than a year after college graduation, Fannie tried to make her way as a writer at home. Her parents made every effort imaginable—a trip to an Atlantic City resort, a weekend with relatives at a Lake Michigan resort—to marry her off. At least one local proposal of marriage in this period came from a much older suitor, withdrawn in haste when the man found out that Fannie was Jewish. Mostly she moped and felt miserable. Despite her passionate love of animals, not even the puppy her house-finicky mother finally relented and bought her eased the doldrums. Fannie did some "light," unsigned work for the *St. Louis Post-Dispatch* but never felt she was really given a chance there and had no luck getting a job at any of the other papers, though she begged. She bombarded the office of the *Mirror* with new manuscripts, but none appeared in the weekly.

Some weeks after graduation Fannie summoned the courage to go to the magazine's office and meet William Marion Reedy himself, "a sage who lived loosely and unwisely" in Fannie's words. Though he may have been a source of gossip for the women of Fannie's mother's circle—she had no personal encounters with his "racy Rabelaisian quality"—he was brilliant at discovering young talent. Fannie had gotten one story past him. Now she wanted to take her place alongside Zoë Akins, Sara Teasdale, and Orrick Johns as a Reedy discovery and protégée. Reedy's most enduring literary find, Edgar Lee Masters of *Spoon River Anthology* fame, would join that list a few years later.

Fannie found Reedy reclining in a swivel chair, his feet high on an incredibly littered desk, "his vast body seeming to run downhill in an avalanche of fat, mussed shirt crawling up out of his low-waisted trousers, a pair of cracked glasses low on his nose, dark graying hair pushed around on his head, eyeshade dangling from his neck like a bib. Books, books, stacked on the floor, on chairs, overflowed the place." To her, he was a "king of greatness . . . kind, stimulating, shaggy, disorderly, lyrical, stunning and reckless."

He was crude but somehow inoffensive. He referred to her "fanny" as he offered her a seat, providing her with yet another wave of resentment against her parents. They had considered naming her Beulah, she mused. At least no one sat on a beulah.

As Fannie remembered the meeting, Reedy read to her from Ovid's *Art of Love,* gossiped about one St. Louis girl who needed to be "bombed out of her virginity" and another who needed to be sealed into hers. He branded Teasdale a middle-western Sappho who bathed under a sheet. He felt that most American writers were wired with suppressed desires but their sex lives took place chiefly between book covers.

He also told her that she might *really* write one day, if she let go—that is, if she had anything *to* let go. Fannie thought she ought to have some sly double entendre in retort. Zoë Akins certainly would have. "My mind doesn't bathe under a sheet," she managed, and Reedy threw his head back and laughed.

It was when he asked about her background that Fannie fell apart. It was not the first time this had happened to her, and the incidents troubled her deeply. Presbyterian? Catholic? "American," she replied. With a knowing look he let the subject drop. Fannie knew, she said, he had seen "the snide person I was. But for the life of me I could not retract or supplement."

She remembered him then telling her to go home and write some "shorts" for the *Mirror.* Sweat for them, he said. "Go home, you nice big healthy girl, and write like hell." The reference to her size embarrassed and irked her. "Hunk of a girl," she thought. "Hunk of a brain."

Reedy actually referred to this meeting in a letter he sent August 2, 1909, to the artist Albert Bloch, a St. Louisian then in Munich who drew caricatures and sometimes wrote for Reedy. Bloch liked Fannie's first story for Reedy and wanted to know more about her. Reedy said she was "fat and pleasant, I understand, and very ambitious." He said he was glad Bloch liked her work because he, too, thought it "had quality to it." Still, eight months passed before Reedy published anything more of Fannie's in the *Mirror*.

It was at this time that Fannie started developing the research technique that would become her signature, plucking her fiction topics from real, hardscrabble lives. She volunteered in the program office of the Jewish Educational Alliance of St. Louis, a settlement house at Ninth and Carr, diagonally across the street from her father's shoe factory. She even put in some time making "heels, counters and top lifts" in a filthy shoe plant and getting to know the young Polish girls doing the work.

∽

As Fannie later told the story, she and her father took a meandering trip to New York for her college graduation present, stopping wherever she pleased. By sheer chance, at the sight of an intriguing billboard they detoured to Mt. Clemens, Michigan, where Fannie became infatuated—"love before first full sight"—with a handsome pianist a decade her senior. He was Jacques, sometimes called Jack but actually Jacob, Danielson, a pianist who also served as assistant to the concert piano virtuoso and teacher Rafael Joseffy.

Fannie first saw Jack "in what might have been the stage setting for a romantic drama by one of those lady writers with three names." As she remembered the day, wandering the vast Park Hotel, exploring the writing rooms, lounges, and solaria, she came upon a small, darkened parlor dominated by a grand piano. Seated before it was a man she could make out only in silhouette. She took in the nobility of his lowered head and the mobility of his hands, playing a Chopin étude under the light of a floor lamp. What she did not realize at the time was that he had chosen the remote room while most of the guests were at the baths or taking naps so that no one would hear him play. Fannie slipped away before he finished and did not see him again for two days.

Through an acquaintance of her mother's who was "taking the cure," Fannie learned that Joseffy was spending time in Mt. Clemens between concert appearances nearby. On a chance meeting the mother's friend introduced Fannie to Jacques. He was impeccably dressed, with heavy, black, groomed hair and the head of a Greek discus thrower. "I was smitten," Fannie said, "to the extent of pain."

Jacques invited Fannie to go canoeing. She babbled on but learned little about him, only that he shrank from public appearances, that he had his own teaching studio but also assisted Joseffy, of whom he was a disciple, that he loved the theater and was an avid "first-nighter," and that this was the first time he had been more than two hundred miles west of New York since he emigrated from Moscow as a boy of sixteen.

The detour to Mt. Clemens had knocked days out of their limited schedule, and if there was to be any time left for New York, Fannie and her father would have to leave the next day. Perhaps it was just as well, Fannie thought. Though his own parents had come to the United States from Germany, Papa didn't like foreigners, especially of the Minsk-Kiev variety. She knew the combination of Moscow and music would upset him. It was better that Papa and Jack not have a chance to meet.

That night after dinner, Fannie dressed in her best and waited in the lobby, not telling even herself for what. After some time she went to bed but then re-dressed, went down to the veranda, and seated herself in a row of empty rock-ers. Jack strolled by. They sat and talked until late but about nothing memorable. He didn't even touch her hand. "I attempted to steer the talk in the direction of girls. . . . There must have been plenty of heart-burning where he was concerned," Fannie thought. Before they parted, Fannie blurted through inhibitions, "Shall we correspond?" Jack replied that he wasn't much of a letter writer. She said she would do the writing if he would send postcards, and he agreed. Back in St. Louis, a card or two arrived. In her autobiography, Fannie reconstructed without quotation marks what happened next. The other speaker is Mama:

> Oh, just a man I met in Mount Clemens.
> It's like pulling teeth to get a word out of that child. What man?
> You wouldn't know. A musician staying at the hotel with Rafael Joseffy.
> Who?
> You wouldn't know. A famous musician.
> Is Joseffy the man who writes to you?
> No, he was with him.
> I asked who is the man who writes to you.
> A musician too, Mama. A wonderful musician.
> That's all we need. A musician. They don't earn salt. Leave it to you to find the men who don't. Did your father meet him?
> No.
> Funny.
> We just met once or twice.
> Mama softened. Who are his people?
> How should I know?
> Well, if I met a young man and corresponded with him I would know. Is he a New Yorker by birth?
> Here it came!
> No.
> Where do they come from originally?
> What difference does that make?
> Kikes? The word that usually went through me like a knife drew blood this time.
> I don't know and I don't care! All I know is his little finger is worth more than all the smug ones in this town put together.
> Where was he born?

I don't know, I lied a little wildly.

I can see now why you didn't want your father to meet him.

Mama, I only met this man a couple of times. He was with a great celebrity. Isn't that enough?

In February 1910, the winter after the Mt. Clemens detour, Reedy published another Fannie Hurst story. She was still in St. Louis, depressed and living at home, unable to convince her parents—or, finally, herself—to let her move on. She called the story "The Dominant Force." It is the tale of a wealthy, elegant, young New York woman who falls in love with a poor musician, a teacher at a noted New York conservatoire. Swathed in furs, she meets him alone in Central Park and vows, at last, to marry him. They speak of their new life together in the genteel shabbiness of his boardinghouse rooms. She adores him. They embrace and kiss. As they part she says a loving good-bye. He thinks she means for now, and so does she. But in another instant she realizes that she means for good. He walks her to her door. She disappears into its liveried entrance. He walks to the corner, searches his pockets for change, and hails a hansom cab.

"Misery and Company"

The *Mirror* published Fannie's first story about shopgirls, called "The Gropers," on May 26, 1910. Legions of young, single American women were joining the workforce in this period, typically in low-paying jobs in retailing. Though Fannie had no need to work for wages, everything about these young women—their style, their grand or limited aspirations, their conflicts and tragedies, their love lives—stoked her imagination. She found herself "bleeding with and for" the single working girl. In the years to come her scores of stories exploring the harsher realities of their lives attracted an enormous readership, largely from these very ranks.

In this era the short story was the home-entertainment equivalent of the evening television series, only the writers—not the characters they created—were the stars. Mass-circulation magazines such as *Cosmopolitan* and the *Saturday Evening Post* at the top and smaller, less prestigious vehicles such as *Smith's* and *Cavalier* ran nonfiction pieces by top writers along with as many as six new short stories per issue. The best were heavily promoted. Editors vied for the work of the most popular writers and constantly sought out new talent to claim as their own.

"The Gropers," Fannie's charming story of the mousy department store clerk and her flashy friend behind the cosmetics counter, even with its neat O. Henry twist at the end, did not turn out to be her career launcher. It took her seven more months even to get another story into the *Mirror.*

Fannie was a year out of college and still in St. Louis, feeling hedged in by her parents "with one of those terrible Chinese walls of flesh and blood and love that are more difficult to scale than stone." She used the "Chinese walls" image more than once over the years to describe how confined she felt. "All my life . . . I've had to struggle against that most insidious of poppy seeds in my potion—kindness," she said years later. "And if you think it easy to straight-jacket yourself to a 'gix' (that is what I call it, that gnawing, aching-void thing which says, 'Write, darn you, write!') with the family tapping its brow over you and urging you to take up china-painting or social work to forget 'it'; with you yourself young enough to feel the play-vitality wanting out like high-power steam, and all outdoors crying, 'Come and live me—I'm immense!'—well, try it!"

By the early fall of 1910, around the time of her twenty-fifth birthday, Fannie finally threw off the family's grip and moved to New York. As a sop to her parents, she claimed to have enrolled in an extension course or graduate school at Columbia University, though no record of either survives. She said she chose her subject not by title but by the earliest offering in the day. This left the rest of her time free to prowl the city for story subjects, to pester receptionists at magazine editorial offices, and to write, day and night. A favorite piece of personal publicity has her doing short stints as a waitress in a Child's Restaurant, as a stitcher in a sweatshop, and as a ribbon salesgirl at Macy's—or was it the old Hearns' Department Store, as related in another telling? She also said she lived in a tenement for a couple of weeks above the shop of an Armenian tobacconist, though none of these could be verified.

Long past midnight, she liked to walk the streets of New York's more desolate neighborhoods alone. A young man who knew Fannie slightly at the time recalled vividly his first brush with "the nobility of the pen" the night he escorted her through the Lower East Side to a settlement house and then on to night court.

Though her parents opposed her move east, they did not stop it. Perhaps, seeing how miserable she was at home, they had resigned themselves to the eventual future of their only child as that dreaded old-maid schoolteacher. Maybe this was easier to palate from more than a thousand miles away. Still, they wrote one another daily, bound as if by stretched rubber band. Her parents provided a generous allowance. In those early years away Fannie returned to St. Louis for extended visits, holidays, and summers. In between her mother lived for the letters, taking them with her to neighborhood bridge games "when her glasses seemed to be misplaced, or [when she] wanted . . . to pour her odd combination of pride and disappointment" into sympathetic ears.

∽

Fannie at first took quarters in a narrow "hall room" within a mile of Columbia. It was "bare to austerity," had "the odor of institution and linoleum," and chilled her "like a wet bathing suit donned at dawn." The loneliness of the experience transmuted into a recurrent detail in both her fiction and subsequent published recollections of early New York life. A favorite, often-repeated passage: "I had no friends and a human voice was seldom addressed in my direction, except to remark, 'Step lively.' " Another: "Not to hear the sound of a human voice addressed directly to you for days, even when your next-door neighbor is within peeping-over-the-transom distance, to find the corner druggist too indifferent, and the street-urchin too wary for even the comforting commonplace of weal and weather, is indeed the jingle of 'Water, water everywhere nor any drop to drink' distilled to its cruelest."

Fannie left that dreary cell for another, a fourth-floor "slit of a room" downtown where for three weeks she never so much as passed a lodger on the stairs. She returned one night to find a patrol wagon backed up against the curb and women in "various stages of blondness, dress and undress" being hustled out and into it. Her fellow lodgers filed into the paddy wagon, and Fannie spent the night riding the subway. An introduction wangled by her mother got her in to see the director of the Three Arts Club, a women's residence for aspiring artists, actresses, and musicians at 340 West Eighty-fifth Street. Though the three arts were not supposed to include writing, Fannie presented herself as an actress, rented a typewriter, and moved uptown.

In those early days Fannie, by letter, regaled her parents with stories of nonexistent success. She mailed home unsigned clippings from the New York newspapers, implying though never saying straight out that the work was her own. Meanwhile, fellow residents at the Three Arts complained that the return of her manuscripts kept clogging their common mailbox. One small success in those earliest months: Reedy, back in St. Louis, agreed to publish a third vignette of Fannie's, entitled "Prose," in the *Mirror's* fiction-filled Christmas issue of 1910. In his acceptance letter he admired her "grim-kind view of life. . . . People *on* just as you see them, a little nasty, a little mean, but good after all."

"Good luck in the fight," he wished her. "You'll win sure. Wish I could help you to an early win, but I can't." His last line was a comment on the push-pull of even minor victory in those first months on her own. "Broke now," he wrote. "Send you small cheque before Xmas."

Fannie returned to St. Louis for the holidays and remained through February of the new year, long enough for a humorous piece she had written called "Home" to be produced at the Columbia, a local vaudeville theater. Her costar was Melville Burke, a fellow Washington University graduate who took the pseudonym Arnold Donald for the production, fearing that "his professional prospects might be injured were his real name divulged." The skit was about the marital complications of a young Englishman married to an American. The local-girl-still-making-good angle provided an obvious promotional opportunity, and the Columbia featured Fannie's playlet on the same bill with "The Sign of the Rose," starring the well-known character actor George Behan.

"It is not Miss Hurst's intention to remain on the stage as her family object to such a course," the *Post-Dispatch* noted. "She will return to Columbia University at the end of her current engagement." Old college friends came to see the performance. Reviewers were kind. "Both the sketch and the acting are above mediocre," said the critic for the *St. Louis Star.* The *Republic* thought it "lacked vitality and action," though Fannie and her costar gave "creditable performances." The *Post-Dispatch* was most effusive. It called the sketch "sincerely worthy" and said Fannie "revealed talents as a player that would justify hopes of genuine distinction." A near stranger who had gotten to know Fannie at the Mt. Clemens resort happened to catch the show while visiting St. Louis. He marveled. "I have often wondered would your modesty hide your light under a bushel basket," he wrote. "Imagine my surprise and gratification upon seeing you on stage. . . . Go to it—it's in you and some day I expect to say proudly 'Fannie Hurst—I knew her when she was a school girl.' " Fannie's mother, on the other hand, found the whole thing "terrible," a complete embarrassment. The show closed after its minimum one-week run, and Fannie headed straight back to New York.

The experience yielded an excellent lead: an introduction to William J. Dean of the theatrical producer David Belasco's organization. Fannie enrolled in acting lessons with Dean as soon as she got back to New York. At about the same time she sold a vignette called "Misery and Company" to Alden Mooch, Sunday editor of *The New York Times,* which was published, as was the custom, without her byline. Mooch even asked by letter if she had any more like it, but it is not clear if he bought others. She secured an assignment to profile William Marion Reedy and wrote the piece, but it wasn't accepted for publication. Reedy foresaw this, even as he obligingly sent her background information about himself. "No disrespect to you, Miss Hurst," he wrote. "There's no one can quite *do* me as I should be done who doesn't know me *well, personally and hasn't had some of my experiences.* Indeed, but for what it may pay the doer—I'd rather not be done at all. The truth about me could only be said and writ by someone who more than half dislikes me, and knows the record."

A story she titled "The Ultimatum" made the rounds of magazine offices but was rejected at *The Delineator, Munsey's,* and *The American Magazine.* Against her better judgment she even revised it along lines suggested by Robert H. Davis at *Munsey's,* but he still turned it down. Fannie vowed she would never again restructure a story to suit an editor or his perception of the marketplace, and over the years when she did give in she almost always regretted it. Oddly, the rejection letters often served as sources of some encouragement. They were personal, encouraging notes, after all, not just preprinted slips of paper.

Fannie's lessons with William Dean led to a bit part on Broadway for several weeks in Leo Ditrichstein's *The Concert,* a major hit of the 1910–11 season. The show was just at the end of its ten-month run. Her five-minute, two-line appearance paid twenty dollars a week and amounted to no more than a fat-girl sight gag; she recalled sitting on an overloaded suitcase to get it closed. The brief appearance gave her plenty of waiting time in the dressing room she shared with four others, three flights above the stage. And so, oblivious to the silent taunts of her colleagues, Fannie, in her terra-cotta-colored dressing gown and blue eyeshadow, hunched herself on a trunk top and bit at her pencil as she wrote to pass the time. In five weeks she had finished a story, "The Seventh Day," a charming yarn about another shopgirl living in a hall room with only her rich fantasy life for company. She had sent the manuscript off to several publications when Belasco announced the show's closing on Broadway and its upcoming national tour, offering Fannie a place in the company. *Munsey's* rejected "The Seventh Day" first, calling it "too crude in workmanship," and *Hampton's* magazine did likewise, finding the plot too much like one they had published a few years back. John Phillips of *The American Magazine* called the story "unusually good," and although he didn't want it for his own publication, he suggested that Fannie try *Ainslee's*. *Ainslee's* said no but passed the story on to its sister publication, *The New Story Magazine,* which in turn sent it to *Smith's Magazine*. *Smith's* accepted it June 20 and sent Fannie a thirty-dollar check. On the strength of her first New York sale, Fannie turned down the Belasco offer to tour with *The Concert*. It would have horrified her parents anyway. Dean told her to keep in touch.

A sale, however, was not the same as publication. *Smith's* held the piece for another six months, and the rejection letters kept coming, finding Fannie either at the Three Arts Club or back home in St. Louis. Her most repeated anecdote on this score is a claim of a total over the years of thirty-five—sometimes thirty-six—rejection letters from the *Saturday Evening Post* alone.

"Power and Horsepower"

The acceptance of a story by *Smith's Magazine* was surely a start, but it was the arrival in Fannie's life of Robert H. Davis that launched her professional writing career. Davis, the chief editor for five of the Munsey magazines, quickly became a beloved friend and mentor. Like Marion Reedy, he had a nose for emerging talent and was the first to publish many of those who would become the most successful writers of the day, among them Mary Roberts Rinehart, Zane Grey, Montague Glass, George Jean Nathan, and Dorothy Canfield. With a simple sentence Davis kept Fannie going during the months she was drowning in rejections. "Fannie Hurst," he declared, "you can write." It was the moment of validation. Suddenly, she stopped wondering whether her passion to write, the "oneness of purpose" still unproven even to herself, was not just some harebrained obsession. Her gratitude for Davis's "unfailing mental searchlight which has made of his skyscraping office a lighthouse for befogged souls floundering about in literary shoals" lasted the rest of her life.

The relationship developed over manuscripts, exchanges of letters, and visits to Davis's office. In November 1911 he criticized a story of Fannie's called

"Dead Sea Fruit," which two other magazines had turned down, but then he bought it anyway for *Cavalier,* one of his lesser publications. Though entirely random, the sequence of events over the next five months worked to Fannie's extreme advantage.

The first story she sold in New York, "The Seventh Day," finally appeared in the January 1912 issue of *Smith's.* Davis bought "Romance en Casserole" for *Cavalier,* calling it "the best thing you have ever submitted." This is the tale of Aggie, the pretty diner cashier who knows how to fend off the advance of every sweet-talking but insincere male customer. She finally receives proposals of marriage from two suitors, one of them a seemingly poor social worker, whom she really loves. When the social worker confides that he is really a wealthy man who has been hanging around the diner badly dressed for the sake of his research, Aggie rolls her eyes in savvy ridicule and shoos him away in favor of the guy she doesn't love who has a steady job. Dejected, the social worker rounds the corner and gets into his limousine. The story prompted Davis to encourage Fannie to produce more fiction "located in the same walk of life. There is nothing like the common people," he told her, "one of which I beg to remain."

Cavalier published "Dead Sea Fruit" soon after, on February 3. Fannie completed two more manuscripts, "Them Incandescents" and "Mere Man." Phillips at *The American Magazine* thanked her for sending them but passed. Churchill Williams at the *Saturday Evening Post* especially liked "Them Incandescents" but said it "doesn't quite get across the line in this office." Davis bought them both for *Cavalier.*

The modest success had Fannie feeling good enough about herself to write a piece for *Student Life,* the Washington University student newspaper, which the editor requested. "I am still in the get-my-start stage," she reported modestly. She gave details of her experiences studying dramatic technique with Dean, claiming that her only reason for doing so was "entirely with a view to my writing." What made every attempt to succeed more difficult, she said, was the competition. "New York is filled with 'Me[']s' struggling toward the self-same goal," she said. What was worse, "The highest attainment is rendered doubtful by the fact that on all sides you are surrounded by those who can do the same thing as well, and are probably better than you." Fannie admitted the appeal of drama writing was its higher remuneration—one week's royalty, "even from a slight thing," could bring in more than the full price of a short story. But she said that fiction was "the real child of my heart." And her efforts—eight to twelve stories a year, she claimed—were starting to pay off. She said she sold less than a third of what she wrote in the first year, and half of what she wrote the next year. So far in 1912, she said, "I have disposed of everything I have turned out since last January."

She ended with a piece of advice:

> Writing is a difficult and too often a thankless game—particu-larly for a woman. You have no idea what a peculiar genius is the "fe-

male writer" (I cannot refrain from the expression). Truly their pens have writ a curious message upon them, they have seemingly turned their own weapons against themselves.

Careers are interesting for your friends, if you must turn your hand to something, well and good; but after all, you know what hand it is that rules the world.

∞

In the months between the publications of "Dead Sea Fruit" and "Romance en Casserole," Fannie circulated a new manuscript, a story she called "The Squall." It made a "very favorable impression" on the editors at both *McClure's* and *Everybody's,* but neither bought it in the end, and at the *Saturday Evening Post,* Williams told her it "just escapes getting across the line." He urged Fannie to be patient, however, adding, "You will yet give us the pleasure of seeing you in print in the *Post.*" Fannie immediately sent off to the *Post* another story, "Power and Horsepower," a piece about Gertrude, the hotel manicurist who— unlike Aggie back at the diner—makes the right choice in love and for the right reason. On May 17, 1912, the week after *Cavalier* published "Romance en Casserole," a letter arrived addressed to Fannie from George Horace Lorimer himself, the *Post's* estimable publisher. He not only accepted "Power and Horsepower" for publication but added: "I am sure from this story that you ought to be a regular contributor to *The Saturday Evening Post.*" Churchill Williams, the editor, wrote the same day, asking for an appointment. Clearly delighted to be giving her good news for a change, Williams began his note, "Bully for you!" She expected a hundred-dollar payment, but he offered her three hundred dollars. Four days later, smelling what was coming, Bob Davis attempted to lock up a year's worth of Fannie's stories for the Munsey group. He asked her for six. Two weeks later, on May 31, Lorimer at the *Saturday Evening Post* again wrote Fannie to override his editor's earlier rejection of "The Squall" and ordered a check for it cut in her name. By that point a Fannie Hurst short story, even one already declined by the reading staff of the *Saturday Evening Post,* had become too important to pass up.

These first six of what would ultimately be hundreds of nationally published stories established Fannie as seer into the hearts of prewar working girls in two basic categories: single, poor, and hoping for something better; married, poor, and desperate for something else. They galvanized a following. Almost instantly Fannie had fans.

"Summer Resources," which the *Post* bought on July 1, took a couple of new, unpredicted, and important turns. It was the first of what Bob Davis later referred to as "them there Hebrew stories." In it the working girl got a new backdrop, one Fannie had only recently gained familiarity with: the veritable marriage mill of an oceanside resort hotel in high season, where Jewish mothers minded their maiden daughters and ferreted out the best matrimonial prospects. Everyone understood the game. In Fannie's story a very chic young woman shows up one day, unchaperoned, and turns the head of one of the most dashing men, a garment importer. She steals his attention away from one mother's daughter, who is furious until she finds another reasonable prospect. The importer fervently courts the chic young woman, even showing her a book of his top-secret new designs from Europe. She promises to meet him the next morning, but she never shows up. Perplexed, the importer remains at the resort another week. When he returns to the city, he goes to see a major client and learns that the client has hired a new designer. It is, of course, the chic young woman he was courting at the beach. She has stolen all his new designs for locally made knockoffs. It is at this point the client turns to the importer and asks, "How's the wife and boys, Arnheim?"

The march was on: "Them Incandescents" ran June 29 in *Cavalier,* and "Power and Horsepower" appeared in the next week's *Saturday Evening Post.* "Mere Man" followed in *Cavalier* on July 13. Three days later Harry Perton Steger of Doubleday wrote Fannie, wanting to "talk book." What about a collection of her stories with a unifying theme or location? "The Squall" made the August 10 issue of the *Saturday Evening Post.* It had seemed like a long slog, but by the age of twenty-six, almost exactly two years after her arrival in New York, the young woman who could have fashioned her rejection letters into an ankle-length dress—even one large enough to cover her substantial frame— had established herself as one of the most sought-after commodities in the world of magazines, then in its heyday. For Christmas she sent Davis a pocketbook. His delight was with more than the gift:

> There is another kind of Christmas that has grown
> out of my acquaintance with you, to wit: your own
> success, your rapid, wonderful, and merited rise to the
> very top of things. It is not my habit to offer the palm,
> but before this year expires let me hand it to you.
> I have a lurking suspicion that the celebrity you now
> enjoy is due very largely to the fact that you are equipped
> with patience and ability in equal proportions. Lots of
> people have one or the other, but few have both.
> And now let me wish you continued and
> uninterrupted prosperity and happiness, and when you
> grow old, which you won't, forgive me if in my dotage I
> should write a story beginning "Once upon a time, there
> was a goil—"

Success came in torrents. Over the next six months magazine editors who had held Fannie at arm's length reached for full-press embrace. "You are coming into your own beautifully," wrote John Phillips of *The American Magazine,* reading her stories in the *Saturday Evening Post* and recalling the "promise of a gifted storyteller" in a manuscript he rejected a year before. "I hope you will go on from glory to glory." In ink he added at the bottom: "I'd be delighted, of course, if you'd let me see a story again sometime." The legendary Ray Long, then the editor of *Redbook,* weighed in, looking for stories; and at least three book publishers—Doubleday and Doran before they merged, and Small, Maynard & Co. of Boston—offered to put her work between hard covers. Everyone seemed to want to publish Fannie Hurst.

Even more impressed with Fannie's accomplishments than the New York magazine publishing establishment were those St. Louisians on the *Post* subscriber list who knew-her-when. A Christmas Eve letter from the man who had been Fannie's revered—and usually very reserved—assistant principal at Central High School said it all. It was certainly one of the most moving tributes she would ever receive. William Schuyler told her he had stopped buying the *Post* when a story of hers wasn't listed in its table of contents:

> What I have hitherto admired in them is your keen and accurate observation of the class you have chosen to depict—the fine humor which pervades the narrative though never destroying the sense of human reality which should be the foundation of all such art. But in your last[,] "A New Year's Adam and Eve," I see something higher than the mere admirable portrayal of a social class—I seem to find a deeper humanity—a *broader* outlook on the fundamental things of life, which give promise of much higher achievement from you in the future. That picture of two simple souls at supper in the midst of the vicious and vulgar dissipation of fast New York is a remarkable piece of dialect. Don't let temporary success blind you to the greater possibilities that are in you. You have the seeing eye and the portraying hand of the true artist and I expect the very best from you.

Chapter 3

"The Key of a Flat"

There was no chance of fooling the Three Arts Club any longer about her professional goals, so Fannie had to find a new place to live. She spent a couple of months in St. Louis and then a brief time at Harperly Hall, the apartment building at the corner of Sixty-fourth Street and Central Park West. By early January 1913, she had moved to 350 West Seventy-first Street, taking a flat right near the railroad tracks just east of the Hudson River that "overhung the New York Central switching yards like a tessellated castle. All night, cattle in process of shipment bellowed in the abyss below." Six months later she moved to 260 West Seventy-second Street, just off West End Avenue.

Cyd Bettelheim, with the help of her sisters, Eva Rosenheim and Rebekah Kohut, operated the Tripp Lake Camp in Poland, Maine, as well as a fashionable girls' school on West End Avenue called the Bettelheim School. They made a nearby apartment available to older girls who were living and working in the city. Fannie moved in along with Bessie Blum, Carolyn Aronsohn, and several others. Fannie remembered three of them as being from Baltimore, all daughters of what she thought of as "well-placed families." The atmosphere of the house—double rooms of bird's-eye maple with cretonne upholstery and curtains, candlelit dinners on lace tablecloths with food sent over from the school—invited intimacy. The girls became friends. This was a more cultivated group than Fannie had known at home or at the Three Arts Club. Most were graduates of schools such as Goucher and Bryn Mawr, and two had been to Europe, one of them several times. More than forty years later Carolyn Aronsohn Lisberger recalled with affection Fannie's "ever bubbling, effervescent humor that kept us girls sitting on the floor hysterical with laughter." But in the presence of these better-bred young women, Fannie mostly felt gauche: "Their manner of dressing bespoke more than words what was wrong with mine," she remembered. Daytime, they almost uniformly went out in tailor-made suits, blouses of fine handiwork, and small fur neck pieces. She, in contrast, liked to swathe herself in an "immense pointed fox." She knew what was wrong with her outfits. She knew what the other girls meant when they offered her a "warmer" cashmere coat to wear instead of her own loud black-and-white check. She knew they laughed at the way she put herself together, just as they had at the Three Arts. But she sloughed it off. "My flair for the flamboyant was as difficult to douse as a forest fire," she once explained. "I am that way, I reasoned to myself. Let them run with the herd." Fannie also knew that these very privileged girls, "with just enough scratching ambition to motivate them to leave sheltered homes," regarded her accomplishments "with frustration and some admiration."

Some admiration? In 1913 their new housemate had stories published under her name in the January, February, March, May, June, September, and December issues of the *Saturday Evening Post*. Eva Rosenheim, who was responsible for public relations for the school and camp, immediately elevated Fannie to the role of showpiece, maneuvering to get her over to the school whenever important visitors or parents were expected. She especially wanted Fannie to meet her stepnephew, Mrs. Kohut's adored stepson, George Kohut, a rabbi by training who ran the Kohut School for Boys in Riverdale and, later, the Columbia Grammar School. Fannie told this story under the thin guise of pseudonyms, but her biographical descriptions leave no doubt as to the actual characters.

Eva concocted a practical joke: Since Dr. Kohut wanted nothing to do with intellectual women, Eva convinced Fannie to pose as a chorus girl named Marjorie Tate for her introduction to him. Fannie arranged through a friend at the Three Arts Club to emerge from the stage door of a Broadway theater along with the showgirls after a performance. When Fannie suggested adding items to her wardrobe to make the ruse more convincing, Eva said it wasn't necessary. Fannie's later read on this was that Eva considered her ordinary manner of dress chorinelike enough. They went to a top restaurant, where, she later wrote, Kohut sat beside her "with a quiet dignity that made his constant pressuring of my knee beneath the table hilarious." Later he took her on a ride around the park, clearly intent on "proceeding with what he thought the occasion required." Fannie at this point wanted to tell him the truth. "I hated being pawed," she recalled years later. "Moreover, something unsportsmanlike in the entire proceedings made me squirm." But she refrained, for Eva's sake.

Dr. Kohut asked her out again, and the second date was a repeat of the first, only this time he asked many questions about her background. He seemed totally smitten. Was she free from romantic involvements? Would she convert to marry a man she cared about if he happened to be a Jew who had once studied for the rabbinate? Did she think a man of thirty-eight too old for a girl in her twenties? The next night Eva organized a family dinner at which Fannie was to meet Kohut, ostensibly for the first time, appearing as herself. Miss Bettelheim was shocked to learn of Fannie's participation in Eva's practical joke. This, in turn, mortified Fannie, who wanted to avoid the dinner altogether. But the sisters thought it best that she go through with it.

Dr. Kohut arrived, and the stepaunts introduced him to Fannie Hurst, the young writer from St. Louis. Fannie remembered the terrible moment: "I could see the flood of delayed perceptions flow into his eyes. The family stood eager for a burst of fun, while I waited, I suppose, for come-what-will." Kohut did what none of them had foreseen. His jaw clamped together, he told his stepaunts that if this was their idea of humor, they should laugh it out among themselves. He turned in quiet fury and left the room. Fannie stood "mute and inglorious," but the family rallied to her defense. No one felt that she was to blame. Dr. Kohut, however, never came around.

Cyd Bettelheim also liked to introduce Fannie to special visitors. One day she called Fannie out to meet her attorney, a rising star in the City Republican Party, "a squat, black-haired sloe-eyed, fiery little fellow" named Fiorello La Guardia, who became a good friend. La Guardia introduced Fannie to the wonders of Greenwich Village, Italian cooking, and New York City politics.

Fannie liked the Bettelheim sisters and felt comfortable in their world. They seemed to feel she added good measure to their "salon," and her presence in this fine home relieved the pressure from her parents to return to St. Louis. It was probably here that Fannie began to cultivate her haughty Middle Atlantic accent. Still, she felt both "miscast" in these surroundings and unable to move on.

She dated a few appropriate suitors. She later identified one of them as a Mr. Rosenstein, though she was never precise in such recollections. The repeated but casual mention of this man's name in letters sent to St. Louis had her sedentary mother on a train to New York in no time. Likewise, his family was making inquiries about the St. Louis Hursts. Fannie hated it when he asked her if she, too, were Jewish, as if that should matter. But it did matter. "Suddenly he had less to explain to me, and I had less to explain to him," she wrote of the experience years afterward. "We were knowing each other with our blood. In a strange way, I felt exultant. For the first time, pride of race, which my snide snobbery had so long denied me, stirred." This was not enough, however, to goad her into what would have been a very appropriate marriage. The day he invited her home to meet his family, she dug out a frequently rejected story of hers in which a young girl faces her fiancé's family for the first time. In this clinical fashion Fannie wanted to pit her actual experience against that of her fictional character. The engagement was not to be. Though she had been given little to go on, and though Jacques Danielson was not yet back in New York, awareness of him floated through her consciousness "like a bit of dragging seaweed."

"The Paradise Trail"

By the beginning of 1913, Fannie had acquired an agent, Galbraith Welch. *Metropolitan* accepted its first story from Fannie, a resort romance called "Home Grown," for which Welch landed an eight-hundred-dollar payment and claimed the standard 10 percent fee. In half a year the value of a Fannie Hurst short story had nearly tripled.

Welch approached Fannie as manager as much as agent and got nervous when, in midexplosion, the new charge gave up living in the flat and took off for a summer holiday in Europe. Fannie always said she traveled steerage on this first trip, just for the experience.

With several stories in a backlog at the *Saturday Evening Post,* Fannie certainly felt entitled to some playtime. Welch, however, thought this unwise. In August he sent a letter off to Fannie in Rome, urging her to send back another story for *Metropolitan* or at least to get to work on a series she could peddle to *Cosmopolitan.* "Otherwise, I'll be in rather bad with the good editorial gentlemen I induced to be patient," he warned. If Fannie stopped working through the summer, what would there be left to print by the middle of 1914? "Your work will be out of the magazines for rather longer than is wise in the case of a reputation, which albeit brilliant, is very young," Welch said, "and when a new writer who has made a hit, produces nothing for a prolonged period, readers and editors are apt to think it's because he 'couldn't keep up.' "

Nevertheless, it took Fannie until the late fall of 1913 to send in another manuscript for sale, this one entitled "A Crimp in Human Hair." In the meantime Paul Revere Reynolds, a well-known agent, cozied up. He urged Fannie to call him, promising "something to say to you that I think might be to your advantage." Fannie had other agent dilemmas on her mind: Her New York mentor, Bob Davis, had begun his own venture in author representation and obviously expected Fannie to sign on with him. This was tricky. Fannie's devotion to Davis was unquestionable, but Welch already was deeply involved in building Fannie's career. In the end, under Davis's direction, Fannie got Welch to surrender dramatic and motion-picture rights to Davis, who in turn assured Fannie he could "offer the best returns."

"A Crimp in Human Hair" didn't sell very quickly. Actually, this is a tribute to the judgment of the top editors of the period. Though Fannie did not openly say so, she had written the story before she achieved celebrity status. Bob Davis had analyzed its shortcomings for her a year earlier. Putting it out for sale at this time was an apparent attempt to unload some mossy inventory, hoping her new star power would mitigate against the story's flaws. No chance. Welch told Fannie that *Metropolitan's* managing editor, Carl Hovey, was willing to buy it, even though it was "not quite commercially on the level of your usual run of work." He suggested she either take the time to repolish the story or reduce her fee. Fannie bluffed and held firm; Welch promised to try to get her market price. It was slow going.

"Breakers Ahead!" however, connected instantly. Welch read the story for the first time on January 29, 1914, and exuberated; he thought it was the best work Fannie had ever produced. This was the story of two small-town sisters, one of whom achieves her dream—at far too high a price—to be a star on the New York stage. Welch advised against placing the story in the *Saturday Evening Post,* where it would "fall in inconspicuously" with the rest of her stories. "It won't make the dent so published that it deserves to make, and I think that you should get from this story not only a good price, but also real attention of thinking people." Welch wanted to get it "attention of the very best kind."

Within thirty-six hours Welch had sent the story over to *Cosmopolitan* and received an eight-hundred-dollar offer for it. Not only that but the magazine promised to trumpet Fannie's arrival on its pages and to announce the story as the first of many. The check arrived within days. In the meantime Welch managed to sell "A Crimp in Human Hair" to *Cosmopolitan* as a follow-up to "Breakers Ahead!" but the magazine passed it to its sister publication, *Hearst's,* which published it in its July 1914 issue. Welch further arranged a meeting for Fannie with the editor of *Century Magazine. Pictorial Review* came after her on its own. Offers just showered in, either through Welch or unsolicited. Welch landed Fannie's first book contract, with Harper & Brothers, for a short-story collection, compiling the strongest of her early works for publication come September 1914.

"Breakers Ahead!" ran in the June 1914 issue of *Cosmopolitan* with major fanfare for Fannie, calling her "a realist—and one of the cleverest and wittiest that American Fiction has produced in many a long day." It said the story would "pull a little at your heartstrings . . . for it gives a true and lasting picture of what many and many an ambitious American girl is up against today in her natural efforts to escape from sordid surroundings and realize her dreams of success." The magazine enraged Fannie, however, by making changes and cuts in the story after she had corrected the proofs. This was something she could not abide. The editor was very apologetic about it and promised it would never happen again. Three years passed before another Fannie Hurst story appeared in *Cosmopolitan*.

In her new guise as literary dervish, she could not have been happier. In the five months between February and June 1914, Fannie had made $5,168 from her writing, including the $800 *Cosmopolitan* paid her for "A Crimp in Human Hair," which she had written a couple of years earlier. To Lois Meier, the most eternally impressed of her college friends, Fannie wrote:

> I am so busy!—so busy and so happy in just a whole raft
> of the most unbelievable new successes! Honestly, I wake
> up mornings pinching myself! Is it all true, say I—then
> thinking back on my dreary weeks of work I begin to feel
> sorry for myself and try to make myself believe I deserve
> what I am enjoying. But in my heart I know I don't. I'm
> meeting the most interesting and fascinating people,
> Lois—this is one day's programme (I just finished a
> story and am loafing this week). Lunch with the Harper
> Brothers (publishers) down in their quaint historic
> offices—in an old shiny mahogany dining room built
> right in the House of Harper—gray heads everywhere
> from the Harpers down to the butler who buttles—then a
> meeting with Tennyson Jesse—the poet's niece and the

girl who's created such a stir with her marvelous
writing—she is blonde—ingenue—and baby-eyed and
writes like Henry James! Then tea up here in my own
apartment with Maude Rutherford Warren, the writer,
and dinner tonight with Oscar Levin, the syndicate
writer—it's all such fun and I am so happy in my new
circle. . . . This letter has been again devoted to the
perpendicular pronoun but forgive!

Despite the very adult situation in which she found herself, Fannie's parents still exercised claim as if she were a schoolgirl, expecting her to spend long periods of time at home in St. Louis. She told Lois she would have liked to have them accompany her to Europe but probably would end up fitting into their plans. As Papa wrote her, "Mama is not inclined to get anything out of life except Cates Avenue." So Fannie spent part of the summer on vacation at the Casco Camps in West Poland, Maine, owned by Eva Rosenheim and her husband, Casper. She then dutifully headed out to St. Louis. Before leaving New York she signed an incredible new joint contract with *Metropolitan Magazine* and the *Saturday Evening Post*. Beginning September 1 she would divide her stories between the two prestigious publications, with *Metropolitan* paying a thousand dollars per story and the *Post* a like amount. As *Metropolitan's* Carl Hovey explained it to Fannie, "The arrangement leaves you free to send what you choose to Lorimer [at the *Post*] and what you choose to us. . . . How about a love story for October?"

Even more was brewing. Davis urged her to keep writing, just as Welch had the summer before. "Fanny [sic] Hurst is now a national institution," he wrote her in Maine, "and you can't spend any time sitting in the garden under a weeping willow, dreaming." American Film Co. made an offer for the film rights to her story "Superman," which the *Post* published June 20. In pencil across the initial request she wrote, "one hundred dollars per reel and 10 per cent of the gross." Fannie thought the producers should pay her the price of a short story for film rights, but American Film scoffed and withdrew the original offer. Hard to imagine, but in 1914 magazines reigned as the larger and vastly more lucrative outlet for fiction.

"Just Around the Corner"

The battles for Fannie's attention escalated. The agent Paul Revere Reynolds surfaced again while Fannie was in Maine during the summer of 1914. He tried to tempt her into his stable with news of editorial developments at *Cosmopolitan* that could work to her advantage. Though she had given him no authority to negotiate, he obtained from Edgar Sisson, the new *Cosmopolitan* editor, an in-principle agreement to pay a thousand dollars per installment for a serial Reynolds seemed convinced that Fannie was writing. She demurred. By the time Fannie got out to St. Louis, Galbraith Welch sent her a note asking if she had ever produced an Irish story suitable for dramatization. The theatrical agents Frank W. Sanger and Walter C. Jordan sought the rights to Fannie's story "The Spring Song." Bob Davis hounded her for new pieces: "What do you know about this war?" he asked, focused like everyone else on the dire events unfolding in Europe.

What Fannie knew about the war was that it had sent "up in smoke" her plan to spend the winter in Italy and Egypt. "Isn't it all too harrowing," she wrote her old friend Lois, "and just a year ago this month I did gaze upon The Hague little realizing it was builded of papier machier [sic]. Meanwhile of course I had sublet my apartment for the winter and here I am high and dry." She moved to the Hotel Brevoort in Greenwich Village for a couple of months, a place she described as "this old pension-like French hotel—much atmosphere (mostly garlic) soot red plush and Ritz-Carlton rates." By October she had rented a wonderful top-floor apartment on East Eleventh Street with fireplace, skylight, a twenty-seven-square-foot studio and three smaller chambers, kitchenette, and bath. "How are you liking my work?" Fannie asked Lois. "I'll have to get busy if I hope to keep up—they are releasing me [her stories] far too rapidly."

Just Around the Corner, Fannie's first short-story collection, came out on September 16, 1914, to mixed reviews. Harpers published it in a flimsy binding with covers of thin cardboard. It had one stock printer's ornament for decoration. Of the stories *The New York Times* said, "The workmanship is uneven and the tales are sometimes too strongly reminiscent of their models; but, if the author would be simply herself, and will avoid straining after effects, she has it in her to do good work in her chosen field." *The Independent* declared (in a sixty-word review), "Brevity would have made the stories better yet." Marion Reedy, understandably forgiving of Fannie's literary deficiencies, lavished praise on his protégée in his St. Louis–based magazine, now called *Reedy's Mirror*:

> There's a core of sound thought back of Miss Hurst's exuberant persiflagitiousness. . . . Her stories have movement and they have endings that arrest you. They tell themselves with a certain seeming flippancy which brings out pathos. . . . As Miss Hurst says I am her "literary godfather," in a personally inscribed copy of the book, I may herewith for her renounce all those traces in her work of the works and pomps of O. Henry, Edna Ferber and the author of "Red Saunders" [Henry Wallace Phillips], to say nothing of one Eugene Manlove Rhodes. But she is not a copyist. She writes like they do because she writes in the spirit of her time and place, in its language—

the language of New York with its connotation of ragtime. But she has a richness in her work those others have not, even when she compounds her adjectives to the fifth or sixth power. Her work pulses with joy and wonder of life, absurd or sad. . . . The Mirror School of Literature is proud of her and sees in her work the promise of yet better things, especially if she will ride her Pegasus and not let him run away with her. There's a peril before her. Too much punch isn't good for anything—not even for a story in these days when all the editors are clamoring for the punch.

The book sold about eleven hundred copies. Frederick A. Duneka of Harpers said that, despite the poor showing, the company was glad to have published it. "The war, as you know, has made everything impossible" was his explanation. Welch, in an aside to Fannie, agreed, basing his judgment on what had happened to other clients. "In practically every case we have had the same experience," he wrote, "that is, that sales have dropped off possibly more than half from what might have been expected if conditions had been normal."

The commercial performance of *Just Around the Corner* had zero impact on Fannie's standing in the magazine world. If anything, it enhanced it. Duneka of Harpers even used the opportunity of reporting the poor book sales to see if Fannie would like to write for *Harper's Magazine*. Welch pestered Fannie for the story synopsis she had promised to send him for possible sale to *Century*. Paul Revere Reynolds wrote again about yet another magazine that wanted stories from her. Welch pleaded urgently for a meeting to discuss serial use of Fannie's stories that would both "interest and flatter." Reynolds was relentless. "You say editors are hounding you for work," he wrote. "I think the time the agent can be of use to the author is when three or four magazines want their stories. Then, by finding out which editor would pay the most, by exciting a little healthy competition, he can get the best price for the author."

Metropolitan seemed displeased with its arrangement with Fannie on one score only: Hovey got miffed every time she offered the *Saturday Evening Post* a story that he wanted. In December 1914 *Metropolitan* put an end to that, offering Fannie a new contract at a rate 40 percent higher than the year before—fourteen hundred dollars per story. What's more, the agreement left her free to continue writing for the *Saturday Evening Post*—but only after *Metropolitan* had received and paid for its requisite six stories. It also forbade her writing for any of the Hearst publications, which included *Cosmopolitan* and *Hearst Magazine,* and other competitors, such as *Good Housekeeping* and *Harper's Bazar* (as the name was spelled then). Further, *Metropolitan* offered to buy and pay separately for any additional stories Fannie might choose to send its way. She negotiated this contract without Welch, indicating that whatever formal arrangement they may have had was over. As for the *Saturday Evening Post,* Bob

Davis, acting for Fannie, smoothed things over with his friend the managing editor, Churchill Williams. Davis told her afterward that the *Post* was "sorry as they can be but delighted that you are still in the family. You are not only forgiven," he wrote, "but I think the whole transaction will benefit you." He predicted that Fannie's star would "rise to the high zenith" in 1915.

Chapter *4*

"Other People's Shoes"

The Greenwich Village experience changed Fannie. By her own description she was never more than "on the rim of it," though the fumes of its rebellious energy and mind-exploding attitudes permeated her—by now—much, much freer thinking. John Reed lived there. So did the photographer Alfred Stieglitz and Max Eastman of *The Masses*, the young propagandist for suffrage and labor. A new radicalism had its center in this warren of close little streets jutting out at odd angles, sometimes triangulating back on themselves. Fannie, enamored of—and indebted to—"the people," embraced Socialism, in her way, on contact; her activism in other causes came more slowly. She had never even heard of the dynamic suffragist organizer Carrie Chapman Catt before she met her at lunch one day with George Lorimer and Churchill Williams of the *Saturday Evening Post*.

Fannie had never really given a thought to the question of women and the vote until her introduction to Catt, who immediately saw the value of recruiting the young midwestern sensation with the growing national reputation. "I had no intention of 'joining up,' " Fannie recalled later. "But in a strange way I could not put this woman all the way out of my mind." After the encounter Catt's name seemed to pop up everywhere, and something in her focus and zealotry awakened in Fannie the notion that she too could play some small part in influencing history.

As Fannie's social circle expanded, so did her social conscience. As early as 1914, and since by then she was starting to have the money to do it, Fannie moved to make her newly developed concern for the masses concrete: When a friendless prisoner at the Montana State Prison wrote her for help via the *Saturday Evening Post,* Fannie sent him enough money for a quilt and fifteen dollars in pocket money in anticipation of his release.

Political and world affairs had been well beyond the scope of Cates Avenue, St. Louis, while Fannie was growing up. Contrasts of wealth and poverty had never particularly disturbed her. "Not even the shantied segregation of the Negroes had risen to smite my consciousness," she recalled. She was too "socially somnolent" even to realize that there were no black students in her high school, which she had always thought was the only one in town. (It would be

1966 before it occurred to her to ask where the black youth of her childhood had studied.)

But New York blasted her out of her smugness "the hurting way." The contrasts were too vivid, their proximity to her daily life unescapable. There was never more than a city block or two between the liveried doormen and luxury shops and "the cats and children among the garbage cans." Experiencing the city was like seeing all the social dilemmas of the human race "written there with the high concentration of the Ten Commandments on the head of a pin."

∞

The filthy tumult of the Lower East Side, where so many immigrants ended up, drew Fannie in. In her words, "Despite the backwash of crime, the hordes of tired old people with prunelike eyes, the flabby-breasted women old at forty, the rickety-looking children, the life and hope of these sodden streets tingled through the soles of my shoes."

Below Fourteenth Street, boys and girls who by day drove trucks and worked in factories, machine shops, and behind counters studied law, vocations, arts, and sciences by night. Fannie once took her visiting mother to meet a family of Polish immigrants she had befriended. The wife had lost one eye in an anti-Jewish riot and fell down a flight of stairs with a baby in her arms. At twenty that child was still in a playpen, but one of the woman's sons had become a dentist; the other, a rabbi. What rich material it all was for fiction. Fannie told an interviewer that she was enamored of this fascinating community's "many loveable traits," yet her mother was mostly appalled by her daughter's fascination with these "foreigners" who took tea from glasses and ate strange saltless pretzels they called bagels. Mama refused to see the connection between them and her own father, David Koppel, who had arrived in America from Germany with a hundred dollars and the address of a cousin in Ohio. Nor could Fannie's mother relate the habits of these foreigners to her own mother's feather beds, homemade candles, barnyard skills, and German accent.

From St. Louis, in January 1915, Fannie declared to a reporter that the two great waves sweeping the working classes toward emancipation were feminism and socialism. (She also let drop that by 1914 she had become one of the three highest paid magazine contributors in the country. In fact, she had just turned down a twenty-thousand-dollar contract because it confined her work to one periodical for three years. Her success she modestly tossed off as "just a matter of grind.")

"I should think that everyone would realize that feminism has arrived," Fannie declared, clearly emboldened with the authority New York liked to bestow on its celebrity authors, regardless of their expertise in the subject matter at hand. Only recently she had lectured to the Suffrage League on polygamy and marriage.

As for suffrage, she told her interviewer, the movement lacked only the enthusiasm, vitality, and brains of American women of every walk of life—

especially those of "the silk and satin class." The wage-earning woman, Fannie predicted, ultimately would "beget suffrage" because "her blood is crying." Those more fortunate, she said, were "unlikely to start proclaiming from the front seats of their limousines." This, she said, reflected poorly on the women of America when compared with their British sisters. In England, she said, suffrage was "a vital, throbbing issue" for "duchess" and "slavey" alike.

The reporter duly transcribed Fannie's diatribe but went to pains to get her to talk about her personal life. Reluctantly, she revealed that she liked "dandy dancing." It was the reporter's own assertion that she was considered one of the smartest dressers in New York.

With her Virginia-bred cousin, the antiques dealer Mitteldorfer "Mittie" Straus, Fannie occasionally went to dances at Webster Hall and on escapades with another friend. She and Mittie liked to snoop about the little corners of lower New York. With Mama nowhere near to complain, Fannie finally could indulge her love of animals and start keeping pets, enough for *Vanity Fair* to salute her for having "the largest private menagerie in New York." Her new pal Fiorello La Guardia provided entrée to places she had not so much as thought about before. She moved from her wonderful studio on East Eleventh Street to an even more wonderful apartment at 126 Waverly Place, said to have been home to David Belasco at one time and O. Henry at another. Though Fannie could not vouch for the veracity of either claim, she delighted in imagining "the grand shade of O. Henry" overhead as she wrote. Mama visited once. She called the place a slum.

Someone else started to appear there, too. Fannie's roommate, Carolyn Aronsohn Lisberger, had the clearest recollection of the tentative first visit of Jacques Danielson, who was on the piano faculty of the New York College of Music at the time, while it was under the direction of Carl Hein and Augus Fraemcke. Years later Carolyn could still picture Jacques, "standing in the doorway . . . refusing to cross the threshold physically or psychologically."

∞

On October 23, 1915, Fannie found herself amid squads of women in military formation, assembling in bracing air for the New York Suffrage Parade. The event drew an estimated twenty-five thousand women and five thousand men. Though the older women, like Catt, were "firm-faced dowagers who caricatured easily," Fannie found in the younger activists a "long-stemmed casual quality." Their modish bobs and simple sporty clothes made her, once again, strangely different and apart from a group of women with whom she otherwise identified. They "spoke the language of lobbies, pressure groups, hearings, resolutions, chairmen, and delegations." All the same, Fannie fell in line, holding up one end of a banner with words she remembered as MOVE OVER, GENTLEMEN. WE HAVE COME TO STAY.

As Fannie recalled the story, Marie Jenney Howe had her hands around the banner's other pole. Her husband, Frederic, who had recently become U.S.

commissioner of immigration at the Port of New York, was marching among the men. Both of them had just read one of Fannie's stories and jumped at the opportunity to meet the popular new author. Fannie, in turn, was glad to befriend this pair of fiery liberals. It was Fred Howe who brought Fannie into the immigrant drama of Ellis Island, allowing her access to its newest arrivals.

For her part, Marie made a decided contribution to improving Fannie's feminist profile. She enlisted Fannie's membership in the Heterodoxy Club, which she had founded in 1912. Heterodoxy was an early bastion of feminist experimentation whose members dedicated themselves to exploring—through their own lives—the personal, sexual, spiritual, and psychological possibilities inherent in being new women. Fannie was never particularly active in the club, but she gladly left her name on its membership rolls. Years later, in 1921, along with other Heterodoxy luminaries such as Charlotte Perkins Gilman, Crystal Eastman, Zona Gale, Susan Glaspell, Fola La Follette, and Alice Duer Miller, Fannie signed the charter of the Lucy Stone League, a society for women who demanded the right to keep their maiden names in marriage (motto: "My Name is the Symbol of My Identity and Must Not be Lost"). Janet Flanner, the *New Yorker* writer known as Genêt, was another charter signatory.

The most delightful things just seemed to happen: Fannie's friend L. H. Bradshaw brought P. G. Wodehouse over for tea one day from his quarters at the Hotel Earle. A summons to tea came by visiting card from Willa Cather. In her tiny controlled hand, she noted that no one else would be present, as if Fannie required any added inducement. When Fannie first met Cather at a party, Cather told her that, if she were still editing magazines, she would want to publish Fannie's stories. Typically oversensitive, Fannie took this to mean that Cather did not personally think much of the work but understood its commercial appeal. "A bleeder under criticism, real or implied," Fannie said of herself, "I was affected by her words as if a buzz saw were cutting me." Cather, who had already published *O Pioneers!,* a work of high literary stature, could afford her wide popularity without fear of "losing caste with the intellectuals." Fannie, by contrast, had only a few short stories to show for her efforts.

At tea in her apartment on Bank Street, Cather was "a gracious woman in her aloof way," Fannie recalled, yet "the icy beauty of her writing, its glacial splendor, in contrast to my own ebullience served to reduce me to self-conscious silence in her presence." Fannie felt vulgar. "Her mind was a porcelain cup that held its content in perfect balance," she mused. "I slopped over into the saucer."

Back in March 1915, *Metropolitan Magazine* had offered Fannie the assignment of a lifetime: to accompany John Reed and Boardman Robinson, the illustrator, to the Russian front to study conditions in the war zone. Nellie Bly's moving and personal reports from the Serbian side had just appeared in the *New York Evening Journal.* Who better to see it from the other side than a writer like Fannie Hurst? Though Reed lived around the corner from Fannie on Washington Square South, the two had never met before the *Metropolitan* proposal. Reed gave Fannie elaborate instructions on how to obtain a passport for this journey, urging her to get a letter from the magazine saying that she was sailing at once and needed the document quickly.

Just before their scheduled departure, the three posed for a photograph, which ran months later in advertisements for *Metropolitan's* September issue, promoting the upcoming report from the Russian front with Serbia. But when the story ran it carried Reed's byline alone. For reasons that became clear only much later, Fannie never made the boat.

"The Name and the Game"

The most successful editors worked meticulously at keeping their best writers happy. They understood how important good editorial relations were to a writer's ability and willingness to produce his or her best possible work. These men—and in Fannie's early experience they almost always were men—harbored no illusions about how they got and kept their own standing. They relied on their writers to keep their magazines competitive. Thus, no birthday passed unshowered with flowers. No story arrived in manuscript that did not get a detailed and enthusiastic critique by return mail. A great one could elicit an appreciative flood.

Carl Hovey, then managing editor of *Metropolitan*, for example, was superb at this. When Fannie's first story under the new contract of 1915 arrived in manuscript, Hovey wrote at once. " 'Ever Ever Green' is great!" he said. "It is real literature. It is big enough to satisfy everybody and fine enough to warm the heart and excite the brain of the eternal seeker of genuine creation." He went on:

> Every sentence pays—out of the details grows a shocking picture, tenderness and humor are natural qualities throughout—nothing is put in for effect—the whole is inbred with a forceful sincerity—it lives—and, as a narrator, how surely you have sustained the innate drama—one reads to the very end with feeling, with intensity. Such work makes measure that the day is coming—I mean the day of first rate writing in this country—you have it—the combination of sincerity with art. What craftsmanship—

In the same mail he had sent a note of abject never-will-happen-again apology (blaming the proofreader) for spelling Fannie's name wrong on an earlier cover. Three days later, in a note about photographs, he felt the need to emote all over again, as if to distance his praise from the apology. "No writer," he told Fannie, "not Joseph Conrad or any other celebrated artist, works on a higher plane than you reached in this story." He said the work had the "profound unconscious reader's interest that you find in Kipling and O. Henry." He assessed its merit against formidable competition. The March 1915 issue of *Metropolitan,* in which it was to appear, also included works by Theodore Roosevelt, Richard Harding Davis, Rupert Hughes, Booth Tarkington, and John Reed.

In "Ever Ever Green," Lola Lalladay, a pretty, wily, very ambitious performer with a traveling vaudeville troupe, has the romantic attention of both the show's producer, Charley Lee, and her partner on the high wire, Al Delano. A trapeze accident paralyzes Al and confines him to a wheelchair. Lola blames herself, even though the accident was not entirely her fault. Without hesitation, though she has the producer's affection and is in line to become star of the show, she quits to devote herself to taking care of Al. They marry and go to live in a cottage provided by Al's old friend Ben, who is their sole support. Though she had teased Al mercilessly before the accident, its impact on his life transforms Lola. She becomes loving and giving. Al, who is dying, lets Lola know that he would like her to marry Ben after he dies. He knows that Ben cares for her and will take care of her.

Soon after Al's death Charley and the troupe return to town for one performance only. They have to take a late train to make their next engagement. Charley comes to visit Lola after the show. He tells her how much publicity her act of sacrifice generated and offers to give her the star spot if she will pack in time to make the train. Lola is tempted. She has no other known prospects, since she hasn't spoken to Ben. But she hesitates; she doesn't want to leave without telling Ben good-bye. Charley berates her. He tells her how trashy it looks for her to be involved with Ben now that Al is dead, as if to suggest the two were having an affair while Al was alive. Lola is appalled and hurt that Charley could even think such a thing, turning both her and Ben's righteous acts toward a dying friend into something tawdry. Charley sees his tactical error and apologizes but at the same time urges her to pack quickly. The opportunity to star in his show, he reminds her, is one she simply cannot afford to pass up. As Charley heads for the station to meet the rest of his troupe, Lola packs. The train whistle blows. As she heads toward the door, she hears Ben's footsteps on the walkway.

The story rated three stars on the honor roll of Edward J. O'Brien's *Best Short Stories of 1915.* O'Brien, a critic for the *Boston Transcript,* compiled a detailed annual assessment of the year's short-story production among the established authors. In all, half the Fannie Hurst stories published in 1915 rated honored mention in the volume.

In his introduction O'Brien wrote, "I must affirm once more the genuine literary art of Fannie Hurst. The absolute fidelity of her dialogue to life and its revealing spirit, not despite, but rather because of the vulgarities she accepts, seems to me to assure her permanence in her best work." Later he made a point of telling her personally that another reviewer for the *Boston Transcript* considered her "T.B.," a story about love and awareness among consumptives, the best in O'Brien's book that year. This was some fine way for a woman author to turn thirty, even if she was only admitting to twenty-five.

Bob Davis was right about Fannie reaching her zenith in 1915. But this was only the first of many and higher ones. Mama would pressure Fannie with her daily letters, making it clear that her New York fling should end, that Papa's patience, as well as his health, was wearing thin, and that Mama was bearing the brunt. Fannie's reaction was to write short stories as if her life depended on their excellence. She raced "against return," against the image of her father asleep with a newspaper covering his face after a heavy midday Sunday meal, against Mama and her kaffeeklatsches, "against the whirring of crickets in the silence after ten o'clock at night," against the woman across the street who did everything at the same hour day after day. "She hated her husband," Fannie remembered, "told Mama so—and there they were, lying side by side in the black monotony of Cates Avenue—there I would be, only lying by nobody's side, and looking into the blackness and wondering."

In letters to Lois Meier back in St. Louis, there were no such confessions, but there were others: "It seems to me that the greatest milestone of my life occurred when I 'broke' away and into this full and busy and happy life. Where folks are *doing*—where one is not smothered beneath the wet blanket of conservatism, where the soil is rich and does not prohibit growth."

Learning of Lois's marriage plans, Fannie bemoaned the entering of her own "twenty-umph" year "unloved, unlearned and unwed!" Even on paper there seemed to be cheer and a wink to this lament.

As Fannie reeled off her social calendar to Lois by letter, it might have occurred to her dazzled friend that a marked elevation had taken place in the cultural caliber of Fannie's evenings, with a distinct musical bias. Fannie wrote of hearing Geraldine Farrar and Enrico Caruso sing *Carmen*; of hearing the pianist Ossip Gabrilowitsch in recital, assisted by his wife, Clara Clemens, the daughter of Mark Twain. "Afterwards, I met them at tea," Fannie wrote. "He is of[-]the[-]world worldly and I immediately found in her a kindred soul. She's the sort of woman whose [*sic*] never quite sure of herself, good-natured enough but stumbling—falls over her words and dress train—blushes too easily—etc., etc."

Fannie even mentioned an important theatrical "first-night" she was looking forward to: the opening of Edward Sheldon's *Garden of Paradise*. It wasn't much of a leap to realize that this shift in interest and Fannie's enthusiasm over it may have had less to do with her ever-advancing status as a New York celebrity than with the man in her life. Quietly and without comment, it appears that Jacques Danielson's duties, by the fall of 1914, had begun to extend well beyond the role of escort. Carl Hovey, in his diatribe about "Ever Ever Green," requested new photographs from Fannie to run with the story in March. He rejected two prints that she had sent over, adding matter-of-factly that they "were not so good as the one I had from Mr. Danielson—what I wanted was that very one."

"Rolling Stock"

By the spring of 1915, six months before her thirtieth birthday and nearly five years into her phenomenal New York adventure, Fannie's literary status had been secured. Elizabeth Garver Jordan, a well-known and respected editor, befriended her and began inviting her to lunch with the likes of Gertrude Atherton, Mary Austin, and Frances Hodgson Burnett. After that Fannie almost always gave a tea for Atherton when she visited New York from her home in San Francisco. Even more gratifying were certainly the extremely flattering references to Fannie in the May issues of both *Harper's Monthly* and *Vanity Fair.*

Vanity Fair nominated Fannie to the year's Hall of Fame "because she has shown us the true heart of the Jewish people. Because in her stories she always combines pathos and humor. . . . Because she has made unhappy shop girls appear as heroines." The caption, which also mentioned her pets, appeared under a dramatic photograph of Fannie in profile by Gerhard Sisters. In it she wears a black drape over her shoulders against a dark studio background, her dark hair softly parted down the middle and loosely drawn over her ears into a low bun. Wisps of hair escape on the side of her face not visible to the camera, the stray hairs blown forward as if by a soft wind. The profile shot and Fannie's sharp and purposeful chin line artfully camouflage the fullness of her face. She is dramatic, beautiful; a presence.

In *Harper's Monthly,* William Dean Howells devoted his "Editor's Easy Chair" column to a perusal of the various portrayers of New York life in fiction. In his view the first rank of writers on Jewish subjects included the English novelist and playwright Israel Zangwill, along with Abraham Cahan and Montague Glass. Quickly, though, he added Fannie, saying she deserved to be named alongside these men for "the same artistic qualities, the same instinct for reality, the same confident recognition of the superficial cheapness and commonness of the stuff she handles" and "for the gift of penetrating to the heart of life."

Three months later *Vanity Fair* also singled out Fannie for recognition in an article entitled "New York Women Who Earn $50,000 a Year." Remarkably, there were more than a dozen New York women who fit that description in 1915. Fannie fell in the much larger group of fifty women earning in the $10,000-a-year range. Her actual earnings for 1915 were $13,200, but $4,200 had not been collected by the end of the tax year. The writer Anne O'Hagan said all of these powerful earners had sent the government a preprinted slip with their tax payment, courtesy of the Suffrage Movement: "I pay this tax under protest," it read, "in obedience to a law in the making of which I had no voice."

As it happened Fannie had enough deductions that year to keep her total tax bill down to $40.65. She spent $400 for the year to rent a writing studio—it appears her apartment had become too crowded—$1,200 for "travel for color," $10 a month in telephone calls, $50 for materials, $75 to buy a typewriter, and $500 in entertaining. By 1916 she had moved out of the Village apartment and returned to the Upper West Side, living for several months at 116 West Fifty-ninth Street and renting a studio at Carnegie Hall before moving on to a brand-new skylit building of studio apartments at 12 West Sixty-ninth Street in December, into a "distractingly attractive" little apartment with "monastery doors, old rugs, steps up and down, Gothic windows and a scatter-brained puppy to amuse her." It would be home for the next seven years. Only two stories high, the structure was built low to keep from blocking the light of the apartment house next door at 88 Central Park West. The 1917 city directory lists Jacques Danielson with an apartment at the same building address.

∽

"Sob Sister" was Fannie's first story about the rotten life of a mistress, this one with armored-tank tracks across the surface of her heart. It so excited *Metropolitan's* editors that they decided to assign the sought-after George Bellows, who taught at the Ferrer School, to illustrate it. Carl Hovey thought the Bellows drawings combined with a Fannie Hurst story would give "a regular predreadnought effect. It will be great!" His boss, H. J. Whigham, wrote Fannie in St. Louis to endorse the idea, saying Bellows's illustrations had a far more powerful draw than those of Fannie's usual illustrator at *Metropolitan,* May Wilson Preston. As an aside Whigham told Fannie it was a good thing she hadn't traveled to Russia with Reed and Robinson. Both had managed to get themselves thrown in prison.

By August 1915, *Metropolitan* had a backlog of Fannie's stories but got huffy every time she wanted to sell elsewhere. Charles Hanson Towne tried to get a Fannie Hurst story for *McClure's.* Whigham opposed the idea adamantly, even though her contract did not expressly forbid her publishing there. He argued that *McClure's* was a class below *Metropolitan* and therefore potentially damaging to Fannie's—and hence *Metropolitan's*—reputation. In addition, its new size made it more of a direct competitor to *Metropolitan* than it had been when Fannie signed her contract. He simply did not like the idea of a writer closely associated with his magazine writing also for a lesser competitor. "And I feel this more strongly in your case than in the case of any other authors," Whigham told her, "because I regard your stories as helping to stamp the character of the magazine more than any other fiction we are now publishing." In the end Fannie declined *McClure's* offer, allowing Whigham to see the gesture as her respectful concession to his wishes. The fact was Towne had been unable to offer anywhere near the amount *Metropolitan* paid per story.

At the same time Whigham encouraged Fannie to think about writing a play or at least dramatizing one of her existing stories, an idea she had long had in the back of her mind. He said a couple of people from the Stage Society of New York had approached him about it. The prospect clearly enticed her; by December she had signed a fifty-fifty collaboration agreement with the playwright Harriet Ford to develop a work for the stage.

Chapter 5

"Oats for the Woman"

*M*etropolitan adorned every streetcar in Manhattan with Fannie's portrait and the announcement that she would write six more stories for the magazine in 1916. Bob Davis thought she looked ridiculous in the photograph, especially the cerise hat, which he likened to "a big German pretzel," or better, "a cross between the wreath set upon the brow of Nero and the hand-chiseled capital on the top of a column holding up the front facade of the Third Presbyterian Church in Yonkers. That certainly is some lid." So much for criticism of his own high amateur photographs of her! Fannie had a steadily growing penchant for extreme and attention-getting hats. All the same, she immediately wrote to the head of *Metropolitan's* circulation department to complain about the posters.

The book publishers were after Fannie again; everyone seemed to think it was time for her to write a novel, though none was forthcoming. She and Harriet Ford were still at work on their stage play. Harper & Brothers contracted to bring out a new short-story collection in the fall, to be titled *Every Soul Hath Its Song.* Surely the prestigious publishing house was lying in wait for a novel, for even with an author like Fannie Hurst a short-story collection was murder to market. Though Fannie had agreed to write for *Metropolitan* for what amounted to another year, she wanted to move on. January was not ten days old when the literary agent Paul Revere Reynolds surfaced again, sending over the draft of a lucrative but limiting agreement for Fannie to write for *Cosmopolitan,* the Hearst magazine. She had long ago outpriced the magazines Bob Davis ran, but their friendship endured, and he took a loving and paternal interest in her affairs, asking nothing in return. "Believe me, you are the limit," he wrote her in St. Louis. She had spent the Christmas holidays with her family and stayed on a couple of weeks into the new year. "It would take you only a few months to so entangle yourself that you or all the lawyers in the world could not possibly extricate the charming Fannie Hurst from the confusion created by her own acts." He urged her to hire the attorney Dennis O'Brien to "keep you immune from the typhus of conversation and the dyspepsia of commerce." Davis advised her to bring back from St. Louis all the documents, papers, and memoranda of the past three years concerning her agreements with agents and whoever else had insinuated themselves into her messy business dealings. Some people were wondering why he had stuck his nose into her business affairs, but he felt he had no choice. "The fact of the matter is, you are the very worst business woman I have ever known," he told her, "and you must be protected against yourself." Fannie hired O'Brien to negotiate a deal with *Cosmopolitan*'s editor Edgar Sisson. It took the better part of the year.

In the meantime there were her social causes to consider. She accepted the Authors' League's invitation to serve on a committee to consider its possible affiliation with the American Federation of Labor. And although she liked to imagine herself as a reliable worker bee, giving tirelessly to a worthy cause like woman suffrage in the way of Carrie Chapman Catt or Marie Jenney Howe, it wasn't really in her nature. In these early days, when suffragist organizers would call on her to make appearances ("Be at the Truly Warner Hat Store on Wednesday") or to perform some lowly task such as selling tickets or staffing a booth at a fair or attending a meeting, she tried to oblige. But before long both the organizers and Fannie herself realized that, although she meant well, too many other demands on her time took precedence. What she did best was to lend her celebrated name to a cause she believed in. She wrote and signed letters of appeal, she spoke in public on an organization's behalf, or appeared for what later would become known as a photo opportunity. This is not to diminish the importance or generosity of her contributions, which the recipients invariably solicited and deeply appreciated. But they also did double service for Fannie, enhancing her image and generating both subliminal and overt personal publicity of the best kind.

About midyear Fannie's editor-friend Elizabeth Garver Jordan came along with a proposition of the sort Fannie did not hesitate to accept: to donate Chapter 3 of a composite novel by fourteen famous authors, based on a theme by Mary Austin. The purpose of *The Sturdy Oak,* a "novel of American politics," was to promote woman suffrage and raise funds for the cause. This was in conjunction with the fall 1917 campaign for the New York suffrage referendum. *Collier's* ran the novel in magazine serial form starting September 22, and Henry Holt & Co. agreed to publish it as a book. Both publishers' checks went to the movement. Austin contributed a chapter, as did Samuel Merwin, Kathleen Norris, William Allen White, Dorothy Canfield, Alice Duer Miller, Leroy Scott, Harry Leon Wilson, Henry Kitchell Webster, Anne O'Hagan, Mary Heaton Vorse, Ethel Watts Mumford, and Marjorie Benton Cooke. All the authors signed over their royalties, for which they were roundly congratulated. Even *Reedy's Mirror* said that, as a novel, the book was "surprisingly satisfactory."

As it turned out *Metropolitan* published only four of Fannie's stories in 1916. *Collier's* ran "Ice Water, Pl———," the first of her many boardinghouse tales, and the *Saturday Evening Post* snared "In Memoriam," a poignant story about German Jewish immigrants who succeed, escaping the Lower East Side for life in a mansion peopled by cooks, housemaids, and butlers commanded in a coarse and appalling English by selfish children and their unselfish and loving mother. Edward J. O'Brien declared "Ice Water, Pl———" one of Fannie's best stories ever. He gave it three stars and reprinted it in *The Best Short Stories of 1916*. Rupert Hughes, a well-established and popular short-story writer, told Fannie the work was simply overwhelming, "irresistibly melting in its pathos and its tenderness," and one of the best stories both he and his wife had ever read. He urged her to turn it into a stage play, though she never did.

Of the stories included in her new collection, it was "Sob Sister," Fannie's first cautionary tale about the life of a spurned mistress, that got the most enthusiastic response. O'Brien credited Fannie for deft handling, saying the story "gains tremendous emotional values without any sacrifice to sentimentality."

Other critics, particularly one for *The New York Times,* were even more effusive. Its reviewer called the story "brutal, but it is also strong, a bit of realism that grips in every line of its tense dialogue, in its impassive objectivity.

> This is the story of Mae Munroe, "herself one of the pink-cheeked grenadiers of that great army whose destiny is as vague as the destiny of pins, and who in more than one vain attempt to climb had snagged her imitation French embroidery petticoats on the outward side of that barbed wire fence." It is a story of raw emotions, with every delicacy shamed; of a woman with mouth too loose and weight too gross; of florid disorder and or sordid situation.
>
> For five years Mae Munroe had lived with Max Zincas. She knew how to broil his steak and how to cook his gravy. She had given him her body—oh, very literally given to him of it. For when burns were like "hell's fire" on his back, she had made the doctors take flesh from her by inches to graft on his burns.
>
> "It was like finding a new way of saying how—I love you, Max. Every drop of blood was like—like I could see for myself—how I loved you, Max."
>
> She tells him this because, after a long absence, Max has come but to leave her. Max is going to marry a decent girl, a young girl because, as he explains, "the world's just built thataway."
>
> In themselves, Death and Birth are not delicate. Nor have any dignity but of the soul they bear with them. And it is the essential greatness of this story that through the grotesqueries and contortions of emotional birth and death pangs we stand in awe before the unveiling of a human soul.

After reading "Sob Sister" in *Metropolitan,* the writer Kathleen Norris, a new friend of Fannie's since *The Sturdy Oak,* wrote to say it was "quite the biggest short story I know about since Kipling was in his prime, and I can't tell you how I hate to read anything so good with another woman's name on it!"

For his part, O'Brien prophesied that Fannie's works "may prove to be the most essential literary documents of our city life for the inquiring literary historian of another century" and then leveled the criticism that would dog her entire career: "Their defect is a lack of economy and selective power."

"Thine Is Not Mine"

What remained of Fannie's Missouri accent disappeared, and the carefully cultivated Middle Atlantic girls' school affectation took permanent hold over her public speech. She had celebrity status; a unique combination of ideas, presentation, operatic appearance, and stature; a knack for the pithy comment and the considered remark, if not the quick, sharp rejoinder. She had drawing power. As early as 1916 she had become a sought-after commentator in both lecture halls and the press, which had the added advantage of creating new and lucrative income streams.

Fannie's subject matter centered on literary topics but also ranged well beyond them. *The Public Ledger,* for example, asked her to write about the dearth of domestic help caused by the slowdown in immigration and the war. The editor supplied the research. Even before the United States entered the conflict, orders for war material from Allied Europe had U.S. factories working at full capacity. The increased demand for factory labor, in turn, drastically reduced the number of workers willing to take jobs in private homes—even at comparable wages. "I presume it may be worth a few cents a week even to the poorest to be called 'Miss Jones' instead of 'Mary,' " Fannie wrote. She argued that homemakers would have a better time finding and keeping cooks and maids if they improved their working conditions, sleeping quarters, and hours. "Women, there are more of you today who want competent and satisfied servants than who want the vote," Fannie said. "Scout out your housemaid's third-floor back. Why is it the mausoleum of her social position, freedom, dignity and ambition? The servant girl problem and the servant girl's problem are Siamese twins, fed by the same arteries."

Fannie raised these same issues seven years later in her novel *Lummox.* The subject also created an impetus for Fannie's eventual and enduring friendship with Eleanor Roosevelt. As for topics closer to her natural expertise, Fannie was every bit as opinionated. To the book columnist John Nicholas Beffel, she decried the public clamor for "punch" in fiction, which editors invariably demanded and which she dismissed as "almost the most destructive requirement in drama and literature in these times.

"It indicates a perverted taste," she said, "a superexcited state of mind and intellect, to be so crazy about the unexpected and weird; to demand such hectic, cayenne-pepper writing." It is interesting that, in roughly the same time period, *The Nation* called Fannie "a mistress of the post-Henry tricks: punch (as her school would say) is her middle name."

The poet Joyce Kilmer, already famous for "Trees," asked Fannie if he could interview her by letter for a series of profiles he was doing for *The New York Times Magazine*. Along with Fannie, Kilmer interviewed twenty-two other big-name authors, including William Dean Howells, Kathleen Norris, Booth Tarkington, Montague Glass, Rex Beach, John Erskine, Amy Lowell, and Ellen Glasgow.

In her responses Fannie again lashed out at magazine editors for preferring "chocolate fudge" fiction to literature. A writer, she added, would be better able to withstand the pressure to pander to the lowest level of popular taste—to keep from "the possibility of 'misshaping' his art to meet a commercial condition"—if writing didn't also have to pay the rent. Of course, since she herself worked best by daylight from 9:00 A.M. until 4:00 P.M. and needed at least twenty days to complete one story, she was first to admit her proposal wasn't very practical.

A critic writing in *The Nation* remarked on how difficult it was to judge Fannie and her most successful peers on merit since they never got a free hand to develop their own style and matter. The necessity to conform to the rigid requirements of popular-magazine writing meant they had to be judged "like public dancers who clog or dip according to contract." Though Fannie always claimed she never shaped a story to meet an editor's expectations but simply wrote as she was driven, the fact is her stories met and continued to meet the expectations of editors with numbing consistency.

She had an opinion about rumblings that the Authors' League might affiliate with the American Federation of Labor. Though Fannie's sympathies were decidedly with labor, she said an author was of a special breed of worker who could not really "lay aside his pen when the whistle blows." Nor, for that matter, could a publisher deal in "open shop literature."

What about the fledgling motion-picture industry and its impact on fiction? So far, nothing good, Fannie said. "Picturized fiction is on a cheap and sensational level. Even classics and standardized fiction are ruthlessly defamed by tawdry presentation." Spectaculars such as D. W. Griffith's groundbreaking Civil War epic, *The Birth of a Nation*, were fine, she said, because in such cases, "the play is not the thing." She ventured no comment on the controversy that film had generated for its derogatory depiction of black people, nor was she asked. But generally speaking, she said, scenario writing was still in too infantile a stage to judge. Fannie did let drop that Frances Hodgson Burnett thought her *Little Lord Fauntleroy* had been so mutilated in F. Martin Thornton's 1914 film version that the author had not been able to sit through it.

Fannie did not support Kilmer's contention that the unsurpassed master of the short story was Edgar Allan Poe. Though she agreed that Poe had formulated a "law of composition" which strongly influenced his successors, she could also name—without thinking very hard—nine short-story writers since Poe who had contributed classics to the literature: Robert Louis Stevenson, Henry James, Bret Harte, Mark Twain, Mary E. Wilkins Freeman, O. Henry, Richard Harding Davis, Jack London, and Booth Tarkington.

Kilmer asked Fannie's opinion of a recent charge by Katharine Fullerton Gerould that O. Henry had left a "pernicious influence" on modern letters— that he wrote incidents, not stories. Fannie argued that although the structure of O. Henry's work was frail and sometimes rested "upon the trick, he builds with Gothic skill and with no obvious pillars of support." And, she said, if O. Henry's facetiousness and structural frailty were at issue, then so were the extravagance of Poe's plots and his "morbid formality."

"Sob Sister"

Not only were Fannie's opinions being solicited but with forty-six stories published in national magazines between 1912 and the end of 1916, opinions about Fannie's work had become stock-in-trade. William Dean Howells at *Harper's* already had classed her in the first rank of writers on Jewish subjects. Early in 1916 a critic for the *Boston Transcript* went so far as to elevate her to the level of O. Henry's successor. O'Brien, in his introduction to *The Best Short Stories of 1916,* went one further, saying that Fannie interpreted "with fine democratic heart the heart of the American people as adequately as Mark Twain or O. Henry." (This utterly delighted Bob Davis, a great friend of O. Henry until his death in 1910. "The Lord knows where you are going," Davis wrote Fannie in a fit of pride. "But I saw you coming.")

With the publication of her second short-story collection, O'Brien set Fannie "among the four or five permanent short story writers of our generation." He also mentioned that the depiction of Fannie on the promotional packet her publisher sent out with the book made her look "like one of them Egyptian empresses." Davis chimed in after his copy arrived, "I never made a single prophesy [*sic*] about you that you didn't fulfill."

The columnist Sidney Baldwin declared straight out, "There is no other writer in Fannie's class, except possibly Edna Ferber, and she [Fannie] has the same trick of elevating a commonplace situation that O. Henry had, though, unlike his terse writing, hers flowers at every point." Through his column in *McClure's,* the magazine's managing editor, Charles Hanson Towne, invited young writers to come forward. "We are all looking eagerly for the O. Henry, the Edna Ferber, the Fannie Hurst who is probably at this moment sitting at a typewriter in some obscure town, hoping for recognition." Even the young F. Scott Fitzgerald, in a letter to his editor, Max Perkins, referred to Fannie and Ferber as "the Yiddish descendents of O. Henry." (Fitzgerald, in *This Side of Paradise,* has his character Tom name an incorrectly spelled Fanny Hurst among the "fifty-thousand dollars a year" literary sensations who had "not produced among 'em one story or novel that will last ten years.")

In a piece for *Cosmopolitan,* her fellow author Kathleen Norris declared Fannie "a genius" who had made the short story peculiarly her own, her work defying analysis like "the old mystery of the flower in the crannied wall." Fannie had written her own appreciation of Norris for the November issue of *Good Housekeeping* a year earlier, and Fannie was developing a friendship with both Kathleen and her husband, the author Charles Norris. Charles wrote Fannie warm, teasing, sometimes fawning letters. When Douglas Z. Doty, the acting editor at *Cosmopolitan*, first read Kathleen's column, he wrote Fannie to say it would make her ears ring. "It's not fulsome praise," he said, "but an understanding and convincing tribute to the lady she regards as master of the short story."

Norris sent on her own final edit to Fannie for perusal. The letter that accompanied the copy is worth quoting at length:

> Here you are, and of all flat sensations in the world,
> the flattest is the one you will have when reading this.
> But I beg of you not to blue-pencil the blarney, I mean it
> all, just because it makes you feel "silly," nobody need
> know that you ever read it, [I mean it all—moved here in
> editing mark] and anyway it's true— . . . Just read it, and
> correct too flagrant errors of grammar and spelling and
> pack it off to Douglas Doty in the enclosed envelope. . . .
> I didn't know whether you were in the twenties or teens.
> I had a lovely time at your house, and told my husband
> that you looked as handsome as somebody's tame
> panther; he was with difficulty kept off the Eighth
> Avenue car—you know these military men! Don't forget
> me the next time you ask Basil King; or I'll learn you to
> let my discoveries alone! Yours for blatant and unladylike
> publicity,
> Kathleen Norris.

In the article, Norris said of Fannie's peculiar method: "The apparently rambling conversations develop the plot in a series of hammer-strokes, and the sobbing ejaculations, in their aimless repetition, have a perfectly human fashion of wringing the heart." She said there were certain of Fannie's stories she could never reread without tears.

The comparisons of Fannie to both O. Henry and Edna Ferber were inevitable, and the similarities, in both cases, were obvious. O. Henry and Fannie both wrote about New York and both sometimes drew their subject matter from boardinghouse and apartment life. Both depended on the manner of telling the story, and both showed, in the words of one latter-day critic, the same fondness for "the trenchant word and the telling phrase." Fannie, however, the critic said, subordinated these values to the development of her theme and the working out of a plot. O. Henry, by contrast, rarely bothered about a plot and instead let his clever words and phrases serve as entertaining interludes.

As for Ferber, both she and Fannie were midwestern Jewish girls who were born the same year. They also sometimes picked similar subject matter, often involving the Jewish immigrant class. Both had "uncommon storytelling powers," which they introduced to readers through the short story. Unlike Fannie, Ferber was always comfortable with, even proud of, being Jewish. Grant Overton, a well-known magazine editor of the time, once explained other areas of "cleavage" between the two. Ferber, he said, was finite in her outlook, able to understand and portray a full range of human emotion. Her perspective, though, was that of ordinary human experience. "When one of her characters suffers racking grief," Overton explained, "it is over the disappointment of some ideal that everybody can grasp." In Fannie's work, he said, there is another dimension, "something not fully comprehended in average emotional capacity, something in excess of the normal."

A critic in *The Nation* saw both women as prime contenders in a crowded field for the crown of leading "feminine O. Henry," but Fannie, who carried to "sublime pitch" the philosophical or descriptive introduction, was the more daring. Over the course of a long writing life, it was one of the few compliments she would ever get for her strange style of wrestling with words, though even this praise included a disclaimer: "She flings herself at language and tosses it about as if it were only her business what she does with it. She has a real instinct for it as a fluid, flexible, living thing. Unhappily, she has also an impulse to distort it for momentary effect."

It was natural that Ferber and Fannie would get to know each other in this period and that they would make the effort to become friends. They had so much in common, and, in Ferber's words, they experienced "something pleasant" when they chanced to meet up. It was also understandable that in their attempts to strike up a real friendship, they would never succeed.

"On the Heights"

*H*arper's made a pass at trying to get Fannie to write for its magazine, and *Metropolitan* did its best to hold on to her. It took a year of negotiation, but *Cosmopolitan* finally brought Fannie Hurst's byline onto its pages with an offer of $1,750 per story, effective January 1, 1917. To give the very high fee, Edgar Sisson, the editor, demanded an exclusive three-year contract, to which Fannie reluctantly agreed, sealing her reputation as the country's "highest paid short story writer." The truth was *Cosmopolitan* had been paying Booth Tarkington $2,000 per story under a nonexclusive arrangement for better than a year.

Though these were momentous events in Fannie's professional life, they happened at a time when they could be no more than white noise to a "breathless period of waiting, with the whole country on tiptoe." This was Fannie's description of the anticipated U.S. declaration of war on Germany during the early months of 1917. "It's difficult to think in any except international terms," she wrote in a letter to Lois Meier Toensfeldt in mid-February. "Each day may bring forth an epoch-smashing decision." It came April 6. Two months later Fannie was promoting the sale of Liberty Bonds. Sisson took a leave of absence from *Cosmopolitan* to serve on the U.S. Committee on Public Information, leaving Fannie and her brand-new contract in the hands of the acting editor, Douglas Doty.

By June the war motif had infiltrated her stories of families and mistresses, shopgirls and immigrant Jews. Now the mistress has a gruff, predatory arms dealer for a lover; now the Hollywood filmmaker lucks into saving his daughter from a heartless gold digger's wedding band when the scoundrel happens to sail off to Europe on the *Lusitania*; now a long-suffering woman can slip her boyfriend out of the tenacious clutch of his widowed mother by convincing him to enlist. The newspaper columnist Dorothy Dix wrote to Fannie to extoll "Sieve of Fulfillment," the story of an earnest and loving woman cruelly abandoned by both her husband and son, and how the simple act of knitting woolen vests for soldiers overseas restored her passion for life. "I do not think any American writer has ever done anything bigger or finer," Dix said, "or that was so photographic of a certain phase of our life."

In July 1917 the immigrant drama Fannie cowrote with Harriet Ford, *Land of the Free,* had its out-of-town tryout at the Savoy Theatre in Asbury Park, New Jersey. It starred the popular Florence Nash and even included a small part Fannie had finagled for an old St. Louis friend, Nancy Saunders.

The producer, William A. Brady, was unhappy with the ending. Fannie suggested an alternative—she wanted to bring an "aeroplane" onto the stage in the last act—but Brady hated that idea just as much. Three weeks before the projected Broadway premiere, Brady insisted the two writers either draft a new ending along lines he was suggesting or allow him to have it written by someone else. Fannie took exception, evidently reminding Brady that he ought not to second-guess a writer whose work always commands thousands of dollars from story-hungry editors.

Brady shot back: "This is my game not yours. I've had thirty years success behind me producing this kind of play and rarely when I am enthusiastic about a play, as I am about this, have I gone wrong."

The show opened October 2 at the Forty-eighth Street Theatre to nice reviews, though some did mention the weak second act. The *New York Times* critic said Nash's performance "seemed limited only by the inadequacy of the scenes she had to work with." Anna Steese Richardson, writing in *McClure's,* celebrated the ascendancy of the woman playwright on Broadway—eight women's plays had appeared in the 1917 season alone. Fannie, she wrote, was so gifted she could walk up to a notions counter, buy a bolt of braid, and find out at the same time all there was to know about the salesgirl's love life. In *Land of the Free,* Richardson said, Fannie had "thrown new light on the character of the Jewish immigrant girl." Nevertheless, the show ran for only thirty-two performances. The experience clearly was unsatisfactory. Fannie and Ford had been under contract since August 1916 to write a dramatization of Fannie's 1914 story "The Good Provider," but it was never produced, and the two women never collaborated again.

Independent film offers at a thousand dollars each came in from Universal Studios for two of Fannie's short stories, "Solitary Reaper" and "Oats for the Woman." Not long after, producers sought the rights to two others, "Golden Fleece" and "A Petal on the Current." The Hearst organization had its own moviemaking division, and the sale of Fannie's fiction to outlets of any kind outside its empire had to be negotiated case by case.

"Golden Fleece" went to Select Pictures, where Charles Maigne adapted the story and changed its title to *Her Great Chance*. Alice Brady and David Powell starred in the production, the first of Fannie's stories to be produced for the silent screen. The plot involves a St. Louis shopgirl who refuses to marry her wild and wealthy boyfriend until she secretly learns—punch!—that his father has disinherited him.

A year later Universal Studios produced "Oats" under the title *The Day She Paid,* with Rex Ingram directing. Fannie ultimately received a $1,750 check for film rights to the story, in which she posed a conundrum: Why do people excuse a man who has sown some wild oats but demand that a woman's indiscretions ruin her life? In the story, Paula is an aging model in a New York lingerie firm who was the proprietor's mistress during a vulnerable period after the death of her mother. (In both a concession to the marketplace and a reflection of Fannie's own prudishness, all heroines "with a past" also required a good explanation for having fallen, one that any moralizing reader could understand if not forgive.)

A widowed St. Louis store owner proposes marriage to Paula. Her boss agrees to keep their past indiscretion secret so that the marriage can take place. The couple live in St. Louis with the widower's daughter, whom Paula comes quickly to love as her own. When the girl turns nineteen, the former boss happens to visit, falls in love with the daughter, and proposes marriage. Paula is horrified. She does everything she can to prevent the marriage without telling her husband the real reason for her objection. He soon figures it out and confronts Paula. For the daughter's sake Paula confesses the truth, and the father forbids the daughter's marriage. At the same time he throws Paula out.

The story appeared in *Cosmopolitan's* June 1917 issue. S. N. Behrman, writing in *The New Republic,* described its plot as an homage to *The Second Mrs. Tanqueray,* Sir Arthur Wing Pinero's play of 1893. It was an unfortunate but fundamental canon of fiction-making in this period, he lamented, that no seduced heroine could be allowed to "come out right."

Universal released *The Petal on the Current* (with the change in article in the title) to theaters in August 1919. "To say that the screen version does not live up to the story by Miss Hurst isn't knocking the picture by manner or means," a *Variety* reviewer wrote of Fannie's tale of the innocent girl whose first glass of beer results in her mother's death and her own near ruin. "Miss Hurst is an unusual person, a genius in her strange, inimitable way, but this does not mean that Tod Browning, who directed, is a genius . . . a Fannie Hurst story translated into ordinary terms [becomes] a very ordinary thing, indeed."

"Hers Not to Reason Why"

Edward J. O'Brien, meanwhile, continued to single out Fannie's work for the highest possible praise. He reprinted a story of hers in his *Best Short Stories* collection three years running, saying he could think of no other author worthy of such a tribute. "Hers Not to Reason Why," Fannie's debut piece under the new *Cosmopolitan* contract was, in O'Brien's estimation, the best story she had ever published. The story also appeared in *Gaslight Sonatas*, a third collection of Fannie's stories, which Harper & Brothers brought out in April 1918. O'Brien predicted it would rank among "the very few permanent short story books."

"Hers Not to Reason Why" records the downward spiral into poverty and desperation of a woman who is determined to live a decent life but who is without husband or the skill to improve her lot. *The New York Times* said the plot of this "gripping little tale . . . would have delighted Maupassant," adding in a pointed aside that Fannie should "shed her ornate, self-conscious style for the stark simplicity of the French master." But the reviewer was complimentary overall, finding in Fannie's work "humanity and lack of sentimentality" and "an antidote for the untruth and sickly sweetness of some of her contemporaries."

Cosmopolitan wanted to send Fannie to Europe to write about the war abroad. So far her war fiction centered on the myriad and sometimes tangential ways the conflict had affected civilian lives. She was enthusiastic about the prospect of going overseas, yet for reasons she elected not to share with her editor, the U.S. government denied her request for a passport. Doty speculated incorrectly that the denial had to do with whether Fannie still had relatives in Germany, and she let the incorrect impression stand. In the meantime she arranged to tour several New York–area army training camps to look into the state of social hygiene among the men for a *Cosmopolitan* article. To her old friend Lois she characterized the trip as a "government job" and also spoke of "stealthy trips to Ellis Island to see the men who have come back to the evacuation hospital." The experiences melted into images, paragraphs, and story lines.

To Lois, Fannie described her encounter with a private whose head had been buried under the collapse of sandbags in a trench for three days with "a little hole of air coming through by accident.

When they found him, his head was turned over his
left shoulder, the position in which he had squir[m]ed for

the hole of air. They have never been able to get his head
back into normal position. The horrors of this war must
be driven home to us more closely. A case like this—and
one would sacrifice his very all to help defeat the hun.

Otherwise, life was a New York whirl into which the war did not really
seem to impinge. Fannie took a weekend place at Cherry Valley, where she installed her maid and her pets, Satsu and Tar Baby. She reported to Lois that she
had spent a weekend at the country place of Representative Julius Cahn, "a day
or two with the self-crowned heads of Provincetown," and, in her continuing
quest for new subject matter, "a hot day in the hot slums." She had befriended
Daniel Frohman, the aging theatrical manager. There were weekend invitations
to his country home in Mamaroneck, and, with Jacques, she claimed a place of
honor in Frohman's private box on opening nights at his theater, the Lyceum.

Marion Reedy had come calling from St. Louis in October 1918. Fannie
shared a secret with him that she had managed to keep from her public and
most of her close friends for three long years. She reminded him by letter afterward not to repeat what she had told him. By return letter, he swore: "I shall
continue to keep quiet as long as I could and to lie if questioned," adding how
fond of her he was and how much he would enjoy a visit from her on her next
trip to St. Louis. There were also special regards to a certain "Russian anar-
chist."

Cosmopolitan paid Fannie two hundred dollars to write a brief appreciation
of the author Samuel Merwin. She had never met Merwin, which she confessed in the profile, though she acknowledged that once when he was editing
Success magazine, "he had the honor to lick the return postage of one of my accompanying manuscripts." Merwin read Fannie's piece and dropped her a note
saying the rejections actually meant something positive for her, since every
magazine he ever edited had failed. "There must have been bad judgment
somewhere," he wrote.

Chapter 6

"I Come Across"

For seven months John Siddall at *The American Magazine* pestered Fannie to write the story of her remarkable rise. Her *Cosmopolitan* contract did not prohibit selling nonfiction to competing publications, and she agreed to his request. Still, the more she thought about it, the idea of telling her own story embarrassed her. Siddall, however, kept pressing. "Let yourself go," he urged, "and come across in the most frank personal way. These are times when that kind of communication is especially acceptable." In another letter of encouragement: "You have an absolute, concrete, definite story to tell—the story of a girl who burst out of conventional surroundings into a field where she could really achieve something. This story, when told simply and directly will be of enormous interest to a lot of people. Young people will see themselves in this story because what is true of you is true of almost everybody—except of course that you got out of a rut and most folks don't. That is why the story is such a corker and why I am so anxious to have it. So please don't give up on it."

And a few months later: "Just sit down and rip it off."

The Jewish News put Fannie on its cover to promote *Gaslight Sonatas*. FANNIE HURST—HERSELF is the headline under a full-page photograph of Fannie, again in profile, again in simple, slenderizing black, again her hair pulled loosely back in that signature bun. This time the pose is more serene and intent than dramatic, with Fannie's eyes fixed on the middle distance in the way of a high school graduation portrait.

For the story inside Fannie told her interviewer that at age twenty-eight she was where she would have liked to have been at fourteen. She repeated this, adding a year to her ostensible age in the essay she finally wrote for *The American Magazine* a year later, under the title "I Come Across." The reference to Fannie at twenty-nine gave Siddall the idea to ask her to write about what it felt like to be Fannie Hurst turning thirty. Of course, Siddall did not know that the dreaded milestone had come and gone unheralded nearly four years earlier. Fannie had absolutely no intention of calling attention to the fact. To Siddall, she simply said she would prefer to keep the business of turning thirty to herself. He clearly did not grasp how deeply this issue cut. "You are a public character," he bullied, "and anybody who is interested can find out how old you are. . . . *Who's Who* contains your name and the date of your birth. It is accessible to everybody." Actually, *Who's Who* confirmed the erroneous birth year of 1889.

Siddall was right about the interest her personal success story would generate, especially the details of her arduous climb out of comfort. "I Come Across" ran in the March 1919 issue of *American*. Details from this article appeared in profiles of Fannie again and again. Her piece exuded the confidence and forced modesty of the comfortably situated:

> My printed rejection slips have become urgent letters of invitation, my two-figured checks have leaped amazingly high up into four; there are those for whom I seem to have a message; and that, even in its lowliest realization, is tinctured with the sublime. And, best of all, what popular success I am enjoying has come not from pandering to popular demand or editorial policy, but from pandering to my own inner convictions, which are little soul tapers lighting the way.

Another avenue of incredibly easy money opened up: second serial rights. The Bell Syndicate started negotiations to buy twelve of Fannie's already-published stories for newspaper reprint. And another possibility emerged: Elizabeth Jordan, then working for Samuel Goldwyn, wrote Fannie to ask if she had ever tried her hand at a motion-picture plot.

Going into the third year of Fannie's magazine contract, Ray Long of *Redbook* replaced Douglas Doty as *Cosmopolitan's* editor in chief. Long already had achieved great stature in the magazine publishing world and for good reason. He moved swiftly to make the most popular and important author on *Cosmopolitan's* roster comfortable with the transition. His first letter to Fannie came on *Redbook* stationery from Chicago. To establish his long-standing and ardent admiration of her work, he reminded her of the times he had tried to get stories of hers for *Redbook*. He said he hoped this admiration would enable him "to give the close sort of cooperation and sympathetic dealing of your stories which has made the regulars in the *Redbook* my very close personal friends."

Masterfully, and without waiting to charm her in a face-to-face meeting, he moved by mail to cast their relationship into the collaborative framework of visionary-editor-guides-celebrity-author. At the same time, subtly but effectively, he placed the power weight on his own side. He made it clear that his first order of business would be to get her to write a serial for the magazine. She shouldn't be limiting her "very vivid power" to the short-story form, he said. "I sincerely believe that you not only can be this country's best short story writer, as I think most people recognize you to be at this time, but that you can immediately take your place among the country's very best novelists."

Five days later Long wrote Fannie again to discuss a story he'd found in

Cosmopolitan's inventory of unpublished work. "Even as You and I" was Fannie's tale of a five-hundred-pound circus fat lady and her friend, the handsome alcoholic glass eater. She loves him, and she saves and comforts him so that he can break her heart into a million shards before he dies.

Long thought the story had a fine theme, contained some of Fannie's best writing ever, and packed "a terrific wallop at the end." Here is how he broached the delicate matter of getting the permission of one who never gave such permission to rework the story:

> I appreciate how great a responsibility it is to edit a manuscript which has been prepared with the care with which you build yours, yet I believe I see so clearly why it was that you and Mr. Doty might have lost interest in this story that I am going to suggest a change in it which I believe will make both of you agree with me, that is, that you allow me to eliminate the first page of the manuscript and begin the story with your description of Coney Island. The reason I suggest this is that it struck me immediately that if you ask for sympathy for this fat woman, you don't get sympathy, but a laugh. If instead of asking you simply let her grow on the reader as you tell the story, he can't help sympathizing with and liking her.
>
> I think, also, that the conversation between the fat woman and the midget just before they leave the show and during their walk back to the boarding house would be improved if you permitted me to tighten it by taking out about half a dozen lines.
>
> Please do not get the impression from this, Miss Hurst, that I am trying or planning to try to teach you how to write short stories. My conviction is you know more about that particular part of this business than almost anyone in the country. What happened in this case was that I received a manuscript by you on which it was reported that you had lost faith. I tried to see why, and I believe I did see why.
>
> I am also convinced that if you will permit me to make these changes, you will come very close to hearing more about this story than any you have ever published.

Fannie agreed to the changes. Five days later Long wrote again: "I have always contended that the bigger a writer may be, the more delightful he is to deal with. You certainly prove my point for me." Five days after that Long pressed again, this time a little more firmly, for Fannie to start writing a novel. And she did.

Long had not yet boarded the train to New York for his move from Chicago, but in Fannie's life he already had assumed the position of Mentor Number 3.

"Humoresque"

The theme music for Fannie's triumphs of 1919 and 1920 was Dvořák's *Humoresque*. In March 1919 *Cosmopolitan* published her most significant Jewish ghetto saga under that title, and just a few weeks later Harpers released a fourth collection of her stories, also calling it *Humoresque*. The story was one of fifteen O. Henry Memorial Award winners for 1919 (Edna Ferber produced one of the others), and O'Brien gave it his highest rating of three stars in *Best Short Stories*. He thought it had "an economy of detail" unusual for Fannie. At the same time he was critical of the other stories in the collection, saying they showed "a certain recession from her previous high standard." Even at that, in O'Brien's view they would have "made the reputation of a lesser writer."

Fannie set her title story in the Jewish ghetto of New York's Lower East Side, in the home of a Russian Jewish immigrant couple with a struggling little brass business and eight children to support. Leon Kantor clamors for a violin for his fifth birthday. His father refuses to buy the boy such an expensive trifle, but his mother understands the urgency of his plea and runs out to get it for him with no thought to the sacrifice. His talent is immediately apparent, and by the time he turns twenty-one he has signed a contract at two thousand dollars per appearance for fifty concerts. He has brought, with unselfish heart, an untold measure of security, honor, jobs, and joy to his family. He loves a young mezzo-soprano named Gina Berg, whom he has known since childhood.

When the United States enters the war in Europe, Leon enlists. His mother silently agonizes. She has already endured the pain of a son going off to war. What helps to cut through the sentimentality is the sense Fannie conveys that a good part of the mother's anguish stems from the enormous negative financial and social impact this particular son's decision will have on them all. For Leon's farewell gathering, he decides to play the favorite melody of his oldest brother, mentally deficient as a result of injuries sustained while the family was fleeing Russia (not unlike the child of Fannie's Polish friend on the Lower East Side). The brother listens in loving rapture. Gina cancels her concert in Philadelphia to be at Leon's side before his departure. As he plays the poem of a dying soldier recently set to music, Gina sings the lyrics: "I have a rendezvous with death." Leon leaves for the station, and his mother retreats to her room, dissolving in pain and tears. The story ends.

In 1947, nearly thirty years after this story first appeared, two high school teachers wrote Fannie to ask if she would tell them what had happened to

Leon Kantor after the war: Did he die, as in the poem by Alan Seeger, or did Leon just have a close contact with death? Fannie replied slyly: "My feeling when I wrote 'Humoresque' was that Leon had a 'rendezvous with death' which he kept. I hope this satisfactorily answers your query."

Many years earlier Fannie had explained that the idea for the plot of "Humoresque" came to her on a Sunday during a sellout concert at the New York Hippodrome. It featured a twenty-five-year-old violin prodigy. An usher showed Fannie to a seat at the back of the stage, behind the performer and facing the amphitheater, with its "expectant, music-hungry, popular-priced audience." She could easily see into the wings as the young performer appeared in the "shadowy aisle" leading onto the stage "like a pale-disembodied spirit, his face and hands and white shirt-front seeming to float in gloom." A row of figures followed: a short, stout, perspiring man of about fifty, carrying the violin like a swaddled infant; a pale, timid-faced, gray-haired woman, and three or four prideful young people, apparently his brothers and sisters. At the orchestra's signal the father removed the folds of silk from the instrument and handed it to his son. For the next two hours, "by the whining, crashing, tremulous, crying, laughing, lilting rhythm of that instrument, [he] kept his vast audience spellbound by his torrential genius." His family stood huddled in the wings. At the end of the concert the violinist left the stage. His father took the violin from his son and rewrapped it. The family surrounded the young star, and they all disappeared into the darkness.

The explanation was a wonderful story in itself, perhaps even true, although the circumstances surrounding Fannie's telling of it leave room for doubt. Fannie submitted the explanation at Ray Long's request for a promotional gift book that Cosmopolitan published for its subscribers in 1928. Long called the volume My Favorite Stories, and in it several of Cosmopolitan's most popular regular contributors selected a favorite story, which each of them introduced with a page or two about its inspiration. Along with Fannie, Sir Philip Gibbs contributed, as well as Ring Lardner, W. Somerset Maugham, Montague Glass, and Robert Hitchens. In such a competitive situation Fannie would find the temptation to resort to artifice irresistible.

And leaving the musical theme aside, the outline of Fannie's story is strikingly similar to the life of the boxing great Benny Leonard, who was lightweight champion of the world in those years. It is hard to imagine that his emotional ghetto-to-celebrity story did not provide some inspiration. Leonard baffled his poor, disapproving, immigrant Jewish parents by sneaking out as a young teenager to pursue a boxing career, but when he triumphed so did they, along with Jewish fans across the nation. He had been "the Great Benny Leonard" for two years when Fannie wrote "Humoresque" in 1919. That year alone, he sent twenty-six opponents to defeat. What's more, Fannie gave her main character the name Leon.

The hostilities in Europe ended some four months before "Humoresque" was published in Cosmopolitan. As American soldiers made their way home,

Fannie noticed a fundamental change in the demeanor of these young men—
"a new and a seer's look in their eyes"—and wrote about it for *McClure's Magazine*. "East and West are as irrevocably East and West as ever, but the twain
have met in the trenches," she said, noting how southern boys had made
friends with westerners and how they had all experienced other cultures.
"What a miracle for America this getting together of her own!" She went on:

> Youth has carried the brunt and reaped the rewards of this War.
> Bill Stiles of Ozarkville has stood surrounded by Titians and Giorgiones, has gazed into the great stone silence of the Coliseum; has
> seen the Pantheon and looked down into the tomb of Napoleon
> Bonaparte.
> "Great stuff!" he says.
> . . . Every so often, like a crack of white lightning out of the
> bloody blackness, comes some sort of justification for the smelling
> butchery of war.
> The quickened brotherhood of man is one!

At about the same time the film director Frank Borzage was looking for a
story to turn into a movie for William Randolph Hearst's own Cosmopolitan
Productions. Years later Borzage told the film historian Kevin Brownlow that
he handed a copy of "Humoresque" to his screenwriter, Frances Marion, and
had her read it aloud. Marion couldn't get through it without choking up—
Borzage's acid test for good material. Marion, who wrote so many of Mary Pickford's films, supplied the happy ending Fannie never would have tacked onto
such a tale. In Marion's version Leon returns from the battles with a shrapnel
wound to the arm. Gina is a childhood cripple, who, in Marion's rewrite,
shows her extraordinary compassion as a little girl by lavishing love and attention on a dead kitten. When the wounded adult Leon becomes despondent at
the thought he will never play the violin again, Gina lovingly tricks him into
full recovery.

Marion justified the changes, explaining that the tastes of the American
moviegoing public simply demanded the happy ending. "The optimism of
hope," she said, drives American audiences to the movies.

Borzage also included a Benny Leonard–esque touch in his movie. Leon, at
the pinnacle of his performance career, is in his tuxedo, violin in hand, ready
to start an important concert in an elegant hall. The camera pans the audience,
a room full of old, sad-eyed Jews, white-bearded men, women in babushkas,
all plucked straight from the streets of the Lower East Side.

The film *Humoresque* was a thunderous success, running for an unprecedented twelve weeks at New York's Criterion Theater. Most critics raved about
it, hailing it as the year's "biggest screen offering and the logical successor to
The Miracle Man," the major hit of 1919. Of its detractors, the Marxist Harry A.
Potamkin called it "an impertinent fable written by a sentimental woman, fur-

ther sentimentalized by the director and almost obscenely sentimentalized by the performance [as the Jewish mother] of Vera Gordon." Nevertheless, *Humoresque* won *Photoplay's* first Medal of Honor, a sort of early People's Choice award with the Oscar's prestige. "The fact that its chief characters were Jewish made no difference to the voters," the magazine reported without irony in announcing the winner. (The next four years' winners had happy endings, too.) Though Fannie initially objected to Marion's changes in plot and characterization, she soon came around. It was, after all, the first enormously successful screen version of a Fannie Hurst story. And though Fannie felt incredibly stupid for "having come in for a couple of thousand dollars on a couple of million dollar picture," she was mindful indeed of the "tremendous exploitation value of the picture to the name Fannie Hurst," which she happily accepted as "value received."

Success for Fannie kept coming, like popcorn kernels exploding in hot oil. She completed the novel Ray Long talked her into writing in a quick nine months. She called it *Star-Dust: The Story of an American Girl. Cosmopolitan* wasted no time in getting it into the magazine; book and film versions quickly followed, bringing Fannie's total earnings for the work to some $50,000: *Cosmopolitan* paid her $17,500 for the serial rights, Harpers gave her an advance for the book, and the film star Hope Hampton paid $30,000 to make it into a movie. The Wheeler Syndicate invited Fannie to cover the Republican Convention of June 1920 in Chicago for a hefty sum, and the *New York American* signed her up for coverage as well. Wheeler tried to get Fannie to release her early "unfit" works for syndication, just as it had done posthumously with the earliest work of O. Henry, but Fannie declined. "Back Pay," another of her significant mistress-and-war stories, caused considerable attention. It would be made into a stage play once and a film twice, as was the case with "Humoresque."

For the New York premiere of the film *Humoresque,* Cosmopolitan Productions sent out formal invitations for a private screening on May 4, 1920, in the Grand Ballroom of the Ritz-Carlton Hotel. If the producers had hoped for a full shot of publicity from this elegantly planned event, they were surely disappointed. But then again, maybe not. There was something suspicious about the timing of the much more startling story that broke that day concerning the lives of Fannie and her sometime escort, the pianist Jacques Danielson.

Chapter 7

"The dew on the rose"

Fannie's infatuation with Jacques so rivaled her professional ambition that she once declined an invitation from Sinclair Lewis to double-date with Carl Hovey and Sonya Levien because Jacques had invited her to dinner first. Lewis thought he and Fannie in combined force could persuade the two *Metropolitan Magazine* editors to fatten their already substantial contract offers. It dazzled Fannie to learn that someone of Lewis's stature considered her not only his professional peer but a negotiating asset. She knew that Jacques would have understood the value of such an evening for her; he would have wanted her to go. But even when the magnetic Lewis pressed, Fannie had little trouble saying no. She knew she would rather be with Jack.

Fannie liked the way her relationship with Jacques had evolved since she had been in New York. Their disparate personal and professional interests and needs allowed her an untold amount of freedom within a committed relationship, especially considering the time frame: 1912 to 1915. And although Jacques's presence in her life had given a certain stylishness to her use of the musical metaphor (witness "Humoresque"), her actual knowledge and tastes were still far too pedestrian for his musically erudite crowd. Jacques, after all, was a very early member of the Bohemians, an elite New York musicians' club whose membership over the years included Jacques's mentor Rafael Joseffy, Gustav Mahler, Rudolph Schirmer, Charles Steinway, Ignacy Jan Paderewski, Sergei Rachmaninoff, Josef Lhevinne, Arturo Toscanini, and George Gershwin. At the same time Jacques's knowledge of the contemporary literary scene was minimal. The couple gave each other plenty of space, so much so that many of their social friends were unaware of the intensity—or often even the existence—of the relationship. Jacques never interfered with Fannie's need for long hours of solitude for writing or with her desire to accept whatever professional or social invitations came her way, and there were always many. She did the same for him. They went their respective ways separately and together. It comforted her to know what his interests and activities were the evenings they were apart. There was a growing realization of their importance in each other's lives.

In this period Fannie was caught between some very traditional ideas spawned and nurtured in the gaze of overprotective parents in provincial, middle-class, Victorian and post-Victorian St. Louis, and the freewheeling, freethinking atmosphere of New York on the cusp of the Roaring Twenties. The hold of home was very difficult to throw off. She wrote her parents every day, sometimes cabling several times. She traveled back to St. Louis to see them four or five times a year, staying for weeks at a time. They had no intention of relinquishing their grip on her, and for reasons as old as her heritage, she gave them this due.

Jacques and she had talked of marriage. She certainly had asserted her independence, but at some level she wanted somehow to please her parents. She knew they would be horrified by the prospect of Jacques as a son-in-law. She could just hear their protests: He wasn't a businessman. He was a musician from "the wilds of Asia," who earned a fraction of what she did and had no real prospects.

She had her own doubts about marrying him, but on somewhat different grounds. Would it matter in the long run if the wife was always the primary breadwinner, as she surely would be? Would marriage distract her and thwart her career climb? Her literary flow? Was a marriage uniting two such divergent and demanding careers really possible? All these were issues on a brand-new frontier in 1915, and Fannie found it easiest to let indecision rule. Secure in Jacques's affection, wary of confronting her family, she let the matter slide.

In time she summoned her courage and went home—alone—to announce her intention to marry Jacques. The family's response was even worse than she had anticipated. Her father couldn't bring himself to utter Jacques's name. Aunt after aunt made a pilgrimage to Fannie's bedroom, pleading with her to reconsider what they all saw as a disastrous course. The relentless pressure left Fannie so drained she finally agreed to wait. Relieved, Aunt Jenny removed her prized string of pearls and fastened it around Fannie's neck. When her aunt left the room, the melodramatist took charge: Sobbing, Fannie ripped off the necklace, scattering pearls everywhere. She gathered them up and placed them in an envelope, on the face of which she scrawled, "Each pearl a tear."

Her first evening back in New York, she went out to dinner with Jacques to tell him the news. He heard her story—she finessed the most hurtful details—and he agreed that they should accede to her parents' wishes. Immediately, Fannie felt the relief of guilt unloaded and absolved. After the meal Jacques walked her back to her apartment. Nothing in his behavior prepared her for what came next. At her corner he doffed his hat and said a quiet, firm goodbye. Before she could unroot herself, he had hailed a taxi and left for good.

She wrote, she telephoned, she found it impossible to work. He refused to see her or even speak to her for eight weeks. Finally, pride undone, Fannie got her friend, Eva Rosenheim, one of the three Bettelheim sisters, to intercede. She reached Jacques by telephone as Fannie stood by. Eva told him that she would go with the two of them to be married at once, that Fannie knew now she had been insane to appear uncertain of what she wanted most.

Politely, Jacques held his ground. He refused to meet Fannie. Though he still had kind feelings toward her, he said, he had work to do and could not have any more disruption. He asked that she leave him alone.

That night Fannie went to his Lexington Avenue studio. He opened the door when she rang the bell, but he did not invite her in. Fannie pushed past him. They struggled through "the emotional labyrinth" for hours. Finally, Fannie talked him into a bold social experiment—a secret, trial marriage. They would reevaluate after a year. They would lead their lives separately and be together only secretly. The arrangement would keep, in Fannie's oft-repeated words, "the dew on the rose."

Forty-eight hours later Eva accompanied the couple to the resort town of Lakewood, New Jersey, on the pine-crowded shores of Lake Carasaljo, where, in this period, the likes of John D. Rockefeller and Jay Gould kept gorgeous estates. Members of Mrs. Astor's select Four Hundred favored the town's vast resort hotels, the Laurel and the Laurel in the Pines, for winter play. For privacy's sake the newlyweds would have avoided the Lakewood, the hotel Nathan Straus (of the Macy Department Store Strauses) backed because the other two did not welcome Jews. The ceremony took place just before noon in the presence of Eva, Police Justice Andrew J. Searing, and his wife, Ellen. Both Fannie and Jacques gave bogus Hoboken, New Jersey, addresses. Jacques told Searing he was thirty-nine, which was true; Fannie said she was twenty-eight.

They broke the news to her parents in St. Louis by telephone, and they, in turn, no doubt passed the word to Rose's sisters and brothers back in Ohio. Other than that, Bob Davis and Marion Reedy were the only people brought in on the secret directly. For five full years Fannie and Jacques told no one else.

"A Bark of Their Own Designing"

The news finally broke the day before Fannie and Jacques's fifth anniversary and the night of the film premiere of *Humoresque*. As Fannie explained many years later, an Associated Press reporter going through the marriage records in Trenton happened on her certificate and called Fannie for confirmation. It is hard to accept, considering the timing, that the discovery was quite this coincidental, but in any event it made the front pages of newspapers across the country. In *The New York Times*, Tuesday, May 4, 1920, it appeared center-page, above the fold:

**FANNIE HURST WED; HID SECRET
5 YEARS**
*Sailed Into Matrimony with Pianist "in a
Bark of Their Own Designing."*

LIVE APART, THEIR OWN WAY
Meet By Appointment—It's a New
Method Which Rejects
"Antediluvian Custom."

Fannie later said the five years of secrecy had not been by design. She often wondered if the decision to keep their marriage to themselves had been as satisfying for Jack as it had been for her. "I had everything," she recalled. "On one hand, freedom to use, not abuse[.] On the other, the silk thread of immense tensile strength that bound me. The paradox of our stolen hours together, when actually they were hours that belonged to us alone! Our secret visits to one another; weekend trips[.] My own happy secure knowledge that I had what I wanted both ways[.] Me Me Me."

To the *Times* she explained more formally that Jacques had undermined her youthful determination not to marry but not her resolve that marriage should never "lessen my capacity for creative work or pull me down into a sedentary state of fatmindedness."

In her observation, she said, nine out of every ten marriages seemed to be "sordid endurance tests overgrown with the funghi of familiarity and contempt." She found that the "high sheen damask" of this most sacred of human relationships too quickly turned into "breakfast cloth, stale with soft-boiled egg stains." She resolved to guard against this happening in her own life.

Fannie emphasized that no fad or "ism" had influenced her decision. She and Jacques simply had worked out a problem "according to the highly specialized needs of two professional people."

Jointly, they decided not to let marriage interfere with Fannie's writing or studies. They lived in separate studio apartments in the same building. Because seven breakfasts a week seemed to be an irksome idea, they agreed on two. Fannie kept her maiden name, since it was "as much a part of her personality as the color of her eyes." And they agreed that any offspring would take the name Danielson until the age of consent, when the child could choose for him- or herself. They also decided that "invariably being invited to the same social functions might eventually resolve itself into the usual married wrangle of dragging one another to places we did not want to go." So they maintained their separate groups of friends. They also agreed not to account to each other for the use of time apart. "For five years [we] have enjoyed our personal liberty precisely as we did before marriage, using rather than abusing, the unusual privileges we grant one another. My husband telephones me for a dinner engagement exactly the same as scores of my other friends. I have the same regard for his plans."

She told the story of a recent evening at the theater with a friend during which she found herself seated next to Jacques and a group of his cronies. Someone introduced them, and they exchanged the formal greetings of strangers.

"I consider 'two souls with but a single thought' a horrible and Siamese state of freak mentality; 'two hearts that beat as one' an anomalous condition, particularly when that single thought so often is of vanished freedom—the heartbeat a heartache," Fannie said before concluding:

> And again, I want to emphasize my freedom from faddism. Neither my husband nor I lives in Greenwich Village or wears horn-rimmed spectacles. My hair reaches to my waist. His is clipped. We believe in love but not Free Love. Rather, we are willing to pay the price in mutual sacrifices toward the preservation of one another's individuality.
>
> On these premises, in our case at least, after a five-year acid test, the dust is still on the butterfly wings of our adventure. The dew is on the rose.

This bark, Fannie told the *Times,* "has not sprung a leak during five years of high seas."

"Mutual and explicit trust"

Fannie's announcement triggered a publicity firestorm. Jacques defended the marriage on page 2 of the next day's *Times.* "It is freedom!" he said, not to have to lie about where he had been on an innocent evening out, or to have to come home to "a nagging wife who either is in a tantrum or in tears, who either upbraids one for brutish selfishness or sobs that one has ceased to love her."

"Mutual and explicit trust" were essential, Jacques told the reporter. "With suspicion and jealousy, this thing is not possible." Fannie, who happened to be at Jacques's studio, then at Carnegie Hall, was asked what would happen if they had children. Though she said that she would shower her children with the full quota of mother love, she would also expect to entrust their practical care to a nanny. "I know dozens of professional women who have kept up their careers yet who have been supremely splendid mothers," she said, "women who have gone on writing or singing or teaching or what not, yet whose love and devotion to their children is undeniable and who have made them better little men and women for their own wide contact with the world."

The *Times* was so taken with Fannie's marital revelation, it ran an editorial about it that day, chiding her for ignoring the current shortage in available housing and nannies. More important to Fannie was the "dew on the rose," the *Times* ribbed, mocking her metaphor. "She has found that which is rarer than the fabled blue moon, the honeymoon that does not wane."

Arthur Brisbane devoted the first half of his column in the *New York Journal-American* to musing on Fannie's model, concluding that her trial marriage actually put the husband on trial—an improvement over the usual situation. Still, Brisbane wasn't recommending the arrangement for any mere mortals; he also thought two breakfasts a week would lead to fewer in no time.

Even George Bernard Shaw weighed in, saying there was nothing new in the thing. Godwin and Mary Wollstonecraft had tried it more than a century earlier, and since then "many professional women in Salt Lake City have shared a husband by living independently and entertaining them when their turn came." Shaw reasoned: "The ordinary routine for married couples is to spend ten hours out of the twenty-four apart, eight in a state of unconsciousness of one another (asleep), and only six in one another's company. That makes forty-two hours a week for husbands and wives. It appears therefore that Mrs. Danielson is only joining the general movement for a reduction of hours."

Marion Reedy, not surprisingly, came quickly to Fannie and Jacques's defense, saying that their marriage seemed to be worrying a lot of people more than it did the couple. "Everybody agrees that a little separation now and then is good for a married pair," he argued. "Why wouldn't a little more be better? What is there immoral or scandalous in two people making a small experiment in the marriage relation, when that experiment involves nothing more than an agreement to occupy separate apartments?"

Reporters sought out the opinions of prominent women. The attorney Clarice Baright accused Fannie of mistaking entirely the fundamental purpose of marriage. "It does not mean a series of appointments," she scoffed. "It is the basis of the family—the family is the basis of the state . . . and the Hurst-Danielson children, poor little mites! What are they going to get out of this magazine short-story plot except their choice of two names?" The patent attorney Florence King was more magnanimous. Asked for comment in her capacity as president of the National Woman's Association of Commerce, then the largest organization of businesswomen in the country, she compared Fannie's announcement to the words of the vaudeville juggler who throws innumerable items into the air but first tells his audience, "This is a good trick if I do it." King reminded her interviewer that Fannie actually was married in the traditional sense and wondered aloud if "she would parade her plans to the world were she not."

Mabel Herbert Urner, creator of the popular "Helen and Warren" series of stories, said her fictional husband-and-wife characters never would have submitted to such an arrangement. In fact, Urner said, "I do not think many women wish to be independent in this way. It is the being 'taken care of' and 'looked after' that every woman craves."

Jacques—though the phraseology sounded more like Fannie's—sent a note and a statement over to the *Times,* which the newspaper printed in full May 7—the third story on the subject in four days. He wanted to "avoid growing misconceptions on the part of that public apparently eager to stamp with sensationalism the slightest departure, no matter how seriously and conventionally undertaken, from the beaten matrimonial trail."

To those who criticized the couple's decision to live apart in the midst of a housing shortage, Jacques said worse economic crimes were being committed in the average married household. Anyway, he said, proportionate to the two incomes involved, "our combined rents and scale of living amount to less than they would otherwise."

Jacques justified himself and his wife on other counts as well: "For those who seem to think that I am being cheated of the carpet slipper, fireside aspect of domesticity, I wish further to make the statement that whenever I find the ache beginning to set in for the comfortable sag of the patent rocker, I need only to drop in at Miss Hurst's for one of the delicious homemade dinners her maid of five years permanency knows so well how to prepare and the deep repose of her studio, which for quiet and comfort is equaled only to the similar hominess of mine own. . . . The worst of this matrimonial alliance of mine is that I like it."

Jacques further argued that his life with Fannie was not "one long rendezvous with alien interests." Rather, he said, Fannie probably was spending more time at home than the average woman, because of her writing schedule and her habit of entertaining friends for dinner three or four times a week. She also was spending three or four months over the course of a year in St. Louis with her parents. "We are both workers and must devote long evenings to study and reading and practice, so all in all, I hardly think we can be classified as a pair that has thrown off the responsibilities of the usual marriage ties in order that we may play promiscuously." Actually, he said, the couple had thrown off some "outworn matrimonial impositions" so that they might "have more liberty to live up to more of the responsibilities of our lives and our work."

The announcement certainly cleared up a few mysteries for those who thought they knew Fannie and/or Jacques well. The editors of *Metropolitan* could now see why Fannie had been unable to make the Russia trip with Boardman Robinson and John Reed in the spring of 1915. And at *Cosmopolitan* the editors could now piece together why the U.S. government rejected her request for a passport to travel to Europe for the magazine in 1918 to cover the war. Under prevailing law, as the wife of a foreign national Fannie would have had to take Jacques's Russian citizenship in order to get a passport. Jacques had applied for American citizenship in September 1917, but the papers didn't make their way through the system until the end of 1920.

Nearly a month after the marriage report appeared, reporters converged on Fannie's parents' doorstep in St. Louis soon after she arrived in town—without Jacques—for a short visit. She was en route to Chicago and then San Francisco for her coverage of the national political conventions. Bristling with hostility, Fannie cried out against the "simply nauseating" amount of publicity the story had caused, not to mention the attendant distortions and falsehoods. The truth, she said, never would have knocked international news off the front pages.

"It is ridiculous to say that I recommend everyone to try the plan that Mr.

Danielson and I have found successful," she sniffed. "We are two people with highly specialized jobs, and we have made the arrangement best suited to our own particular needs." She went on:

> We all know how marriage actually operates in the majority of cases. It is not surprising that those who have made a failure of it, resent anyone else beating the game. The timid and the unimaginative naturally do not applaud anyone who breaks away from their hampering fears and deadly monotony. We all know how hoary institutions, regardless of how ineffective[ly] they operate in modern life, are worshipped by the conventional masses. Marriage is no exception.

In no time the phrase "a Fannie Hurst marriage" entered the national vocabulary.

PART 2

Preceding page: Corbis/Underwood & Underwood

Chapter *8*

"The glittering circus"

When Fannie thumbed through her mental snapshots of the 1920s, she saw a nation enthralled with the autosuggestive, psychotherapeutic technique of Émile Coué, the French pharmacist who claimed he could effect organic change by having a patient repeat the words "Every day, and in every way, I am becoming better and better." She saw men in derby hats, women in knee-high skirts with hip-hugging waists, sinuous dancing, and necking as "the new name given to an old technique." Chaperones no longer shepherded young ladies around, and the lending libraries had long waiting lists for *Alice Adams, Miss Lulu Bett, Main Street,* and *If Winter Comes.* Reserved for another of her mental albums were shots of the "lost men of the Bowery," made beasts by the grade of bathtub gin they favored, and the young people who "necked and smoked, drank and soaked their share of names into police blotters."

Experimentalism reigned. "Sex is a discovery," Fannie recalled. "The word, which had lurked so long in the nasty silences, becomes usage. *Lady Chatterley's Lover* is carried in public, without a book cover. *The Well of Loneliness* and *Damaged Goods* are as discussable as *Rebecca of Sunnybrook Farm.*"

Fannie bobbed her hair, tried cigarettes and cocktails, but none of it took. She certainly had open access to members of the era's "fabled minority," but she never really connected with most of them. Young Scott Fitzgerald spoiled one of her dinner parties, but only once. She saw herself as "one of the millions who lived on, worked on, outside the glittering circus [of those] who aimed for the roof of the world but compromised by swinging from the chandelier."

Fitzgerald, Maxwell Bodenheim, Floyd Dell, Edna St. Vincent Millay, George Bellows—of these, Fannie said: "I would have been tongue-tied in their company, overwhelmed by their status, lacking their powers to extend their exhilarations by way of the cup that cheers. Or, rather, the demitasse that cheers, since part of the technique of the Prohibition era was scotch, gin, or what you will, served in demitasses." To the vast majority, she said, the era was neither riotous nor fabulous. Willa Cather's Bank Street apartment in Greenwich Village, for example, "was no more a part of Fitzgerald's twenties than Mars."

The Algonquin crowd Fannie saw as "a loosely assembled group of pundits, wits, wags, versifiers, critics and a minority of literary figures of stature." All the same, Fannie considered the group New York's intellectual focal point. Yet the smart talk that out-of-towners seated near the "Round Table" strained to overhear consisted largely of "witticisms of local vintage, epigrams, and sophisticated patter, gone now with the wind of that day's repartee and reportage."

Fannie shied away from a coveted seat at the Round Table, though the critic Alexander Woollcott invited her to stop in whenever she pleased. Her instincts were sound. Margaret Case Harriman, whose father managed the hotel, remembered that whenever Edna Ferber showed up to take her infrequent place at the table, Woollcott "peevishly" called her by Fannie's name. In telling this anecdote, Harriman gently described Fannie as "a popular writer for whose style the Round Tablers felt less than reverence."

Fannie's own recollection of what kept her away: "This was the glib, smiting-word-at-any-price set, for which I had no talent."

Looking back on her life, Fannie had the image of herself as someone inept at cultivating friendships with the most interesting personalities in her field. "Some of them were more than my peers, and perhaps a sense of inferiority froze me," she said years later. "But even where I was not disturbed by any such feeling, I did not seem to know how to fraternize." Of course she also acknowledged readily that these same people did not seek her out, except in cases of requests for support for one of their pet social causes, as Dorothy Parker would in the late 1930s and 1940s, when she was involved with the relief effort for Spanish refugees. If New York literary life had a center in the 1920s, Fannie felt quite outside it.

All the same, she had a more than passing acquaintance with most of the day's literary and social paragons. The sheer force of her fame made her a must-invite to the kinds of social gatherings that made the newspaper columns. A sampling of her lunch and dinner partners in 1925: Ellen Glasgow, Horace Liveright, Fola La Follette, Rupert Hughes, Zona Gale, Rutger Jewett, Kathleen Norris, Inez Haynes Irwin, Lillian Gish, Nellie Revell, Mary Pickford, Theda Bara, Charles Roy, Louise Dresser, Bessie Love, Lois Weber, Elsie de Wolfe, Noël Coward. Of those, she had warm relationships with Gale, Irwin, and de Wolfe.

Fannie befriended the powerful literary agent Elisabeth Marbury in this period, and Charles Hanson Towne, the editor and bon vivant, was a favorite and frequent escort. Through such associations Fannie got to know Henry and Agnes Leach, the John O'Hara Cosgroves, Wallace Irwin, Mary Austin, Gertrude Atherton, Cosmo and Clayton Hamilton, Carl Van Vechten, Edna St. Vincent Millay, Elinor Wylie, John Farrar, Irvin Cobb, Glenway Wescott, and Christopher Morley. Theodore Dreiser struck up an acquaintanceship after Fannie wrote him in 1917 to congratulate him on a story of his in *Cosmopolitan*. Fannie's own favorite Dreiser anecdote had him following her all the way from the New York Public Library to St. Louis(!) to finish a particularly provocative conversation. By the end of the decade she was on his party guest list for a time. Van Vechten and his wife, Fania Marinoff, were great friends of Fannie's who swept her onto their self-styled social carousel. Van Vechten was an early white support force for the many talented members of the Harlem Renaissance, and Fannie quickly came to share in his advocacy and concerns.

"Star-Dust"

Fannie named the lead character in *Star-Dust,* her first novel, Lilly Becker. Lilly is a St. Louis girl from a middle-class German, probably Jewish, background at the turn of the century. As Lilly comes of age, the values of her close-knit, small-minded community begin to suffocate her, as does the need of her overbearing parents to see their own limited lives fulfilled through hers. There is mastery and unmistakable firsthand knowledge in Fannie's depiction of boardinghouse and ethnic German neighborhood life. Her portrayal of Lilly's anguished struggle to break free from her background and her ignorant abhorrence of sexual intimacy ring familiar. So do many of the names and some of the characterizations, particularly those of a boardinghouse matron and her disturbed and wayward grandson, which Fannie wholesaled from her own childhood experience.

As *The New York Times*'s critic pointed out, Fannie's "widespread and well-earned" reputation as an artist of the short story made her first venture into novel writing "a more or less breathtaking experiment." An established writer's first crossing from one literary form to another could be treacherous. Though all the reviewers had criticisms, the consensus seemed to be that Fannie's first novel was flawed but worth reading.

Even those critics unfamiliar with the autobiographical source of much of Fannie's inspiration admired those passages lifted directly from her own life most. Although the *Times* thought the book needed some judicious weeding and pruning, it ventured that "one would have to go very far indeed to find a better drawn, more lifelike picture of this particular kind of existence." *The Literary Review* found the novel "full of observation of human nature in its daily way, vividly written, emotionally all there." *The Bookman* admired *Star-Dust*'s many " 'pulse beats of life,' " though its critic complained that they were often "so violent and prolonged as to lead one to suspect heart trouble."

In the story young Lilly's sense of entrapment is so extreme that only three weeks into her marriage to a steady, boring, but up-and-coming second assistant of a hardware emporium she flees St. Louis for New York. Alone in the larger city she hopes naively and in vain to turn her parlor talent into an operatic career. This plan fails immediately, and Lilly comes to the even more devastating realization that she is pregnant, and has been since before she left home. She tells no one, and she does not turn back. Instead, she manages, against extraordinary odds, to keep her child and raise her well. She makes a professional success of herself in a theatrical booking agency, but not without painful sacrifice.

The novel unfolds in episodes clearly tailored to the monthly serial format in which *Cosmopolitan* published it between March and December 1920, paying Fannie a handsome $17,500 for the ten-part series. In the meantime the production company of the actress Hope Hampton bought the film rights for an additional $30,000. R. L. Giffen of Alice Kauser's agency handled the negotiations, telling Jacques that Fannie's novel had commanded the highest price paid for any story in quite some time. Jacques thought it should have fetched more. All told, between the magazine, the film sale, and the book version Harper & Brothers published on March 25, 1921, Fannie took in some $50,000 when that amount could buy a five-story, twenty-family apartment building in a middle-class neighborhood in the Bronx.

Fannie saw a private screening of the film in December 1921, two months before its First National Pictures release. It sent her into a rage. She found Anthony Paul Kelly's ordinary and highly sentimentalized screenplay so removed from her own story that she issued a denunciation of the film to the national press. The *St. Louis Post-Dispatch* ran the statement in full, explaining in a preface that authors routinely complained about the liberties film companies took with their stories. However, no one before this had ever gone so far as to do so formally and for publication.

In her statement Fannie likened the cinema to a gifted but very spoiled baby in the family of arts, a child in dire need of a good spanking. The film version of *Star-Dust,* she charged, was "neither true to my theme, my idea nor my story." Her purpose, she explained, had been to explore the idea of vicarious fulfillment. In her conception the protagonist fails to achieve the professional and romantic ambitions she has for herself but ultimately realizes them both through her child. In the screen version, Fannie complained, the heroine ultimately fulfills "through a series of tawdry and trumped-up situations, her ambition to become an opera singer." Furthermore, Fannie said, while in her novel the child "grows up into a vital young womanhood and motivates the entire story," the child in the film is a boy who dies in infancy.

"By what dictatorship is the author made subservient to these intolerable conditions?" Fannie asked. "Allowing for the bow to the censor and the inevitable mechanical demands of translation from written to acted word, whose ultimatum is responsible for the liberties taken with the author? It is high time that the reputable author put in a claim for the integrity of name and work against the present abuses of the screen."

Fannie's objections forced the producer to change her screen credit: "Adapted from the novel by Fannie Hurst" quickly turned into "Suggested by . . ." Nonetheless, Jules Brulatour, Hope Hampton's wealthy manager (and much older lover), threatened Fannie with a quarter-of-a-million-dollar libel suit for her public repudiation of the film. Fannie's attorney, Benjamin Stern, saw the move as a scare tactic and urged her to stand firm. She could set a valuable precedent by insisting that literary properties not be "garbled and mangled and misinterpreted beyond recognition in translation to the screen." This, Stern said, "will cause the next man who attempts to spoil the literary reputation and the work of an author to sit up and give long attention to the work in hand." It could even mean that authors would begin to see screen interpretations of their work instead of money paid for the use of their names and the titles of their works in order to mislead patrons into the theater.

The out-of-court settlement took three years to reach. No money exchanged hands except from client to lawyer. Hope Hampton Productions won from Fannie a public apology for her damaging remarks. Her contract, she acknowledged, permitted the production company to do whatever it wanted with her story and its theme, "and they may have been better qualified technically than I to decide whether the changes they made were necessary or desirable," she wrote. "In view of these facts I now realize that my criticism transcended the limitations of my contract and I cannot do less than retract it."

It would be Fannie's last such display of high-minded petulance. The film industry was simply too powerful, the cost of attorneys too high, and the monetary rewards for keeping silent too great. On top of that, her subsequent triumphs made even her own version of *Star-Dust* too embarrassing to defend.

The Marbury

Fannie reaped many rewards from her coverage of the 1920 national political conventions in Chicago and San Francisco. She established herself as an observer of current events, she heightened and refined her interest in the political process, and, best of all, she befriended the dowager queen of New York literary-theatrical agents, Elisabeth Marbury, one of the city's most original and fascinating personalities.

"The Marbury" was how Fannie came to refer, with deep affection, to this three-hundred-pound, "five-by-five" monolith with bright blue eyes, some thirty years older than Fannie. The age gap had absolutely no impact on the friendship the two women quickly forged. For years Marbury and two of her audacious and successful friends—the interior decorator Elsie de Wolfe and the financier J. P. Morgan's daughter Anne—went through life in an entrepreneurial triumvirate of exceptional power and panache. They established salons in Irving Place and Sutton Square in New York and, for a time, as residents of the historic Villa Trianon in Versailles. Fannie's fascination with these three women's lives and accomplishments—as well as the endless curiosity about their sexual preferences—was more than evident. It found its way into her fiction. Fannie transmuted the story of Marbury's astute real estate speculation, which made exclusive and fashionable Sutton Square of an East River slum, into an important episode in her 1933 novel, *Imitation of Life*. A decade later, long after the Marbury's death in 1933, Fannie cut the main characters in her 1942 novel, *Lonely Parade,* straight from the unique pattern for living that Marbury, de Wolfe, and Morgan had so boldly established.

The Marbury—in *Lonely Parade* Fannie dubs the corresponding character the Charlottenburg—crossed Fannie's visual plane during both women's first half hour among the Democrats in San Francisco. Fannie duly noted this in a paragraph of her very first—and not particularly distinguished—column for the *New York American* containing names-cum-comment of significant personalities who had arrived for the convention that day. "Elisabeth Marbury," Fannie wrote, "who speaks for herself."

As Fannie remembered their actual meeting, Marbury stared at her for several days before sending over a note saying, "I like you," with an invitation to lunch. "From the moment I met the lady," Fannie recalled, "the relationship was to mean one venture after another into experiences identified with a personality so pungent that even small details of the ten [actually thirteen] years of subsequent friendship I was to enjoy with her stand life-size in my memory."

The Marbury's social contacts, ranging from the Prince of Wales to Sarah Bernhardt to George M. Cohan to Oscar Wilde to Frances Marion and Marie Dressler, "were astutely tied to business," Fannie realized, "and vice-versa." "The plays, novels, musical compositions that were to make name and fame for their creators were sometimes born over her teacups. The stimulus of her personality, salty wit, dry sardonics, generosity and human warmth were electrifying to the artists in one field or another who crowded about her."

She once told Fannie, "I create the compulsion in creative people to utilize their great gifts to the limit. You'll know that before you're through with me."

By January 1921, Elisabeth Marbury's agency, the American Play Company, had started to represent Fannie in a nonexclusive arrangement. The movie deal for *Star-Dust* already was in the works with another agent at the time, and Bob Davis had finally stirred up interest in a stage version of "Humoresque." Marbury advised Fannie to leave the property in his hands and thus liquidate her obligation to him.

The new agent wasted no time. In January she started with "Back Pay," Fannie's 1919 story for *Cosmopolitan* about the mistress of a wealthy wartime arms dealer with the *"crepe de chine* soul." In the end she forgoes the wages of sin and returns to her hometown sweetheart when she learns he is blinded and dying in a veterans' hospital. By March, Marbury had sold the stage rights to "Back Pay" to the theatrical impresario A. H. Woods—*Cosmopolitan* irritatingly controlled the movie rights—and had negotiated a second deal under which Fannie would collaborate on a new play for David Belasco. Two weeks later Marbury sent over a third contract—this one with Sam H. Harris for the dramatic rights to "Roulette," an eighteen-thousand-word novelette in three parts which Fannie had just sent over to *Cosmopolitan.*

Verne Porter, the editor, thought so highly of this tale of Russian twins separated at birth (and reunited in what *The New York Times* considered far too strong a chain of coincidence) that he decided to run the whole story in the May issue. To readers the magazine bragged in a banner headline: WE EN-LARGED THIS MAGAZINE, AT A COST OF THOUSANDS OF DOLLARS, SO WE COULD PUBLISH THIS POWERFUL STORY COMPLETE IN ONE ISSUE. It was by far the longest short story *Cosmopolitan* had ever published in its entirety. The expensive decision was clear indication of the value of Fannie's stock with Porter and Ray Long, the Hearst magazine group's *über*-editor, but no more so than her unconventional choice of subject matter for stories in this period.

The Bookman celebrated Fannie's achievements with the third in a series of literary portraits. The writer and her admiring friend Inez Haynes Irwin wondered where in Fannie's "cool forest mind" lurked those crowds of old Jewish mothers and fathers "whose sorrows wring our hearts," where a woman in her twenties had learned so much about old age. She wondered too where such a sumptuous girl had gained such an intimate knowledge of the poor, of the criminal mind, "of violent impulse . . . heaving hope . . . quaking regret."

The stories got more daring. "She Walks in Beauty," in the August issue of *Cosmopolitan,* recounted a daughter's devotion and sacrifice to her drug-addicted mother. The magazine called it "a great masterpiece and one of the most impressive stories published in years." Another story, "Guilty," was even more controversial. This was the strange tale of a fishmonger whose wife goes mad and dies in childbirth. Years later the fishmonger pleads guilty to murdering his beloved and beautiful daughter, whom he fears has inherited her mother's mental illness, after she reveals her plans to marry. Long later said that if Fannie had discussed her idea for this story with him beforehand, he would have urged her not to write it. As it was, it contained so many elements verboten in magazine fiction convention that it seemed as if Fannie had lined them all up and compressed them into this one piece of work. Mindful of how objectionable her story might be, Fannie called Long before she turned it in to tell him to feel free to reject it if he found the subject matter too unseemly.

Porter read the story first and kicked his questions upstairs to Long. Long said it "contained frankness about prenatal influence and about obstetrics of a sort which no magazine ever had published up to that time." Porter's concern was that readers with any knowledge of psychoanalysis might get the wrong idea. Long had no such qualms. The story, as presented, had him "clear up in the air with enthusiasm." In the end the two men agreed they liked it too much to let any such consideration get in the way of publishing it.

"You are the only writer in the world who could have handled the story so that I would feel that I could publish it," Long told Fannie, adding, "And I believe I'm safe in saying that I'm the only editor living who'd have the courage to print it, now that it's written." (Of course, six years later he had lost that bravado. When Fannie submitted another gruesome short-story synopsis, Long begged her not to write it: "The hell that we both got for 'Guilty,' " he said, "would be nothing as compared to the hell from this.")

The editors led *Cosmopolitan's* February issue with "Guilty," heralding it as "the most daring piece of fiction published in years." It precipitated subscription cancellations and advertiser protests but also praise. Blanche Colton Williams, the Columbia professor and eminent short-story critic, told Fannie, "This fishy thing . . . held me spellbound." And *The New York Times* said it "sends a real chill shuddering down the reader's spine."

The Marbury's ever-present walking stick seemed to be tapping out its compulsion-inducing magic on Fannie's creative impulse.

"Back Pay"

The new association with Elisabeth Marbury, plus the lucrative sale of *Star-Dust* to the movies, pointed up how shortsighted Fannie had been in agreeing to tie film rights to her *Cosmopolitan* short-story contract. True, her stories were now commanding an enormous two thousand dollars apiece. But the film rights for the five stories her 1917 contract required her to sell to William Randolph Hearst's organization every year netted only an additional twenty-five hundred dollars each. Against the thirty thousand dollars she had gotten for *Star-Dust,* the figure now seemed ridiculous. Worse yet for Fannie, of the dozens of her stories which Hearst's International Film Company had at its disposal, it had produced only *Humoresque* since 1917, and had repeatedly refused to resell any of the others to prospective buyers. Not only did this rob Fannie of the 50 percent share of the resale profit to which the contract entitled her but the slow release of her stories to the movies was, she felt, "in these heyday years of my output . . . keeping me under a bushel basket, so to speak."

There was another situation Fannie had not anticipated when she signed her contract with *Cosmopolitan.* Broadway theater managers, as a rule, were far less interested in securing the dramatic rights to short stories for which the film rights were unavailable. Hearst controlled all the best ones. So it was not surprising that Fannie fired off an angry telegram to Hearst himself the minute she read of his plans to begin production on a film version of "Back Pay"—just as her stage play of the same story went into rehearsal. She urged him to delay the film release until the play could get off the ground. Marbury offered to intercede with Hearst directly in the matter. To oblige Fannie, Hearst postponed the release date of the film twice but then argued that he could not wait any longer. He didn't really accept her reasoning. The film version of *Humoresque* had been released in 1920 with no adverse effect on Fannie's ability to sell the rights to the stage play a year later. Furthermore, he said, the play's producers had probably secured the commitment of the sought-after Laurette Taylor to star in it on the strength of the film's huge success. In Hearst's view Fannie was benefiting from their contract every bit as much as he was, and in any event he had the right to film and release *Back Pay* whenever he pleased.

Posturing aside, in the end Hearst did exactly as Fannie asked. Famous Players–Lasky held off release of *Back Pay* until February 1922—the play premiered the preceding August. At the same time, it put two more Fannie Hurst short stories into film production. "Superman," a 1914 story renamed *Just Around the Corner* for the screen, premiered six days into 1922, and "The Good Provider," published in 1915, appeared under that title four months after *Just Around the Corner*. In further testament to the value the Hearst organization put on keeping Fannie happy, Ray Long arranged a bonus payment of seventy-five hundred dollars for the rights to "The Good Provider." This was on top of the twenty-five hundred dollars she already had received for it.

As it happened, none of the three new films came anywhere close to the popular appeal of *Humoresque,* though each had its charms. Frances Marion again wrote the screenplays for both *Back Pay* and *Just Around the Corner,* and she directed the latter. Frank Borzage directed both *Back Pay* and *The Good Provider.*

Variety said the best thing about *Back Pay,* which starred Seena Owen and Matt Moore, was its title. The trade paper dismissed the film's "old oaken bucket story about the country gal who goes to the big city and goes wrong all along." All the same, it held water well enough for William Seiter to remake it as a talkie for First National in 1930, starring Corinne Griffith and Grant Withers. *Variety* effused over Sigrid Holmquist's ingenue performance in *Just Around the Corner,* which also starred Margaret Seddon and Lewis Sargent. And although he was respectful of Marion's direction and story adaptation, the reviewer thought the film fell short of "special." *The Good Provider* starred Vera Gordon of *Humoresque* fame and Dore Davidson. William LeBaron of Cosmopolitan Productions rushed the cutting and titling to get it into the movie houses ahead of a new Goldwyn production of the Rupert Hughes story "Pop," which had a very similar story line even though its characters were not Jewish.

Fannie, at the production company's request, sent out her own set of screen titles, which arrived the last day before deadline. "We are using your 'lingo' all through," LeBaron wrote her in Paris, where she was vacationing in the spring of 1922. "Everyone who has seen the picture as we delivered it Saturday night, is crazy about it and I really think we have a big hit." Three weeks later he wrote again to report that her titles helped tremendously and that the film was a "corking, artistic, commercial success." *Variety* gave it the most enthusiastic notice of the three Fannie stories released as films in this period but predicted it would not gross as much as *Humoresque.* Fannie, who had caused such a ruckus with her repudiation of the film version of *Star-Dust,* told a reporter for Hearst's *New York American* how pleased she was with the movie, and that it showed how a story could be transferred successfully to film. Though the article was a shameless bit of self-promotion on the part of the Hearst organization, it probably did reflect Fannie's feelings about the production.

As for the play, it ran for two and a half months at New York's Eltinge Theatre in the early fall of 1921 after a mixed critical reception. Helen MacKellar played the lead. The *Times*'s Alexander Woollcott heralded the first appearance of "the prolific Fannie Hurst" as a "full-fledged, unassisted dramatist," then wrote that although the language was sometimes "incredibly gaudy, and with scenes that quite slosh about in sentiment," she had written an essentially interesting story, despite its "timid and spurious conclusion." Though it would "offend the fastidious and . . . make the intellectuals a little sick," he said, it was going to "thrill the multitude of simple and sentimental folk who will not care a rap that the truth is not in it."

Brutalizing, but the *New York Sun*'s reviewer made Woollcott seem kind. "During one of the intermissions someone in the fourth row was heard to call loudly for the author," the reviewer wrote by way of snide conclusion. "The audience regarded him curiously and waited patiently for the lights to appear."

Soon after this unexceptional Broadway production, Sam Harris let the theatrical rights to "Roulette" lapse. A year later A. H. Woods picked up the option for a thousand dollars—Harris had paid the same—but a stage version was never produced. First National Pictures released it as a film directed by Alfred Santell in June of 1928. *Wheel of Chance* starred Richard Barthelmess and Lina Basquette and was adapted for the screen by Gerald C. Duffy.

At the end of 1921, Ray Long anxiously waited for Fannie to decide if she would renew her agreement with *Cosmopolitan* for another two years. In the end she did. However, her price per story went up to three thousand dollars starting in 1923. And she held very tight to her film rights.

Chapter 9

"The Vertical City"

At about the time Fannie signed on for another two-year hitch with *Cosmopolitan*, Harper & Brothers brought out a fourth collection of her stories, this one called *The Vertical City*, from one of the story titles. The book includes "The Smudge," Fannie's first story with black-white racial overtones. It is the tale of the single mother of a child who does not know that her parents were never married. The mother, a white actress, makes a good enough living in blackface, portraying maids, that she has sent her daughter to the best schools and set her up for a more promising future. For extra income she has developed a small but lucrative side business making a unique dark-tone theatrical makeup that does not smudge or run.

The daughter comes of age and falls in love with a young man from a very good family. It is the life her mother wants for her. Just as it appears that the young man will ask for the daughter's hand, her scoundrel father appears for the first time in the girl's life. He accosts her mother at the theater just as she has come back to her dressing room. He offers to marry her—and legitimate their child before her background ruins her chance to marry well. In exchange for this belated and self-serving act of gallantry, he wants control of her makeup business. The actress is so revolted by the prospect that she wrestles with telling the child the long-hidden truth, hoping her daughter will understand the choices her mother has made and be proud of her courage. The father demands to meet the child, and the mother agrees. He waits downstairs in her home while she goes up to wake her daughter. The brush of her dark makeup on her daughter's skin leaves a small smudge. At this moment the mother realizes a confession from her will ruin the girl's life. Instead, she resolves to marry the father.

The idea for "The Smudge" came to Fannie at the theater one night, as she was watching a white woman perform in blackface. For Fannie, a character always suggested a possible plot—never the other way around. As always, it was "little unknown people" with "drab little tragedies" that intrigued her most, "those who have passed the zenith of expectancy and are on the down hill side of the road."

Though Edward J. O'Brien was highly complimentary of the stories in *The*

Vertical City, newspaper reviewers tore into it. "Miss Hurst's worst vice is senti-mentality," the *New York Times* critic said. "Her worst fault is cheapness. Her greatest art is her fresh and vivid phrase; her greatest talent is her ability to de-scribe to her readers things they do not know in terms of what they do." The *Boston Transcript* compared Fannie's "crude and chaotic" style to "the flashy news reports of yellow journalism. . . . We read her in the same state of mind that we listen to 'jazz music' or cast our eyes over the latest manifestation of 'free verse' poets." N. P. Dawson in *The Literary Review* of the *New York Evening Post* said Fannie's imagery "is as lively and hardhitting as ever, the floridity of her language does not droop, nor do the wells of her ever-gushing sentiment show any signs of drought. . . ."

Fannie was so upset by the reception she advised Harpers to lay low on publicity "placements." Her publicist, Ruth Raphael, was an old family friend from St. Louis who immediately wrote Fannie in Paris to ease her mind. Raphael said Fannie's relationship to the Hearst empire, which counted the *New York American* and *Evening Journal* among its holdings, was the real reason for much of the nastiness being printed in rival papers. According to Raphael, both the literary editor of the *New York Sun* and the features editor of the *New York Evening World* refused to touch a story or photo of Fannie's for their publications because of her association with their reviled competitor. In spite of that, Raphael reminded Fannie that she was still getting more and better coverage than most writers, and anyway an insulting review at half a page was preferable to a paragraph of flattery. She dismissed the motivations of each of the critics on grounds such as "cattiness" and bitterness over unrelated publishing disputes of their own. From this dubious company she made an exception of Heywood Broun, "who at least thinks for himself—you know what sheep I've told you the critics are."

"I am aghast," Raphael wrote Fannie, "when I think how several little re-viewers who perhaps only get a free copy of the book for their criticism, can represent big newspapers—just a thirty-dollar a week reporter can speak for the *Times,* for instance, and make trouble."

Nevertheless, she told Fannie she would not disseminate any personal sto-ries about her to the press until Fannie got back from Europe. Fannie's editor at Harpers, William H. Briggs, felt strongly that the publishing house needed to counteract "the two-breakfasts-a-week-stuff and the Hearst touch." For that reason Raphael was not even mentioning that Fannie was with Jacques in Vi-enna, hoping to stave off another round of gossipy speculation about the na-ture of their union. Harpers hoped to cast Fannie in her most literary and un-Hearstian light.

Raphael was reassuring despite the critical blows: "You get across better than anyone," she told Fannie.

"Forty-Five"

The White Star steamer *Olympic* carried Fannie and Jacques to Europe in the late winter of 1922. Fannie told a shipside reporter she would stay six or seven months, mostly in Italy, to complete her new novel. As it happened she was back by June. Jacques planned to spend the time in Vienna studying music, but Fannie's itinerary included stops in Paris, Rome, Vienna, Munich, Stuttgart, Berlin, Frankfurt, and London.

There were literary demands on her more pressing than the novel. Ray Long wanted at least one of the stories she owed him for *Cosmopolitan* (CHILDREN ARE CRYING FOR STORY, he wired. WHEN MAY THEY EXPECT ONE.) And she was already a year late with the play David Belasco had advanced her money to write. He had just granted her a year's extension and already was gently pressing for progress.

Fannie certainly spent time working on her novel, but what most directly came to mind during the trip was the inspiration for "Forty-Five," a novelette she submitted to Long soon after her return. He decided to run the whole story in one issue of the magazine instead of splitting it into two parts. Unsolicited, he offered a thousand dollars for it on top of Fannie's then standard two-thousand-dollar fee.

"Forty-Five," the story of an American mother and her daughter on an extended visit to Paris, certainly ranks among the best stories Fannie ever produced. On reading it the author Charles Norris wrote her in a burst of uncontrolled enthusiasm: "My knee in the dust to you! I abase myself before your genius . . . that one person, six feet one, 175-stripped—could be so deeply stirred by the art of merely putting words together, should repay you here and now for all the struggle and fight of early years. You etch into the brain with a steel pointed dagger a picture of Paris that is unforgettable."

This is how she began:

> There is the Paris o' your heart and my heart, the Paris of Little Billee, Hugo and Maupassant, and the Paris to which George Moore confessed.
>
> There is the Paris that butters its radishes and eats its crabs with the whiskers on.
>
> There is the Left Bank, that on Quat'z Arts nights paints its slim body Tuscan bronze and walls up its eyes in gold-leaf, but of any morning, except the morning after, carries home its breakfast bread by the yard, and cuts its cheese with a palette scraper. There is Montmartre with a court plaster lizard on her shoulder, red heels, no stockings, petticoat ruffles not always fresh, but all the passions smoking to slow flame in her come hither eyes, and the soot reservoirs in half shells beneath them.

There is the terrible Paris of Zola, the harlequin Paris of Merrick and the Baedekered Paris of Cook's.

The Paris that smells of chypre and of closed plumbing; of cognac and sawdust; of love and of too few baths.

The Paris of Comédie Française and the Folies Bergères [sic]. The Paris of undraped dancing girls, their beautiful bodies revealing and disclosing in just the proportion to make that beauty horrid. Paris with her thumb to her nose.

Paris at sunrise with the wagon-loads of carrots coming into market, little pink tongues sticking out. . . .

Then there is the Paris of Edith Whatley and her daughter, May.

In the story Edith is forty-five years old to her daughter's twenty-three. Though born and reared in Muncie, Indiana, she is a New York sophisticate who has just had her face lifted by Paris's premier plastic surgeon. The operation has wiped a score of years off her face but has also turned what was once a calling-card beauty into an expressionless mask. At her daughter's insistence the two of them bob their hair, dress as flappers, and diet themselves down to the girth of skinny, twelve-year-old boys. They adopt the bored stance and sardonic wit of the flapper. They take eyelids-half-mast pleasure in speaking and thinking contemptuously of all the less savvy American tourists they pass, Baedekers in hand.

One day, by chance, they run into one of Edith's fondest high school friends. She is in Paris, Baedeker in hand, with a daughter May's age. The surgery and Edith's style have so effectively concealed her actual age that the friend—a graying, matronly forty-five—doesn't recognize her for several minutes. The friend's daughter is youthful, plump, and Muncie-dowdy in dress. The two old friends pick up where they left off so many years before, and all four share their time in Paris. By further chance they run into Edith's high school beau, Bob Pennyrich, who is now a very successful Muncie businessman. He immediately steps in as Paris escort for the quartet. In taking the reader to the story's conclusion, Fannie sweeps through a woman's every pressure point in her slow dance with aging—trying to look too young, the limits of plastic surgery, what constitutes a well-spent life, the emotional and physical discomforts of menopause. Pennyrich and May fall in love. Pennyrich explains to May what attracts him to her: ironically, it is those fetching crinkles around her eyes, like the ones that drew him to her mother so many years ago but that no longer sweeten her face. Edith, whose heart had swollen in a vain and mistaken hope for a rekindled relationship with Bob, finds herself saddened, foolish-looking, and alone.

It was the second time in Fannie's published fiction, Star-Dust being the first, that a daughter competes for and wins the affection of her mother's undeclared but obvious love interest. The theme clearly fascinated Fannie—she used it several more times.

"*Ravella*"

From Rome, Fannie detoured southeast to tiny Ravello on Italy's Amalfi coast, a postcard-perfect village on a hilltop overlooking the Gulf of Salerno on one side and the Mediterranean on the other. The ideal place to write. In a descriptive reverie many years later, Fannie cross-dressed the village and turned it into "Ravella," but her recall of the visual particulars was more precise. Her hotel "hung like a crag from a mountain . . . I could look down upon a fishing village at the base of the vineyards, the old colors of its roofs like faded calico. A slightly curling sea. Horizon."

There, in the dining room, amid the "elderly English ladies with dyed hair and old-fashioned jewelry, set with small dirty diamonds . . . rickety Englishmen with stained goatees and window-glass monocles, German tourists inseparable from guidebooks and rucksacks," Fannie met the eminent Arctic explorer Vilhjalmur Stefansson.

Lean and rugged-faced, Stef at the time was forty-three to Fannie's actual thirty-six, and already well-renowned for his exploration of vast areas of the Canadian Arctic, his ethnological study of the Eskimo, and his part in the discovery of the last unknown islands of the Canadian archipelago, Borden, Brock, Meighen, and Longheed in the Canadian Northwest. He had published *My Life with the Eskimo* in 1913 and his second book, *The Friendly Arctic,* had only recently been released. His interests also extended over vast unrelated expanses. "Never before," Fannie later recalled, "I may even say or since, had I been in close contact with an intellect that flashed its lightning over such farflung territories." She found herself "suffering a fierce jealousy of his vast self-acquired knowledge which highlighted my lack of it." "Ravella" became the starting point for an important and enduring friendship.

Fannie had kept Belasco primed, writing him from the steamer and then again from Munich to congratulate him and tell him how inspired she felt after seeing *Kiki,* then in its twenty-third week at the Belasco Theatre and sold out for weeks ahead. "I hope that the spell of the inspiration is still with you," he wrote back. "We must repeat this success—you and I—in a play of Yiddish life, such as only you can write." For good measure she had enclosed a photograph of herself, taken with the well-known German actor Anton Lang.

London, this visit, meant a series of lunches and dinners with such impressive British literary figures as Sheila Kaye Smith and G. B. Stern. But the introduction that flowered into a friendship of consequence was to the combustible Rebecca West, who was building herself up to a breakup of her long affair with H. G. Wells. West quickly made Fannie her mother-confessor. She saw Fannie as "a Jewess of the most opulent oriental type," to whom she would soon begin to pour out her heart in detailed letters over the next thirteen years or so.

Once back across the Atlantic, Fannie went straight to the Adirondacks to write. Though she went quickly on to St. Louis to visit her parents, they complained bitterly that she had not come to see them directly when she got back from Europe. Her typewriter took the place of command in their second-floor living room.

When the *St. Louis Globe-Democrat*'s reporter came calling, Fannie disingenuously explained that she did not consider herself a success. She said she was still waiting to scale "the pinnacles not yet sighted" in the form of a much better novel than *Star-Dust* and "a really great short story."

The reporter found her "altogether an attractive figure" in her black crepe size-camouflaging gown with the bat-wing sleeves lined in "orange so deep it was almost henna." She parted her long black hair simply down the middle and gathered it in a low knot. Her two ivory bracelets on the left wrist got a mention, as did her necklace—"bizarre but effective."

As for her time abroad, Fannie told the reporter that too much time in Europe made her desperate for home soil. "Europe," she said, "is tired, effete, decadent, and we are now and vital. That's the difference."

Chapter *10*

"The chastening influence of failure"

New gusts of possibility blew into the fall of 1922. *The Delineator* asked Fannie to consider doing some short stories for its pages. This was surely a gratifying request from the magazine Theodore Dreiser had made great before moving on, but Fannie never got around to responding. The Wheeler Syndicate bought thirteen of her already-published short stories to recycle to its newspaper clients. And John Farrar asked for a contribution to his "Parody Outline of Literature" series for *The Bookman*. "Naturally," he wanted Fannie on the list of contributors since he already had asked Floyd Dell to retell *Hamlet* in his own style and modern setting; Dorothy Speare to do *Romeo and Juliet*; Rupert Hughes, *Circe and Ulysses*; Ring Lardner, *Enoch Arden*; Will Irwin, *Cinderella*; John Dos Passos, *Henry IV*; and Louis Untermeyer, *Hero and Leander*. Farrar gave her a few suggested subjects: *Lancelot and Elaine, The Lady of Shalott, Pygmalion,* or *Galatea*. The series ran but with no contribution from Fannie, or many of the promised others for that matter.

McCall's Magazine began courting Fannie madly, for, as its associate editor Adele Miller confided, it was essential to any magazine's future to have both Fannie and Booth Tarkington in its stable of writers. The magazine invited Fannie onto its "Christmas Tree of Stars" for the December issue, a promotional message inviting readers to enjoy the authors *McCall's* planned to feature in the months ahead. Fannie appears not to have acknowledged the magazine's request for a piece comparing and contrasting the effects of war on the women of Europe and the United States. But she seemed eager to contribute three hundred words to a spring symposium entitled "Does a Moment of Revolt Come to Every Married Man?"

Meanwhile, the Authors' Guild nominated Fannie to serve on its permanent council, along with George Ade, Gertrude Atherton, Irvin Cobb, George Creel, Edna Ferber, Montague Glass, Rupert Hughes, Mary Roberts Rinehart, and Tarkington. From the standpoint of her peers, she had most assuredly arrived.

CONGRATULATIONS ON THIS YOUR BIRTHDAY, said the cable from her mother in St. Louis on October 18, the day before she turned thirty-seven. MAY YOUR PROGRESS CONTINUE TOGETHER WITH YOUR PRESENT GOOD HEALTH THROUGHOUT A PERIOD TO A RIPE OLD AGE WILL BE OUR CONSTANT WATCHFULNESS AND

88

PRAYERS[.] WE ARE ENJOYING YOUR REGULARITY IN KEEPING US INFORMED[.] ARE
FEELING ALL RIGHT[.] POP GRADUALLY IMPROVING.

The only burned patch on life's vast green lawn was the stage version of
"Humoresque." Fannie returned to New York when rehearsals started in September, then traveled with the company for the out-of-town tryouts. Against
her better judgment the producers had talked her into writing a much stronger
"war note" into the second and third acts. She felt that the family story ought to
predominate over the war motif, which by 1922 had certainly played itself out.

She also had deep reservations about the very lovely, very Irish Laurette
Taylor in the lead role. Though Miss Taylor's star power was calculated to be a
draw on Broadway, she was "no Jewish mother" in Fannie's view. She seemed
unable to move the audience in her big scenes. Worse, Fannie thought, "she
has a cold, almost a vindictive manner and none of the heart-swelling appeal
[that is] necessary to the role. . . . Non-Jews seem uninterested [sic] in her performances and the Jews themselves, antagonistic." Fannie hoped the star
would show the good judgment to abandon the part before the main premiere.

It also unnerved Fannie that the production company was thinking about
moving the play's major opening from New York to Los Angeles. To her mind,
New York was the only possible venue for the opening. As she saw it, New
York was where "the types flourish in such abundance" and where the field for
casting and firsthand observation was widest. But her main concern was the
star. Fannie thought it was essential for the actress's first surroundings and opportunity to be in a place where she would not "get set" wrong. "The role is so
foreign to anything in her previous experience and her mind is such a delicate
plate for impressions," Fannie wrote, "that I tremble."

For months Fannie endured the torment of abetting a show she felt sure
would be a flop, especially after it became clear that Miss Taylor intended to
stay in the part. In letters to Elisabeth Marbury and to Stef, Fannie confided
her deep distress and steeled herself for the failure ahead.

At the same time she felt driven for the first time to lose weight. Fannie had
always been uncomfortable with her size, but until new scientific and aesthetic
information became widely available in the 1920s, it hadn't seemed possible to
do anything about it. Now the relationship between calorie intake and fat was
clear. The 1920s ushered in a new, much, much slimmer conception of beauty.
Up to this time reporters had routinely described Fannie in newspaper and
magazine profiles as beautiful, attractive, and chicly dressed, even with accompanying photographs that emphasized her lovely but very full face and her
wide, blocky frame. Size simply did not seem to play much part in the aesthetic judgment of feminine beauty. But that was changing. Fannie embarked
on a rigorous campaign of diet and exercise.

The play *Humoresque* opened in New York on February 27, 1923. Contrary
to Fannie's predictions, Laurette Taylor was brilliant in the part, even without
benefit of insights into her character that Fannie's mother easily could have
passed along. The critics could not have praised the actress more. Alexander
Woollcott, for example, writing in the *New York Herald,* exalted in a "perfor-

mance of moving beauty by one of the first ladies of the land." John Corbin in the *Times* found her portrayal of Sarah Kantor "incomparably subtle and beautiful." As for the play itself, reviewers seemed to like the first act and find the second one passable but hated everything else about the production—especially the script. Woollcott said the play had him "snarling with resentment at its downright incompetence." Corbin was more specific: "The play as Fannie Hurst has written it goes wrong," he wrote. "An audience that thrilled and melted to the beauty of the first act, and warmly applauded the second act, turned cold at the final curtain." Twelve days later the critics Percy Hammond and Heywood Broun had gotten wind of Fannie's dissatisfaction with it all. Hammond claimed that when Laurette Taylor refused during the out-of-town tryouts to be "limited by an author's lines," Fannie packed up and left the set. On opening night fellow novelists such as Wallace Irwin, Irvin Cobb, Edna Ferber, and Ring Lardner amused themselves at intermission, trying to pinpoint which lines bore the Taylor touch and which, the Hurst. When the audience called for the author after the final curtain, Fannie declined to take the stage.

Broun examined why, despite the star's performance, the play was, in his words, "not prospering." He did not agree with the prevailing argument that neither Jews nor Gentiles enjoyed seeing a Gentile play a Jew. In Broun's view the war theme was the problem. When Fannie wrote her original story, it was essentially a call to service, an effort to express through her hero the emotion of the youth of the country toward the war. "History," Broun wrote, "has conspired to defeat [the] dramatic aspirations of Miss Hurst. A good many in the audience are not stirred when Leon Kantor says that he is going to fight to end oppression. As a special favor to Miss Hurst, the French should have kept out of the Ruhr." Broun argued that Americans had dramatized their emotions at the height of hostilities; now Fannie was in the impossible position of dramatizing a dramatization. After four short weeks at the Vanderbilt Theatre, the play closed. *Clipper* magazine summed up the reason with the words "lack of public support."

Stef, who was traveling, had written Fannie back when she told him how worried she was. This was his idea of solace: "Should it be merely the play that goes to pot (through fault other than yours), the chastening influence of a failure to one used to success may pay you handsomely in the end."

Later he reminded her it was "only an episode, and will have its value. But I shall be very glad to hear it is over—preferably through a success that can go on with its own momentum."

"The summer of anxiety"

Somehow amidst all that was happening in Fannie's life, she carved out the time necessary to finish her second novel, initially entitled *Bertha* but renamed *Lummox*. She tried *Cosmopolitan*, *Redbook*, and *Metropolitan* magazines—Fulton Oursler said it was certainly "the book of the year"—but none thought the manuscript lent itself to publication in serial form. This did not surprise Fannie, but it disappointed her greatly, and she confided as much in a letter to her peripatetic friend Stef.

Stef's letters to Fannie were growing steadily more personal. In one, written en route to London aboard *The Empress of Scotland*, he told her that she might be experiencing a "rise above temporary marketability" as she grew toward greatness. He sympathized, however, with her frustration at losing out on the possibility of an extra forty thousand dollars, Fannie's going rate for first serial rights. The money would have been a welcome protection, he said, against "the blandishments of literary tradesmen."

Stef also asked Fannie for letters of introduction to her new London friends. "Your friends are like your books," he wrote, "apart from their intrinsic worth, they tell me about you." No packet of introductory letters arrived, but Stef did not hesitate to look up Rebecca West, who graciously invited him to tea. "If you value your place in my heart," he wrote to Fannie afterward, "you needn't fear she will ever usurp it. I should never feel her attraction across a room, as I did yours. It doesn't carry men across a tea table."

When all hope of serialization was lost, Fannie sold a chapter of the new manuscript to *Cosmopolitan* as a short story entitled "Seven Candles." The magazine paid a fabulous short-story rate of three thousand dollars, the same price Fannie received from Ray Long for a story she had sold him a few months earlier. That story, "The Brinkerhoff Brothers," was the tale of two aging, persnickety, companionate brothers and what happened to both of their lives when one of them fell in love and married. It prompted Long to repeat to Fannie the assessment of another *Cosmopolitan* editor: that she was "the only American writer who can put the same thrill in details of human life that Dickens did." To this he added, "And you never did it quite so well as you did in this story." Long had every reason to be passing along any flattering comment about Fannie that came his way. She had declined to sign a new contract with *Cosmopolitan,* and he very much wanted her back under exclusive arrangement. The accolade may have overstated the case, but Edward O'Brien also seems to have been taken with the story, awarding it his highest ranking in *Best Short Stories of 1923*.

Fannie's apparent dissatisfaction with the preexisting arrangements in her life extended to her book publisher. Her friend Charles Norris, husband of Kathleen, a best-selling author who liked to advise Fannie whenever she gave him an opening, encouraged her to shop the new manuscript around. His sense was that whichever company got hold of *Lummox* would probably become her permanent publisher and thus have the opportunity of promoting her into a best-selling author. "I do hope you'll remember that what you want is sales and not big royalties," he said, "these will come fast enough once you achieve the other." Norris already had *The Amateur, Salt,* and *Brass* to his credit; *Bread* was just about to be released. He described it to Fannie as a study of the woman who elects to achieve economic independence. "It seems to me that the girl who goes out and becomes financially independent and acquires a profession by which she is always able to earn her living, eventually 'gets it in the neck,' " he said. "At any rate, that's my theory, and I am going so far as to advocate keeping the unmarried woman out of business or if she decides to accept the office life, she must renounce at the same time all thoughts of marriage."

There is little doubt that Fannie rejected Norris's conclusions if not his theory, but she happily accepted his business advice and began casting around for a new publisher. Knopf expressed keen interest; Macmillan, Harcourt, and Bobbs-Merrill all quickly offered contracts. In the end she stayed with Harpers, for lack of an offer exciting enough to warrant the jump. The company set a publication date of October 5. Jonathan Cape agreed to bring out a British edition.

Efforts to sell the movie rights to *Lummox* went nowhere. The film agent R. L. Giffen suggested that Jacques's interference was part of the problem. "While I am sure that Mr. Danielson is very successful in his own profession," he said, "it has not been my experience that he is a good businessman, insofar as the handling of motion picture negotiations are concerned." Jacques had full charge of Fannie's business dealings and their personal fortunes. At the financial end of her creative endeavors, she retained the prerogative to react and intervene whenever she pleased. But she relied on him to clean up the messes.

From every perspective it was Fannie's "summer of anxiety." Her mother took sick and spent five weeks under care in St. Louis before Fannie brought her to New York for three and a half months of medical attention. The nearness of daughter seemed to work. "Finally, she is responding to treatment," Fannie wrote to her old friend Lois Meier Toensfeldt in St. Louis in late August. "Papa is here and of course it means about 98 percent hospital duty for me." Nevertheless, and however complainingly, Fannie was willing to do what was required. As her friend Sam Shipman, the theatrical producer, pointed out: "Children, after all, are only so many banks where parents deposit their sacrifices," expecting at some point to make drastic withdrawals upon demand.

Stef wrote from London, "However do you manage to write me so often and kindly with all your work and worries?"

"A pig for success"

The New York newspapers carried word of the publication of *Lummox,* making a point of saying that Fannie had forgone a huge cash offer to publish it first in serial form in order to protect the novel's artistic integrity. The concept of spin was nothing new to the publicists of 1923. Harpers' publicity department also admonished editors everywhere to destroy the many photographs they had on hand of Fannie. The lady author was now "shorn of many pounds," and replacement images were on the way.

The book was a sensation, and reviewers gave Fannie the literary reception of her dreams for her empathetic survey of the life of a domestic servant. With noble soul Fannie's Bertha silently endures a rape by her employer's son, a false accusation of theft, and because of it the loss of references. Her life is one of endless drudgery, unpleasant departures, and no security or respite, crowned by Bertha's diminishing value in the marketplace with every passing year.

There was criticism, to be sure, tough criticism, but the nature of the praise overpowered it. Most gratifying of all was surely a note of peer acknowledgment from Maxwell Perkins, the paragon of editors, whose author list included Ernest Hemingway, Scott Fitzgerald, and Thomas Wolfe. From his office at Scribner's, Perkins took the time to send Fannie a copy of Edith Wharton's 1911 novel, *Ethan Frome,* calling her attention to Wharton's introduction. In it Wharton explains the issues she faced in bringing an inarticulate protagonist to life on the page. One can sense the blush of pride in Fannie's note of thanks. "Mrs. Wharton's preface is more than pertinent to my own difficulties with *Lummox,*" she wrote. "It is reassuring to know that even a goddess has her tussles."

The reviewers took Fannie as seriously. *The New York Times,* unsigned, said that although *Lummox* was not a great story, Fannie had done much that was fine, touching "the deepest wells of human emotion. With a certain diaphanous and almost mystic skill she has fashioned a heroic character from indifferent material." To J. W. Krutch in *The Literary Review,* she was a writer with more talent and force than taste, which was the only way to account for "so much bad in the midst of so much good." Her tendency to fall into bathos in some critical scenes was regrettable, but that should not stop the reader from staying with it. "One must merely resign himself to take the gold and accept the heavy alloy as best he may," Krutch said.

Heywood Broun in the *New York World* admired Fannie's ability to "make an emotion rise and stalk before the reader" and found her mastery of dialogue "often almost magical." However, he said, "Someone ought to speak to her severely about adverbs. Far too many things in *Lummox* happen goldily." He also was struck by how strong an influence Gertrude Stein had on Fannie's writing and quoted a particularly Stein-like passage: "It was good to set out the milk bottles. Six in a row. They were so there. Quarts. Bulge. Dimension." He also fixed on Fannie's uneven use of simile. He could accept the unfathomable "Gladnesses that were as easy as spinach" from an author who also produced so fine a phrase as "the air was like a lady with a slow fan," or "tired Old Testament-eyes" or "eye slits, like wise, smiling old buttonholes." John Farrar in the *New York Tribune* called *Lummox* "annoying, offensive, puzzling," but with a great theme superbly handled.

Fannie's good pal Charles Hanson Towne did not recuse himself from reviewing *Lummox* for the *International Book Review,* and his assessment, not surprisingly, reads more like a blurb than criticism. Rebecca West, however, did not hesitate to criticize the book in print. She didn't like the "exuberance" of what she otherwise considered a "very striking piece of fiction." West said that Fannie had done the story "with too many applications of her painter's brush, or with too coarse a brush."

Other British critics, however, gave Fannie and her publisher cause to rejoice. Harper & Brothers found the reviews in the British press fantastic enough to trumpet in a full-page ad in *The New York Times* a year after the American publication date. *The Times* of London declared the book "great art . . . ugly as Abraham Lincoln was ugly, great in the way he was great." And from the *Observer* of London came the pronouncement that it was "the best novel we have had from America for at least a decade." Every bit as gratifying was the response of friends genuinely moved by Fannie's brainchild and without any evident ulterior motive for telling her so. Marie Jenney Howe, one of the first people she got to know in New York, was awestruck. "It does seem remarkable," she wrote, "that after achieving so much popularity you have gone on still farther until you have outdistanced your already successful self. . . . I wish I could understand that urge in you that holds you up and presses you on."

An early mentor, Rabbi Leon Harrison of Temple Israel back in St. Louis, wrote to say that he had always felt the best was yet to come. He was delighted to have heard from Fannie how much of the "soul and self" had gone into the work. Of her previous efforts he said, "The worker has always been much bigger than the work."

Total strangers weighed in, too. Stanley F. Babb, literary editor of the *Galveston News,* proclaimed it literature with "all the immense power of Dreiser without his sometimes wearisome verbosity. I tell you frankly that it interested me much more than any book I've read since Hardy's *Tess of the D'Urbervilles.*"

The literary critic Joseph Collins included Fannie and *Lummox* in a psychological study of life and letters entitled *Taking the Literary Pulse,* published a year after the novel's release. Collins said Fannie had borrowed with "skill and dexterity" "from the painter, the musician, from the cubist and the impressionist, from the symphonist and the sonatist." *Lummox,* he said, recalled something of James Joyce, Guillaume Apollinaire, and Paul Morand. He called Fannie "a fiction architect who has designed and constructed a building not so attractive in appearance as many of those built by her competitors, but with some features that make it more acceptable to tenants; it is adapted to present-day needs, and to personalities."

Perhaps the most amusing tribute of all was Fannie's inclusion in Christopher Ward's series of parodies for the *Saturday Review* and the *Literary Review* of the *New York Evening Post.* Along with entries by "Tooth Barkington" and "Calla Wither" was one titled *Stummox* by "Fannie Wurst." Hers appeared first in the hardback compilation.

Unqualified rapture was Fannie's response to the novel's reception. "I am so happy that I walk on air," she told her uncle in Cincinnati by letter. "Every day is so full of excitement that I am on tip toe day *and* night. *Lummox* is *the* literary sensation of the year and has brought me *artistic* acclaim that is as great as any popular acclaim has been. That's what I wanted—being a pig for success. *Both* kinds of acclaim—popular and *artistic* and now I have *both* crowds and I'm the happiest person on earth. Just fancy—write a book which is the literary sensation of the year and *then* losing 29 pounds. O it's a glorious old world!"

To Bob Davis she gave due credit, inscribing his personal copy of *Lummox* with gratitude for planting the idea in her head:

> One day you said to me: "The story of the domestic
> servant is yet to be done. You write it!" I wonder if that
> remark wasn't the genesis of this book which I am so
> affectionately inscribing to you. I am pleased to think
> that it was. The warmth and inspiration of your
> personality have had such an influence over my entire
> writing experience that again you must carry the burden
> of some of the blame for this my newest and storm-born
> [?] brainchild.

Life had reached the apogee of perfection. There was nothing left to do but complicate it.

Chapter *11*

"Happiness Dwelt Here"

Despite Fannie's complete satisfaction with the success of *Lummox,* the apparent restlessness of the past few years had not subsided. She still wanted change. Even without the financial cushion of a magazine serial or movie sale ("*artistic* successes don't pay as well a popular ones," she realized), she arranged to move house.

The time had come to vacate the "apartment of laughter" on West Sixty-ninth Street, the Gothic-style set of studios that she and Jack had shared, in their peculiar fashion, for seven years. For years afterward, Fannie thought the building should have a plaque that read, "Happiness Dwelt Here." Indecision made a mess of the transition. Fannie let matters drift so long that she ended up paying rent for a time on both the old space and the grander new one in the studio building two blocks away at 27 West Sixty-seventh. It was a perfect metaphor for what was happening in her love life.

Jacques and Fannie still granted each other the complete freedom of their original covenant. Their idea had been to protect each one's ability to function professionally at the highest possible level and for neither to subject the other to people to whom he or she felt no connection in interests or friendship. Three years earlier, as they had announced their marriage to the world, they'd made a point of telling the readers of *The New York Times* that they were not wild Greenwich Village faddists; they believed in love but not free love. Their unique union had been designed to accommodate disparate careers, not dalliance.

In December 1923, more than eight years into the marriage, a *New York Times Magazine* reporter interviewed Fannie on the state of her novel union. The tone of apologia which had so dominated the original announcement of the marriage was gone. Now Fannie spoke in broad generalizations and with absolute authority. Her marriage was no experiment; it was a demonstrated success. Fannie was the voice of possibility for any others daring enough to try. Her observations for publication included no specific references to her personal situation. But the writer pointed out that Fannie's conclusions and deductions came directly from her own experience.

"Monogamy has to be pampered a bit," Fannie said. "It has to be made to appear like a many-faceted jewel. A woman must be new to her mate, a man must be a not altogether known quantity to his. Neither can afford to let all the barriers fall." She said her experience had convinced her that "actual freedom is more likely to be used than abused." A relationship of mutual trust keeps both partners "on the *qui vive* for each other," she said, unlike the "old-fashioned good-wife-and-mother" type, which she felt was "contrary to the biological instincts of the human race." Fannie repeated her position soon afterward in a cover essay for *Liberty* magazine titled "Propinquity," in which she made a strong case against too much letting down of the guard in marriage. She offered this summation of her philosophy:

> Wise is the man or woman who does his mental, spiritual and physical valeting in propinquity to no one. How much of heartache, private misery, public divorce scandal might be spared if only people who are forced by circumstances of marriage, money or relationship to live under the same roof could realize that the perils of propinquity lie in moral, mental and physical unfastidiousness.

What she did not mention to her *New York Times* interviewer or in her *Liberty* essay was how the spacious union she and Jacques had devised was roomy enough for her to have embarked on and sustained a parallel love affair, the record of which she clearly intended to remain sealed forever.

Fannie, without Jack, was often in the company of other men. Her assortment of regular escorts included elderly admirers such as Daniel Frohman, the legendary theater manager, and the philanthropist August Heckscher, and bon vivants like Charles Hanson Towne. Vilhjalmur Stefansson fell unremarkably into this group of readily available crooked elbows, but his relationship with Fannie quickly took on much more significance.

Fannie retained enough of the St. Louis prude never to face her desecration of the oath of trust she and Jack had proclaimed to all the world. Nor did she ever feel sufficiently liberated to be open about or comfortable with her choice. She was comfortable with secrets. And so the relationship remained a secret, just as her marriage had, so oddly, those first five years. It does, however, seem probable that some of Fannie's friends or Stef's (among her papers there are invitations to country weekends, such as one from Maxwell Anderson and his wife, at which Stef was also expected to be a guest) might have been wise to it.

Fannie never spoke about the relationship directly and went to great pains to code her veiled references to it in her memoirs. She did confess to the awkward situation in which she found herself. But she told the story as if it had occurred at a point in time well before she and Jacques were married, as if it were the tale of a young coquette's inability to choose between two ardent and worthy suitors. By such camouflage she cast away all intimation of impropriety. But she also offered far too elaborate a defense for what she had portrayed as an attractive young woman's rather ordinary dilemma—a situation that would not require any particular defense. As was her pattern Fannie let indecision rule. She said she did so because she wanted Jack and marriage and she wanted to be free. She needed more inner satisfaction with her work, and she wanted to experience whatever she could of life. The flattery of romantic attention from a dashing bachelor explorer also figured, as it satisfied a craving to be desired that had churned inside since her overfed high school days. And though she felt enormous affection and comfort in her relationship with Jack, she also coveted Stef's self-actuated scholarship, even as she deprecated it. She seemed to need the intellectual affirmation that his admiration of her represented. As she put it, "I am bulging with greed to see and be and do, even at the expense of those I love. Even, alas, at Jack's expense."

There was another possible element that she did not mention. At thirty-seven Fannie likely was coming to terms with the realization that she and Jack would never have children. She claimed, in a totally different context, that when children "did not come," in her phrase, she and Jacques "felt little of the frustration usually attributed to the childless." She thought the creative aspects of their respective careers had provided the compensation, but she was never really sure. It is not much of a leap to say that the relationship with Stef, like her menagerie, helped as well.

Many years after the fact, Fannie insisted that her attitude toward Stef never collided with her devotion to Jack. It is a dubious claim, and there is evidence to the contrary. Hers was a marriage she repeatedly insisted was idyllic, to a husband she insisted she made happy, to someone she had pledged a radical and very explicit trust.

True, in the eight years since she and Jacques exchanged vows in Lakewood, New Jersey, a new decade had brought in a far more sexually charged atmosphere. There was a much freer morality afloat, the sort of environment that might have led one not otherwise so inclined to stray—especially someone like Fannie, who had the pained, affair-strewn letters of Rebecca West for bedtime reading. Still, such long-term and angst-less duplicity is difficult to explain away.

There was a new apartment to furnish. Fannie would not for a moment have considered using any of that awful "manufactured Grand Rapids stuff." That was for the provinces. The rest of sophisticated New York at this time was opting for the era's modernism in interior design. And although this pared-down version of Fannie adopted the new look in jewelry and clothing, for the furnishing of her new home she unearthed "two glorious Spanish beds made out of church altars and a few choice pieces besides."

"The Literary Spotlight"

Fannie capped her most literarily brilliant year by shunning the high-paying, high-circulation magazines that gave her stardom in favor of more intellectually positioned outlets for her stories. "The Spangle That Could Be a Tear" went to *The Bookman,* and *The Forum* bought "White Apes." As was the habit with erudite journals, neither could make more than token payment. Henry Goddard Leach apologetically told Fannie that he knew the $500 he had offered for "White Apes" was only a seventh of her usual asking price. But it was twice what *The Forum* had ever paid for a story before. Besides, he said, telling her what she already knew, she would gain the advantage of a more critically tuned audience and the appealing company of writers such as Agnes Repplier and Anne Douglas Sedgwick. *McCall's* kept trying to put Fannie's fiction onto its pages, offering her $3,750 for the opportunity. But the editor, Harry Burton, was after a story "more magazineable" than "White Apes." Tempting as the proposition must have been, Fannie resisted this one time.

To secure her immediate financial future, Fannie turned to nonfiction to make up the slack. She prepared four sample editorials for the McClure's Syndicate before the year was out. This was in anticipation of a lucrative weekly column for the agency's newspaper clients in the new year. By June, thirty-four papers had signed on to run it. Burton of *McCall's* also confirmed a long-standing offer of ten thousand dollars to send Fannie to Russia in 1924 for a series of articles.

Still, it would have been foolhardy for Fannie to forgo a magazine sale of her next, as yet unwritten, novel—especially after learning how *The Forum* planned to publish "White Apes." "Breaking a short story into two parts is the sin unforgivable," she told Stef. "But I suppose they simply did not have the room." She discovered that she did not very much like the idea of a small audience either.

So much for the high road. Only twenty days after Fannie began very halting work on her next novel, *McCall's* bought first serial rights to it on the basis of a brief written outline. It was to be the story of a Roman Catholic girl who both panics and experiences a—hysterical?—religious epiphany before her impending marriage. She breaks her engagement and decides to enter a convent. The subject matter could not have been more problematic for a mass-market women's magazine, but Burton's greater concern was getting the name of Fannie Hurst onto *McCall's* pages as he had promised his readers. He immediately met her asking price of forty thousand dollars. He also took the precaution of insisting that she stick to the idea exactly as outlined and agree to delete or change to the magazine's satisfaction any passages it might deem offensive to readers. Burton, whose wife was a zealous writer of novels with Roman Catholic themes, advised Fannie to keep a "rocking chair position," to tell the story but not to discuss it in her text.

To Stef, Fannie confided that she disliked the magazine but agreed to publication because its large but very specific audience would not diminish book sales. In addition, forty thousand dollars was "a whopping serial price." Given her financial drought of the preceding two years, she was enthusiastic about the sale. "With anyone else I should feel a sense of braggadocia [sic] in telling you my affairs," she wrote to Stef in the uncharacteristically confidential vein she reserved for her closest relatives. "Not with you. Only a sense of the joy of taking you into my confidence."

She also expounded on what money had come to mean to her, refusing to see it as a goal in itself, except insofar as it provided freedom, and even that was of dubious benefit. "Money can make life so complex," she said. "I've never known what it means to have it in fabulous sums . . . but after one has more than enough to keep the ugly things of life pretty well out of the vista . . . it can become a task master. That is, unless one knows the secret of being perpetually debonair with money. Spending it—giving it—being wise with it—never canny. In my case the money value of my stuff is rather ironical. I honestly and sincerely care so little . . . except that I must earn if I would live."

Fannie was finally feeling comfortable in her newly positioned literary crown. *The Bookman*, after all, had honored her with its first "Literary Spotlight" of 1924, replete with a William Gropper caricature. The unidentified author of the appreciation proclaimed Fannie the reigning master of the short story, whose genius lay in "a marvelous knowledge of human nature, a marvelous feeling for the exact and subtle values of words—perhaps no other writer today can use a single word, or a brief phrase, with the stunning force and power she displays." Her technique was likened to that of the baseball pitcher who "winds himself up into various contortions and bowknots before he lets fly the ball." But unlike the pitcher, "she almost inevitably delivers a strike." And of her appearance, the author gushed about her opulence, her Oriental beauty "with very black hair and very red lips, a creamy skin and magnificent dark eyes. She dresses characteristically, in daring tam o'shanters, in gorgeous brocades and heavy embroideries." Still, the writer found her almost girlish in manner, even a little shy. "Modest and tongue-tied about her own work, she is full of enthusiasm about that of others. Her friends are almost all women—one feels that she has but small interest in men."

When Rebecca West came to town, Fannie sensed immediately how exhausted, ill, and unhappy her friend was and provided welcome serenity and comfort. Rebecca often looked to Fannie as an oasis of sound-mindedness. In this instance she found Fannie's patience and generosity "things marvelous to recall." Rebecca had planned her U.S. tour in large part to finalize a break from her deteriorating ten-year affair with H. G. Wells, with whom she had borne a son. She was suffering coughing fits and colitis and had been the object of much moralizing gossip. To Fannie she confided that she had been revisited by the newspaper magnate Max Beaverbrook, who had proclaimed love to her twice, made love to her this time during a brief but intense affair, then cut her off with a perplexing, agony-producing abruptness.

"Things are difficult for Rebecca," Fannie wrote to Stef. "She has been openly snubbed by the Woman's City Club and a speaking engagement canceled there. I burn with the injustice of it. But there is so little to do except by one's own puny and individual attitude refute the nagging, carping, stone-throwing world in which we live." Fannie hosted a tea in Rebecca's honor and sent invitations out to her most literary list. Zona Gale, celebrated author of the 1920 best-seller *Miss Lulu Bett,* attended, as did the screenwriter Anita Loos and John Emerson, and Fannie's old friends Bob and Madge Davis, and Carl Hovey and Sonya Levien. The Hoveys brought Emanie Sachs, a first-time novelist whose stories had been appearing in *Smart Set, Pictorial Review,* and *Hearst's.* Levien told Fannie that Sachs thought *Lummox* was the best book she had read in twenty years, but it was Sachs and Rebecca who forged the close friendship to follow.

Week followed week in unabated delight. There was tea with the film star Gloria Swanson and a private dinner with Zona Gale and Rebecca before she resumed her tour—Fannie liked writing Stef about that one—and then an appointment with the young literary sensation F. Scott Fitzgerald.

"I loathe agents"

Fannie's only professional difficulties in this period came from attempts to sell the film rights to *Lummox.* Movie producers were as hesitant about its prospects for the big screen as magazine editors had been about its serial publication. On top of that Fannie, again because of indecision, confused the matter totally and strained an important friendship by putting the property into too many hands.

More than a few agents liked to think of themselves as Fannie's sole representative. Fannie, for her part, was convinced that she needed none of them. It was true that R. L. Giffen of the Alice Kauser agency had closed a lucrative film deal for Fannie with the sale of *Star-Dust* back in 1920; it was also true that Fannie's friend Elisabeth Marbury had arranged her most recent sales of theatrical rights. Both were within reason to think they might have fair claim on *Lummox.* But as it happened Fannie firmly believed that the novel was hers to dispose of however she pleased—with or without an agent's assistance—and to the highest bidder.

"I loathe agents," she declared in a letter to Stef, dismissing them all as an annoying, pestering, competitive lot whose services she felt were largely superfluous. They were good at creating a market or enhancing a present one—two services for which Fannie had absolutely no use. Fannie felt that her commitment to Giffen ended with the conclusion of the *Star-Dust* deal, to be revived only with a new and attractive offer on another property. As for the American Play Company, Fannie had allowed the agency to intercede for her out of friendship to Marbury, its vice president, and to Charley Towne, who was heading the agency's literary department at the time. In Fannie's view she was without obligation to any of them, free to accept the best offer that came along regardless of how it got to her. Her loyalty went no further than the 10 percent she willingly paid for presentation of the highest bid.

And so, when Marbury originally asked Fannie about film rights to *Lummox,* Fannie told her that she would be happy to entertain any reasonable offer Marbury might bring. Marbury, operating as she did with other important authors, took this to mean that *Lummox* was hers to sell. As she later explained to Fannie, she had no written agreements with Oscar Wilde, Somerset Maugham, or Eugene O'Neill, but all of them got her agency involved from the outset whenever the subject of selling the dramatic rights to one of their literary properties came up.

At about the same time Giffen called Fannie to say that he had heard over the transom that *Lummox* had been sold to the movies. Fannie assured him this was not the case. He asked if she would give him permission to squelch the rumor and bring her a good offer. Fannie instantly said yes. Giffen took this to mean that she had granted him exclusive right to the property and immediately had a notice printed up which read:

LUMMOX
THE SENSATIONAL BEST SELLER
BY
FANNIE HURST
HAS NOT
BEEN SOLD FOR PICTURES
DESPITE REPORTS TO THAT EFFECT
AND IT WILL NOT BE
UNTIL I SELL IT, AS EXCLUSIVE AGENT FOR MISS HURST

Marbury saw the notice and wrote to Fannie at once. The insult was surely intensified by the fact that Giffen worked for Kauser, who had learned her craft over many years as Marbury's "brilliant" assistant.

"Of course, it is quite alright [*sic*] for you to do anything you please with your material," Marbury sniffed in a formal letter to Fannie. "Only I wish that such friends as Charley Towne and myself were not obliged to learn this kind of thing second hand instead of from you personally."

Fannie found Marbury's attitude bewildering and felt no embarrassment for her actions. She explained to Marbury how she viewed what had transpired and then told the agent that all of her dealings with the American Play Company had been out of friendship alone. By way of example Fannie cited the McClure's Syndicate arrangement. She said she had declined the exact same offer that Charley Towne presented to her when the syndicate approached her directly several months before. It was just that Charley had approached the syndicate without checking with Fannie first. "Sooner than disappoint Charley after all his effort," Fannie explained, "I signed without further ado."

Fannie sent all the correspondence to Stef, obviously under the baffling impression that its contents fully vindicated her. She felt blameless in the matter and thought that Marbury had behaved with shocking avarice. "I know it isn't the immediate money, but just part of the campaign of her life," Fannie said. "I cannot seem to get past bewilderment."

To Marbury, she wrote, "If you feel that our friendship has been violated, I assure you that I am even more deeply hurt than you, whom I have loved, must be."

Marbury let the matter drop. She wrote back to Fannie at once, offering congratulations to Giffen on his exclusivity and adding "in all sincerity" that she hoped the eventual deal would be lucrative. In her own hand she added, "Let us lunch together a day next week!" All was soon forgotten, and the friendship endured.

As it happened, it would take another four years to get a movie deal for *Lummox*. Neither Giffen nor Marbury negotiated the eventual sale.

Chapter *12*

"A torment of restlessness"

Fannie and Stef sustained and perhaps even heightened the intensity of their affair with cryptic letters and cables, punctuated by furtive, usually failed attempts to meet up on road or sea. Both of them traveled frequently for the greater part of the time they were romantically involved. As it happened, the long separations worked to the relationship's advantage; they increased the sense of longing and reduced the chance of discovery. More important for Fannie, they protected her need for distance, freedom, and privacy. Stef probably would never have understood this need of hers as well as Jack. Even at her most impassioned, Fannie remained somewhat remote.

This is not to say that the affair lacked intensity. By the time Stef left on a lecture tour starting in early January 1924, Fannie was finding his absences more difficult to endure. She wrote him almost daily, even though there was doubt the letters would reach him. She complained of experiencing "unexpected bad places," "staring, sort of vacant days," and "the curious gone feeling that I have when I talk over the radio—of no audience. Except that I know our radio is almost infallible." She spoke of the Sixty-sixth Street elevated train station and the Gotham Hotel—two venues of obvious significance to the two of them—and of "a torment of restlessness." His letters, she said, went "so deeply into the meaning of things, even when they seem most casual. It makes everything easier and less as if we were dressed up in Benda masks."

On her new diet and exercise program, she walked in the park for nearly two hours each day. She started work on her novel at about 9:00 A.M., sometimes blocking things out in her mind as she sat on a park bench. But progress was terribly slow. "I have the idea firmly in hand but it won't fit into a setting," she said. "I cannot seem to mount it. Places don't seem real to me yet and my characters are all jammed back in the fog." She wondered if the "burning restlessness" she felt was the cause. The work simply had not yet gripped her enough to make her "a little mad with the joy of the job. Or does that kind of madness seem suddenly pale."

She said she was able to concentrate, even though she was encountering "bad places"—bad meaning bad for concentration because her thoughts had a new "—a happy—hunting ground! And yet I know that I must not be lured into the intoxicating ether except when the daily stint is done and that somehow helps the doing of the daily stint."

She spoke wistfully of the "lovely" reason she had been experiencing intermittent insomnia "for some time past," which a recent night out to the theater to see Max Reinhardt's *Miracle* had exacerbated. "You who analyze beauty so relentlessly will, I think, succumb without mental reservations to this. I did. I came home dazed and thrilled and a little drunk and with a tingling kind of excitement that somehow now I am more capable of than before." She offered to go see it a second time with him, even though she made a point of never seeing performances twice. She said she found her entire chemistry had quickened. "Sharper more stimulating reactions. Isn't that what Byron called the intensification of his capacity for life." Of course, the corresponding penalty was depression of equal magnitude. "But it's worth it!" she said.

At Stef's gentle prodding she also had taken to reading over his manuscripts and helping him with editors in whose magazines he wanted to see his work published. She spoke to one of the syndicates about getting him a column like her own. Stef was never bashful about requesting this kind of assistance from Fannie. Access she could arrange, and she did so willingly and freely. But Stef's work apparently did not meet the commercial editorial standard in the way that hers did, and she was unable to get him any financially meaningful assignments.

By the end of January a St. Louis stop had been added to Stef's lecture tour. He wanted Fannie to try to meet him there, a place she could travel to without raising suspicion. But Fannie could not rearrange her schedule to go on such short notice. She already had committed to address the combined English classes at Columbia University on the afternoon of February 8 and to be honored by the Barnard Club that night. The National Women's Painters Association was honoring her the next day at the Cosmopolitan Club, and Judge Samuel Levy had arranged for her to sit in on a number of children's court cases in the afternoon. February 10 she was addressing a mass meeting of the National Health Circle for Colored People, a visiting nurse association for indigent black people in the South that Fannie had started to support actively.

"Does this sound feverish?" she asked Stef. She assured him that she never interrupted her workday for such events, scheduling them all after four o'clock in the afternoon. And anyway, she told him, "—they help the Restlessness!"

She went on: "Do you know the art of rereading a letter until it doesn't have to be read off the paper at all but has burned itself into the consciousness. Sometime I shall instruct you."

Ruth Bryan Owen

Fannie eagerly anticipated Stef's return to New York on March 7. Ironically, his arrival roughly coincided with publication of the

McCall's symposium "Does a Moment of Revolt Come to Every Married Man?" Fannie contributed along with Somerset Maugham, Joseph Hergesheimer, Gertrude Atherton, Charles and Kathleen Norris, Will and Inez Haynes Irwin, Zelda and F. Scott Fitzgerald, and Mr. and Mrs. Wallace Irwin. Her answer, like most of the others, was yes, that a moment of revolt comes to "practically every occupant of this draft-ridden, leaky, old-fashioned and defective institution." Divorce courts housed the explosions, the active revolts, she said, but there were also "moments of passive revolt . . . the dynamite sticks that never go off. . . . Latent world-smashing power that men (and women) carry under their hearts!" Indeed.

She postponed her departure for Russia twice; once probably to leave time to spend with Stef on his brief stay in New York between the end of his national lecture tour and his trip to Australia, and a second time because her father suddenly took ill, necessitating another trip to St. Louis. The delay also enabled her to see the premiere of the screen version of her ten-year-old story *The Nth Commandment.* This was another Cosmopolitan Productions release of a Frank Borzage–Frances Marion collaboration on one of her early works. Again, the screen plot varied widely from Fannie's original story. In Fannie's version a beautiful, married salesgirl cleverly outsmarts and takes full financial advantage of a rake who wines and dines her with the clear expectation of sexual favors in return. Only at the end of the story does it become clear that she has led him on for a higher purpose: to save the life of her tubercular husband and provide for her infant child.

While in St. Louis, Fannie addressed the Chamber of Commerce, prompting a graduate school professor at Washington University to tell her how much he enjoyed *Lummox* and how it had, finally, made him a believer in her work. Despite the left-handed compliment, his note was one of the few affirmations of any kind she had received from her alma mater in the fifteen years since graduation. This was a major and enduring irritant for her. College had been one of her most happy and important experiences, and she dearly coveted a spot among Washington University's distinguished alumni. How was it possible that the administration and faculty seemed so pointedly to ignore her lengthening list of extraordinary accomplishments? Anything that reminded her of this slight rankled.

Fannie finally set the time of her Atlantic crossing for mid-June, even though her father's condition had not improved. The doctor advised that to change her schedule again would only cause her father further worry.

The delay had one fine advantage. It created an opportunity for Stef, once back in New York, to introduce Fannie to a visiting acquaintance of his. Ruth Bryan Owen was an attractive, talented dynamo who also was bred in the Middle West. Yet unlike Fannie, Ruth, the daughter of William Jennings Bryan, grew up among the powerful. Political activism and access were second nature to her. Even in the complacent, apolitical St. Louis neighborhoods of Fannie's childhood, Ruth's father's fame had penetrated. Everyone, Fannie said, spoke of "free silver" and "The Cross of Gold." Ruth herself had been an early source of fascination for Fannie and her St. Louis pals. For while Fannie wallowed in the fat-teenager doldrums, Ruth was upsetting her parents by marrying a well-known painter twice her age. They soon divorced. Fannie still remembered how national reports of Ruth's bold and rebellious act "had the small girls of my world goggle-eyed." Actually, Fannie, never missing an opportunity to make herself seem younger, was not so small at the time. Like Ruth, she was eighteen years old.

Fannie's new friend was also a woman of limitless energy. During the war she had become one of twelve members of the American Women's Relief Fund, helping to establish a hospital in Paignton, Devonshire, for the care of three thousand soldiers. She was cosecretary of the fund's Economic Relief Committee, which helped women in need in London to find regular employment. She also helped organize the Woolwich Girls Club, a settlement house for factory girls in southeast London.

In 1915 Ruth went to Alexandria, Egypt, as a nurse. In that time she progressed from ward nurse to surgical nurse to nurse in the front-line hospitals. When it became too dangerous for outside entertainers to enter the battle zone, she put her rich contralto voice to work entertaining the troops after grueling days caring for the injured. More recently she had been living in Florida with her four children and second husband, Reginald Owen, a British army officer who had contracted Bright's disease during the conflict and became one of her patients. A later attack of scarlet fever affected his kidneys, and he was left an invalid. Ruth tried her hand at filmmaking but relied most heavily on the lecture circuit to supplement the family income. Unsurprisingly, she was a phenomenal public speaker, especially on the subject of peace, civic responsibility, and the horrors of war.

In letters Ruth had been prodding Stef to arrange an opportunity for her to meet Fannie, and she could not have been more effusive in her thanks for the introduction. She found Fannie delightful and "fell in love with her at first sight." Fannie quickly took Ruth under her wing, inviting her to a dinner party at home and then to the International PEN benefit, where she introduced Ruth to Herbert Swope of the *World*, whom Ruth had wanted to meet. "So you see I am indebted to you, indirectly for all sorts of pleasant things. I hope that I may keep Fanny's [*sic*] friendship as a permanent possession."

This she did. From the evidence of the reams of correspondence in Fannie's files, and the scores of women with whom Fannie shared warm and important friendships, no other such relationship compares. Fannie simply adored Ruth Bryan Owen, and the feeling appears to have been mutual. Ruth opened the world of political power to Fannie and clearly was instrumental in her political education and evolution. She never hesitated to ask favors of Fannie in return—big ones—to which Fannie always generously and happily responded.

"*Abie's Irish Rose*"

The PEN banquet to which Fannie took Ruth Bryan Owen was cause for a small contretemps between Fannie and her fellow novelist and essayist Mary Austin, both of whom were active in the writers' rights organization. Newspapers had picked up on Fannie's dismay over the choice of the evening's entertainment, a benefit performance of *Abie's Irish Rose*. Austin then had called on Fannie to express her feelings about the work in remarks before the performance.

"Perhaps if I were a Mary Austin and sufficiently secure in my remoteness from the feeble aspects of the play in question, I might not feel as I do," Fannie wrote to Austin. "It may be just that sort of inferiority complex, although I will never admit that my work at any time had any of the qualities that make *Abie's Irish Rose* a travesty on life."

This particular "travesty" had opened on Broadway two years earlier. The author, Anne Nichols, Georgia-born and Philadelphia-bred, was neither Jewish nor Catholic and had never met a member of either group until she was fifteen. Critics despised the play, dismissing it immediately as vulgar, unoriginal, and sentimental. Robert Benchley of *Life* even went so far as to run contests for his readers to send in capsule criticisms of it, declaring Harpo Marx's quip "No worse than a bad cold" the winner. Nothing, however, stopped the play from achieving overwhelming popular success. The original production ran for a phenomenal 2,327 performances and subsequently enjoyed countless road shows and a long-running radio adaptation. It made Nichols a millionaire.

Fannie, like other PEN members, had wanted Reinhardt's *Miracle* to be the choice for the benefit presentation, but Austin had championed *Abie*. She felt that it represented American folk art drama in much the way Mutt and Jeff represented the folk art of the day. "That does not mean that I am pleased with it, or that I would not much rather have a higher kind of folk art," Austin said. It was her view that tastes in folk art seemed to run to the farcical and grotesque because "the folk of America, being mostly transplanted, find it easier to get rid of the racial or group peculiarities that they find hampering them by laughing them off." Fannie, in turn, said she had nothing positive to say about this story of a Jewish-Irish courtship and marriage. She did not think it represented folk life in America, and she certainly was not prepared to do the playwright the discourtesy of saying so in her presence. Besides, to say anything at all on the night of the performance, Fannie thought, could be construed as support for the work. This she could not allow.

Clearly Austin thought no less of Fannie for her refusal, for it was only a few months later that she asked Fannie to expound on the nature of her creativity for her latest book, *Everyman's Genius*. Fannie offered her reflections but asked specifically that she not be identified by name in print.

Fannie told Austin that she found herself relying more on her subconscious, which was not to say the conscious processes of writing were any less difficult. Any idea, Fannie said, almost always came in the identical way. She made the debatable claim that, with one exception, she had never taken an incident, character, or situation directly from life. Instead, she said, "there usually arises in my mind, apropos of nothing in so far as I am able to directly trace, the beginnings of the idea, some such question as this: Given a combination of certain conditions, how will a given human being react to them? The story then builds itself around this central query." As her career had progressed, she said, she found herself less and less dependent on concrete examples of human behavior. Instead, she said, "combinations of facts present themselves to me from some no-man's land of my consciousness." She explained more fully: Psychologically the facts actually represent "composite subconscious impressions that have got themselves caught in my brain-grooves, but there are times when these impressions seem to march themselves out, reluctantly it is true, onto my typewriter roll in a fashion over which I have no particular jurisdiction." Sometimes she found herself wondering if "that mysterious force in the unchartered areas of my brain was reliable, or was only a madness lurking there."

Austin included Fannie's remarks under Fannie's name—she wasn't sure if she or the publisher was to blame—but told her she was in very good company and hoped she wouldn't mind being identified. She said both she and May Sinclair had the same experience as Fannie of being able to describe things and places they had never seen. "You are so innocent of the mystical technique," she said, "and yet evidently so intelligent an observer of yourself, that I am sure it would be very much worthwhile to study you."

Chapter *13*

"Mr. and Mrs. Ivan Doe"

Long before Harry Burton put up the ten thousand dollars to send Fannie to Russia for *McCall's*, she had wanted to go. Besides her abortive attempt to make the trip with John Reed for *Metropolitan* back in 1915, Ray Long had offered to send her for *Cosmopolitan* in 1922, but she couldn't get a visa. The same thing happened when Burton first made the offer for *McCall's* in 1923. It was just as well that her travel plans fell through that time, because the general feeling was that it took until 1924 for anti-American sentiment to soften up enough for it to be a better time to try.

Giving such an assignment to Fannie meant the plus of Jacques, who spoke fluent Russian and could demystify the local culture. According to several profiles of Jacques in various music periodicals, his grandfather Roman Danielson was a well-known artist, and his father, Samuel, was an important sculptor, decorated by the czar. Jacques himself was said to have studied at the prestigious Moscow Conservatory of Music until he immigrated to the United States with his father and brothers in 1891. Jacques, then known as Jacob, was seventeen at the time. Fannie seemed delighted to be making the trip with him— even going to quite some pains to find out about and book a lovely French hideaway for them to enjoy en route. Stef had taken off for Australia a month before she and Jack sailed.

Burton's idea was to have Fannie write a three-part series on the lives of "Mr. and Mrs. Ivan Doe" in their "falling civilization," and she had enormous enthusiasm for the plan. Ever since Jacques had come into her life, and the Russians had embarked on their grand experiment in socialism, Fannie, like so many Americans, had wanted to know everything about the changes revolution had wrought. She told a reporter she wanted "to see what has happened to the people, to study them sociologically, in the hamlets and in the country—to see what is their reaction, and what is coming out of all that blackness and illiteracy." The "Slav temperament" simply fascinated her. "Think what it is bringing to this country, what it is giving us!" she told a reporter. "Russia is the theater of the world today—a potential country to be mined intellectually, actually, literally and figuratively."

Their visit lasted a full three weeks, ending in mid-August of 1924. Before she left Moscow the *New York Times* correspondent Walter Duranty interviewed Fannie. She told him she was most profoundly struck by the country's emphasis on youth. It gave her the feeling that the entire nation had been put into the hands of its emerging generation. "There is all of youth's crudity, ignorance and recklessness, youth's restiveness and contempt, even toward elders and older ways. But there is also youth's tremendous vitality, youth's hopefulness and youth's power to work miracles because it does not know that impossibilities are impossible," she said. If America was a melting pot, Russia was "a mess of chemicals fizzing and bubbling together. What the final precipitate will be it is impossible to conceive."

In Paris she was interviewed again, by a correspondent for the *International Herald Tribune*. This reporter quoted her—she claimed erroneously—calling the Soviet experiment "a great beast, half-stupid, half-mad, on its back in death agony." Leon Trotsky was "the only white light of inspiration," and Petrograd and Moscow were horrible places, whose inhabitants lived in deepest poverty and overwhelming fear. The visit had convinced her, the *Tribune* reported, to "climb down from the soapbox forever."

Strangely, *The New York Times* ignored its own reporter's story and commented editorially on the *Herald Tribune* interview. The *Times* likened Fannie's change of heart to that of Emma Goldman, "a woman much more red than Miss Hurst ever was." The *Times* said Fannie had left home believing Russia's rulers were making a "highly laudable reform in the conduct of human affairs and that they deserved the sympathy and encouragement which, with grief, regret and some indignation, she saw so many people here refusing to give them."

The Nation found the whole subject interesting enough to cover and picked up Fannie's original Moscow interview while ignoring the more damning comments in the subsequent report from Paris. Later the editor explained that the choice was made because Duranty's work was usually reliable and appeared in this case to reflect Fannie's general attitudes. Fannie wrote the editor to thank him for his good judgment, saying that the report from Paris had been "grotesque."

"It is true that I have come out of Russia with certain disillusionments, but not the hodgepodge of cheap, sensational catchphrases calculated to make headlines," she wrote. She said she had commented at length on both the favorable and unfavorable aspects of Russia, as she saw them, and certainly hadn't leaped to any "hysteria of condemnation." She went on: "Convinced as I am that the Russia I beheld is far from the goal her well-wishers have set up for her, my faith in the ultimate success of the experiment has not wavered."

McCall's ran Fannie's three-part series in January, February, and March 1925. McClure's Syndicate serialized the work as soon as it ended in *McCall's,* and newspapers such as the *New York World* ran it in full. The *World* heralded the report as a close-up view of the Russia of today "in a way that gives an insight into his hopes, ambitions and fears as nothing else ever has done." There was much less clearing of the throat in the edited-down version for the *World*, which began like this:

I have been to Russia.

The Russia I have seen is the Russia of flux. The laboratory whose floor is slippery with blood is also befogged with fumes. But when you stop to think that it is the largest laboratory in the world and the most combustible experiment in all the history of mankind, the eight years of its duration are scarcely more than a month as computed on the calendar of empire-building.

Fannie chronicled her travels alone by train from Berlin to Riga, where Jacques, traveling from Vienna, met her. Together they went on to Moscow, where she browsed and ambled and visited "not with the Leon Trotskys but the John Smithskys." Actually, though she did not say so in the article, she met Trotsky as well, simply by writing a letter to him and asking for an appointment. He received her at the far end of a ceremonial room then furnished with only his desk and yellow oak office chairs. The walk to the other end was "a grilling mile to traverse," she recalled, "reducing the visitor to peanut proportions." The top of his desk was swept clean, except for a book—her own *Lummox,* from which he began to recite from memory. He said it was one of his favorites. Trotsky was enough taken with Fannie that they met again, in August 1938, when she was vacationing in Mexico and he was living out his last months in exile before his assassination. A writer acquaintance of Fannie's, Leone Moats, arranged quietly for Fannie to visit both Trotsky and the painter Diego Rivera.

In her article Fannie described the Russians she had gotten to know. There were "the A's," a family whose breadwinner was a hundred-thousand-dollar-a-year consulting engineer before the revolution and now earned thirty dollars a month as superintendent of a farm implement factory. "B" was a deported Russian-born West Broadway furrier who with his sisters and brother-in-law lived in two rooms in the center of Moscow. The entrance to their apartment had fallen into such disrepair that the only way in was through a kitchen courtyard. Six families shared that kitchen, including one that kept kosher, necessitating a separate oil stove, which they propped on a soap box in the corner.

A fairly recent Jackie Coogan movie was playing at the local cinema, and B's married sister told Fannie how horrifying it was that poor little Jackie's Hollywood bosses drove him "to the last breath of his tortured body"—this she had read in the Moscow press—and what a pernicious and horrible example he was of American child labor practices, of the babies "being broken across the wheel of capitalism." Fannie reported at length on her teatime with "The Lady of the Chocolates," a member of the Russian theater movement, and introduced to American readers characters such as "Girl with Red Heels," the product of New Russia, a sixteen-year-old who had forsaken the Old Testament Judaism of her forebears for a magazine called *Bezbozhnik*—"Atheist," or literally, "Without God." Fannie pictured the girl's mother, a tram car driver she dubbed Old Woman, wringing her hands in fear of the return of pogroms and persecution as Girl with Red Heels, cigarette at her lips, crossed her feet, dangled her red heels, and shrugged her insolent young shoulders. Before leaving Moscow Fannie posed for a photograph laying a wreath at the grave of John Reed.

Harry Burton could not have been more pleased with Fannie's report. "Not since I have been editor here," he said, "have I received any articles having as much vitality, clearheadedness and charm as these."

The access Jacques provided to Moscow's "Smithskys" was unparalleled, and Fannie was clearly grateful for what he had made possible. She dubbed Jacques "Himself" in the series, the name by which she ordinarily referred to him in letters, and complimented him warmly. Before leaving she sent a copy of Stef's most recent work, *The Northward Course of Empire,* to Trotsky.

"The awfulness"

It took Fannie a year to write *Appassionata,* and at the beginning of January she handed in her completed manuscript to the editors at *McCall's,* fully expecting her forty-thousand-dollar payment. Instead, the editors claimed that what Fannie had produced deviated dramatically from her initial outline and was sure to offend the great majority of *McCall's* readers. They demanded drastic changes, and despite deep reluctance Fannie made them, as she said, "reducing my script to pulp." When the magazine still declined to publish the serial, Fannie saw no recourse but to sue. It took two years for her attorney to negotiate a settlement, but in the end she walked away with a check for twenty thousand dollars from the magazine. She never wrote for *McCall's* again.

The temporary setback did not impair her generosity toward her friends. Stef sent Fannie a check for $1,040 to repay, with interest, a $1,000 loan. She sent back his check uncashed. "I know you are in rather a financial jam right now," her dictated letter read. "Jack and I don't want you to feel hurried about paying off this little debt." Besides, she said, the idea of taking interest from a friend gave her a "de Medici, three-ball feeling."

Slyly, Fannie conducted much of her correspondence with Stef offhandedly through her secretary, sending friendly but formal notes in the nature of those she might send to Charley Towne or Carl Van Vechten. There were other letters which she wrote privately, however—handwritten in her unmistakable, unbeautiful script or badly typed with the equal giveaway of stray asterisks and missing apostrophes. They often bore no salutation, complimentary closing, or signature, and she marked the most personal with the word DESTROY.

There was money to be made on the book-publishing rights to *Appassionata.* Unhappy with the way Harper & Brothers had handled *Lummox,* Fannie again decided to change publishers. It could not have escaped her that Edna Ferber's *So Big,* published by Doubleday, was the number one best-seller of 1924, while *Lummox* had not even cracked the top ten for the year before. She placed the blame on Harpers. Horace Liveright of Boni & Liveright got wind of Fannie's dissatisfaction and immediately made an offer for *Appassionata,* but Fannie had other plans. Only recently she had befriended Blanche Knopf, who with her husband, Alfred, owned the prestigious publishing house Alfred A. Knopf. Fannie accepted an advance of three thousand dollars against royalties of 15 percent on the first thirty thousand copies and agreed to rework the manuscript by late summer. Knopf planned to publish the book in January 1926. Liveright played the jolly good sport. "Hell," he wrote, "life's much too short and too long, too, from another point of view, to let immediate selfish interest dwarf all of the much more lovely things." Again, Jonathan Cape agreed to publish in Britain.

Fannie was generally open to less than literary propositions that could enhance her celebrity and replenish her bank account. For someone of her reputation and popularity, the national lecture circuit was a natural. For years, agents had been hounding her to sign on for extended tours. The problem was that Fannie loathed public speaking, even though she happened to be exceptionally good at it. What she described as "the awfulness" engulfed her in the hours before she approached a lectern. Not only that but such tours required booking a year in advance. Almost as a matter of principle Fannie resisted any commitment that did not leave her free to change her plans on a whim. She also, as always, bristled at the idea of working through an agency. Nevertheless, at fees of four to five hundred dollars for a couple of hours' work—plus expenses for her and a secretary and all that good publicity—she found a way to endure it. The scent of Stef and Ruth Bryan Owen, who were annual diehards on the lecture trail, must have lain heavily over Fannie's decision to overcome her dread. She signed on for a monthlong national speaking tour for the Louis J. Alber agency in March 1925.

What she could not have anticipated was that her father would take ill again just as she got ready to pack. Fortunately, she had arranged her schedule so that she had a few days in St. Louis before heading cross-country to Pasadena, and that put her at ease. Just before her first appearance Bob Davis happened to cable that he had arranged for all of her books to be housed at an O. Henry Memorial in Asheville, North Carolina. The news, she said, in her answer to Davis from St. Louis on March 9, "shamed me into success. Anybody lucky enough to receive a wire like that would have to justify it." She went on:

> And strange as it may seem, I did go over! But then—
> all buoyed up of the one success, and ready for the cross
> country dash, I've run into a tragic denouement. I
> managed my schedule so that I might have a few days
> visit en route to Pasadena with my father in St. Louis.
> The morning of my arrival he was taken with such a
> severe heart attack that it is out of the question for me

to continue my journey. I have wired ahead
cancellations. It looks as if my father will not emerge
from his state of coma.
    What a stern affair the merry business of life suddenly
becomes when it presents its unfathomable side.

Sam Hurst died that day at the age of seventy-six. In the moments before his death, Fannie said he thanked her for enriching his life and prayed that her husband would never fail her—though he still could not bring himself to say Jacques's name. He also implored her to humor her mother, who would have no financial worries since he had left his wife with an estate worth some one hundred thousand dollars, substantial for the times. Still, Fannie said of her mother, "Her life line was too fused with Papa's to bear the severance. . . . Mama's face became an empty house, all the windows dark because the lights in her eyes were out."

On March 13 Fannie wrote Bob Davis again:

Dear Bob,
    My Father is dead.
    And one takes up and carries on.
    The matter of the O. Henry Memorial in Asheville
will be attended to as promptly as I can send for a batch
of books, autograph them and send them onto F. Roger
Miller.
    It will be good to see you when I return in April.
    Fannie.

In no other surviving letters to her friends does Fannie express more sentiment than this about the death of her father. Rabbi Leon Harrison of Temple Israel replied in kind to her "mournful note [which] awakened poignant emotions in my sensitive soul. I felt for you deeply for I have been through all that, and worse."

Stef cabled, too. AWFULLY SORRY. YOU HAVE TO KEEP TO THE TASK. Dutifully, Fannie resumed her tour on March 16 with an appearance in Kansas City. She headed west the next day.

Her letters to Stef in this hectic period are consumed with the immediacies of the tour. She conveys no trace of grief, no anxiety about her mother, whom she had left in the care of a devoted neighbor, Julia Browne. She complains of a lack of positive feedback from the lecture agency and of the "awfulness." She also delights in a *Houston Chronicle* reporter's description of her as "slender," which the photograph illustrating the article confirms. "SPINACH IS JUSTIFIED," she scrawled happily in pen across the margin of the clipping. There is no mention of Pop.

"*Are a Woman's Secrets Her Own?*"

Back in New York while Fannie was on the road, Jacques completed an article about his wife for the British book journal *Now and Then.* He sent a copy to Blanche Knopf. "I am anxious for you to read it," he told her, "because it reflects so many of the things I feel about Fannie and which I want in time to see the American public appreciate even more than it does at present." Unfortunately, no copy of the manuscript is known to have survived.

On their tenth anniversary, May 5, Fannie and Jack went back to Lakewood, New Jersey, the scene of their marriage, which *The New York Times* duly reported. Was it true they had an agreement to renew the relationship annually or declare it void by separation? Fannie would not answer. Jacques said it had been true when they first married, but now they were renewing at five-year intervals.

It was not Fannie's talent as a writer but her talent for making the public care about whatever she was up to that fascinated B. Z. Goldberg, the Jewish intellectual and writer. In an article for the Yiddish newspaper *The Day (Tog),* Goldberg mused on this "art in itself." Theodore Roosevelt had it, as well as others much less prominent or talented. "Nobody knows just why."

Goldberg was equally struck by the atmosphere in Fannie's studio, a place that reminded him, on entry, of an old church archive, an old monastery, and at times even the Tower of London. In it he found old furniture and statues standing under mounted heads of both the Virgin Mary and Jesus, as well as the covers of old Torahs. The candle-lighting of an elderly maid, the screeching howl of a puppy, and a monkey's rasps heralded Fannie's entrance. She appeared in a simple yet elegant dress. He noted her figure—"of the Jewish type, medium height, rather broad and stout"—and her "considerable face," with hair carefully glued back at the temples. "She speaks rather affectedly, careful how the words leave her mouth, and says very little. . . . There is not even the pretense of a seeking, a longing, a groping in her soul, a reaching out into the beyond. You do not feel like talking to her of *Weltschmerz* and *Weltanschauung* and a philosophy of life. You are more inclined to talk of simple home affairs."

And yet, he said, he very much had the impression that Fannie considered herself an artist. Her theory, he said, was that popular success need not preclude the creation of good literature. No great writer ever ran away from popular success once he saw it coming, she said. To this last Goldberg offered no comment of his own.

As it happened, popular success was serving Fannie very well—at least financially. Much to Ray Long's relief she started selling short stories to *Cosmopolitan* again, now at a fat $3,250 per story. Of the two that appeared in 1925, "The Gold in Fish," the saga of the Goldfish family, had significant afterlife in the form of a play and then a film.

Fannie's weekly articles for the McClure's Syndicate had created a welcome revenue stream, only they involved a lot more work than she had originally contracted to do. Newspaper editors, it turned out, were far more interested in getting minifiction at about a thousand words instead of the "soapbox speeches" Fannie had agreed to produce. The problem was, to write even very short fiction took much more time and effort. Her feature was popular with editors, and Fannie felt she had the leverage to ask for some special consideration: intermittent relief from her obligation, additional compensation for the work she was putting in, or at least a return to the easier "soapbox" format. She understood that Clinton Brainard, the syndicate's chief, might think she could easily turn these short fiction pieces into more elaborate and polished stories for more money later. But this was not the way her mind worked. "Once I have used the germ of an idea in 'editorial' form, it is second hand and [I] am no longer interested in it for future use," she told him.

She said her complaint was about the burden the assignment had become. But she also was quick to mention that enlarging any three or four of these ministories to four thousand words would pay as much as her whole year's contract from McClure's, which guaranteed thirteen thousand dollars for 1925, fifteen thousand for 1926, and eighteen thousand dollars in 1927. There is no indication that Brainard released Fannie from the contract, nor that he made the deal any easier or sweeter.

She did have another outlet for less taxing writing assignments. An informal arrangement for nonfiction articles from *Liberty* magazine began in 1924. Fannie picked very general topics for these occasional essays, which appear to have required little or no research. "Are a Woman's Secrets Her Own?" (Absolutely. Tell nothing of the past after marriage.) "Ain't Human Nature Human?" (Indeed. People are finally the same whatever the culture.) "Which Would You Rather Be? A Man or a Woman?" (A woman. Born into a time of new and pioneering possibilities. What's exciting anymore about being a man?) "The American Husband" (Neither couth nor scholarly but kind, loyal, sacrificial, devoted to wife and children. The lady writer salutes him. Was this a paean to her own father?)

But *Liberty* had bigger plans for Fannie in preparation for its May issue of 1925. The executive editor, John Wheeler, asked her to write a promotional introduction to a contest the magazine had decided to sponsor. From a dark and dramatic photograph by Nickolas Muray, Fannie looks off the page and into the eyes of readers, urging them to submit ideas for "Liberty's Greatest Contest." These were to be suitable for both a serial story for *Liberty* and a motion-picture screenplay. First prize? An unbelievable fifty thousand dollars.

"A person who has never written a line of fiction in his life may carry around a brain teeming with ideas, plots and situations and characters and never dream of getting them out," Fannie wrote, "until an idea contest such as *Liberty*'s throws the stick of dynamite necessary to stimulate him."

Wheeler, the novelist Rex Beach, and Jesse Lasky of Famous Players–Lasky Productions, judged the hundred thousand entries. Imagine the swell of hope in the hearts of would-be writers across the country. And imagine then the cynicism that greeted news that the contest's celebrity introducer, Fannie Hurst, also had produced its winning entry.

"I Have Been to Hollywood"

By July, Fannie took up residence in a bungalow in Beverly Hills and was hard at work on the serial story for *Liberty* to complement the upcoming screenplay she had outlined in detail to Jesse Lasky. She had to wait around for weeks for film production to begin, and since *Liberty* did not plan to announce the prizewinner until mid-August, Fannie had to keep her reason for being in Los Angeles secret. The magazine, however, wasted no time spreading the word to potential advertisers: "Would you object to saying your winning scenario was written on a Corona typewriter?" John Wheeler queried.

Wheeler, Fannie, Lasky, and even the magazine's owner, Col. Robert R. McCormick in Chicago, got into the back-and-forth over a title for the serial and movie. "The Moving Finger Writes," à la Omar Khayyám, "Orchid," and "Song Without Words" were Fannie's early suggestions for her highly melodramatic tale of the beautiful young store model whose half-witted nursemaid kidnaps her from a good home in infancy and brings her up in poverty and drunken squalor. In a triumph of good breeding, the child, Orchid, rises above her surroundings. The director, James Cruze, wanted to call the picture "That Elegant Flower." McCormick favored "The Moving Finger." Fannie offered "Baby Bunting" and "Girdles of Garlands," which no one liked, before a consensus formed around "Mannequin." Though the title had been used for a movie before (and would be several times after), the legal department declared it an acceptable choice.

Fannie could not have been more delightedly disdainful of the whole Hollywood experience. "The cinema way of doing things," she wrote to Elisabeth Marbury before a dinner engagement with Mary Pickford and Douglas Fairbanks, "is to bring the author out here in luxury, run up enormous expense of upkeep et al., and then after six or eight weeks of that kind of performance, get down to the business of production." She had Alice Joyce, Gloria Swanson, and Lillian Gish for neighbors, "but in California, Movieland, one dare not gratify one's Middle West instinct by running in next door for a chat," she explained. "One communicates entirely via secretary and carefully typewritten note. One makes very elaborate and grand gestures with one's next door neighbor for a dinner engagement six days hence." Fannie said she expected to come "blazing home upon you draped in something or other that cost $41,500. I don't know what it will be, but one cannot go home from these luxurious parts without being draped in something or other that cost at least that sum."

She never managed to see Frances Marion on that trip and mentioned it to the Marbury, who was Marion's good friend. "I imagine that about forty-eight shining black slaves with turquoise studded into their flesh and emerald beaded eyelashes, must protect her from the motley herd, of which I form so small a part," Fannie teased, adding that she didn't know how much more of all this "gorgeousness" she could stand.

Of course the proximity to Jesse Lasky and Gloria Swanson got Fannie a twenty-five-thousand-dollar deal to write a modern version of *The Taming of the Shrew* for the movie star. She also hand-delivered a copy of the manuscript of *Appassionata* to Mary Pickford, who Fannie said had the "golden, spiritual, luminous quality that I feel the role requires." Pickford was polite though she showed no particular interest in playing Fannie's controversial Roman Catholic heroine, but she used the opportunity of her letter of regret to invite Fannie to dinner with Lillian Gish on the twenty-seventh. (Fannie had approached Gish about doing the film before she got to L.A.) Over a casual lunch Fannie excited Lois Weber, the director, about the prospect of making a movie of "The Gold in Fish." That project foundered a few months later, however, when, according to Weber, the Motion Picture Exhibitors and Producers nixed her choice for the lead, Alla Nazimova. Norma Talmadge would have made a good substitute, Weber thought, but said Talmadge did not want to play a Jewish role.

On it went. Fannie's appointment calendar for lunches, teas, and dinners reads like a rollout of screen credits: Theda Bara, Bebe Daniels, Louise Dresser, William de Mille, Charles Ray, Lillian Gish. Fannie bought a police dog for companionship.

The whole experience put her in "a merry sort of stupor," with more "pep de vie" than she had ever had before. "People have always told me that with my superabundance of vitality I should seek out a tropical clime," she wrote to her old friend Ruth Raphael, still a book publicist at Harper & Brothers. "But what the tropical clime is doing to me is only to speed up my merciless speed." In her two months in California, she polished the manuscript of *Appassionata* and delivered it to Knopf, she offered *Cosmopolitan* a short story and wrote it, and she wrote an essay for *Liberty* entitled "I Have Been to Hollywood," in which she gave her impressions of that "potpourri of a civilization that has sprung full-grown out of the bulging brow of an art-industry.

> I have dined with "Doug and Mary," young Olympians, in their home on the top of the world. I have walked with Lillian Gish, who is herself moonlight, in moonlight. I have stood in a ballroom with the matchless Pola and beheld the gilded, the shellacked, the No. 2 grease-painted, the manicured, the pedicured, the celluloid youth of this Athens-on-the–Santa Fe vie for the privilege of hanging their patent leather scalps about her fair and Polish waist.
>
> I have beheld Valentino at close enough range to set the composite flapper spine of America to ringing like a bell. I have dined at Hollywood's Montmartre beside Adolphe Menjou straight "off the

set" and still in the make-up and silk dressing gown demanded by his role. I have sat between Ramon Novarro and Rod La Rocque at luncheon and enjoyed the ecstatic and vicarious indigestion of all their fans.

She also started work on a stage version of *Lummox,* telling David Belasco she hoped to greet him by fall bearing the play she still owed him.

Foremost, of course, she accomplished her primary purpose: the scenario outline and full book-length magazine serial of *Mannequin* for *Liberty.* Knopf was to have first option on publishing the serial as a novel, but Fannie assured Blanche: "Be of good cheer. The idea will never be novelized. It will live and die a serial." Nevertheless, Knopf bought it and scheduled publication for August 1926, seven months after it planned to publish *Appassionata.*

Actually, Knopf's response to Fannie's involvement in all the anticipated prize hoopla allayed her biggest worry: how her new publisher would react to the "musical comedy farce" in which she was involved. "If I were to tell you the conditions under which it was written, etc., etc.," Fannie teased Blanche Knopf, "and all the amusing performance that went with it . . ." She offered to soft-pedal her involvement in "the enormous amount of exploitation that will necessarily follow in the wake of this fantastic performance." There was no need.

Fannie's concern about the Knopfs led her to ask Ruth Raphael, who knew everybody in and around publishing, if she happened to discuss the prize, not to refer in any way to her original reluctance to be part of the competition. Fannie wanted Ruth to emphasize how thrilled she had been with the whole performance.

The situation had Fannie bursting with bons mots. "Your letter finds me out here in this curious world of bungalows that look like six-tier birthday cakes," Fannie wrote Rebecca West. "In one of these bungalows, myself, surrounded by movie queens, raspberry-colored Rolls-Royces, and sheiks that on a close inspection turn out to be bell boys from the hotel adjoining." Rebecca wrote back from Constantine Bay, where she was vacationing with her son Anthony "in a bungalow facing the austere scene on the other side, not a bit like your bungalow." West was planning another trip to the United States in the fall but had taken such blows on her lecture tour the previous year that she planned just to "creep over," she said. "I am never, never going to be in the limelight again."

By mid-August, Fannie had enough of the "movie queen of Grade X intelligence [who can] . . . move the Kingdom of California by one thrust of her heavily insured hand." She longed for her New York existence. Her mind drifted—or so she wrote—to thoughts of Thomas Hardy, Marie Curie, and Albert Einstein, living "in their fine kind of simplicity." This also summoned the specter of Stef, from whom she had not heard in some time. Fannie told Marbury she had "neglected him most awfully, poor old Stef." She went on: "I suppose because there is nothing much to be done about him, I do the cowardly thing and hide my head in the sand. I hate to think of him, sort of down and out and lonesome and bored, but hang it, what is there to do about it? . . . He has mental magnificence to fall back on, and that, after all, is about all that matters."

She wrote him the next day, through the deliberate distance of a secretary's dictation. From the text of the letter, it is obvious there had been a falling-out between the time she returned to New York in April and her departure for Los Angeles in July. She told Stef she had managed to emerge "from the state of inferiority complex into which you have succeeded in throwing me. I don't care a hang for the herd instinct, whether I have it or I haven't it. I refuse to cerebrate about matters at all and get all jammed up with self-consciousness. I are what I are." Clearly for the secretary's benefit, she added, "I hear from Jack regularly and he always sends messages to you, which I always forget to pass on."

A few weeks passed before Stef wrote back. He reminded Fannie of their plan to read each other's favorite books and then discuss them. He clipped some articles for her from *The New Republic* and *Vanity Fair,* one by Van Vechten, who was then leading the charge into Harlem, popularizing its proliferation of talented writers, artists, and musicians with discerning white audiences. Stef had just learned that Van Vechten and his wife were new friends of Fannie's. Had he known that in time, Stef said, he would have accepted a recent invitation to accompany Van Vechten on one of his raucous tours of Harlem nightlife. Stef said he declined, "because I had heard he usually gets drunk and I dislike drunks, or at least am uncomfortable with them." Sweetly, he added, "But I would have taken the chance for the sake of listening in on something about you."

To Jacques, Fannie cabled on July 30: I AM SCARED. JUST THIS MINUTE FINISH FIRST DRAFT OF MY SERIAL. ISN'T THAT TERRIBLE. FANNIE. Jacques cabled back with incredible news of his own for a change. He had just been paid fifteen thousand dollars—a huge sum in his professional universe—for participating in an important lecture series. Fannie was genuinely thrilled for him and said so in her birthday telegram, adding, THINKING OF YOU EVERY MINUTE and I HAVE TO ADMIT I MARRIED SOMETHING and I WISH WE WERE TOGETHER.

Three weeks later, in care of the Harvard Club, she also cabled Stef: HAVE NO MAILING ADDRESS BETWEEN NOW AND RETURN TO NEW YORK ON SEPTEMBER 6. HELLO. F.

Chapter *14*

Zora

In the months approaching the fortieth birthday she didn't tell anyone about, Fannie wore the mantle of prominence and authority with a regal air. Though she still claimed to be four years younger than she was, she had otherwise dropped all pretext of youth. She positioned herself as what she had become: a famous, established personality, her status earned over fifteen years of impressive achievement and high national standing. She had a fair and generous nature and enormous clout to wield. And she enjoyed both the gratification and the affirmation of having these to dispense.

Like so many of her liberal and socially conscious contemporaries in the 1920s, Fannie actively began to lend her name and what energy she could spare to what she filed in great bulk under the folder heading "Negro Matters." In addition to her support for organizations such as the National Health Circle for Colored People, Fannie joined a fair cross section of influential white figures, many in the literary world, in encouraging parity for the emerging black literary stars of Harlem and beyond.

It was in this status and spirit that Fannie became one of twenty-four judges in the first *Opportunity* magazine literary prize competition, sponsored by the National Urban League. Eugene O'Neill was among them, as were Zona Gale, Bob Davis, Henry Goddard Leach, Dorothy Canfield Fisher, James Weldon Johnson, Alexander Woollcott, and Robert H. Benchley. More than seven hundred entrants competed for the eight hundred dollars in prize money in the categories of best short story, poem, play, essay, and personal experience sketch. John Erskine, the eminent author and Columbia University professor, a good friend of Fannie's, presided over the awards dinner on May 1 at the Fifth Avenue Restaurant. It was a signal gathering, a mixed-race crowd of 316 people, which the *New York Herald Tribune* celebrated as a sign "that the American Negro is finding his artistic voice and that we are on the edge, if not already in the midst, of what might not improperly be called a Negro renaissance."

Top honors in the short-story category went to a West Virginia writer named John Matheus; G. D. Liscomb won for a play called *Frances*; and first prize for poetry went to "The Weary Blues," the work of a young talent from Washington, D.C., named Langston Hughes.

But Fannie's attention was turned to the second-prize winner in short story, a woman, new to New York, to whom she personally handed the award for a work entitled "Spunk" and who also shared second place for her play called *Color Struck*. She was Zora Neale Hurston, who, through her student stories in the literary magazine of Howard University, had come to the attention of Charles S. Johnson, *Opportunity*'s editor. Johnson had already published another story of Zora's in his magazine, and with his powerful imprimatur she had immediate entrée to New York's most significant black literary circles. This recognition of her talent at the most prestigious interracial literary event ever held cemented her place.

Here was a personality with flamboyance and genius in equal measure, a self-confident native daughter of a unique set of circumstances for a black woman growing up in the South at the turn of the last century. Not only was she reared in Eatonville, Florida, regarded as the first incorporated all-black township in America, but her own father, a minister and carpenter, served the town as mayor three times and drafted many of its laws. She internalized her mother's maxim—to "jump at de sun"—and that most assuredly had gotten her off the ground and rising.

Many years after the fact a woman—not Fannie—present at an after-party the night of the *Opportunity* dinner recounted the way Zora had stopped the room, announcing her own entrance with eyebrow-raising flourish. She lifted from her shoulder a flowing bright red scarf and swept it theatrically across her neck. With the gesture came the name of her prizewinning play, *"Cullah struu-uuuk,"* lest anyone forget the place she had come to take among them.

It is easy to see why Zora and Fannie became friends. Fannie came to see in Zora someone who "lived laughingly, raffishly . . . with blazing zest for life," even as this played into Fannie's own desire to be of service to a highly talented emerging black—woman—writer who could use her good offices. Zora, for her part, encountered in Fannie "a stunning wench," a real "Somebody" with "a rainbow wrapped and tied around her shoulder that glints and gleams." Zora also needed no prompting to understand the value to her career of cultivating a relationship with the great Fannie Hurst, once proffered.

∽

Fannie was not the only significant white female connection Zora made at that dinner. Annie Nathan Meyer, an author, philanthropist, and trustee of Barnard College, found the younger woman's brilliance captivating. Meyer saw the possibility of doing a good deed for Zora and crossing a college color barrier in the process by offering her the chance to go to Barnard and finish the work she had started at Howard University toward her degree. Barnard's dean, Virginia Gildersleeve, overlooked Zora's uneven transcript from Howard—below Barnard's usual admission standard—and recommended her for transfer on the strength of "Spunk," which Gildersleeve considered "distinctly promising." Zora's grades, however, were not at university scholarship level, so both

Meyer and Zora began casting widely for funds, contacting anyone they thought could be of help, including Carl Van Vechten. Van Vechten, too, had been at the May 1 dinner.

Meyer helped Zora come up with seventy dollars toward the full tuition, and Zora registered at Barnard in the fall of 1925 as a twenty-six-year-old transfer student. She became, in her own Zora-esque fashion and phrase, "Barnard's sacred black cow." What she did not share with the college registrar or anyone else at the time was that her actual age was thirty-four.

She still needed $117 to satisfy the first term's bill, not to mention what it took to keep her clothed, fed, and housed. Classes kept her in school most days until five o'clock in the afternoon, and she needed time after that to study. Odd jobs were the only solution, but with the going rate for waiting a dinner party only $3, it was nearly impossible to stay afloat. This was nothing new for Zora, who had been fending for herself since the age of thirteen. While in Washington studying at Howard, she had worked variously as a manicurist in a black-owned barbershop that served only whites, as a waitress at the Cosmos Club, and as a maid for distinguished black families. The need to work had nearly doubled the time it took her to amass two years' worth of credits.

There was no further contact between Fannie and Zora until the end of September, when Fannie wrote Van Vechten to ask for "Miss Hurston's" address. It delighted Zora when she received Fannie's invitation to tea, and she promptly told Meyer about it. Meyer, in turn, offered to write Fannie on Zora's behalf to see if she would help with a scholarship. "I am sure she would help," Zora told Meyer, "but I felt a little 'delicate' about asking her." That was October 17. On November 2, Meyer wrote to Fannie in ecstatic gratitude: "I was tickled to death when Zora told me," she wrote. "*So* kind! I'll work hard to get the rest of the money I need for tuition." Two days later Zora had moved into Fannie's apartment and started helping her with secretarial chores after study hours. Meyer immediately told Gildersleeve of Fannie's interest in Zora's writing and what Fannie had done for her. This so impressed the dean that she promptly told Meyer about a student loan fund and the possibility of a scholarship for Zora in the new term if her grades were high enough. It had taken the advocacy of Fannie Hurst to bring either of these possibilities to light. Not long after Zora's fellow students began taking an interest in her, too, inviting her to teas and otherwise making her feel welcome.

The full nature of Fannie and Zora's financial arrangement is not known. Perhaps Zora bartered secretarial services for room and board. Perhaps Fannie paid part of the tuition debt, which Zora worked off in this manner. Maybe the deal was a straight salary-for-hours arrangement.

What is certain is that Zora was at work at a desk in Fannie's apartment on November 4, helping with her correspondence and telephone messages and running errands whenever asked. The arrangement pleased Zora, but it turned out to be problematic for Fannie. For all Zora's many talents, and "the shine" they had taken to each other, Zora had no discernible secretarial skill. "Her shorthand was short on legibility, her typing hit-or-miss, mostly the latter, her filing a game of find-the-thimble," Fannie later recalled. "Her mind ran ahead of my thoughts and she would interject with an impatient suggestion or clarification for what I wanted to say." As if in evidence, among Fannie's papers remains a poorly typed carbon of a very short letter dated November 10, 1925. This was a week into Zora's tenure as Fannie's assistant. The keys were weakly struck, and there were too many typeovers. It bears the end notation "FH/ZH."

A month after going to work for Fannie, Zora took a room in Harlem on West 131st Street. She told Meyer she thought she had found a way to earn her expense money and raise more toward the next semester's tuition. "On the whole, I am not distressed," she wrote to Meyer, who subsequently arranged some part-time work for Zora at the home of a friend, helping with dinners and apparently some housekeeping two days a week. Though the myth holds otherwise, the month between November 4 and December 6, 1925 seems to have been the full extent of Zora's tenure in an early-day work-study arrangement at the home office of Fannie Hurst.

Nonetheless, the friendship grew in the coming months, and Fannie was generous with her introductions, both to her celebrity friends and to editors. She offered to take two of Zora's articles and a story on rounds to editors, including Ray Long at *Cosmopolitan*. Fannie had suggested some changes in the story, which Zora made reluctantly. "I do not wish to become Hurstized," she told Meyer. "There would be no point in my being an imitation Fannie Hurst, however faithful the copy, while the world has the real article at hand. I am very eager to make my bow to the market, and she says she will do all she can for me with her editors. Victory, O Lord!"

On January 5, 1926, Zora wrote to her prospective sister-in-law, Constance Sheen, bragging about working for the famous Fannie Hurst, whom Sheen greatly admired. In the letter Zora describes a December evening she spent at Fannie's—this was after she had taken the room in Harlem. Present was such an impressive array of household names that she sent along the matchbox she shared with Fannie, Stef, and Charles Norris in testament. (Irvin Cobb was also present, Zora wrote, but he used another pack with Jesse Lasky and Margaret Anglin.) Zora told Sheen that she "thrilled at the chance to see and do what I am. I love it!" She liked being able "to actually talk and eat with some of the big names that you have admired at a distance if no more than to see what sort of a person they are." At the same time she assured Sheen that all this exposure had not gone to her head, and that she enjoyed receiving a letter from her old friend as much as any celebrity encounter. "They are *often* insincere," she said of her new big-name acquaintances. "Their show of friendship mere patronage." The comment did not seem directed at Fannie because Zora offered in a postscript to ask "Miss Hurst" in a moment of relaxation to send Sheen her autograph. Her sister-in-law admitted she would be pleased to hear anything Zora might care to share about Fannie "from Dan to Beersheba." Zora reported, "She is working on a new novel now, and is consequently digging in quite furiously. But she will write you, watch and see."

Despite Zora's financial struggles, the term at Barnard went reasonably well, though she continually had difficulty with the bureaucratic folderol. She managed to get the time wrong and missed her history exam and had problems completing registration for the next term's courses. Dean Gildersleeve found it a bit exasperating. "I wonder whether we really ought to encourage her to remain in college," she wrote to Meyer. "Does she get enough out of it to compensate her for the difficulty and annoyance of trying to fit into the administrative machine? We have given her a grant from the scholarship funds, but I feel a little uncertain about her."

Zora wrote Fannie on March 16 to apologize for having been a no-show on Washington's Birthday, when Fannie had expected her to drop by. "I got a call to wait a dinner shortly after," Zora told her, "and $3.50 is not a sneezing matter."

"You must allow for my mental mixups," Zora wrote. "This year has been a great trial of endurance for me. I don't mind saying that more than once I have almost said that I couldn't endure. I shall hold on, but every time I see a cat slinking in an alley—fearing to walk upright lest again she is crushed back into her slink—I shall go to her and acknowledge the sisterhood in spite of the skin." She expressed deep gratitude to Fannie for taking her "under your shelter" and making it easy for her to make friends. "Your friendship was a tremendous help to me at a critical time. It made both faculty and students *see* me when I needed seeing."

Many years later Fannie told the story of an invitation Zora once extended to visit one of her classes. It is interesting that Zora's March 16 letter to Fannie includes an invitation to visit one of her classes at Barnard and then have lunch together. Fannie replied that she would be pleased to come on Thursday, March 25. And indeed Fannie's appointment book for that date shows the entry: "Zora—108 West 131 Student Hall Noon."

In her recollection of the episode, Fannie showed up at Barnard on the appointed day, but Barnard was closed for the spring holiday and Zora had left town. The behavior ordinarily would have infuriated Fannie, but almost never where Zora was concerned. "She was casual about it all," Fannie said, "and strangely and uncharacteristically, so was I." And in fact, "Zora—noon" reads Fannie's appointment book entry for the following Thursday, April 1.

It seems unlikely that Fannie and Zora ever revealed to each other their respective age finesses. Fannie was maniacally secret about hers, and Zora had good reasons—in Fannie's and everyone else's presence—for posing as a very young comer. As a woman of forty Fannie saw Zora as a college student. As a woman of seventy-five Fannie still referred to her old friend quite pointedly in print upon her death as the newspapers did, as a woman of fifty-five. This perpetuated the fiction of the wide age disparity between them. They always related to each other as if a generation separated them, in the manner of adored teacher and beloved student, older protector and brilliant younger protegée. The relationship never settled into either of these forms, though Fannie and Carl Van Vechten would cheer Zora's every achievement for years to come with the style and enthusiasm of pride-filled parents. To the childless Van Vechten and Fannie she was "our Zora," even though Fannie and Zora were only five years apart in age.

The two women never gave up the role-play, but their actual commonality of age may account for the warm and easy familiarity they quickly achieved despite the formal boundaries imposed on the relationship and never crossed. These boundaries persisted even after the two had known each other for many years and had shared a couple of long road trips. They persisted even after Zora had attained a high enough level of publicly acknowledged stature as a writer and folklorist to be Fannie's absolute peer. The deep financial disparities never changed, of course. When Fannie's novels commanded publisher advances of five thousand dollars, Zora, as a black author, could expect advances of a tenth of that amount or less.

Neither woman could have missed the kindred spirit in the other. They shared passion for their craft, striking and original presence, fierce determination and ambition, and, in a favorite phrase of Fannie's that easily applies here, an unwillingness to "run with the herd."

But it was within the circumscription of their differences that the friendship took shape and hardened. With the notable exclusion of sheer raw talent, Fannie and Zora stood on unequal footing in every practical regard: needs and nature, personal burdens, professional power, financial status, the ostensibly wide difference in age, and, of course, color. In the year 1925, for any or all of these reasons, Zora would have assumed a deferential posture toward Fannie, who was, by turns, a girlhood hero, employer, advocate, benefactor, and fixer. Other young men and women, black and white, whom Fannie helped along the way did likewise, though no other such relationship really compares. She conducted her relationship with Zora more in the sphere of friendship than she did her dealings with other "young" people she chose to help, but not in the manner of her friendships with the women she considered her peers. When Zora was in town Fannie regularly invited her to tea alone but never included her on the invitation lists for large cocktail parties or intimate dinners, as she did so many of her other women friends.

After that initial note to Van Vechten, in which Fannie asked for "Miss Hurston's address," between them it would always be Fannie's "Dear Zora" to Zora's "Dear Fannie Hurst." Later, as contact grew more intermittent, Zora would address Fannie even more formally as "Dear Miss Hurst."

It fell to Fannie to offer the use of her first name to Zora, and the perplexing fact is, Fannie appears never to have done so. Zora and Van Vechten moved to the familiar form within a year or so, but with Fannie that boundary remained fixed. This was likely a reflection of offensive conventions that even some of those bent on undoing the injustices of segregation and inequality observed, consciously or unconsciously.

Fannie was in a position to help Zora in significant ways, and over the years she invariably did. As for Zora, she enriched Fannie's life. On the road and otherwise Zora had a way of turning life's kaleidoscope a twist to the right or left, exposing Fannie to new ways of seeing the world. To Fannie, Zora was someone "awash in splendor"; splendor irradiated her personality and her work. Nonetheless, their relationship never shed its senior-junior casing, nor the distasteful fallout of racially divided times.

Chapter *15*

"Who Are You?"

The fall of 1925 went quickly. Fannie produced five new stories for *Cosmopolitan* and another Hearst magazine, *Harper's Bazar*, all of which she had ready for publication in the new year. Fannie had left standing orders for the immediate return of any story she submitted that editors were not prepared to publish exactly as received. (Virginia Woolf had recently described her as one of the American writers "whose aim is to write a book off their own bat and no one else's.") But she agreed to accept Ray Long's suggestions for revising the one for *Bazar* titled "The Smirk." Long, with his usual deft touch, helped work on the rewrite along with the magazine's editor, Arthur McKeogh. He then sent Fannie a copy of the revised version in a neat typescript alongside her original. This, in turn, induced her to make changes of her own following the editors' lead. Everyone was pleased, including Edward O'Brien, who gave the story three stars in *Best Short Stories*.

"The Smirk" was Fannie's first offering for *Bazar's* expanded new fiction program. In announcing the plan the magazine said it hoped to include "a smart bit" from Fannie at least every other month. For the January issue, in a little over two thousand words, Fannie again hit on the horrors of the face-lift. She told the story of Alicia, who submits to the surgery at the age of forty-two as she anticipates the arrival of a returning ambassador and recent widower—whom she loves—and his young daughter. The surgery has restored her youthfulness but left her face with a permanent smirk that neither the daughter nor the father can get beyond. In her effort to attract the man, she has managed to scare him out of her life.

Madeline Borg, a wealthy charity patron, had befriended Fannie and convinced her to write a pageant for presentation at the Jolson Theatre for the Federation for the Support of Jewish Philanthropic Societies. The effort represented Fannie's first public support for a mainstream, high-profile, specifically Jewish cause. It probably spoke more to her friendship with Mrs. Borg than to any growing passion for the welfare of her people, however. The next year, when Fannie addressed the Women's Division of the United Jewish Campaign, it was certainly at the urging of her friend from early New York days, Rebekah Kohut, the chief organizer. In 1927, when Missy Meloney asked Fannie to write about the Jews of New York for the Sunday *Herald Tribune,* Fannie replied that she was not informed on the subject. A year later and again in 1931, she did not hesitate to express her complete lack of sympathy with the Zionist movement in general and Palestine in particular on the ground that she opposed all forms of segregation. On this score, like all others, Fannie continued to keep her own counsel.

Knopf had not yet published *Appasionata* or *Mannequin* but already had plans to follow the two novels with its own collection of Fannie's short stories, scheduling release for early in 1927. This easily accounts for why, in this period, Fannie produced so many stories so fast.

In late October the always robust Fannie complained to Stef about an attack of "nervous indigestion" that sent her off to see a doctor, but it didn't last long. She was under some pressure to produce the long overdue plays she had contracted to write for David Belasco and Sam Harris. She seemed disinclined to return the two advances but even less inclined or able to get the work done. By December, Marbury's American Play Company, which had negotiated both deals so many years earlier, was chasing her for scripts. From Belasco, Fannie obtained yet another year's reprieve.

There were private pressures, too. By the end of the year Fannie's affair with Stef seems to have devolved into a struggle of wills. As he wrote her from the Harvard Club on the penultimate day of the year, "I have been going on the theory that only those things mattered which seemed important to me. But now I realize that while many things may seem important only one is important. So hereafter I shall not attempt to judge the things you want me to do, but shall do them in so far as either instinct or reason enables me to judge your real desires."

This was not what Fannie wanted at all, and she told him so in a return note written on the back of his letter. He must continue to pass judgment on whatever she wanted him to do, she said, and save her the burden of having authority over him. "Giving in between people like us amounts to giving up," she wrote. "Either I must come to see with my mind (and not with words from the teeth out) that the things that matter most to you are as big or bigger than the things that matter most to me, or I must find a way to grin and bear these rather rudimentary differences between us, our ideas and ideals. This applies both ways. We have to cerebrate our way out."

Encouragingly, she added: "I am willing to try."

"Appassionata"

Knopf wisely released *Appassionata* in January 1926, while Fannie's serial of "Mannequin" was still running in *Liberty* and the film was appearing in theaters across the country. This did its part for bookstore orders.

Readers, it seems, had made their peace with Fannie's jerky, quirky, overladen writing style, forgiving her technical deficiencies and irritants in the interest of a good story. In the words of one reviewer, her storytelling had the power to exonerate her books from "abundant faults of taste and eccentricities of style." Nearly thirty thousand copies had been sold by March.

In *Appassionata,* a work she remained proud of, Fannie conceived a heroine who totally loses interest in the prospect of marriage and the doings of the secular world. This is partly out of "love of her own intact loveliness" and partly because she cannot bear to let marriage make the mess of her life it has made of the lives of her mother and sister.

Grant Overton, the editor and critic, said it "unites the mystical and sensuous elements of human existence in what is often far from being a balanced ration," with sensuousness predominating.

In *The New York Times,* Henry Longan Stuart seemed to like the story but could not have been more disparaging about the writing style. He called the work "a sheer triumph of matter over form," poking fun at Fannie's "turgid, choral and ecstatic stream of trivialities that is prose only occasionally." He chided her tendency to let pleonasms and tautology become "the very stuff and substance of the uncanny medium in which a single phrase, sometimes a single word, is made the motif for variations that run through paragraphs without any sensible advance being registered in the progress of the idea." He predicted that she would face censure for her "mingling of the pagan and the orthodox Christian motive" in her account of Laura's call to celibacy and Christian service.

Actually, Roman Catholic readers were enthusiastic about the book. A priest whom Fannie had asked to read the manuscript for errors could find only the smallest mistakes. He marveled at how one "not of our faith has been able to penetrate the soul of a young girl, beautiful, open to temptation and yet keeping her face turned to the great goal of Religious Vocation." *Catholic World* praised the novel for having an "infinitely greater delicacy" than *Lummox.* Frances Stirling Clarke of the *Weekly Film Review* found it so "poignantly beautiful and true," so "truly Catholic, rarely and exquisitely mystical," that in appreciation she sent Fannie her own little medal of the Sacred Heart and Our Lady of Mt. Carmel. One Boston reader claimed Fannie had penetrated Catholicism's "essential secret." Two Jesuit priests wrote independently to laud her "inner, intimate knowledge of the mystic workings of grace upon the soul of Laura Regan" and her "beautiful, reverent and accurate treatment of things Catholic." At least two readers, one not even Catholic, saw themselves in the characterizations.

Even seventy years after *Appassionata's* publication, a devout Catholic reader reencountered her parochial school days in the 1950s through Fannie's early-twentieth-century characters. "How confusing for a young woman to be presented with the romantic mysticism of being a Bride of Christ just as she is becoming sexually awakened," the reader mused. "How could she escape the suffocating presence of the men in her life? Of course, the convent."

Other readers were less impressed. The author Lloyd Morris, writing in the

Saturday Review of Literature, was so merciless that the magazine's editor, Henry Canby, apologized to Fannie for having published his review. Morris considered the book "a serious insult to the intelligence of readers" and advised Fannie to take an elementary English course, buy a dictionary, and make expiation with fasting and prayer. *The New Yorker* dismissed the work as a "decidedly and characteristically secondhand, third-rate piece of business" though the magazine did give Fannie credit for "a glow, an *elan,* a volubility of expression that many an author might envy." The reviewer was Harry Esty Dounce, who liked to sign himself Touchstone. Dounce went on to complain that he was tired of stories "cats-cradled with Oedipus and Electra complexes" and "exceedingly tired of principal characters always designated as You and not greatly thrilled by contemplation of a girl whose incomplete transferences have landed in perverse love with Christ, as visualized in the head with the trick eyelids."

In *The New Republic,* Robert Littell acknowledged that Fannie seemed constitutionally incapable of letting well enough alone. However, he said, it was probably that very trait which left the reader "breathless with her roaring power and erratic beauty." She rubs the idiosyncrasies of her characters into the reader's consciousness "like an overdose of salt until we want to scream," he said. "But they live and that's what counts." Fannie, he declared, was "a magnificent, inexhaustible, maddening, helter-skelter, unfastidious talent."

As the sales push continued, Paramount Pictures released *The Untamed Lady,* based on the screenplay Fannie had written for Gloria Swanson. The film fared far less well than *Appassionata.* If *Mannequin* had paid Fannie fifty thousand dollars, *Variety* said, *Untamed Lady* merited about a dollar and a half. "It's a bad picture. Strictly mediocre stuff that won't help Miss Swanson a bit."

"Mannequin"

Mannequin turned out to be an all-around embarrassment, which is not to say that Fannie regretted collecting all that money for what amounted to a few weeks' work and a summer in Beverly Hills. Letters flooded her mailbox from countless among the nearly one hundred thousand contest entrants. Aspiring writers from across the country used the cover of congratulations to curry favor with Fannie, to seek her help in getting to publishers, to ask for critiques of their own work, and to offer plots for her to develop. There were those who acknowledged defeat at the hand of one so accomplished and those who grumbled about why someone already so rich and famous would enter such a contest in the first place. There were mudslingers and crazies and those who cried robbery. Famous Players–Lasky fended off the lawsuit of one Olivia W. Seymour, who accused the studio of plagiarizing the plot of one of her stories. A sympathetic fan wrote to commiserate with Fannie, as if she were an old friend. "There have been many instances of thought transference," the woman wrote, "that even though the stories might be somewhat alike, Miss Seymour should realize others might get the same thought, and it was only your good fortune to have yours accepted first." She also could not resist asking Fannie if she would help her in her own career climb. In pencil at the bottom of this letter is a note in Fannie's handwriting, clearly intended for her secretary to transcribe and mail on to the letter writer as if it were her own. It said that the "large number of unfortunate aspirants for the Liberty prize who seem to harbor delusions of plagiarism" had forced Fannie to suspend temporarily her helpful activities on behalf of all others. It was, she said, "a regrettable case of when the many may suffer for the few."

On the record, Fannie told *The New York Times* that Miss Seymour was among dozens of "poor, disturbed souls who harbor the hallucination that their literary masterpieces lie unhonored and unsung while unscrupulous lady writers climb their windowsills and steal ideas and manuscripts." She felt sympathy, she said, "but what a nuisance they are, these wronged geniuses whom the world ignores while the few wicked and selected writers sit back and eat peach melbas all day on the ill-gotten gains of stolen ideas!"

The inevitable solicitation letters arrived, too. "When I tell you that requests come in to me at the rate of an actual average of ten or twelve a day," Fannie told Margaret Sanger, the birth-control crusader, "I think you will understand my inability to meet specifically even those that lie close to my heart, and certainly yours does." Fannie tried to explain that although her stories had "a pretty stiff market value," her output was simply too limited for her to be as rich as people seemed to think.

To Washington University's request for help with a new women's building, she used the moment to express years of smoldering rage. It took two drafts written a day apart to get it just right: The effect of the college's "vast, impersonal mien" had made Fannie feel like a graduate without a school. "Chilled silence" had greeted her efforts to keep in contact when it would have mattered most, when she could have used the cooperation, sympathy, or guidance of her alma mater. "I had only the chilled silence which in turn has chilled me into silence," she wrote. "So far as I am concerned, every emotion of mine toward Washington U. may be dead of the frost—except deep down within me—in spite of everything are affectionate memories of days that were dear."

Mannequin was so blatant a commercial undertaking that Fannie took preemptive steps to stave off a literary setback. As soon as the prize money arrived she tithed 10 percent of it to the Authors' League for the benefit of indigent writers. That gesture also created a ready excuse for turning down other compelling requests for money. Before she had even handed in the full manuscript of *Mannequin* to Knopf for publication in hardback, she asked Blanche to flag the book jacket with words to this effect: "*Mannequin*: In which the author of *Lummox* and *Appassionata* indulges in a literary adventure. *Mannequin* is a rattling good yarn and proves that this author can make herself at home in hunting grounds of widely varied character."

Fannie tried to stop a British magazine from buying the serial rights to *Mannequin* for fifteen hundred dollars, ostensibly because she objected to that publication's editorial policy. The new executive editor at *Liberty,* Harvey Duell, was not sympathetic to her position. He exposed what was really troubling her when he told Fannie he was going to have to ignore her protest. Surely she would not have produced for *Liberty* something below her usual standard.

Liberty appears to have had good success with the serial itself, though the timing of John Wheeler's departure as executive editor to start a vague entrepreneurial venture does raise questions. Wheeler told Fannie that he had made a swing through the Midwest while the serial was running in *Liberty* and couldn't find a copy of the magazine anywhere. The film was released in January 1926, as the fifth episode of the serial was on the newsstands. The movie appears to have been reasonably popular with audiences. Among the stars, Dolores Costello as the ingenue and ZaSu Pitts in the role of the half-witted nursemaid got outstanding notices from the reviewers, who had less to say about the other three principals—Alice Joyce, Warner Baxter, and young Walter Pidgeon. Walter Woods and Frances Agnew had adapted the prize story for the screen. "Fanny [sic] Hurst hasn't anything to be proud of in turning out this yarn," *Variety* sneered. "It is a wonder [the director] Jimmie Cruze managed to turn out a picture as interesting as it is with the material at hand." The trade paper rated the picture average and cautioned exhibitors to make their own judgment as to whether *Liberty*'s advertising splash would translate into added box-office dollars.

The book version of *Mannequin,* when it finally appeared in September 1926, was an all-round disaster. Serious reviewers were universal in their disdain. Not many years later Fannie went so far as to try to excise *Mannequin* from the list of her literary credits, referring to both it and *Star-Dust* as "the dark ages of my work." She told *McClure's* to leave it off the introductory line of her weekly feature. In 1930, when a bibliographer for *America's First Editions* sent a complete list of Fannie's works for her to cross-check, she crossed *Mannequin* out. How, the bibliographer asked, could he keep his reputation if he turned in the list without it? "It is really a scenario," Fannie wrote back, "and as such, won a prize. I hope this will cover you in any difficulty you mention." She got Grant Overton, in a 1928 book of literary criticism entitled *The Women Who Make Our Novels,* to explain *Mannequin* away. He told of how Fannie had entered the contest in a playful moment and then found herself in "a trap that was promptly sprung" with no control over her story. "It can be said," Overton ventured, "that she did her best to redeem what had begun as a joke and continued as a torture."

It certainly was not lost on Fannie that the year she followed *Lummox* with *Appassionata* and then, seven months later, with *Mannequin,* Edna Ferber followed her best-selling *So Big* with *Show Boat,* a sensation of comparable (and certainly more lasting) magnitude. That said, by the time Knopf's edition of *Mannequin* came out, Fannie was ensconced at the Villa Cristina in Florence, furiously at work on "an antidote that matters." Her new novel, she told Blanche Knopf, "has taken on qualities that amaze and delight me.

"Even if the public decides to hate it, nothing can take away these weeks of excitement and thrill," she wrote. And, in another letter, "Suddenly, the entire idea seems to drench me . . . no matter what happens later these have been weeks of genuine elan over the job."

Chapter 16

"No Food with My Meals"

The first time Fannie published her personal diet and exercise program, her point was to explain how someone in a sedentary, solitary profession could stay fit. She was remarkably up-to-date in her approach. As early as 1923, for example, she had a personal trainer (whom she loathed and called Simon Legree) knocking on her front door every morning at half past six to put her through an hour's workout.

Fannie confided these details to the readers of *Liberty* magazine in a piece cleverly titled "No Food with My Meals." In it she explained what made a person like herself, with no physical complaints and no really compelling need to worry about her appearance, decide to "keep fit through fit."

It was easy, she said, for a Gloria Swanson or a Pola Negri or a Douglas Fairbanks to be conscientious about her or his physical condition, with the whole world watching for the "ever-lurking second chin" or evidence of diminishing agility. But a public figure like the virtuoso violinist Jascha Heifetz had no such concerns; his technique would be the same however he looked. "There is no ferret-eyed public to count the crow's feet or sagging face muscles of Thomas Edison or Thomas Hardy, or Madame Curie, or Orville Wright, or Mary Roberts Rinehart or Rose O'Neill, or James Smith of the Equitable," Fannie said. And so it was for her. "No editor has ever said to me, 'I can't use your story. I need a younger author with a more athletic figure,'" she said. And neither her husband nor her friends seemed to mind what might otherwise be unwanted extra pounds.

Despite her remarkably robust constitution, Fannie found herself intrigued by the increasing number of stories appearing in lay publications about the need for both city and country dwellers to "offset the artificial scheme of everyday life" with better diet and exercise habits. Articles that lionized the men and women in public life who were growing old with intelligence and grace made her realize that she wanted to be counted among them one day. She had observed "the effect of daily habits upon the mind and the health and the appearance of the people about me." And she had gotten fed up with her own "creature habits of undisciplined eating and general routine."

In addition, Fannie said her conversations with "scientific men of eminence" had helped her better understand the latest thinking on what it took to keep the human machine cranking. Though she didn't say so, this group of scientists would have included Stef, who had developed his own theories on longevity, fitness, and survival based on his firsthand experience with the Eskimo. One of Stef's convictions that she clearly rejected was his emphasis on the importance of a diet high in proteins and fats. In 1928, in fact, he submitted to a hospital-supervised experiment during which he ate and drank as he had in the Arctic. The diet consisted of nothing but water and meat—80 percent fat and 20 percent lean—for an entire year. In the end doctors had to concede that the regimen had no ill effect on his robust health. For obvious reasons, Fannie did not mention to the readers of *Liberty* that her interest in fitness coincided almost exactly with the start of her relationship with Stef.

Fannie's first step was to go to the doctor for a full-scale physical checkup. She checked out fine, save a somewhat languid blood pressure and a slightly elevated pulse. Her physician recommended weight reduction, exercise, abstinence from sugar and starchy foods, fresh air, light clothing, and no excesses of any kind. From there Fannie began to design a fitness program to suit her high vitality and scheduling needs. "I know I have an enormous resistance to fatigue," she said. "A capacity for sustained effort. An endurance that I can test to a greater limit than a person with a lesser resistance than mine." She put it to work.

The job of "Simon Legree" was to lead an hour of arm, leg, and torso exercises each morning, replete with deep breathing and rolling and rowing movements. About the trainer she confessed: "I may say right here that if I were a person of the fine and high resolve I seem to have implied from time to time in this article, the paid services of this trainer would not be necessary."

Bathtime followed the trainer, "warmer than a less robust constitution could stand it, and then letting it come cooler and cooler and end in an invigorating cold shower." Actually, the elaborate bath ritual was one of Fannie's long-standing joys incorporated into her fitness package. Only recently Lois Meier Toensfeldt reminded Fannie of her college-days habit of splashing around endlessly in the bathtub. She quoted back to her: "I bathe me early I bathe me late—I splash around at a furious rate—from one to the next I can hardly wait—from the sole of my feet to my raven pate—I'll be clean when I enter the Golden Gate."

From 7:30 to 8:30 A.M., Fannie answered her mail and made telephone calls and then sat down to breakfast. This consisted of the juice of one lemon and one orange, a slice of dry whole-wheat toast, and a cup of half-and-half coffee substitute and hot milk without sugar or saccharin. For a waffle lover like herself, Fannie said, the first 620 of these meals were the hardest. From breakfast Fannie went directly to her desk.

She made snacks of a raw apple at eleven o'clock and again at three, just before stopping work for the day. For lunch her maid would prepare a bowl of hot soup composed of fresh tomatoes, cabbage, celery, and green peppers, boiled together in plain water without meat stock or any fat at all. "This," by the way, she offered, "makes an excellent soup."

After work she would go for an hour's walk in the park and another half-hour walk before dinner. At teatime she allowed herself a cup of weak, sugarless tea and nothing else. Before dinner at 7:30 P.M., she would take a ten-minute nap.

Her evening meal consisted variously of the following: once a week the white meat of a chicken and once a week a white-meat fish. Five meatless meals composed of a good variety of vegetables. Salads with lemon juice for dressing, cooked fruits. No bread at all after the breakfast slice, and sometimes a couple of water crackers with a little morsel of cheese.

Fannie said the new regimen had her feeling better than ever. There was only one further step on the path to moral courage: to "go through this routine without the flayings of this trainer . . . a goal to which I am still traveling."

In fact, by the end of 1928 she had replaced Legree with a daily trip to a gymnasium. The idea was so novel and so threatening to Fannie's mother back in St. Louis that when she heard about it, she cabled her daughter at once in panic: TAKE MY ADVICE STOP GYMNASIUM WILL WRECK YOUR HEALTH I WORRY VERY MUCH BE SURE AND STOP IT I AM FINE BE SURE AND STOP IT.

Though Fannie was now noticeably thinner than she had been as a younger woman, she remained on the plump side when compared with the famished flapper ideal then very much in vogue. In the essay, written in 1926, this fact does not seem to concern her much. For Fannie, having a good appearance was at this point not particularly tied to being superthin. That soon changed. By the end of 1928 Fannie was intrigued if not convinced by the salon theory of a woman acquaintance about the new ideal of the slender silhouette. Slender, the woman said, reflected the spirit of the automobile, the airship, and the wireless and therefore represented an evolution and not a passing fad. These were not times, she argued, when the feminine ideal could in any way suggest "bovine satisfaction, sodden repose, placid perfection."

Perhaps it was coincidence, but almost immediately after this exchange Fannie complained to her old friend Lois, "My lean and meager diet seems to do little for me. My face is as round as a moon and my all too solid flesh, all too solid. As always, I nibble lettuce leaves and at the moment, at least for the last two months, steal two precious hours for daily gymnasium work (do not by any chance pass this last on to my mother who imagines exercise is dangerous)."

She repeated the "all too solid flesh" refrain in a letter to Rebecca West a few weeks later, bemoaning the fact that Rebecca had decided not to visit that winter. Fannie was sorry she was going to miss out on an opportunity "to gyrate semi-occasionally in the name of the reductions of certain 'buxom parts' " on the new "torture-machine" she had installed at home. "My handsome and expensive machine yearns for you," she said.

"A novel aborning"

Despite Fannie's protests to the contrary, her datebooks for the years 1926 to 1930 indicate that either she had taken a job moonlighting as a compiler for *Who's Who* or she was very busy cultivating just about anyone who mattered. Rebecca West whips through town a few times and is frequently on Fannie's schedule when she does. There are lunches, cocktails, teas, and/or dinners with the Sinclair Lewises, Blanche Knopf, Mischa Elman, Efram Zimbalist, Will Rogers, Elisabeth Marbury, Anne Morgan, Elsie de Wolfe, Sam Goldwyn, William Randolph Hearst, Carl Van Vechten, Pauline Lord, Condé Nast, Maxwell Anderson, André Maurois, Somerset Maugham, the Booth Tarkingtons, the Jesse Laskys, Lord and Lady DuVeen, Dr. A. A. Berg and his brother, Charles and Kathleen Norris, and Marie Curie—a partial list. Fannie's rival Edna Ferber suddenly begins to appear at her top-list dinner parties, then disappears again, and there is even a "nine A.M." with her old college nemesis, Zoë Akins, now a highly regarded playwright.

Political figures appear for the first time. Theodore Roosevelt is present on one or two occasions, as is the distinguished presidential confidant and aide Colonel Edward M. House. Ruth Bryan Owen, victorious in her second run for Congress from Florida in 1928, writes frequently, grateful for Fannie's enthusiastic support.

Interspersed are theater first-nighters with Jacques and Daniel Frohman and high-spirited evenings at the star-strewn Greenwich Village restaurant of Romany Marie on the arm of Stef. Fannie kept trying to help land him some lucrative magazine work. In May 1926, as she and Jacques prepared to sail for Naples, she told a shipside reporter that their eleven-year marriage "has been a success in every way."

At the time of that trip, Fannie oddly announced a plan to go to Oxford from Italy and write a thesis on Anglo-Saxon languages. By the time she got to Europe, she later explained, the professor with whom she had intended to study had died suddenly, dashing the plan. Once back home in the fall, though, she held tight to the notion. She told another interviewer that she hoped to give up fiction writing for five years so she could "go in for study and anthropological research . . . I like the cloistered life. I want to go to Oxford." Perhaps Zora Neale Hurston's work with the brilliant anthropologist Franz Boas at Columbia had inspired her. Fannie's own intention, she said, was to prepare to write a serious book about women. In another interview some years later she described her dream project as a multivolume study of women in the history of the human race.

"That's what fame means to me now," Fannie said to the writer from *Success,* whose assignment was to ask that very question. "It means that I have arrived at a point where I'm able to drop out of creative work for a time, so that when I come back, I'll come with a book that is bigger and more real than anything I have ever done."

There were shades of hoped-for triumph over the old slam "Better a classical failure . . ."

Even as Fannie spoke the words, it was clear to her interviewer that her schedule for several years ahead was far too packed for this to be a realistic yearning. The reporter was struck, as all reporters seemed to be, by the impeccable stage set of Fannie's life: her cathedral-like surroundings, her menagerie of pets, her unrepeatable personal style. The writer pondered

> this pitched battle going silently on between sincerity and theatricalism. It is as if the reality in her were symbolized by the striking beauty of the black-and-white in her color-motif—black, shining hair, black, straight brows over shining eyes, black, simple frock. And there comes the theatrical—that high, insistent blare of cardinal-red, a red that is at once bright and soft, passionate and thrilling and gay. The long flowing silk smock is of that red. It is repeated in the great knobbed comb thrust low into the knot of her hair, and again on the lips painted carefully and exactly to match the smock, the comb, the sofa. It is beautiful, striking, undeniably effective. Would she wear the cardinal red smock, one wonders, and the comb and the lips to match, at Oxford? And would the red sofa go too?

Zora once observed that no one ever used those three colors in juxtaposition to greater effect. Fannie, she added, "will never be jailed for uglying up a town."

Fannie renewed her acquaintance with Theodore Dreiser in this period, and he began putting her on the guest list for his Thursday at-homes. She was frequently called on to speak at venues as diverse as dinners for the United Jewish Appeal and luncheons of the League for Political Education. In fact, she started speaking out quite a lot. She could be counted on for something striking, unexpected, and newsworthy to say. *Redbook* described her as "one of America's keenest minds." She joined the board of directors of the National Health Circle for Colored People and replaced Theodore Roosevelt as appeal chairman. Though she willingly drafted that organization's annual mail request for money and spoke on its behalf when called upon, she was lax at best about attendance at board meetings. This was no slight to the National Health Circle: it was the same with virtually every organization with which she allied herself—and there were dozens—over the rest of her lifetime. It was so valuable to have her name in prominent display on an organization's letterhead, and the access to call on her for radio and other public appearances, that no one seemed to mind.

In January 1927 Fannie thrilled the ever-thrillable Lois with a detailed

140

glimpse of her daily routine. It was surely an intake of helium for the St. Louis housewife and mother of one: "I am deep in the throes of a metropolitan winter," Fannie wrote.

> I have two Cambridge University professors as
> houseguests. An anthropologist and his biologist wife.
> A play about to burst into rehearsal. A novel aborning.
> A growing menagerie to be tended. Lectures looming.
> Tonight I turn back the scene of my childhood and
> deliver the commencement address at one of the city
> high schools. And from there to be thoroughly
> incongruous I rush off to attend a party given by Ethel
> Barrymore which is known as an inhibition party. In
> other words, what is your pet inhibition. It doesn't mean
> much of anything to me but in the parlance of the times
> that sort of phraseology seems to matter to those who
> have just sufficient smattering of their Freud and Jung to
> know nothing about it. I think I've misnamed the party!
> On second glance at my card, I see it is to be a
> "suppressed desire" party—I didn't think those things
> were of a sufficiently conversational nature to be aired at
> parties.

All the while Fannie added research, writing, and polish to the novel in progress she had been so enthusiastic about the previous summer in Europe— "the most American thing I've ever done." She managed to slip in a few more short stories for *Cosmopolitan*. The one titled "Give This Little Girl a Hand" was a fictional takeoff on the life of the legendary New York nightclub hostess Texas Guinan. Fannie called her heroine Rodeo West.

☙

Knopf brought out *Song of Life* as a short-story collection in March 1927 to the usual mix of push-pull, have-to-hate-her-have-to-love-her reviews. "I confess that I always wince at the prospect of new books by her," wrote H. W. Boynton in the *New York Sun*. "There is something in her manner, at once acrid and unctuous, sentimental and naturalistic, that makes the flesh shrink and the gorge rise. . . . She has, at her worst, the most distressing style of all our popular storytellers. Yet she is among that company unmistakably a storyteller, as well as unmistakably popular." He added, "In these stories . . . she is at her best."

As for the play she wrote to Lois about, it was Fannie's own dramatization of her short story "The Gold in Fish." The play was nearly a year in preparation before its December 26, 1927, premiere at Broadway's Eltinge Theatre, with staging by Rollo Lloyd. As early the April before Fannie was musing in print on the pain a writer endures as his or her brainchild gets "mauled and reshaped, and, to him, it seems cruelly mutilated" for the stage. "The author sits far back in the theatre," she wrote. "Timid invader of a strange land. He thinks of the quiet hours of gestation, the painful hours of the child's birth. He quivers, for he hears, as I have heard from [an] . . . actress, 'I can't say it that way.' "

Her reference was surely to the tussles with Laurette Taylor over *Humoresque,* but the staging of the Goldfish family saga, now titled *It Is to Laugh,* came with its own set of agonies. The story chronicles a Jewish immigrant family's rapid financial rise thanks to an enterprising son bent on full assimilation. He moves everyone uptown to a palatial apartment but rejects his background, changes his name, and alienates the family he now considers an embarrassment even as he works devotedly to improve their common lot.

Fannie had first offered the play to David Belasco in fulfillment of their 1921 contract for her to produce a vehicle for the actress Lenore Ulric. Belasco rejected the idea, so Fannie arranged production with Barbour, Crimmins, and Bryant with Edna Hibbard in the starring role. Yet early in 1929, a year after *It Is to Laugh,* Belasco's organization again was asking for its promised play. This flabbergasted Fannie, who thought she had satisfied her obligation to Belasco "to the letter of the law . . . It is extremely uncomfortable to have Mr. Belasco feel that I have not," she told the agent who had replaced Elisabeth Marbury, "and I am eager to know on what basis he reaches his conclusions." Belasco let the matter drop.

Fannie finished her novel and delivered it to Harpers under the title *A President Is Born,* but she found its aftermath "none too lustrous." She usually looked forward to the playtime she always granted herself, but for some reason this time she did not welcome the respite. "Leisure gives me too much awareness to keep me happy," she wrote Rebecca West in London in a rare moment of candor. "I dare not let the anaesthetic wear away sufficiently to get on to myself . . . and the damn stupid things I've done to and with my life. I could forgive myself easier if they were anything more than stupid things . . . having long ago decided that stupidity is the one cardinal and unforgivable sin." West, whose own life was in its usual disarray, couldn't bear the thought of ever-controlled Fannie in such a state. "Why in the wide world should you feel unhappy about your life?" she asked. "You who have managed everything so well, who get on with your work, who never do anything ungraceful! What is this fantasy? I wish I could come over. I wish, I wish! The only thing is I should be as miserable there as anywhere else."

It Is to Laugh certainly did nothing to improve Fannie's state of mind. The critics gave it the usual mixed reception. At least one reviewer thought that Fannie had "wielded her pen deftly" to concoct a "charming, light and rather loving little story that raised its voice in protest against the bigotries and snobbishness of suddenly acquired pomp and circumstance." Audiences apparently disagreed, as did Fannie herself. She seems to have made a point of not turning up on opening night, when audience members stayed in their seats for at least five minutes to shouts of "Author, Author!" hoping she could be found. She considered the whole experience "an abortion." The show closed after a month.

"Damn it!" she told Rebecca in a subsequent letter, writing about the play. "I'll make the grade yet!" But in fact it was the last stage production she ever attempted.

Chapter *17*

"From the teeth out"

Not only did Fannie have an opinion about everything but she had an opinion that newspaper reporters seemed hungry to quote. Sometimes, given the content of her remarks, the honor is a testament more to her pervasive celebrity than to the brilliance inherent in what she had to say. On some occasions, however, even out of her depth, Fannie was surprisingly astute.

At Christmastime in 1925 she wrote for the *New York American* a heart-twisting story, clearly at the newspaper's request, about its annual distribution of goods to some eighteen thousand needy families. The piece duly appeared in two prominent columns under Fannie's portrait on the *American's* front page.

Returning from Europe in 1926, she assailed that summer's annoying crop of "arrogant, bombastic, boastful" American tourists, saying their presence in France was as responsible for the current anti-American agitation as the debt question. She proposed travel quotas for the next five years to cap their numbers.

A few months later she told the Associated Press that she favored a bill passed in the British House of Commons prohibiting newspapers from publishing the sensational and sorbid details of divorce cases. She thought similar legislation would have merit on this side of the Atlantic.

In the spring of 1927, when she advanced the notion that economic independence for women would end the rising divorce rate, the *Journal-American* bannered her thoughts across the top of the front page in double-sized type. If women earned their own money, she argued, they would have choice. "It saves them from early marriage for protection, support or escape from an unhappy home. When they are free they won't have to see divorce as the only way out. They'll marry carefully, thoughfully and stay married." This is how she summed up her argument: "If feminine means dependent and weak, then the sooner they get unfeminine the better." She would elaborate on this theme for years to come. "Modern from the teeth out" was how she described her own modernism. "Inside of me are hundreds of grandmothers, influencing me, holding me to old thoughts, old ways, old traditions which I have constantly to argue and combat."

Not long after, when the bleached-blond Ruth Snyder went to trial for bludgeoning her meek and sleeping husband to death in their Queens Village cottage—with the help of her lover—Fannie joined the frenzy of comment in the pages of the *Journal-American*. Midtrial, well before the handing down of the sentence that would make Mrs. Snyder the first woman put to death by electrocution in New York State, Fannie posed a question to the paper's readers:

> Suppose Mrs. Snyder were suddenly to cast aside the rather holey, faultily knitted fabric of her cell-made tapestry of the story, and lay out frankly on the table, so to speak, the sorry medley of actual facts that lead to this sorry tale.
>
> Would not the people, who are made of the same flesh and blood that Mrs. Snyder is made of, somehow feel sympathy for that flesh and blood instead of the antagonism her present attitude builds up[?]
>
> Would not the people in the end be more lenient than under the present conditions of pretense, evasion, rebuttal and re-rebuttal[?]

In this same period Fannie dealt just as persuasively with more mundane fare—snaring newspaper space for doing little more than opening her mouth in a public forum. In an address to the women's organization of the Free Synagogue, just around the corner from her apartment, she assailed the man who avoids high culture because he is too tired. That same fellow is never too tired for "baseball, golf, prizefights and three-hour lunches," she scoffed, leaving women to be the "cultural, intellectual and spiritual white hope of the United States." She repeated this theme in a speech to a convention of women's clubs, rating a headline for the Hearst empire acolyte even in *The New York Times*.

She wasn't any easier on the women. *Redbook* devoted some four thousand words to her attack on how little women had managed to accomplish since getting the vote. Despite the election of three women to Congress and thirty to state legislatures, the emancipation, she said, had not come off. "The golddigger of one form or another is rampant on every social plane," she harangued. "Women who have their political and social and industrial emancipation live as never before upon the privileges of their sex." She even cited the Snyder case by way of example. Ruth Snyder wanted no women on her jury. "Talk to almost any employed girl and see how she regards her job. As a stepping stone to a new world of new opportunities? Not so, usually," she lamented. "As a bridge of sighs that leads to marriage."

She charged that the middle-class woman who stays at home was more of a chattel than ever before. Her grand- or her great-grandmother at least worked the farm to earn her keep and had legitimate entitlement to her share. By contrast, the woman of 1927 in comparable circumstance was little more than a consumer, surrounded by laborsaving devices, schools, and nannies. In short, a taker.

What about the so-called emancipation the 1920s had precipitated in

Fannie at her desk, circa 1915.
New York Public Library Manuscripts and Archives,
Robert Hobart Davis Collection

Above: Fannie, in plumed hat, and fellow cast
members of a student production of Oscar
Wilde's *An Ideal Husband* at Washington
University, December 1908. Fannie played
Mrs. Cheveley. *Washington University Archives,*
St. Louis, Mo.

Right: Fannie, a sometime fashion victim, was
notorious for refusing to "run with the herd"
when it came to clothing. Some, however,
thought she dressed wonderfully.
Corbis-Bettmann-UPI

FANNIE'S EARLY MENTORS

Above left: William Schuyler, assistant principal at Central High School, St. Louis, Missouri. *St. Louis Public School Records and Archives*

Above right: William Marion Reedy, editor of the *Mirror,* which first published Fannie professionally. *St. Louis Mercantile Library*

Above: Robert Hobart Davis, who first declared "Fannie Hurst, you can write!" *Harry Ransom Humanities Research Center, Fannie Hurst Collection*

Right: Ray Long, editor of *Cosmopolitan,* who urged Fannie to turn her efforts to writing serials and novels as well as short stories. *New York Public Library Picture Collection*

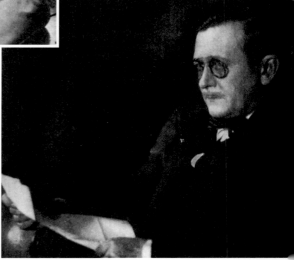

Right: Young Jacques.
Harry Ransom Humanities Research Center,
Fannie Hurst Collection

Below: The interior designer
Elsie de Wolfe, Anne Morgan, daughter
of the financier J. P. Morgan, and
producer Elisabeth Marbury, whose
lives as successful single women
fascinated Fannie and became the
inspiration for her novel *Lonely Parade.*
Pictured here December 2, 1915,
on board the S.S. *Imperator.*
Corbis-Bettmann-UPI

Left: Fannie and Jacques, caught on Fifth Avenue, May 6, 1920, the day their secret five-year marriage made front-page news across the country.
Corbis/Underwood & Underwood

Right: Fannie and Jacques, June 13, 1924, as they sailed for Europe. They spent three weeks of that trip in Russia, which Fannie wrote about for *McCall's* magazine, with Jacques's help as translator.
Corbis-Bettmann-UPI

Above left: Fannie seemed ready to leave Jacques before they set sail for Europe in June 1931. Instead, they made a return visit to Russia, which Fannie described as "strenuous and rather heart-breaking." Pictured here in Stockholm, August 1931, on their way home. *Corbis-Bettmann-UPI*

Above right: Fannie and Jacques were avid first-nighters, and are pictured here at the premiere of *The Hurricane* at the Astor Theatre, November 9, 1937.
Corbis-Bettmann-UPI

Above right: The Arctic explorer Vilhjalmur Stefansson, December 1921, shortly before he and Fannie met. *Dartmouth College Library*

Above left: Stefansson on the Canadian Arctic Expedition, 1913. *Dartmouth College Library*

Right: Fannie's friend Zora Neale Hurston in a photo taken by their mutual friend Carl Van Vechten. *Carl Van Vechten Papers, Collection of American Literature, Beinecke Rare Book and Manuscript Library, Yale University*

Above: Fannie, with the German shepherd she bought for company, in Hollywood during the writing of her serial *Mannequin* for the *Liberty* weekly. The magazine awarded her a $50,000 prize for the scenario of *Mannequin,* which was made into a film; Knopf published it in book form. *Corbis-Bettmann*

Below: A display of Fannie's titles published by Alfred A. Knopf: *Appassionata* and *Mannequin* (1925), and the short-story collection *Song of Life* (1926). *Harry Ransom Humanities Research Center, Fannie Hurst Collection*

Fannie campaigned for Ruth Bryan Owen and then chaired the farewell dinner on May 9, 1933, before Owen sailed for Copenhagen to assume her post as minister to Denmark, the highest diplomatic rank a woman had ever held. Left to right: Ruth Owen's youngest daughter, Helen Rudd; the aviator Amelia Earhart; Ruth Bryan Owen; Otto Wadsted, Danish minister to the United States; and Fannie. *AP/Wide World Photos*

Fannie was instrumental in getting Mayor Fiorello La Guardia and Governor Herbert Lehman to the dedication ceremony of the A. A. Berg Collection at the New York Public Library. Left to right: Frank Polk, La Guardia, Berg, Fannie, and the governor. Fannie's handwriting identifies each person. *Harry Ransom Humanities Research Center, Fannie Hurst Collection*

Fannie and columnist Walter Winchell at the trial of Bruno Richard Hauptmann, the accused kidnapper of the son of Charles and Anne Morrow Lindbergh, in the Hunterdon County Courthouse, Flemington, New Jersey, January 30, 1936. *Acme, AP/Wide World Photos*

Above: Fannie and First Lady Eleanor Roosevelt with Ruth Bryan Owen Rohde and her new husband, Capt. George Rohde of the Life Guards of King Christian of Denmark, after their wedding at St. James Episcopal Church, Hyde Park, New York. President and Mrs. Roosevelt hosted the reception, July 11, 1936. Fannie is wearing her hat with the glassine visor that caused such a stir at the Democratic Convention in Philadelphia.
Corbis-Bettmann-UPI

Right: Fannie and Ruth Bryan Owen Rohde strut through the lobby of New York's Hollywood Theatre at the world premiere of *The Life of Emile Zola,* August 11, 1937. *Corbis-Bettmann-UPI*

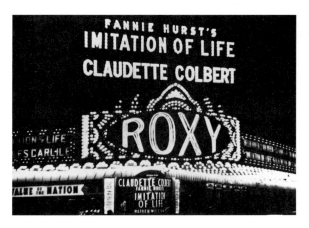

The Roxy Theatre marquee for the 1934 version of *Imitation of Life,* just the way Fannie liked it.
Harry Ransom Humanities Research Center Fannie Hurst Collection

clothing and hairstyle? Fannie said women were spending more time in beauty salons having their hair bobbed and marcelled than they ever did when they wore it long. As for the supposedly freer new style in clothing, she noted "the elaborately simple woman of today whose single sheaf of frock, single sheaf of silk underclothing, flat sheaf of hair and sheer stockings bespeak the last word in complex concentration of effort." She called it "an elaborate and subtle and expensive simplicity, this, that enslaves even while it liberates." But when the fashion arbiters introduced a return to the long, ultrafeminine styles of the 1890s in the fall of 1929, Fannie's protest of what she saw as an effort to force women back into an outmoded pattern became the basis of a *New York Times* editorial.

Redbook's editors were positively thrilled with the piece and asked Fannie for another right away. She accepted, then did *Cosmopolitan* the courtesy of asking Ray Long how he felt about it. Even though Fannie was free to write nonfiction for other magazines, Long asked her to reconsider. "Competition in the magazine field is so keen that anything of yours to appear there really hurts us," he said. Fannie told Edwin Balmer at *Redbook* she would have to renege, and he graciously accepted her "fair and frank" explanation of why.

In the fall Fannie endorsed by letter a campaign to organize Metropolitan Life Insurance Company's ten thousand office workers into a clerical union, moved by knowledge that many of the company's female workers still earned wages as low as twelve dollars a week. Even *The New York Times* thought Fannie's support for the cause worthy of reporting. Through her fiction, after all, she had been the champion of the working girl for years. It might have startled those fans to learn that she paid her own secretary even less.

Fannie brought 1928 in on a lighter note. At Adelaide Stedman's Fortnightly Forum, an event at the Park Lane Hotel that probably merited coverage only because of the speakers, Fannie told the audience that the twentieth century had not really killed romance. It was true that Thomas Edison had replaced Santa Claus, she said, but it also had turned out that the new truths with which people were forced to deal were "vastly more interesting than the romantic concoctions of the past."

∽

Forty-eight hours later Fannie was in the singularly unromantic environs of Pittsburgh, visiting mining towns, miners, and their families in the throes of a devastating coal strike. Hearst's *Pittsburgh Sun Telegraph* had offered her fifteen hundred dollars to tell its readers what she thought about it all. In a series of four articles splashed across its front page and picked up by Hearst papers throughout the chain, Fannie examined the situation from the perspective of the outsider. She wrote "with a fresh eye and a mind unbiased as yet with the factional aspects of this great dispute." Her conclusion in a sentence: "Regardless of who is right and who is wrong in the issues at stake—this uncivilized spectacle of families living like dogs among slops in kennels opposite the very thresholds of their vacant homes is wrong." She called for a U.S. Senate investigation to "unearth the forces of transportation, competition, interstate-commerce, overproduction, etc., which are the real roots of your evil." She warned Capital not to force Labor to its knees. "The day that this industrial fight is lost to Capital, spells ultimate peril to your democracy, your well-being, your prosperity," she said, urging an immediate truce and government intervention.

"No one can look upon a situation like that and not decide on a personal responsibility toward doing his bit to alleviate so glaring an example of man's inhumanity toward man," Fannie told the editor, H. M. Bittner, as she turned in the last piece. Some days later, when *Cosmopolitan* pressed for a short story she was late in delivering, she told an editor that the desolation she had witnessed in Pittsburgh had gripped all her time and interest.

In March the Senate Interstate Commerce Committee summoned Fannie to testify. The suffering was more desperate than what she had seen in Russia, she told the senators, and neither the Pittsburgh Coal Company nor the city's wealthy class had shown any inclination toward alleviating it.

Bittner wrote Fannie afterward, enclosing a check to cover the costs of her Washington trip. He told her what a fine impression she had made. "As a matter of fact," he added, "you started a pretty big thing when you came to Pittsburgh. I have hopes now that a solution will be found as a result of the present inquiry. If it happens, certainly a great deal of the credit will go to you."

"A President Is Born"

A President Is Born was the book with the impact to follow *Lummox* even though five years and two other novels, *Appassionata* and the embarrassing *Mannequin,* fell less convincingly in between. No wonder the process of writing *A President Is Born* had gotten Fannie so excited. Bob Davis read the book and predicted a Pulitzer Prize. So did her fellow author Inez Haynes Irwin. "I wonder. I wonder . . . ," Fannie wrote to Rebecca West on publication day, as if she were keeping her fingers crossed. Rebecca read the book twice and said it gave her that "prairie feeling" she always got on a visit to the Middle West. "Bless you," she wrote Fannie. "Bless you."

President was Fannie's story of the making of a president. Her narrative sticks closely to the first seventeen years in the life of one David Schuyler and his Illinois farm family. By using the device of footnotes that refer to the diaries of Schuyler's older sister, Fannie is able to reflect on the years of the narrative while at the same time tracing Schuyler's political journey toward the White House. As *The Nation* pointed out, this device allowed her to handle two eras side by side and tell the straight story in one while commenting on it with the perspective of history in the other. The format was so convincing that even two years after the book was published, readers wrote Fannie asking for details of the Schuyler family, whom they clearly believed to be real. Even the niece of Fannie's beloved high school teacher William Schuyler, whose last name she had given to her fictional hero, wrote to ask if any of the incidents she had used in the book had actually come from the St. Louis Schuylers. Other than the name she held dear, Fannie replied, the answer was no.

"The fact that the most casual exertion of so-called human intelligence should indicate the fictitious character of the family described in my novel does not seem to come to the rescue of my readers and save them the expenditure of postage," she wrote to Harry Hansen of the *New York World.* "Either they are incredibly dumb or I am something powerful authentic."

Even H. W. Boynton in the *Sun,* who had to mention Fannie's usual propensity to get the reader's gorge rising with her "distressing fondness" for the physically disgusting and her dreadful use of English, had to admit that this book was of substance, fine and sound.

Henry Canby was less appreciative of Fannie's imaginative method but still said the book was "a considerable story not to be missed in the season's reading." This he offered despite his strong sense that through "punch, push, repetition, even footnotes that tell you what to believe, she has turned a good novel into the feature story of the making of a President."

The critics, for the most part, had their usual complaints—Fannie had a way of providing opportunity for witty, snarly comment at the expense of her writing—but nearly all had to concede the book's inherent merits. Not so, Dorothy Parker of the "smiting-word-at-any-price set" Fannie always found so daunting. "I can find in *A President Is Born* no character or any thought to touch or excite me," said Parker in a sarcastic review of the book in *The New Yorker.* "I am awfully sorry, but it is to me a pretty dull book."

Clearly, readers couldn't have disagreed more. By the fourth week of publication, *President* had sold nearly a hundred thousand copies. Best-seller lists across the country in those early weeks had *President* positioned third behind Booth Tarkington's *Claire Ambler* and Thornton Wilder's *Bridge of San Luis Rey.* Harper & Brothers was surely as pleased as Fannie. The publisher had wrested her back from Knopf with the offer of a seventy-five-hundred-dollar advance, but there seemed to be no hard feelings. The friendship with Blanche and Albert continued as warmly as before. There was no Pulitzer for Fannie in 1928; if she was disappointed, no one would ever know.

By prize announcement time the following year, Fannie was on to the next thing. A new collection of her short stories called *Procession* was in the bookstores as of January 17, 1929. Unfortunately, the reviews could not have been worse. Tess Slesinger chided Fannie in the *New York Evening Post* for writing about the "peepul": "Our Fannie Hurst has gone sentimental. Not that she had far to go, but she has gone the whole distance this time, and the result is a sickening performance." *The New Statesman* was most cruel. Fannie, the reviewer said, "knows as well as I do that she is forsaking a distant and doubtful but once desired objective for one more immediately profitable. I do not take upon myself to say that she could ever write a great novel or a great short story. I am quite certain that it would have been worth her while to try, and that she is, in consideration of magazine fleshpots, throwing the chance away."

Chapter *18*

"Hollywood, Hollywoodn't"

One spectacular benefit of being a famous writer in the early years of the twentieth century was the cooperation of technology in providing unexpected and lucrative new markets for existing work. Simply by writing stories with staying power in the early years of her career, Fannie was able to see return on her best properties, in her lifetime, as many as four, five, and six times. The only effort on her part was yet another endorsement of yet another check. She would hate this characterization of her literary output, but there is no ignoring the place natural timing played in her phenomenal success. A magazine story that reasonably could have been expected to sell again for the stage, for newspaper reprint, or for inclusion in a hardback short-story collection suddenly became fodder for the silent screen, then for the "talkies," then for radio dramatization, and before too long for television programming. Especially in the years of the Great Depression, this versatility provided a welcome financial cushion. Each medium required its own surrender of rights, a new set of contracts and payments of fees to the author. By 1929 only silent films had left the list of outlets.

Fannie managed to produce three more short stories for *Cosmopolitan* in 1928 in addition to her Texas Guinan–inspired tale, "Give This Little Girl a Hand," which ran in February. "Hossie Frossie" won praise from newspaper reviewers for Fannie's undiminished ability to "recreate the deadly, maddening monotony of a narrow household." Ray Long called it a "bearcat"; he didn't think she had ever before written a story so emotionally packed. The *New York Times* reviewer, however, mused on how much more poignant "a little refining and restraining artistry" would have made this tale of a mother's futile attempt to save her daughter from her own mundane fate.

Reviewers saw little merit in the third story, "The Young Prince," though they seemed to appreciate its basic premise. Fannie originally had chosen "Sissy" as the title of this look at the interior struggles of an effeminate and sensitive teenage boy named Bernard. Though *Best Short Stories* gave it only one star, the response it elicited from at least two young male readers was downright eerie. Both thought Fannie had spoken to them personally, with telling details from the minutiae of their own lives. One of them was even named

Bernard. With "The Third Husband" Fannie upped her price per story to four thousand dollars. A *Herald Tribune* reviewer would later describe it as a good story gone wrong for want of effort.

☯

As it turned out, none of these three stories sold to the movies, but Fannie did usher in 1928 with a check for forty-five hundred dollars for silent film rights to "Roulette." This was the six-year-old story for which she twice had sold dramatic rights although no play was ever produced. With Alfred Santell directing, First National Pictures released the film in the summer of 1928 to excellent reviews. It starred Richard Barthelmess in a widely praised dual performance as a set of twins thrust apart in the Russian pogroms. The two-roles-in-one device already was familiar to movie audiences. Gerald C. Duffy adapted Fannie's story for the film, which also starred Warner Oland, Lina Basquette, Margaret Livingston, Sidney Franklin, Martha Franklin, and Ann Schaefer.

Columbia Pictures bought the rights to Fannie's play *It Is to Laugh* for an unimpressive thirty-five hundred dollars, which she was forced to accept in arbitration of a dispute over the purchase. Another new title—*The Younger Generation*—replaced *It Is to Laugh,* which had replaced Fannie's original, "The Gold in Fish." Columbia hired Frank Capra to direct, and Fannie's old friend Sonya Levien wrote the screenplay. The picture was shot without sound, but the sensation created by Warner Bros.' first half-talkie, *The Jazz Singer,* shook up the industry, and Columbia rushed to catch up. Capra reshot enough of the sequences so that every second reel of the film could have dialogue. For him, it was an "etude in chaos" as crews accustomed to hammering, sawing, yelling, and howling with laughter during filming had to learn for the first time how to be *really* quiet on the set. Sound engineers recorded the track on wax discs, then distributed these to theaters on records that played alongside the sound portions of the film. Symphonic music provided background for the silent reels. Even with good technical work in the studios, much rested on the competence of the sound projection systems in the theaters. Flubs with synchronization of the records to the film could make the picture look pretty silly, as happened at the New York opening in March 1929.

Lois Weber offered a hollow apology for not making "The Gold in Fish" into a picture herself, as she originally had planned. She told Fannie that "the Columbia people" had called her in at the outset, but she claimed that she had refused to touch the story unless the studio agreed to leave Fannie's plot and characters intact. "I have never had the courage to see what was finally turned out in about three weeks' time," she sniped. Actually, the plot and character emphasis seemed to follow Fannie's story fairly closely, although how she felt about the picture is not known. *Variety* could not have been more disparaging—"sentimental oil has been spread on thick and often spills over . . . another insincere attempt to sell sympathetic syrup to the Jewish public." The

New York Post pronounced it "a pretty dull effort, but it may interest those who have never heard of *Abie's Irish Rose* or any of its dramatic descendants." Even Hearst's *New York Evening Journal* was unsupportive: "Another one of those ultra sentimental and rather trite yarns about the East Side." Yet Capra's biographer Joseph McBride thought the picture, which starred Jean Hersholt, Lina Basquette, Ricardo Cortez, and Rosa Rosanova, had more emotional power than anything else Capra directed in this period. The *Boston Herald's* reviewer, however, complained that Capra had rearranged the material so "injudiciously and so willfully" that he had lost all sense of proportion.

After five long years a director came forward with the passion to get Fannie's beloved *Lummox* produced, signaling the start of what would be a decade of exciting and lucrative deal making for Fannie with Hollywood. He was Herbert Brenon, the versatile Dublin-born filmmaker whose most recent silent film credits included *The Alaskan, Beau Geste, The Great Gatsby, The Breaking Point,* and *Peter Pan.* Fannie was ecstatic with the prospect, for it gave her the opportunity to work with a director of high caliber on her most beloved project and to witness firsthand the advent of the sound era in film.

Brenon was unlike anyone in Hollywood that Fannie had been connected with before, and she was perfectly smitten. In her words, Brenon squeezed her novel dry of its essence and stormed her brain for information. "His intellectual curiosity about an author's meaning is without limit; his respect for the author's ideas as wide as his intelligence," she said. He corresponded with her for months before production began and visited New York several times. He sent his screenwriter and chief collaborator, Betty Meehan, to spend days with Fannie working on the project. They became great friends. Fannie had begun to lose a dramatic amount of weight at this time, and Meehan, dazzled by the success, started disseminating Fannie's eighteen-day diet up and down the Malibu beach. This created dinner-party havoc for household cooks, who posted the regimen on refrigerator doors and tried their best to accommodate dinner guests with what the meal called for, depending on which day of the diet the various invitees had reached by party night.

In April 1929, as filming was about to begin in Hollywood, Brenon sent for Fannie. She was eager to participate in the production process, despite the fact that her mother in St. Louis was in rapidly failing health. As was her habit Fannie wrote her mother every day—though frantic telegrams from Rose crowded her mail slot whenever the postal service failed her. It was Fannie's old friend and neighbor Julia Browne who took it upon herself to look after Mama lovingly and dutifully. At first Rose had thrown a fit about Fannie's decision to go to California while she was so sick. The guilt assault forced Fannie to offer to cancel her trip, but then Rose backed down. Julia said Rose was contrite about her bad behavior. Though Fannie debated bringing Rose to California to stay with her, she was really too preoccupied with the film to make that an attractive proposition. "I work all morning with a secretary, rush to the studio about eleven o'clock and am constantly 'on the lot' until day is done," Fannie told Julia. "I am constantly needed in the production of this picture . . . The demands on my time are just incredible, socially and professionally." Rose would have been terribly bored.

Even with Rose ailing Fannie remained in California for almost two months. This time she found life in Hollywood "a series of exclamation points . . . gay, gaudy, giddy beyond the telling." When Elisabeth Marbury invited Fannie to visit her farm in Maine on her way back, Fannie teased, "What could you do for me in the way of sunken gardens, carrara [sic] marble swimming pools, Egyptian bathrooms with mirror ceilings, cream-colored Hispano-Suiza motor cars, trained leopards and golden swan bedsteads?"

∞

Nevertheless, it was about the even more fascinating sound revolution in film that Fannie wrote in a piece for *Redbook* cleverly titled "Hollywood, Hollywoodn't."

The change to sound affected everyone, she said, "from the set-dresser who finds that glazed chintz is not acoustically desirable, to the property man who must supply for the dinner table scene soda crackers with a noiseless crunch." The proliferation of "voice culture," diction and articulation experts, amazed her, as did the sorry exodus of foreign- and Brooklyn-accented stars of the silent screen. The sound department, she said, had abrogated the director's power. "Take that scene over," the engineer barks. "Miss G. swallows her vowels and you cannot have your love-scene played at that acute angle to the microphone." Directors had to relearn their craft, forced to silence for the first time while cameras rolled. Broadway's top talent—actors who already knew how to talk—suddenly developed West Coast appeal. In the lobby of her hotel one night, Fannie ran into at least ten Broadway fugitives: Willie Collier, Irving Berlin, Bob Milton, the Nugents, Ina Claire, Ruth Chatterton, Sophie Tucker, Gus Edwards, and George Arliss. The talkies, she predicted, would kill the road show. What now could justify a small-town fellow paying three dollars and thirty cents to see a third-rate road company when for sixty cents he could see and hear the cinematic version with the original company?

Having someone like Brenon make a film of her prized literary creation was "balm on old wounds" for Fannie, who had so often protested the "machine-stitched, third-rate hokum that has been dished out in her name." She went one further: the first rank of directors—she cited Charles Brabin's work on Thornton Wilder's *Bridge of San Luis Rey*—were men who believed in holding tight to the author's fundamental idea. If *Lummox* failed on the screen, she said, it was not going to be Brenon's fault.

United Artists held up release of *Lummox* until February 1930, nearly a year after the filming. Box-office draw the first weekend in Detroit surpassed five of UA's previous seven pictures. Winifred Westover had come out of an eight-year retirement and gained forty pounds to star as Bertha. Reviewers considered the detachment and world-weariness she exuded "singularly convincing." The picture, they noted, offered "no promise of customary entertainment." Its technical deficiencies were explained away by the fact that it had been filmed in those long ago days when sound was still in its infancy. The delayed release meant that the film was being screened alongside more recently produced works, in which the technology had been put to more sophisticated use.

Both Brenon and Meehan thought United Artists had treated the film like "a stepchild" even though Brenon's work on it was widely acclaimed. "I don't think I've ever read more superb reviews," Fannie told Meehan in a letter. She was perplexed by United Artists' apparent reluctance to release the film in New York. "It does seem to me that after a work has received the dignified applause and approval and recommendation of every city in which it appears, the producers might not be so cagey."

There was no years-long wait to see a film version of "Give This Little Girl a Hand." The story promptly sold to the movies for $10,500. Millard Webb ended up directing the "all-dialogue" picture with five original songs. This was another time that the film's producers sought Fannie's counsel instead of keeping her at frustrating bay. With the suggestion "The Painted Lily," she provided the inkling that became the actual title, *The Painted Angel*. The film, released in January 1930, starred Billie Dove, Edmund Lowe, Farrell MacDonald, and Peter Higgins. It introduced the device of the "talking reporter," one of the nightclub guests whose job it was to take the audience quickly through Rodeo's early life with a series of fade-outs. *Variety* thought the movie had a monotonous "revue-grind" element, which high-perched camera and underleg lens studies helped to relieve, but found it well-staged and coached all the same.

There was resurrection for Hester Bevins, the mistress of "Back Pay" with the crepe de chine soul. Since her debut in 1919 she had made appearances in a magazine short story, in a book of short stories, in a play, and in a silent film. First National Productions decided to remake *Back Pay* as a talkie and hired William Seiter to direct the new film, which starred Corinne Griffith, Grant Withers, Montague Love, Louise Beavers, and Louise Carver. Francis Faragoh adapted the story for the screen. In this instance Fannie's only involvement was as recipient of a check for five thousand dollars for sound rights. At the same time, she got the same amount for the sound rights to "Humoresque," even though its talking remake was a good eighteen years off. The new "all dialogue" *Back Pay* opened at the Strand in New York the week of May 30, 1930. "Miss Hurst . . . wrote this one for the five-and-ten counter girls," *Variety* complained. "The producers attempted to expand the territory, but the story held them back. So let the Woolworths worry."

Fannie reassured her readers that, unlike so many of her literary contemporaries streaming to Hollywood to write for the movies, she would have no part of it. "By no stretch of the imagination can I conceive of myself as ever writing, or desiring to write, directly for the motion-picture screen," she declared. This already was untrue when she said it; for in the blush of romance over her involvement with United Artists through the making of *Lummox,* she had informally submitted a story to the studio intended as a film vehicle for Fanny Brice. She called it "But I'm Good Company." The studio responded with what Fannie considered a humiliating dismissiveness, as if she were some rank amateur. This snapped her back to the reality of doing business with Hollywood, and she responded immediately, firmly but politely demanding that any future discussions be conducted in a businesslike manner. Fannie never allowed anyone to diminish her earned standing with insult more than once. United Artists responded, and at the organization's prompting she resubmitted the story, rewriting the Brice-tailored role so that a more general personality could be cast in the part. Hollywood—Hollywoodn't. The only thing to come of it was a little publicity. A newspaper reported that Fannie turned down a million dollars to write a talking picture for Fanny Brice so that she could go back to New York and finish her next novel.

"Five and Ten"

*C*osmopolitan bought Fannie's novel *Five and Ten* for thirty-five thousand dollars to run as a serial chronicling the life of John G. Rarick, a self-made dime-store chain magnate and the thirteenth richest man in the world, whose money brings him no happiness. His wife, Jenny, mired in the pursuit of the next acquisition, is involved with a gigolo. His daughter, Jennifer, is arrogant and superficial, and his son, Avery, despondent despite the speedboats and roadsters he collects for toys, commits suicide. In atonement for all the unhappiness in himself and around him, Rarick gives all his money to benefit science so that he may die poor.

When the first episode of the serial ran in *Cosmopolitan* in April, Ray Long wrote Fannie at once. "I can't tell from where I sit whether it was you or Coolidge that sold out the issue," he said. "But I'll say this. You certainly make a *great* team." The last installment ran in the September 1929 issue of the magazine, and Harper & Brothers timed the release of the book version to coincide. How prophetic that *Five and Ten* should have come out in hardback the month before Black Monday, 1929.

Reviews were generally positive, winning Fannie praise for "her usual deep perception and genuine ability to invest relationships with significance and poignance." The book was not considered as powerful as *Lummox* or *A President Is Born,* but as Alice Parsons Beal put it in *The Nation,* "Here is emotion. Here is good red blood. Here is, or are, guts." There were also, of course, the usual complaints: "Pages of impressive narrative are sandwiched between long-winded stretches of pretentious exposition," said the *Saturday Review,* "but nevertheless the narrative as a whole somehow manages to come out on top." Fannie sold the film rights to Metro-Goldwyn-Mayer, which planned to star Marion Davies as Jennifer. Fannie's push for her friend Robert Milton to direct the film was ignored, and the job went to Robert Z. Leonard.

Between Fannie's Hollywood sojourn for the filming of *Lummox* and a preoccupation with her mother's illness, she managed to turn out another story, "grim as fate, but powerful as the devil," in Ray Long's view, though others disagreed. "Carrousel" was the tale of two sisters triangulated to the same man, whom one of them—but which?—stabs to death with a pair of sewing shears. It ran in *Cosmopolitan's* January issue of 1930.

For Fannie the overriding preoccupation of 1929 was her mother. The four years since Sam Hurst's death had been dreadful for Rose, who had never had real interests outside her home, her husband, and her daughter. Though Fannie tried to bring her to New York to live, it was pointless. Rose had nothing in common with the mothers of Fannie's friends and always ended up feeling like a fifth wheel, a burden. "In a tragic and irrefutable way, that was partly true," Fannie later reflected, "and the louder our contradictions, the stronger her intuitions."

In the years after her father's death, Fannie yearned for her mother to display a flash of her old naughtiness and spirit, but Rose was listless, in Fannie's words, an empty cocoon. Fannie began to think of her as an object lesson in how not to meet the disaster of the death of a spouse. Rose's generation, Fannie said, had neglected to take out insurance against old age.

With Fannie in New York and what remained of Rose's family in Ohio, most of the local burden fell on Julia Browne, who actually moved into the Cates Avenue home to look after Rose, even though she was in her sixties at the time and had no identifiable illness. Yet she was constantly sick. Fannie's debt to Julia was enormous.

By letter Julia urged Fannie to stop in St. Louis and stay for a while on her way back from California, but Fannie couldn't bear the prospect. "The series of hideous experiences I have had while there makes the very sight of it almost unbearable," Fannie wrote. Instead, she planned to stop long enough to pick up her mother and take her—plus chauffeur, cook, maid, and secretary—to Windrose Farm, a country place she had been renting for a number of years in Westchester County. She wanted to devote the summer months to pampering her mother.

Julia warned Fannie of how impossible Rose had become and tried to free Fannie of any guilt she might harbor for her failings as a dutiful daughter. "I have lived around you all too many years to believe that," she said. "I have only to point to the fact that your mother fights with everyone for you to be convinced that she is not faultless. . . . She is mentally alert all right, but not a well-balanced woman. You couldn't convince me there is anything wrong with her mentally except that she's just been indulged and given into until she can't understand why everything and everybody will not bend to her will."

Julia said that while Sam Hurst was alive, he was the target of Rose's periodic "antics" but now she—Julia—had taken his place. "She would fight with him," Julia said, "just as I can read between the lines and know that she is fighting with you. With me it has been the most biting sarcasm and an ugly domineering attitude. You have indulged her since she has been sick so long until she is the worst spoiled person I know anything about. She is just like a bad child without the beauty." Julia said Rose was cursing at telephone operators when they couldn't find a number she needed and fighting with her friends when they did call and when they didn't. This was especially true during her hospitalization, even though she had instructed Julia not to tell anyone where she was. Charitably, Julia excused the erratic behavior as part of Rose's sickness.

Julia warned Fannie not to let Rose abuse her during their summer together, nor to allow her to make Fannie feel that she was mean and unsympathetic. "All this business of putting aside your work is very nice, but she wouldn't feel even that you had done one thing," Julia said. It hurt Julia that Rose felt resentment toward her after all she had done for Rose. She had humored her more than she had her own sweet mother, who didn't require it. All the same, Julia said, "I believe I know her better than anybody—every angle to her nature—and I know that after all is said and done, she is pure gold." Julia also warned Fannie not to let her mother interfere with her marriage. Rose was deeply resentful of Fannie's life, Julia said, with "a feeling of jealousy and that life is too easy. Do you understand me? Bear that in mind."

Fannie resolved to show her mother complete attention and to make her feel totally adored. "I am really hopeful that after a summer together, I will have succeeded in helping her to help herself mentally, without in any way crossing or aggravating her," she said. "Yes, I realize my job!"

Fannie knew that Rose's "high-voltage temperament" obscured her richness and generosity, but in spite of it she had managed to endow her daughter with a warm and cared-for childhood, employing no technique beyond her vast mother love. "No doubt psychiatry could detect in me deep fissures in character and scars across my memory that need to be diagnosed in order for me to understand myself," Fannie later reflected. "If that be true, they are benign scars, because with all her storminess and even on occasion her terribleness, I loved her and was loved."

Once, when Fannie was just out of college, Rose got so tired of the endless stream of rejection letters from editors, she offered to pay the magazines to publish Fannie's stories. Sam told her she should be ashamed to suggest such a thing; Fannie was appalled. Rose theatrically claimed she wished she were dead, for all the abuse her family gave her. "These ridiculous moments live on in heartache and regrets," Fannie wrote later. "Mama meant so well. She would have schemed to get me the moon had I expressed a wish for it. Yet time and time again I turned on her: Oh Mama, please keep out of it."

Fannie often wondered if her success had given pleasure to her parents. There was gratification, to be sure, but Fannie's fame had also meant her swift departure from their lives in any meaningful way. Nothing had meant more to her mother than when Fannie came home to be with her father when he was dying. To neighbors Rose bragged about the demonstration of devotion, calling Fannie a child in a thousand.

"Oh yes, I was a child in a thousand," Fannie wrote in reflection. "Caught in the paradox of loving these two, yet like a hunted animal, eyeing every egress from their home."

Since no record or mention of the trip survives, it is not clear if Rose actually made it to Windrose Farm with Fannie in the summer of 1929. What is known is that she died of a cerebral hemorrhage, on October 2, in her bed on Cates Avenue. Julia called Fannie with the news at 3:00 A.M.

Lois Toensfeldt thought Fannie had risen nobly to the sad and trying experience of Rose's funeral, showing herself a model of poise and efficiency under terrible stress. Grieving, Fannie told Lois she did not seem to be able to reconcile herself to a world in which her mother wasn't. She repeated this theme often over the years, in her memoirs and in letters to close friends and relatives who knew her mother well. To Bob Davis, she said that life without her mother in the world was like living with a shell hole in her center. Yet there was no obvious manifestation of such pain, certainly nothing akin to the pain that Jack's death would later cause her. Davis understood it as grief, however, and urged Fannie to take comfort in the fact that for Rose Hurst her daughter had been "the Celestial Choir . . . the very breath of her existence; the overtone, the undertone and the Cosmic chord. What more there is to be said cannot be said by mortals."

However intense her grief or guilt, Fannie gave herself no time to wallow. She settled immediately back into her high-energy routine. Grant Overton got her to agree to write a "serialette" for a magazine he was editing in the Collier's group called *Country Home*. He offered her twenty thousand dollars for twenty thousand words. Paul Palmer, Sunday editor at the *New York World*, engaged her for a newspaper symposium on divorce. The idea was to respond to a recent resolution passed in London at the International Congress for Social Reform. It called for an end to inhuman and vindictive divorce laws and customs, and support for an attitude more conducive to freedom and individual happiness for all involved parties, parents and children alike. It further pressed for each of the marital partners to have the freedom to dissolve the marriage so that no one would have to remain in an unhappy relationship against his or her will. Other contributions came from Bertrand Russell, H. G. Wells, Theodore Dreiser, Warwick Deeping, Rebecca West, André Maurois, and Lion Feuchtwanger. The collection of essays was later published in book form in both the United States and Britain.

A friend of Zora Neale Hurston stepped forward, asking for Fannie's assistance. This was young Dorothy West, who had shared second prize in the short-story category for "The Typewriter" with Zora's "Muttsy" in the second *Opportunity* awards competition back in 1926. West was staying at Zora's apartment while she was living on West Sixty-sixth Street, not far from Fannie's home. Fannie willingly advised and encouraged West, looking over her stories when asked and helping her with introductions to editors.

After four years with the McClure's Syndicate, Fannie was ready to give up the weekly grind. Too many newspaper clients had canceled her, the sleazy *New York Graphic* repeatedly embarrassed her by taking liberties with her copy, changing headlines, and supplying illustrations that often didn't match the text. On top of that, the contract prohibited her from working for any other syndicate for twelve months after she stopped writing for the McClure's organization. Fannie tried everything she could to get out of the pact—especially with John Wheeler of the Bell Syndicate bearing down with what may have been a better offer. But, like "a chicken-hearted jelly fish," she conceded to Wheeler, purposely mixing her biology and metaphors. She reluctantly signed on for another stint with McClure's when the syndicate met most of her conditions. Again, she tried the "soapbox" format, but within a month she was back to the grueling task of short-short fiction week after week. Editors couldn't seem to think of Fannie as anything but a fiction writer. She quit McClure's at the end of 1930 for a lucrative contract offered by King Features Syndicate for 1931 and 1932, up nearly three thousand dollars, the Depression notwithstanding. On top of that, the new editors agreed to let her write soapbox.

Who did seem to see Fannie in a new light was Stef, who called wistfully for her from his travels in ways he had never before expressed. "You will be forty when I am fifty," he wrote her on his return from England aboard the SS *Majestic* (even he didn't know she was nearly forty-four), "and life so short even when we were thirty and twenty. Fannie!" The stay in England was brief, he said, "but one long longing for you." He bemoaned the fact he would have six—maybe only three—hours in New York before traveling on to his next lecture site. "Don't let that prove symbolic of the future," he said. "We are both in the hands of fate, in one sense. In another, I am in yours. I could influence you, I suppose. But it is you who are at the helm."

3

Preceding page: AP/Wide World Photos

Chapter *19*

"Back Street"

The year Fannie turned forty-five, she showed the same disdain in
life as she did in fiction for the work of plastic surgeons but none for
New York's elite new cadre of obesity experts, whose strict and expensive super-
vision could mean weight loss in the double digits. This was worth the price.

Dr. Henry James Spencer put Fannie on the most draconian diet regimen
she had ever attempted, which, over the course of a year and a piece, radically
transformed her appearance for the first time in a decade of trying. Even before
the last ten pounds were off, the effect was staggering. "Oh Betty, you simply
won't know me," she wrote to her Hollywood friend Elizabeth Meehan in February 1931, urging her to come to New York for a visit before she could "blow
up again like a balloon." In fact, she fought with those last ten pounds for years
to come but never again could be described as fat, or even plump. In January
1931 Bob Davis wrote that he hoped she wouldn't let her "thirst for the svelte
line interfere with your grandeur as a woman. The less there is of you the
worse it is for this generation." (Davis's gratitude to Fannie at the time was as
immense as his affection. She had mobilized a group of prominent authors including George Ade and Montague Glass to write Davis's column at the *New
York Sun* while he recuperated from a disabling accident. The stunt promoted a
flood of attention. "Good Lord how the animals woke up when the pinch-
hitters started," Davis crowed.) As Fannie got thinner and thinner over the
next year, Davis warned her to stop before she had to "cross the sunlight twice
to make one shadow."

But the most amusing by-product of Fannie's intense focus on restricting
and controlling her intake of food was the leitmotiv it produced for her seventh novel. At the time she was well into the writing of the work she had titled
"Grand Passion." It tells the story of a soon-to-be powerful investment banker
named Walter Saxel, who marries the appropriate woman instead of Ray
Schmidt, the inappropriate but more intriguing woman he truly loves. Six
years later Walter and Ray meet again by chance. Their love is instantly rekindled. Very discreetly, or so Walter thinks, he keeps her in the shadowy corners
of his life from then on. (Actually, the investment banker had come into
Fannie's imagination as Walter Sax. When she realized how close the name was

to that of her friend Emanie's husband, Walter Sachs, she changed it at his request. Schmidt happened to be the last name of Dr. Spencer's secretary.)

Over time, Ray Schmidt gives up her own successful career, as well as her family and friends, so that she can be totally available to Walter. This means days and weeks of waiting with nothing to do, since Walter's crowded schedule of business, travel, and family obligations makes it impossible to predict when he can steal the time to be with her. Nevertheless, he wants her waiting when he can.

Walter is the quintessential "miser lover." He keeps Ray in almost monastic simplicity, which, he once self-servingly explains, is his effort to preserve the dignity of their love and to elevate Ray above the tawdry taint of the arrangement. The result, however, is that the once-accomplished Ray is reduced to china painting and some small-stakes gambling on horse races to fill her days. Walter sees these as acceptable pastimes, oblivious to their role in supplementing Ray's subsistence allowance. Still, it is a reasoning she accepts. She pampers Walter with wise counsel about his work and family life—she does research for him and writes and coaches his speeches. She never nags; she never whines or complains. Lovingly, she prepares him perfect meals of the rich and fat-laden German foods he adores, elaborately described by Fannie.

In their late middle years, they travel as they have many times to Aix-les-Bains—Walter and his family, as always, in the most lavish hotel and Ray around the corner in a simple pension. His older two children have known about the affair for years and hatefully resent the woman they deride as the Saxel family shadow. Walter's older son, concerned about embarrassment to the family as his sister becomes engaged to marry, decides to confront Ray. He goes over to her pension to have it out. Walter walks in on the scene. In fury, Walter defends Ray and his love for her and orders his son to stay out of this sacred corner of his life. Walter and Ray dine alone, as always, on one of her particularly rich meals. He tells her without rancor that he has been passed over for a prestigious diplomatic appointment, which he coveted and expected to get. It is obvious from the circumstance that wide knowledge of his relationship with Ray has sullied his reputation and lost him the chance.

During the dinner Walter has a severe attack of apparent indigestion. When the pain eases he heads back to his family at the hotel and there, surrounded by his wife and children, suffers a paralytic stroke. Once alone in his room with the older son, Walter, barely able to speak, implores the young man to dial Ray's telephone number. Ray answers, and Walter faintly repeats her name into the receiver as he dies. The receiver drops from his hand and dangles from its cord with the line still open. In agony, Ray listens to Walter's final moments and the gathering of his family in panic and grief.

The untimely death may or may not have been the reason, but Ray is left with nothing except a few mementos, a few of Walter's belongings and the memory of her selfless love. The older son, in remorse and out of reluctant respect for his father, goes to see Ray again. He offers to continue her support payments, the minuteness of which surprises him. But he is killed in a racing accident before he can make good on the promise.

To survive, Ray turns to gambling. Ultimately she returns to the casino at Aix-les-Bains and for some years manages to get by, sometimes off the largesse of big winners whose custom it is to toss a large bill over their shoulders to the waiting hands of the slightly shabby, birdlike group of older women who gather in the casino night after night. One by one Ray sells off her possessions, keeping for last a handsome pair of Walter's dress shoes. She hasn't eaten for days. The day she sells the shoes for three francs apiece, enough for casino entrance, she has the luck to catch a five-hundred-franc note tossed into that scrawny swarm without a backward glance by a handsome young American. From the comments of his friends, she realizes her unknowing benefactor is Walter's youngest child. Elation fills her. Faint with hunger, clasping the note to her heart as if it is "from Walter's dead hand," Ray returns to her room. She is found three days later, dead of starvation, the five hundred francs clutched to her bosom "like a porous plaster."

Ray Long called the novel "gorgeous" and paid Fannie forty thousand dollars to run it as a *Cosmopolitan* serial. He didn't think "Grand Passion" was a dignified enough title for the story and pressed Fannie repeatedly to agree to call it *Back Streets*—plural—the name it eventually bore over seven voraciously read monthly installments in *Cosmo* from September 1930 through March 1931. The fan mail poured in. "As a picker of serials," Fannie told Long, "you are 'hot.' "

For the hardback edition of *Back Street,* Fannie once again changed publishers. The Hearst Corporation, at this time, decided to start its own imprint, the Cosmopolitan Book Corporation, and lured Fannie to sign on with the promise of a $16,500 advance—more than twice what she had ever received before—an advertising budget of $10,000, and "publication on a scale which never before had been attempted." In the meantime, with her usual but no less remarkable energy, Fannie turned out the promised novelette for Grant Overton at *Country Home*. It began running in the February issue under the title "Local Girl."

Fannie returned from a trip to Cuba with Davis, his wife, Madge, and Daniel Frohman in time for *Back Street's* hardcover release on January 17, 1931. Though Pearl S. Buck topped the best-seller lists for fiction with *The Good Earth* that year, *Back Street* took eighth place and provided Fannie with her first and only showing on a list compiling best-seller figures nationally for a novel over an entire year. Still, she accused the new publisher of waging a disappointly ordinary campaign. The sales manager assured her that everything possible had been done for the book, that forty-five thousand books in such a depressed economic climate was like selling 60 percent more in normal times, and that she should be pleased. *A President Is Born,* for example, which sold much more than twice the number of books as *Back Street* in 1928, never made the annual best-seller list.

She did what she could to stir up publicity on her own. When the British author J. B. Priestley traveled to America for the first time and poked hostile fun of everything around him within hours of his arrival, Fannie fought back with a statement to *The New York Times*. Priestley complained about the "nightmare" of New York City and its spoiled women. He scoffed at the population's tendency to overeat and the national curse of indigestion. He accused Americans of having more interest in buying books than reading them, repeating the report of a friend who found Sinclair Lewis's *Main Street* out on the coffee table of every home he visited in the United States. In every case, Priestley declared, the leaves of the books were still uncut. Fannie sentenced Priestley to be "court-martialed by laughter" for his "hot-off-the-griddle" appraisals, pointedly adding that the only existing edition of Lewis's novel had its pages precut by machine. She was sick of pompous foreigners looking down on the United States. (More than a decade later, after Fannie wrote Priestley to compliment him on an article he had written, he recalled their contretemps and explained that shipside reporters had taken his "few little jokes" out of context and magnified them into a "gigantic, virulent attack upon the United States." The result, he said, was that for years he, "who had more fondness for and knowledge of America than almost any other English author . . . was known as the 'man who disliked America.' " He mused on the mischievous role the press has played in Anglo-American relations.)

As for *Back Street,* Fannie understood enough about market conditions to be well pleased with the novel's performance. As she told Betty Meehan, it was "all too thrilling and exciting the way the book is behaving and I sort of wake up pinching myself." The strong word of mouth and relatively good sales steeled her against another run of disappointing and downright insulting reviews. Even her good friend Rebecca West couldn't resist a sideswipe. Of Fannie, she wrote, "She is naively unaware of the traditional ideals that have governed English prose for the last three hundred years or so. . . . But if she learns nothing from outside, she has wisdom within." (No doubt it was West's willingness to wrap her compliments in such scratchy flax that eventually caused Fannie to question the sincerity of her friendship.)

These were momentary hurts, easily soothed by the balm of fan letters that arrived by the score. "*Back Street* has left me with anguish that still hurts." "I was wrung to the heart by *Back Street*." "I have eaten, dreamed and slept *Back Street* till I was scared of meeting the ghost of Ray Schmidt face-to-face." From Cleveland, Ohio, came a letter addressed to "Fannie Hurst, Genius."

Studio executives were with the fans on this one. Here was a story with such power to imprint on the consciousness, its future in celluloid was guaranteed. Response was immediate. How fitting that Universal Studios bought the movie rights for thirty-five thousand dollars on Valentine's Day, 1931.

"*A summer's diversion*"

Flush with *Back Street*'s raging success, Fannie didn't waste a minute. She started thinking out her new novel and wrote "Funny Face," another four-thousand-dollar short story for *Cosmopolitan*. She kept turning out her weekly syndicated column for King Features. In Hollywood, MGM got ready for an April release of the movie *Five and Ten,* and the film version of *Back Street* went into production at Universal. RKO offered Fannie an unrefusable thirty thousand dollars to write a story directly for the screen. She signed that contract April 17 and worked "with unabated zeal" to turn in the first draft of "Night Bell" three weeks later. Yet even before that submission she had signed a five-thousand-dollar contract with Columbia Pictures for an original screen story with the working title "Park Avenue." Had only two years passed since Fannie announced to the readers of *Theatre* magazine that she could not imagine herself ever writing an original screenplay? Never mind; that was before the stock market crash had made any and all income sources appealing. Suddenly Fannie was describing screenwriting as a "highly special technique" all its own. "Life's old bandwagon moves fast these days," she told an important film reviewer, "and I find it's rather thrilling to be aboard."

Clearly, amid all that activity Fannie's decision to upend her personal life in the summer of 1931 had nothing to do with a professional lull. The love triangle had long been the central theme of her fiction—girl-suitor-suitor, mother-son-girlfriend, sister-sister-husband, brother-brother-wife, and the husband-mistress-wife of *Back Street*. Triangulation was also a major theme of her own life—mother-father-daughter, parents-daughter-writer, parents–daughter–unacceptable suitor, and, most recently, wife-husband-lover. The time had come to do something about it.

Fannie had long been comfortable with the ambivalence she felt about her two main men—her easy, undemanding marriage to Jacques and Stef's acquiescence to the furtive liaisons, the one-ring telephone signals to announce his impending arrival, the dash into the bushes on the way to Fannie's apartment at the end of the day to avoid her secretary's passing glance. Fannie was thoroughly reliant on Jack in her business dealings, and despite the separateness with which they seemed to function, their lives were more intricately intertwined than most people realized. Jack handled all their money, made every investment decision, rode herd over all her contract negotiations, chased collections when necessary, and soothed, comforted, and supported Fannie whenever things did not go her way. His even, elegant temperament, his devotion, his apparent ease with the freedom she required and demanded, both to engage in the world and to retreat from it into solitude, all left her very comfortable with the marriage. Her worry for and devotion to Jacques during his several bouts of illness in these years attested to the deep affection and attachment she felt, even her love.

Something every bit as compelling, however, drew her to Stef. Another woman with firsthand knowledge has confided that Stef was an unusually gifted lover, but Fannie claimed it was the overpowering intensity of his intellect that attracted her so. Of course, she makes this claim in the same autobiography in which she admits to *no* affair after her marriage, let alone a sex life. "I was jealous of him," she said of Stef, "but only of his learning; jealous of his mind." She loved the affirmation of having such a man's love. The summer of 1931 was certainly what passed for anguished indecision in a life as cool and controlled as Fannie's, but she showed no outward manifestation of the internal conflict. It was a time of intense creative and social engagement, and, thanks to Dr. Spencer, she had never looked better.

☞

On June 1, Stef left New York on a lucrative but dreaded eleven-week lecture tour with the Chautauqua circuit. His affair with Fannie was nearly a decade old by this point, and long separations had been part of the configuration since the outset. This time, however, Fannie found the prospect of being away from him unbearable. Stef had agreed to the tour with the idea that it would help him raise the money to buy a farm in Vermont to which the two of them could retreat in privacy. Fannie wanted to help any way she could. She wrote an article to twin with one of his so that he could get the money for both from *Redbook*. This was generous of Fannie, except the plan fell apart. Ray Long took a stand against her writing for the competition, and *Redbook* had no interest in a story from Stef without one from Fannie.

Over the coming three months Fannie committed herself to finding the most amicable and publicly undamaging way possible for her and Jacques to part. Fannie and Stef made their plans in total secrecy. Record of the episode survives only because Stef ignored Fannie's admonition marked in capitals across the face of this series of letters: DESTROY. He did, however, keep them separate from his other papers.

"Dearest, dear," she had written him as soon as he left town.

> Every dream and every hope and everything that makes life rich is on a train tonight bound for Canada.
> My dreams have chiefly to do with enriching that richness—for you and for me. My happiness lies in seeing you as happy as you deserve to be **** which means all the happiness there is, for us both.

Twenty-four hours later she wrote again. "My universe is shot to pieces but I shall not sit in it and mope. There is *work to be done!!!!*"

Fannie called Zora Neale Hurston, who was living in an apartment around the corner after several folklore-finding expeditions to the South. Casually, Fannie suggested a trip up north in Zora's car. She said she wanted to see some farms for sale in Vermont, but more important to visit Elisabeth Marbury, who had asked to see Fannie urgently, at her summer house in Maine. Zora, who had recently engaged Marbury as her own agent, was game. The two women made plans to leave on Sunday morning, June 7.

Stef, in the meantime, casually arranged for the Chautauqua program director, Nola Erickson, to invite Fannie to see the program up close. UNDERSTAND YOU WILL BE MOTORING NEAR BUFFALO WOULD BE HAPPY TO HAVE YOU MOTOR ACROSS INTO CANADA AND SEE OUR PROGRAMS ALSO WOULD ENJOY ANOTHER VISIT WITH YOU, her June 6 cable read. Stef sent his own cable to Fannie, making it seem as natural as possible that such an invitation would be forthcoming, that she could get a copy of the whole Chautauqua schedule from his office, and that she should keep him in mind if she went farm hunting in Vermont.

Fannie and Zora left as planned. An anecdote Fannie told years later could easily have happened at this time and along this route. According to Fannie, she and Zora stopped at a well-known Westchester County hotel, Zora draped in a red head scarf and garbed in "one of her bizarre frocks of many colors." Suddenly Fannie had an idea. She pushed ahead of Zora at the dining room entrance and urged her not to ask questions. When the headwaiter appeared, he glanced at Zora and then looked, in Fannie's words, "as if a window-shade had been drawn over his face." Fannie went on: "Before he could come through with the usual 'Sorry, everything reserved,' I announced, 'The Princess Zora and I wish a table.' " The women were shown to the best spot in the room. Back on the road, Zora remarked, "Who would think that a good meal could be so bitter?" They headed north to Albany, then east to the area around Putney, Vermont, to look at farms. But instead of heading toward Maine at that point, Fannie had Zora turn due west. By Tuesday afternoon, June 9, Fannie had Stef on the telephone from the Waverly Hotel in Herkimer, New York. The plan was to leave for Canada the next morning.

Zora also memorialized that trip in a profile of Fannie she wrote for the *Saturday Review* in 1937, six years after it took place. In the piece Zora playfully describes the contradictions in Fannie's character, the self-possessed, intelligent woman who is nobody's fool in business; the submissive coquette who runs purring to Jack for comfort over every annoying, petty incident; the powerful, no-nonsense celebrity who enjoys "playing at the little girl who runs away from home."

As Zora told the story, she serviced her little Chevrolet and arrived at Fannie's door first thing in the morning. In no time the two women were driving up the Boston Post Road. In Zora's version there is no mention of the Vermont farm hunting but a stop at Saratoga Springs in the afternoon. Fannie went off to make a telephone call, leaving Zora in front of a bubbling fountain where she could taste the fresh spring water. She gave Lummox, Fannie's two-pound Pekingese, a chance to stretch. This is Zora's re-creation of what happened when Fannie returned:

Miss Hurst had that look in her eyes that a child has when it is about to tell its mother that it has seen a fairy.

"Zora, your getting that drink of water reminds me to ask you if you have ever seen Niagara Falls?"

"No, I never have, Miss Hurst, but I have always meant to see it some day."

"Oh well then, you might just as well see it now. Everybody ought to see Niagara Falls as soon as possible. Suppose we go there right now?"

"Fine, but what about Miss Marbury?"

"Oh, she can wait. I couldn't think of letting you go back to New York without seeing the Falls."

So we pointed the nose of the Chevrolet due West with my foot in the gas tank splitting the wind for Buffalo. And next afternoon we were there before sundown.

At the falls, which Fannie had seen before, she stood by the car while Zora rushed up to the rail in wonder. She marveled at its "monstropolous" proportions, "the Pacific Ocean rushing over the edge of the world." Soon Fannie called to her, "mouth all primped up again.

"Zora, you must see this thing from the Canadian side. Let's go over there and get the view. They light it up at night, you know."

In five minutes we had crossed the international bridge and I had to go into a little building right close there to register the car. When I came out, Miss Hurst was almost dancing up and down like a six-year-old putting something over on its elders.

"Get in the car, quick, Zora. I think we can make Hamilton before dark!"

So we saw Hamilton, and Kitchener, and Gault, and many another town in Ontario. It took us two weeks, not a minute of which was dull. I cannot remember in which town it was, but in some town in that part of Canada we saw a big sign that said that Vilhjalmur Stefansson, the great Arctic explorer and lecturer was speaking on the Chautauqua. So we hunted him up and he gave us free passes to the lectures and they were fine. All about mosquitoes practically eating up dogs beyond the Arctic circle and how wolves don't go in packs.

What Zora remembered as a two-week trip actually was only nine days, the time in Canada amounting to no more than three. In her story for the *Saturday Review,* Zora wrote that in the last days of their trip Fannie's attention had shifted to her notebook, in which she was busy scribbling. "She had had the fun of running away," Zora said, "and she had had the fun of fooling me off to go along with her."

That Zora remained so truly ignorant of Fannie's covert purpose for this trip is hard to imagine, even if Fannie did not take Zora into her confidence when the two of them set out. But even more intriguing is that Zora would choose to embarrass Fannie by telling the story—with its potentially compromising references to Jack and Stef—in print as if she were just that ignorant. If Fannie never confided in Zora, what possible objection could she have to Zora's decision to retell such an innocent yarn? Maybe this was Zora's way of having the fun of fooling off "Miss Hurst." It may be no more than a fluke of rewrite and editing, but Zora's repetition of the story in her 1942 memoir, *Dust Tracks on a Road,* omits the playful references to Jacques and Stef entirely.

Zora and Fannie headed back toward Rochester in heavy rains. En route they rescued a little Maltese kitten on the verge of drowning, and Fannie got home at two o'clock on the morning of June 16, kitten in tow. Fannie wrote to Stef at once. "Have seen no one [Jack] as yet. Not even Clara [the housekeeper]. A mountain of mail stares at me and there is much to do and yet I have only one inclination and that is to write. I feel precisely as if only a small part of me has returned but that small part must*** must*** must act. . . . I am so homesick that I can scarcely bear it." "Homesick" was Stef and Fannie's code word for missing being together.

Three days later Fannie wrote Stef that she could "bear no longer delay." Again, she begged Stef to destroy her letters. Fannie kept trying to bolster his spirits. Stef found the Chautauqua circuit demeaning and degrading, despite the money it paid. "Try draining your sense of humor to capacity and if that doesn't work, cancel!" Fannie told him. "We'll arrange funds somehow. I'll either go ahead with my plans if they seem the inevitably right ones or rearrange according to yours. In the event that you discontinue, advise me at once." Her plan was to sail in a week for Paris or Sweden, "depending on the outcome of a certain conversation which I shall have either this evening or tomorrow. . . . Oh, how much I want to be with you to help you through these days."

Fannie had made tentative plans to join her friend Ruth Bryan Owen in Denmark on an eight-week camper trip she was taking with her children, though the prospect of Fannie in a camper is truly comical. Instead, as it turned out, Fannie boarded the *Gripsholm* June 27 on "an innocuous little visit to Scandinavian countries." With Jack. How symbolic that on a canal trip from Gothenburg to Stockholm, they got caught in a storm and narrowly escaped drowning. But by the time the story made the newspapers, her traveling companion erroneously became Ruth Bryan Owen. "The whole world seems to have been exercised about your shipwreck," Ruth told Fannie, "and I have been kept busy explaining that my part in it was greatly exaggerated. It reminded me of the story of the man who said to an acquaintance, 'I hear you made $100,000 on oil shares.' His friend replied, 'It was not $100,000 it was $10,000 and it was not oil shares it was railroads, and I did not make it, I lost it. Otherwise, the story is accurate.' "

From Sweden, Fannie and Jack made a "strenuous and rather heartbreaking invasion into Russian territory." Fannie told a friend it was "hardly what you would call a summer's diversion." Once there she saw "much squalor, much misery, much joy and exaltation" and wrote about it in the *Saturday Evening Post* for a handsome two-thousand-dollar fee. Her story included mention of her chance encounters in Moscow with George Bernard Shaw. At a lecture Shaw told his audience that he found conditions in Russia so excellent and food so plentiful that he had thrown out a train window all the provisions his concerned English friends had sent along with him. Jacques translated for Fannie the after-comment of one Russian audience member, that a thousand empty stomachs must have constricted in horror as Shaw uttered the words.

There is no known documentary record that even suggests what transpired between Jack and Fannie to make her change her mind and spend the summer not only in his company but on a return journey to his birthplace. One version, attributed to Stef, who presumably got his information from Fannie, held that Fannie remained in the marriage because Jack demanded a million dollars from her to end it. (Referring to wives, she had devoted more than one column to her aversion to "alimony leeches.") This may have been only what she told Stef. There is no way to know the reason she gave Jack for wanting out of the marriage, or even if she ever let him know she wanted out. Nor is it known if Fannie ever made Jack aware of the place Stef held in her affections, or if it even concerned him if she did. What is known is that on Fannie and Jack's return from Russia, life went on as if the summer of 1931 had never happened, the old triangle still in place.

⌒

Little wonder how the plot for the short story "God Made Little Apples" came into Fannie's head. The wife of a doctor nine years her senior falls in love with an architect who is eight years younger. The lovers plan to sail away together on the *Ile de France* to Paris in adjoining suites. The day before the planned departure, the husband calls out for the wife in his sleep. The tenderness of the moment affects the wife deeply and makes her realize that she cannot hurt him in this way. Though she is in love with the architect, she also loves her husband and realizes her future is with him. She breaks the architect's heart. Meantime, unbeknownst to the wife, the doctor has been having an affair with his much younger nurse. He too comes to the realization he needs his wife and cannot hurt her in this way. He breaks up with the nurse and in recompense offers her ten thousand dollars and a trip to Europe. She agrees to go, but the ship on which she wants to sail is fully booked. The girlfriend ends up on the *Ile de France,* for there has been a last-minute cancellation. *Cosmopolitan* published the story in May 1932.

For public consumption and in loving admiration, Fannie reflected many years later on the forbearance Jack had shown. "Only the most subtle and giving nature could have fathomed or tolerated what I myself did not, and do not yet, understand," she sighed. "Deep in my heart I am sure I never hesitated between the two widely different men. But . . . I must face up to my guilt in lingering by the wayside between the two whom I had allowed to meet but cursorily, all the while avoiding decision."

Once back in New York, Fannie was at her desk, thinking out her new novel, revising "Night Bell," which she had started to call "Symphony of Seven Million," tinkering with "God Made Little Apples," and writing her piece on Russia for the *Saturday Evening Post*. Surely there was no intended double entendre in the choice of title: "Russian Goose Hangs High."

If Fannie needed affirmation of her literary merit at this time, and like all writers she probably did, it came in early August in the form of an incisive four-page portrait in *The Bookman,* which, when she was forty-five, enshrined her place in American letters. The writer, Harry Salpeter, gently but not uncritically dubbed her "the sob-sister of American fiction." He did not intend this to be the contemptuous moniker it quickly became. "As a story-teller," he explained, "her chief problem has been to make the reader shed the tears from which she has forced herself to refrain. She is the sob-sister of American fiction in the sublimated sense of that vulgar phrase. I use that phrase not as a literal characterization, but only for the most human connotations that are to be extracted from it."

Salpeter saw in Fannie a portraitist and advocate for women "whose advocacy is none the less forceful for being oblique and suggested within the confines of the portrait." He felt certain if she ever attempted a work of "pure—sexless—art," the warmth of her own sex would thaw through it, "converted into sexual advocacy of woman, as woman and of woman, as a minority in a world made by and for men." Fannie had to equivocate when Salpeter asked her to spell out the message in her novels beyond the stories, because it was a notion she had never consciously considered. "I must have a message," she finally conceded, "because I am so passionately anxious to awake in people in general a sensitiveness to small people. . . . I have a great respect for 'just a life.' "

Fannie said she had never pandered to a public or a policy. "If I write down," she said, "it is because I am down. If I write low, I am low. . . . If I have achieved a popular success it is because I am the stature of my work."

To Salpeter, *Lummox* still stood as her "most valid claim to recognition and distinction." He acknowledged, however, that *Five and Ten* and *Back Street* had also managed to resonate most potently with readers and critics because, like *Lummox,* these works contained within their pages "the *echt* Fannie Hurst."

Chapter *20*

"Command me"

The Great Depression quickly smote the insouciance that had made the 1920s roar. Throughout the decade Fannie postured as a person of seriousness and purpose, albeit with a dramatic flair all her own. She had long been an opinion maker on the rights of women and their changing relationships with men; this was a natural outgrowth of the topics she addressed in fiction and the way she lived her own life. True, editors for years had resisted her weekly "soapbox" essays, and King Features had let her contract lapse at the end of her two years with the syndicate. But those same newspaper editors readily gave her a platform for opinions in response to any number of issues. Even *The New York Times* repeatedly headlined her statements on matters of public concern. "Fannie Hurst Opens Drive for Signers to Geneva Petition" on disarmament. "Stage Censor Fails, Fannie Hurst Says," when she declared to the Theater League that taste, morality, and ethics could not be controlled. "Aided by Fannie Hurst" referred to her speech at a Roxy Orchestra concert to benefit unemployed musicians. "Miss Hurst Aids Pacifists" confirmed her endorsement of the Griffin Bill, which supported the immigration of conscientious objectors from foreign countries. "Noted Writers Aid Textile Strikers" referred to a group formed by Fannie, Theodore Dreiser, and Sherwood Anderson to help striking textile workers in the South. Over the years the usual impetus for Fannie's activism, outside a rather generalized but no less heartfelt humanitarianism, was a request for assistance. She honored requests from causes and organizations she felt comfortable supporting and— not so incidentally—for public exposure she greedily welcomed. In his portrait for *The Bookman,* Harry Salpeter found her among the "most publicized, most ubiquitous" of authors, "often rushing into print where authors more discreet fear to tread." Until the 1930s were well under way, however, the Pittsburgh coal strike of 1928 would remain her only experience of bona fide power wielding on a national level. But even in this instance Fannie's interest stemmed from a request for coverage by a newspaper with a checkbook, not from any particular passion for the cause itself. As Salpeter put it, "She is healthily opinionated; she does care about a lot of things, even if she does pretend to care about more, for purposes that are tinged with publicity motive.'"

What changed the timbre of Fannie's involvement in the 1930s was not the disastrous economic crisis brought on by the stock market crash of 1929. She made her concern for the suffering of others concrete with discreet but generous loans to good friends and warm acquaintances when they found themselves in dire need. "Most of the time, the depression that is abroad over the land seeps in and bears one down," Fannie wrote to Blanche Knopf in November 1930, "the rest of the time, the whole aspect of hunger and degradation and unemployment makes one feel a little insane."

Incongruously, for Fannie personally the 1930s turned out to be a time of professional exhilaration and power, the highest-earning years of her career. ("You didn't mention the Depression," Lois Toensfeldt quizzed at the end of 1932 after Fannie's return from a summer in Greece. "Do you know there is one?")

Her involvement in civic and national affairs in this period continued to have the feel of a somewhat random willingness to respond to whatever compelling requests for help came her way. And many did. In March 1932, without apparent prompting, she took a front seat at the Samuel Seabury hearings into Tammany corruption, warranting her own newspaper headlines for doing so, photograph and all. She said it was time for Americans to show genuine civic concern. A year earlier the same corruption inquiry had brought down Fannie's friend Magistrate Jean Norris of Woman's Court, the first woman to hold judicial office in New York City and the first to lose her job for official misconduct. She was accused of altering a trial transcript. Fannie had mined Norris's courtroom many times for story inspiration and felt a strong sense of indignation and obligation as the slung mud started to splatter the magistrate's robes in the late fall of 1930. "If at any time you want a public statement from me or an expression of my deep-dyed and justified admiration for you and your big work—command me," Fannie offered. She poured tea at a reception in Norris's honor and fired off a letter of support to *The New York Times,* but it never saw print. She did excite the interest of the House of Harper to publish a book Norris wanted to write about the whole sorry mess, but Fannie's editor at the time talked her out of ghostwriting it, and the idea fizzled. In time, so did the relationship.

Judge Norris's misfortune did not dampen Fannie's new enthusiasm for her own brand of political engagement, spurred by the ambitions and political fortunes of Ruth Bryan Owen, Fiorello La Guardia, and New York governor Franklin D. Roosevelt. Through Stef, Ruth and Fannie had already been friends for many years; La Guardia, one of Fannie's earliest New York buddies, resurfaced in her life as he embarked on his mayoral campaign, and the Roosevelts began cultivating a friendship with her a good two years before their move to the White House.

When requests for help came from these quarters, Fannie responded with the gusto of genuine commitment. It was the friendships themselves that motivated her, not the issues or causes any of these friends espoused individually. Through these associations, and others that developed because of them, Fannie fashioned a style of activism as peculiarly her own as the way she wrote and the way she dressed. It exploited her celebrity aura and status, her access and influence, in support of those who mattered to her and the issues they championed. Conveniently for her and her political friends, Fannie's sensational new novels and film deals during the decade renewed and aggrandized her already formidable popularity and renown. She was a welcome presence.

"Command me," she repeatedly offered. When called upon, she provided loyal, straightforward, and generally effective public support. This did not extend to requests for her to submit to the organizational-administrative grind of routine board meetings and the like, even though she sometimes accepted such appointments with earnest intent. Fannie's real value to her friends lay in her public appeal. She was a suction cup for publicity. Newspapers and magazines welcomed her remarks and any carefully posed photograph in any manner of deed. She had a unique radio personality, and broadcasters seemed to want to air whatever she had to say. As she helped others, she enhanced her reputation as a right-minded, do-gooding social activist and good citizen. The perception and the reality served her well.

Adamantly, Fannie remained unaligned with either major political party and refused ever to speak on partisan matters. During the Roosevelt administrations, she became so closely identified with the Democrats that her refusal to declare outright allegiance to the party was likely a way to avoid making large financial contributions. Fannie was always happy to give of herself but generally less interested in parting with money, even for things she believed in. At the same time, she was always willing to enlist the help of the powerful for an issue or individual that she felt merited attention. Though she was a formidable public speaker, she wisely knew her limitations and declined to range into subjects too far beyond her depth. For example, when Theodore Dreiser asked her to serve on a small committee to preview and critique Paramount's film of Dreiser's novel *An American Tragedy,* she readily agreed. But when he asked her to address a rally on behalf of oppressed miners in Harlan, Kentucky, she declined. "I fear," she said, "that unless I felt sure of doing it supremely well, I might work more to the detriment of the cause than otherwise." This happened more than once.

The coincidence of Fannie's friendships with Ruth Bryan Owen, La Guardia, and the Roosevelts, and her lifelong helpmates—charisma, timing, and fate's own luck dust—put her in a unique position astride the incoming administrations in New York City and Washington, D.C. Her celebrity had long ago given her powerful voice. Now the combination of that celebrity and powerful friendships gave her a behind-the-scenes political standing of her own. Unlike so many others with such direct access to the center of power, she asked little in return. Vainly and quietly, however—and perhaps this was the key to her enthusiasm for the process—she dreamed of much.

"I want your mighty arm"

R uth Bryan Owen's 1928 campaign for election to Congress on her second try had Fannie in total and vicarious thrall. Ruth's ambition reached beyond a seat in the House of Representatives, to as far as the vice presidency of the United States. And from the outset of her late-life political career, she was wise to the power of a Fannie Hurst in her camp, if not among her constituents. In 1928 Ruth was campaigning from Florida, a southern state that never ratified suffrage "with all that implies politically." She got more explicit in her requests for help from Fannie in the weeks leading up to the primary. "I would be so grateful for any gesture which you find it possible to make," she wrote, "and a resounding word from you would certainly go a long way just now." In the days before the final vote: "I want your mighty arm extended in my behalf."

Fannie cabled her congratulations for Ruth's nomination victory from Paris in the midst of a summer in Europe. Ruth approached the November election campaign with dread, because of her personal complications with the Democratic presidential candidacy of Alfred Smith. "The placing together of the names Bryan and Smith has a very bad effect on party psychology," she explained to Fannie. "It seems to rouse all the old traditional struggles between Father and Tammany and Father and the liquor interests, etc., and plenty of people who would themselves accept Mr. Smith are roused to fury by the thought of Father's daughter espousing his cause." She found that the best thing she could do for Smith's candidacy was keep quiet. She wanted Fannie's help in making sure that her campaign for Congress was seen as something separate and distinct from the presidential contest.

Once she was elected—there were seven other women in the Seventy-first Congress—new complications surfaced. Ruth's Republican opponent, William C. Lawson, challenged her victory on the ground that this descendant of soldiers who fought in the Revolutionary War had not been an American citizen long enough to take a seat in Congress. He argued on the basis of the Constitution's requirement that a representative had to have been a citizen of the United States for seven years. Sections 3 and 4 of the Congressional Expatriation Act of 1907 had revoked Ruth's citizenship when she married her British husband in 1910—this was the same law that had kept Fannie from getting an American passport after her marriage to Jacques. Ruth had gone abroad to live while the law was in force, requiring the actual surrender of her American status. The Cable Act of 1922 restored Ruth's citizenship, but Lawson based his argument on the fact that seven years had not elapsed since. "First the government takes away my citizenship on account of marriage—a discrimination against my sex," Ruth complained to Fannie. "Then they force me to go through naturalization proceedings—an absurd indignity—and then after this, which no man is called upon to undergo, my opponent attempts to assert that I have not been an American citizen long enough to hold office. Ye gods—"

Fannie immediately offered "to lift a loud voice as well as enlist the emphatic denunciation of the important men and women in my community." At the same time she assured Ruth that all the attendant publicity would do her more good than harm. Ruth was grateful for the offer of help and thought that she and Fannie could "stir up some real interesting excitement" if Lawson pursued the matter.

In response to the challenge, Ruth encouraged Fannie to gather a group of her writer friends for Ruth to meet in New York in March to "arm them with the things we want said." In May she got Fannie to frame a question explaining Ruth's case to Representative John L. Cable, who had prepared the act that restored Ruth's U.S. citizenship. In the meantime Cable released a statement on Ruth's behalf, and Ruth saved Fannie's salvo for the floor of Congress, "at which time," she said, "I would like a howl of righteous indignation to rise from the women of the United States, with you as their spokesman." In the end she successfully argued that her citizenship had been restored as if she had never lost it.

Fannie was more than happy to oblige every request Ruth made and, in return, asked a few very small favors of her own: help with naturalization papers for a chauffeur she had hired, confirmation that her own U.S. citizenship was secure, and support from Ruth for a bill that interested her. Ruth, in turn, asked Fannie's help with her own bill to create a centralized federal department of home and child, for which Fannie offered to "cook up some kind of synchronization of your thunderbolt and my clarion note. Have you any suggestion as to just how and when I should release a statement?"

The friendship extended to travel plans. In London in the summer of 1930, Ruth and Fannie sublet the flat of Stephen Coleridge from Stef, who had been renting it for some time. The two women entertained often during their stay, widening each other's acquaintance circles and deepening their bond.

Fannie welcomed Ruth into her closet for the borrowing of elegant clothes and also was free with diet tips. "Which are the 5 per cent vegetables and which the 10 per cent," Ruth asked in one letter. "Peas are out, okay. What about potatoes? Turnips?" Fannie warned her to get a physician before she started reducing since "indiscreet diet undermines health."

With a public servant's sense of entitlement, Ruth felt no shame in bothering Fannie to meet with sundry constituents who were fans of Fannie or harbored visions of a writer's future for themselves, and Fannie repeatedly and graciously obliged her. When the Roman Catholics opposed Ruth's push for a federal department of education, she approached Fannie "for any clarion calls you may emit."

Fannie, meanwhile, found her own political reach lengthening. "I've just been wallowing in your world," she wrote casually in a letter to Ruth on November 9, 1931. "—Visiting the Roosevelts at Albany and Hyde Park."

"*Women in Washington?*"

By way of a short note, Fannie came to the direct attention of Eleanor Roosevelt, first lady of the Empire State, in the spring of 1931. The reason for Fannie's note has not survived, but Mrs. Roosevelt's response was immediate and warm, including an unspecified but explicit invitation for an overnight stay at the Governor's Mansion in Albany or at the family estate in Hyde Park. "I think you can probably give me very many more ideas than I can give you," Mrs. Roosevelt said. "I am delighted to know that we have someone who can render us such valuable assistance on this particular topic."

That September there was lunch with Mrs. Roosevelt at her New York home on East Sixty-fifth Street and then, in November, the long-desired invitation to Fannie and Jacques for a night in the Governor's Mansion, when Roosevelt was expected to be "home for dinner though very busy with the budget." For Fannie the Albany visit was "unforgettable" but more remarkable was what happened next. Roosevelt himself, with Missy LeHand at the wheel of the car, took Fannie farm hunting in his beloved Dutchess County. They stopped for lunch at Hyde Park, where Fannie also got to see Mrs. Roosevelt's furniture-making shops at Val-Kill and wrote her enthusiastically about them. The governor seemed to take a personal interest in Fannie's desire to purchase a farm in the area and pursued the matter for some months after their Sunday outing. "Why not go look again?" he urged her in a note after that delightful afternoon's drive.

Jacques's emergency appendectomy forced cancellation of Fannie's lunch for Mrs. Roosevelt on December 10 as well as her plans to go farm hunting from Hyde Park again with the governor that weekend. The lunch was rescheduled for December 21. Fannie invited John Erskine, Daniel Frohman, Eleanor Robson (Mrs. August) Belmont, Charles Hanson Towne, Millicent Hearst, the wife of the publisher William Randolph Hearst, and Jacques. The octogenarian Frohman couldn't have been more honored by the invitation to such an occasion and only wished he "could have heard all the nice things that were talked about, around the table, by those brilliant people." Fannie's unfailing friendship, warmth, and kindnesses toward Frohman in his increasingly deaf and disheveled, though still active years, were particular testament to her loyalty to loyal friends at high moments and low. It was one of her most admirable qualities.

Six months later, at the Democratic Party Convention in Chicago, Roosevelt became his party's landslide nominee to challenge President Herbert Hoover in the November election. Fannie immediately cabled her congratulations, swiftly followed by a note: "This is just to say that if in the next few months you would like for me to raise my pen in any way you would consider specifically helpful to you, please command me." Both the governor and Mrs. Roosevelt immediately and separately acknowledged the offer, holding it open for future claim.

In the meantime Ruth Bryan Owen lost her bid for reelection to Congress in the primary ballot. Fannie commiserated, telling her friend—and meaning it—that she was "too important, too precious and too needed to be even temporarily shelved. Everyone who knows you and your talent and equipment for the affairs of state must share with me the feeling that this is only a temporary lull in your constant strides forward." Ruth was clearly of the same mind and already planning her next strategic assault. She was campaigning hard for a Roosevelt victory in November. In fact, she was banking on it. To Fannie, she confided, "Roosevelt has intimated that he thinks the time has come to put a woman in the Cabinet and that he thinks highly of my qualification." She told Fannie their task was to get Roosevelt elected and at the same time to create "a regular clamor for RBO as Secretary of the Interior." Ruth felt that a portfolio of education, conservation for forests, care of Indians, national parks, and the general safeguarding of natural resources could be sold as women's work. Already she had begun mobilizing support from the myriad women's organizations to which she belonged "to back us up." She asked Fannie's help enlisting the endorsement of the Hearst newspapers, which already had thrown support to the Roosevelt campaign. She planned to be in New York soon, she said, "to see that doctor who gave you that sylph-like figure. That and a judicious face-lifting are needed to really restore the morale." Instead, she took to the campaign trail, stumping for Roosevelt from town to town.

In early September the Roosevelts made their first request for help from Fannie. "I wonder if you will do a really big thing which we want done now," Mrs. Roosevelt wrote, "and which we feel only someone with your experience and ability can do successfully." This was a probable reference to a radio broadcast Fannie ultimately made on Roosevelt's behalf in the weeks before the election. It elicited lavish gratitude from both the governor and his wife in separate notes of appreciation. Fannie also got wide coverage for her announcement that, because of her commitment to Roosevelt personally, she would vote for a major party candidate for president for the first time in her life. She called the Roosevelts " 'just people'—charming, informal, cultured and without the slightest show of pretense" in an interview with Hearst's *New York American*.

The Roosevelts would continue to value the visible presence of a Fannie Hurst among their vocal supporters, even though it invited scorn from high-minded intellectuals like the poet Marianne Moore, who also had St. Louis roots. In a letter to the critic and philosopher Kenneth Burke, Moore rolled her eyes at Roosevelt's decision to flaunt the support of someone like Fannie, seeing it as indicative of "an inharmony" in the man "which nothing but death will cure." Fannie's hated old theme music was playing again, "Better a classical failure."

Shortly after Roosevelt's election Fannie spoke at the Women's Arts and Industries exposition at the Hotel Commodore, along with Mrs. Roosevelt. Fannie again decried the fact that too many women thought of business as a bridge, a "temporary makeshift" en route to marriage. "The Alice Foote

MacDougalls, Elizabeth Ardens, Mary Woolleys, Jane Addamses, Dr. Sabins and Amelia Earharts are all too few," she said, listing the nation's highest order of female achievers with household names. It was a refrain she would repeat often over the next thirty years but an odd choice of subject matter for a program that had included, earlier in the day, an auction of the precious family heirlooms—even a Russian wolfhound—of a once-successful businesswoman who had fallen victim to the Depression, left idle, unemployed, and desperate for money for the week's food and rent.

Ruth Bryan Owen, meanwhile, also campaigned vigorously for Roosevelt and, more subtly, for her personal cabinet ambitions. On Halloween, by which time a Roosevelt victory seemed secure, she wrote Fannie encouraging her to seize every opportunity after the election to go on record in support of putting a woman in the cabinet "coupled with the name R.B.O." She saw a challenge coming from the nation's second woman governor, Nellie Tayloe Ross, then out of office in Wyoming. Ruth told Fannie it was "going to take something to off-set this."

Within days of the Roosevelt victory, Ruth was at the Hearst estate at San Simeon, California, getting Hearst to back the general concept in all his newspapers and hoping for his personal endorsement. She asked Fannie to organize a symposium on the subject. She also asked Fannie to ease her approach to Elisabeth Marbury, a formidable force in the woman's division of the Democratic Party, and to other powerful party voices who could throw support her way.

On December 6, Fannie arranged a lunch at which Ruth had the chance to display her wares and state her case informally to some of New York's most prominent social figures: Anne Morgan, a daughter of J.P.; Mrs. Oliver Harriman; Helen Rogers Reid, a director with her husband of the *New York Herald Tribune*; and Millicent Hearst. Fannie scheduled lunch the next week with The Marbury, presumably with the same agenda. Two days later Fannie wrote to Ruth to tell her of some "encouraging indications" growing out of the efforts, including petitions Fannie had helped circulate. Fannie had even gotten Colonel House, who had known Ruth since childhood, on board. "Hurrah for our side!" Ruth cheered by mail, apparently unperturbed that Frances Perkins had emerged as another possible female contender for cabinet consideration, and one with the most impressive credentials. Perkins, a longtime social reformer, had most recently served as Roosevelt's commissioner of industry in New York State, with responsibility for the enforcement of workers' compensation, occupational health and safety codes, and an end to child labor. Before that she had been a member of the state's Industrial Board, forerunner of the Labor Department, under then Governor Alfred Smith.

Fannie nonetheless remained hopeful, especially after the author William E. Woodward, quoting an "indisputably accurate" confidential source, said that Roosevelt was not yet committed to Perkins. Woodward endorsed Ruth's plan to have Colonel House submit her name to the president-elect and told Fannie to be very careful that any publicity—and there should be as much as possible—not bear the mark of press angentry. "Presidents-elect are quite sensitive about this," he said, and told the story of someone Woodrow Wilson had selected for his cabinet but dropped because the man's friends were "too organized and too vociferous." The publicity, he said, "ought to be directed but it ought to appear to be spontaneous." He thought newspaper editorials would be important, along with authentic letters from women across the country urging Ruth's appointment, as well as "Old Bryanites," those people who thought her father, the Great Commoner, was right all along.

Woodward very much wanted to see Ruth get the job but, because of his own identification as a Socialist, had to stay in the background. "I'm writing all this to You, Fannie, because you're a doer not a dreamer." He also reminded her that even if Ruth did not get the cabinet job, the momentum from all the attention would put her in line for something else. "Ruthie is, I suspect, faint-hearted over this Cabinet business," he said. "She always brings the conversation around to the chance of getting a second place. . . . If you're faint-hearted, you're licked before you start. You tell her that, will you, when you see her. She may not get what she wants, but there is no harm done in hoping for the best."

On January 17, Fannie cabled Ruth: GOOD PORTENT SEEMS TO BE IN THE AIR. INTERNATIONAL NEWS PHOTO JUST TELEPHONED—WANTED NEW PICTURE OF YOU, NOT "IN CASE OF" BUT BEFORE YOUR APPOINTMENT.

A week earlier Millicent Hearst had arranged a dinner party at which both Fannie and James Farley were present. Farley, the newly named chairman of the Democratic National Committee and head of the state party organization, was receptive to talk of a woman-occupied cabinet post. He advised Fannie to put together all the data she could relating to Ruth's career in public and political life, which he offered to put "under the President-elect's thumb" at the appropriate time.

On February 8, Fannie and Ruth sat together at a tribute dinner at the Waldorf-Astoria in honor of the incoming first lady, at which both were asked to speak. Fannie entitled her remarks "This Shifting World," and Ruth expounded on women and politics. Two days before the dinner Fannie had hosted a luncheon with a very select guest list in Mrs. Roosevelt's honor, to which she had invited Colonel and Mrs. House, Ida Tarbell, Jacques—and Stef. At the time Stef, through his Nordic connections, knew of an opening for a diplomatic posting in Denmark. He told Ruth he could "possibly help a little" if she was interested, but for the moment she was holding out for better.

Mrs. Roosevelt, meanwhile, recruited Fannie to help her put together a committee to foster the establishment of recreational centers—"rest rooms," she called them, for unemployed girls. "You will not be asked for money on the spot," she told Fannie in a December 1932 letter, "but I do want a nucleus to discuss a project which will be really individual work, and I hope very much that you will feel like joining with us." Fannie was far too enamored of the Roosevelts to ignore such a summons. Dutifully, she helped recruit Millicent

Hearst and Helen (Mrs. Vincent) Astor to serve as cochairs for a "May Ball" at the Armory to raise funds for the centers. Mrs. Roosevelt, who was to be the honoree, expressed effusive gratitude. "You have been a very dear friend and have helped me a great deal," she wrote Fannie. Subsequently, however, and in her usual style, Fannie did little for the project beyond lend her name, recruit committee members, and appear at the fund-raiser. To a direct letter of request for funds, she replied, that she was "financially not in the running." Word of her involvement, however, sparked interest from other writer friends. Hollywood's Adela Rogers St. Johns, who had experience with the concept, offered assistance, as did the author Anzia Yezierska, but for more desperate reasons. Yezierska, sadly, had fallen victim to the economic crisis and was desperately seeking an appropriate job for herself. The staffing of the rest rooms was to be by volunteers, so that would not have been an employment opportunity for the author. But Fannie wrote letters to other mutual friends on Yezierska's behalf.

Once Roosevelt named Frances Perkins to the post of secretary of labor, Ruth seemed to defer graciously to the stronger candidate. In any event she felt confident of what lay ahead since the president-elect had twice assured her of a good post. She told Fannie she was hoping for either the presidency of the civil service commission or assistant to Secretary Cordell Hull in the State Department. "Please burn all the candles you have in front of your shrines and icons in the interest of the State Department appointment," she urged. After a subsequent conversation with Ruth, Fannie again wrote to Farley, who himself had been named postmaster general. She appealed to him once again to make Ruth's wishes known: that she would be pleased to serve as undersecretary of state, undersecretary of the interior, or assistant secretary of the interior. Farley replied that he was not sure Ruth would get any of those assignments, "but I know that the Governor has her in mind for a very substantial place in the Cabinet. I am sure she will be satisfied."

Fannie and Jacques made the invitation list to the inaugural festivities, including the absolute thrill of a buffet lunch at the White House on March 4 and a White House tea the next afternoon at five. Ruth got Fannie an extra ticket for the inaugural ball. After the glittering weekend Fannie wrote to Mrs. Roosevelt immediately, again offering "to perform any services in your behalf for which you think I may be especially fitted. This is not just a rhetorical offer. Feel free to command me to jump into any breach you think I may successfully manage." A week later Fannie was at lunch with the first lady in New York, and soon after she found herself marginally involved with the tribute dinner being planned to honor Frances Perkins.

As it turned out Roosevelt named Ruth to what Stef had referred to as "the Denmark job." She was to head the U.S. Legation to Denmark and Iceland, not quite the rank of ambassador but still the highest American diplomatic post a woman had ever held. From a publicity standpoint its import had more appeal than a secondary or tertiary appointment within one of the departments. Ruth asked Fannie to put together a farewell tea before she sailed, but Fannie thought better of it. She immediately took charge of organizing a testimonial farewell dinner for her good friend on the scale of those that already had been given for the first lady and for Perkins. "I do not know the technique of these occasions," Fannie confessed, "but I do know people who can instruct me. . . . Just a private shin-dig with a group of people for tea is not sufficiently in key with the importance of the thing I want to stage."

And so, with fine seat-of-the-pants finesse and little time, Fannie set about organizing a fitting departure tribute to Ruth on May 9 at the Commodore Hotel, arranging newspaper coverage, guests of honor (including Mrs. Roosevelt and Amelia Earhart), speakers (among them Henry Goddard Leach, Governor Herbert Lehman, Secretary of State Hull), a strong Scandinavian presence, complimentary hotel rooms, Eleanor Roosevelt on the dais, and Dr. Leach as dinner chairman. Stef, who was at odds with Fannie at the time, declined the invitation to be a featured speaker at the dinner. Fannie cabled back at once: URGE RECONSIDERATION OF WITHDRAWAL ON BASIS OF DESIRABILITY OF YOUR PRESENCE AT OCCASION OF THIS PARTICULAR NATURE. F HURST. Stef answered by return cable: YOUR TELEGRAM HAS WESTERN UNION'S LABEL SAYING DO AS YOUR HEART TELLS YOU AND ON THAT ADVICE I WITHDRAW MY WITHDRAWAL YOU OUGHT TO WITHDRAW A FEW THINGS TOO. STEF.

Just in time for the dinner, a suspiciously well-timed article on the notion of women in high government office titled "Women in Washington?" appeared in the May *Cosmopolitan,* written by none other than Colonel House. He said it was time for women to get their due in government. Men, after all, had not made such a conspicuous success of it to be allowed to continue in sole responsibility. Women might not do better, he reasoned, but they certainly couldn't do worse. His list of possible contenders started with Eleanor Roosevelt, then moved to Ruth Bryan Owen, whom he said he would not hesitate to trust "with any office from the Presidency down." He then named Frances Perkins, Eleanor Robson Belmont, Esther Everett Lape of the American Peace Award, Jane Addams, Nellie Tayloe Ross, Helen Reid, Olga Samaroff, and nine others, including Fannie.

The *Alumni Bulletin* of Washington University asked House to amplify on his reason for including Fannie in such a list, and he explained: "She is an outstanding figure in the United States and no woman is more widely read or has greater influence. Any university might well be proud to reckon her among its alumni." Fannie could not have been more thrilled with the article—not to mention the attention it got from her errant alma mater—and she told the colonel so. "You are the godmother of my article in the *Cosmopolitan,*" he replied. "I never enjoyed anything more than writing it for my heart was in it."

Through the rest of the spring and summer, Fannie kept in touch with Mrs. Roosevelt, but at a respectful and appropriate remove. The first lady invited her to lunch in New York in May, and Fannie sent occasional notes off to Malvina Thompson, Mrs. Roosevelt's devoted secretary, and copies of her radio addresses and lectures with their promotional references to the New Deal. In

August, *Cosmopolitan* ran a blatant paean to Ruth's diplomatic appointment, "Woman into Diplomat." By Fannie Hurst.

There was a return visit to Hyde Park in September for a luncheon with the president and first lady, and soon after came Mrs. Roosevelt's thoughtful note about a Dutchess County farm that had come on the market for twelve thousand dollars, though she happened to know that the owner would take nine thousand dollars. But the first of Fannie's thrilling and numerous White House overnights came December 5, 1933, and included Jacques. Fannie told the first lady it was a "high-water experience" for them both. In a lifetime of so many high-water marks, it was clear that she meant it. To Rosamond Pinchot the day she returned to New York, she swooned, "I am more than ever convinced of the grandeur of the Roosevelts." The sensation never went away.

That is how the friendship of Fannie and the Roosevelts was forged and sealed. Before long and because of this association, Fannie's political circle would grow to include Molly Dewson, Nancy Cook, Mary Dreier, and Frances Perkins in national Democratic Party circles, as well as a group of earnest professional women of serious purpose who were active in social reform and jurisprudence, such as Henrietta Addition and Charlotte Carr, Lillian D. Wald, and Judges Anna Kross of Women's Court and Jeanette Brill. The most intriguing of Fannie's new friendships grew out of her White House visits. It was with Roosevelt's closest political aide, Louis McHenry Howe, and in these final years of his life, it assumed much the style of a schoolboy crush. The ailing Howe took to slipping amusing, adoring poetry into the mail to Fannie in New York or under her door at the White House when she spent the night. He liked to call her by the pet name Circe.

Chapter *21*

"Symphony of Six Million"

Fannie spent little more than a month on the first story she ever wrote expressly for the screen, and that included the rewrite. Amazingly, the project survived a change of leadership at RKO. After David O. Selznick replaced William LeBaron, Fannie's "Symphony of Seven Million" became *Symphony of Six Million* and Gregory La Cava was named director. Her scenario chronicles the life of a brilliant young Jewish doctor from the ghetto who devotes himself to serving the poor until the material desires of his beloved family sidetrack him.

La Cava's assistant came to New York to meet with Fannie about the script. He alarmed her with talk of adding such artifice as chair-ridden cripples and teachers of the blind, and Fannie wrote to Selznick directly to complain. She warned him off the "cheap poppycock," imploring him not to let the picture fall into such a passé, sentimental mold. As to the casting, Fannie felt strongly that conventional Jewish types in the lead roles would kill the picture. In fact, when Vera Gordon, whom Fannie had handpicked to play the mother in *Humoresque,* asked for her help with getting the mother's role in *Symphony,* Fannie told her quite flatly that the production team had screened *Humoresque* as an example of what to avoid.

Fannie wanted the film to show the travails of any family against an American background instead of a particular type of family against a Jewish background. She thought the story should be Jewish incidentally—"a story of human beings rather than a story of Jewish human beings." In Fannie's conception the doctor, Felix, should be a man "unconsciously possessed with a Christ-like instinct for service—his love story is a love story of humanity—as superb a theme as a picture can carry." She saw him as a fanatic, an idealist, a man devoted to service, around whom flow the love lives of the members of his family and his tender relationship with his mother. She begged Selznick not to "doll him up in a machine-stitched love story."

Selznick assured Fannie that every effort was being made to avoid those pitfalls, especially in the casting of the mother, a role that went to Anna Appel. Yet even with Ricardo Cortez and Irene Dunne in the romantic leads, the comparison to *Humoresque* came immediately. "It has precisely the same pattern,"

Variety pointed out, "with the scalpel replacing the fiddle, the father instead of the mother the champion of the protagonist, but the same trek uptown, the same success and the same breakdown: shellshock in one instance and broken confidence in the other." Fannie's hoped-for universality was lost. *Variety* branded it "an all-Jewish film which could have stood more attention as to racial contrasts for general appeal."

Once in the theaters the film got largely enthusiastic reviews, which, in the opinion of RKO's sales promotion manager, were more generally constructive than any he had seen about a film in a long time. RKO exploited Fannie's connection to the movie at every opportunity and in every mention, a strategy that pleased her greatly. In fact, when Universal released *Back Street* four months later, Fannie tried to strong-arm that studio into doing likewise. "Do you agree with me that in a book as widely known as *Back Street* and with an author whose name has draft with an enormous public, the playing of that name conspicuously in all advertising matter, in lights, in announcements, in all matters pertaining to the picture, is important?" she asked. "Naturally, this aspect of it will help determine my future moves with regard to future manuscripts. I hope Universal will see fit to handle this matter as brilliantly as did RKO."

What infuriated Fannie, however, was RKO's decision to produce a novelization of *Symphony* with her name above the title in type larger than that of the actual writer's name, a move she considered misleading, unethical, and certainly against her best interest. RKO apologized, cajoled, fawned, then quickly took Fannie's name off the book entirely, making the only author of record the pseudonymous John Adams. But much to her distress, when A. L. Burt published the novelization in book form, Fannie's name was back above the title.

"Park Avenue," the scenario Fannie had sold to Columbia, went nowhere. Columbia did produce a film called *East of Fifth Avenue* in this period, but it bore so little semblance to Fannie's original idea that the studio declined to give her the opportunity to rewrite it, even after she inquired. She did not receive a screen credit, nor would she have wanted it. She wrote another scenario, titled "Ladyship," but was unable to ignite studio interest in it, and the property languished in her dead file. In September 1932 Paramount hired her to write a screenplay for America's most popular songstress, Kate Smith. *Hello, Everybody!* was Smith's first and only starring role in a movie, a lucrative embarrassment for Fannie and a disaster for Paramount. It cost more than $2 million—the most expensive musical ever made at the time—and also had the poorest box-office showing during the first week of its release, early in 1933. It provided little more than padding to justify nine songs for Smith. (No one at the time had much to say about the disjointed inclusion of a scene in which Smith sings "Pickaninny Heaven" over the radio to shots of smiling, orphaned black children in dormitory beds. This was nowhere in Fannie's screenplay.) Paramount, like RKO, advertised the film as "Fannie Hurst's *Hello, Everybody!*" which in this instance she may have regretted. *Variety* said she must have pounded out the story in a weak moment "while commerce had a half-nelson on art."

By contrast, the film version of *Back Street* was a clear winner, "a tear-jerker, without being artificially sentimental . . . a human document faithfully translated into celluloid and sound, which rings true from start to finish."

Though Fannie had nothing directly to do with the film's production, it was steadfastly faithful to her story. The director, John Stahl, did leave out the gorge-starve and gambling motifs and therefore altered the ending to suit. In the film Walter's son comes to visit Ray after Walter's private funeral and offers to continue her small monthly support payments. As he leaves Ray thinks back to what might have been if she, as a young woman in love with Walter back in Cincinnati, had been able to meet his mother before he married and gain the older woman's approval as planned. Through her reverie, weak, tired, and suddenly very old, Ray calls out, "I'm coming, Walter," then collapses. Irene Dunne and John Boles starred.

Variety couldn't have been more effusive in its praise, especially noting how "all the variegated highlights and shadows" of Fannie's novel had been fully transmitted to the screen without eclipsing the basic romance.

Fannie herself felt "pride and gratification in Universal's accomplishment" and adored Dunne's portrayal of Ray. The film, Fannie said, was a sincere and faithful interpretation of her novel, which meant a new standard for the industry. "It means," she said, that "the screen and the author are becoming more compatible."

But this new compatibility apparently did not extend to author and fellow author. Well after the film's release Theodore Dreiser became convinced that Universal had stolen parts of his 1911 novel, *Jennie Gerhardt,* for the screen version of *Back Street* without paying or crediting him. Dreiser claimed that the preempting of material from *Jennie Gerhardt* for *Back Street* had brought down the purchase price on his property when Paramount decided to make it into a movie a year after *Back Street's* release. Yet given the time sequence, it is more likely that *Back Street's* success prompted Paramount Studios to buy the more-than-twenty-year-old *Jennie Gerhardt* in the first place and so to capitalize on the public's apparent appetite for fallen women on the screen. Dreiser's work may have commanded ten thousand dollars less than Fannie's, but that was found money, for which he should have thanked her.

Instead, Dreiser got ready to file a lawsuit in January 1935 and had his lawyer advise Fannie's attorney that she too would be named in the action. This was not because Dreiser was accusing her of plagiarism, which he wasn't, but because *Back Street* the film had made use of her copyrighted material and therefore involved her. As it happened, he never brought the case. That did not stop him, however, from firing off an angry letter to Universal's Carl Laemmle, Jr., seven months later, still fuming over the perceived injustice. He responded just as angrily to the "attempt at nonchalance and persiflage" in the reply he got from another Universal executive, who accused Dreiser of "shallow and bitter envy of Miss Hurst."

Though Fannie never commented on the matter, it was shortly after this time that she had a new take on Dreiser. The man she had once flattered as "the white hope of the poor old Great American Novel" became "that hateful hyena."

"Creed, race mean nothing to me"

Without fail, starting in the mid-1920s, Fannie took the progressive position on matters involving discrimination, prejudice, segregation, and equal opportunity for America's black population. Even when the subject was her own Jewish background, she would say, "Creed, race mean nothing to me. We are human beings. This is my creed." She was consistent enough and public enough in support for progress on this front to warrant repeated expressions of appreciation from prominent members of the black community.

Charles S. Johnson of *Opportunity* magazine wrote her on sending her a literary collection in 1928: "You have been such an unfailing friend of the young writers."

Ivy Bailey of *The American Public Opinion,* about to launch a weekly newspaper in Harlem in 1940: "You have inspired and helped thousands of our Negro women."

James Hubert of the National Urban League, imploring her to remain on his board of directors, even if in name only, after she asked to resign for lack of time in 1942: "You, Miss Hurst, are one of those friends and one whom we as Negroes in America have confidence in."

Fannie shared Carl Van Vechten's interest in the subject but not his relish or passion for it. As early as 1926 she got so tired of his Johnny-one-note involvement with Harlem that she asked him if they could have a "taboo-tea. Taboo—just for once! The Negro. I want to know some of the things you think about striped peppermint candy, aziolas [sic], Al Jolson and mugwumps." At the same time, she was always willing to blurb good books by the most talented black writers and often sent them encouraging letters of support. She facilitated access to powerful white agents, editors, and publishers for Zora Neale Hurston and for Dorothy West. She judged competitions and made radio appeals, speeches, and public statements whenever called upon by just about anyone until the 1940s. At that time, when several organizations to which she had blithely lent her name were singled out in the press as Communist fronts, she became more discriminating in her causist choices. Probably because of her trips to Russia, the FBI had been keeping tabs on her for years, but from the perspective of the Communist hunters, her file was not particularly damning.

Her earliest recorded thoughts on race appear in a newspaper article published around 1928. She told the reporter that her contacts with the Negro race up to that point had been "varied" and "something I don't particularly think about one way or the other." She thought both whites and blacks treated the race question too self-consciously. "Negroes nowadays resent being studied by whites and the whites are a bit too patronizing in their manner," she said. By way of example, she told of a ball in Harlem she had recently attended at which blacks and whites mingled freely. "It should have been just a gala occasion, but it wasn't," she said. "One could detect a feeling of aloofness on the part of the whites, a kind of feeling that one race was among another watching it at play." She said she had no particular likes or dislikes about black people as a group but did offer that she knew some "lovable characters" who were black and numbered them among her friends.

The blind spots that appear in Fannie's fiction are mirrored in the wince-worthy attitudes that show up even more distinctly in both her nonfiction and some of her well-meant private efforts. However confusing and offensive they seem now, they cannot be judged accurately by looking backward with knowing hindsight through sixty-five years of turbulent social history into a world that no longer exists. They cannot be explained away, either, nor can they be ignored.

They appear most vividly in the appeal letters she wrote in the late 1920s on behalf of the National Health Circle for Colored People. She wrote or sometimes ghostwrote these letters, guided in both format and specifics by the organization's executive secretary, Belle Davis, a black educator turned fund-raiser who kept the organization going. In 1927 the missive went out under the photograph of an adorable, impoverished, crippled black child. Fannie reports that the child is outside the reach of the nation's social machinery because not only is he poor and crippled but he is black, poor, and crippled and therefore *"needs you so!"* In fairness to Fannie, it was what she was asked to do, and this part of the letter is very much of a piece with the heart-tugging, individualized prose that some relief organizations still favor for their fund-raising campaigns. But Fannie also throws in an utterly gratuitous reference to "the nice little chap with a happy friendly nature which is the heritage of a happy friendly race." And this was for the letter especially geared to black recipients.

The letter aimed at a white audience, with its references to blacks as a "languid-minded" people, was every bit as ill-considered. It is not just reading with enlightened hindsight that gives this impression. As it was sent out at Eastertime in 1927, this letter caught the ire of one recipient, a man named Devere Allen, who took offense at many of Fannie's references, especially her mention of the emergence of previously "unsuspected qualities" in the American Negro, which she intended as a compliment. He also objected to her imputation that poor southern blacks endured unsanitary hygienic conditions, improper housing, and general violations of the laws of health as a result of ignorance and lack of desire. "Unfortunately," Allen rebutted, "it is not only the ignorant but also the comparatively well-educated Negro in this country who is obliged to use his ingenuity in the search for decent living conditions."

Fannie thanked Allen for his frankness but suggested he had let "exaggerated race consciousness" influence his point of view and that his attitude amounted to "my race right or wrong." All the same, she was quick to apologize—"to both you and your race"—if she had been guilty of "well-meaning patronage toward the Negro, an attitude I abhor as much as you do."

Allen had to agree with Fannie that black people were often as guilty of exaggerated race consciousness as other minorities tended to be. But he told her that he personally would have to be exculpated from such a charge. The executive and literary editor of *The World Tomorrow,* a Christian socialist magazine that soon would publish "How It Feels to Be Colored Me" by one Zora Neale Hurston, was white.

Imitation of Life, the novel, drew attention to Fannie's high-heel prints on the road to improved race relations. She became an important white face to call on, and her response almost invariably was to help out whenever she could. In November 1933, when Langston Hughes asked her for a check and a public statement on behalf of the trial of black teenagers accused of rape in Scottsboro, Alabama, Fannie readily replied: "I feel that not only are nine human destinies involved, but the entire nation is on trial along with these young Americans. Hasty and unfair trials for human beings in general, must not be tolerated in America. Hasty and unfair trials for Negroes in particular can only grind a very black mark into the face of America for tolerating any form of injustice against a minority race." "Very black mark" was, perhaps, an unfortunate choice of imagery but certainly the mildest in a series of such blunders Fannie seemed incapable of avoiding.

That same month the John Simon Guggenheim Memorial Foundation asked Fannie for a "full and frank" but confidential assessment of Zora Neale Hurston, who had applied for a fellowship to go to Africa to study the origins of juju, African music, and primitive medical practice. Zora had provided the list of references, which also included Franz Boas, her mentor in anthropology; Ruth Benedict, another Columbia University anthropologist; Carl Van Vechten; and the writer Max Eastman. Although Fannie enthusiastically described her friend as a "talented and peculiarly capable young woman" with "individuality and a most refreshing unself-consciousness of race" and "a well-trained mind," she also said she was "an erratic worker" and an "undisciplined thinker." This Fannie tried to cast backhandedly as an asset, saying it would benefit Zora greatly to have an obligation to a sponsor such as the Guggenheim to fulfill. Fannie clearly also thought she was doing Zora a favor to point out that her friend was "a rather curious example of a sophisticated Negro mind that has retained many characteristics of the old fashion and humble type," that she had not sacrificed her "natural characteristics" by trying to strain for social and intellectual sophistication as had so many of her peers. "For this reason," Fannie concluded, "I think she is rather importantly fitted for research of the nature she describes." Zora told Fannie she loved the letter.

Zora was not awarded a 1934 grant from the Guggenheim Foundation, though it was more likely the pointedly disparaging assessments of Boas and

Benedict of her ability to accomplish the goals set out in her very ambitious proposal that spoiled her chances that round.

In the fall of 1933, Zora sold *Jonah's Gourd Vine,* her first novel, to the publisher J. B. Lippincott, who asked Fannie to write the book's preface, a request she agreed to "with gusto and pleasure." On her own, Fannie spoke to Jonathan Cape, her British publisher, to urge the firm to buy the British rights to Zora's book. Fannie wrote to Lippincott numerous times and met with him, using her formidable clout to urge the publisher to give the book and Zora the attention they both deserved. After Fannie finished the preface, she sent it off to Lippincott with a carbon to Zora in February 1934. It began:

> Here in this work of Zora Hurston there springs, with validity and vitality a fresh note which, to this commentator, is unique.
>
> Here is negro [sic] folk lore interpreted at its authentic best in fiction form of a high order.
>
> A brilliantly facile spade has turned over rich new earth. Worms lift up, the hottish smells of soil rise, negro toes dredge into that soil, smells of racial fecundity are about.
>
> As a matter of fact, not even excepting Langston Hughes, it is doubtful if there is any literary precedent for the particular type of accomplishment that characterizes *Jonah's Gourd Vine.*

Whatever Zora may have had to say to Fannie about the preface is not known. The message would have been delivered in person since only three days after Fannie sent the preface to Zora the two women were on the road together again. What is known is that Lippincott published the preface as written, "brilliantly facile spade" and all.

That same year, as a member of the executive committee of the Writers Campaign Against Lynching, Fannie joined the call for specific federal anti-lynching legislation. She was a featured speaker at the NAACP's twenty-fifth anniversary dinner and became a patron of its exhibit on lynching the next. "It becomes grotesque," she said in a statement for the association's magazine *The Crisis,* "to contemplate our country rising in righteous indignation against the atrocities tolerated by a Hitler, when hundreds of our own wayside trees are jibets from which have dangled the broken necks of men who have been strung up there by the bestiality of unpunishable mobs." Her vocal involvement in these matters continued—and was welcomed—for years to come.

"The last carbon copy of that Jewishness"

In time both Fannie's involvement with black-white relations and the rise of Hitler's regime in Germany would force her into confrontation with her ambivalence about being Jewish, starting with the reticence she had exhibited in St. Louis about exposing her religious identity. Once a New Yorker she never again actively tried to hide her background. Both the press, which invariably mentioned it, and her choice of short-story subject matter saw to that. Even the earliest critiques of her work often identified her flat-out as a "Hebrew" writer or as the able interpreter of the Jewish immigrant class that she turned out to be. All the same, she almost seemed to enjoy taking positions unpopular with the Jewish establishment, such as her opposition to Zionism.

Fannie felt in 1925 that Zionism only "segregates us, raises barriers or creates race prejudice." Three years later she was even firmer in her opposition. She gave an interviewer the impression that she lacked even academic interest in Palestine. "She speaks decisively and forcefully enough to discourage debate. She pleasantly drops the hint with all answers that you can take it or leave it," wrote Maurice Bergman.

Fannie thought there was a "deathless quality" to "Jewish racialism," something that pulled and gnawed at her in a way she could not control by reason. She had grown up in a milieu in which the greatest crime a child could commit was to go against the wishes and concepts of parents. She thought her generation represented, perhaps, "the last carbon copy of that Jewishness" since rituals, ceremonies, and dogma had started to lose their hold. Gradually, she had managed to liberate herself from "this oppression," she said, but not from "the racial affiliation with its invisible taboos, invisible and intellectually unjustified." In the world of her parents, she said, the sequence was first Jew then man. "To us, the last carbon copies," she said, "it is first man then Jew." Assimilation, she felt, was the answer to the Jews' problem, and, as she told the *Jewish Tribune,* it need not mean a loss of what she called a Jew's racial characteristics. "True, he is breaking away from the old traditions, beautiful in themselves. But he still has to be reckoned with as a Jew."

Though she herself could never have considered marrying outside her religion—"a whole line of invisible ancestors were clutching at my freedom"—she would have had no such objections for a child of her own. She expressed the belief that the Jew "stands conspicuously in the front of the thin ranks" representing America's intellectual life but did not believe that the rest of American Jewry was free from criticism. She also agreed that "the type of Jew who deliberately apes the Gentile is a pretty bad sort." But this was only in response to the interviewer's assertion that this was the case.

As Adolf Hitler came to power in Germany in 1933, Fannie was quick in vocal condemnation of his policies in general but not with specific reference to his assault on Germany's Jews. That year she chaired—which is to say she signed the appeal letter for—the American Committee for the Relief of Victimized German Children "without distinction of race or creed." It was the kind of cause that appealed to her, supported by a group of literary activists from many religious backgrounds and aimed at helping German children of all types. Her appeal letter expressed alarm over the torture under Hitler of some sixty thousand Jews and Gentiles to date, as well as the wave of hunger, despair, suicide, and degradation afflicting Germany. It provoked at least one German sympathizer to accuse Fannie of being the unwitting pawn of an anti-German campaign masquerading as a charity.

"I have been in Germany recently," the man reported, "and I have seen no degradation. On the contrary, I have seen a new spirit and a new faith, which was in itself a miracle." It is not German children who have been victimized, he said, "but the American people, including high-minded women like yourself, who fail to detect that they are being exploited for political purposes." The reaction was not an isolated one; pro-German sentiment ran strong in America at the time.

Fannie replied to her critic that she was aware of too many "first-hand evidences" to share his benign attitude. She realized that hysteria could easily distort the truth in stories of physical atrocity, so she was not laying emphasis on those reports. However, she said, "intolerance, as indicated by racial hatred; bigotry, as indicated by such sophomoric follies as the burning of books, and now the final item of shunting women back to the kitchen, convince me that here is a situation that must not be endurable to those of us to whom tolerance, emancipation and justice are matters of paramount importance."

Early in 1934, beleaguered as she was with requests to put her name to "use and abuse" for good causes, she acceded to a school friend's request for public support for a group aiding German refugees. She felt the significance of the cause outweighed the embarrassment of overexposure. Her anti-Hitler statements flashed on the screen in an anti-Nazi propaganda film entitled *Hitler's Reign of Terror* released at about the same time.

Cosmopolitan sent Fannie to Berlin that September to gather material for a piece examining how the composite Herr John Doe was faring under Nazism.

Her article appeared in March 1935 alongside similar efforts by three other correspondents examining how the various John Does of the world coped with Fascism in Italy, Communism in Russia, and the New Deal in the United States.

> There is much to be said for this man Hitler and his regime, and Herr and Frau Doe wish it were easier to separate the grain of the good from the chaff of the evil. It is all so terribly confusing to be the man in the street like John Doe. He has the evidences of his customary good sense. He sees unemployment seeming to dwindle, but without comprehending how.
>
> He feels himself, as never before, an entity, social, industrial, economic. His business is careening to the debit side but his hopes are soaring above it. He is not at all sure he would exchange one hour of it for all the Germany that has gone before.

That is what is bewildering him so. That is what finds him in a borderline state between fear, hate, rebellion, hysteria, allegiance, confidence.

He feels that his last vote of yea for Hitler was due to coercion, and yet he is beset by the maddening consciousness that, without that coercion, his vote would nevertheless have been that same Yea. He is a man torn. A man doubting. A man trusting.

It was an insightful analysis, in which the word *Jew* did not appear once.

Fannie's unwillingness to press the Jewish case was not unique among prominent American German Jews. The *Herald Tribune* columnist Walter Lippmann, for instance, opposed any sort of official American protest on the ground it could undermine liberal opposition in the persecuting country. Others felt American Jews had no right to disrupt the diplomatic strategies of the U.S. government and that, in any event, a low-profile approach was best.

But there was a different slant to Fannie's resistance to supporting Jewish-specific causes growing out of the crisis. She expressed it most clearly when Louise W. Wise, the wife of Rabbi Stephen Wise, approached her in 1935 to ask that she host a meeting of Christian and Jewish women "to take up the question as to how we can meet the Nazi inroads into America, as well as to come to the rescue of those Germans, Christians and Jews alike, who have come to this country fleeing from Nazi persecution." Mrs. Wise headed the women's division of the American Jewish Congress, which was behind the effort.

The ecumenical coating on Mrs. Wise's request did not persuade Fannie. She responded flatly that she thought such a meeting was inadvisable. Even though it called together a group of Germans, Christians, and Jews, Fannie said, the problem was it emanated from a Jewish source.

"I have bitter reason to believe that this in itself is of an antagonizing nature to various important sources," Fannie told her. "I think the psychology of it is dangerous, and as you know, feel strongly that a movement of this sort would be [sic] many times more potential should it have its germination in non-Jewish circles." There is little doubt that although Fannie probably spoke the truth, her reasoning stemmed as much from her abiding discomfort with the organized Jewish community. Like so many others with high-level access and influence, she stood back and waited for germination from some other source.

Chapter *22*

"Sugar House"

"An acute case of the heebie jeebies" accompanied Fannie's delivery of her new manuscript in the spring of 1932. To close friends she spoke of the work as if she had a grudge against it.

She had put a scant and distracted year into the writing, though long after the book was published she would describe that process as fourteen months of pain. "I hated it," she said. "I didn't want to write it. . . . Again and again it defied me. But I always came back to it."

The novel started to form in her mind before and during her road trip to Canada with Zora Neale Hurston in June 1931, but Fannie did not get down to writing until fall. By mid-October it was still developing slowly. Though she told a friend that the effort was so consuming her "time was in no sense [her] own," she allowed the constant disruption of her usual round of private lunches, teas, and dinners as well as public appearances on behalf of everything from disarmament and the wane of puritanism in American literature to the Salvation Army. Her fascination with the Roosevelts took hold during these months, and she lost time in December for hospital duty during Jack's confinement after his emergency appendectomy.

There were unsettling developments in her professional life. Hearst had brought in Richard Berlin as general manager of his magazine empire to quell some internal turmoil. One of Berlin's first acts was to oust Ray Long, a Hearst—and Hurst—favorite but Berlin's only rival for full control of the operation. Hearst didn't stop him. Harry Burton of *McCall's* came aboard as Long's successor, an understandably uncomfortable development for Fannie. True, Burton once had paid her handsomely to write about Russia, but it was also on Burton's watch that *McCall's* had refused to honor its agreement to serialize *Appassionata*. Not one to harbor grudges with potentially deleterious economic effect, Fannie took an open-minded attitude about the editor's arrival at *Cosmopolitan* and waited for a first move from him.

Cosmopolitan Books collapsed, a victim of its impossible economic timing. That sent Fannie right back to Harper & Brothers, where her longtime editor, William Briggs, welcomed her with the offer of a five-thousand-dollar advance for the new book. This was before she was even very far into the writing. She sold her story about the doctor's wife and the architect, "God Made Little Apples," to Burton's stand-in at *Cosmopolitan* before his arrival and managed to resell it later in the year for another thousand dollars for radio presentation on the Standard Oil program. Though Fannie still owed *Cosmopolitan* several short stories under an unfulfilled 1928 agreement, she sent her next new short story to the woman's magazine *Pictorial Review.* For "One in Three Thousand" (she had wanted to title it "Soiled Dove") *Pictorial* paid her the *Cosmopolitan* rate of four thousand dollars. The sale resulted in a fortuitous new business connection, for when it came time to present her new novel for serialization, *Pictorial's* editor, Theodore Von Ziekursch, outbid *Cosmopolitan* with a forty-five-thousand-dollar offer too good to refuse. It was the most Fannie would ever receive for a serial.

Von Ziekursch scheduled the first installment of the novel for December 1932 and settled on "Sugar House" for the title. Harper held off publication of the book version until February 1933 but liked Fannie's other title suggestion better: *Imitation of Life.*

None of this did anything to allay Fannie's doubts about the manuscript. It never occurred to her to stop publication in *Pictorial Review.* These were times in which once-successful businesswomen admitted in newspaper interviews to sleeping in subway cars. It was unthinkable to turn so much money down. But with Harper & Brothers she took the high road and offered to return the advance; at least that's what she told Bob Davis. Not only was the publishing house against the idea but it already had pegged *Imitation of Life* to lead its spring 1933 list. Fannie did not know what to do. She felt the need of wise counsel and asked Davis to read her saga of white Bea Pullman and black Delilah Johnson of Atlantic City, New Jersey, and their two daughters.

The story in brief: Bea, left penniless by the death of her husband, starts peddling maple syrup to support herself, her infant daughter, Jessie, and her wheelchair-bound father, the victim of a paralytic stroke. She hires the "enormously buxom" Delilah, "with a round black moon of a face that shone above an Alps of bosom," as live-in housekeeper, agreeing to take in Delilah's very light-skinned baby girl, Peola, in the package. They form a household with Bea as breadwinner and Delilah at home, but they barely manage until Bea comes up with a plan to commercialize Delilah's fabulous recipe for waffles and her delicious maple-sugar-candy hearts.

With Bea on the business end and Delilah in the kitchen, the women parlay the dream into a coffee shop with its own product line, then several coffee shops, then a chain of coffee shops and the status of millionaires. Delilah, trademark of all the B. Pullman & Co. products, becomes a national icon. She opens each new coffee shop until she can no longer take the physical strain and grooms legions of Delilah look-alikes to run the restaurants. Even after their huge success Delilah, a woman of limited education who is filled with selfless devotion and not an ounce of personal ambition, insists on staying with Bea and taking care of her, by then with a lieutenant maid to do the heavy lifting. In the end the daughters for whom the two women have worked so hard and sacrificed, and because of whom they have come together, cause them both misery.

∽

Davis was getting ready to sail for southern Europe when Fannie tracked him down. In her letter she did not specify where she thought her novel had failed, but she told him she thought the gap between her conception and her execution had been too wide.

The reaction to the manuscript at Harper had gratified her. "Naturally, I want to think they are right," she told Davis, "but as I see it, 'Sugar House' didn't jell. I would rather not have publication than put forth an effort which does not advance me a notch on the hickory stick or at least permit me to hold my own."

Fannie said she was willing to call the book a year's apprenticeship, throw it out, and start over again. She did not see any way to improve it. "I have shot my last bow there," she said. "It must stand or fall as it is." She asked Davis to help her decide what to do.

His reply came in cable form:

NO.

DAVIS

DO YOU MEAN NOT PUBLISH?

FANNIE

NOT PUBLISH.

BOB

He was brutal, but Fannie thanked him for being a good enough friend to be so direct and honest. The work, he said, "in no particular rises to the heights of your abilities or discloses the power present in your previous books. The incontrovertible evidence of true genius that marks 90 per cent of your output with a pen is not in this manuscript. . . . This book flashes with intermittent lights. It is not the beacon that you have kept alive since you lit the lamp on the Peninsula of Manhattan."

He told Fannie she had created no character that a reader could truly love, except Delilah, "and even she crashes to her doom with no reward save placing her dark lips upon the knuckles of her benefactress." (Actually, Delilah, prone on a floor stretcher at the end, reaches for Bea's ankles to kiss.) As for the two daughters, "I can't help but feel that the two brats . . . are terrible symbols," Davis wrote. "Peola, the sterilized, had a good idea and if Jessie's children are stillborn, it will be a damned good thing for posterity."

Davis gave the manuscript to three fellow travelers aboard ship. One pronounced it the autobiography of an unhappy businesswoman. Two male readers found the ending a disappointment, and a fourth reader couldn't get through it. "None of those who were privileged to examine know who wrote the book," Davis told Fannie. "I have kept that a secret, to be revealed when the volume appears and is a whale of a success—to the joy of my heart, and the confusion of my critical powers."

That much he got right. Fannie agreed to let Harper publish *Imitation of Life,* and the book was released February 1, 1933. Within three weeks, with its serial version still running in *Pictorial Review,* the book was in its eighth printing and ninth on the best-seller list for the month. It was a credible showing, even though book sales never came anywhere near those of the year's best-selling works of fiction. Three months later Fannie sold the movie rights to Universal, which again put her property in the hands of the director John Stahl.

Bea and Delilah

*P*ictorial *Review* promoted "Sugar House" as "the romance of the American woman's coming of age during the turbulent twenty years between 1912 and 1932—told in the story of Bea Pullman as a girl, a bride, a mother and finally, as herself." The racial subplot clearly was not a selling point for the series. When the book came out *The New York Times,* by no means complimentary, fixed only on what its anonymous reviewer saw as Fannie's unfortunate resolve to have it "enormously read."

"She never leaves out anything," the reviewer wrote, "not a thread, not a bead, not a ruffle, rat or hairpin. And when the story comes to nothing but a dramatic cipher, her semblance of vigor seems a febrile and rococo to-do." Archer Winston, in *Booklist,* found *Imitation* to have the compel-repel mechanism so common to Fannie's work: the "sloppy, verbless prose" and "sentimental hokum" somehow producing "strange vitality" and "honest reportorial observation."

Fannie's lead character, Bea Pullman, is an amalgam, a pastiche of bits of the lives of the most successful women Fannie knew. There is the scent of Ruth Bryan Owen, who largely supported her four children and incapacitated husband by absenting herself on long lecture tours and later in Congress and diplomatic service. She is part Alice Foote MacDougall, the Depression-era widow–turned–coffee-shop tycoon and millionaire with whom Fannie often shared tea. Elizabeth Arden, another friend, transmutes into Virginia Eden in the story. Both the fictional character and Arden turn small skin-care salons into multinational enterprises. Fannie even borrows an episode from the life of Elisabeth Marbury, in her bold development of Sutton Square.

On first reflection Bea Pullman's story seems to be at odds with Fannie's own oft-stated position on women in the professions. Her complaint in print was always about the tendency of modern women to squander the gains of suffrage and equality by seeing their careers only as bridges to marriage and family rather than as end goals. It is obvious that Fannie personally felt women could succeed in both work and love at the same time. "Gone are the days when Margaret Deland's *Iron Woman* was the prototype of the woman who achieved success in business," Fannie told an interviewer at the time. "Competent women of the modern day affect filmy draperies as well as tailored suits. They play not a single but a dual role. Their downtown manner may be a deft blend of competence and dignity, but at home they can shed that manner like a cloak." Fannie not only espoused this modern attitude; she lived it.

In the novel she chose to deal with a tiny, elite subset of the female population, especially in the 1930s, the woman who has achieved phenomenal success, for whom career is everything, the woman who has unwittingly estranged herself from family and any hope of romance. She sees career not as a bridge to marriage and family but exactly the opposite. Bea is a woman who out of necessity finds herself in a career that she allows to become all-consuming. In the end this blinders-on immersion in business leaves her empty, bored with her work, loveless, and terribly alone. By the time she is ready to embrace life more fully, there is nothing much left to embrace. Fannie's point was not to caution against professional success. How prescient: She was preaching balance.

In the story Bea's daughter, Jessie, is a vapid girl sent to boarding school at age eight, who returns after years away to fall in love with her mother's business manager before Bea has revealed her own feelings for him. In this Fannie redeployed the theme of older woman involved with younger man, which had so recently reappeared in the short story "God Made Little Apples." But in *Imitation of Life,* just as in *Star-Dust* and the short story "Forty-Five," the triangulation involves a relatively young mother and grown daughter both in love with the same man. The reason for Fannie's fascination with this device remains a mystery, but in every case her mothers sacrifice their own shots at happiness.

The racial subplot of *Imitation of Life* got scant attention, but a few reviewers did remark on how it represented the best part of the story. *The Christian Science Monitor* loved the character of Delilah, though its reviewer thought Fannie had "overcolored" her. Mary Ross, writing for the *Herald Tribune's* book section, saw the book as "a triumph of the black woman more than the white." The *Cincinnati Enquirer* called Delilah "one of the most magnificently drawn characters in all the great store of literature depicting Negro life," and Helen Wolff of the *San Francisco Chronicle* said she had never been more stirred than at the moment when Peola cries out to her mother, "Let me pass!" Only Robert H. Wilson, in the Chicago *Herald Examiner,* went so far as to declare *Imitation* a book that would last, "one of the most human documents written on the race problem that is the penalty of slavery in a free country."

⚭

The origins of Fannie's black characters? Certainly not in the person of Delilah but in her verbal imagery, superstitions, and voodoo potions—"light of full moon, shank bone of mule . . . hog teeth, buzzard feathers"—there are at least the fumes of tales Zora Neale Hurston brought back from her folklore-collecting expeditions. Zora repeatedly urged Fannie to visit during her teaching stints and folklore sojourns in the South and the Caribbean, trying to tempt her to travel with word of how ripe the region was for material for fiction. Their occasional teas for two back in New York were ideal private settings for Zora's legendary acts of storytelling.

But the car trip to Canada, at the point when Fannie was thinking out her novel, surely represented something more. On that nine-day excursion through resort and rural New York in 1931, Fannie and Zora repeatedly encountered "the ogre of discrimination" in hotels and dining rooms. Fannie recalled her own refusal of accommodation whenever their chosen hotel assigned Zora to the servants' quarters or pretended there were no more available rooms. But Zora would not allow the protest. "Zora's attitude was swift and adamant," Fannie recalled, quoting her friend saying, " 'If you are going to take that stand, it will be impossible for us to travel together. This is the way it is and I can take care of myself as I have all my life. I will find my own lodging and be around with the car in the morning.' " And that is how they went on.

Neither Delilah nor Peola is anything like Zora, nor, probably, do they accurately represent any figure Zora might ever have described to Fannie. That said, in Fannie's view Zora did exhibit "that recurring and puzzling trait, lack of indignation," which Fannie made intrinsic to Delilah's personality.

Delilah, however, springs more readily from her stereotypical roly-poly plantation mammy predecessors of stage, screen, and popular fiction, not to mention "Aunt Jemima" of the pancake-mix box, already a staple in American pantries. Fannie may have had other stores to draw on, too, such as her impressions of the black housekeepers she had known growing up. "Miss Fannie" was a name by which even the bank clerks she had known since childhood still called her.

Still, it is possible to imagine how the long car trip with Zora played into the development of Fannie's plot for *Imitation*. Fannie had often stated that her story ideas started with snapshots from real life. Her method was to take these static images, then devise for her readers how such a set of characters would react within a set of conditions of her imagination's choosing, often quite unrelated to the circumstances at hand. In this instance Fannie appears to have stepped outside of herself to take the mental photo. The picture she had to contemplate was of two women, one black, one white, happy companions on a long, carefree road trip, barreling through the otherwise segregated world from which they have both sprung. (Did they share the front seat? There is no way to know, although Fannie's later recollection of Zora as having once been her chauffeur makes it seem doubtful.)

The "tragic mulatto" had been a stock figure in fiction for years by the time Fannie created Peola, but it is also possible that she pulled the idea for her from the recesses of adolescent memory. There had been a very light-skinned black student who passed for white at Fannie's own segregated high school back in St. Louis. Fannie claimed not to recall the story when a school friend reminded her of it well after the book came out, but then she virtually never admitted to her real-life sources of inspiration. It turns out this classmate had walked partway home from school with Fannie's group each day. The young woman managed to graduate from Central High undetected and to go on to a teachers' college, also segregated. It was only when she landed a teaching post in an all-white public school that she was found out. Chronologically, this would have happened during the period Fannie was spending several months each year in St. Louis, with access to the local gossip mills.

Peola ultimately rejects and denies her devoted and self-sacrificing mother, crushing Delilah's heart. Peola has had herself sterilized in order to keep the secret of her race from the white man she loves desperately and intends to marry. (He is an engineer who was gassed and lost half a hand during the war.) Peola finally returns to New York after many years away, but only to extract a pledge from Delilah and Bea never to reveal the truth. She argues her case, and they both protest vehemently. Reluctantly, however, they give her their promise. Peola moves to Bolivia with her beloved and never sees her mother or Bea, as far as we know, again. Delilah, heartbroken and ashamed for her child, knowing this can come to no good, dies of cancer with Bea at her side. A tumor had been growing in her stomach for three years, but she never spoke of it—nor did Bea happen to notice that anything was wrong. Bea honors her friend's wishes to the fullest, staging for Delilah the most elaborate funeral imaginable, replete with white horses and carriages, to carry Delilah to glory in the world beyond.

For Bea, Delilah, and their daughters, Fannie creates a black-and-white household with as full and unself-conscious an attitude of racial equality as the self-effacing Delilah and Bea's unexamined but earnest sense of tolerance allow. When the widows join forces, Bea, Delilah, the two babies, and Bea's invalid father all live together on the ground floor of Bea's parents' modest bungalow, in quarters tight enough to hear one another breathe as they sleep. When the upstairs renters vacate and Delilah needs more room to bake her sugar hearts, all five of them move to the upstairs bedrooms without a second thought. The babies share a nursery "in the sublime democracy of childhood." Even after their finances improve and they move to New York, it is to a six-room apartment they all share, the only room with a view of Central Park given to Bea's father, not to Bea. Delilah does take the worst sliver of a bedroom for herself, but any other arrangement would have gone against type. (It is also obvious that Bea's character would never have insisted otherwise.)

Even when Bea is barely earning enough to keep them all in food, she does not hesitate to call the best doctor for Peola; she offers Delilah's child the same security she offers her own. At a time when Fannie was paying her own college-educated secretary forty dollars a month, and a maid's monthly wage was eight to ten dollars, Fannie has Bea pay Delilah a hundred dollars a month—and it is the most she can get Delilah to accept. Delilah also has shares of stock in B. Pullman & Co., which Bea has stored in a bank vault. The reader is never told what percentage of the company the shares represent.

Delilah has no head for business and no real interest in money other than for what it can do to help someone else. The first time the business shows a profit that does not have to be plowed back into the company, Bea presses Delilah repeatedly to tell her what she would like for herself. Delilah says she wants nothing. When pressed again she wants things for Bea, then for Bea's father, then for the girls. Pressed a third time, she expresses her wish for the elaborate funeral. And until that time? Delilah wants to move out of the New York apartment to a home with a garden that they can all share. Repeatedly, Bea offers Delilah whatever she wants, but Delilah always refuses, preferring to stay in the role in which she feels most comfortable, as domestic helpmate to Bea.

In the household, only Delilah ever raises the specter of black subservience. She dwells on the subject, accepting, even glorying in it. She struggles repeatedly to force the rebellious and headstrong Peola into the same mold. She sees the situation as God's will, but she also voices the more practical concern of teaching Peola these deferential ways in the interest of her safety. Delilah doesn't hesitate to tell Bea that both girls are equally guilty after she catches them sticking pins into Bea's father's arms for sport. But she adds that Peola might as well learn already that "what's jes' naughty for a white chile, can be downright agin' de law if a black one does it."

Through the years Peola is growing up, repeatedly and damagingly Delilah humiliates the child in front of her white "family," trying to force her to learn "her place," trying to convince her of the sinfulness of ever trying to pass for white, of not accepting and loving who God put her on earth to be. Delilah carries this to such extremes that when she disciplines both girls for the pin-sticking incident, she makes Peola wait for her punishment—a twist of the ear—until Delilah has twisted Jessie's ear first.

When Bea demands the girls' account for their actions—and clearly places the blame where it belongs, on Jessie—Delilah won't even let Peola express to Bea the apology that springs to her lips before Jessie has come around to admitting her own wrongdoing. "Ain't you got no way of keepin' yourself in your place?" Delilah scolds Peola. It is Delilah's refrain. She knows how miserable the "white horses" raging in the blood of Peola's very light-skinned father made his short life. She wants to spare her child the same fate. Yet Peola's resentment rises with Delilah's every repetition.

Because Bea happened to be the one to take Peola to enroll in the neighborhood public school, Peola has her first chance to allow her ambiguous appearance to reinforce the prevailing assumption that she is white. She separates herself from the school's other black students and keeps up the ruse for two years. That is, until Delilah shows up in the classroom one day with her raincoat and galoshes, exposing her daughter's deceit. Peola goes into a hysterical rage; Delilah is bereft. It is at this point that Delilah makes one of her only personal requests of Bea: that she send Peola away to study as she has Jessie. They find a place for Peola in Washington, being privately tutored in a cultured black household by the daughter of a Howard University professor. Without discussion Bea readily agrees.

It is little wonder that in the end Peola rebels so completely against the injustice she experiences, her loving mother's unquestioning acceptance of it, and her own denigration in her own home at her own mother's hand. It is not that Peola longs to be white per se; it is that she will not accept being denied for no valid reason what life might otherwise offer her. She has trained as a librarian—the fulfilled promise of her experience with the Howard University family—and moves to faraway Seattle. But to get a good job in her field, she is back where she started, seeing that her only choice is to pass for white. Within an unjust and evil system that offers her no fair alternatives, a system supported and perpetuated by the attitudes and actions of her only living parent, the accident of Peola's light coloring has afforded her the possibility of what she sees as a better life. By the chance meeting of two lonesome souls, she falls in love with a white man. She realizes, for both their happiness in an uncomprehending world, she will have to protect him from knowledge of her race. That settles the matter in her mind. She knows she must "pass all the way."

∽

Bea is fair by nature but unmistakably a product, like her creator, of her place and time. Fannie's depiction of Bea in these instances reveals much about the giant blind spots that too often got in the way of her own otherwise well-intentioned efforts on behalf of black causes and friends.

Bea Pullman is by no means a crusader for civil rights in the world at large. From the outset of their unique relationship, Delilah worries about what will happen as the two children get older and Jessie figures out that Peola is black. Bea tells Delilah not to think about it, that they can cross that bridge when they come to it. It is Bea's position that northern whites do not feel the way southern whites do, that the world has changed and people are broader-minded than they used to be. "Yas'm," mocks Delilah, "broad-minded as mah thumbnail." Yet when she makes Delilah the company trademark, Bea has Delilah pose for a photograph in her work clothes, in the style of the "mammy" logo she knows will work best to sell their product. Delilah faintly protests that she wants to be photographed in her Sunday best, but she goes along with Bea's wishes. As the company succeeds, and newspapers want to photograph Bea, she demurs. It is unladylike to have one's picture in the newspaper. Even though it would be excellent publicity for the firm—just like Delilah's mammy portrait—Bea refuses.

When Jessie finally does learn the word *nigger* on the playground and hurls it at Peola, Bea's shock is genuine. She gives comfort to Peola's gush of tears and reprimands Jessie sternly, demanding that her daughter apologize to her friend. Delilah objects. She tells Bea that she thinks it is as "natural as tides" for a white child to call a black child by that name, and that Peola needs to get used to it and learn to be proud of the fact that she is one, or brace herself for misery. Bea, who is always respectful of Delilah's wishes, ignores her this time and keeps after Jessie to apologize for having uttered the horrid slur.

Yet in the instance of a more subtle demonstration of bigotry Bea behaves quite differently. Bea calls the pediatrician whose office is on the ground floor of their New York apartment building to come up and see Peola when she is ill. He treats Peola warmly and compassionately until he learns—actually Bea doesn't hesitate to tell him when he asks—that Peola is Delilah's child and therefore "colored." At that point he abruptly leaves the apartment. Bea neither comments nor makes so much as a grimace of recognition of his unacceptable action. Then again, Fannie's purpose in including the episode may not have had anything to do with Bea's bigotry. It may have been more to reinforce the raincoat-and-galoshes message of how perilous Peola's future posing as a white person would be—that even those closest to her, black or white, could unwittingly expose her to harm.

Repeatedly in Bea's presence, Delilah tries to impart the lesson of place and subservience to Peola. In every instance throughout their growing up, she puts Jessie, "ma white chile," ahead of her own. Bea never comments in these instances either, nor does she suggest the inappropriateness of Delilah's behavior or the damaging effect it might have been—was—having on Peola. It is Bea who has insisted that the world has become broader-minded; yet to Delilah she suggests no broader-minded vision for Peola's training. Delilah certainly puts no stock in trying to change the way things are outside the tight little shelter they have built for themselves, and neither does Bea. But at the same time Delilah is ever-vigilant about preparing her daughter for what she knows she can expect from the world outside.

∽

Bob Davis was right. The novel flashed with only intermittent lights, its characters and plot twists somewhat sloppily worked out. Latter-day critics have repeatedly criticized Fannie's inadequacy in interpreting black culture and character, folkways and sensibilities, not to mention the faulty dialect. Although the book was widely read, it generated little significant literary comment in its own day and no particular controversy.

The fan mail, however, was enormous and overwhelmingly favorable. "I know Peola. I am Peola, for I am a Negro," wrote a woman from Indianapolis. "Sometimes, when I feel as though I cannot stand this agony, this torture, this scorn, I'm utterly glad that Peola did what she did. Sometimes when Fannie Hurst is engraved deeply in my mind, I say to myself while I am washing dishes or getting dinner, 'I wonder how Peola and her white husband got along. I wonder if he ever found out.' " A white New York reader who worked with young black women thought the story had revealed for them through the example of Delilah how "living content to do one's best at the lowliest task can achieve the finest of friendship and loveliest of lives."

"Your vivid pages are worth more than reams of statistics and bundles of tracts in promotion of better feelings between white and black," wrote Edward F. Murphy, a Josephite professor at Xavier University in New Orleans, who described himself as a devotee of higher education for blacks. "Here is the 'touch of nature' that renders north and south, American and Afro-American kin. You have given us a new kind of *Uncle Tom's Cabin,* as epochal in its way as the old, and certain to enhance the trend that H. B. Stowe began."

The priest said he never had seen a black character more beautifully depicted than Delilah, "or the rich possibilities of interracial cooperation so strikingly suggested as in the arm-linking of Delilah and Bea in business." Through Bea's "bereft and pitiable" end, he thought Fannie had shown that blacks had no monopoly on misery, and that Delilah, by contrast, had been "borne in Harlem grandeur to glories in the realm where everything is prospectively so right." He went on: "If anything, the Negro, with a simple triumphant faith, has an edge on earthly happiness; certainly at least, a priceless salve for sorrow without which the rich and privileged are poor indeed."

Knowing that a film of the book was in production, Murphy rejoiced in the advantage this was sure to mean for the black talent of Hollywood by providing a serious and interesting treatment of the race question and the chance for black actors to play roles other than flunkies or clowns. "Black America," he predicted, "will rise up and call you blessed for that!"

Despite the disappointment in *Imitation of Life* Fannie expressed privately to her friends, she told the priest she could not help but feel that the book, "in its small way, has been a certain boon to the Negro problem here in America, and every notch on the hickory stick of tolerance, enlightenment and man's humanity to man is a notch worth striving for."

Chapter *23*

"*Imitation of Life*"

It flashed in bright white lightbulbs on the face of a dark marquee on opening night: FANNIE HURST'S IMITATION OF LIFE, just the way she liked it. And judging by the "stentorian sobbing of the ladies in the Roxy mezzanine" that November night in 1934, the picture was going to be a runaway success. Fannie wrote John Stahl immediately to gush over the way he once again had interpreted her work with "insight, sympathetic understanding and a quality too subtle to analyze." The level of her sincerity is difficult to judge since Fannie by this time had completed her next novel, *Anitra's Dance,* and would have liked Stahl to direct it.

The director did not involve Fannie in the making of *Imitation of Life,* and many of his departures from her original story had to do with the mechanics of translating a work written for the page to film, a fact of life Fannie long ago had learned to accept. In June 1934, while production was under way, Hollywood adopted a new and more stringent censorship code. This, as it happened, had no discernible impact on the making of *Imitation,* yet other considerations with equal ability to convolute did. *Variety* alluded to *Imitation's* potential problem: "Its reception in the South can, of course not be judged or guessed by a northerner," the reviewer cautioned. "Exhib[itor]s below Mason-Dixon will have to make their own decision."

The admonition was a reflection of times in which the managing editor of a Louisiana newspaper thought nothing of warning Adolph Zukor in 1937 either to stop producing films that crossed the color line by showing racial mixing or promoting social equality or to risk jeopardizing the future of his industry in the South. Dolph Frantz of the *Shreveport Journal* wrote to warn that there would always be a bad reaction when "Negroes and white persons act together" on the screen. (Frantz described himself in the same letter as a "genuine friend of the Negroes.") Actually, he was wrong. *Imitation of Life* held the number one or two slot in southern theaters throughout its run.

Still, concern over the film's reception in the South no doubt explains some of the pointed visual appeasements added to the script, none of which appear in Fannie's novel. In the movie Delilah's bedroom is clearly down a flight of stairs in the town house while Bea's is up. At a lavish company party at home,

Delilah and Peola never enter the upstairs ballroom filled with white guests, even though they are both beautifully gowned.

This wasn't quite enough for some viewers. The Knights Templar complained bitterly to Joseph Breen of the Motion Picture Production Code Administration about what appeared to be the order's masonry uniforms on black members of the procession in Delilah's funeral scene. The order charged that using the Knights Templar uniform in that manner offended its members, cheapened the order's image, and confused outsiders. Breen explained that no offense had been intended, and that an actual fraternal order of Negroes from Los Angeles, wearing their own uniforms, had marched in the procession.

Reviews of the film in the white press were mixed, although, as Andre Sennwald in *The New York Times* pointed out, "the most shameless tearjerker of the Fall" seemed destined for commercial success. All the major white commentators seemed disappointed in the film's treatment of the race question, even though they acknowledged it had gone further than any film before it. Richard Watts, Jr., of the *New York Herald Tribune,* thought the film so missed coming to grips with its moving and underlying idea that he wasn't even sure the producers had figured out it was there. There was no exploration of Delilah's willingness to "keep her place" in Bea's presence, for example, or of why she seemed to be so happy in a relationship of friendly servitude. It is a question Fannie answered—Delilah was content to await gratification in the next world—but not very well.

Everyone seems to have had problems with the depiction of Peola but on grounds that were more Stahl's fault than Fannie's. In the book, after Peola denounces and rejects her mother in her quest to pass for white, she leaves for good, never made aware of her mother's death. But in Stahl's version Peola returns for the most heart-wrenchingly memorable scene of the film, wailing in grief and remorse over her mother's casket. Peola sobs uncontrollably as she sits herself in the front seat of the family car for the procession from the church, next to the black chauffeur. Bea, Jessie, and Steve, the mother-daughter love interest, take the mourners' seats in the back. Nowhere in the script does Stahl give Peola a love interest, black or white, and the viewer later learns that after the shock of her mother's death Peola mends her ways and decides to continue her studies at a good black college. Through both this act of submission and the scene in the funeral cortege where she accepts her place without so much as a bitter glance, the viewer knows Peola has come around, has given up the fight, as her mother always wanted. She will perpetuate the status quo.

The reviewer William Boehnel thought the film went timid on the tragic theme of Peola's passing, saying it carried the idea to a certain point but then dropped it in favor of one of its more conventional subplots. The unnamed reviewer in *Literary Digest* thought Delilah "had a way of forcing herself on her daughter." Watts thought the treatment of Peola was just plain cavalier: "The film looks upon her with considerable distaste and scolds her for being unkind to her mother," he wrote. "The story seems to tell us she is cruel and selfish in not being willing to keep her place meekly. It seems the film's indignation in the matter should not have been extended entirely on the unhappy daughter." Sennwald also was struck by the film's apparent suggestion that "the sensitive daughter of a Negro woman is bound to be unhappy if she happens to be unable to pass for white."

Aside from Fannie's fawning letter to Stahl, she had little to say about the film, that is, until controversy over it broke out in the black community early in 1935.

"A Sensation in Harlem"

If the response in uptown Manhattan was any barometer, Stahl's *Imitation of Life* was a major event for black America. "A Sensation in Harlem," declared the *New York Amsterdam News* in a headline over a photograph of the film's exceptional black actors Louise Beavers and Fredi Washington in January 1935. *Imitation* played almost every local movie house that month, and Beavers mesmerized audiences of all backgrounds with her Academy Award–worthy performance. *California Graphic* magazine's editor, H. O. Stechan, reported on the many in the film community who felt Beavers had turned in the best screen performance of 1934. "But of course the Academy could not recognize Miss Beavers," he said. "She is black!" Claudette Colbert, who played Bea, did receive a nomination that year, but for her work in another film. The movie itself received a nomination for Best Picture.

Beavers's role in particular and the film in general provoked waves of pride and fury. Articles and letters to the editors appeared in all the major black newspapers and magazines. There was a Harlem symposium to discuss its pros and cons; opinions everywhere ran hot. The movie had the effect of those dimensional twelve-line boxes schoolgirls like to draw, the ones that the blink of an eye can animate to turn inside out. Perception depended entirely on the blinker.

There were those like E. Washington Rhodes, the young black editor of the black *Philadelphia Tribune,* who thought the film was "the greatest condemnation of American racial prejudice ever screened." Others, like the intellectual Sterling Brown, condemned it as an insulting rehash of the "old stereotype of the contented Mammy, and the tragic mulatto; and the ancient ideas about the mixture of the races."

Black supporters of the film saw in Delilah a fair representation of the "polite sincere attachment" of a white employer to a "veteran Negro servant." While one letter writer considered the film a worthy tribute to black motherhood, another thought Delilah "showed the tendencies of a cheap prostitute," and helped paint "a whole race as degenerate." West Indian and African-

American blacks squabbled over the film's value. A Harlem resident acknowledged, "We have our Delilahs and we have our Peolas, here in New York, as elsewhere in America." Yet others saw these depictions as representing nothing more than a shallow, insulting, unknowing misinterpretation of type by poorly informed whites.

☙

The Crisis, magazine of the NAACP, ran a justified and flattering profile of Beavers by the Los Angeles writer Chauncey Townsend, its release timed to the film's screening in black communities. But the article brought on the ire of one Pauline Flora Byrd of Kalamazoo, Michigan, who decried how intolerable it was that actresses of the caliber of Beavers and Washington should have to appear in a picture "so full of vicious anti-Negro propaganda" and so insidious that it "deadens the discriminatory faculties of those who see it." The theme, she said, was one dear to whites and bitter to blacks, "namely, that they are a sort of god in our eyes, that we find our greatest satisfaction in their company, that we are irresponsible children dependent on their superior intellectual acumen for our well being, that we not only cannot think for ourselves but do not care to do so, that we as a race are clinging to ancient superstitions which are just beneath the surface waiting to crop out." A Baltimore letter writer, Frank T. Wood, Jr., responded that the lady from Michigan was wrong, that the film plainly represented two different stages in the development of the race: "the docile type which has played on the feelings of our Nordic friends and caused them to spend vast sums of money for high schools, colleges and universities which now open wide their doors to us" and the modern type who has "seen the advantages of being able to pass, or to cross the color line." The two hardly represent the whole race, Wood said, "but that does not destroy the fact that they do exist."

Louise Beavers herself thought all the controversy was pointless. "Why not regard the picture as it was intended? As a story—a story about human beings?" she asked in the *New York Amsterdam News.* She said she could imagine a character like Delilah, one untempted by money, content to "go along her way as long as she was assured of a place to sleep, enough to eat and a big funeral at the end." She said she personally would never sell out her race "for a dollar" and revealed that she had forced deletion of certain lines from the original script by refusing to deliver them. "I knew that Negroes would not want to hear them," she said. "I have always tried to protect my people and to show directors that they are just as sensitive and particular about their race as whites are about theirs." Beavers by then was a beloved and established Hollywood figure, the personification, in Donald Bogle's words, of the "ever-enduring, resourceful mammy goddess." In all, before her death in 1962, she appeared in some 125 films.

Mercer Cook, a respected black educator and writer with degrees from Amherst and Brown, saw *Imitation* in Paris. He had not been privy to the debate at home but thought the picture, even with its obvious defects, had been more effective than any other film as propaganda favoring the American black in pursuit of recognition as a human being.

Rhodes reflected in the *Philadelphia Tribune* on the film's extraordinary appeal with black audiences. Blinking twice at the box, he saw in some of *Imitation*'s most offensive scenes a deeper and more positive intent. "The play shows that even the deepest of human emotions, love and devotion, are unable to surmount the American custom of keeping separate the colored and white races," he wrote. In Peola's bitterness, disillusionment, and desire to pass for white he saw the unavoidable outcome of her frustration. She had a wealthy mother who had made a white woman rich, but something as disrelated as her skin color prevented her from having the full value of her mother's labor and sacrifice.

"This angle is in the picture," Rhodes said. "But one must find it. The producer for business reasons did not make it clear that the colored girl's anguish of spirit was not due to any desire to be white and associated with white people because she was ashamed of her race, but rather because she observed from her earliest youth that white folk had most of the opportunity to get ahead."

Likewise, he saw deeper purpose in the scenes that seemed to make such a point of segregating the races, the ones that had other black viewers bristling. When Bea and Delilah frantically drop everything to go after Peola, who they learn is passing for white as a restaurant cashier (another scene not in the novel), Rhodes wrote that Bea got in the backseat and Delilah rode in front with the driver. Rhodes saw this as the director's decision to offer viewers a glaring reminder of how "the color bar operates when two anguished souls with but a single thought must observe the custom of separation or suffer the agony of ostracism." But this is not what happens on-screen. Stahl actually shows Bea and Delilah riding together in the backseat of Bea's limousine when the two women go to find Peola. The driver, in this instance, is white. Rhodes obviously confused this with the later scene at Delilah's funeral.

Here is Rhodes's explanation for Delilah's fixation on a big and lavish funeral: "Perhaps Delilah realized that the only way for her struggling soul to find solace was in death. After all, that might be the reason why colored people have big funerals. In life they are hedged in and segregated. In death they have an opportunity to approach equality and they take it." In this connection, though, Rhodes couldn't help but mention the prohibition against black cremation in Philadelphia, designed to keep black ashes from ever accidentally mixing with white.

Speaking of Peola, Rhodes said, there were those who accept their fates and quietly "recline on the stone floor until the end comes," and there are those who will "bat their heads against the cold, grimy walls and tear out their fingernails seeking a way out." To Peola's credit, he said, "the latter type is the one which makes progress and causes the advancement of civilization."

Rhodes published his praise of the film at about the same time Sterling Brown let loose in *Opportunity,* under the headline "Once a Pancake." The reference is to a scene in the film that doesn't exist in the novel. In the film Delilah's waffles are pancakes and, instead of through a chain of coffee shops, Bea makes her millions packaging Delilah's special mix. When they finally have money, Bea offers Delilah 20 percent of the company—Fannie never mentioned a figure—and explains to Delilah that she can now have a home of her own. Delilah's reaction is to refuse the offer, fearing that Bea is throwing her out, that she no longer wants her service. Bea reassures Delilah she can stay as long as she wants and offers to put the money and shares in the bank for her. Bea's business manager shakes his head and comments, "Once a pancake, always a pancake."

Though Delilah also remains with Bea in Fannie's version, insisting on a tiny wage, Bea reminds her she could be working "for me under any financial terms you name." Early on in the relationship, while they are still struggling and Bea finally has enough to pay Delilah her arrears in wages, Delilah refuses the money until they can better afford it. She explains her position: "We's partners in this shebang, Miss Bea. Never did have no truck with money-suckin.' " She does not forget that Bea has given her food, shelter, work, and a home for her baby when no one else would consider such an arrangement. Delilah's responses to Bea are more akin to those of a wife than to those of a partner or employee.

Sterling Brown was a poet, anthropologist, folklore expert, author, educator, and critic whose driving concern was for the reliable portrayal of the black character. He acknowledged the differences in plot between Fannie's novel and Stahl's film. But he felt the characterization and ideas were about the same and directed his criticism at both. There was no "true folkeloquence" in either depiction of Delilah, he said, snidely listing her "passion for rubbing 'dem white little dead beat feet,' the inebriation of her language, too designedly picturesque, her unintelligible character, now infantile, now mature, now cataloguing folk beliefs of the Southern Negro, and now cracking contemporary witticisms." Some of the words Fannie put in Delilah's mouth appalled him: *"It's de white horses dat's wild, a'swimmin' in de blood of mah chile. . . . I wants to drown dem white horses plungin' in mah baby's blood."*

"Can one reader be forgiven," scoffed Brown, "if during such passages there runs into his mind something unmistakably like a wild horse laugh?"

He did think the film, probably as a result of Louise Beavers's intrinsic dignity, had "less of Octavus Roy Cohn" than Fannie's book, and he acknowledged that the film, at least, managed to carry the subject some distance from the stock Stepin Fetchit characters, cabins, and cotton fields of previous efforts. "All of these things are undoubtedly gladdening to our bourgeois hearts," he said. "But that doesn't make them new."

To Brown, Delilah was straight out of southern fiction, a woman whose creed is resignation to injustice. "When she refuses her 20 per cent (not because it was too little) she is the old slave refusing freedom," he said. When Bea stops Peola as she is finally leaving her mother, Brown says Peola logically should have erupted in a tirade of bitterness, but she is silent. Surely, she should have seen through Bea's "condescension and the gentle exploitation" and responded at the moment.

There were truths about American life in the picture, Brown said—a partnership in which the white member "gives the real power behind the enterprise a paltry 20 per cent," that the white partner would live upstairs and the black partner down, that they would not ride side by side in the same automobile, and that the prodigal daughter would ride up front with the chauffeur in the family car at her mother's funeral. He went on: "And it is true that for Jessie, business success would mean horse-shows, Switzerland, and finishing schools, where she could learn to stretch her eyes and simper, whereas for Peola it would mean a precarious future, remorse-ridden and threatening. All of this is true to the ways of America," Brown said. "But it hardly seems anything to cheer about."

Fannie thought Brown had missed the forest for the trees and told him so in a letter to *Opportunity,* which the editor ran the next month. She made similar statements in private letters to questioning fans. For her the dilemma was how to defend her literary standing with black intellectuals, whose affirmation she coveted, while at the same time taking her full measure of credit for the story's tremendous popular appeal with audiences of both races—not to mention maintaining her good standing with Universal Studios.

To Brown she said she realized the inevitability of any race being merciless about its interpretation by an outsider, and that it was also true that many aspects of the film "fall short or deviate or even malign my original theme." Still, she said, the movie "practically inaugurates into the important medium of the motion-picture, a consideration of the Negro as part of the social pattern of American life." Brown, she said, had concerned himself with the "superficialities of idiom and the shape of the cook's cap" while ignoring the film's larger social value. "The attitude is ungrateful," she charged, "but what is much more important, it is also unintelligent."

Opportunity got Brown to respond on the same page of the magazine. He said he had no general complaints with outsiders interpreting his race and that they often had produced the finest interpretations. "But I do not consider Miss Hurst's book, or the picture, to belong with these." He had no objection to the depiction of highly exceptional characters, but he thought it was clear from Fannie's letter that she intended Delilah and Peola to be considered typical of black life and character, a position he could not accept. Fannie never responded to this point of Brown's, but in that she depicted Bea, the single mother and phenomenally successful businesswoman, as a highly exceptional character, it seems logical that she would have conceived of Delilah and Peola as equally out of the ordinary.

"This picture breaks no new ground," Brown said.

> The beloved mammy is a long familiar darling in the American con-
> sciousness; vaudeville headliners, song-pluggers, after-dinner speak-
> ers (especially Southern), moving pictures and novels have placed
> her there. The tragic mulatto, who adds to the cross borne by the
> long-suffering saintly mammy, is likewise a fixture. She is so woe-
> begone that she is a walking argument against miscegenation; her
> struggling differentiates her unpleasantly from the self-abnegation of
> the mammy; her cheap yearning to be white is a contemptible sur-
> render of integrity. Like her mammy, she contributes to Anglo-Saxon
> self esteem.

Brown felt the only social value the picture conveyed was the negative one suggested in the title of his review: "Once a pancake." He said he would accept
Fannie's pronouncement on his intelligence—"far be it from me to dispute
such a trivial point with a lady"—but as for her charge of ingratitude, "I cannot
imagine what in the world I have to be grateful for, either to Universal Pictures
or to Miss Hurst."

Zora Neale Hurston and Langston Hughes

Curiously absent from the public debate over *Imitation of Life* was
Zora. No surviving letters or documents give any indication of
what she had to say about the magazine serial or the novel when they came out
in 1933, while she was living in Florida, nor after the film was released in
1935. It is certain that Zora had done nothing to antagonize Fannie. In the period between the book's publication and the movie's release, Fannie happily
wrote the letter of reference for Zora's first Guggenheim application and the
preface to *Jonah's Gourd Vine,* then took a second car trip with Zora in Florida
in February 1934. At Zora's urging Fannie had accepted an invitation to speak
at Rollins College during its Founder's Week celebrations and used the opportunity to deliver her first major "Here Comes Mrs. Roosevelt" address. Fannie
asked Zora to meet her at the Breakers Hotel in Palm Beach, where she was
staying with her friend Helen Worden, the *New York World-Telegram* columnist
who later married John Erskine. Fannie had invited Worden to travel along
with her and Zora, "my cafe au lait–learned-and-native-Georgia-cracker-Ph.D.-
author-vagabond-friend-and-crack chauffeur." In anticipation of the release of
Jonah's Gourd Vine, Fannie encouraged Worden's interest in Zora, for which
Zora expressed deep gratitude to Fannie. The women meandered four days en
route to Winter Park with a memorable visit for Fannie in nearby Eatonville,
Zora's hometown. After the trip Zora wrote Fannie her most moving letter of

gratitude, pledging "that which I know you value most. I promise to work, and to turn out the best literature that I can; to keep my perspective wholesome and not to descend to deceit in literature no more than I would in friendship. In other words, not to blind myself nor attempt to create the artificial concerning my people for outside consumption, however much I am tempted."

A year later, when the controversy over the film version of *Imitation* broke out, Zora happened to be back in New York in short-lived pursuit of a Ph.D. at Columbia. She and Fannie were together on several occasions. It is likely that whatever Zora had to say to Fannie about the film at that time—they could not possibly have ignored it—she expressed in person.

After that what is known for certain is that Fannie continued to relate to Zora in the same responsively enthusiastic and helpful way she always had. Fannie made brief remarks at two teas in Zora's honor in 1935, one in February, just as Brown's first article appeared, and another in May, while the controversy was still bubbling in the black press. Six months later Fannie happily wrote another—this time unequivocal—letter of support for Zora's application for a Guggenheim fellowship to study folklore in the Caribbean. On this second try the fellowship came through.

There are two surviving pieces of correspondence, both written well after the controversy had died down, in which Zora expressed opinions about *Imitation*. The first is on a postcard she wrote to Fannie from Port Maria, Jamaica, in July 1936, on the first leg of Zora's Guggenheim research trip. "Do you know they banned the showing of your *Imitation of Life* here?" she wrote. "The shoe pinched too much." The second was written early in 1940 from Durham, North Carolina, a full five years after the film's release and at a time when Zora was inviting Fannie to come to Durham to speak. Zora assured Fannie that *Imitation* had "a grand set of admirers" in that part of the country, and that Sterling Brown, who was also teaching nearby, apparently had not spoken for the majority when he wrote against the film and book. Zora went on to say that Brown had accused her of furnishing Fannie with the material for *Imitation*. "I let it stand without contradiction," Zora wrote, "because I feel he does me honor. In so saying, he pays you an unconscious tribute because he is admitting the truth of the work. What he and his kind resent is just that. It is too accurate to be comfortable."

Latter-day Hurston scholars contend that Zora's comments in this letter cannot possibly be taken at face value; that entries in her slang glossary and the way she drew her own characters in subsequent fiction represent veiled responses to *Imitation* and make clear how little regard Zora would have had for Fannie's feeble attempt at an authentic depiction of black characters. The reasoning goes that because of Zora's deep indebtedness to Fannie, not only would she have refrained from expressing her true feelings about the work but she may have felt obliged to flatter her to her face.

It is also possible that Zora simply disagreed with Sterling Brown. In the case of her 1940 letter—which is as much about Zora's antagonistic relationship with Brown as anything else—there was no real value to Fannie in flattering her about *Imitation* five years after the fact. But Zora did have reason to assure Fannie that she would be well received should she decide to come to Durham to speak.

A similar argument is made about a 1937 note to Fannie from Langston Hughes, well after all the controversy, in which he expressed to her his gratitude, "as a Negro," for her having helped to bring "the first serious treatment of the Negro problem in America" to the screen. A year later Hughes wrote a biting parody of the film entitled "Limitations of Life" for the opening of the second season of the Harlem Suitcase Theater. It was the "sensation of the evening," the *New York Amsterdam News* reported, "fairly replete with keen, incisive satire on the race question" and "literally rocked the house." Hughes had cleverly reversed all the roles, so that a black Claudette Colbert figure got her feet rubbed by a white mammy to hilarious and very pointed effect.

The playlet does not appear to have resulted in any animosity between Fannie and Hughes, and there was no particular reason it should have. Fannie, who had written blurbs for Hughes's books and supported his causes in the past, gladly offered comment for publication when *The Big Sea* came out in 1940. A later missive from Hughes—a seemingly unprecipitated cablegram in 1949 that congratulated Fannie on a radio appearance he enjoyed—is warm and friendly. HOW NICE TO HEAR YOUR VOICE CHARMING AND DELIGHTFUL INTERESTING THIS MONDAY ON MARY MARGARET'S [MCBRIDE'S] PROGRAM is all it says. "How lovely of you!" came Fannie's reply.

Chapter *24*

La Guardia

There is little doubt that Fannie would have endorsed the candidacy of Fiorello La Guardia for just about any office. By the time the Democratic landslide of 1932 brought Franklin Roosevelt to power and swept the Republican La Guardia out of Congress, he and Fannie had known each other for more than twenty years. Even at those evenings at Cyd Bettelheim's house, Fannie had seen in the young reformer "a magnificent unrest, coupled with a desire to be a leader on his own terms." How well she remembered his diatribes in training, lashing out at the intolerable levels of corruption and disgrace in city government. Though the two had very little direct contact during La Guardia's years in Washington, this in no way diminished their sense of connection. La Guardia, for example, thought nothing of asking Fannie for a statement of support during his 1921 congressional campaign, and Fannie made him the subject of a column in the *New York World* when he made his first disastrous run for mayor against the Democratic incumbent, James J. "Jimmy" Walker, in 1929. She made plain she had no plans to vote for La Guardia; she supported the Socialist leader Norman Thomas. But she created an irresistible portrait of a "blazing rebel" moving through New York "like a doctor with a stethoscope," which he pressed against the hearts of passersby to better understand their human, social, industrial, and political pain. A man who cared.

Because of their long friendship, the relationship had a much more familiar and insistent style than Fannie's more recent bond with the Roosevelts. With Fannie, La Guardia lapsed into good-natured teasing without much provocation. THANKS FOR YOUR LETTER FANNIE, he cabled, in asking her to introduce him at a town hall meeting called to protest the election fraud he alleged had cost him his seat in Congress. I WAITED FIFTEEN YEARS FOR A KIND WORD FROM YOU STOP NOW HERE'S A CHANCE TO TELL THE WORLD THAT WE ARE FRIENDS. On another occasion, we can only wonder what bile she had spewed that prompted him to send her a tiny box of Carter's Little Liver Pills accompanied by a handwritten note: "I hope your liver is better."

Twice in the days before his election as mayor on the Fusion ticket in November 1933, Fannie reassured La Guardia of her full support and offered to write a magazine profile of him. "I feel so strongly that you have superb equipment for this high office and I am behind you in spirit, enthusiasm and good will," she wrote, signing herself "your old and devoted friend."

La Guardia had not yet taken his New Year's Day oath of office when Fannie wrote to ask him to give Cyd Bettelheim a city job. "I would not for worlds suggest a name to you on the mere basis of friendship," Fannie said. "I am too eager for the kind of brilliant and outstanding success you are sure to make, to even attempt to impede your road with sentimental appointments." La Guardia clearly had no problem telling Fannie when she was off base. He said that Cyd's heart was too big for her to be able to keep control in office, and that he cared too much about her to cause her such a public form of embarrassment.

On a February morning in 1934, the coldest day on record with the temperature at fourteen degrees below zero, Fannie went down to City Hall. She wrote to Ruth Bryan Owen in Copenhagen about her day watching "the Napoleonic little dynamo" at work. She thought he was "a breath of clean air through the foul atmosphere of what have been previous atmospheres," she said. Excitedly, she added, "Things are stirring in the old town."

There were new stirrings in Washington, too, she told Ruth. She reported on her lunch with Eleanor Roosevelt just a few days earlier. The first lady, Fannie said, was "winning the entire nation and breaking down the silly inhibitions of inhibited women." As for FDR, the public had already canonized him. "Certainly the period in which he lives, as well as his own magnificent potentialities, have made him *great*," she reflected. "But it is a curious and exciting phenomenon, and one is prayerful even as one cheers. He has it now, he must hold it and I firmly believe he will."

Even with Ruth in Copenhagen, she and Fannie remained as tight as the sides of a laced corset. The nervy requests from Ruth kept coming, to which Fannie invariably responded with the fullest of hearts. At the height of the Depression, Ruth wrote Fannie with a bright idea she wanted her to champion. She asked Fannie to get Millicent Hearst and Anne Morgan behind an all-woman drive to raise the money to buy the rented building then housing the U.S. Legation in Copenhagen for the "fantastic bargain" price of thirty-five thousand dollars. Ruth thought this could be a powerful symbol of female backing for the first appointment of a woman to the U.S. diplomatic corps. By the time "pangs of conscience" hit Ruth over the wisdom and timing of her self-serving brainstorm, Fannie already had dutifully carried the embarrassing idea on to her wealthy friends.

As La Guardia settled into office, Fannie dropped him a line whenever what was going on in the city moved her to comment. She loved the decision of Parks Commissioner Robert Moses to establish a popularly priced restaurant on the Sheepfold in Central Park, despite some snobbish opposition in her neighborhood to the riffraff it would attract. (Tavern on the Green, which charged twice the going rate for a cup of coffee, could not exactly be called popularly priced. But when compared with the ten-dollar dinner tab at the casino Moses planned to tear down, it met the criteria.) And she pushed the mayor to overlook the unwarranted Tammany taint on her great friend Henrietta Additon, commissioner of the Crime Prevention Bureau. Fannie assured him Additon was not a Tammany loyalist at all, that she saw things much as he did. She also cautioned that it was not in his interest "to antagonize the many individuals and organizations watching Miss Additon and her bureau with the greatest interest." In a lighter-hearted mood she opposed his decision to ban organ-grinders on the city's streets. "Women in tenement kitchens can stir up tastier stews to the tune of 'O Sole Mio' from the court beneath," she complained. "Pedestrians with faces like vinegar pickles can be made to smile and lady writers in their studies like the merry racket as the melodies spill in the street under their windows. . . . Such homely pleasures do not come under the heading of 'nuisance,' " she said. "They help the city day to shine." Only a form letter came back, explaining the mayor's rationale: radios, phonographs, and frequent public concerts had made organ grinding obsolete; exploiters were renting out the instruments at exorbitant fees, and in any event organ grinding was begging.

By September of that first year in office, La Guardia got around to offering Fannie a chance to perform a public service in his administration. In the year plus since Colonel Edward M. House had named her to his list of top women contenders for high government office, she had become quietly anxious for an opportunity to serve in some fitting capacity. What a letdown the rather formulaic letter that arrived from City Hall must have been, offering her a place on a city committee, working under a state committee, "in the tremendously important undertaking of promoting a greater consumption of fresh milk and cream."

She told the mayor that if it were important to him personally for her to get involved with "Milk Month," she would accept the appointment. Otherwise, she preferred that he save her for better use. "As I've told you," she wrote, "I'm eager to be of help in this tangled civic pattern of ours and I feel that one of these days just the right opportunity will present itself." She couldn't have been more pleased with the offer in 1936 of a spot on the New York City commission for the World's Fair of 1939 and said an eager yes to serving as its secretary. Fannie considered the fair such a noble endeavor that she was determined to take the appointment seriously and engage fully in whatever was asked of her. In fact, it was the only committee assignment she responded to in this way to date, and she actually was disappointed when she realized the commission had no particular duties. In 1937 La Guardia also asked her to serve on a committee to correct "the evils" of the substitute-teacher system in the New York public schools, and again she accepted but had little to do. In 1939 he made her a consultant to the municipal radio station but told her he thought it would be too much to ask her to serve on the board.

"No Food with My Meals" Redux

Fannie delighted in being "full of ribs and hip bones and curious unprecedented phenomena such as angles and plane surfaces" for the first time in her life. The initial year's weight loss had lightened the load on her scale by forty pounds. Standing before the bedroom mirror had become an exercise in glee. She delighted in the reflection of her 145½–pound self, pinning in her waistband or twisting the slightly loosened flesh on her neck to achieve "the Jean Harlow angle or the Hepburn line of jaw." Her weight would eventually go as low as 133 pounds—later even lower, to 128—for the times and her large frame, truly thin. In public the effect was of breathtaking physical transformation.

"What are the plans, aside from starvation, that occupy your mind?" Bob Davis asked her at Christmastide in 1932.

At somewhere in the neighborhood of five feet six in height (measured variously at five feet five and a half inches and five feet seven), tall for the times, Fannie projected a commanding presence, even with what her doctors considered poor posture. The new sleekness added dramatically to her stature, at least in the estimable view of the lady editor Anna Steese Richardson, whose opinion Fannie valued. O. O. McIntyre, the columnist, declared Fannie "a vision . . . not that you were not always easy on the eye." Her longtime acquaintance Irvin Cobb walked behind her for several blocks before he recognized her. When she finally demanded a greeting, Cobb asked if the woman before him were really she. "The same Fannie Hurst," came her reply. "No, no," Cobb said. "The same Hurst I will concede—but definitely not the same fanny." The anecdote was so good that by the time it made Fannie's obituary, it went, "The Hurst may be new, but it's the same old fanny," and the attribution elevated from Cobb to FDR.

La Guardia was equally in thrall to Fannie's new shape and implored her to share her secret. She told him the key was learning to shake the head violently from left to right whenever someone passed the starchy, sugary foods. But she also warned: "Be as conservative however, when it comes to overdoing self-denial, as you are liberal-minded in your policies." In this she declined to take her own advice.

Nevertheless, the visual effect of her efforts was so stunning, and such a source of New York chatter, that *Liberty's* editor got Fannie to write about how she had done it. This reprise got the same catchy title that had worked so well back in 1926, "No Food with My Meals." Fannie even got Harpers to publish a reprint of the extended essay in hardcover.

The essay showed Fannie at her absolute best: wordy, as always, but insightful, self-deprecating, and thoroughly lucid about her own complicity in this ludicrous societal phenomenon. The piece could have waited sixty-five years for publication and no one would have guessed that it was written in

1934. The one exception would have been Fannie's description of the affirmation she received in childhood—she was eleven pounds at birth—for being so heavy. "Guess how much she weighs!" her grandfather would proudly challenge his cronies, even as she approached adolescence. Fannie explained that, while she was growing up, people never dwelt "upon the flesh or lack of it" since weight was not something over which anyone was expected to have control. She also was oblivious at the time to how her family's eating habits contributed to her size. Her mother's idea of breakfast consisted of oatmeal, bacon and eggs, toast or hot biscuits, griddle cakes with apple jelly or molasses—all at the same sitting. This, she said, created a lifelong susceptibility to "the tickling of the nostrils at the smell of frying bacon."

Fannie claimed always to have had a latent unease with her size, but it was only gradually and insidiously that she began to see herself as "an unedifying spectacle." She pinpointed 1922 as the year when "the first whirrings of the dietary chant of the dieting women began to assail my ears." Suddenly, she said, "the biology of my entire sisterhood seemed to have undergone an evolution" as "female silhouettes began to take on the concavity of the letter C." New industries emerged. Restaurants started offering melba toast, spinach, and saccharin. Spas catered to obesity—"real or imagined"—ahead of liver complaints and gallstones. Public opinion started to demand that even the divas of grand opera "be able to look down and see their toes."

"Such diet-derivative phrases as incompatibility, mental cruelty, fanaticism, irritability, cussedness began more and more to creep into the phraseology of the divorce courts," Fannie ventured.

The new crop of young men, "a generation born and reared in the slimming era, by now are trained to like their fair sex . . . slablike, flat-chested, hipless and with skin tones of emacia carefully smeared over with sunburn, real or artificial." Then, she said, "the nerve-racking noun of the age burst explosively upon the scene. Calories!"

She gave this description of the day it struck her. She was out having lunch in a hotel with a young friend who, at five feet, nine inches and what she remembered as 109 pounds, was complaining about a large weight gain. Fannie looked down at the lunch she had ordered—creamed celery soup, grilled chop rolled around a kidney, green salad with oil dressing, a sweet, and coffee. The friend ate steamed spinach and nothing more. "I died that day," Fannie recalled, "of shame."

She began her serious diet having already abandoned her much-touted walks in the park, not to mention the dumbbells, static bicycle in its sweat cabinet, vibratory machine, rowing machine, and electric horse. "Exercise may aid and abet its construction or destruction, baths massage, health waters, and what not be its handmaidens," she concluded (and this was a revelation in its time), "but fundamentally, chemically, irrefutably, it is certain foods which make fat!"

She turned down several other obesity specialists in favor of Dr. Henry

James Spencer, who taught her all about her metabolism from a contraption in his office. He diagnosed no glandular alibis or "pathological peculiarities" as her basic problem, rather a lifetime of too much food in the wrong proportions. He restricted her to twelve hundred calories a day, but once her waistline started contracting she began to eat even less. She developed new forms of self-torture, visualizing creamed soups instead of her soulless, fatless broths; pressing her nose against the plate-glass windows of lunchrooms that served all manner of tempting foods. Then came the perversities: "I began to take on a quite horrible and private pleasure in watching other people eat, or preferably overeat," she confessed. "I importuned, nay commanded, my futilely resisting guests to more of this and that richly devised concoctions; pressed upon them the au gratin potato, the sherry-flavored tart. . . . I schemed for the obesity of my lean friends and the greater obesity of my obese ones."

The momentum of the weight loss had so consumed her that she consistently lied to Dr. Spencer about how little she was eating in order to speed the reducing process. She was giddy with the admiring responses her new shape prompted and furious when there was no reaction. Only later did she realize that in the year she defied her doctor's warning about temperance she had become "a narrow-looking bony individual with a disproportionately large head, wide uninhabited-looking shoulders, old-looking hands and a cold kind of chic."

Her first thorough physical examination after the initial forty pounds records no complaints other than a couple of boils and "flabby musculature." Though she continued to feel robust, she started resorting to laxatives several times a week to relieve chronic constipation and was subject to repeated skin infections, rapid tooth decay, and later recurring problems with her cuticles and fingernails. The health guru Bernarr Macfadden heard about the trouble with Fannie's teeth and wrote to urge her to change her diet radically and come spend a month at his spa or risk losing her vitality, not to mention her creative genius. Fannie assured him she was trying to "supply nutritive sufficiencies that may be causing the trouble" and was widening the scope of her diet. What she added to help her teeth was calorieless bonemeal, which Stef checked through his food researcher friends at Stanford and the Mayo Clinic and confirmed could cause her no harm. None of this did she impart to her *Liberty* readers.

"The miracle of it, cheating my doctor as I did, was that I had not lost my health," she wrote instead. "Perhaps the spectacle on all sides of women almost deliberately throwing the incomparable asset of their health away upon the absurd altar of slimming, for no other reason than the desire to be slim, helped . . . to snatch me from the jaws of a dieting lady novelist's more or less untimely death."

Still, she never evolved enough to give up the fight, or her propensity to go frantic over the smallest gain in weight. She thought it noteworthy enough to include in a letter to her uncle an incident at a 1937 party at which Mayor La Guardia was her dinner partner. Knowing her abstemious reputation, he expressed surprise to see her indulge in a madrilene. Actually, Fannie was under the impression that the delicious consommé consisted of nothing more than frozen tomato juice. In fact, she was eating it for dinner several times a week. La Guardia set her straight: it was full of calves' hooves and other animal fats. Suddenly she understood how she had put on that inexplicable pound and a half. "That's the way I'm built, and that's what I've got to face all my life, I guess" was her lament. "Damn it!"

To the readers of *Liberty,* she acknowledged a new trend away from adoration of women with boyish figures but didn't take it very seriously. "The Mae West atavism seems to be little more than a half-hearted fad," she said, adding that millions of people still seemed to be waiting for the miracle of a slimming serum.

She also warned all dieters of "the dangers of the short-cut food fad; of following any diet regime outside a physician's prescribed one; of succumbing to the perils of the pineapple-and-lamb-chop group of fantasies; of the terrible risks involved in accepting what is almost certain to be the he-says and she-says dietary word of their not always thoughtful dieting sister; of the falseness of current aesthetic values as they fluctuate to the season's fashion; of the absurdity of a woman weighing 109 pounds undernourishing herself on boiled green tissue paper."

Fannie's personal dietary obsessions made her funnier in her own mind than any character she ever put into a novel or short story, which was not to say she had the strength of character to give them up. "Slimming is a battle that is never won. But at least I am on to myself," she said. "I can laugh it off."

But not convincingly. When Harpers presented her with a book-jacket design based on a fat lady for *No Food,* Fannie refused to approve it. And when the *Milwaukee Journal* ran before-and-after photographs of Fannie with its 1937 reprint of the essay, she was furious. Not only did it put the article in a "ridiculous light," she told John Wheeler, whose Bell Syndicate was distributing the essay as a short series, but it was in the grossest possible taste. In fact, she went so far as to demand a stipulation that no newspaper could illustrate the article with before-and-after photographs of her.

In the meantime Fannie's weight had edged back up to the 150-pound range in 1936, but she did not become alarmed enough to call in another specialist until the summer of 1940. At that time Fannie underwent a hysterectomy, the shock of which brought her weight down to 133 pounds. She, of course, was enthusiastic, but Dr. Benjamin Shallett, the new specialist, immediately increased her intake of fats, carbohydrates, and salt and urged her to bring her weight to what he considered the more desirable level of 135 to 140 pounds. "Do not worry about your recuperative processes," he told her. "They will return to normal, but please eat all that which I prescribed and don't worry about any weight increase. In the treatment of obesity, particularly in women, I am mindful not only of the anatomy of the body, but of the anatomy of vanity and I correlate the two, so don't worry."

She stayed under Shallett's care for several expensive months, then decided to go it alone. In November she wrote him: "I am two pounds up. Then two pounds down. The ups seem to have it a little more frequently. But so long as I remain in the safety zone of the gay 130s, all's well. Should 140 rear its ugly head, you will be seeing me."

Shallett responded with news of a visit from Fannie's friend "the voluble" Adele Nathan, an author of children's books. He said she "ran the gamut in nothing flat from Venus through Astarte, Cleopatra, Helen of Troy, and a few other mythical and historical symmetrical cuties, ending with you as *ne plus ultra.* I seined such piscatorial fry as 'flower-like,' 'beauteous,' 'dainty,' 'willowy,' and so on into the *ad infinitum,* glimmering wistfully to the plaint, 'Why don't you make me like Fannie Hurst?' "

"Anitra's Dance"

The process of creating *Anitra's Dance* had Fannie in the same state of high anticipation she felt for *A President Is Born.* By mid-March of 1933 she was confidently predicting a "humdinger" of a book even though she had not progressed beyond the point at which it was still "the novel I mean to write—not the poor thing that may limp inarticulately across paper." Unlike Bea or Delilah, Anitra was a character Fannie really liked, a woman born after the war who knew nothing of prewar standards of life, a creature of "the New Day." Once she got down to the writing, it came into form "not only quickly and easily—but completely—according to my standards."

"One strives to believe that another novel on the already mountainous heap of them is worth any conceivable sacrifice," she reflected in a letter to her good friend from Heterodoxy days, Zona Gale. But something more had happened to her during the writing of *Anitra.* "The madness was upon me," Fannie said, "and I felt that it really mattered, which is in itself compensation." The work went so well that within three months Fannie was two-thirds of the way through it. In the end she could not be sure if it was her best book or her worst, but to an interviewer she said it had been written "with the greatest facility I have ever shown in writing."

Harry Burton at *Cosmopolitan* was so anxious to see the manuscript that he convinced Fannie to show it to him two months before she finished it. Betty Meehan wrote from Hollywood to talk about the buzz it already had stirred. Twentieth Century–Fox asked Betty to pry an advance copy out of Fannie and William LeBaron, who had seen a synopsis and thought it was amazing, different and greater than anything Fannie had done before. Fannie quickly sent off copies of the manuscript to Paramount Studios and to Twentieth Century–Fox, where Ray Long had temporarily ended up, and there was a flurry of back-and-forth but no deal. Fannie pictured Katharine Hepburn in the leading role and wrote to the actress to ask if she would like to see the script. Nothing came of the overture.

Though Burton read the manuscript right away, he held off deciding whether to serialize the novel until he saw the completed version in November. "Well, you've done it," he wrote Fannie then. "*Anitra's Dance* is far and away the best piece of writing you have ever done, and you are going to wake up to find yourself the crowned and feted of the critical boys the morning after it is published." All the same, he said, the cutting necessary to fit it into the magazine's format would prove fatal to its "beautiful writing and subtle characterization," so he decided against publishing it, emphatically reassuring Fannie of her importance to *Cosmopolitan*—"her natural home"—and reminding her soon after of the six short stories she still owed him.

None of this dampened her spirits. With her first invitation for a White House weekend in hand, she made sure the press was clued to report on the grand Gay Nineties party she staged to herald the imminent repeal of Prohibition. She chose the popular Billy the Oysterman's restaurant for the site and a guest list that reflected not only her social command but the many worlds in which she had established a valued presence by the end of 1933. It included the philanthropist Millicent Hearst, wife of the publisher; Walter Damrosch, the orchestra conductor then hosting a music-appreciation program on radio; the longtime public official Grover Whalen; Roy Howard of the *New York World-Telegram*; the columnist O. O. McIntyre; Elizabeth Arden of the beauty products empire; the editor Henry Sells; the critic William Hawkins of the *World-Telegram*; the actress Francine Larrimore; Lawrence Langner, founder of the Theatre Guild; Rosamond Pinchot; Charles Hanson Towne; Daniel Frohman; oh, yes, and Jacques and Stef, of course.

Harper & Brothers thought enough of the new manuscript and the profitable performance of *Imitation* to increase Fannie's book advance to seventy-five hundred dollars. The publisher also agreed to insert bars of music throughout the text, despite the added production cost. An encouraging preliminary order of four thousand books came in from one distributor before publication. That, and Bob Davis's effusive response to this book after the way he had reacted to *Imitation,* surely heightened Fannie's expectancy. Davis said *Anitra* was "perhaps the best presentation of the panorama of domestic activity as it uncoils in American life, thus far offered by a novelist."

It was a heady time for Fannie, attributable in large measure to her burgeoning friendship with the first family. The more she knew of the Roosevelts, the more she liked them all. "The President continues to astound, stun and impress the populace with his incredible performance of continuing to pull bunnies out of high hats," Fannie told Ruth Bryan Owen in a letter to Copenhagen early in the year. "He is without doubt proving himself to be one of the superb executives and statesmen in the history of our country, and on top of it all his personality has entrenched him warmly in the hearts of millions." As to the first lady, Fannie reported, she "has had to contend with superficial inhibitions that exist chiefly by reason of race [gender?] memory in the heads of the women of this country, but I firmly believe that they are at last beginning to realize that she is one of the great events that has happened to them."

Fannie developed the theme more fully in her Founder's Day address at Rollins College during the trip with Helen Worden and Zora Neale Hurston in February 1934. It would be Fannie's first high kick in her personal crusade to interpret Eleanor Roosevelt to the nation's women. To Fannie, Mrs. Roosevelt was a revelation, something "new under the sun," a "First Lady without precedent," and what the American people exposed by their attitudes toward her was either "their tight-mindedness or their right-mindedness." She warned that those who question or would curb the actions born out of her fine intellectual curiosity, those who "fail to comprehend the releases which she spells for the entire sex, wear upon their sleeves the symbol of their own limitations."

Shortly after her return from Rollins, Fannie was back at the White House for another night in the Lincoln Bedroom. The invitation came informally, after the first lady learned that Fannie would also be attending the Women's Press Club dinner, an event that attracted five hundred women, howling with delight to the writer Dorothy Ducas's send-up of Mae West.

Fannie was busy with her own small-scale political agenda, too. On the day of *Anitra's* release Harpers informed reporters of the intimate luncheon Fannie had scheduled in honor of Colonel House and his wife, at which President Roosevelt's mother and daughter were expected along with Charles Hanson Towne, Jacques, and Stef. Quietly, Fannie had approached Colonel House about recommending Stef for an appointment to the government committee named to study the army's operation of the airmail system, and House had followed up with Secretary of War George Dern. As for Sara Delano Roosevelt, she immediately edged Fannie to the top of her list of ripe new charitable solicitation prospects. Over the next two years the president's mother invited Fannie to join the board of the Visiting Nurses' Association, give money to Camp Herbert Parsons for needy children—in this case, Fannie actually sent a seven-dollar check—and join her special table at a fund-raising dinner for the Henry Street Settlement House.

Fannie understood the inevitability of these ancillary obligations, as well as what she was thankful turned out to be the rare requests of close friends for her help in getting onto the president's or first lady's appointment calendar. It was small pay for the access she had gained to such an urgent and vital universe. "I can't so won't begin to tell you how I loved every moment of my visit," she wrote the first lady on returning to New York after the March overnight. "I'd like it a lot if one of these days you would command me to do something that would help or please you."

The affairs of state in the mid-1930s were surely more valued contemplation than the battery of bad reviews in March and April brought on by the publication of *Anitra's Dance*. Fannie's private hope that this book would compensate her for the disappointment she had experienced with *Imitation of Life* was quickly dashed. The crowns and fetes that Harry Burton had predicted instead took the form of tar and feathers. Yet even as the critics slammed her once again, they acknowledged how close she'd managed to come to being really good, even great. In *The New York Times*, Louis Kronenberger praised Fannie grandly for undertaking such "a large-scale and ambitious piece of work, requiring very powerful abilities," something that a writer who was merely clever or competent could not even have begun to attempt. He lauded the inspired way in which she had brought her two main characters—the musical genius Richard Bruno and his genius of a late-life daughter, Anitra—"almost to life." He also was impressed with Fannie's skillful creation of the "mad, topsy-turvy atmosphere" of the Bruno family menage. Fannie, he said, set all this in motion, "violently, imaginatively, galvanically."

But, like so many critics before him when the subject was a work of Fannie Hurst's, he could not resist dipping his broad, stiff brush into the sticky, black ooze:

> All this that is so exciting and saturating, comes in the end to nothing at all. Every foe of art manages to creep inside the gates: melodrama, lushness, sentimentality, solecism, false values. Miss Hurst tries to sustain the pitch to which she has raised herself by every sort of frantic gesture. Anitra loses her strong, unique personality, becomes silly and storybook, has a flapper's idea of grande passion, a muddle-headed idea of a great renunciation, and finally, an operatically managed death. At the very moment of her release into the Great Beyond, her father crashes through with the long-sought theme for his symphony. And at the same moment of maudlin bathos, the story ends.

Put simply, Kronenberger said Fannie lacked taste and restraint, likening her to someone who needed to have her arms tied behind her back to stop her from gesturing so wildly.

The Harpers publicity department moved to blunt the blows with more benign and cheerful references to Fannie dropped to reporters and columnists for newspapers and magazines. Her decision to take driving lessons made the columns, as did her appearance at Leonebel Jacobs's studio party in honor of Margherita Sarfatti, the mistress of Benito Mussolini and an acclaimed Italian writer and critic. Fannie attended most of the scheduled events in Madame Sarfatti's honor and struck up a warm acquaintanceship with her in the process. Two of three pieces of short-short fiction that *Collier's* had gotten her to write appeared in the magazine, though Fannie begged off writing any others because she didn't like the format. A well-timed profile appeared in the May issue of *Psychology* magazine, written by Fannie's good friend Ada Patterson, and *Literary Digest* featured Fannie on a page with five other notables under the heading "They Stand Out from the Crowd." A newspaper photographer caught a shot of her partnered with her fellow writer and friend George Hellman at a crowded open-air dance in Central Park. Fannie, too, would join in the Swing Era passion for social dancing. By 1936 she was among the throngs at cocktail lounges and nightclubs just after teatime several times a week, putting the world's growing troubles behind them to the rhythms of the big band sound. She even took lessons from her greengrocer's handsome young son. She had no shortage of willing dance escorts, often young ones, but never Jacques or Stef.

Chapter *25*

"Beating the drum"

If Fannie was to be of real use to the Roosevelts, she was going to have to come up with the big idea herself. Her growing passion to serve was not going to be satisfied by accepting yet another request from the first lady to put her name on the dinner committee for the campaign for rest rooms for unemployed girls.

A bigger idea was brewing: The positive response to her speech at Rollins College made Fannie think that perhaps she could be of unique use to the administration by waging a one-woman "beat-of-the-drum" crusade to extol the first lady's virtues, to interpret her to the masses. Fannie started with an address over the radio station WABC in May 1934, hoping it would lead to sponsorhip for a national tour. The first lady seemed amenable to the plan, yet Fannie ran into roadblocks. "Although radio and press seem responsive to the idea," she wrote Mrs. Roosevelt, "in every case it would be necessary for me to adhere to a policy of the sponsor, and of course, complete freedom is the fundamental prop of my idea." The first lady thought surely someone would be willing to leave Fannie "a free hand as they do me." Martin Aylesworth at NBC had seemed receptive enough to the idea for Fannie to postpone a planned trip to see Greenland with Ruth Bryan Owen, hoping he would come through or "somehow, someway" she could find a way to make the plan come off. In the meantime both she and the first lady found themselves in good company on a list of the nation's most dangerous radicals in *The Red Network,* a "red scare" booklet by a suburban Chicago housewife named Elizabeth Dilling. Among the other luminaries in its pages were La Guardia, Dreiser, Heywood Broun, Edna St. Vincent Millay, and even Mahatma Gandhi.

"Ridiculous as it is, laughable as it might be under the circumstances," said the *New York Post,* "this nightmarish hodgepodge of jittery Red snooping is no more ridiculous than the propaganda used by European Fascist leaders such as Hitler. From it, in New York City, springs the campaign of police brutality and suppression of civil liberties, the effort to draw a red herring across the problem of unemployment relief."

By late July, Fannie had given up on her promotional plan for the first lady and had to content herself with being photographed sewing a National Recov-

228

ery Administration label into a garment for the *New York Evening Journal*. Two weeks later, on a day's notice, she boarded the SS *Ile de France* for the trip to Berlin that resulted in her "John Doe" piece for *Cosmopolitan*. When she returned, shipside reporters were eager to know her reaction to what she had seen. Things in Germany were simply too complicated for an on-the-spot comment, she told them, but she was willing to venture that America had underestimated the situation. "I will say this," she added. "Beware of singing countries. They sang in Russia before the Revolution. They are singing in Germany now."

Louis McHenry Howe

There was another White House visit for Fannie in May 1934, and a return in October for the small dinner held in honor of Eleanor Roosevelt's fiftieth birthday. Politely, Fannie told the first lady she would gladly return to New York on the last train after the dinner so as "not to indulge in my usual rapacious usurpation of the Lincoln Suite." But Mrs. Roosevelt would have none of it. Fannie saved with her papers the printed program from the evening's performance by an Italian string ensemble. No wonder Daniel Frohman teasingly referred to Fannie that year as "My Dear White House Darling."

The phrase certainly characterized her relationship with Colonel Louis McHenry Howe, the president's close adviser. It began over lunch at the Roosevelts' New York town house one day early in the administration. Fannie found herself seated next to this "strange and exciting little man" with the "atrocious health," a self-described kingmaker whose dedication to the Roosevelts was "nothing short of superb fanaticism." Howe told Fannie it was he who had flung Roosevelt the challenge that led to his run for the presidency and it was also Howe who had pledged to stay beside him until victory. He even moved into the White House with the first family to be at the president's beck and call. Fannie's own White House overnights strengthened their connection, as did Howe's frequent trips to New York for radio broadcasts on behalf of the administration, which often included a stop at Fannie's.

Bent, his face lined with physical suffering, he was a man who looked many years older than his sixty-odd years. In ways beyond the incessant coughing and labored breathing, Fannie found him tortured and frustrated, but with an indomitable sense of humor, fed by the happiness his chosen work brought him. He once told Fannie: "I am a minstrel, singing outside the window of beauty." And on another occasion, "I am a minstrel without even a singing voice."

The friendship between Fannie and Howe seemed to emerge full-blown. His clear enchantment with her no doubt sealed it. This is a poem he slipped under the door of a White House bedroom on one of her early overnights:

"Why the Author Will Never Dare Call on F—— H——," cleaned of spelling mistakes and typos:

> Animals behave their worst
> Beneath the spell of Fanny [*sic*] Hurst
> The dog that smoked—the cat that drank
> And into Drunkard's madness sank—
> If such as proved the dreadful fate
> That smites the *minor* vertebrate—
> Predict the awful end, who can,
> Of that poor, inoffensive man
> Who—passing by the lady's door
> Ventures to step the threshold o'er?

And another time: "Dear Circe—The glacier lies—God knows how thick—But—is it safe to use a pick?"

On one of Howe's New York visits, Fannie found him looking so feeble and ill she begged him to have some cognac. She served it in a tiny ruby glass, one of a beautiful little set she had picked up in Venice. Howe held the glass up to the light, remarking on how much the first lady would love it.

"Oh, please," Fannie remembered saying to him. "Let me give you the set. And you present it to her." An awkward silence followed before he replied, "No, no, please! I never accept gifts. In my position, I make it a rule."

Realizing she had offended him, Fannie made light of the incident but afterward sent him a note: "That I dwell too far outside diplomatic circles to be adept in diplomacy is apparent," she wrote. "But how was this gal to know that a colored glass bauble could possibly accomplish so complex an end. Of course I will not press it upon you, but next time you come, I will ask you to drink a toast to my newer wisdom out of the colored glass." Howe dissected himself mercilessly. "I am a thick-skinned boor," she recalled him saying, "to have injected a political philosophy into this situation. Please give me the set. I am ashamed of myself." Fannie said his misery was abject. "I don't deserve your forgiveness but give it to me—along with the set. Please." In the end, "grateful and chastened," Fannie said, he carried it away. A thank you to "Circe" again came in rhyme: "In your Christmas gift to me/Two old friends transformed I see/Well I know them both, alas/General *Glass*ford—Carter *Glass*."

By 1935 Fannie reported to Ruth Bryan Owen that her contacts with the White House were "for the most part chiefly through Louis Howe, and as always, interesting." But soon after Howe's health took such a serious downward turn that Fannie wrote to his daughter to see if there were anything she could do to help. Mary Howe Baker wrote appreciatively to Fannie and asked her to write her father cheery letters to keep him amused. In late March, Fannie confided to Zora Neale Hurston that Howe, "one of my closest friends, is so near death that it is just a matter of hours." To her aunt and uncle in Cincinnati the same day: "I guess you are reading in the papers the hour-by-hour bulletins concerning Col. Louis McHenry Howe at the White House, who may even at this writing have passed on. The country is certainly in a chaotic and unsettled state. I have no idea from hour to hour how my affairs stand, so I am just sort of sitting in the lap of the gods, and hoping that they stand at all."

Miraculously, Howe survived another year, bursting with plans and projects between painful wheezes. Fannie went to see him at the U.S. Naval Hospital in early February 1936, while she was in town to participate in a platform discussion exploring the question "Should Women Be Allowed to Work?" The beard made Howe look strange to her, and although she found him emaciated, he was alert and full of ideas, "playful, amusing and rather pathetically gallant." He was eager for her to cooperate with the administration in publishing a series of articles for a magazine that would interpret in a simple way such complex matters as taxes, government loans, and the Works Progress Administration, better known as the WPA.

After leaving the hospital Fannie returned to the White House for a "pleasant, chatty" dinner with the president and first lady, two of their sons, and two other guests. Then Fannie and the first lady dashed over to the Shoreham Hotel for the panel discussion. The next morning, both in kimonos, Fannie and Eleanor Roosevelt took breakfast in the first lady's sitting room, joined by the Roosevelts' son Elliott. Fannie then met briefly with the president to talk about Howe's idea before heading out to the Senate Gallery in the White House car. There she ran into New York senator Robert Wagner, who urged her to "do some radio work with him on the subject of housing." Two weeks later they were on the air. She returned to the White House for a lunch with cabinet wives before catching the three o'clock train. It was all "the usual White House thrill," made even more memorable this time by Mrs. Roosevelt's mention of it in her newspaper column, "My Day."

Back in New York, Fannie thought about Howe's idea and the enthusiasm the president had expressed for it. What he had in mind was to appropriate well-known fictional characters and have them present the explanations in an amusing way. Fannie warned him off asking her to borrow someone else's conception of a character. If she was going to do the articles, she said, she would have to "draw the bunnies, such as they are, out of my own high hat." At the same time she floated an idea of her own that appealed to her more: it would involve the White House in a twice-weekly women's coast-to-coast radio program for which she already had been approached to write the material.

"I would like to have a group of three or four women, allegedly a club group, meet twice a week to discuss over the air and interpret in a dramatized, colloquial fashion (interspersed with comedy) matters that pertain closely to the idea and ideals of the Administration," she offered. The idea—for an outstanding woman in one field or another to be a guest of the club at each meeting—was similar to one Ruth Bryan Owen had tried unsuccessfully to sell to the networks a year earlier. Ruth's idea was to host a series of radio broadcasts with ten "first ladies"—women outstanding in their own fields—who would discuss an important issue over the air with Ruth. When she wrote Fannie about it in March 1935, she had not yet figured out who would represent screen, stage, art, or music, but her choices for the other "first ladies" spoke loudly for how well women were doing in the world. Eleanor Roosevelt already had confirmed she would participate; in addition, Ruth wanted Amelia Earhart for aviation, Florence P. Kahn for legislation, Judge Florence Allen for the judiciary, Dr. Mary Harris for prison wardenship, Mary E. Woolley for education, and—what other choice could there be?—Fannie for letters.

Howe did not respond to Fannie's radio idea. He was too focused on what he was now calling his "Bug Town Women's League for Political Education" series, but hoping for a better title. He went into more detail on his concept, wanting his women characters to discuss "many non-partisan facts concerning how the government works and in particular the Good Neighbor idea which the President has encouraged." The Good Neighbor policy was Roosevelt's 1933 attempt to end all artificial trade barriers and commit the country to cooperation with all the American republics, a subject in which Fannie had absolutely no expertise.

"They will not be controversial, merely facts," Howe explained, "but that they will be interesting is assured by the fact that Fannie Hurst has consented to prepare this series." He asked her to prepare a sample column at five hundred to a thousand words. "Be a good child and try it out," he urged. "—an imaginary summary of the meeting, bringing in these characters and making them distinct entities."

Fannie spent two more weeks thinking about Howe's proposal, maybe even trying to fulfill his request. Yet, when it came to the writing, she had too much trouble working with a fictional concept she hadn't thought up herself. Fannie could not even bring herself to produce the prototype for the sake of fulfilling the request, or even just humoring a dying friend. For a writer so often accused of overweening sentiment, her own behavior was equally devoid of it.

"I have been thinking a great deal about your suggestion," she wrote to Howe, "and have come to the rather woebegone conclusion that I am not your author. I don't think I have the kind of humor that can make these articles as amusing as I think they should be. And I also think it is important that someone write them who is close to the factual end of the Administration. From this long range, I would need to be fed my facts, rather than gather them at first hand."

The next communication was a cable, inviting Fannie to Howe's White House funeral, April 21, 1936. From Mary Howe Baker came a note of thanks for Fannie's own telegram of sympathy to the family and the roses she had sent to his wife. "Father often spoke of Circe," Howe's daughter wrote, "and her many kindnesses to him for which we are thankful."

"How the other sex shall live"

This was the Day of the Woman as Fannie saw it, an era "pulsing with change" that she predicted would mean "an amazing liberation of the energies of women" over the coming fifty years. Publicly, what concerned her most in 1934 was how women could hold on to the phenomenal gains they had made thus far. So many forces were working against them at a time so soon after she and her peers had climbed "out of [their] swaddling clothes" and incorporated themselves into what they thought was the permanent economic pattern of American life.

Privately, she was deeply frustrated by the slow sweep of progress. As she wrote to Inez Haynes Irwin in turning down an invitation to address a regional conference of the National Woman's Party in Boston in 1931: "Where are those dreams that actuated us during the years when we were struggling for the power to inject ourselves into the government of our country? Just think of the last decade! It does seem that no decade in the entire history of our country could have given women greater opportunity to inject new idealisms into our national picture. In almost every way it seems to me we have failed, not only in the general workings, but from prohibition on down to the sorry state of our city government in its handling of the woman situation."

Irwin helped broaden her perspective. She reminded Fannie that it was one thing to get the key to the house but quite another to contemplate entertaining in a place that was inundated in dust, rubble, rubbish, and filth. Since women got the vote, Irwin said, the Woman's Party had put its energy into examining how the laws of every state affect women, and she reeled out the horrors: in some states it was still legal for a man to will his children away from his wife, to claim all her earnings, including money resulting from a lawsuit she brought. There were states where a married woman was not allowed to sign a legal document. In South Carolina a man could beat his wife and refuse to support her, have as many mistresses as he pleased, and even bring them into his wife's house and bed without giving her grounds for divorce. Irwin said the Woman's Party believed that the legal injustices had to be addressed first, hence its priority focus on the Equal Rights Amendment.

To the magazine *Independent Woman,* Fannie opined that "beautiful but dumb" was over, that women were giving more attention to "the human envelope," to varying their experiences, and that along with loveliness they "seemed to have enhanced their brains."

Before an elite women's group of fashion industry executives in November 1934, she warned her audience to be wary of those forces in society that were working as deterrents to women's progress. Some had been brought on by the "calamity of 1929," such as the Depression and the policies of Hitler and Mussolini, which had relegated women back to the kitchen, "thus settling this vexatious question of how the other sex shall live." The respected journalist and lecturer Dorothy Thompson, wife of Sinclair Lewis and a social friend of Fannie's, reiterated this concern two years later when both of them were honored by the New York League of Business and Professional Women, along with twenty-two other women of exemplary achievement in dozens of fields. Thompson added that any move to take away the gains of women put men in equal jeopardy. The social order that rises against one group, she said, will rise against another.

But for Fannie, another, every bit as insidious issue was the undoing of the advancement of women by their own actions. She referred to this as "the languid psychology of the hordes of women who still observe the twenty-four hour a day working hours of the industry of gold-digging." Nothing could put Fannie in fuller self-righteous swagger than the specter of a woman who made a profession of getting a man to take care of her.

At the same time Fannie exalted in the fact that the United States, despite more than a hundred laws that discriminate against women on its books, could still produce a group such as the one she was addressing, which "simply has no counterpart, Russia included, in the world today, nor has it ever had." But it was Fannie's opinion that the women of the United States were oblivious to their jeopardy at the hands of those who wanted them "jammed down like jacks-into-the boxes. . . . The time has come for us not to relinquish our clutch on the sides of the boat," she warned. "There are hands ready and eager to hack at our hands, to make them release hold."

Ironically, it was Fannie's friend Ruth Bryan Owen who unwittingly played out this distressing scenario. By February 1935 rumors had started to circulate that Frances Perkins would leave the cabinet to become president of Wellesley College. Fannie immediately reported the potential opening to Ruth, who did not respond to the challenge. That July she also ignored the suggestion of Postmaster General James Farley that she quit her Danish post and take a responsible position in one of the government departments. He wanted her back on home soil to be available as the Democratic Party geared up for new elections.

Yet when Ruth returned to the United States on home leave in October, audiences at every stop on her lecture tour seemed to raise the idea of her running for president. "Of course you and I weigh all this at its correct net weight," she wrote to Fannie from the road, "but it is interesting as an indication that the times [femininely speaking] have changed faster than I had realized. A woman for President was fantastically impossible in public thought a few years ago. Now it is discussed in all seriousness." Fannie, too, felt that the idea of a woman in the White House was still far off, but, as she told an interviewer, she could think of a half dozen women who already had the equipment to run. She did not name them, but Ruth was certainly high on her list. Ruth, by this point, had lost such aspirations. She had her sights set on the Court of St. James's, which, until the lecture tour, she considered well out of reach. The response of her audiences had gotten her thinking that the London ambassadorship was "not as far away as it was even a week ago."

Back in Copenhagen a year later, news reports of the preelection campaign attacks on President Roosevelt had Ruth in fighting spirit, anxious "to plunge into the fray." She again planned her home leave for October, when she could be of the most use to the president in the final weeks before the ballot. "When one thinks of the amount of sterling Goodness which is represented by our White House family, and the amount of courage and intelligence and vision," Ruth wrote, "one cannot help feeling annoyed at the misrepresentative attacks, but it is a joy to realize that the President does not let any of it hurt or annoy him." Fannie spoke of how beleaguered the run of strikes and social disorder in New York had left her, and how passionately she felt the need to "to fix our broken economic and industrial machinery within the framework of democracy." She had accepted a two-year term as president of the Authors' Guild, but her overriding involvement at this time was with her writing.

Fannie's commitment to the Roosevelts had not waned, however. She remarked to Ruth on "the extraordinary strides" the first lady had made in both public confidence and admiration. "Of course she is too definite a personality not to accumulate large numbers of enemies on both sides," Fannie acknowledged, "but they are in the enormous minority, and I think that the end of the first four years in the White House will be remarkable for her achievement as much as for any other."

As for the administration, Fannie said, even when it errs, "one has the feeling that the President is looking up the right street and sooner or later will find his way into it." She was supportive of his approach to labor. "Revolution in America is something I do not wish to see," she said, "and without seeming to be too sanguine, I don't think either of us will live to see it, Allah be praised."

Reporting on the Democratic National Convention in Philadelphia that June, *The New York Times* cited Fannie as "one of the striking figures in the convention throng" and quoted her praise of the first lady at length. "When you get a woman who destroys the pastel and mauve traditions surrounding women in the White House, in the face of the most appalling criticism," Fannie said, "it is the kind of emancipation that is a tremendous advance for women. . . . I'm confident there will be no going back to the pastel tradition." The reporter had trouble concentrating on Fannie's statement, distracted by her "amazing chapeau . . . as radical a sartorial innovation as the introduction last year of Schiaparelli's 'glass' dress." The close-fitting cap of gleaming black ciré with its broad glassine visor "drew astonished glances everywhere she passed."

As it turned out, Ruth precipitated her planned October leave by several months, partly to help with the election campaign but more specifically for personal reasons. In July 1936 she arrived in New York shortly before the considerably younger Danish army captain she had decided to make her third husband. The Roosevelts offered their Hyde Park estate as the wedding venue, and Fannie, thrilled for her friend, donned the glassine hat again to be Ruth's sole attendant. Only Fannie and the chauffeur rode in the car with the betrothed couple en route from a prewedding lunch to the ceremony. "They were hilarious," Fannie wrote to Ruth's daughter, Kitty, who was confined to bed with a difficult pregnancy and unable to attend. "They were two lovers off on a jaunt, they were Romeo and Juliet with a sense of humor. . . . We might have been any gay, carefree party of youngsters eloping from a girls' school instead of the participants in a wedding of international importance, en route to the home of the President of the United States." Newspapers reported that Fannie had gone through the ceremony with one glove off, attributing her action to the extreme heat. The truth was she was concentrating on keeping a grip on the wedding band, with which she had been entrusted. "I had the horrid hallucination that it had rolled away from me to underneath the President's pew."

Not long after Ruth resigned her Danish post under pressure, even though she had wanted to stay on in the job until after Roosevelt's reelection. She wrote Fannie that this was to avoid any accusation that she was campaigning for Roosevelt on the taxpayers' money and also because of new citizenship issues. Her marriage to Rohde—Borge was his actual given name; Mickey came from his Danish nickname, Migge—had given her dual Danish-U.S. citizenship, with the attendant appearance of a conflict of interest. But, more pressingly, the fact that he was eight years younger than she had arched too many State Department and Democratic Party eyebrows. Even Fannie thought Ruth had lost touch with what was happening in the United States and said as much to Molly Dewson. Dewson, in turn, asked Eleanor Roosevelt to have a talk with Ruth before she set out on the campaign trail.

Nevertheless, with her new husband and youngest daughter, Helen Rudd, Ruth barreled through New York State, Michigan, and Ohio, making two to five speeches every day. An accident in Indiana left her laid up for a month with a broken leg—too long to be of any further use to the reelection effort. But almost as problematic was the spectacle and ridicule to which her marriage had subjected her. Once recovered she traveled to London with Mickey and wrote Fannie repeatedly of how deliriously happy the marriage had made her. It seemed to relegate everything else in her life to the background. She and Mickey went on to Copenhagen again to see if the dual status could be eliminated by royal decree. But it turned out to be more complicated a process than Ruth thought, and she began to wonder if it were really worth the trouble. She told Fannie she was having new thoughts about her future, but even before the wedding she had confided to her good friend Bess Furman—if not to Fannie—that she was in love, dog tired, and wanted out of public life.

"With European war clouds hanging low," she told Fannie, "I do not like to think of my dear Mickey remaining in the Army and he is anxious to become an American citizen without delay. His dream of bliss is an apartment in New York high up in the air as possible." Her thoughts had turned to other prospects: writing for Hollywood, perhaps, or finding a part-time job within the administration that would give her more leisure time.

Ruth's change of heart must have been terribly disappointing to Fannie, who had placed such store in her friend's drive and prospects. It probably explains Ruth's delay in confessing her actual plans. Yet Fannie responded to Ruth the way she always did, with a full-hearted and ready willingness to help out in any way she could. She had advice on how Ruth might go about selling a new manuscript and ideas on how to find a reasonably priced apartment in New York. (Fannie volunteered that her own six-room studio at 27 West Sixty-seventh cost her $266 a month, reduced from an original price of $375.) She also promised to snoop around for appropriate job possibilities for Ruth within the administration. As it turned out, Ruth went back to lecturing.

Chapter 26

Diversions

Whatever disappointment the reviews of *Anitra's Dance* may have caused Fannie, she did not waste a moment brooding. Her one-woman shop was back in production immediately with the energy and diversity of a major industrial complex. In the space of a few months she had delivered four of the six short stories she owed *Cosmopolitan* and by the beginning of 1935 had gone on to the ambitious new novel she planned to call *Great Laughter*. In that same time frame she also managed to wedge in a new film scenario titled "Once upon a Time" and to think out the plot for a new serial novel.

Inspired by the birth of quintuplets to the Dionne family of North Bay, Ontario, and the sideshow their lives had become by the time they were toddlers, Fannie collected her thoughts on the subject for an essay for *Cosmopolitan* in April 1936. Since by that time the girls had been removed from their parents' home, Fannie advocated rearing each of them in a separate environment to ensure their distinct identities and some degree of normal development. But this is not what her imagination produced in the way of a fiction. Just as the quintuplets were being born in 1934, Fannie inverted the idea and wrote "Five Fathers," the story of a woman who dies in childbirth, leaving her daughter to be raised by her husband and his four brothers. And two years later she pondered what would happen in the lives of a set of beautiful quadruplets who as young women all fall in love with the same star boarder. She put the emphasis on what was normal about them rather than what was freakish.

In other works of short fiction at the time, Fannie produced three female-angled thrillers. There was the battered wife of "Hattie Turner versus Hattie Turner," who finds her husband slain but can't remember if she is the killer; the nanny of "Nothing Ever Happens," who gets involved in the kidnapping of her young charge out of boredom and bad association; and, a bit later, "Elaine, Daughter of Elaine," about the husband who kills his second wife for physically abusing the child of his first marriage. "Home, James" was the tale of an aging wife whose husband stops her from pursuing an attractive younger man—not out of jealousy but because his love and gallantry extend to wanting to stop his beloved from humiliating herself with advances he knows will be spurned. Though the thrillers and the multiple fathers story appeared in *Cosmopolitan* within a few months of delivery, "Home, James" collected dust in the magazine's inventory for more than a year.

∞

Fannie allowed several diversions from her writing. In June 1934, though still edgy about the way Washington University had treated her since graduation, she returned to St. Louis for the first time since her mother's death and stayed for her twenty-fifth college reunion. That and the realization that her fiftieth birthday was looming had started her thinking that the time was right to begin collecting material for an autobiography. She had not kept a diary since high school—and who knew where that had ended up?—but she resolved to start recording her experiences with 1936. In the meantime, with the help of her secretary, she began soliciting reminiscences from old school friends, neighbors, and her few living relatives.

In January 1935 Fannie pinch-hit for Kathleen Norris at the trial of Bruno Hauptmann, the accused kidnapper and slayer of Charles and Anne Morrow Lindbergh's twenty-month-old son. She made her appearance in the Flemington, New Jersey, courtroom the day Hauptmann's wife testified. Among the many stories *The New York Times* ran about the case the next morning, only Fannie's syndicated piece focused on the transcendence of an otherwise plain and uninteresting woman in her moment of valiant devotion to a husband accused of so heinous an act. It was vintage Fannie Hurst. One fan wrote to declare the column "an inspired, impassioned, rhythmical thing—one of the things read once in a lifetime and always remembered." In a later symposium on what would be known for at least the next sixty years as "the Trial of the Century," Fannie decried the shameful national display it had triggered of "vulgar, sensational, wet-lipped, insensitive and even vicious curiosity concerning the heart-rending tragedy of two of its most deeply revered citizens." At that time Fannie still held out hope for the future political prospects of Ruth Bryan Owen and deftly worked the diplomat's name into her two-hundred-word comment.

There was pleasure travel: Derby Week in Louisville, Kentucky, in early May and a two-month, all-expense-paid junket to Hawaii with Jacques in July and August, courtesy of a promotional campaign for the U.S. territory. Sidney Bowman, a Los Angeles publicist, had arranged an exquisite itinerary and attended to every detail. Within a month of her return, Fannie produced the supposedly optional quid pro quo of the arrangement, a detailed article on her travels for a major publication. As a courtesy she sent the piece off to Bowman so he could have a look. "I hope you are not going to find 'Belle of the Pacific' too analytical to suit your purposes," she wrote. "I have tried to celebrate her matchless charms and also to scrutinize some of her problems."

Bowman was shocked at what he read and cabled her immediately in complete distress. In terms as polite as fury would allow him to muster, he told her she had inaccurately interpreted the territory's racial situation, had improperly analyzed its industrial and agricultural progress, had insulted the princess and industrial leaders, and generally had seemed to ignore Hawaii's accomplishments while magnifying minor, negative incidents. Though he realized it wasn't pertinent to her, he told her that if she published it, it would seriously injure him.

As soon as Fannie received the cable, she wrote to assure Bowman that she had killed the article, even though a major magazine had agreed to publish it. Her decision was based "solely on one clause in your message to me which reads: 'publication present form would seriously injure me.' " Fannie reminded Bowman of the hesitancy she had expressed when he proposed the trip and the "untrammeled freedom" to record her honest impressions that he had promised, should she write about Hawaii at all. She refused to engage him on the particulars of their differing points of view, but she did point out that he operated from the angle of a promoter while she stood as impartial observer. "I personally think that the efforts to suppress honest discussion of the Hawaiian picture will, in the end, be about as futile as trying to close up a bursting dam with a cork," she said. Bowman then reversed himself and urged her to change her mind and publish the piece. But Fannie stood fast. Ultimately, she appears to have submitted something entitled "Hawaii, Crucible of Peace Psychology" to a small specialty journal. But when it came to trying her hand again at the big-circulation splash Bowman originally had hoped for, Fannie found that her muse had moved on. Bowman kept pressing gently, and Fannie finally did cobble something together for *Cosmopolitan*. It ran in the magazine three years after the junket.

In the spring of 1935, Henry Morgenthau, Sr., father of the U.S. Treasury secretary, invited Fannie to speak at a tribute dinner for Albert Einstein held at the Waldorf-Astoria for the benefit of German refugees. It was probably on this occasion that Fannie found herself seated next to the great scientist on the dais. Thrilled as she was to be in his company, she couldn't help but notice his discomfort mount with every new accolade. Suddenly, Einstein leaned toward Fannie to hiss something softly into her ear. "Do you know that I never wear socks?" he offered and poked a naked ankle out from underneath the tablecloth.

Later in the year she experienced her own discomfort with a tribute dinner she was asked to chair, in honor of her dear old friend Rebekah Kohut, Cyd Bettelheim's sister and a paragon of the Jewish community. Clearly Fannie agreed to accept the post because she had no delicate way of declining. But given the insulting lack of enthusiasm she showed for the task, it might have been better if she had. First, as Fannie explained to the honoree herself, she objected to the too-Jewish composition of the preliminary committee, ostensibly because so many of Mrs. Kohut's activities were nonsectarian. Actually, it embarrassed Fannie to have her name on so Jewish a list. Second, Fannie did not want to sign the initial letter asking people to join the committee because it put her in the uncomfortable position of having to beg. And, third, she did not want to be seen as having initiated the idea of honoring Rebekah Kohut when, in fact, the idea had originated with others. Fannie thought they should be the ones to take the lead. By way of planning for the dinner, Fannie had someone else put a request to Mayor La Guardia to speak, even though she had gotten to know him through the Bettelheim sisters. When Frances Perkins declined the invitation to attend and a zealous committee member asked the labor secretary to reconsider, Fannie wrote Perkins a letter of apology for the disrespect her fellow committee member's action had shown.

From someone as well accustomed to the favor-trading ways of politics as Fannie, her behavior could not have been more pointed. Fannie knew what was expected of her. She had instigated and organized her tribute dinner for Ruth Bryan Owen with the fullest possible involvement. She certainly had no desire to insult Rebekah Kohut, but her lifelong discomfort with being Jewish—exacerbated by the chilling developments in Europe—simply overtook her.

As the situation in Germany worsened—Hitler's introduction of the Nuremberg racial laws made a mass Jewish exodus from Germany inevitable—Fannie's old feelings of ambivalence about her religious background persisted. In February 1936 she politely but swiftly declined the vice presidency of the United Palestine Appeal, using her workload as the excuse. But when the organization approached her again six months later, she was more forthright in explaining her reticence to get involved. She realized the value of Palestine as a haven for Jewish refugees, but her long-standing intellectual opposition to the idea of segregation for Jews—which she took to be the larger meaning of Palestine—left her "puzzled, bewildered, frantically anxious to help, and yet because of my doubts, impotent."

A major analysis by *Fortune* magazine of "Jews in America" at this time gave Fannie pause. "Instead of first and foremost being concerned with the place of the Jew in certain important walks of American life," she wrote an acquaintance, "I am instead overwhelmed by his achievements, even as they are negatively presented in the article. Also, I am torn between pride in those achievements and fear because of them."

In March 1936 she declined to support a fast to protest the Polish pogroms, even though she was sympathetic with the idea of taking some action. She said she preferred to "save my voice for even a more vigorous form of protest." This never materialized.

By early 1937, as the situation in Germany became more desperate, Fannie had not budged. Rabbi Stephen Wise approached her for help with some of the initiatives of the American Jewish Congress, but still she begged off. "This is such a strategic moment in the troubled history of our troubled people," she wrote, "that I pause to analyze with what may seem painfully minute detail, the wisdom and safety of every step we take. Until I feel sure of the wisdom and the safety, I continue to mark time."

"Sister Act"

Fannie was a full year into the writing of *Great Laughter* by January 1936 and still had further to go. She knew the book would not have serial possibilities, so she set it aside as the year got under way. "Sister Act," by contrast, was tailor-made for the monthly format that invariably meant a welcome income injection, so Fannie began knocking out a first draft of her tale of grown-up quadruplets. With fifteen thousand words written, she went to see Harry Burton at the Hearst offices to pitch her story.

Burton seemed enthusiastic but stopped short of offering Fannie a contract. Instead, he asked her to show him what she had written thus far. In the office Fannie agreed, but she thought better of it by the time she got home and the insult had time to take. "I don't think it's fair either to you or to me to submit anything less than my best," she told Burton in declining to send over the pages. She was angry. He had pushed her to get the story into talkable shape and then, when she did, treated her as if her twenty flawless years writing for *Cosmopolitan* counted for nothing. She certainly had never given the magazine a reason to exercise such caution and couldn't resist reminding him of the stacks of "unused and unusable manuscripts" that had been lying around the *Cosmo* offices when he took over. Not one of them was hers.

Her letter, however, presented her position less stridently, and Burton didn't hesitate to ask again about seeing the pages a few weeks later. This time Fannie told him she had put "Sister Act" aside when he did not make a definite offer and had turned her attention back to *Great Laughter*. But she assured him that "Sister Act" was next in her production queue. In the summer, when he asked a third time to see the manuscript, she told him she could not risk a rejection from him midway through the work. "It would do something to the mental machinery of me," she said, "and thereby jeopardize the high degree of enthusiasm with which I am moving along in this story."

Perhaps it was the energy required to have two major projects going at once, but Fannie seemed to be allowing less intrusion into her daily schedule than she normally did. Though her commitment to the Roosevelts had not waned, she had only the most modest involvement in the reelection effort. She had written another tribute to the first lady, this time for Molly Dewson's *Democratic Digest,* back in March 1935 and had agreed to write for the book being put together for the June 1936 Democratic Convention. Fannie's assignment was to catalog the administration's efforts in behalf of all arts. For a piece for *Forum* magazine entitled "Where I Should Like to Live," she managed to work in a reference to her day farm hunting with the president, and she considered "quite a startler" another convention piece she wrote which cataloged all the various responses to Roosevelt, pro and con ("He's a mother's boy. He's Messiah. He's hooey. He listens to everybody. He's a dictator" and so on).

But with great embarrassment she had to refuse the one direct request from the president himself in the campaign season. She was his personal choice to write a "colloquial survey" of the administration's achievements to date and have it ready for publication within two months. However, with so many obligations pressing down on her, she had to tell his staff that she did not feel she could spare the time. Roosevelt was understanding about it and wrote her personally to tell her so. He said he would spare her having to deal with the kind of factual and comparative material that required travel and research but was sure there was plenty of human-interest material around that she could handle perfectly. He wanted her to try to place some magazine articles in the lead-up to the election.

∞

Some days Fannie was at her desk from seven in the morning until seven at night. "Stef and a newsreel" was not an uncommon way to spend an evening in this period, though the majority of her evenings were spent at home with Jack. In the celebrity realm there were numerous dinners with Jacques's famous musician friends Mischa Elman and Jascha Heifetz. One surprising entry appears in the agenda-style diary she started keeping in these years: "Had dinner with Jack and Stef. Fritted away an evening without any work. Shocking!!!" It was the only recorded episode of a gathering à trois—the other known encounters of Jack and Stef were in larger groups—but Fannie made it seem to signify nothing in particular.

Fannie shirked her obligations as president of the Authors' Guild, even referring to herself as "the absentee president." And although she despaired at having gotten herself roped into chairing the Women's Round Table Committee of the National Public Housing Conference, she had gotten firm assurance that the group would make no demands on her time.

In early April, *Pictorial Review* offered "such fantastic terms" for a short story that Fannie had to agree, taking four weeks out to write "Candy Butcher." The story used as its starting point the real-life adventures of Gertrude Ederle, the first woman to swim the English Channel, in 1926 and in record-breaking time. The magazine never sent Fannie proofs of the story, and by the time she saw what the editors had done to it, it was set in type. Never had she been more furious over editorial handling, calling it "the cruelest butchery of my material that I have ever encountered." She could not get over what she considered the gratuitous and insulting scalpel that had been taken to her prose and offered up just one example. Her words:

> suddenly outside her tightly locked self, her pain. It lay instead upon the waters. It ran out on them, to the horizon. Her pain was on the wavelets that were hurrying toward Tavvy lighthouse. They rose and with them she rose. The currents ran, and with them, her recumbent, plying body.

The edited version:

Suddenly the pain that had been locked inside her escaped and
lay upon the waters.

Fannie wailed there was "not the slightest justification for paraphrasing my
writing or making substitutions that happen to be more to the liking of the
person who did the job." Perhaps this was open to question, but not to
Fannie's mind. Fannie liked her work the way it came off her secretary's typewriter in final draft, and that is the only way she wanted to see it on a printed
page. Her inflexibility, even at this late date, was indicative of how deadly serious she was about both her art and her literary placement, critics notwithstanding.

It was just as well that Fannie never saw the diary entry of her fellow writer
Dawn Powell that February. It would have sent an icepick through her soul. At
a party at the home of Will and Inez Haynes Irwin, Powell was surprised by
how the aging crowd of writers present continued to view themselves as the
"backbone of American *belles lettres*," discussing the respective talent—or lack
of it—of their friends and peers. Fannie was mentioned, as were Charles and
Kathleen Norris and Edna Ferber, "as if these names still had meaning in a literary sense," Powell sneered, adding that it was her assumption that most people had written off those names as "either dead or hacks." "Certainly," Powell
ventured, "they never represented anything but normal, average intelligence
and some hard work."

Chapter *27*

Rosalie Stewart

For copyright protection Fannie had taken the precaution of having Harper & Brothers privately publish her scenario "Once upon a Time" in booklet form before she started shopping it around to her many studio contacts. She also gave it to R. L. Giffen, the New York agent she sometimes used, but he, too, was unable to move it. Given the film successes of *Back Street* and *Imitation of Life* as recently as 1932 and 1934, it seemed strange to Fannie that her manuscripts were not in more insistent demand, but they weren't. Enough self-doubt set in that she finally succumbed to the determination of Rosalie Stewart, a Hollywood agent who had been pursuing Fannie for several years. Fannie agreed to have Stewart represent her exclusively for film deals under a twelve-month contract.

The decision was a major departure for Fannie, who over the years had not changed her mind about agents. She used their services only when they brought her an unsolicited deal or, as a last resort, when she had failed to sell a property herself. Her agreements were always case by case. This time Stewart managed to convince Fannie that a longer-term arrangement would pay off in earnings. She felt sure she could bring in a buyer for "Once upon a Time," even though it already had made the rounds, and she was equally confident that she would be able to move some of Fannie's older works.

All fall and winter Stewart blazed through Hollywood packing Fannie's stories and novels. Sale of *A President Is Born* to Universal looked so likely that Fannie converted it into a scenario and gave it a new title, but in the end the studio changed its mind. There was not much market for politics in Hollywood. Stewart then thought she had studio interest in Fannie's 1930 short story "Carrousel." Fannie could not remember if she had sold the sound rights to "Humoresque"—there was a good bet—and Stewart dusted off "The Hossie Frossie" for RKO to read as a possible vehicle for its seventeen-year-old child star Anne Shirley. Again, in each case no sale.

Six months into the contract, Fannie began to regret having made it and composed a letter asking Stewart to loosen up the arrangement. "As opportunities from time to time come along for me to negotiate elsewhere," she wrote, "I naturally find myself bound by our year's agreement, so that instead of our contract proving the boon I had hoped it would, it is actually a deterrent." She decided against mailing the letter, however, and let the months pass. By July 1936, a month before their agreement ran out, Stewart got Metro-Goldwyn-Mayer interested in "Once upon a Time" for John Stahl's unit. The offer was half the minimum fifteen thousand dollars Fannie wanted for it. Stewart cabled Fannie she thought she could get the studio to pay ten thousand dollars but not more. Fannie asked her to try for eleven thousand dollars, so that she would have ten thousand dollars left after paying the commission. MGM refused to budge, and Fannie finally agreed, but only because Stahl was her first choice to direct it. By the next day Stewart had concluded the deal, and not a moment too soon. YOUR STORY AGAIN PROVES THE POINT I MADE IN NEW YORK THAT UNLESS A GOOD STORY SELLS FOR PICTURES IMMEDIATELY ON RELEASE . . . AN AGENT CAN BY FIRST LIKING IT TREMENDOUSLY SECOND WORKING ON IT CONSTANTLY GET AN OFFER, she cabled. The check and contracts were in the mail August 12, 1936, two days before the agent agreement ran out. Fannie signed on with Stewart again, and a strong working relationship developed.

As for the film of "Once upon a Time," by March 1937 George O'Neil was reported hard at work on a script, and the expectation was that a movie would be out by late summer or early fall. But that was the last Fannie heard of it.

"Great Laughter"

The hundred-year time span of *Great Laughter,* Fannie's tenth novel, made her decide for the first time to hire a skilled editor to go over the pages before she turned them in to Harpers. Given the repeated bruisings she had endured over a quarter of a century at the hands of reviewers—the nastiest criticism of her novels had a very consistent ring—it was probably wise for her to submit to a rigorous line-by-line edit before turning in her manuscript. But this turned out not to be her intention at all. Instead, Fannie instructed Vera Ballou to root out her "exaggerated tendency for repetitiousness, redundancies and inaccuracies with regard to the age of my characters" but to leave the expansive "stylistic license" she allowed herself alone. She was willing to have Ballou bring questions of grammar, rhetoric, and syntax to her attention, but no more. She wanted her work to stand essentially as written.

At the same time Fannie asked Bill Briggs, her editor, to schedule *Great Laughter's* publication to coincide with a lecture tour she had signed up to make in late October. In this way, she implied, she could gracefully manage to be out of New York when the reviews started to surface. She had great confidence in the book, but she was just as certain of the critical dissent sure to follow its publication. And in all these years, and for all her popular success, nothing had inured her to the written lashings. In another context she once admitted, "It was and remains my unhappy faculty to remember verbatim the beatings, no matter how slight my regard for the appraiser, and to forget the praise." Her habit was to read a bad review, let the words "eat in and sear in," then retire to lick her wounds, hoping no one close to her—especially not her parents when they were alive—had seen the hurtful words. "I am a bleeder under criticism," she said, "and I have not done too well in the matter of controlling this mental hemophilia." She could have avoided much of the most hurtful criticism altogether with the help of a good editor's sharp red pencil. But at some level she seemed to invite the biennial opportunity to hemorrhage. Perhaps it was a way to bring back the verbal lashings of her St. Louis childhood.

Fannie submitted the manuscript to Harpers in early July, feeling strongly enough about it to go over the head of her editor and write directly to Cass Canfield, Harpers' publisher. She told him how important she thought *Great Laughter* could be if it was handled "a little specially and brilliantly." It was more than " 'just another book,' " she told him. "Even if the critics (perish the thought!) should gum up its road a bit, I have the feeling that if we stand by, the book can be pushed through to success." Canfield assured her the House of Harper would do "everything we can to put it over in the most effective and original way."

The rest of the summer passed quietly. At her annual physical exam, Fannie's doctor handed down a sentence of "flabby" and sent her back to the long daily walks in Central Park, a routine she had started to consider a "misery" but one she submitted to nonetheless because of a few returned pounds. Sometimes she eschewed the park for nighttime meanders through neighborhoods she had yet to explore; other days she did both. The city had emptied out, but no matter. Fannie enjoyed her own company as much as anyone else's. There was a day trip with Stef followed by dinner at home with Jack, and a June lunch under the trees at Hyde Park with the first lady and friends. Still, Fannie spent as many days in "blissful solitude" as not.

Rosalie Stewart concluded the sale of "Once upon a Time" to MGM in late July, and within weeks word of the charms of Fannie's new novel in production at Harper & Brothers had started to filter west through the New York offices of the various Hollywood studios. These representatives made a point of keeping in close touch with Fannie between books, always ready to pounce when she had something new to show. In New York, William Fadiman of MGM was first to ask Fannie for a copy of the galleys for *Great Laughter.* Merritt Hulburn at Goldwyn Productions made the same request of Rosalie Stewart out in Los Angeles, which prompted her to cable Fannie for a copy. Stewart also used the opportunity to explain to Fannie that she would be able to do much better in the way of price if she could read the whole manuscript through before the New York studio representatives started mailing synopses back to Los Angeles. Fannie thought *Great Laughter* should be worth a lot of money and didn't want Stewart to think small because of the ten-thousand-dollar payment she had accepted for "Once upon a Time." Stewart was suffering from no such confusion. She was raring to break new ground. If it turned out to be true that the film rights to Edna Ferber's *Come and Get It* had fetched sixty thousand dollars, Stewart said, there was no reason *Great Laughter* couldn't top it and then some.

Fannie sent Stewart a set of galleys, admitting in her note that she already had slipped a copy to Fadiman at MGM. Bill Lengel of Columbia Pictures and David Selznick also asked for copies, but Fannie held them off because she had no more available. Fadiman read the manuscript quickly and responded to it in a detailed letter to Fannie on August 20, the same day Fannie mailed the galleys out to Stewart in Los Angeles. Fadiman's response, Fannie told her, was "quite extraordinary," to say the least.

The book, Fadiman said, was rich in characters, authentic background, and fundamental emotional conflicts. He said it was rich in that "all of the characters are really only microcosmic; tiny, strutting reflections of an era that witnessed a complete psychological re-adjustment in America, a post-war period of uncertainty and lack of balance." He saw the novel's protagonist as time itself. From a screen perspective the story offered any number of possible plots, since each of Gregrannie's progeny formed an independent plot and unity and symbolized another aspect of the century the book covered. He captured each character study in a couple of words. In Chauncey he saw the "groveling opportunist" and in Josie, a woman fearless and proud. Carmella was "cleverly clinging and soft in a hard world" and Louis, a maladjusted introvert. Cassie was "pathetic in her deformity" and May, "modern and limited in her narrow-horizoned objectives." There was Wallie, the murderer and misfit; John, "vain of his small talents"; Linda, "feckless and repressed"; Hearn, a "pompous politician weakened by sentimentality"; and, of course, Gregrannie, "wise, tolerant, sympathetic and masterful." From a cinematic standpoint the book presented obstacles, to be sure, but Fadiman said it was important enough to demand serious and immediate consideration. He assured Fannie he would do all he could to push the book at MGM.

Fannie began responding to the other requests for galleys. On August 21 she sent copies to the New York office of Paramount and to Charlie Beahan at Universal. Wanting to escape the mounting tension, she and Jack took off for a short holiday in Margaretville, New York, near Saratoga. They left Fannie's secretary, Ethel Rabin (actually Rabinowitz, but Fannie asked her to shorten her name on the job), back at the apartment in New York to play traffic cop to the studios, but with her role carefully orchestrated by Fannie. When Columbia Pictures called again for a copy of the galleys, there was none left to be had. Tuesday, a "vastly excited" Beahan returned his copy and cabled Fannie that he needed to speak with her urgently. On the telephone he pressed for an asking price, but she held off.

"Thirty-five thousand?" she remembered him asking.

"No," she replied.

"Fifty?"

"No."

"I'll try and get you sixty and let you know," he tried.

"Well, let me know," she said.

"I can get you sixty," he said. "I can get you something that would interest you."

"No offer no longer interests me," she said to end the conversation. "I'll be in town in a few days and we can talk further if you desire."

"Well," he said, "don't close with anybody else meanwhile without letting us know."

"I'll think it over" was what Fannie remembered saying to end the call.

That was Wednesday, the twenty-sixth. Since the U.S. mail had only gotten a copy to Rosalie Stewart on the twenty-fifth, the same day Beahan made his offer, Stewart begged Fannie not to close with Universal until she could get the galleys around to the other studios in Los Angeles and give them adequate time to respond. Fannie agreed. Also on the twenty-fifth, Fadiman's copy of *Great Laughter* arrived at MGM's Hollywood office, where an executive read through the whole thing by midmorning and pronounced herself "terribly enthusiastic," according to Stewart. Stewart then took her only set of galleys to Twentieth Century–Fox and after that to United Artists, where Bill Hawkins cabled Fannie urging her to keep the deal open until he had time to get it through UA's hierarchy.

Stewart also made arrangements to present the story to Paramount at noon on Thursday. She thought prospects there were excellent. Paramount, she reminded Fannie, had directors like Frank Lloyd, Wesley Ruggles, Leo McCarey, Ernst Lubitsch, who all "practically buy their own stories." Paramount also had Frank Capra, she said, "considered by many [the] greatest director here." Capra, she said, was in search of the next important subject matter to follow *Lost Horizon* and was prepared to "pay anything for the next great story." She urged Fannie to sit tight for a week and leave the negotiation to her so that the best price could be obtained from one studio without angering all the others.

Wednesday the telephone in Fannie's apartment rang like a bell concert. "Twentieth Century is hysterical," Ethel reported. "Mr. Beahan is a wreck—and probably because he is aware that other studios are angling so hard for it. He tried to remind me that it was Universal that did such a good job on *Back Street* and Universal that did wonders with *Imitation of Life.* And what Universal would do with *Great Laughter*!! They want it very badly that's easy to see." As if in response to all the excitement, Fannie's monkey escaped from its cage in a wrecking spree down the halls of the apartment and onto the balcony. Miss Rabin said the episode nearly caused Clara, the elderly housekeeper, to die of fright.

On Thursday nine telephone calls came in from Hollywood and fifteen more from the studios' New York offices. "Universal leads the pack of wolves with an *offer* on one man's reading, but the others [are] clamoring for the right to read and overbid," Fannie told Miss Rabin. "I simply don't know where to turn. I hope this hysterical enthusiasm means what it seems to portend."

Paramount turned out to be so enthusiastic that Fannie said the reaction made Fadiman and Beahan seem only mildly interested by comparison. "I've had experience in competitive bidding," Fannie puffed, "but this, on my 'white elephant' is the climax I think."

Whatever the outcome of the bidding war, it was all good news for the novel, especially if some of the excitement could spill into the newspaper columns. Fannie scripted a call she instructed Miss Rabin to make to the publicist at Harpers, now Ramona Herdman. Fannie wanted the call to appear as if Miss Rabin was telephoning of her own accord since Fannie was on holiday and out of touch. Fannie told her to emphasize how the various studios saw "not only the immense dramatic values of *Great Laughter,* but its literary importance and beauty, etc., as a book, etc. etc. This may pump a little knowledge into her as to what it is all about." She told her to head down to Harpers' offices on Friday with the movie correspondence and cables. "You can talk with less reserve than I could," Fannie said. "Phone, just to make sure she'll be there. . . . If Miss Herdman is clever, which she is not, she ought to get a good story out of the made story of 'Hollywood Goes to Market.' " Fannie had made unbreakable plans to be some seventy-five miles away in Hyde Park on Friday for another Roosevelt lunch.

Miss Rabin dutifully headed down to Harpers on Friday. "I expected a whopper," she told Fannie of the news release the publicist prepared on the spot, "but in essence, she said, 'Heavy bidding going on in Hollywood for Miss Fannie Hurst's forthcoming novel, *Great Laughter.* It is reported that a considerably greater sum is being offered for this book than any other.' " Miss Rabin reported that, according to the publicist, Margaret Mitchell's best-seller *Gone with the Wind* had commanded only sixty thousand dollars for its film rights. "Isn't that great?" she enthused. Actually, though sixty thousand dollars was the asking price, David O. Selznick's production company paid fifty thousand dollars for the film rights when the book was well on its way to best-sellerdom. At the time of its sale, *Great Laughter* was still in manuscript.

Meanwhile, Harry Burton of *Cosmopolitan* called Fannie to say that another writer was stealing her plot for "Sister Act." Fannie couldn't figure out why someone in *Cosmo's* offices would leak her nifty plot idea, but Miss Rabin ventured another thought: "What would be the point of their giving away this theme—knowing that you were working on it. . . . How about the possibility of their wanting to hurry you a bit? Or put the fear of the Lord in you?" Hmmmm. Fannie turned some concentrated attention to finishing "Sister Act."

On her return from Hyde Park on Friday night, Fannie learned from Stewart that Irving Thalberg at MGM had come in with an offer of seventy thousand dollars for *Great Laughter,* "with bidders on the horizon to top him and heaven knows what Universal will do, so it becomes incredibly grotesque." The excitement had even overtaken the telegraph and telephone stations of Saratoga and Margaretville in a way "that has to be seen to be believed." Fannie thought it was funny how no one at Harpers had sensed the picture in the novel, but then she considered the staff at the publishing house "four-fourths dead anyhow."

By Saturday morning it got quieter in New York, but not so in Margaretville. Fannie was still fielding calls from Hollywood. On Friday, while she was in Hyde Park, eight more Hollywood calls had come in. "When they wear down Rosalie Stewart, they start on me," she told Miss Rabin, adding that Thalberg had upped his offer to eighty or eighty-five thousand dollars—"I'm too dizzy to know." West Coast executives from Goldwyn, Paramount, Universal, Selznick, and Fox were in the game, as were Frank Capra and several others. Her voice wobbling with enthusiasm, Stewart told Fannie that the negotiation was making Hollywood history. Never before had there been such a bidding war for an unpublished novel. The response was so overwhelming, Stewart had started wishing for someone *not* to like it, just to contain the chaos.

Fannie was glad she had gotten out of New York before Universal pinned her down to sixty thousand. Meanwhile, she told Miss Rabin, "The telegrams continue to pour in and life in the country is just one merrie hell, although it is quite perfect here."

Fannie began to prepare Miss Rabin for a second strategic assault on Harpers, where the reaction so far had been "just as slow and dull as everything else about them is." As soon as there was an agreement, Fannie wanted her secretary to load the Harpers publicist with ideas for handling news of the sale. "Tell her that it is a good chance to put very interesting vibrations at work regarding *Great Laughter,*" Fannie told Miss Rabin.

> It is the first time a novel has been bid for and bought at so vast a price from galleys, long before publication. If she had guts and imagination, neither of which she nor her organization possess, she could get good yarns out of it all: My reluctance to show it. The fact that *Great Laughter* has none of the usual motion picture appeal, but is a study of a period and characters rather than a novel of rapid action. As Fadiman says, its real hero is the last twenty years. Oh, a clever mind could bite in and whet an appetite in the public for this novel and get it tip-toe awaiting it. School yourself in what I am saying in this letter and try and convey it to her.

Fannie thought the events had given Harpers "a chance to sow some exciting seeds and if they muff it, I won't be surprised, but I will be if they don't, so hoping for a surprise." Fannie wanted the movie deal to be an "open secret— will tell everybody once it is consummated because we might as well put success vibrations in motion before the book is published and get people expectant. Ha ha—perhaps only to be let down. Hope not. . . . Miss Stewart said last night over the phone she feels sure of $85,000, as Thalberg is like a mad man."

There was another exchange of phone calls between Fannie and Rosalie Stewart and then, around midnight Sunday, August 30, another cable arrived in Margaretville from Stewart. It stated that at 11:00 P.M. Thalberg had purchased the film rights to *Great Laughter* for one hundred thousand dollars, a record-breaking price for an unpublished manuscript, and asking Fannie to confirm the sale in a telegram over her signature to arrive at the MGM studio offices the next morning. Stewart informed the other studios, whose representatives bowed gracefully out. That is, with the exception of Charlie Beahan at Universal, who was firing off cables of his own the next morning. One went to Fannie. He said he could not understand how she could say Rosalie Stewart was handling the manuscript when he had already closed with her at $60,000. To Stewart, he also insisted that the deal was his and that Universal intended to hold the property BY EVERY MEANS POSSIBLE. Stewart reported that the same message had gone out from Universal to MGM by cable but that Thalberg appeared unconcerned by it and was certain that Fannie had acted in good faith.

SUGGEST YOU AND I DO ABSOLUTELY NOTHING ABOUT IT LET THALBERG HANDLE THE MATTER IN HIS OWN WAY, Stewart advised. But Fannie couldn't resist. Beahan had defamed her, she felt, and she cabled him in fury the next day: YOU ARE WRONG BOTH IN YOUR FACTS AND YOUR CONCLUSIONS. SORRY YOU SHOULD APPEAR SO DUMB. FANNIE HURST. In spite of all the excitement over the deal, she couldn't let the impugning of her good name go. The remark had caused her "untold mental anguish," she told Stewart. After a subsequent telephone conversation with Beahan, Fannie reported to Stewart on September 2 that Beahan claimed Universal had not been given a last look-in before the deal was closed with MGM. "I hope that is not true," she wrote, "but in the event that you were forced to conclude with Mr. Thalberg without reaching Universal, the slip up was not due to my failure to keep my word, but I imagine to mechanical processes in the way of your getting to Universal from your end."

Stewart, in a later postmortem, explained that Universal in Los Angeles had declined to communicate with her all week, likely because Beahan had told the studio to stay out of the negotiation because he had the matter in hand in New York. Beahan also denied that a threatening telegram had been sent to MGM from Universal but acknowledged that someone from their office in Los Angeles might have telephoned to "verbally register resentment."

Fannie said Universal was prepared now to let the matter lie, and not to take legal action, even though the studio would have been willing to pay

$125,000 for the story. "I have no desire to establish a spirit of antagonism with them," she said, "but I do feel that if I concede [sic] to their request now, it will look as if I am throwing them a conciliatory bone, or have been guilty of what they accused me. Since this is so emphatically not the case, I feel the need of stepping very carefully at this time." Universal had tried to flatter her with the argument that because of *Black Street* and *Imitation,* she was its star and should give all her material to the studio. Fannie quickly countered that Universal hadn't felt that way when she tried to sell the rights to *A President Is Born* and "Once upon a Time." In those instances she had been no star at all. She thought perhaps the real purpose of all the insisting was to line her up for her next piece of work.

That was going to be "Sister Act." Harry Burton's well-placed words had gotten Fannie back to work on the serial again, but now her mind danced with more remunerative reasons for finishing the story. With the *Great Laughter* contract with MGM in hand by September 11, Stewart would soon need another Roman candle to launch in its sky path.

Fannie—even O. Henry—could not have written a more stunning end to the real-life story of "Hollywood Goes to Market." Two weeks after the deal was done, on September 14, Irving Thalberg died at the age of thirty-seven, succumbing to the effects of a congenital heart condition complicated by an attack of pneumonia. Fannie got all of the money due her—for tax purposes in two fifty-thousand-dollar installments, one in 1936 and one in 1937—and sent a copy of her novel to Thalberg's widow, Norma Shearer, as a memento as soon as the book was published. *Great Laughter* has languished unproduced ever since.

As for the book, the *New York Herald Tribune* trumpeted *Great Laughter's* appearance with a full-page review. *The New York Times,* however, again was "on the debit side," as Bill Briggs delicately put it. Other reviews of significance were equally disappointing. The Ballou edit had done little to tame the customary indictment of Fannie's work on charges of repetitiousness and careless writing, "hard to forgive in a novel as seriously designed as this one," snipped Margaret Wallace in the *Times.*

All the same, the advance sale had been excellent, and the buzz from Hollywood outpaced whatever damage the reviews otherwise could have done. Six weeks after publication the book had sold nearly twenty thousand copies and was still moving. On a five-thousand-dollar advance, both Fannie and Harpers were well into profit and greatly pleased before the year was out. Canfield sent Fannie a celebratory note, and the first royalty statement on *Great Laughter* showed nearly three thousand dollars in net earnings for Fannie by year's end. Fannie wondered if her lecture tour through Detroit, Columbus, Indianapolis, Kansas City, and Fort Worth had accelerated sales in those cities. Briggs did not have a direct answer to the question, but the tour already was behind her when he reported that the week of December 3 had been *Great Laughter's* best, and that response was well-scattered geographically. Word of mouth also must have been strong because sales kept percolating well into February, giving *Great Laughter* the longest sales run of any of Fannie's books. Ramona Herdman dropped Fannie a line asking if there wasn't some news about her that Harpers could break to help keep sales going into spring.

"Show Business"

F annie was soaring so high during the fall of 1936, she asked Bill Briggs not to send over the clippings of her *Great Laughter* reviews. "I'm working pretty grand now," she told him, "and don't want to wilt."

Why should she wilt? It may have been only popular success, but all of Hollywood seemed to have gone mad for Fannie's work. Heading into her fifty-second year on earth, she was producing with the energy of a hopeful novice and making money like a master. Instead of taking time off to play, as she usually did between serious novels, this time she considered her respite a working holiday, tinkering with "odds and ends which amuse me, and which I take none too seriously." Trying to generate more big income was another way to put it. Fannie had no delusions about the permanence of her earning potential. Even before the windfall of 1936, she had explained as much to a wealthy friend she approached for investment counseling. "My only security against the future is all tied up in a delicate instrument known as the human brain," she wrote. "If mine wears out, nobody can carry on my business without me."

With Stef off in Iceland, he had missed the excitement of the MGM deal, and Fannie sat down at once to write him the good news. Miss Rabin filled in all the specifics. "Now that this matter is out of the way," the secretary wrote, "Miss Hurst has been devoting herself to the quadruplet serial for *Cosmopolitan*. She is now in the rewrite stage and working very rapidly. What with an address on the 22nd of this month before the Kiwanis Club, two radio speeches in one day on September 28th, publication date of *Great Laughter* the 15th of October, the future seems to be quite full. However, as you probably know, that is the only kind of future Miss Hurst seems to like."

Ethel Rabinowitz was a young twenty-one when she went to work for Fannie. She had trained to be a teacher, but passing by the bulletin board at the Young Women's Hebrew Association on 110th Street one day in 1932, she saw a notice that Fannie had posted seeking the services of a competent stenographer and typist. Intrigued, she applied for the job. Fannie hired her on the spot at a salary of ten dollars a week and in the course of four years only granted one raise, bringing the weekly wage to fifteen dollars. This was no reflection on her value to the author, because in no time Fannie developed a dependency so complete that when "Miss Rabin" suffered a severe attack of appendicitis, Fannie suggested she "freeze it," so as not to have to take time off.

"Madam," Miss Rabin was forced to tell her as she left for the hospital, "this is beyond freezing."

The two women traveled together when Fannie lectured or had to go to California, yet they remained on a "Miss Rabin–Miss Hurst" basis even while sharing berths on long train trips. Still, they managed to achieve something approaching familiarity. In quiet moments Fannie would ask Miss Rabin about her love life, and Fannie, in turn, would tell tales from her glamorous evenings out. On these frequent occasions Fannie was always marvelously dressed, Miss Rabin remembered, often in garments provided by a buyer-friend at Klein's Department Store who would bring the gowns to Fannie's apartment for her to try on, then sell them to her at prices even Miss Rabin could have afforded. Whenever the conversation was personal, Fannie spoke briefly but always with good description and enthusiasm. "Always with spirit," Miss Rabin recalled, though she could remember no stories with any intimate details.

In four years of working with the author day in and day out, Miss Rabin had the impression Fannie was a person without strong family ties. Though she kept a picture of her late mother in the her workroom, she rarely mentioned her, and her father, not at all.

These were the years of Fannie's dramatic weight loss, and Miss Rabin remembered her as slender and corseted but somehow uncomfortable with her flabby body, which never really adjusted to its new reduced size.

The days at Fannie's apartment were long and active. Miss Rabin would arrive at nine in the morning, just as Jacques, perfectly groomed and perfumed, prepared to leave for his studio. He projected an air of great virility. Miss Rabin said there were rumors of another woman in his life, and she often wondered what he kept in his Carnegie Hall studio besides the grand piano. Though he and Fannie had their own bedrooms—Miss Rabin worked in Fannie's—they had the possibility of sharing. Miss Rabin's sense was that Fannie loved Jacques deeply and depended on him, and that their relationship was warm and companionate—a real friendship. Although Fannie never took her young secretary into her confidence, Miss Rabin was also very well aware of the other "real thing" going on in Fannie's life—with Stef. But she kept it to herself.

Every morning the secretary found Fannie dressed in exactly the same white-patterned black dress (Miss Rabin often wondered if or when she found the time to have it laundered) and the same worn-down shoes. Bruno, Fannie's Yorkshire terrier at the time, would have been walked before Miss Rabin's arrival, and Fannie already would have several pages ready for typing. A bit later Fannie would sit down to mumble dictation. Despite her excellent public speaking voice, she always mumbled dictation. Sometimes, when she was deeply in a novel—and Miss Rabin enjoyed this most—Fannie would send her to the library to research historical episodes or places she wanted to include in the narrative.

There was nothing mythic about reports of Fannie's boundless energy. It was real, as was her clear exhilaration in long hours of hard work. "Her hunger was to sit in that room and work," Miss Rabin said, remembering how Fannie hated the interruption of a telephone call and with what discipline she rewrote and rewrote and rewrote. "I think those were her happiest hours."

The complete version of "Sister Act" was on its way to Rosalie Stewart by October 5, and three days later, with an impromptu telephone assist from Fannie ("You were simply marvelous," Stewart flattered, "but then you are one of the smartest persons I have ever met"), Warner Bros. paid a very impressive sixty-five thousand dollars for the film rights. Harry Burton paid another ten thousand dollars to run it in condensed form as a novel-in-one-issue in *Cosmopolitan*. And somehow, in the midst of all that activity, Fannie managed to slip in the short story "Elaine, Daughter of Elaine," which Burton snapped up at the usual four-thousand-dollar rate. Fannie also pitched yet another serial idea to him, inspired by the Aga Khan, whom *The New York Times* had profiled in March 1936 soon after his followers had presented him with his weight in gold to celebrate his fifty-first year on the throne. The story, datelined Bombay, made note of his immense wealth and popularity, his interest in horse racing, his social connections, his French wife. When Burton heard what Fannie was cooking up, he committed to buy the story—in writing and promptly this time—as soon as she could get it to him. A contract for the serial was signed the first week of the new year.

In the meantime another highly remunerative opportunity surfaced: Paramount wanted Fannie to rewrite and fix a skeletal story idea of Lew Lipton called "Show Business" that would follow the lives of a group of children growing up on the Lower East Side who each become famous in a branch of show business. She wired Stewart to explain her reservations: CONFIDENT MY VALUE LIES IN ORIGINAL WORK. CAN TAKE CUE GENERAL THEME BUT "SHOW BUSINESS" IS A SKELETON PLOT. SAVE ME FOR CREATIVE JOB. Stewart kept pressing, though, and Fannie began to warm to the plan. Much as she tried to resist thinking about it, "certain ideas sneaked in through the crevices" on her morning walk. Paramount sent an emissary to talk the story through with Fannie, after which she realized that "the idea he brought me was practically my own 'Humoresque.' " No wonder Paramount had her in mind.

Election Day, November 3, brought the chance to see "a page of history in the act of turning." The Roosevelts invited Fannie to join a select group at Hyde Park awaiting election returns that night. At 9:15 P.M., in light rainfall, she boarded the train along with Marion Dickerman, Nancy Cook, Frances Perkins, the George Backers, Caroline O'Day, and Agnes Leach. White House cars whisked them from the station to the brightly lit mansion, where the group was greeted by the president's mother and daughter-in-law along with Frank Cooper and Secretary and Mrs. Henry Morgenthau. Guests wandered from room to room in fine humor, snacking on light refreshments and drinking cider. The first lady, in white chiffon, arrived an hour later, at half past midnight, and the jovial chatting went on, punctuated every so often by the announcement of returns from one state or another over the radio.

"Of course, long before this, it was obvious that the landslide was happening," Fannie wrote in her diary the next day, "but the radio kept delivering the news of the great success." At 1:15 A.M. Fannie was summoned into the dining room, where the president was ensconced. "Panic-stricken but eager," she encountered an unforgettable tableau, suggestive of an old woodcut commemorating a moment of major significance. With candles flaring in old silver holders, the president sat at the head of a hard old wooden dining table, flanked by his children and bodyguards, his mother and wife. He looked happy, flushed and boyish, his soft collar rumpled and his smile unfailing. He offered her his hand and plenty of casual exchange. In the midst of his personal excitement, it impressed Fannie that he greeted her by name and showed the interest to ask her any number of personal questions. He was smiling, relaxed, and good-natured, "probably the secret of his great endurance," she thought, marveling at her good fortune to be in "the most important home in the world that day, talking with probably the most important man in the world."

After that Fannie was in and out of the dining room at will, being called upon from time to time to convey various messages. At about 3:00 A.M., with the rain coming down in torrents, Fannie and her party loaded themselves into automobiles to be taken to the cottages to spend the night. Fannie's private chauffeur for this occasion was the first lady herself, who dropped her off as she, alone, headed out for Newark airport, where her son James was expected to arrive at 5:00 A.M. She had kept this information from the president, she told Fannie, because he worried so whenever his children traveled by air. "It seemed most disturbing to think of her riding alone through the rain-swept night," Fannie wrote afterward, "but anyone who knows her, soon learned to think of her under all sorts of extraordinary conditions, chiefly because she is an extraordinary woman."

The rain was still pouring the next morning but could not possibly have soaked any spirits on the Hyde Park estate. There was a big family breakfast, served informally. New guests arrived by train for lunch, which was served on little tables "catch-as-catch-can" in a spirit of buoyant festivity. Everyone then sat around and talked and played "just as though the whole nation was not waiting and hanging on news of the Roosevelt estate."

A month later Fannie was back in Washington for the first lady's "Gridiron Widows" party. Her stay that night in a "huge and beautiful pink room" meant that, since Franklin Roosevelt took office, she had managed to sleep in every bedroom in the White House with the exception of the first lady's and the Presidential Suite. The first lady presented each guest with a copy of her new autobiography that night. In Fannie's the inscription read: "To Fannie Hurst, offered in humility and with much affection."

⬯

Between Hyde Park and Gridiron, Rosalie Stewart closed the deal for "Show Business" and, after much back-and-forth, got the studio to agree to Fannie's difficult terms. Paramount already had paid out ten thousand dollars to Lipton for the original idea and another ten thousand dollars to Bartlett Cormack for ten weeks' work on a script. To Fannie, the studio offered a two-day, all-expenses-paid trip to Hollywood for her and her secretary (Fannie took Jack instead), five thousand dollars for signing the contract, and thirty-five thousand dollars six weeks later on delivery of a "master scene screenplay with dialogue." Within two weeks of receipt the studio would let Fannie know if revisions were necessary, in which case she was obliged to provide one week of rewrite without payment. After that, if the studio still wanted more of her time, it would come at five thousand dollars a week. Her minimum payment then would be forty thousand dollars from Paramount, meaning that her contracted earnings in the last four months of 1936—counting a projected forty thousand dollars for the "Aga Khan"—came close to a quarter of a million dollars at a time when that amount of money could buy a thirteen-story downtown hotel. Fannie boarded the cross-country Superchief for Los Angeles on November 21.

Nine days later she was back in New York, full of ideas for the "Show Business" project. But Fannie's first visit to Hollywood in seven years had not changed her mind about its excesses. "The first 48 hours in Hollywood were the longest," she told Bill Briggs at Harpers when she returned. "Fortunately they were the last."

"Had I cared to succumb to its golden lure," she went on, "I could have remained and enjoyed what seems to be my present vogue out there. In that event, I could have invited the entire House of Harper out to week-end with me in one of the simple little forty-room chalets dear to Hollywoodians, and every Harper one of us could probably have enjoyed his own individual swimming pool, patio and Rolls Royce. Now, aren't you sorry I came home to settle down in my 67th street tenement?"

Christmas Eve, Fannie had three copies of the screenplay in the mail to Stewart. A week later, as Stewart delivered the manuscript to Paramount in Los Angeles, Fannie and Jacques prepared for a breakfast of champagne-bathed eggs at the postmidnight New Year's party of the *New York Times* publisher, Arthur Hays Sulzberger, and his wife, Iphigene, who had become social friends.

It took only a week for Paramount to ask for radical revisions in the screenplay—the changing of two or three of the characters and "more solid story written in place of the present episodic form." Stewart told Fannie the studio wanted her to come out to Los Angeles to "whip the story into shape" but did not want to pay her any extra money. Of course, in Fannie's view, "an episodic story not too burdened with plot" was what Paramount had ordered up in the first place. She reminded Stewart that Lewis Gensler had even told her to "beware of 'too much story' since this picture was to have an entertainment value;

that is, artists of the first rank were to be presented in their various fields of work." However irritated, Fannie controlled herself and told Stewart she was more than willing to cooperate in giving the extra time needed, only "not there and not for free."

Cosmopolitan, meantime, was pressing for Fannie to commit immediately to a timetable for the new serial, to which her attention had turned. But mollified by news from Stewart that Paramount had delivered the rest of the initial forty thousand dollars owed, Fannie met with Russell Holman, the studio's representative in New York. After their talk she agreed to write a whole new version of the screenplay at no extra charge. If the studio wanted revisions after she turned the new version in, it was agreed she would charge an additional five thousand dollars a week for the work.

Gensler, Holman, and William LeBaron prepared a detailed letter explaining exactly what they wanted from Fannie in the second round, and she got to work as soon as she received it. The writing did not come easily, however, and well into February, Fannie started to regret having started all over again "the Fannie Hurst way." She felt she had given Paramount "the bargain of a century" since she could have finished an entire serial novel in the time this screenplay was taking her.

She submitted her rewrite to Paramount at the beginning of March. Within days the studio rejected it. From Fannie's end there was nothing more to be done. She had written it twice "from the ground up" after all. Still, her reputation in Hollywood mattered to her, and, having accepted forty thousand dollars for rejected work, she was concerned about her standing for future projects.

"Paramount is at full liberty to use any parts of the draft I have written," she wrote Stewart's boss, Harry Edington, "and if there is anything I can do, even though I have previously indicated that I have already given them double time on this story, I will be glad to lend them whatever efforts my time may permit." All the same, Fannie wanted to make it clear that her name could not now be connected with the project in any way, which was agreed.

With that Fannie took off on a five-month journey to Europe and the Middle East, where her stops included Cairo, Luxor, Damascus, Baghdad, and even Jerusalem. She worked on the serial in Florence but "with the glorious speed of a snail." Paris was the highlight, this trip. She told Bob Davis she had finally "cracked through the social, diplomatic and literary life" of the city, though she wasn't specific about whom she had met. As for her Aga Khan–like yarn (Fannie finally settled on "Lamb of the West" for its title), it took nearly another year for her to have it in shape, and then even more time for Burton to be satisfied enough with it to put it in the magazine. Stewart had no luck peddling it in Hollywood.

"What's what?" Fannie wrote Stewart on her return from the Middle East in early August 1937. "Are any of my pictures, *Great Laughter,* 'Sister Act,' 'Once upon a Time,' 'Show Business,' scheduled or in production? I'm both mis- and uninformed."

Of the four, only "Sister Act," now called *Four Daughters,* turned out to have a future in film—a long and successful one, too, including its two sequels, *Four Wives* in 1939 and *Four Mothers* in 1941, and the 1954 remake, *Young at Heart,* which starred Gig Young. The 1939 *Daughters Courageous* reassembled the cast but put them in a different family. Fannie had to threaten a lawsuit to wrest more money out of Warner Bros. for the reuse of her characters. In the end the studio paid her an additional $12,500.

As for the other stories, Paramount concluded that "Show Business" would never jell properly into a film; even if it did it would cost too much to cast. Thalberg's death had caused interest in *Great Laughter* to evaporate completely, and "Once upon a Time" also seemed to vanish from consciousness. Early in 1938 Stewart had luck again with an idea of Fannie's for a script based on the life of Jascha Heifetz, but much to Fannie's consternation the deal she struck with Goldwyn Pictures blew up before any money changed hands. Stewart hawked every new story Fannie produced through to 1940, but without luck. At least as far as her new work was concerned, Fannie's meteoric streak through Hollywood was over.

Chapter 28

"We Are Ten"

Harpers brought out a new collection of Fannie's short stories in September 1937, just before she and Jacques moved into a grand, new white elephant of a triplex at Sixty-seventh Street off Central Park West. The decision actually made the newspapers: ten thousand square feet on the top three floors of the Hotel des Artistes. The rent, which did not make the papers, was in the neighborhood of five hundred dollars a month. The new book, the eighth published collection of Fannie's short stories, would also be her last of this ilk. It included all but four of the stories she had written since the release of *Procession* back in 1929. True, she had written fewer short stories in these years, but her overall production had not really slowed. It was just that her more consuming focus had been novels, serials, and screenplays, not to mention her fascination with politics.

At Fannie's insistence the new book bore the title *We Are Ten,* for the ten stories it contained. Annoyed with the publicity apparatus at Harpers, she hired her old friend Ruth Raphael to keep the book from being "stillborn"— Fannie's word. Almost invariably Fannie lapsed into birth imagery to describe the process of bringing one of her ideas from conception to publication—an interesting choice for someone childless. Ruth did her best with *We Are Ten,* starting with a major mass mailing—fourteen hundred cards—but the effort netted only one response.

Reviews of the book were respectful, for the most part, except in *The New York Times.* There, the critic Edith Walton mercilessly condemned the "sheer badness and mawkishness" of the writing, "the garishness of her plots," "the obviousness of her themes," and the way Fannie seemed to be writing "transparently to order," "carelessly and tritely and with so little of her original zest." The critique was about as nasty as they came, made no easier to take by its proximity to the profuse praise for Zora's new novel, *Their Eyes Were Watching God,* one turn of the page beyond. "Indeed, from first to last this is a well-nigh perfect story," wrote Lucy Tomkins, "a little sententious at the start, but the rest is simple and beautiful and shining with humor." Fannie herself already had declared this first novel of Zora's after her Guggenheim fellowship to be "shot through with the lightning of an authentic talent." She meant it, too; Fannie never endorsed a book on its dust jacket that she didn't feel strongly about.

Fannie thought Harpers should have followed her *Times* review with a strong advertising campaign. But when none was placed she called off Ruth's efforts, which she was paying for herself, since "the necessary pumping of oxygen could not be accomplished without a closer cooperation."

Zora, however, was getting serious promotional attention from her publisher for *Their Eyes Were Watching God.* Somewhere between the publicity departments of Lippincott and Harpers came a bright idea to double-service Fannie's and Zora's publicity needs. The *Saturday Review* assigned Zora to profile Fannie, providing an opportunity to showcase Zora's fine writing for white readers at a time when Fannie, too, could benefit from the attention. The sidebar to Zora's article was a review of *We Are Ten*—a complimentary one. Her fellow author Isabel Wilder said Fannie's "curiosity about life and her zest for it are almost overwhelming and very contagious."

But the angle that clearly sold the *Saturday Review* on the idea was suggested in the headline editors chose for the piece: "Fannie Hurst by Her Ex-Amanuensis." Never mind that Zora had spent a scant part-time month in this capacity. That very taut stretch was sufficient to clinch the assignment, and Zora certainly knew Fannie well enough to provide an insightful piece of writing. To her credit, Zora never mentioned her tenuous secretarial connection to Fannie in the text. That was supplied only by the editors, who put it both in the title and in a biographical sentence about Zora in italics at the very end: "Zora Neale Hurston, for many years Fannie Hurst's amanuensis, has written several books about her own people." As it turned out, those three words *for many years* became the starting point for decades of skewed facts about the two women's relationship. Twenty-four years later Fannie herself supplied others.

To Zora, Fannie was someone who could make a person "hop from one emotion to the other so fast that not one suspicion of sleep will dim your eyes." Even though Zora found Fannie's moods and statements more contradictory than those of any other person in public life, "if you study her out, she is the very essence of consistency."

In Zora's view Fannie was someone who wrote because she was driven to, never on demand. "If everything she writes is not a *Humoresque,* a *Back Street,* a *Lummox* or a *Vertical City,*" Zora said, "it is not a play to the gallery. It is because the gods inside have failed her for the moment." The very significant omission in Zora's list of Fannie's best work was *Imitation of Life.*

Zora saw in Fannie "a little girl who is tall for her age. You can just see her playing doll-house with grown-up tools. One moment a serious worker controlled by her genii; the next instant playing make-believe with all her heart. Playing it so that it is impossible for you to doubt that for her it is true while it lasts." She went on:

> You can just see the child in St. Louis wandering around in the
> big house with no other children to play with. She could not run
> loose in the streets because her people were never poor. There were

too many good carpets and lace curtains in her house for it to be over-run with just anybody's children, either. She did not even have a cousin near her own age. She was the little girl with the long curls who looked out of the big window until she got tired. Then she would fiddle with the lace curtains until she was told to stop. She put up with adult company as long as she could stand it, and you can see her when she hit upon the glorious device of making up her playmates out of her own head.

Not all of these details of the St. Louis background were accurate. For a time there was a playmate, for example, and there were not so many good carpets and curtains in the Hurst household as Zora imagined. For more than a few years there was not even a house. But Zora was right about Fannie's love of beauty, "the air of the Medicis" in which she surrounded herself, both at 27 West Sixty-seventh Street and in the new place, with "bits of this and that from here and there in the world, but mostly from Italy and Italy of the great art period." And she picked up on the incongruity of Fannie's miserly quirks amid all that opulence: "She might seek here and there for a bargain in soda biscuits to eat with cheese, and then pay an enormous sum for a beautiful plate to eat it from" was how Zora described it. Miss Rabin remembered Fannie buying gnarly apples from the greengrocer at bargain prices, ostensibly for her monkey, only to put them in a bowl by her desk and eat them herself.

It was also in this article that Zora revealed the details of the long road trip to Canada when Fannie decided to have "the fun of running away." Six years had passed since the drive that sped Fannie to an emotional precipice, only to make her back away just as fast. The clash of egos with Stef would have been too calamitous for a satisfying life together; Stef needed to be the center of things as much as she. She also had come to think of him as arid in places—a gorgeous sunset, she recalled, would bring on only an expatiation on the laws of refraction. "As if bogged down by facts, his imagination scarcely left the ground," she later reflected. "He had the scientist's dedication to truth, but he was earthbound, lacking the wing-lift to put what he knew to work."

There were other, overriding issues, too. Who would have managed Fannie's money? Certainly not Fannie, who had no head for it. Stef never could have filled Jack's shoes as a careful and conservative financial manager, nor would it ever have interested him to do so. The accumulation of money had no appeal for him; he was constantly short of funds. Fannie gave him loans with some regularity over the years of their involvement. Once, Stef even turned over a thousand dollars that she had loaned him to a needy tenor he felt could use it more. Although he was judicious about repayment, if sometimes slow, the very fact of these awkward transactions had to have muddied the road.

Fannie's very cryptic diary entries for the only years of the relationship for which she kept personal notes, 1936 to 1939, give the vaguest traces of the change in her feelings as the long affair sputtered to an end.

February 28, 1936, watching Stef among a theater box full of southerners at the Savoy in Harlem, she thought he looked "about as out of place as one of his Eskimos." She witnessed his naturalization ceremony that June, but two months later canceled a dinner plan with him and cousin Mittie because she was "out of mood for either of them," choosing to dine with Jack instead. She gave Stef a birthday party in 1937, but the next year noted only that she had been "nice to him" when he came calling in the afternoon that day. In February 1939, she helped him celebrate the publication of his new book and noted seeing him several times over the summer. But on each of those occasions she remarked on how "heavy and dull and tired" she found him. Their last recorded dinner was on October 22, 1939, not alone but at a Polish restaurant with their mutual friends Henrietta Additon and Charlotte Carr. In December, Stef sent Fannie money in partial repayment of an outstanding loan. "True, I have been earning," he explained, "though not enough to meet expenses." He said he was five months behind on his room rent because of payments from the summer that had not yet come through.

By the time he repaid that loan in full the next year, the two were not seeing each other at all. Stef had become deeply involved with his adoring, much younger assistant, whom he would soon marry and to whom he would remain happily married until his death in 1962.

By the spring of 1942 Fannie and Stef had become so estranged that she told an acquaintance who asked her for an introduction that she was not the right person to make it. "However," she assured the man, "he is a kind and amenable person and will, I feel sure, give you consideration."

At the start of her secret marriage to Jacques, Fannie celebrated with a printed inscription of *Every Soul Hath Its Song* that read, "To J.S.D." Now she marked the end of her other secret union in the same code. *We Are Ten* bears the dedication line "To Stef."

"Do Re Mi Fah"

Everything about *Cosmopolitan*'s handling of "Lamb of the West" irritated Fannie, though with a contract signed and forty thousand dollars at stake, she held her tongue until the end. At the time she probably had not fully absorbed what was happening to her standing at the magazine, because Harry Burton kept sending her mixed signals. But there were clues as early as 1936, in the way he had balked before committing to "Sister Act" and in the overly long wait to see "Home, James" in the magazine's pages.

Fannie may have sloughed off these two incidents at the time, attributing them to the quirks of Burton's personal style. He had none of the exquisite grace of his predecessor, Ray Long, who had the ability to make her feel flattered even as he asked for major revisions in a story. Though Burton was always attentive, respectful, complimentary, and friendly toward Fannie on the surface, his actions betrayed his real intent.

By the time "Lamb of the West" was being edited in 1938, the shift in Fannie's status was unmistakable. It incensed her when Burton's minions intruded "beyond editorial comment into structural and character discussion that must primarily rest with the author." She remained adamant that she would make only those changes that suited her own sensibilities about the work. But even more galling was the new title the editors slapped on the serial and used to promote it without consulting her. She thought the choice—"Bride of the Rajah"—had the appalling ring of bad turn-of-the-century pulp fiction and demanded the right to choose a substitute. "Not only do I dislike 'Bride of the Rajah,' as 'my' title," she snipped, "but it becomes nothing short of absurd in view of the fact that, at your request, I altered the manuscript in order to remove the implication that Barron [the Aga Khan–inspired figure] was anything but Aryan." (So much for her repeated claim that she never changed a plot to suit anyone else.)

By way of apology Burton sent her crowds of flowers and put his assistant to the task of appeasing her. She, in turn, expressed sincere gratitude in a note of thanks: "Even when the going is rough and tough, I am fortunate in my editorial relationships," she wrote Burton. "You 'took it' and helped me 'take it' and as for that Hawley youth in your office—he is an *ace*." All the same, the title "Bride of the Rajah" stayed.

For some time after she finished the serial, Fannie continued to offer her new short fiction to Burton first, even though she was no longer under contractual obligation to do so. When the clean copy of "Rhinestones Preferred" came off her secretary's typewriter in the spring of 1938, Fannie sent it right over. This is the tale of a woman from the wrong side of the tracks who marries an astronomer, but their disparate backgrounds soon cause him to lose interest in her. So as not to interfere with his plan to divorce her, she does not tell him she is pregnant until the papers are signed; but she continues to love him and raises their son alone. He, on the other hand, decides to marry a former girlfriend of his own class. He maintains relations with his son through visits and gifts, and the ex-wife agrees to a plan for the son, starting at age six, to live with his father six months a year.

Just before the child's move, a sharp-tipped compass arrives as a gift from the father. Accidentally, it pierces the boy's cornea, and he is rushed to the hospital. Doctors advise they can save the eye, but only with a transplant. The mother does not hesitate to offer her own. While both mother and son prepare for surgery, the ex-husband unexpectedly arrives. The indifferent embrace of his second wife has brought him to realize how much he lost by giving up the mother of his son. He knows now that she is the woman he truly loves. Unaware of the unfolding tragedy caused by his own gift, he has come to ask for her back. She does not tell him how the boy was hurt but explains that he needs her eye and that she is giving it to him—and if her disfigurement is not a problem for the husband, she will happily have him back.

Burton accepted the story but immediately started asking for changes. In most instances Fannie obliged, but she held her ground on refusing to have the reason for the husband's return be the wife's impending sacrifice. Though Fannie had always been paid promptly at *Cosmopolitan,* it took more than a year for the four-thousand-dollar check for "Rhinestones" to be cut. And there was an interminable wait for publication—this time a year longer than for "Home, James." Never before had the magazine treated her work with such disregard.

"Do Re Mi Fah" was an ill-fated effort. It was the next story Fannie sent to Burton, and he turned it down immediately. He gave budgetary restraint and her high fee as his primary reasons this time but in the same letter asked her to consider writing a group of stories for him. If he bought "Do Re Mi," he explained, it would only clog up the story queue in the event that she took on the series. Again he caused confusion with his reply: "But don't run away from me" was his reassuring addendum. "This is *no* precedent."

Fannie saw this as the perfect opening to pitch her own idea for a group of stories to Burton. These were sketches more than stories actually and centered on the turn-of-the-century boardinghouse of a fictitious Mrs. Leland. They were to be narrated by Lora, her star boarder, who was a thinly disguised Fannie retelling actual episodes from her childhood with fictionalizing finesses. "Comedy, tragedy, defeat, success, hope, frustration, birth and death play their roles at Mrs. Leland's," Fannie explained to Burton, and it all unfolds as the American scene "moves in its artificial security toward the End of an Era."

The idea had bubbled up from the letters and reminiscences of old acquaintances and relatives, which Fannie had been collecting since 1935. This was when she started to toy with the idea of writing her memoirs. The first two stories, in fact, offer a perfect portrait of Fannie's parents—her complicated mother, her parents' complex relationship with each other, and her equally complicated love for them both. In passing she had mentioned the autobiography idea to Bill Briggs at Harpers; he in turn told the publisher. Cass Canfield was enthusiastic and wrote Fannie at once to urge her on. The reason was obvious: Who better than she to tell her own story? She had the unique perspective of someone with a fascinating personal history who also could interpret the social scene. In 1937 Fannie held Canfield off, telling him he would have to be patient. The idea was still in the "think-out-loud stage, no larger than a man's hand." For the moment she was quite content to let her memories take the more guarded form of new short fiction, safe stories about people long dead, stories that could be told without adverse repercussion, stories that pulsed with realism but that couldn't hurt anyone else.

Burton looked over the first Mrs. Leland story and then the second. The writing, he flattered, maintained "a high level of excellence—perhaps the best actual writing since *Lummox*." All the same he declined to buy the stories either individually or as a prospective group. As a reason he gave his reluctance to commit to a series with the magazine still operating under the Depression-imposed restraints of a smaller budget and fewer pages per issue. This rang particularly false since it was Burton who had proposed the idea of a series. The truth was, he had no interest in publishing wistful recollection. Burton wanted "dramatic newsiness" and a "sensational circulation angle," something that would grip young readers with its contemporary edge. A nostalgic romp through boardinghouse life at the turn of the nineteenth century was not what he had in mind.

His attitude also explains the long delay to publication of "Rhinestones Preferred." In January 1938, for example, the short stories *Cosmopolitan* published bore titles such as "Unto Us," by Adela Rogers St. Johns, described as "the miracle of Christmas and how it came to a couple who were desperately in love," and Alberta Hughes Wahl's "Everyone's Hungry in Hollywood," which bore the tag line "Lo—the poor screen star! She can't eat her cake and have *it* too." Fannie, for the first time in a quarter of a century of one of the most illustrious and profitable magazine fiction writing careers in the heyday of magazine fiction, was out of sync with the marketplace.

She tried "Do Re Mi Fah" out on *Pictorial Review,* whose editor Mabel Search had been courting her anxiously for some time. Fannie's query letter to Search exuded her usual confidence, despite the recent blows. "I am sufficiently ahead on commitments to my editors who are well supplied with serials, short stories and articles to hold them for the next little while, and I now have a short story to show you." As sincerely as Search wanted a Fannie Hurst byline over a story in *Pictorial* again, it was not going to be this one. "When a story makes an editor so unhappy that he can hardly finish it," she mused, "I wonder what it will do to readers? Frankly, I haven't the courage to find out. Will you forgive my cowardice and do something else for me soon?" Fannie didn't hold the rejection against Search, though; the two women soon became fast friends.

Fannie bypassed Burton on her next effort, "Play That Thing," and sent it directly to Search, who paid four thousand dollars for it. "I checked with Harry," she told Fannie, "and he said that was what he paid for your short stories." Actually, Search would have been wiser to check with George Bye, the literary agent with whom Fannie had just decided to sign on. With the souring of her relationship with *Cosmopolitan,* Fannie was going to need more new outlets than *Pictorial Review.* Bye could save her the discomfort of having to peddle her own work around town. He started inauspiciously with "Do Re Mi," which piled up nine more rejections on top of the two Fannie already had received for it. But he did better with the boardinghouse series, for which she would write five stories in all.

⌒

As if to signal that her career was coming full cycle, Bye sold the first two stories in the series to the *Saturday Evening Post,* the home of Fannie's first big break twenty-six years earlier. The downside of this nostalgia-laden transaction was that the *Post* would not pay more than three thousand dollars per story. It was quite a comedown; *Cosmopolitan* had been paying Fannie at the four-thousand-dollar rate since 1928—before Black Monday—and had continued paying it without complaint straight through the cash-poor decade that followed. The rest of the series commanded even less. *Woman's Home Companion* bought "Sunday Afternoon" for two thousand dollars, and the *Chicago Tribune* syndicate bought up the others for fifteen hundred apiece. To have sustained her high rate throughout the Depression and to have her work devalued just as the economy was turning around must have been a terrible embarrassment. Without Bye's help Fannie managed to slip two stories into *Good Housekeeping* but likely only because Mabel Search had moved on to a new job there and their friendship was very thick at the time.

Still, the fact was that the long, long reign of "one of the highest paid magazine contributors in the world's history" had come to an end. Bye and the frightening crush of world events helped ease Fannie's personal transition. Still, she began to manifest an oversensitivity to perceived slights. In March 1939, when *The New York Times* left her name off a list of speakers at a major rally on intolerance, Fannie had her cousin write a letter to the editor to complain. Fannie herself followed up with a letter to Arthur Hays Sulzberger claiming that the newspaper seemed to have been deliberately excluding her name from lists of "those present, those speaking, those participating, etc.," at major events in the city for at least two years. "This happens practically without exception, and since I am more or less active in the city picture, very frequently," she wrote. "Now I ask for no change of behaviorism [sic] on the part of your paper toward me. But if there is a reason for it, I do ask to know." Fannie was assured there was no deliberate attempt to omit her name, and indeed a review of the *Times's* pages for the years in question shows repeated, lengthy, prominent mention of Fannie's appearances and comments at a wide range of civic events.

Bye drummed up new outlets for her stories and articles—*Reader's Digest* was one of his personal favorites—and both her new stage of life and the war in Europe supplied the others. *This Week Magazine* of the *New York Herald Tribune* took an essay titled "I Wouldn't Go Back if I Could," in which Fannie surveyed her journey as a member of a generation that had straddled four worlds—"the pre–World War era, the World War era, the post–World War era and now Hitler's War era." Just before the 1940 general election, *Liberty* magazine gave her a platform to say why she thought Roosevelt deserved a third term in the midst of "This Urgent Now." For the piece she borrowed shamelessly from Democratic Party campaign literature, feeling the obligation to acknowledge this straight out to party leaders but not to *Liberty's* editors or readers. As she told the presidential campaign staff, she "felt the statements would be more forceful if I did not acknowledge their source."

She also—finally—took a stand, albeit wobbly, on allowing more refugees from the war in Europe into the United States, again for *Liberty*. She obscured her purpose in a thicket of elaborate metaphor and imprecision, presumably so as not to come down too hard on the administration's foot-dragging. But she urged all Americans to "help light the way for those outside in the wilderness of darkness, where men are fighting and grinding down one another into the muddy face of Europe." It was America's job, she said, "to guide and comfort the anguished hordes who are looking toward it. It is as if this house of the American family were almost the last frontier of hope for those war-ridden, driven, forgotten, and banished souls who look so pleadingly toward it." In a speech to the Flatbush Council for Religious Goodwill, she urged the nation to immunize itself against "the terrible mental, psychological and spiritual sickness" that had Europe in its grip. "We can close our port of entry to any type of citizen provided such an act lives up to our sacred tenets of the democratic way of social behavior toward our fellow human beings. What we cannot do, however, is to close our ports of entry to dangerous germs of thought, which can enter on the polluted, poisoned ether that blows across the Atlantic."

For *This Week* she marveled at how much of the history of humanity had been crammed into her own lifetime—nearly fifty-five years by this point, though she was just as happy to give readers the impression that she was closer to thirty-nine. She had traveled by horse and buggy and airplane and lived in homes lit by kerosene and electricity. She had seen ice cut out of lakes, bought from an iceman, and manufactured in her own kitchen. She had listened to music from boxes, phonographs, and radio and watched magic-lantern shows and movies. She had been warmed by open fires, base burners, hot-air furnaces, steam and electric heat, and cooled by palm-leaf fans, electric fans, and air-conditioning.

"Today a world, seemingly taxed to its limit of endurance, is confronted with crisis, bloodshed, emergency, insecurity, fear, jeopardy and terrorism in a manner without precedent in human affairs," she wrote. Yet that same world brought with it the opportunity, the "mental adventure," of trying to fix it. "We need not be filled with pity for the children to whom we are passing on this heritage," she said.

For all the world's problems, Fannie was happy to live out her destiny in times that allowed her to "fly through the clouds at sunrise" in the age of "x-ray, anesthesia, air conditioning, radio, clipper ships, dental hygiene, democracy and insulin." She liked living in a world that was "thinking about and doing something about the exploitation of human labor, social diseases, intolerance, housing, freedom of speech, civil liberties, cancer and man's inhumanity to man."

∽

Cosmopolitan had dealt Fannie a setback, but she bore no apparent grudge. Graciously, Burton's successor turned down another couple of short stories she offered, and she simply let Bye peddle them elsewhere. She did manage one more sale to *Cosmo* in this period, though it would be her last for the next twenty years. The new editor bought an essay from her in 1941, and without a reduction in her long-accustomed nonfiction rate of $750. That was certainly reaffirming. "Sweet Are the Uses of Maturity" was what she wanted to call it.

Still, there were signs of readjustment. It took her nearly four years to write *Lonely Parade,* the novel she had begun after "Bride of the Rajah" in 1938, but the period included both personal and public upheaval: the hysterectomy in the summer of 1940 and the unsettling developments on the national and global front as the United States prepared to enter World War II. At about the same time Fannie let it be known that she was finally hard at work on that long-planned autobiography. It was going to be "completely, absolutely, fearfully truthful," she promised. Expressions of interest came immediately from *Cosmopolitan,* the *Saturday Evening Post,* Fawcett publications, the Metro-Goldwyn-Mayer office in New York, and, of course, Harpers. Fannie told an interviewer she was going to expose all the "vulgarities" of her family history and did not really care what people thought of the approach. "I have a scalpel in my hand," she said. "Fortunately, I have no living relatives. I can speak out with absolute frankness and not hurt."

PART *4*

Preceding page: Harry Ransom Humanities Research Center

Chapter 29

Sam, Rose, and Edna

It was through her supposedly fictional account of life with teenage Lora in Mrs. Leland's boardinghouse that Fannie first venerated the memory of her parents. Lora's parents, Fred and Clara Kirk, are not easily distinguished from the Samuel and Rose Hurst who once lived at Mrs. *Cleveland's* boardinghouse with their own teenage daughter. And Fannie's tales of life with the Kirks read like anecdotes that could easily have been interchanged with those in the autobiography she began writing at about the same time. In fact, some of them were. There is no sugarcoating on the personality portraits in either format, and in both Fannie makes much of the deep affection in which she held her parents, in spite and because of their flaws.

The spur for both portraits came from recollections Fannie solicited from longtime acquaintances many years after the deaths of Sam and Rose. To his neighbors Sam was "big, dignified, silent," "so quiet," "so good to my blind husband . . . just a businessman and a gentleman . . . upright, gentle, but terribly strong in his convictions." To Fannie's friends he was "warm-hearted" with a "kindly smile" and a wife who harassed him into putting on his overshoes. By contrast, Rose glistened. "How many ways I think of her! What a character"; "she said such funny things"; "so interesting to talk to . . . wonderful descriptive powers . . . must have been very pretty . . . playing duets with her sister Bettie . . . delightful guest and hostess"; "unique in the real sense of the word. So fun-loving, so understanding, so big-hearted!"

As parents the Hursts were obsessively focused on Fannie in the manner of people fearful of loss. But this was not at the expense of their couplehood. As Fannie put it: "Mama and Papa, to be sure, had their private existence together, shutting me out in to an arctic loneliness when they retired to their bedroom at night, closing the door behind them." It was something that must truly have bothered her as a teenager, because in her autobiography she mentions her feelings about the door shutting three times. It also resonates with that recurring theme in her fiction: mothers and daughters in competition for the love of the same man. In Fannie's fiction, however, the man in question is never the father; her mothers are always widowed, separated, or divorced. And it is always the daughter who prevails.

Fannie described her mother as a woman who could walk into a room filled with women and douse them "like so many candles on a birthday cake," as a quick-witted "extrovert" in a community that had never heard the word. But Rose also harbored a temper as "fiery as lightning, terrible as thunder," that often left Fannie and her father "huddling and waiting for the storm to pass like a pair of wayfarers, our mute surrender to her fury serving only to increase the gale which could rage out of a trifling or fancied hurt, and a clear sky." Rose's pattern was to emerge from her outbursts as if they had not happened, turning instantly back into her warm and loving self. Fannie saw her as a " 'natural,' " a woman who wouldn't hesitate to issue forth with an "ain't." To Fannie's mind, she sparkled with "a wit both unique and exhilarating."

By reaction as much as in contrast, Fannie and her father shared the tendency to withdraw into themselves, Papa to a more extreme degree than Fannie. Neighbors remembered him walking home from work on a hot day waving a palm-leaf fan, white handkerchief tied around his neck, coat over his arm, and an umbrella in his hand. To Fannie, he was "soft as silk and as gentle to the touch." He rarely reached out for her to offer as much as a hug, and even in young childhood she held back as much as he did. To his own brother Henry in Memphis, Fannie described Sam after his death as "an extremely reticent man, undemonstrative and not given to retrospection." She could not remember him referring to his boyhood more than a half-dozen times. For that reason, and because her little family so naturally gravitated toward the more effusive Koppels, Fannie knew little of her paternal origins. She could remember the funeral of her grandfather Hurst, a grocer, and her grandmother as a "small, dynamic woman who handled her children . . . with vigorous authority," but almost nothing else. Even those family members who lived in St. Louis while she was growing up—her father's brother Benjamin for example—she mentions without comment, including them on a long list of those close to her and departed.

In the evenings at home, Fannie remembered her father changing from his double-breasted business coat into a black "seersucker," as if he found shirtsleeves too vulgar. She never once saw him in an undershirt. "I always felt that he must have been a thoughtful and studious lad," Fannie wrote to her uncle Henry in Memphis, "but if he ever had unrealized ambitions, I never heard of them." Though Sam's formal education did not extend beyond two years of high school, he gave off an air of sensitivity and refinement, his nose forever in a newspaper. "Knowledge is power" is what he liked to tell Fannie, over and over again. But he also had a rigid list of credos, in which he encased his family:

> Liberals and Socialists were anarchists.
> The theater was Bacchante in pink tights. Artists, long-haired depraved
>   Bohemians.
> Russian Jews were "kikes."
> Negroes, all right in their place.

Keep our national nose out of international affairs.
See America first and, possibly, only.
Foreigners beat their wives and wear small collar sizes.
Modesty is a girl's finest raiment.

In fiction Fannie's alter ego, Lora Kirk, described her parents like this:

> Pretty nearly everybody adored, and after a certain manner, feared Mamma. Except me. Her sharp tongue sometimes hurt, but never left a scar. Even though I was off the piece of my father's nature of measured restraint, I understood the volatile quality of Mamma's too well to fear it. From the day I was old enough to appraise her with what I guess was nothing more than my intuition, her immense maternity, blind as a bat and warm as heaven, enfolded me like some sort of celestial eiderdown, secure and without weight.

Rose Koppel was nineteen and ripe to marry when she went to St. Louis to visit her "rich relatives" and met the thirty-two-year-old Samuel Hurst, soon to become the mate she would badger, henpeck, and stand fiercely beside until the day he died. Though the Koppels were from Hamilton, Ohio, and the Hursts from Memphis by way of Simpson County, and then North Hillsboro in Scott County, Mississippi, the two families had much in common from the standpoint of background. Both were highly assimilated ethnic German Jews—Sam's father actually was born in France—who arrived in the United States before the Civil War. Though Rose and Sam would prove to be absolute opposites in temperament and style, their match was a good one on paper. Their brief courtship climaxed in a wedding ceremony at Rose's home on Central Avenue in Hamilton on January 11, 1885, with Rose dressed in "an elegant traveling suit with diamond ornaments and the groom in conventional black." The Reverend Rudolph Pollock of Hamilton's small reform Jewish temple officiated. Toting what the local newspaper described as their many expensive presents, the newlyweds left immediately for St. Louis, where Sam and one of his three brothers, Benjamin, had started a canning business. There was financial promise, but money was extremely tight.

Fannie must have been conceived on Rose and Sam's wedding night, because she was born nine months and ten days later, forty weeks to the day. Actually, Rose had named her daughter Fanye; the anglicization was not supplied until Fannie started school.

Clearly, Rose's pregnancy had not been planned. Fannie learned this fact by chance one day when she overheard Rose telling a friend how devastated the news had left her. She and Sam were still virtual strangers, after all, unprepared both emotionally and financially to start a family. Even so, Rose was pregnant again eleven months after Fannie's birth.

Back in Hamilton there was great anticipation of the first Koppel grandchild. It made sense for Rose to choose Hamilton for Fannie's birthplace, isolated as she was in St. Louis from the comfort of her large and boisterous family. It would remain an important part of Fannie's self-story that she and her mother had been born in the same bed—she twenty years later, on October 19, 1885. At the time Rose's parents—David, a successful cattle dealer in his fifties, and Caroline, her quiet, unsmiling mother—were both alive. Fannie remembered her grandmother as "a spare, mirthless woman . . . lusterless as her husband was gusty, she mended, baked, scrubbed, laundered, reddened the brick sidewalk, did menial work in the chicken house and nurtured an angry kind of self-pity because of overwork which Grandpa, like Papa, neither encouraged nor desired." Grandpa, by contrast, was "roaring, vulgar, packed with native wit, unlettered, high-minded, foul-spoken, generous."

All of Rose's siblings—she was the second of three daughters—were living at home when Fannie was born. Her sisters, Bettie and Jennie, were there to fuss over Rose and the baby, and Rose's brothers, Charles, Abraham, Gustav, and twelve-year-old Kaufman, better known as Kutty, eagerly welcomed their first niece. Rose was the only one of the Koppel children to have married by this point, so in those early years it would fall to Fannie and the little sister named Edna, born a year and a half after Fannie, to be everybody's babies. As it happened—and this was not for several years—Abe was the only other Koppel sibling to produce an offspring.

Despite her initial misgivings Rose took to mothering with ferocity. "I may not have been wanted," Fannie later reflected, "but, once arrived, love, security and more were my portion." Surely this was true for little Edna, too.

Fannie gives a scant four pages of her autobiography to the story of the little sister who died of diphtheria in July 1891 at the age of four. Fannie could recall what she looked like because of a studio photograph of the two of them that her mother kept. It highlights Edna's small-boned frame against Fannie's larger, fleshier one, and Edna's sweet, heart-shaped face against the rounded fullness of Fannie's. Fannie acknowledged that the child who, "like a butterfly, alighted in our house for a brief four years" had a strange effect on her life, not admirable. Years later Lillian Becker, a childhood friend of Rose's, could still remember the visits of the two little girls to Hamilton each summer and how angelic a creature Edna had been—"not only lovely to look upon but lovely in manner—we all adored her." Fannie, because she was more bashful and reticent than Edna, got less attention. Lillian surmised that "probably this caused a little jealousy," because she could remember Fannie pinching or slapping Edna whenever Fannie felt provoked and thought she could get away with it.

The events surrounding Edna's fatal illness were harrowing for her five-year-old sister, to whom little was told. The extent of the impact on her parents can only be surmised. Fannie could remember the doctor coming and going from the house and being barred from the bedroom that she and Edna shared. She remembered being sent away to stay with elderly family friends in their apartment above a grocery store. Though Rose and Sam would stop by to see Fannie every couple of days, fearing the risk of infecting her, too, they never came inside. Instead, they would call to her in an upstairs window from the sidewalk below.

"Mama always cried and said Edna was a very sick child and that I was her life and it was terrible to be away from me," Fannie wrote of those strange, confusing days. " 'Sweetheart,' papa called up to me, using one of his rare endearing terms, 'be good and say your prayers for Edna'; and then he too cried and held Mama's hand, and I stood at the window, silent but with a tight feeling and remorse for all the times I had taken things away from Edna and secretly drunk her condensed milk."

After the death Sam, looking big and helpless, and Rose, draining tears, brought Fannie back to the darkened house still fragrant with the scent of roses. No one mentioned what had happened. Fannie asked no questions. Upstairs in the room where the two girls had slept, every trace of Edna had been removed, except for her rocking chair and two dolls seated upright upon it.

Among Fannie's papers the photograph of the two sweet Hurst girls remains. Shirtless, they stand cheek to cheek, with Edna a bit in front of Fannie, each angled slightly toward the camera. In a second print of the photograph, there is only Fannie's image and an airbrushed space where Edna stood, her only vestige a disembodied shoulder, superimposed on Fannie's chest like a tiny phantom.

Fannie remembered her mother up at dawn, scraping the quarantine sign off the front door. She remembered her mother's eyes filling with tears for years whenever Edna's name came up. Sam nursed his grief even harder and longer. Did he love Fannie that much, too?

Fannie never asked out loud the questions that haunted her in the aftermath: Had Edna been their parents' favorite? Would they have rather Fannie died instead? Would Edna have turned out prettier? Smarter? Was Fannie sorry to be left an only child? Or glad?

Though Rose's tendency to overindulge and overprotect Fannie got even more pronounced after Edna's death, she still adamantly opposed Fannie's longing for a pet. One day Fannie enraged Rose by bringing home a kitten. Rose gestured violently to keep the stray off her sofa, frightening the little creature so that it shot down the back stairs in search of refuge. It would be several days before a handyman found the kitten dead in the basement rafters. Little wonder that when Rose finally broke down years later and let her daughter have a dog, Fannie named it Fury.

Rose cried over the kitten she had scared to death that day, but for Fannie the episode caused weeks of abject misery. She said it also taught her "something secret and, I supposed, rather terrible" about herself. Later she confessed, "The kitten hurt worse than the dying of a little girl named Edna."

"The snags of circumlocution"

Despite Fannie's pledge to write a frank and tell-all account of her life, the disingenuousness crept in. She had been reinforcing her widely disseminated public story for a good twenty-five years by the time she sat down to put her autobiography on paper; it was far too late to start contradicting it. How then to honor her pledge of forthrightness? Fannie resorted to what she called "the snags of circumlocution which autobiography so often imposes." The result was the subversion of an otherwise straightforward reflection on her life and times.

The issues presented themselves on several fronts. Fannie's long-standing desire to appear younger than her years caused one set of complications. She was approaching fifty-five when the idea for an autobiography started to attract her, and by then the four or five years she had been slicing off her actual age since young adulthood she sometimes stretched to ten or more. To maintain this younger facade, which she felt was important professionally, Fannie armed her narrative with a rather poetic disclaimer: "With no notes to guide me, not a scrap of diary to refresh me, my chronology wide open to challenge, the memories spill as if from a cornucopia of time."

She also obscured any too-obvious parallels between events in her life and identifying moments of national significance for which the dates were too well etched in collective memory. Thus, for example, she made it a point to station major occurrences of the first or second decade of the century alongside defining moments in her own life that occurred as much as ten, even twenty years later. She left the World Exposition of 1904 out entirely. Fannie would have been nearly nineteen when St. Louis hosted the World's Fair. It is nearly unimaginable that the fair was not part of her experience, falling just as she was about to graduate from high school. Perhaps it seemed wiser to omit reference to it than to try to explain how she happened to be old enough to have enjoyed it at such an early point in the century.

As for St. Louis itself, Fannie described it as a place both snug and smug while she was growing up, watching it compete vainly with Chicago for preeminence as the "Gateway to the West." Fannie thought of her hometown as an island of "stability and conservatism," an outgrowth of its early French and German settlement, into which her father, with his "capacity for monotony," fit "like a round peg in a round hole." To explain how the city managed to remain so insulated and parochial, Fannie reminded her readers that "radio and television were not yet common methods of communication." The only flaw in that logic was that for the years in question, 1885 to 1909, neither medium yet existed, at least not for household use.

Fannie also did a little tap dance around World War I. Keeping up her personal age ruse required giving the impression that she had been young and single when the United States entered the war in 1917. Actually, she was thirty-two and already married to Jack. Her tack was to position Jack as a love interest caught in Europe by the crisis while on tour with his mentor, Rafael Joseffy. The caught-in-Europe story actually might have been true, except Joseffy was already dead at the time. Jacques, for his part, was still a Russian national in 1917, over forty years of age and living in the apartment on West Sixty-ninth Street just above Fannie's, teaching piano from his studios at Carnegie and Steinway Hall, which she shared with him for a time.

Other snags: In literally hundreds of interviews over the years, Fannie insisted that beyond the point of a snapshot of inspiration, she almost never drew her characters from real life. The fib should not have posed difficulties for the memoirs, but it did in the case of one character whose inspiration Fannie must have thought it inappropriate to share. This was her uncle Kaufman's wife. Fannie adoringly described the woman she called Aunt Selene as a stylish, chic, fun-loving department store buyer who endured the abiding disapproval of her sisters-in-law because of a lingering girlhood reputation for being "fast." It turns out the aunt's name really was Ray, just like that of the heroine of *Back Street* she seemed so strikingly to resemble.

Stef also got a pseudonym. Though the name Vilhjalmur Stefansson appears benignly on a list of friends, male and female, he also appears in the guise of Hugh MacDonald, an ardent suitor who had vied for Fannie's affections but as mentioned previously, at a time well before her marriage. The dodge saved her the awkwardness of having to explain how, in spite of a prolonged extramarital love affair, she could consider her "Fannie Hurst marriage" such a total and blissful success. It also protected her moral standing along with her well-kept secret. More to the point, it provided a way for Fannie to confess in a style of full disclosure while she actually disclosed nothing. References to Stef are couched, camouflaged, and scattered throughout the narrative in a way that makes them nearly impossible to pinpoint or follow without prior knowledge of the actual circumstances. So artfully did Fannie place her decoys that Stef's widow did not recognize the references to him on first reading, even though she was well aware of the long-standing liaison, which had predated her marriage.

Fannie's subterfuge solved the problem of any possible censure from her public, though at one point in the narrative she got so bold as to declare that "three quiet and memorable men, Papa, Jack, and one whom I shall not mention, stood at my elbow." The statement appears in the text at a considerable remove from any discussion of Hugh. Fannie leaves her reader ignorant of her actual situation all those years, but she gives a vivid sense of her ambivalence and how she reconciled these simultaneous commitments in her own mind.

Jack, of course, was too intimately involved with the actual chronology of Fannie's life to be fooled by her typed acrobatics, and she would never have hurt him intentionally at this point in their lives together. This is as good an explanation as any for why, though she worked on the manuscript between 1938 and 1945, she did not complete it until well into the 1950s. By then

Jack, too, had joined the ranks of family members whom her words, thoughts, and past actions could no longer hurt.

"Boardinghouse trash"

One other snag in the autobiography needed clipping. Fannie's well-worn success story had portrayed her as the girl who broke free from an excruciatingly ordinary, prosperous, and stable middle-class background to create her own destiny. "Barring a few sporadic ups and downs in Papa's business life," she finally wrote, "my childhood was spent in middle-class well-being, nice home, and after I had begun my teens and Papa's factory prospered we moved from better house to better house to better house, from Morgan Street to West Belle Place to Cates Avenue." In the memoirs she does acknowledge a two-year boardinghouse stint at Mrs. Cleveland's but then explains it away as an economic move necessitated by a serious but temporary reverse in Sam's otherwise successful business. The family simply needed to scale back expenses so that Sam could pay off his creditors instead of declaring bankruptcy. In Fannie's published version the Hursts rented out their family home for that period, then returned to it as soon as the crisis passed. The problem with this explanation is that there was no family home to which the Hursts could have returned. Sam and Rose, like Fannie after them, never owned any place they lived. In fact, not only were the Hursts renters but by the time Fannie turned fifteen they had changed addresses at least ten times.

Under cover of fiction in the Mrs. Leland short stories, Fannie explains the Kirk family's situation with more candor. Though many of the identifying details clearly stem from fact, she changed her father's second business venture from shoes to buttons and put the home from which the Kirks had to retreat on one of St. Louis's most elegant avenues. Even in the best of times the Hursts never had a home address as lofty as that of the fictional Kirks:

> During the period of my childhood, storms aplenty assailed our little family of three. Business collapse, the result of panic years, which drove my father from the canning industry into the button business, and which had necessitated our removal from our own private home on pretty Westminster Place to Mrs. Leland's Boarding House, had hit us broadside.
>
> But through it all, the even keel of my existence had never shown tremor. I remained the most overdressed small girl in school. I continued to have a fancy purse full of pocket-money. I attended Mr. Mahler's dancing school.

Though neighbors and friends bear out Fannie's report of beautiful clothes, loving parents, and ample money to spend, the family's frequent moves in those first fifteen years were not always "from better address to better address." Not one but at least three of those addresses were boardinghouses. In addition, for a period of about a year—not long after Edna's death—the family either went into hibernation or disappeared from St. Louis entirely. Fannie entered the first grade at Stoddard School in the fall of 1892 but transferred out after twenty days. She does not appear on the enrollment register of Stoddard or any other school in the district for the rest of that year or for the next. She returned to Stoddard in the fall of 1894, but her record shows no local public school attended in between. She remained at Stoddard through eighth grade, graduating with her class, but in that six-year period both the city directory and Fannie's school records list six more home addresses for Samuel Hurst.

The city directories also indicate that Sam's business difficulties were of a much more sustained nature than Fannie wanted her public to believe. The Hurst Packing Company that Sam started with his brother failed around 1890—after five years in operation. Subsequent to that Sam is listed as a manager or clerk of two other canning concerns, then in 1894 (this would be the directory compiled in 1893, while Fannie's name does not appear on a local school registry) Sam's name does not appear in the directory at all. By 1895, when Fannie was ten years old, Sam takes his place as secretary, and later president, of the Standard Heel and Counter Company. This is the shoe-manufacturing firm that eventually prospered, but not before Rose and Fannie were subjected to yet another boardinghouse stint.

For an only child, the boardinghouse experience opened up whole new universes. Fannie had live-in playmates, including older, more experienced girls who shared their titillating confidences; a boy to be stuck on, even if he returned the compliment by calling her "Fatty Show-off"; and Mr. Cleveland, the retired professor who spent most of his time in his basement study while his wife slaved away for her boarders.

However adventurous these periodic forays into cooperative living were for Fannie, they were horrid for Rose. She made the best of it, hosting card games and kaffeeklatsches for her fellow boarders, but she never stopped complaining to Sam. What kind of a man would put his creditors before his family? "Both Papa and I realized that Mama's barbs came at you with speed," Fannie explained, "but, like theatrical rapiers, were made of rubber."

In Fannie's Mrs. Leland series, the Kirks, like the Hursts, get extra closet space in the boardinghouse and special consideration at every turn. In the memoirs Fannie reports that her mother demanded milk, bread, butter, and applesauce for her after-school snack each day, and extra towels and a daily breakfast of three eggs and grits for Sam. To the annoyance of the other boarders, special dishes always seemed to find their way to the Hursts' table, not to mention a better quality of ketchup and coffee, specially brewed. With Mrs. Cleveland's permission, Rose usurped a common hall closet for her private stock of foodstuffs, and in both the fiction and nonfiction versions it was Rose who inevitably bailed the beleaguered Mrs. Cleveland/Leland when out she ran short of money to pay her bills. Both versions also describe at length Mr. Cleveland/Leland, the former college professor whose underground study ignited Fannie's fascination with literature:

> It was in Mr. Cleveland's dark cave that I first encountered the name Plutarch, whose chief virtue according to Mr. Cleveland was that he had never heard of Christianity. From those same shelves Lecky's *History of European Morals* and Gibbon's *Decline and Fall of the Roman Empire* soared above my head like skyscrapers, with me absorbed and scarcely able to get my feet off the ground floor. Novels were there too, which Mr. Cleveland allowed me to carry up to our room. *David Copperfield, Père Goriot, The Scarlet Letter.* Norse mythology in the form of a huge book, *Twilight Tales,* which had been removed from the kitchen chair to make room for me. I thought the title *Anatomy of Melancholy* the most wonderful brace of words I had ever heard. Mr. Cleveland read me parts of it, translated the many Latin phrases, and explained Robert Burton's analyses of love and art, tearing to shreds his ideas on religion. Benjamin Franklin's *Autobiography* was there, unexpurgated, which I drank in while Mama still spoke such words as pregnant and prostitute in German in my presence.

In one of Fannie's Mrs. Leland stories, titled "Mamma and Her First National Bank," Lora's father comes home from the factory distraught with news that a valued employee, age sixty-two, has gotten his hand caught in one of the machines and will have to stop working. "Look here, Fred," Lora's mother says, "there are limits to everything. If you think more of the Sanbornes than you do of your own family, you take yourself over to the South Side to them. I'm as sorry as the next over what has happened, but after all, the Sanbornes aren't kin and you're covered by accident insurance . . . the man has got insurance doctors to take care of him, and there's many a poor devil gets hurt and nobody to pay his sick leave." Papa explains that Sanborne was trying to hold on long enough to pay off his little home. These are fighting words to Mamma Kirk. "All I'm good enough for is to bear the brunt when you come home upset over a man whose family live better than yours does! . . . If you'd come home some night, Fred, sick to your stomach over your own family, instead of your factory hands, I'd say you had reason!" And on and on.

The story ends with the Kirks calling on the Sanbornes, only to learn that because of the accident Sanborne's daughter will have to postpone her already long-delayed plans to marry. At that Mamma absents herself from the group. Privately, she bends down and reaches up under her dress to her "First National Bank" deposited inside the top of her stocking. Quietly she slips a wad of money to Sanborne's daughter, telling her not to let her father's accident stand in the way of her future. In a separate gesture, Papa discreetly hands money to Sanborne's wife. And then all the way home Mamma complains to Papa that he cares more for his workers than he does for his own blood.

"What a woman," Fannie sighed, recalling the way her mother could spread both warmth and chill. "Naughty, difficult, darling" were the adjectives that came to mind. "I yearn for the power to write her in full dimension," Fannie said, "but my pen clogs."

By the time the Hursts moved out of Mrs. Cleveland's and down the block to an attached seven-room house they shared with Sam's brother and his wife, Fannie was sixteen. It was not until her third year of university that they could afford the house on Cates Avenue in the Cabanne district, one of the city's more fashionable residential areas. It was this house that Fannie later wrote about most vividly, endeavoring to give the impression that it was where she grew up.

Though Fannie felt the need to play down the highly transient aspects of her childhood, her boardinghouse experience was clearly central to her imagination. It created the backdrop for dozens of her early stories, as well as the Mrs. Leland series. And however annoyed Rose may have been about having to live in "family hotels," she put the best possible face on her situation for family and friends back in Hamilton. One reported later to Fannie that Rose had told her that boarding was "quite the fashionable thing to do." Lillian Becker had no reason to doubt Rose, but, she and other friends liked to tease her anyway, jokingly referring to the Hursts as "boardinghouse trash."

From Fannie's own description, there does not appear to have been anything fashionable about Mrs. Cleveland's "gloomy hall" that led to the "second floor front and alcove" inside "two shabby red brick residences joined by a bridge" on a street that had seen "better days, its one-time fine residences converted into piano showrooms or boarding houses." The serving staff consisted of "old black Kate," the one-eyed cook, a tall, good-looking waiter who slept on a cot behind the furnace, and the maid with the razor-scarred face.

Lillian Becker's good-natured teasing in Hamilton each summer must have cut a little deeper than any of Rose's old friends knew.

Chapter *30*

"Summer palace"

In the neighborhood Fannie was remembered as a "little role-poly school girl" with two "long fat braids" who craved books and dill pickles and rode her bike to school. Stoddard, at the corner of Lucas and Ewing Avenues, was one of the largest elementary schools in the district. At twenty-five rooms it was overcrowded and impersonal in Fannie's recollection, and although outstanding students managed to be singled out for special attention, Fannie was not among them.

With all the moving around the Hursts did, it was natural for Fannie to consider Grandfather Koppel's house in Hamilton a haven, her "summer palace." Every year as soon as school was out, she and Rose packed up two enormous trunks, a wardrobe, and a flat, and boarded the train east. Fannie's finery took up most of the space. Rose could not bring enough clothes in which to parade her little Fannie at the kaffeeklatsches sure to be held in honor of the annual homecoming.

Fannie liked everything about Hamilton. For one thing, it was a place where she did not have to worry about being fat. ("How much do you think she weighs," Grandpa proudly asked his friends as he trotted Fannie out to the town's two taverns so that their "beer-smelling, tobacco-stained denizens" could admire her. "She's a good one, not?" Fannie remembered him saying, adding the comment, "I was a good one in Hamilton.") For another, her aunts and uncles allowed her to have pets—even such exotica as goats, rabbits, and ponies. More than half a lifetime later, Fannie still could savor the tastes and smells of Hamilton, the market wagons piled high with produce, "live fowls, fresh country butter wrapped in cheesecloth, watermelons that you plugged before purchasing." How fine were her memories of afternoons spent roaming meadows and pastures, the acrid smells of "heat into vegetation, weeds and cow droppings. The sounds of bell-sheep, of frogs plopping into the creek, cattle lowing in a motionless scene, and that throat-catching whistle of a distant train." She could still taste the dill pickles, peaches, and tomato preserves she used to sneak from her grandmother's cellar.

Sam always joined his wife and daughter for a shorter visit later on in the summer, though his stiff formality had a way of altering the atmosphere, as if someone had removed a whistling kettle from the stove. The house got a new hush. Fannie's aunts abandoned their household "wrappers" in favor of proper day dresses. Sam would try to ease the tension he inadvertently created by joking, but it was really no use. "Persiflage," Fannie said, "sat on Papa like a ton of coal."

Even after Grandma Koppel's death when Fannie was eleven, the atmosphere of the household stayed the same. Bettie, Fannie's spinster aunt, replaced her mother as woman in charge and managed the place so effectively that Grandma was hardly missed. Fannie's *jolie-laide* Aunt Jennie also remained in the Central Avenue house after her marriage to Joseph Levy, a handsome and successful businessman. To please his wife (Fannie said Aunt Jennie was so plain she fascinated), Uncle Joe commuted twenty-five miles to Cincinnati for work each day. As for Fannie's uncles, Gus never married and was "quite a beau, chiefly among farmer maids," Fannie said. "You could trace his course by [following the] odor of bay rum with which he doused himself. But even then it did not quite cover up the strong effusions of Grandpa's cattle." Uncle Charley, she said, was "urban and urbane"; Uncle Kaufman, "sporty"; and Uncle Abe, as "stormy looking as a young Beethoven, of no earning capacity and with an immense fascination for women." Abe had married Rose Kahn but was divorced after the birth of their daughter, Ruth, Fannie's only first cousin on her mother's side. The Koppel house rang with German and Grandpa's broken English. "Lazy louses!" he would roar disapprovingly at his stalwart sons.

"We were bourgeois through and through," Fannie said, "and the bourgeois in me must have responded. I like the coarse texture of life at my grandfather's. Even while I was already rebelling against the fate of having been thrust into a world so alien to my yearnings, I felt at home there."

Back in St. Louis, Fannie's friends remembered her as "jolly, genial, unpretentious," despite Rose's propensity to dress her for ostentation. In early adolescence, she slept in a teeth-straightening device that the former Rosa Lee Einhorn remembered as a "baseball mask, Sir Galahad contraption." The Einhorns also lived in the boardinghouse with the Hursts, and the two girls would often sleep together on Saturday nights when their parents went to bridge club. Rosa Lee said she stayed with Fannie because Fannie was afraid to stay alone or, more likely, because Rose was afraid for Fannie to stay alone.

Along with piano lessons ("Fannie, practice!" was Rose's constant cry), Fannie endured the mortification of a ballroom dancing course at Mr. Mahler's. It was hard always to be the last, or next-to-the-last girl chosen to dance. Once Mr. Mahler had to offer to be her partner when no one else came forward, and then deepened the humiliation by marveling out loud to the rest of the class at how light she was on her feet. It was as backhanded a compliment as she ever received. Rose arranged for elocution lessons, taught by a three-named teacher "of Aubrey Beardsley slenderness, thyroidic eyes and many scarves." From her Fannie learned voice placement and a rendition of "The Rosary" to music. "She stoutly insisted that I was exceptional," Fannie later reported, adding in dead-pan: "Mama paid her one dollar an hour."

Still, the Hurst household could not have been more humdrum. "There was little talk to which a child could listen to her cultural advantage," Fannie said. "No one ever read a book or attended a lecture or a concert, although come evenings, while waiting for Papa, Mama in her crisp 'dressing sacque' would seat herself at the upright piano in our reception hall and render—yes, 'render' is the word for it—her repertoire, tried and true." Fannie went on:

> I would sit on the stairs and let the tunes infiltrate while Mama pounded at the keyboard, the bisque girl and boy on top of the piano rattled, and the odors of pot roast and German fried potatoes drifted into the sounds; and fantasy had its way with me: I visualized myself as beautiful, slender, and desired. Older men were in love with me. My essays were read at teachers' meetings as the finest that had ever been done. I was voted the most popular girl in the school . . . teachers singled me out . . . my dance program was the first one filled.

One day a chain of girls walked in the school yard at recess and one thought to ask each of them to shout out her religion. "Instantly," Fannie said, "the line took it up like a singing regiment. Left foot, right foot, each girl snapping in turn: Lutheran. Catholic. Baptist. Lutheran. Presbyterian. The exception was the girl at the far end. Me." When Fannie opened her mouth to speak, no sound came out, and in the silence that followed, she loosened her arm from that of the girl next to her and stood aside. "Suddenly," she said, "I had become different."

That night she asked her parents what being Jewish meant. "It was difficult to be what no one else was, even though it was never talked about," Fannie explained in her memoirs. This was a family that never observed a holiday—not Thanksgiving or even birthdays—and never went to temple. Sam suggested that perhaps the time had come to join a congregation and send Fannie to Sunday school, but Rose objected for her own reasons: "I don't intend to join the temple and be stuck in the back pew so I can see my rich relatives up front. Besides, aren't you the one who always says you can say your prayers as well at home as in temple?"

Sam, who was about as ignorant as Fannie on the subject, encouraged her to check out books about Judaism from the library. All he knew, he told her, was that being Jewish was both a race and a religion and that she should be proud of both. But she wasn't.

The feelings came back again when Rose decided Fannie should have a private school education for high school and enrolled her in a school Fannie identified as Harperly Hall. No school by that name ever existed in St. Louis, but there was a day and boarding school for girls at the time called Hosmer Hall, housed in a beautiful West End mansion on Washington Avenue. Its college preparatory program was of such caliber that a Hosmer certificate guaranteed admission to Wellesley, Smith, Vassar, Mount Holyoke, Chicago University, and the University of Michigan. The Mary Institute, however, was the local private girls' school with greater prestige.

When Fannie applied for admission, she and Rose went to meet the head-mistress, who reviewed a list of standard application questions with them. Name. Address. Age. Grandparents' names and places of birth. When she asked about "religion," Rose replied "as if she were biting off a thread." On hearing the word *Jewish,* Fannie was sure she saw the principal's pen pause in midstroke. Rose smelled prejudice but still paid the sixty-five dollars first-term tuition when Fannie's letter of acceptance arrived and registered her for the ninth-grade class that fall.

"It proved a heartbreaking experience of short duration," Fannie said. "From the beginning, my separateness from the Harperly girls, even though it had nothing to do with creed, asserted itself."

To start with, Fannie had little in common with these girls from "good" St. Louis families, and her own self-conscious aloofness didn't help to bridge any gulfs. These girls did not go to Mr. Mahler's for dancing lessons but got their coaching in the private ballroom of the home of one of the girls. They did not spend summers at their grandparents' in Hamilton but vacationed in a short list of tony resort towns. They probably wouldn't have understood a childhood of Saturday nights with Rosa Lee in the alcove of the second-floor front.

Fannie's choice of clothing did nothing to help her blend in. In contrast to the plain choice of dress these girls favored, Rose had Fannie outfitted, even on her first day, in a plaid skirt that was ruffled to the waist and an enormous hair-bow of the same plaid accenting her high pompadour. She had patent-leather shoes with plaid tops to round out the ensemble.

Both Fannie's experience at Mr. Mahler's and her first term at private school exacerbated in her a feeling of separation. The major frustration of her youth—"feeling out of the herd"—bore in deeply. Every given of her life became prob-lematic. She was fat and everyone else was thin. She was an only child and all the other girls had siblings. She was Jewish and . . .

It was not long before Fannie and Rose agreed that private school had been a mistake. In January 1901 Fannie enrolled one term late at what was St. Louis's only white public high school at the time, Central High.

Central High

The poet Orrick Johns was a schoolmate of Fannie's. He remembered Central High School as a place that brought all the burgher and professional classes of St. Louis together, along with some children of working men. From the north, south, and west ends of the city they gathered in that

Victorian pile on Grand Avenue—fourteen hundred Germans, French, Jews, and descendants of the old South. Among the teachers only the assistant principal, Will Schuyler, stood out. As for the rest there were "no peaks and no depths," in Johns's view, the only objective of this faculty being "to make the average American, Western style, according to a local image long recognizable."

Both Fannie and Johns, in their respective memoirs, honored the special place that Schuyler had occupied in each of their lives. Fannie got to know him by being sent to his office one day for punishment. She found "a slightly built man, humorous and grave," who never referred to her infraction and barely looked at her file. Instead he spent two hours with her, wanting to know about her and her family. He showed her his collection of handmade little clay animals. Framed poems and quotations covered his office walls—a far cry from the wall decor at her home on West Belle Place. "People who seemed to live on another plane from us were strangely depressing," Fannie said years later. "Here was someone with framed poetry on his walls and Mama's laundress stole soap." Although Schuyler was in his sixties at the time with three grown children, he was Fannie's first major high school crush.

Throughout her years at Central, Fannie talked with Schuyler as she had never talked to anyone else. Of course this did not include any revelations about how fat she felt or how lonely when her parents shut their door at night. She certainly did not mention her humiliations where boys were concerned, nor her revulsion at the thought of anything sexual—an aversion that took her years to overcome. But she did talk to him about other, less revelatory confusions and her unguided adventures into reading, which had taken her into either "shallow literary waters or those beyond my depth."

Fannie's parents found the subject of sex impossible to broach, so Rose came up with the idea of having a slightly older neighbor girl bring Fannie out of the "rigid and ashamed silence" that seemed always to cloak such matters in those days. What Rose had not anticipated was that "Mama's harbinger of the facts of life" would come at Fannie "with the vocabulary of the abattoir, conditioning [her] with a kind of revulsion against most physical manifestations, including those of persons indisposed or ill."

Back at school Will Schuyler encouraged Fannie's writing. Later he followed her career with great interest. "Do you remember you asked me to let you out of school early one Christmas Eve—'to keep you out of mischief?'" he reminded her eight years after graduation, after her New York career had taken off. "And how I didn't let you go but occupied you in writing for me a Christmas story? I saw your capabilities then—what you are doing today is but their natural development but what you will do tomorrow must be much greater—don't rest satisfied with present achievement—you have power for finer things than any you have yet published."

Despite the mediocrity of the rest of Central's teachers, Fannie's greatest preoccupation during high school was figuring out how to get their attention. Classes were huge. Teachers called on pupils impersonally from a stack of cards on which a grade was marked each time they recited, and those marks would be tallied up twice a year to produce the term report. A teacher in whose presence a student might sit five hours a week could pass her on the street without a glint of recognition. Central High School made Fannie feel "as anonymous as a prisoner behind his number."

"No matter how I strove, chiefly without study but by what I considered personality, I seemed unable to arouse interest, except in the form of an occasional rebuke for violation of a rule or careless preparation of an assigned lesson." Though she did well enough in English and history classes, she failed her French exams twice, Latin and chemistry once, and got an "incomplete" for her Spanish and geometry reviews. Clearly scholarship was not going to be Fannie's ticket to recognition, so she joined Rose on her legendary shopping sprees, hoping to find another way to make her presence felt. Red shoes? Won't they get too scuffed at school? How about a red dress to match? Classmates years later could still picture Fannie bobbing down the halls of Central under a massive pompadour and a bow of multiple loops of taffeta standing six or eight inches high instead of the standard two that all the other girls seemed to favor.

This need to draw attention to herself did not diminish her popularity. Friends saw in Fannie a good and fun-loving nature, a sense of humor, and an "understanding of and kindness to those who were not so fortunate." They also found her sincere and deep, provocative and endearing, along with "a lot of other superb qualities." Fannie's fame and literary success notwithstanding, she was sure to be the best remembered of the class at any reunion.

Fannie was a strong but not particularly passionate athlete. She played girls' basketball for Central and was "probably the best forward the team ever had." It was Fannie who had the ability to keep the girls together when tempers would fly, and in recognition of this talent teammates elected her their captain. She also later became president of the girls' athletic association. She played on the tennis team, often practicing with her friends at 5:30 in the morning (even then her vitality was dazzling), then raiding a nearby vegetable patch for snacks.

Though Olna Hudler would become her best friend at Washington University, Frances Windhorst and she were inseparable while all three were classmates at Central. Others referred to Fannie and "Frank" as "the heavenly twins." It was not the calla lily, the signature flower of Fannie's later years, but a huge chrysanthemum that each of them would pin on her left shoulder every school day from the first day of mum season to the last.

Sometimes they liked to pull pranks. When visitors from Boston sat in on an English class, Fannie and Frank had secretly placed on the head of a bust of Shakespeare a red velvet hat at a very jaunty angle. This horrified the teacher, but she never managed to identify the culprits.

When another English teacher assigned the class to write original stories,

Fannie offered to compose them for her friends in exchange for chemistry homework. Even then her writing style was distinctive; the teacher immediately recognized it and scrawled across each paper, "Written by Fannie Hurst." Fannie's recollection was that her punishment was a refusal to allow her to deliver one of the commencement addresses, though this seems doubtful, since her transcript shows she took chemistry in her sophomore year. It may have been another of her envious recollections, since both Frank and Olna appear on the program reading their graduation essays, while Fannie had no role in the ceremony at all. Frank recalled the ghostwriting incident and remembered that Fannie had to "pay the piper," but she did not record what the punishment had been.

The West Belle Place neighborhood of Fannie's high school and early college years was full of teenagers whose idea of fun was climbing up and down the fancy surreys, carriages, and such at the Harrigan Carriage House, sharing hot dogs and chocolate eclairs, and snacking at the Hursts', where Rose always had something good to eat. The Hursts also had that "funny maid who went around without her shoes on when she was tired." It was also in the West Belle house that Rose finally broke down and let Fannie have the dog named Fury. Fannie's neighbor Lois Wilkes delighted in evening walks with "Fury My Love" pulling wildly at his leash. Fannie got to keep him until he bit a man and had to be sent away. That was a truly terrible moment, for having a pet, Fannie said, "released something hard and tight" in her. It gave her freedom to retire to a dark storeroom, "free to coddle and pronounce unrestrained endearments." She felt the way the poor dog looked, "chilly and alone inside, as when Papa kissed Mama, omitting me, or when they closed their door at night, or when I came out of Central High into a group of boys waiting to carry some girl's books, not mine, or even when I read a book or a piece of poetry, or thought something lovely and there was no one to tell about it."

Fannie's typically adolescent unhappiness stemmed largely from her being fat, lonely, and Jewish yet, in the manner that was her lifelong hallmark, she concealed these feelings from even her closest friends. "Favorite classmate" is her term for describing her best high school friend—a revealing choice. Olna searched her memory for signs of this teenage despondency Fannie confessed to nearly half a century later but could retrieve little evidence. It was true that sometimes Fannie had said disparaging things about her weight—and Olna's too—"but it was always in a laughing mood," Olna recalled. "You laughed so easily and so spontaneously and you were so lovely when you laughed." Fannie's discomfort with being Jewish also passed Olna by. "It just never occurred to me it was an occasion for unhappiness," Olna wrote. "A little inconvenient perhaps, at times, but I was brought up to think that people were people. . . . You joked about the Jews (to me alone, I think) but I joked about southerners and I felt those two activities were on a par."

As to the loneliness, Olna, who came from a big, "freewheeling household," always thought Fannie's life was practically ideal. "To me, going to your home was like going into a quiet cool park. Everything was so orderly, so peaceful—so I thought. You seemed to have all any girl could wish for. Of course I did not realize how shortly I'd begin to miss sisters, brothers, arguments, sacrifices, etc., but at the time you got little sympathy from me, only admiration." The fact is, Olna said, "I was asleep to most of your troubles." And in another letter, "Never did I dream that circumstances weighed so heavily upon you. To me, you were an only child with plenty of money and *the world* and anything you could wish for was yours." All Olna could remember was Fannie's "laughing, lighthearted" way. Mildred Hoyle was more struck by Fannie's beautiful voice, deep laugh, and challenging mind. And Bernice Kieffer, another one of Fannie's West Belle neighbors, remembered what a "tease machine" she used to be and how once, in anger, she called Bernice's home an orphan asylum because the Kieffers had so many children.

Looking back on her adolescence, Fannie concluded she was "just another squirmer with an itch I could not scratch." She was inhibited and an exhibitionist at the same time. "Psychiatry has new names for the same old adolescent symptoms of cosmic itch, frustration, yearning, intimations of sex, depression, elation, despairs, egocentricity, love, infatuation, crushes, passions unrequited. Naturally, I knew them all, shame, secrecy, self-pity, forbidden thoughts, family antagonism, fear, envy, preoccupation with death, the slow demise of innocence, budding maturities—the flowering."

Years after most of the West Belle Place neighbors had moved on, one of the women from the old neighborhood, by then married and living in an upscale suburb, decided to host a reunion of the "West Belle belles." Three times Wilma Robi Hailparn wrote Fannie, urging her to make the effort to come. The year was 1945.

"All kinds of nostalgias move about within me as I look backward over the years," Fannie wrote Wilma. "And how helpful it would be to me just now as I write my Self-Portrait. . . . Unfortunately, the affairs of this troubled world are ganging up to such an extent that government is using me as a handmaiden, and of course I am eager to be what small service I can. Needless to say, I realize what I am missing."

PART 5

Preceding page: AP/Wide World Photos

Chapter 31

"Decade of destruction"

Of the war years Fannie said, "I barged through that decade of destruction, despairs, national crises, and literary unrest in order not to sit through it." She wrote regularly to the few young soldiers she knew personally and lent her name to or made broadcasts for a new array of war-related causes. At the behest of the U.S. Treasury Department, she made four multicity tours, some with Louis Bromfield, General Carlos Romulo, Clifton Fadiman, Ogden Nash, Mark Van Doren, and Van Wyck Brooks, and offered manuscripts for auction to promote war bond sales. She also did her very small part in President Roosevelt's campaign for a third and then a fourth term. But it was on the subject of women and the war that she was most articulate.

Fannie's attitudes were a natural progression of twenty-five years of reflection and expression on the subject. She had no problem getting attention for her ideas, via newspapers, magazines, public speeches, and broadcasts, and she never hesitated to be as hard-hitting as possible. She also knew it was on this subject that she personally was most effective. It is interesting that she always directed her criticism at women themselves and not at men or society at large for victimizing them in any way.

Before the war, at an annual conference of the American Ethical Culture Union late in 1937, Fannie accused modern women of contributing inadequately to modern cultural life. Though women had proven to be the most stalwart supporters of the arts, their numbers were far too few in the ranks of world-class artists, musicians, and writers. "Creative art demands a relentless forfeit, merciless self-denial, rigid asceticisms, loneliness," *The New York Times* quoted Fannie as saying. "To what extent women are not capable of paying that forfeit is controversial." Laborsaving devices had started to eliminate some of the drudgery of housework, Fannie said, and it would be telling to see how women handled the increase in leisure time. "The home as an alibi is threatened," she said, bemoaning the great waste of a national resource already represented by time spent at beauty parlors and bridge tables.

A year later Fannie saw no need to be polite when she found herself on a prestigious panel of judges for the "Ideal American College Girl" without having been informed that the contest parameters precluded finalists from expressing interest in any career other than that of housewife. Fannie expressed her outrage to reporters, who duly printed her remarks.

But by June 1940 Fannie's attention, like that of everyone else, had turned to the prospect of American entry into the war in Europe, and she called on women to take a firm stand for peace. That December she urged women to assume their rightful place in national life, to protect peace in the way that European women had failed to do. "I am convinced," Fannie told the *New York Journal-American,* "that it lies within the future composite power of American women to educate our next generation to tolerate nothing short of a world in which wars cannot occur." She urged a radical overhaul in the nation's educational system so that girls could be made aware of their equality with boys. It was also time for women to realize, she said, that "indirect power hasn't real validity."

"Our intelligence and intellectual curiosity should stack up to more than they do," she said. Sadly, since the status of women had changed, she could see no appreciable difference in American life. If anything, things had gotten worse. "The greatest wars in the history of the world have happened since women have come into their own," she noted, adding that she was especially upset by the women of Germany and Italy, who had gone "gratefully back into passivity. At the command of dictators, they popped back like jack-in-the-boxes."

Knowing she was never going to be successful as a committee member or parachute packer—though at one point she did put in some time (and lost ten pounds) grinding nuts in an airplane factory—Fannie tried to propose a special wartime role for herself in January 1941. She started with a letter to Florence Kerr of the National Advisory Committee of Community Service Projects of the Works Progress Administration. (Kerr's committee was another of the many obligations Fannie accepted at the behest of Eleanor Roosevelt but fulfilled in name only.) Kerr had been quoted in the newspapers urging that the government draft its "women power" to help meet the national emergency. It was a position Fannie heartily applauded. "What ringing challenge can be sounded through the nation to awaken women to their important part in the crisis days ahead?" Fannie asked her. "How can we best bring about immediate legislative acts that will regiment them into formation for helpful action? I am willing to lift my pen or lend my presence in any way you can suggest." No response was forthcoming.

In March she told Roosevelt's secretary, Steve Early, of making her own plans to go to South America, where she was well known through the Spanish translations of her books and the distribution of films. She wanted "important credentials and, if the State Department desires, would be willing to play my part in a good-will mission." Early passed her letter on to Charles A. Thomson, chief of the State Department's cultural relations division, and to Nelson Rockefeller in the Commerce Department, who was coordinating commercial and cultural relations among the American republics.

∽

By May, still casting around for a meaningful role for herself, Fannie approached the first lady directly with an offer to help induct women to their new role in the nation's defense program by means of a nationwide speaking tour. She felt that women still had not grasped how much the daily pattern of their lives had been altered. "Even those who have already deserted the bridge tables for the bandage tables, do not as yet comprehend what has happened to them," she lamented. "They need to be aroused to their emergency! My time and service to this end are at the government's disposal." The first lady concurred and said she would put Fannie's letter in the hands of whomever was to be put in charge of home defense.

In October the State Department assignment she had requested to South America finally came through, but Fannie started having misgivings before she attended the first of two lengthy briefings in Washington. "I don't know what to say to the State Department at this time," she wrote Mabel Search, "but I certainly do not feel that I can go, since I am breaking ground for a new book and am finally face-to-face with what I have long planned—a winter that is going to be fairly quiet, free of speaking engagements, etc." Otherwise, Fannie said, of course she would be interested.

"Flew to Washington for more South American conference," her diary entry for October 12 reads. "Still vague. Trying to offer substitute services."

Just after the Japanese attack on Pearl Harbor in early December, Fannie revived her offer of a nationwide speaking tour to Mrs. Roosevelt, but nothing came of it.

In the meantime Fannie waged an ultimately unsuccessful but no less vigorous one-woman campaign to promote Ruth Bryan Owen, now Rohde, for the position of U.S. archivist. In the process Fannie urged and got the support of every influential person she knew, from the health guru Bernarr Macfadden to FBI Director J. Edgar Hoover. The effort was stillborn, however, because the president already had decided to appoint Dr. Solon J. Buck to the post.

Locally, Fannie pursued Mayor La Guardia repeatedly to give special consideration to her casual friend Judge Jeanette Brill of Magistrate's Court. Brill, in order to ensure her eligibility for a government pension, needed a term extension of at least two years in the event that La Guardia decided not to seek a third term. Were she not reappointed in a new administration, Brill would have served only twelve of the fourteen years necessary to qualify. "I have neither political nor for that matter highly personal reasons for interesting myself in this situation," Fannie told the mayor, "except an ordinary layman's desire to see the magistrate, who has served conscientiously, reap her pension." In the meantime, as U.S. director of civil defense, La Guardia urged Fannie to make herself available to speak in support of U.S. foreign policy and put her on his "Women in Literature Committee," which also included Leonora Speyer, Rachel Crothers, Blanche Knopf, and Lillian Hellman.

He annoyed Fannie the following summer, however, when he ignored her offer to raise the money to turn the once again "idle and useless" Tavern on the Green in Central Park into an outdoor summer canteen for the legions of "sailors and their oddments and endments of girlfriends" who were roaming the park at all hours "with results that show up startlingly in high schools and juvenile court rooms." She claimed to have rounded up some twenty-five thousand dollars in commitments to ready the space for this purpose, but by July 11, with no response from the mayor, it was too far into the summer to proceed. "I can understand your possible reason for not being interested in this enterprise better than I can understand being ignored," she told him in a letter she did not mail.

⌾

The lack of Washington credentials did not stop Fannie from sounding off to the nation's women, however, whenever she had the platform. "We women are no longer the waiting Penelopes of war," she told some two thousand Jewish convention women at the Hotel Astor in January 1942, adding that women were "a vital, needed and perhaps even a drafted part of it." A month later, in a commencement address to Hunter College graduates, she urged the young women to see themselves as "a new species of frontierswomen." She said they should be poised to seize their opportunities and hold on to their gains after the war, unlike women after the First World War, who "managed to get a foot inside the door" but then retreated.

"This time I hope they will swing it wide open," she said. "Opportunity has knocked twice at the same door in a quarter century. Of course, there will be some retrogression after the war, but don't let the door swing back too far."

To Julia Browne, her old friend in St. Louis, Fannie wrote: "My life has changed in countless directions. I still hold down my desk and work at my specific job. But the demands on all sides are manifold and nowadays, of course, so many things that used to be a matter of choice now come in the form of a command, because after all a request from the government in wartime is that and one responds gladly." Actually, there had not been as many government commands as Fannie might have hoped.

With eleven other women leaders, she did address a national women's conference under the auspices of *The New York Times* in April 1943 and elaborated on the same theme in remarks considered significant enough for reprint in the magazine *Vital Speeches*. "Do we, as in the last World War, step aside when our men come home and resume economically, industrially, almost w[h]ere we left off?" she asked. Since World War I there had been more "commotion" than "promotion" where women were concerned, she said, noting too that it had even been "controversial up to almost this very moment whether women doctors are eligible for Army or Navy service."

Some months after that conference, Fannie appealed to the wife of the *Times*'s publisher, Iphigene Sulzberger, to consider an idea: "It occurs to me that you have both the intelligence and power to launch what can be an historic and constructive enterprise," Fannie wrote. "I feel sure that now, as never before, is the moment to harness the enormous untamed woman power in our country and direct it into new and important channels. It is empire building of a sort, because women today are pioneers confronting a universe of new conditions." Fannie's idea was to start with New York City, then establish a network of centers "where women can meet, confer and determine on their post-war mass behavior in industry, economics, civics, politics and government." The *Times*, Fannie ventured, could be "an invaluable springboard by way of which we might awaken a national consciousness concerning this vast discussion. I have a driving urge to sound this call to the women of America at this strategic moment." The *Times* continued to run symposia during this period in which experts gathered to discuss the role of women after the armistice and other postwar themes. But Fannie's driving urge did not drive her idea any further than the letter she dashed off to the publisher's wife.

The fact was, Fannie was quick with an idea or a polemic—even a one-shot mailing to dozens of prominent people in support of a friend. But she was very weak on long-term follow-through, except in the case of her writing. Though she craved the validation of a significant role bestowed on her by the significant people she knew in the significant events unfolding, her friends had already figured out that she was too caught up in her own universe to extend herself very far beyond it.

"Seriously, Fannie, do write some script for us," La Guardia wrote her in March 1943. "Do not say I never write to you. I am always writing to you. The trouble is I always get a negative reply." Fannie protested that she had never once refused him in the six years of his administration, especially since he had only asked for "trivialities" and "window-dressing," from her—hardly the stuff to warrant a negative reply. As someone with "no partisan axe to grind: a concern for the social and civic stamina of this unparalleled city; and a deeply rooted desire to see it become the industrial cultural colossus it should," Fannie felt she might have been an asset to the mayor, but he never looked her way. What she could not figure out was whether he continued to overlook her because he regarded her "as the gal from back there" or because he had "not the interest nor the evaluation" to permit her to "cooperate more vitally."

This letter got his attention. Not two weeks later he dropped in on Fannie, unannounced, and stayed for three hours, offering her the position of deputy commissioner of corrections, which she declined because it held no appeal. In the days ahead, however, he extended the term of Magistrate Brill so as to assure her pension and he involved Fannie in the creation of a citywide "Unity at Home, Victory Abroad" committee aimed at promoting tolerance. This was a task she decided to take more seriously than usual. A year into the project, after the assembled committee had met three or four times, she wrote the mayor with the candor their long-standing friendship had fostered: "Your shadow looms over these meetings. I respect the shadow, but I am not afraid of it. Some of the members are, which is style-cramping." She was just as direct with him on another occasion, after hearing what she considered justified criticism of his policies from the city's teachers. *The New York Times* reported her comments on the matter, and she explained herself further to him by letter. To La Guardia's credit, he thanked her.

∞

There was no letup in Fannie's personal crusade to help chart the future course of the nation's women. When a reporter asked her how well she thought American women had done in industry since Pearl Harbor, Fannie demurred. Until women in nontraditional workplaces ceased to be a curiosity, she said, there would be no way to tell. For the time being the female welders, crane operators, bus drivers, defense workers, bacteriologists, airplane detectors, air wardens, pilots, motormen, taxi drivers, and lookouts, were only "cute news," worthy of celebration in songs like "Rosie the Welder"—she meant "Riveter"—and uniforms designed by the nation's smartest couturiers. "Case in point—farmerette," said Fannie. "The very label is sufficient commentary."

At the same time she expressed distress over the conservative attitudes of many of the women she had met in her travels around the country. She got the strong feeling that both for women in uniform and for the daughters of career women, security after the war was going to mean "four walls and a man coming home with a pay envelope." Sadly, Fannie predicted, "Home fires are going to roar after the war.

"Too many of the women who have come into their own in such dramatic ways . . . are ready to give it all up," she said. "They have had their cake and eaten it. Now they feel frustrated. They lack resiliency." Her prediction was that an inevitable revival of the old hearthside era was going to have to run its course after the war. Then, sometime later, women would finally be prepared to claim the legacy of their rightful wartime gains. "We all know what happens to the town pump after we are away from it," Fannie said. "And then after we've been back awhile we begin to wonder. 'Wasn't that pump bigger?' "

The postwar world, she said, will give women new status "if we want it and will use it." Her concern was whether they were really going to want it.

Chapter *32*

"Back Street" Remake

Universal released a remake of *Back Street* nine years after John Stahl's version and a decade after Fannie's novel first appeared. Unlike Stahl, neither the new director, Robert Stevenson, nor the screenwriter, Bruce Manning, showed any interest in discussing the project with Fannie, but finally, at her insistence, Manning dropped her a note saying that the picture would stick closely to the 1932 version, albeit with Margaret Sullavan and Charles Boyer in the starring roles. Dismissively, Manning offered to send Fannie a copy of the screenplay if she really wanted to see it.

Although he gave her no opening, Fannie could not resist telling Manning that she found the choice of Boyer for a role "so essentially Middle West" perplexing, especially considering his French accent and exotic personality. She also let Manning know that she had plenty of ideas for the production but had not been given any route for transmitting them. "I do not think that I display undue author's ego in manifesting a profound interest in a picture which has gone as deeply into the public mind and memory as this one," she wrote him. "I will be eager of course for any additional information you find time or impulse to pass on." Evidently he had neither, perhaps because one uninvited kibitzer was enough. He had to contend with Joseph Breen of the Production Code Administration, the self-censorship arm of the motion-picture industry.

Breen maintained that the 1932 film had stirred up so much controversy over the moral rectitude of glorifying adultery that it had come to symbolize what was wrong with Hollywood. For that reason alone Breen thought it was imperative that the remake raise "not the slightest valid objection . . . even in the most remote detail." To wit: No intimate love scenes involving Walter and Ray and no dying "I love you" over the telephone. Ray had to be depicted in a state of total degeneration caused by poverty and loneliness and could not be referred to as Mrs. Schmidt (Schmidt being her maiden name) for appearances' sake. There could be no suggestion that Walter held any sort of official appointment, nor could Walter's son in any way be seen to condone his father's extramarital affair. Between Ray and Walter no money could change hands. In short, nothing could be done to point up the illicit relationship, which, in Breen's view, was obvious anyway.

Manning's office told Breen that he would tell the story as a tragedy in which Walter's sin ruined an important career opportunity, destroyed his daughter's marriage prospects, and brought shame on his innocent family. He set Ray in a life of dullness, boredom, isolation, and futility—without the role of essential helpmate to Walter that Fannie had conferred on her and that gave the character a measure of worth and fulfillment—not to mention plausibility.

This round, the film created no moral furor. In fact, the only protest on file came from the Investment Bankers of America, who objected to the depiction of a member of their upstanding profession in this derogatory way.

Fannie attended the February premiere in New York with Jack and afterward had nothing good to say about the film. "Terrible" was the only comment in her diary, though she was amazed by the "extravagantly enthusiastic" audience response. "The story seemed to have retained its old hold on the public," she said. As for a coast-to-coast radio broadcast of the story two years later, which featured Boyer and Martha Scott, Fannie thought it also was terrible. "Boyer ham acting and Martha Scott, excellent," she wrote in her diary.

"Lonely Parade"

*L*onely Parade took Fannie an uncharacteristic four years to complete because her manuscript got "badly stuck" along the way, requiring more rewriting than she had ever done before. She wrote only a few articles and short stories in this period, including one, White Christmas, about the White House which Doubleday, Doran & Co. published in a gift-book edition for Christmastime sale in 1942.

"I can't explain it to myself," Fannie told Robert Van Gelder of The New York Times, in trying to understand why Lonely Parade took so much time. "I had that novel all planned—I knew where all the plumbing was—that's what I call the main outline, plumbing. I knew where the pantry was. Everything was perfectly clear in my head, just where I was going." Though Fannie never said so, she got her inspiration for the novel from aspects of the lives and friendship of Elisabeth Marbury, Elsie de Wolfe, and Anne Morgan. In Fannie's story any one of her three heroines gladly would have traded her seemingly glamorous single life for matrimony on any terms.

Confident about the novel's sales prospects, Fannie used that leverage to wrest some concessions from Harpers before she agreed to allow the house to publish her again. She was convinced that blame for her inability to match sales with those of, say, an Edna Ferber or a Pearl S. Buck, lay with her publishing house. She was continually disappointed in the way Harpers treated her. It irked her no end, for example, that the publisher had allowed Lummox, which with Back Street was to her mind one of her "two most important books"—to go out of print, and she expressed this in no uncertain terms. Bill

Briggs pressed and pressed to see the manuscript of *Lonely Parade,* but Fannie played coy. First, she wanted Harpers to find a way to put her old titles back in print. After some back-and-forth the publisher arranged for P. F. Collier to release new copies of a six-volume reprint collection of her best titles: *Lummox, Great Laughter, Imitation of Life, Five and Ten, Anitra's Dance,* and *Back Street.* That settled, she sent the new manuscript over.

Briggs emoted over the size, scope, and drive of the story and the "skillful fullness" of Fannie's writing. He thought the book was a "noble monument" to Marbury, nearly a decade after her death, noting how much Fannie must have admired her. "I know that Hurst and Harper have the big spring novel here," he said.

But the more insightful analysis of the work came from William James Fadiman at MGM, to whom Fannie slipped a copy of the proofs once it was set in type. Though Fadiman believed it presented certain obstacles for filming, he thought it was a "unique and intensely original novel in its re-creation of that vanished era when one century ends and another begins." He thought the book "ingeniously denies the implications of Lesbianism among the three heroines" even though the "very core and strength" of the narrative was partially dependent on that assumption. "The frustrations and inhibitions of the three girls, the pulsing tension of the mood which pervades them collectively and individually, the psychological motivations which permit them to substitute monetary and social success for domestic and sexual satisfaction—these are all integral and essential elements in the cumulative effect you achieve," Fadiman told Fannie.

Other problems from a film perspective were the lack of a hero and a satisfactory romance, not to mention the "censorable nature" of many key scenes. "But weighing heavily on the other side of the scale are three full-length three-dimensional portraits of vital, absorbing women, magnificent creations. They remain completely and intriguingly alive." Though some might see the book as a defeatist work, Fadiman saw it otherwise: "These three women attained a kind of spiritual glory in defying tradition, in living their own lives as they believed they should be lived, and in their striving to compensate in every way for those personality defects that denied them sex and marriage and motherhood. It is this element of bravery and ennobling courage that I am endeavoring to stress in my report . . . to the studio." There was no offer for the film rights.

There had been much back-and-forth with Harpers about the title. Fannie already had reluctantly given up her original idea, "High Sierra," when Knopf came out with a book by the same name. Before a consensus formed around *Lonely Parade,* Fannie and Harpers had rejected "Trilogy," "Virgin Territory," "Ancient Eyes," "Three Women," "Three Wise Women of Gotham," and "Prologue to Now."

In the run-up to publication Fannie did all she could to get the publishing house to put its enthusiasm behind the book. She sent the publicist Ramona

Herdman a list of story ideas for the mass-circulation magazines, such as "Do men really want a woman who works?" and she drafted a letter with a pregame locker-room pep talk addressed to the publisher, Cass Canfield, himself. The book had to be handled, she told him, with "a new mind and point of view."

"I cannot feel that this is just another Fannie Hurst book," she wrote, adding that it was imperative for Harper & Brothers to treat her "as if I were a brand new author—come to you from a rival concern." Not to do so, she said, would surely "invite a licking." She reasoned that since it had been four years since *Great Laughter,* Harpers would have to invest in a bang-up promotional campaign in order to get the attention of dealers. Without it they would take a ho-hum, just–another–Fannie Hurst–book attitude toward *Lonely Parade,* and place orders in the same numbers they had for *Great Laughter.* But she felt *Lonely Parade* deserved better.

"I could have turned out a book a year during the last several," Fannie said. "Instead I worked steadily on the one book. I believed I had a timely message. I think I should be handled in that mood." Book advertising had made new and important advances in the years since she last published, Fannie argued, and she wanted *Lonely Parade* to benefit from these changes. For books, she said, the right advertising campaign had become every bit as important as publicity. To Briggs, her longtime editor, she raised the specter of hiring an outside publicist but held off when he expressed disapproval.

Harpers published *Lonely Parade* on January 6, 1942, a month after the attack on Pearl Harbor. Even with the nation in full mobilization for war, Fannie's attention was focused on how her publisher was handling Novel Number Eleven. On the day of publication she fully expected to see big advertisements in the New York daily press to herald the novel's arrival in bookstores. When she realized that none had been placed, she wrote to Canfield at once. "There is nothing to do now, of course. Had I anticipated that anything like this could have happened, I would have covered the situation out of my own funds." Her next call was to Constance Hope, a well-known publicist who also was an old friend of Jacques. Hope had been after Fannie's account for some time, and Fannie signed her up immediately.

Reviews of the novel, as it turned out, were solid—less insulting than usual. "Interesting character drawing; skillful writing," Catherine Van Dyne remarked in a trade review for *Library Journal.* "The story is lustful with unfounded but repeated suggestion of lesbianism. Not for the young or perhaps for the average reader." Margaret Wallace in *The New York Times* was not without criticism but liked the way the novel was "spiced with sharp observation and lively originality." She said Fannie "[cut] a wide swath through the goofier manifestations of café society, knocking over fads and foibles with hearty and informed ill will." As a problem novel, though, she thought it fell apart, "perhaps because the problem is not stated in sufficiently general terms."

Publicity for the book positioned it as Fannie's attack on society's attitude toward career women, which caused one reader to wonder: "Couldn't she have

Above: *Thinking Out Loud,* Fannie's radio program for the NBC Blue Network, lasted only its initial ten broadcasts, two weeks in June 1942. A permanent sponsor could not be found. *Temple University Libraries Urban Archives*

Left: Rose Hurst.
Harry Ransom Humanities Research Center, Fannie Hurst Collection

Fannie (right) and sister Edna, ages approximately five and three.
In the second photo, Edna has been airbrushed out.

Harry Ransom Humanities Research Center, Fannie Hurst Collection

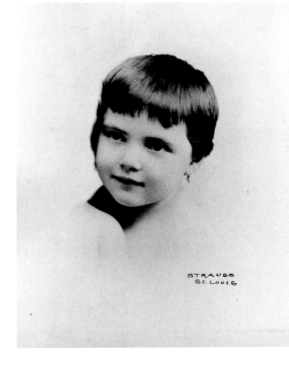

Above: Fannie was an avid tennis and basketball player during her high school days. She is pictured here (top left) with the Central High School Girls' Tennis Team, 1903. *St. Louis Public School Records and Archives*
Below: Fannie was a frequent Washington visitor during the Roosevelt administrations. She is seen here walking with Eleanor Roosevelt.
Harry Ransom Humanities Research Center, Fannie Hurst Collection

Above: Fannie's "house within an apartment house," the fabulous Gothic-style triplex in the Hotel des Artistes. Photographed (with Fannie at right) October 20, 1944. *Temple University Libraries Urban Archives*

Right: At Fannie's birthday dinner for two dear old friends, Daniel Frohman, the well-known theatre manager, and August Heckscher, the philanthropist, Ruth Bryan Owen Rohde listens while Frohman (right), who was turning eighty-seven, tells a story. Heckscher was eighty-nine. The party was August 25, 1937. *AP/Wide World Photos*

Ronald Reagan substitutes for Ralph Edwards on this February 6, 1957, episode of NBC's *This Is Your Life,* which honored Fannie's publicist and friend, Constance Hope, shown seated next to Dr. Milton Berliner. Standing, left to right, are Reagan, the actor Gregory Ratoff, the Begum Aga Khan, opera stars Lauritz Melchior, Lotte Lehman, and Rose Bampton, and Fannie. Baritone Robert Merrill also appeared on the show. *Harry Ransom Humanities Research Center, Fannie Hurst Collection (photograph identifications courtesy of Curtis Stallworth, Museum of Television & Radio)*

Above: Fannie between writers William Saroyan, left, and Louis Bromfield, on yet another dais, circa 1950. *Corbis-Bettmann*

Right: Fannie and Jacques aboard the Moore-McCormick luxury liner *Brazil* at Pier 32, North River, New York, before their departure on a twelve-day cruise to Bermuda and the West Indies, May 5, 1948. *AP/Wide World Photos*

Below: Fannie went head-to-head with Mike Wallace on the popular New York City television program *Night Beat*. *Harry Ransom Humanities Research Center, Fannie Hurst Collection*

Fannie and Marlon Brando.
Harry Ransom Humanities Research Center,
Journal-American *Collection*

Above: From right to left, actress
Lana Turner, producer Ross Hunter,
Fannie, and Turner's daughter,
Cheryl Crane, on hand for the
premiere of Hunter's remake of
Imitation of Life, February 19, 1959.
Corbis-Bettmann

Left: Fannie with Sandra Dee
on the publicity circuit for the
1959 version of *Imitation of Life.*
AP/Wide World Photos

Above: Fannie in Central Park, telling stories to children, August 8, 1959.
Corbis-Bettmann-UPI

Below: The Missouri Society presents Fannie with its annual Silver Mule
Scroll and Award Present at the event in New York, April 17, 1963, are
(left to right) Langston Hughes, Miller Moore, president of the Missouri
Society, and Thomas H. Eliot, chancellor of Washington University.
Corbis-Bettmann-UPI

Fannie returns from the Hollywood premiere of *Imitation of Life*,
February 1959. *AP/Wide World Photos*

based her book on three women who were happy?" Fannie's reply reveals a lot about her attitude toward this work and stories past. She felt the need for happy endings was an unfortunate American preoccupation, since only by understanding unhappiness could humankind develop the "compassion and capacity for tolerance and humanity." The story was not a morality tale, warning women off the career path because of the unhappiness it was sure to bring. Quite the contrary. It was simply the story of what had happened to three individual women at a time—as suggested in one of her rejected titles—that was a "prologue to now." Fannie's "timely message" came in the form of testament, not treatise; stories, not standards; a jumping-off point for discussion, not an admonition.

By the end of its first month on the market, *Lonely Parade* was in its fourth printing. In another month it crossed the twenty thousand sales mark "very handsomely." Everyone, including Fannie, was pleased, even though she once again had failed to edge into the realm of best-seller. Briggs nudged her to finish her autobiography at long last, but again she held him off. "A strange thing has happened!" Fannie wrote him in April 1942. "I am suddenly 'in' a novel, something I hadn't planned for quite some time to come. But apparently it was ready even if I wasn't so the 'Self-Portrait' remains secondary."

"Fannie Hurst Presents"

By the early 1940s Fannie wanted her own radio program—not a show that would fall under the rubric of "a morning 'bathroom curtains and baby's bib' hour," but a bona fide "soapbox," even if the medium did seem to do such "excruciating things to the average female voice." As Fannie told her literary agent, George Bye, with so much drivel being poured "along the ether," why shouldn't she be able to add to it? "A woman's place on the air need not be confined to discussions of bathroom curtains; how to remove inkstains; fashions in broccoli," she wrote a CBS executive when she first became enamored of the idea in 1939. "Neither need they go to the other extreme and confine themselves to politics, domestic or political economy." Fannie's idea was to talk about "ivory, apes and peacocks; a social angle of life suggested by the day's news; the care and feeding of pandas; why I do not read James Joyce; cops I have known; the lady of the house. In short, any subject that interests me enough to want to talk about it."

By the time this came up, Fannie had been making guest appearances on radio programs for nearly twenty years. In November 1922 she broadcast from Newark on the Marguerite Mooers Marshall program in what was described at the time as the first interview with an author ever conducted over the airwaves. In the literally hundreds of appearances that followed, Fannie cultivated a distinctive radio persona, replete with those *veddy ameddican* Middle Atlantic pronunciations she had not come by naturally. As a mainstay of women's radio programming, she appeared repeatedly on such shows as Claudine MacDonald's *Women's Radio Review* and Mary Margaret McBride's extremely popular daytime hour, both broadcast over the NBC network. But she was also a sought-after guest on programs of more general interest. For years she was an arbitrator for the WMCA show *Labor Arbitration.*

As early as 1932 Margaret Cuthbert, NBC's public affairs director, had commented on Fannie's "unusual radio personality" and certainly meant it positively, for it was Fannie she chose seven years later from a wide and impressive field to present Anne O'Hare McCormick with a special award from the American Women's Association during a live broadcast. Afterward Cuthbert told Fannie her presentation had "splendor. . . . It couldn't have been done with more distinction and feeling." She thought Fannie had something special for radio and that she should come to see her in a week or two to talk about it. That was in 1939, but nothing came of it.

So Fannie contented herself with invitations from other established female show hosts, all the while wondering why it wasn't she doing the inviting. Dorothy Gordon, for example, had Fannie appear on her NBC Blue Network program, *Yesterday's Children,* first interviewing Fannie for five minutes, then having her read two of her favorite childhood stories over the air. Occasionally there was call for a radio adaptation of one of Fannie's earlier stories, notably "Madagascar, Ho!" in 1941 and "Dolly and the Colleagues" in 1942, but this was no substitute for a show of her own.

Bye did not have the contacts to make it happen, but Fannie's new publicist, Constance Hope, did. In 1942, with *Lonely Parade* still in the bookstores, Hope brokered a deal for Fannie to make ten broadcasts over NBC's Blue Network under the title *Thinking Out Loud.* For two weeks in June, Monday through Friday, the program aired for fifteen minutes at five o'clock in the afternoon. *Variety* said it was "frankly an attempt to see how [Fannie] and radio take to each other" and pronounced the program fairly good, even though the reviewer suggested that Fannie adapt some of her vocabulary to suit the ear. Fannie gave the network a three-week exclusive right to sign up commercial sponsorship for the program, but the sales department found no takers and the program died.

The same thing happened in the fall of 1943 with another format entitled *Sunday Evening at Fannie Hurst's.* In this concept Fannie, John Erskine, and Carl Van Vechten discussed literature informally over coffee in Fannie's salon for the benefit of radio listeners. Fannie was hopeful after the first recording. She thought the show was "alive and interesting and civilized. Good talk which I think was sufficiently human to be understandable to large numbers." But when several months passed without word of a sale, she was filled with self-doubt about her prospects in the medium. She told Erskine she thought potential sponsors probably liked everything about the program except her part in it. Of course, Erskine assured her this was far from the case, but for whatever reason no sponsor was found.

Later that year the agent Thomas Stix did manage to put together a deal for Fannie to appear over NBC's Blue Network with the Borden Company as sponsor in a program called *Fannie Hurst Presents.* This was a series of half-hour radio programs featuring Fannie as narrator and mistress of ceremonies for a thousand-dollar fee for every appearance, less the 20 percent commission paid to Stix. For thirteen weeks starting July 8, 1944, against a background of organ music and sound effects, up to eight actors dramatized one of Fannie's best short stories, excluding "Guilty," which the network banned.

Fannie panicked when the program did not generate any fan mail in the first few weeks and even got some of her friends to write in as part of a "mail-puller," though Stix advised against it as far too transparent and ineffectual a tactic. He told her not to worry about the seeming lack of public response, since even popular dramatic shows rarely brought in much fan mail. All the same, the program was not picked up for another season, and Stix did not have any better luck with it the following year.

By January 1946 Fannie was ready to give up. "Now that we are entering our second year of trying to place this piece of excess baggage known as Fannie Hurst," she wrote Stix. "I am convinced that I owe it to both of us to hurl myself out in the wide-open spaces known as 'public domain.' " She reiterated her appreciation for his efforts, "but not least my resentment that I wasn't a better product."

There was hope by fall. Stix managed to sign Fannie for the position of "first night" theater reviewer on the ABC affiliate station WJZ. She jumped into the assignment with great enthusiasm, starting in January 1947. The brief reviews aired in "the wee small hours" after the final curtain, and Fannie started off the year with her opening-night impressions of such new productions as *Love Goes to Press, The Big Two, Street Scene, Finian's Rainbow,* and *All My Sons.* She soon realized that the time slot was impossible, however, and couldn't get the station to change it or at least to do a better job of promoting the late-night feature. It wasn't long before Fannie began to feel too unheralded and unappreciated, and she quit the job before the first three months were up.

Chapter 33

"Hallelujah"

In the spring of 1939, Fannie summoned her courage to return to St. Louis for the first time in a decade, presumably to gather atmospheric material for her autobiography. As she told Julia Browne, the devoted friend and neighbor who had moved in with Fannie's mother after Sam's death, it was taking "a bit of artificial self-stimulation" to bring herself to go home again because, aside from Julia, there was no one left in the city who mattered much to her anymore. (The statement would have shattered Lois Toensfeldt, Fannie's other remaining faithful pal from the old days, but Lois was never the wiser.) Hoping vainly to elicit a rousing response from city leaders, Fannie made a national broadcast about St. Louis from New York in advance of her trip, but it garnered only one piece of fan mail—from Julia, a jabbing reminder to Fannie of her marginal standing as native daughter. "I am neither disappointed nor surprised" was her disingenuous claim, "because where you expect nothing you cannot feel let down when you receive it."

By this point in Fannie's life, recognition and accolades had come often and from enough quarters for the silence from St. Louis to startle. "That darned old 'home town' froze my spirits again," she wrote Julia a month after she had announced her imminent arrival, "and I just can't muster up sufficient impulse to make the visit I contemplated."

Fannie did slip in and out of town a year later for a speaking engagement and on that occasion described St. Louis to a reporter as a "good but somewhat reserved parent" whenever her children came home. This grouse passed unnoticed, but a couple of ill-placed comments to a reporter on her first war bond trip to the city, in October 1942, did not. When a *Globe-Democrat* writer asked Fannie how she felt about a proposed twenty-five-thousand-dollar-a-year spending limit, she kiddingly told him that she thought it was going to be tough, what with her being down to her last yacht and all. "Either my humor was pretty heavy or the reporter's sense of humor was somewhat dull, or both," she said later. "In any event my ironical remark was cruelly misstated." That, and her published slight of the once elegant St. Louis mansion district, Vandeventer Place—she said it was tending toward shabbiness—brought on a barrage of angry mail. "Every time I open my mouth in St. Louis I seem to put both feet into it," she wrote Lois afterward. "The cure for that dilemma is obvious." Lois tried to mollify Fannie, but she wouldn't have it. "I am convinced I have sort of a senile sensitivity to the town which seems to invite the kind of thing which happens to me on the old home soil. Somewhere within me the fault lies rooted. So please forget it."

Still, the city was very much on her mind; in addition to the memories flooding back for her memoirs, she had planned to make it the setting for much of her new novel, *Hallelujah*. In fact, her side purpose for the war bond trip was to rediscover the city for the novel's sake. One of her main characters is even a brilliant poet-drunk with a taste for prostitutes named Florence Wooley of *Wooley's Weekly*, unmistakably inspired by Fannie's late mentor of *Reedy's Mirror* fame, William Marion Reedy. "Urbane troglodyte that he was, his mind flowered into shapes and colors, showering stars that sometimes you could capture for the instant. No matter if they died at your touch like snowflakes, something of Wooley's imagination laid itself upon you."

After the fits and starts of work on *Lonely Parade,* the new novel poured out in one continuous stream. The inspiration for *Hallelujah* came not long after *Lonely Parade's* release in January 1942, and Fannie already was into a second draft by the time she made the pilgrimage home that October. There she told a reporter that her story would revolve around the time leading up to the war but would not include it.

> "Do you think that fellow Hitler is hell-bent for a war Nella?"
>
> "I'm afraid I don't know as much about European affairs as I should. I'm so sorry for France and Poland and for all those Jews—"
>
> "I hope to heaven it doesn't mean we are in for years of wholesale murder."

It was as much as she ever had to say specifically about the plight of her people in Germany. Fannie told the reporter she could not write about the war just yet because it was too close. "You can't evaluate it correctly," she said.

Briggs thought Fannie was breaking all speed records for producing *Hallelujah* and wanted to push it through for Harpers' spring 1943 list. But in the rewrite Fannie slowed things down. Both she and Briggs agreed it was time for Harpers to produce an updated monograph about her career but ran into trouble finding the appropriate person to write it. No one with sufficient literary credentials and a positive enough viewpoint was available to take on the task. Fannie's good friend Mabel Search made an unsuccessful stab at it, then Briggs recruited Charles Hanson Towne, who was more than glad to oblige. Towne had reread the novels and got ready to put his thoughts on paper when Briggs called him off the project, citing paper shortages, manufacturing, and general financial restrictions brought on by the war.

Fannie was not going to trust Harpers with promotion this time around. She rehired Constance Hope a full three months before *Hallelujah*'s release in January 1944. Fannie's secretary immediately sent Hope Fannie's schedule for the last days of September 1943. It was the same week that Fannie and John Erskine were making sample recordings for their prospective radio show and Jacques was in the hospital with heart problems. Fannie let nothing slide: speech for the opening meeting of the American Women's Association on the twenty-first; two "monster mass meetings" in Providence to auction off manuscripts for war bonds along with Clifton Fadiman, Arthur Train, and Christopher La Farge on the twenty-third; judge at the first dog show ever held in Harlem on the twenty-fifth, a plan of the ASPCA's to lead "Negro children away from the wide open roads to delinquency"; a broadcast over station WQXR for the U.S. Treasury on the twenty-sixth; broadcast over CBS at the Brooklyn Paramount Theater for another huge war bond drive on the twenty-seventh; and another war bond manuscript auction on the twenty-ninth, this time in Pittsfield, Massachusetts.

Not only did Hope place more than one hundred and fifty stories, interviews, and column notes around the country between October and February, including the first word sketch of Fannie ever published in *The New Yorker*, but she even got the glove designer Merry Hull to name her latest model *Hallelujah* after the book. Hope's fee for her services: a thousand dollars.

Lois told Fannie that all St. Louis was furious that she had chosen the city as a backdrop for such a book. "Nothing was further from my mind than 'stabbing my hometown with pen point,' " Fannie replied. "On the contrary, a submerged nostalgia and affection must have been responsible for my choosing it as background to a story which could have been laid anyplace else just as conveniently." The blast of negativity prompted Fannie to ask the war bond committee to excuse her from the next St. Louis appearance, but they were convinced she was good for the program and insisted that she go. "Anyway, I imagine the majority of the people who attend the rally are more interested in the bond issue than the literary issue," she said. "I hope so."

Harry Burke, a stylish writer who knew Reedy well, examined *Hallelujah*'s St. Louisian aspects in a major feature for the *St. Louis Globe-Democrat*. Though Burke was less convinced by Fannie's portrayal of the Reedy figure, he commended her for recalling so many old St. Louis memories and scandals as " 'diffused images,'—always a little out of focus," creating the "feeling we have been through that present circumstance of place, or event sometime, somewhere before, but never identifiably."

The publicity campaign did not bring about a movie sale for *Hallelujah*, however, though all the major studios looked at the galleys. It also did nothing to stop a gush of insulting, truly terrible reviews, probably the worst ever. "It is an extremely bad novel, but Fannie Hurst writes for the bad novel market,"

wrote Katherine S. Rosin in the *Saturday Review.* "In a way, it is both impertinent and pointless to review her. She is, I am afraid, as much of an institution
as chewing gum and soap operas. . . . One can only accord to her the tribute
that she sells plenty of books for herself and her publishers and provides pleasure for her followers." *Time* said Fannie somehow managed, without specific
descriptions, to make the novel's "superheated atmosphere quiver with a heavy
middle-aged eroticism." Paragraphs such as this one come to mind:

> On those early occasions when Johanna was first beginning to
> feel the inexplicable lure of this untidy and somewhat monstrous
> young man, she had crowded her pillow up about her ears at night to
> shut out the sound of the soprano laughter that more or less habitu-
> ally emanated from the Wooley apartment. Sometimes the pressure
> of emotions unrequited became more than she could bear, and in the
> darkness and silence of her maiden's room, she sobbed into the pil-
> low. The years had adjusted, but not reconciled, Johanna.

Newsweek said the book involved "the weirdest array of phony characters
ever assembled." And Rose Feld, writing for the *New York Herald Tribune,* said it
added up to "a magnum of saccharine fermentation that never quite turns into
wine." Feld, who had profiled Fannie at her pinnacle in 1923 and 1926, clearly
had altered her once-admiring view. She remembered Fannie's stories in *Metropolitan* around 1915, and how, along with Theodore Roosevelt on politics, the
cartoonist Art Young, and the book reviewer Clarence Day, Fannie had "struck
the same keynote of trenchant awareness of the decade." In Feld's view Fannie
had then established herself as "an articulate and new voice in what was
known as the period of 'flaming youth.' When she laughed, she laughed loudly
and joyously, when she wept it was with copious tears." Acknowledging that it
was unjust to fault a writer for remaining in the framework of a past era, Feld
still thought that *Hallelujah,* even with its present-day background and problems, "dates like the hobble skirt." Fannie's style, she said, "seems irritatingly
and monotonously flooded in a tide of ancient treacle."

The most brutalizing review of all appeared in *The New York Times*—not in
the weekday section, where Orville Prescott poked fairly good-natured fun at
Fannie's writing and softened the blow at the end of the piece: "Is it long-
suffering virtue in distress you crave? Cute crippled tiny tots? Gallant and
good-hearted prostitutes? Or do you like vice among the millionaires? Dypso-
mania, hysteria, sadism, incest, pathological cowardice and lechery? It's all here
just waiting to be snatched up by an appreciative public." The book had "surprising vitality . . . pace and drive and a certain gruesome force," he added.
Fannie might plumb the "depths of plush-lined bathos" but "at least never for-
gets to tell a story."

It was Edith Walton's critique in the *Times's* Sunday book review that sent Fannie to the telephone on a Saturday night to complain directly to the newspaper's publisher, something it would never have occurred to her to do before, even though the Sulzbergers were social friends. Someone at Harpers had seen an advance copy of the review a week before publication and alerted Fannie that not only was it bad but it had been written by the same woman who had been reviewing Fannie repeatedly and negatively in the pages of the *Times* for years. *Hallelujah,* Walton wrote, contained "the same flamboyance, the same emotionalism, the same sloppy writing" as all of Fannie's books, even the same "golden-hearted Hurst heroine" in the character of Lily Browne. "The only difference is that Miss Hurst seems to have forgotten how to tell a good story. Her books, in the old days, were never so devastatingly dull."

Sulzberger heard Fannie out and decided, on the basis of what she had told him, to take action. He managed to reach one of the assistants of editor Robert Van Gelder, who, on the publisher's instruction, rushed back into the office and pulled the review, substituting for it one for another book. Sulzberger took pains to explain to Fannie that doing this required etching a whole new copper cylinder, containing eight pages of next Sunday's book review, and that the cylinder had to be etched twice—once for type and once for illustration. Further, he instructed the editor to scrap the eight thousand advance copies of the book review that already had been printed for separate circulation. He also made a point of telling Fannie that all of this took him until eleven o'clock Saturday night, with two more calls necessary on Sunday. It was not until he got to the office on Monday morning that he learned that Fannie had been mistaken. Edith Walton was not the writer Fannie's informant at Harpers had in mind. Walton had reviewed only one other book of Fannie's, her 1937 short-story collection, *We Are Ten,* albeit harshly. Walton had been confused with Margaret Wallace, who indeed had reviewed at least four of Fannie's major books for the *Times*—*Five and Ten, Back Street, Great Laughter,* and *Lonely Parade.*

"I am told that the present review is not favorable, and about that I am sorry," Sulzberger wrote Fannie. "But in view of the fact that the reviewer is not the person you believed her to be, we are going ahead with the original cylinders and the review will appear this coming Sunday."

Fannie was mortified over the misidentification and the trouble she had caused. She assured the publisher that he had been "considerate, fair," and told him, "The integrity of your point of view I will not soon forget." She did not know how Harpers could have gotten the two reviewers confused and regretted the error "beyond the telling," adding, "If the forthcoming review were twice as bad as it apparently already is, that arctic fact would be mitigated by your sense of justice." She offered to cover whatever costs she had forced the newspaper to incur but also related a sidebar to the drama to him, which she had learned about only in a subsequent telephone call with Harpers. When Walton's *We Are Ten* review appeared back in 1937, Harpers had complained about it to a predecessor of Van Gelder, who agreed that the critique was "more vicious than logical" and promised never to let Walton review another one of Fannie's books. Van Gelder, Fannie conceded, could not have been expected to know of the promise when he assigned Walton to review *Hallelujah*. "It goes without saying that under ordinary conditions I never would have sanctioned a protest," Fannie wrote Sulzberger. "But I am further told that Miss Walton publicly celebrates the fact that she abhors my work. This, you will agree, is something of a liability to an author who works for years on a given piece of work. However, as stated above, I repeat that as much as I regret your decision to scrap the substitute review, I respect it."

Sulzberger wrote Fannie once again, thanking her for her note without further comment and enclosing a copy of the one he sent Van Gelder:

> It is too bad that things in life are so rarely 100 percent. If Miss Walton had confined herself to reviewing Fannie Hurst's book instead of reaching out and reviewing Fannie Hurst herself a bit, our position would have been perfect.
>
> As it is, I am unhappy—not because the book was unfavorably reviewed, for I haven't read it and know nothing about its merits—but because I think the nature of our review would give anyone who was looking for bias some right to claim that bias was indicated.
>
> Books should be reviewed on their own. It is all right to say that a book is poor; it is not all right to say that the author has forgotten how to write a story.
>
> Miss Walton's point of view is indicated to me in her statement that she desires to be "meticulously fair to Miss Hurst." That is what she is expected to be. Why should she emphasize it? AHS.

Despite the disastrous reviews, the book did fine, with a short stay on the best-seller lists of both *The New York Times* and *Publishers Weekly*, when it was selling at a rate of a thousand books a week a good month after its release. Total distribution, according to the publisher, was more than twenty-seven thousand copies.

Chapter *34*

"A bit of an inferiority complex"

Fannie faced both her sixtieth and sixty-fifth birthdays in the five years immediately following the war. Jacques had been on slow-down alert since 1943, when an apparent attack of indigestion turned out to be a stoppage in one of the very minor rear arteries of his heart, and although Fannie reasonably could have been expected to use the excuse to lighten her own load, she kept moving at her customary whiz-by speed. Through a winning combination of Jack's prudent investments, Fannie's sustained earnings, and their careful spending habits, the couple had amassed far more money than they could go through in a lifetime. Yet Fannie worked without letup.

This did not mean that nothing had changed. Those whose own political aura had enhanced Fannie's national stature died during these years and the period just before: Louis Howe in 1936, Roosevelt in 1945, and La Guardia in 1947. Although Fannie continued to exchange notes and very occasional visits with the former first lady, and Mayor William O'Dwyer called on Fannie for civic duties in much the way La Guardia had, she had lost her direct line. The best of her old-time friends and literary boosters also were gone—Elisabeth Marbury, Rutger Jewett, Bob Davis, Charles Norris—and with them, logically, a sizable portion of the ardent but nameless fans who had been buying her work for thirty-five years. Fannie's response to the changes was to behave as if she were still a neophyte intent on building her reputation. In a sense she *was* still building her reputation, but this round, for this and later generations.

By 1947 Harpers had published Fannie's next two novels, *The Hands of Veronica* and *Anywoman,* bringing the number of her published books to date to an impressive twenty-three: fourteen novels, including the disavowed *Mannequin;* the eight short-story collections; and her extended essay, *No Food with My Meals.* She also finished work on the childhood portion of her autobiography, which she began to think of as "Volume One," with the next parts to follow when she felt comfortable enough to tell the story.

Seeking more new outlets for her magazine work, Fannie hired yet another handler, the agent Jacques Chambrun. He negotiated contracts for a year's worth of feature articles to run in the *American* weekly during 1945 and 1946 and for a special "Fannie Hurst Page" in *Saturday Home,* the weekend supplement of the *New York American,* for the better part of 1947.

To Chambrun, Fannie once mentioned with mock facetiousness that she was developing a bit of an inferiority complex over the now frequent refusals from publishers who once had clamored for her work, and she was positively outraged when he allowed *McCall's* to take two months to say no to one of her stories instead of the less-than-a-week turnaround she had gotten since her earliest days in the business. But there was no false pride. The kind of stories *Cosmopolitan* once bought for four thousand dollars she now sold to the likes of *Canadian Home Journal* for four hundred without comment. And she complained just as haughtily and bitterly as she always had when those new, unknown editors took liberties with her manuscripts as if they did not know whose work they were handling. Her novels, the steady income from her weekend supplement contracts, the occasional page or story in *Good Housekeeping,* and her endless public appearances all helped maintain her sense of purpose, achievement, and equilibrium. Age was not going to be her barrier. Fannie seized every opportunity, large or small, to put her name before the public in whatever form that opportunity came and for whatever payment.

"I am vital vital VITAL"

In the 1940s Fannie added the postwar problems of American youth to her grab bag of topical subject matter, urging after-school and other such programs to hold down delinquency, and La Guardia snapped her up for his Problems of Youth Committee. The future of women in American culture, however, remained her most insistent theme. When Margaret Pickel, the dean of women at Columbia University, asked in a magazine piece why there were no jobs for women, Fannie congratulated her at once for writing an article so balanced and free from "reckless recrimination." Fannie reminded Pickel of how strategic a moment they were living through, when women would "either lose what ground they have gained during the inevitable change years that come with war, or use that ground as a springboard into a future worthy of their potentialities." Pickel thanked Fannie for her thoughts, adding it was her own sense that some women were doing themselves unnecessary harm by making "wild accusations" about the "professional jealousy of men." In Fannie's standard speech to women's groups during the latter part of the decade, she leveled harsh criticism at women for their failure to prove to men that granting them the vote had brought appreciable gifts to the nation, and for their further failure to do anything to forestall the Second World War.

"Until women learn to use politics for the purposes for which politics is intended, no woman in this room, or in this nation, is entitled to self-satisfaction over our achievements, notwithstanding our present spiritual, artistic, intellectual or ethical achievements," she said. Women could not leave their clocks eternally stopped at "sex o'clock," Fannie said, "an hour which, to be sure, has its place on the dial, but twenty-three additional hours also have their places."

The interests of men and women were starting to merge, she said. "Women will and must play a role not only in the home, but in the political, economic, and social life of tomorrow."

As La Guardia entered his third term of office, he gave Fannie a position on the executive board of the City-wide Citizens' Committee on Harlem. She had addressed the National Urban League dinner in 1938, urging members of the black community to think of themselves as Americans first and to lift up a single mass voice demanding the rights and privileges of their citizenship. The organization put her on its board in 1939, but even as she accepted the post, she explained that she could be counted on for vocal support but neither time nor money. By 1942, embarrassed by her lack of involvement, she willingly offered her resignation, but the director, James Hubert, wouldn't hear of it. "Your contribution to our whole problem, not only by appearing for us at gatherings, but by speaking out generally, is immeasurable," he told her. Hubert's departure from the organization a few months later gave Fannie her opening to resign for good, and she did.

She took the same stance toward her membership on the board of United Neighborhood Houses, but her involvement with the deteriorating conditions in Harlem was more wholehearted, showing up even in her private correspondence. Daily trips to St. Luke's Hospital to visit Jack during his heart episode in 1943 had heightened Fannie's concern about the area. "Almost daily the buses are scenes of unpleasant episodes between colors," she told Carl Van Vechten in a note, saying that "a more and more undisciplined Negro press" apparently was responsible for "inciting the Negro-in-the-street to open hostility. I am concerned," she said, "although this is only a deduction from a highly local observation. However, there is no doubt that it is symptomatic of impending events which, if controlled in time, can be handled to the advantage of the minority."

In 1946 she wrote an article for The New York Times Magazine titled "The Other and Unknown Harlem," in which she made a point of featuring several of the area's many fine homes and upstanding residents. Though she acknowledged Harlem's burgeoning social issues, she deliberately presented a picture that did not synchronize with what she called the "popular whoop-'em-up, shoot-'em-down, race-rioting, zoot-suited, bear-greased, white man's version" of Harlem life.

Asked earlier that same year by Negro Digest to contribute to its "If I Were a Negro" series, Fannie outlined her cautious strategy for the pursuit of justice and equality—quite akin to the way she approached Jewish matters throughout the war. She also displayed some of the fixed ideas that she had been harboring about black people since the 1920s.

Fannie said as a Negro she would want to achieve awareness of the plight of her people without bitterness, that she would want to be "capable of a sense of high pride in those singing qualities of heart and spirit; those rhythms of mind and body, which have helped the race survive. I would want to experience gratitude for the godliness, the friendliness, the joyous perpetual adolescence of the Negro. Qualities which have enabled him to laugh off, sing off, pray off, some of his gargantuan social burdens. That would give me courage and self-confidence." She said she would carefully guard against "inciting within myself, or within the members of my race, a belligerent assault upon the situation, because by the very nature of the minority's dilemma, my cause would be doomed by the power of the majority."

Fannie was particularly indignant over the way the U.S. military had treated its black soldiers, segregating them from white soldiers and discriminating against them even as it sent them into battle. She said her strategy would be to "bore from within," to "go out after the indignation of the growing number of white allies" to help effect change.

"I would teach my children their unassailable right to the liberties of the democratic way of life," she said. "I would teach them to rely upon the integrity and the dignity of their own spirit. I would teach them that by affiliating themselves with the labor movement, by demanding economic equality, by realizing their right to reap the benefits of a peace which they helped achieve, they are leading their people, the bloodless and the victorious way, out of the jungles of inequality."

This was a daughter of smug and segregated turn-of-the-century St. Louis writing, a girl whose parents thought Negroes were "fine in their place." For someone who had grown up too oblivious to notice the absence of black students at her high school or university, she had come far. But for a woman who had benefited from more than twenty years of adult immersion in the issues at the highest level—writing about them, speaking out about them, lending support to talented black writers, forming friendships, serving on boards and committees, and having social and professional access to black people of every sphere—old St. Louis still clung to Fannie's thinking as she puzzled things out.

Despite her reputation for aloofness, Fannie was generous, loyal, and caring in friendship, until she had reason to change her mind. This was true even when the relationship grew out of professional necessity; the friendship went on long after the usefulness of the relationship to her career had disappeared. People like Daniel Frohman and August Heckscher remained priority friends for Fannie, even as they doddered into their nineties; she would never have risked hurting either's feelings. And although her interests had long sinced diverged from those of her good friends from high school and college, she answered their letters promptly, paid courtesy visits, and showed the requisite concern about their lives and children. Her few remaining relatives got the same respectful treatment.

She didn't offer friendship indiscriminately. Molly Dewson, the clever editor of the *Democratic Digest* and a fellow dog lover, tried for years to get closer to Fannie but never succeeded. Dewson pondered Fannie's remoteness in deeply psychological terms, at least in a poem she dashed off one night. She saw Fannie as someone in pursuit of life at full speed but at the same time unwilling to engage at an intimate level. She pointed to the fact that Fannie surrounded herself with animals—likely because they asked less of her than the people she knew. "Not an emotion shall escape I will seize each last one in my inky fingers," Dewson wrote of Fannie. "I am vital vital VITAL / yet why are my finger tips so cold / everyone else is so warm."

Neither Fannie nor Ruth Bryan Rohde spent a minute analyzing each other's behavior, but then they were so similar in vitality, ambition, self-possession, and external focus. That relationship never faltered. Long after Ruth's political potency was behind her, Fannie still delighted in cohosting a huge New Year's Day reception with her when appropriate during the war years, in Fannie's spectacular cathedral of a gallery. Twice they honored General and Mrs. Hugh Drum and other top military personnel stationed in the city.

Fannie never stopped giving credit to Bob Davis for all that he had done for her in the early days. Six months before his death in October 1942, she began soliciting tributes from the writers he had "discovered"—thirty, by his count, including Fannie, Mary Roberts Rinehart, Dorothy Canfield Fisher, Montague Glass, Octavus Roy Cohen, Zane Grey, George Jean Nathan, Rex Stout, Katharine Brush, Ward Morehouse, and Conrad Richter. Fannie's plan was to put together a special volume in tribute to his remarkable career. Davis was deeply moved by the gesture, even though the war made it impossible to interest a publisher in the project.

Fannie did not hesitate to pressure Mayor La Guardia to speak when her friend and personal physician, A. A. Berg, dedicated his collection of nineteenth- and twentieth-century manuscripts at the New York Public Library. But more significant for Berg, Fannie enabled him to attend an important medical conference in Italy by looking after his ailing sister, writing him detailed letters daily about her state of mind and health.

She was also prepared to go just as far out of her way for a nobody. Fannie exhausted every possible contact until she found a job for the glib and handsome son of a neighborhood shopkeeper who had become her ballroom dance instructor and sometime escort. Fannie adored the young man and dutifully wrote him while he was in the military—until she caught him in what she considered an unforgivable act. He had asked her for an eighty-dollar loan to cover money he said was being garnished from his wages because of an airplane instrument he had ruined. Fannie sent the check to his commanding officer along with a letter asking for verification of the story. Exposed, her young friend then confessed to Fannie that he actually owed the money to a civilian who lived near the base in Pecos, Texas, whose car he had damaged. He said he had only concocted the military dressing to give his request more urgency, in the way an author like herself might add a detail to improve a story she was writing. With this last, he hoped to tease Fannie into a smile of forgiveness.

It was a gross miscalculation. "It is rather ironic that on D-Day, when my heart was pretty full of the sense of the deeds of our boys, this wretched exploit should have fallen into my lap," Fannie finally told him after he wrote her twice. She had never signed on to be his mentor, she said. "I do, however, insist upon saying in the plainest English at my command, that I think it was a genuinely secondary performance and I have not yet reached the stage in my mental plans where I am content with anything less than first-rate friends." From that moment, and though he continued to try, there was no way back into her life.

∞

Money was also at the base of other episodes that shook or shattered long-term relationships in Fannie's life. In the matter of unpaid debts, Fannie trusted her friends to behave as she would, as her father always had. If she gave a loan, she did it generously and without hesitation or deadline for repayment. But she expected the money back as soon as the borrower was able to repay, and without a reminder from her. She gladly lent five hundred dollars to Helen Worden and John Erskine, for example, when Erskine was in frail health and the couple was desperate for cash. When Erskine recovered, and Helen blithely reported to Fannie that their finances had improved, no check followed. Fannie was stunned. "My budget isn't so flexible now as I could wish," she wrote them. "I am repeatedly having to postpone writing people with a real 'need.' Five hundred from you would help me not to have to turn away so many 'needers.' "

Fannie kept the Erskines in her life, but Mabel Search was not so lucky. Their ten-year friendship, littered with letters from Mabel apologizing to Fannie for letting her down in one way or another, finally faltered over an unrepaid loan of twelve hundred dollars. And after an even longer friendship, her relationship with the director Robert Milton cooled when she had to badger him for the return of silver flatware he had borrowed, which finally came back minus one mother-of-pearl-handled fork. Fannie enthusiastically received the emerald calla lily her friend and frequent escort Albert Richter Rothschild had made for her but did not hesitate to let the friendship cool over a loan of twenty-five hundred dollars. In that case, Fannie gently threatened legal action.

For Fannie displays of poor character from a friend were far worse crimes than social slights, which seemed to roll off her. She herself made and broke plans so often, doing so was hardly something that would make her think less of others. When too much time passed between opportunities to see valued old friends, she was quick to take the initiative to reestablish contact. In her confident way she would drop a note of reminder that she could not be gotten rid of so easily.

Fannie claimed that major social occasions always gave her the "got to go home blues," but worse was her dread of missing out on something significant—so she would go anyway. It was a "teasing conflict" she never got beyond. She attributed her discomfort in high-powered social situations to two sources: first, her feeling that she was too bumbling with repartee to engage comfortably with New York's "eclectic world of sophisticates" and, second, that she did not like the feeling of being held in judgment by the "man-eaters" in the room "who cared little for or even disliked my writing, and who probably also disliked me for the seemingly chilly reserve which coated my unease."

Yet this did not stop her from feeling perfectly comfortable writing fan letters to perfect strangers whose work had thrilled her: the painter Grant Wood got two ("You are the new, the challenge, the ringing note in America today!"), as did Thornton Wilder, whom she declared "the new high water mark in our American theater" after she saw *Our Town.* She often dashed off a note to the commentator Charles Edward Russell after one of his broadcasts and struck up a lively correspondence with him that continued until his death.

Among the friends she considered her "prized possessions" were unknowns like Lois Toensfeldt and Julia Browne, David and Uranie Davis, and Fannie's dressmaker, Ethel Shanley, alongside the bright and once-brighter lights: Bob Davis, Fiorello La Guardia, George Hellman, Carl Van Vechten, Elisabeth Marbury, John and Helen Worden Erskine, Ruth Bryan Owen Rohde, Mischa Elman, Harry Herschfeld, Charles Hanson Towne, Francine Larrimore, Mary Margaret McBride, Henrietta Additon, Anna Kross, and Stef. Although Fannie liked to think of herself as "a die-hard where friends are concerned," the fact is she dropped or was dropped by many and never seemed to look back. She lost patience with Rebecca West around 1937, and the relationship with Kathleen Norris seemed to run its course at Charles Norris's death in 1945. Though Fannie's papers show decades of warm and intense correspondence with both West and Norris, neither got more than the most perfunctory mention in her memoirs—and then as literary notables of the era, not on the lists of her important friendships. Mabel Search, who had been Fannie's constant companion throughout the 1940s, does not even rate an offhanded mention. Nor, oddly, does Zora Neale Hurston, with whom there was no known falling-out.

Fannie's own explanation for her discomfort with intimacy, as well as her inability to cultivate friendships with those she admired most, was probably too facile. She was "happier in the surging swarms," she said. "The bluish dead-faced murals of people with the unseeing stares, sitting in rows in subways, were more eloquent, it seemed to me, than the processed epigrams of the wits of the Round Table could ever be."

Her metaphoric summation of why she was the way she was got closer to the reality: "I had chosen my jungle," she said, "or perhaps it had chosen me."

Zora

In 1943, the year after the tribute to Fannie in *Dust Tracks on a Road,* Zora invited her old friend "for old time's sake" to see her to be honored as a distinguished alumna of Howard University. Fannie wrote Zora back at her Daytona Beach, Florida, address: "I don't think you want me at Howard University on March 2nd, because I might 'burst' with pride and that would mess up the ceremonies," she teased. "A bursting lady author is never pleasant." Actually, Fannie said, she had a government commitment in Detroit that day, otherwise nothing could keep her away.

Fannie also congratulated Zora on the publication of her memoirs, though she erroneously called the book "Footprints in the Dust." She told Zora how thrilled she had been to open the book to the chapter about herself and Ethel Waters but that she had given her copy away to the son of the author Julian Street before she had a chance to read it. She said she had been very anxious to introduce Street to Zora's work and was ordering another copy that day.

From Fannie's and Zora's papers, there does not appear to have been much contact between the two from that time on. Although Zora moved back to New York for several years during the 1940s, the two women do not appear to have exchanged letters or visits, at least none is noted in Fannie's appointment books, until February 10, 1949, when Zora was mired in legal troubles. "Please help me," she wrote Fannie in desperation. "You know that I can take it and would not cry out for help unless I was really desperate." She needed an urgent loan of seventy-six dollars for "room rent and other things" resulting from her legal difficulties. The preceding fall Zora had been falsely accused of molesting a young boy and had been embroiled ever since in trying to clear her name. She told Fannie she had exhausted every other resource—including the pawning of her typewriter—before appealing to her old friend. It appears from Zora's letter that Fannie already had been of assistance in a second small-claims court case brought by an accuser named Richard D. Rochester. "I know that I am indebted to you and Mrs. [Helen Worden] Erskine and to the archangel James McGurrin," Zora wrote of her victory in court that day.

It is not known how much, but Fannie sent Zora money at once. In thanking her Zora swore, "by anything and all things that I hold sacred," that she had never committed a crime that would have been "against everything in my soul and nature." What shocked her further was that "both my race and my nation have seen fit to befoul me with no excuse whatsoever. . . . And do not forget that this foul thing did not happen to me in the deep South, but in enlightened New York City, so it seems that even here, there are those who care nothing about fair play where a Negro is concerned."

The next letter from Zora to Fannie came six months later, from Beaufort, South Carolina, on word that Fannie had been hospitalized. To Zora, such a thing was unimaginable. "I see you always swirling the waving veils of space like a spear of flame," Zora told her, offering to come take care of her. "I am at your feet and at your service. There is nothing that I would not do for my benefactor and friend. You know that I can type now. I can cook as always. I can do many more things than I could when you scraped me up out of the street. If there is anything that you feel that I could do to please you, you must let me know. I should pay back for all that I have received somehow."

Fannie thanked Zora warmly for her offer but asked nothing other than a visit on her planned trip to New York over Labor Day, a few weeks hence. "In this torn and harassed world," Fannie told Zora, "the stability of friendship is about the only staff of life we have left." It is the last surviving piece of correspondence between them.

Fannie did not attempt to contact Zora after the wire services circulated the gossip-provoking news that she had gone to work in Florida as a household maid. Convinced that Zora had staged the incident for attention, Fannie told Van Vechten so in a postcard. It was in Zora's "fine old tradition," she wrote. "Naughty but nice." Fannie signed the handwritten note as she did all her more personal correspondence since the 1930s: in red ink with a hand drawing of her signature flower, the calla lily, and often a smiley face.

Chapter 35

"The Hands of Veronica"

Within a year of the release of *Hallelujah,* Fannie had her new novel about an agnostic but spiritual healer ready to sell, but she didn't like the suggestions her new editor at Harpers made about altering the plot. Although Frank MacGregor left the final decision about whether to make the changes to Fannie, she thought this showed lack of interest on Harpers' part, and her response was to relegate the book to "cold storage." MacGregor accepted her decision at face value and removed *The Hands of Veronica* from Harpers' fall 1945 list.

When months passed without any further word from MacGregor, Fannie tried an end run. She showed the manuscript to her longtime British publisher, Jonathan Cape, asking for his "ruthless judgment." Cape was enthusiastic about the novel and said so in a cablegram, offering to publish it at once. It was the kind of response Fannie was looking for from Harpers, and she sent the cable to MacGregor. This time she explained herself fully, laying out in detail why she had decided to withdraw the manuscript, even though he never really asked. Though Harpers had been gracious about offering to publish the book, she said, she had gotten the feeling it was a grudging response to please a longtime author but without enthusiasm for the manuscript.

She did not want to put the publisher in that position, so before deciding what to do, she needed Mac to tell her the truth: What did Harpers *really* think of the book? Had she imagined the reservations on his part, or were they real? "I realize it could have been just a combination of my attitude and paper shortage that is responsible for the fact that there has been no further comment from Harpers about the possibility of my changing my mind and publishing *Veronica,*" she wrote him. "It will help me in my ultimate decision if you will give me the honest-to-goodness sum-total decision at Harpers as to whether it is better in their opinion to let the book go unpublished."

To this she added, "Please understand, dear Mac, that this is written in all good will and without an iota or reproach, since I have absolutely no basis for such an attitude." MacGregor responded within a few days that Harpers would be happy to go ahead with publication. He did not comment on the manuscript directly but threw in the encouraging inducement of continued interest in her autobiography as soon as she was ready to present it.

There was no Hollywood interest in *Veronica,* but because of Hollywood there was modest good news on the reprint front. Popular Library bought thirty-five thousand copies of Fannie's early short-story collection *Humoresque* to release in paperback in conjunction with a new movie remake of the 1919 story. And at about the same time, Enterprise Pictures bought the film rights to "She Walks in Beauty," Fannie's 1921 short story about a daughter and her drug-addicted mother. World Publishing Company bought the reprint rights.

Harpers planned the release of *The Hands of Veronica* to coincide with the film's debut in January 1947, in apparent hopes of capitalizing on the association in the public's mind of Fannie with *Humoresque,* but the new film story had little resemblance to her original. Clifford Odets and Zachary Gold had eliminated the war motif, turned Leon into an ambitious violinist with a ghetto background (John Garfield played the part and Isaac Stern, the violin). They also added the dominating element of the violinist's love affair with an older, sophisticated, then suicidal music patron played by Joan Crawford.

As with the remake of *Back Street,* Warner had no interest in exploiting Fannie's now tenuous connection to the film. It already had annoyed her no end that the studio ignored her offers to help with the production—gratis. ("Legally, I made a stupid contract on the original story years ago," she complained to the columnist Dorothy Kilgallen.) No one even thought to invite her to the premiere until Fannie requested an invitation herself.

When Kilgallen neglected to mention Fannie in her review of the movie for *Modern Screen,* Fannie decided to drop her a note—she denied that her purpose was to complain about the omission, but that was exactly her intent. Instead, she based the comments in her letter on what she saw as the omission's larger significance. "I think the manner in which *Humoresque* has been handled points toward the need to arouse a state of indignation in the minds of those who help shape public opinion with regard to Hollywood ethics or lack of them," Fannie said. "There is a certain inherent *noblesse oblige* in the situation." Although it was too late to do anything about *Humoresque,* she added, "In the name of authors in general, I do urge your future awareness of this type of abuse."

Fannie may not have gotten any promotional benefit from the *Humoresque* remake, but the film's release did prompt Warner to pay her for the right to broadcast a radio adaptation of the new movie version of her story. And the interest in *Humoresque* in paperback prompted Popular Library to request the rights to *Lummox, Five and Ten,* and *Great Laughter* as well as options on her other Harpers novels.

On January 6, 1947, Harpers delivered the first six copies of *Veronica* to Fannie. She was so pleased with how it turned out that not even the misspelling of her name on the inside jacket flap upset her—though she did mention it to Mac. Even *The New York Times* reviewer was reasonably kind. "Miss Hurst's Streamlined Healer," read the headline. Nona Balakian said Fannie must have had Hiroshima in mind when she set out to grapple with trying to reconcile science and religion. "As always, her success depends on her ability to absorb and reduce to simple emotional terms, the moods and attitudes of the moment. Reading her is a little like seeing a quick review of the year in 'March of Time': you know it has nothing to do with you, but a surface, wholesale reality makes it seem authentic." Balakian said that in Veronica, whose pseudoscientific mysticism allows her to effect cures for everything from acne to a misplaced vertebrae, Fannie had produced "one of the most remarkable heroines of the season: a present-day Bernadette who, professing to be an agnostic gains the support of medical science in her miracle cures."

The book got off to a decent start, with sales of six hundred copies the first week along with the nineteen thousand copies that had been ordered before its release. Harpers placed ads in the major New York daily newspapers, including a sizable one in the *Times*. When Fannie told Mac she had the feeling the book was "on the stillborn side," he assured her it was "not doing badly at all," with total sales by the end of February at twenty-one thousand copies. This was "somewhat under the sale of *Hallelujah,*" he said, "but don't forget that when that was published there was a real boom in book buying, and today, while buying is not bad, it at least is not on the level of three or four years ago."

"Anywoman"

After *The Hands of Veronica,* Fannie had half an idea to write a series of articles, or perhaps even a book, about forbidden Russia, but her many efforts to secure a visa failed. Instead she settled in to work on her autobiography, at least the part of it she felt comfortable enough to write at this time, and it was with no small anxiety level that she sent "Volume One" over to MacGregor at Harpers in February 1948. He let weeks go by without commenting on it, an inconsiderateness Fannie responded to by asking for the manuscript back. She told MacGregor her decision to reconsider stemmed from the response of another reader. That person, whom she did not name, had told her that it was too much of a tease for her to cover only the first twenty years of her life and end her saga so abruptly. Fannie thought this made sense. "I think I knew all this subconsciously, but was lazy-minded and wanted to feel finished for the time being at least," she explained.

When MacGregor still did not write to comment on the manuscript, Fannie telephoned him to complain. She was brusque but then softened her tone in a subsequent note, excusing him. She acknowledged how difficult he must have found it to be honest, given the personal nature of the material. Even this did not elicit a response from MacGregor. In fact, his only written communication with her in this period was to report that Popular Library, after republishing *Lummox,* had reneged on the rest of the deal to bring out several other of Fannie's old titles in paperback.

Once again Fannie put the autobiography aside. She headed a few hours north for a summer in the Catskills, which provided inspiration for a new novel, and in a little more than a year had the manuscript for *Anywoman* ready to submit. This time MacGregor quickly accepted the book for publication, passing it on to Fannie's old editor, Bill Briggs, for handling.

Briggs brimmed with his usual enthusiasm. *Anywoman,* he said, was a "full-sized, completely developed Fannie Hurst novel," which drove him, as it would its eventual readers, immediately into the atmosphere of the Catskills. He assured Fannie that she again had produced "another very fine piece of storytelling."

Fannie thought she again should engage an outside publicist. Her choice this time was Dick Hyman, whom she had met on her long walks in Central Park. His role, she told Mac, "would not be book publicity so much as a sort of side campaign to announce the coming of the book," and she promised he would stay well out of Ramona Herdman's way. Hyman's plan was to start promoting Fannie two months before the book's release in April 1950 for a thousand-dollar fee.

∽

Fannie did her own part in getting her name before the public. She accepted what turned out to be a three-week assignment from International News Service to cover the murder trial of Dr. Hermann Sander, a Manchester, New Hampshire, physician accused of injecting air into the vein of his cancer-ridden patient Abbie Borroto in an act of mercy. Fannie's impressions ran in the *New York Journal-American* and other newspapers across the country daily until Sander's acquittal.

This round, when *Anywoman* came out, Fannie had no direct complaints with her publisher, even complimenting MacGregor on the ad Harpers ran on publication day in *The New York Times Book Review.* She even had much better luck than usual with the book review itself. Wilbur Watson wrote positively about her story of a girl from a tradition-bound Catskill village who falls in love with the wrong man—"the Brooklyn sharpie who teaches swimming at the luxury hotel across the valley"—and whom she grimly follows at summer's end, then waits for patiently through his marriage to a flamboyant widow and the loss of both his legs in a plane crash. "As is always the case with this novelist," Watson wrote, "a wealth of absorbing detail enriches every page. Miss Hurst's streets are as vivid as ever—the pulse of life is always there, under the drabness. . . . It goes without saying that her loyal public will follow her to the last page."

Unbeknownst to people like Watson, that loyal public was dwindling. The sales in advance of publication of *Anywoman* were well under half those of Fannie's previous two books, and the first-week sales were even more abysmal. MacGregor gallantly blamed the shrinking market for fiction—not Fannie—and assured her that Harpers would do what it could to come up with a sizeable total.

Fannie's proud, even radical response was to offer a refund to Harpers of the unearned portion of what she had been paid in advance for the book. She was serious about it, too, because she reiterated the offer in August: "I don't want the advance to cause publishing loss to Harpers and will therefore dig down and refund the difference if you get what I mean, which I Do mean," she wrote MacGregor. Eventually he accepted, without as much as a mention of the mutually profitable history that Fannie Hurst and the House of Harper had so long enjoyed. Fannie's air was pleasant, businesslike, and matter-of-fact as she sent in her check for the outstanding amount early in 1951. This while Edna Ferber was finishing her next novel, *Giant,* which would sell 3 million copies the following year.

In 1953 Fannie completed her next novel. Her retaliation was to send the manuscript directly to Jonathan Cape in London for the British edition to be published first, which it was. Her strategy did not entirely work, however. For although *The Man with One Head* was soon released in England, as planned, a U.S. publisher for it was never found.

Jacques

The unraveling of Fannie's status at Harpers matched her plummet a few years before in the world of magazine fiction. By 1951 the editors at such high-end women's magazines as *Ladies' Home Journal* and *Good Housekeeping* who once had vied for Fannie's short stories (or at least rejected them with fawning deference and trepidation) now passed up her work with a flip "not up to the author's usual standard" or "too much old age in it." New stories such as "Abe Adolphus" kicked around New York for more than a year before ending up unimpressively in *Canadian Home Journal* for five hundred dollars American, and others, such as "Grapevine," never saw print. It had gotten to the point where a *Reader's Digest* editor thought nothing of patronizing Fannie with suggestions of how she could improve a profile she had written of Elisabeth Marbury for the magazine. Fannie responded to neither the letter nor the request, and the profile never ran.

Yet Fannie had been such an important figure and force on the national scene for such a long time that, outside of a handful of editors and agents, the diminution in her literary capital was not widely known. This gave her an amusingly bifurcated standing in the world at large. In a note to a young friend of his, the editor John Farrar described Fannie around this time as "gorgeous and indestructible." A little wrinkly but still striking and chic at sixty-six, she had the name recognition and visual appeal—yes, these were different times— to be sought after repeatedly for appearances in the fledgling medium of television. In October 1951 NBC named her a permanent panelist—at eighty dollars per appearance—on the host Ben Grauer's daytime half-hour television program *It's a Problem.* The show aired daily for a year. Fannie's appointment books in these years show regular appearances on Mary Margaret McBride's radio program as well as numerous one-shot appearances on other popular television and radio shows, such as *The Tex and Jinx McCrary Show,* which gave an annual "Woman of the Year" award in which Fannie participated (young William Safire was a producer), and Fred Friendly's *Who Said That?* Warner paid a two-thousand-dollar fee for the rights to release "Sister Act," this time in some yet-to-be-determined television format. Even Edward R. Murrow featured Fannie on his prestigious live interview program, *Person-to-Person,* in June 1954, following an opening segment on the bandleader Guy Lombardo.

There was no letup in the crush of Fannie's daily activities: animal welfare, mayoral committees, public speeches, board meetings (she had joined the Heckscher Foundation board), cocktails, theater premieres, dinners, and when *Life* magazine wanted an incisive commentator to applaud the recently released female part of Alfred C. Kinsey's landmark study of American sexual practice, the editors turned to her.

Money per se was certainly not a problem for Fannie and Jack, but with his having closed down his Carnegie Hall studio in 1951, and her income prospects less assured, they looked into trying to reduce their overhead by giving up the top floor of their gargantuan triplex. This included Fannie's Gothic chapel–like writing studio overlooking the apartment's crenellated stone terrace. Ultimately, however, the potential savings in rent was not worth the aggravation, and they held on to the extra space.

Doors close, windows open. A new income infusion turned up in 1952 in the form of a weekly opinion column, "From My Window," which ran for a time in *American Weekly,* the weekend supplement of the *Journal-American.* Life rolled along in its usual way.

On Monday morning, March 3, 1952, Fannie awoke at the stroke of 5:30, and Jack turned on the radio for the weather report so that Fannie could dress appropriately for her ninety-minute morning walk. The couple had been to a dinner party at the home of Ethel Shanley the night before. Jack had been in fine form, telling light jokes in the pleasant company of old, good friends. Shortly before midnight, as he and Fannie prepared to leave, Ethel wrapped up a piece of Cornish hen for them to take home to their latest Yorkshire terrier.

In the morning, through the sound of running water as she prepared her bath, Fannie thought she heard a call. She paused a moment, heard nothing more, and went on with her morning routine. She heard the call again, turned off the water, and went into the hall. "Did you call me, Jack?" she asked. There was no response. Fannie flew in terror to his room to find him writhing in pain. "Don't leave me," he begged as beads of perspiration appeared on his forehead. "Don't leave me."

"I had to!" Fannie recalled in deep regret of the moment she ran for help. "I had to!" When she returned Jack was dead at age seventy-six.

In the reams upon reams of Fannie's personal, social, and business correspondence during the thirty-seven years of her marriage, her references to "Himself" are strikingly few. With the exceptions of their wedding anniversary and his few hospitalizations, Fannie moved through her extremely active social calendar as a woman without encumbrance or attachment—independent, single. There is little in the constant "I" and "me" of her expression—when giving or accepting invitations to dinner or cocktails or travel—that even remotely suggests the presence of a significant relationship in her life, let alone a marriage. More to the point, there is nothing in, at least, the outward way she conducted herself during these thirty-seven years to presage the impact of Jacques's death on her sense of self.

Jacques may not have seemed to be much on her mind in the years they were together, but she certainly moved to correct this in the time that followed. In her daily appointment book, every Monday after Jack's death Fannie marked the passing of another week without him.

March 3, 1952: "My darling left me at 6:30 A.M." March 10: "My darling, My darling died one terrible week ago this sad day." March 17: "Second week of intolerable living with out my dearest." March 24: "Third week of I am alone." Four years later: "The 203rd Monday, February 6th, 1956. 'Passed away' is the phrase they use. I could never use it for you, dear love, you have never passed away from me and never will." February 20: "You were my all when you were with me. You will continue to be my all, as long as I live." Over sixteen years of Mondays, until the day she died, she never missed one.

In her memoirs Fannie mentions this ritual in the most offhanded way. "Every Monday morning—Jack died on that day—I write him a short letter, chattily, not in grief and with no feeling that he knows about it in an afterlife. It is a self-indulgence I allow myself. Frequently I dwell on: We had it nice."

To Fannie, Jacques in death was someone "who proved the grandeurs of which quiet men are sometimes capable." He had been her "remote control," which Fannie claimed promptly to have realized, even if Jacques did not. The marriage, she said, was built on mutual respect for each other's freedom, a condition, in Fannie's appraisal, neither of them ever violated. Throughout their long years together, Fannie claimed that, despite outward appearances, her "busy and many-sided life was to be activated by my desire to keep myself intact in his regard."

Jack was a man of inner gravity, despite his humor and nonchalance, harboring "the melancholy of one who suffers with and for whoever suffers." Fannie said she felt his eye upon her at all times, even when it was least apparent, "not wanting me to spoil myself in the eyes of others, even in superficial matters."

The tempo of his life was slower than Fannie's, especially after he had stopped teaching. But he loved his music and a slew of diversions from theater to travel, even to light sports such as ice skating, handball, and canoeing. He was a prodigious walker and liked the stock market and games of chance, but at the center, Fannie felt, was herself. "My domination of him," she said, "was only exceeded by his domination of me."

A year after Jacques's death Fannie prepared a column that was released to newspapers across the country and broadcast on the radio program *This I Believe,* presented by Murrow. In her statement of some five hundred words, she said she had never been good enough for Jack, who was noble, pure, and selfless, a man of "wonderful goodness" who lived a "stainless life." "He's gone now," Fannie wrote. "But his life has taught me how the good that men can do can live after them." A year later, when she was asked to participate in the Murrow series for the second time, again the subject of her statement was Jack. "Now, personally," she wrote, "I aspire to live by the precepts of my husband's wonderful goodness and stainless life, to earn the right to live comfortably with myself and to pass on as he did inspiration for better living to those who are left behind."

The response to Jacques's death of at least one student bore out Fannie's testimony. "He was one of the greatest influences in my life," wrote Martha Ellen Wenz in a letter of condolence. She said he had a way of giving her confidence in herself, unlike any of the five teachers she had before him. She found him calm, serene, and understanding, never praising too much, just offering a smile when the lesson was good. The smile, she said, stayed with her.

Jacques's estate, once settled, amounted to some $423,500, to which Fannie was sole heir. She donated the bulk of it to the Albert Einstein College of Medicine of Yeshiva University for the establishment of a cardiac laboratory in Jacques's name. At the dedication ceremony Eleanor Roosevelt was at Fannie's side.

Surely a measure of Fannie's pain was guilt. Had she kept Jack from pursuing a more public career in music? Had he fallen under the spell of her swollen ego? Her admittedly endless "Me. Me. Me."? With full conviction and stream-of-consciousness punctuation, she declared, perhaps as much to convince herself: "Jack had a happy life with me. Time and time again he told me so He acted so He told others so He looked and was so."

There was also the ear-piercing silence of her sudden aloneness, a condition she now shared with friends such as Helen Worden, whose husband, John Erskine, died at about the same time, and Inez Haynes Irwin, whose husband, Will, had died a few years earlier. It was from Inez that Fannie got the most unsentimental but meaningful advice:

> For awhile sympathy glides off that encasement of
> glossy adamant in which you live a prisoner. All one
> really wishes is coma. Then one by one the thousand
> hands of life reach out and clutch us to her. And
> although ourselves still not alive, we accede to her
> placements. Sympathy then is ineffably tender.
>
> Only one thing I can tell you and of this, I am sure.
> The only—not cure—anaesthesia for grief is work. Work
> more work and still more work.

These were words she seems to have taken to heart. For although Fannie's grief appeared to be profound—"Monday since life lost its loveliness for me." "Fourteen Mondays ago, my agony fell upon me." "Fifteenth Monday of my tragic widowhood." "Twenty-fifth Monday since the blackest day of my life"— it was perfectly controlled. Her calendar, even in the days immediately following the one-woman funeral she staged for Jack—she said it was his request that only she be present—was as full as ever, including previously scheduled broadcasts she did not cancel. At the first of May she was off to Geneva as planned as a U.S. delegate to a major World Health Organization conference, and on her return she was ready for full engagement. To the U.S. surgeon general, Dr. Leonard Scheele, she offered to mention her "small identification with W.H.O." on a couple of upcoming broadcasts and any other services from her in this regard he might welcome. "I hope you will call on me," she wrote enthusiastically, "because my interest does not cease with the conclusion of The Fifth World Health Assembly."

Four years later, on Monday No. 208, the diary entry reads: "Dearly beloved, We are almost two weeks into the fifth year of your going—if only I could become more reconciled to it . . . but I can never be without this great and redeeming thought to cheer me on—I have had you in life and I still have you in death, my love. How can I complain?"

And in her memoirs, reflecting on the marriage that involved a parallel relationship of like intensity for sixteen of its thirty-seven years, she wrote: "It would seem that our sea of matrimony was full of treacherous archipelagoes. But we sailed it for wonderful years of blue waters, blue sky."

Chapter 36

"Classical Success"

In the years after Fannie's graduation from Washington University, she never stopped feeling that the school had turned a "granite shoulder" of indifference toward her. She responded with hurt feelings, which she never hesitated to express, and a closed purse. What intensified her embitterment over the years was the respect she received from colleges with which she had a much more tenuous connection. Faculty and administrators at Columbia and Barnard, Hunter and Vassar often called on her expertise. And by the time *Lummox* had fixed her place in the literary cavalcade, Fannie could practically taste her desire for recognition from her alma mater, and she wasn't embarrassed to say so, especially in response to specific requests for funds.

"In the fourteen years since 1909, I have had neither encouragement, cooperation, nor exhibition of interest from either the university or the alumni association," she complained in the period when she was still returning to St. Louis to visit her parents several times each year.

By 1933, with *Lummox, Appassionata, A President Is Born, Five and Ten, Back Street, Imitation of Life,* and dozens of textbook-quality short stories to her credit, Fannie felt the beginnings of a new attitude forming. Washington University's recently hired news director, Raymond Howes, assigned a student to do a profile of her for *Student Life.* How fitting, given how many of Fannie's apprentice pieces had appeared in the magazine, and the prospect of the story delighted her—until she saw it. "Not only from the angle of old-fashioned journalism should such perennial stuff be anathema to you young comers," she raged in a letter of complaint, "but the lazy and uninterested and uninteresting saying of stale things without even the gesture of pretending to check up on the life and contemporary doings of the alumna under discussion, adds just one more sense of disappointment, not to mention other emotions, to an alumna who by now should be immunized to the attitude."

Imagine her embarrassment when Howes informed her that her own secretary had provided the information. "We had the choice, therefore, of printing no story at all or a hackneyed one," he explained. "We chose the second alternative because we felt that no series of biographical sketches of important graduates would be complete without something about you."

By way of apology Fannie offered to help Howes in any way she could. He countered with an invitation for her to open the university's annual fall lecture series. This he followed up with the flattering article for the school's alumni bulletin heralding Colonel Edward M. House's inclusion of Fannie on his list of American women capable of holding high government office.

Fannie was finally starting to get her due when a new level of unpleasantness struck her like a whack in the stomach. A representative of an organization that wanted Fannie as a speaker contacted Washington University's New York alumni group hoping the connection would provide some leverage in getting her to appear. The caller was told that Fannie had broken ranks with the group some years earlier after she "applied" to the university for an honorary degree that the college declined to confer. Mortified, Fannie wrote Lois Toensfeldt at once to ask her help in squelching the story, which she insisted was "untrue just one hundred percent." And despite Howes's continued solicitousness toward her, Fannie petulantly declined the lecture invitation with an obviously transparent excuse and got angry with her alma mater all over again.

In 1935 the brouhaha over *Imitation of Life* brought out of the woodwork an old college friend, Henry Carter Patterson, who was living in Philadelphia. He and Fannie commiserated in letters about their disillusionment with the school, but Patterson's objections were on an entirely different score. "I have no heart for its consideration as long as I know that no Negro applicant, no matter how brilliant a person he or she might be, would be considered by our alma mater," he wrote Fannie. Patterson admitted he had gone easy with a visiting assistant chancellor on the subject, "being only too aware that we Quakers, despite our professions, have not yet seen fit to civilize our own colleges (Swarthmore, Haverford, Bryn Mawr, etc.) in this respect." Fannie took another thirteen years to register her objection to the policy, a response that can only be interpreted as very little, very late.

At about the time Arthur Compton became university chancellor in 1945, Patterson and other old friends of Fannie's led a charge for her to receive the honorary degree so long denied her. Fannie, of course, welcomed the initiative but carefully took pains to distance herself from any appearance of collusion with the efforts on her behalf. Instead of offering her a degree Compton began making periodic requests to Fannie to represent him at various important ceremonies on campuses in the New York area, which she happily agreed to do. He also sent special words of congratulations when she was named to a distinguished group of St. Louis Women of Achievement in 1947, adding his regrets that she did not come to town to receive her award.

Yet the thaw in Fannie's relations with the university did not stop her from a public lament of the "granite shoulder" in an article of reminiscence she wrote for the February 1950 issue of the *Alumni Bulletin*. In it she called for "tighter and righter" relations among the alumni, faculty, and student body. Her article elicited several favorable responses, notably one from a professor in the electrical engineering department who happened to have been a neighbor of Fannie's when her parents were living in the boardinghouse on Laclede Avenue. "I don't mind telling you in confidence, that I believe the university should have recognized your contribution in the form of an honorary degree," he wrote. "There were others that believed likewise. But you must know that recommendations for such recognition must in every case run the gauntlet of departments directly concerned, and that in the field of literature some of the specialists are convinced that literature ceased with Shakespeare or Addison or Meredith, or whom-have-you depending upon their particular little potato patches. So these awards are apt to reflect the personal bias of a few individuals, and do not necessarily represent general opinion." So there it was. That dusty indictment from college days stood: Fannie Hurst, Classical Failure, even after all these years.

In 1951 Fannie's lawyers sent a copy of a will she had prepared to the chancellor's office. It left half of her estate to Jack, who was still living at the time, and the rest for the establishment of a proposed "Fannie Hurst Literary Awards of the Year." Though her alma mater was surely honored to be named among the three permanent members of the prize committee—Columbia and the University of Illinois were the others—the implicit information in the document may have given some pause. It included no direct financial bequest.

The following autumn the university again invited Fannie to open its annual lecture series and then, at long last, in February 1953, came Chancellor Compton's long-awaited invitation for her to receive the honorary degree of doctor of letters, to be awarded June 10 during the university's centennial commencement exercises. Better at sixty-seven than never. In baking heat Fannie stood in the august company of T. S. Eliot, retired Judge Learned Hand, and seven other figures of national renown. To the outside world it amounted to no more than a couple of paragraphs of newspaper filler and grist for items that Fannie's new four-thousand-dollar-a-year public relations consultant, Alix Williamson, could slip into New York newspaper columns. For Fannie it was a moment of supreme vindication, the symbol of authenticity she had coveted for the better part of forty-four years.

There was no one with whom to share it. "Three who would have cared most, Mama, Papa and Jack, were gone," Fannie recalled, "and so I stood alone but deeply grateful that aloneness has no terrors for me." After the ceremony she stole away to Cates Avenue, just to see the old house again.

That fall Fannie asked her attorney to look into establishing a scholarship fund in her name for needy and worthy students at Washington U, then she took off on a monthlong jaunt to London, Paris, Rome, Athens, Istanbul, and Jerusalem.

It was in Jerusalem that Fannie finally came to terms with her Jewish heritage. She was not proud of her "mental processes or lack of them" on the subject. In her memoirs she admitted that, over the years, even discussing the problem embarrassed her. "Generations of the hunted and driven seemed to rise in me; a cold resentment toward the world that had driven them, mingled with a sense of humiliation at belonging to an unwanted people." She couldn't look at a Hasidic Jew without a "snide sense of embarrassment for him and myself!" In a group of women of all persuasions loaded down with jewels, it would be the Jewish woman Fannie would single out for criticism. She remembered her father's strenuous objection when her mother had wanted to buy her an expensive baby-lamb coat, saying Jews had to be more careful about ostentatious display. "Papa must have known why he despised ostentation and preached the cult of modesty almost to the point of obsession."

Though the subject of anti-Semitism was painful for Fannie, it always seemed "somewhere out there" in the way of a malaria epidemic in Asia. "I hold no brief for the fact that I was one of those for whom it took a Hitler to blast out of regarding the Jew and his problems objectively," she confessed. The rituals of the faith held no special meaning for her, no more so than those of the Greek or Episcopal church. But in Israel the realization of who she was came upon her. Seeing the "tribal men and women out of Yemen and the long-eyed Sephardic Jews, and Jews who for the first time in their history were not walking the desert sands but the storied streets of the homeland to which they had returned, it came to me as if up from the Biblical soil: These are my people, and Mama and Papa and I from Cates Avenue in St. Louis are their people."

She wondered out loud what had compelled her to reveal these secret places in her life in her memoirs. "They do not enhance me," she wrote. "Nor do I do it in the spirit of confessional. I do it because I feel lighter and perhaps a little nicer."

"Anatomy of Me"

"*Anatomy of Me*—JUST PUBLISHED," the ad copy read, "—The lyrical, sparkling autobiography of Fannie Hurst."

Doubleday & Company was where Fannie's memoirs ended up early in 1958, but only after she had signed and reneged on a contract to have the book published at Henry Holt & Company. At Doubleday the editor Ken McCormick and staff received the manuscript with enough enthusiasm for Fannie to think she had finally found the right publishing home. That lasted from January until October, when the book actually came out.

Then, as usual, she was distressed over what she considered a lackluster promotional campaign. She assessed Doubleday's effort against those being given to the books such as those of Sheilah Graham, whom even McCormick considered a fair comparison, and found her new publisher's effort wanting. She mentioned that she had a new novel almost ready to deliver, but in view of the way Doubleday was handling *Anatomy*, she thought perhaps she should take it elsewhere.

McCormick took her at her word. "I've no way of knowing whether this new novel is good, bad or indifferent," he wrote to his promotion department, explaining why he thought extra effort was in order to try to keep Fannie on Doubleday's list. She wasn't the first lady novelist to go into "minor eclipse," he reasoned, and still had the potential, in his view, to "come back full strength."

In an effort to convince Fannie to stay with Doubleday, McCormick tried to impress her with news of a recent increase in the company's sales force, but she could not have cared less. What she wanted to hear about was paid advertising with her name on it. McCormick told his colleagues that he thought she could be convinced to reconsider with at least a small, visible campaign in the New York area before Christmas. "There's no question that part of the cost of publishing is author vanity advertising," he said. Hence, the beautiful ad mock-ups.

Just in time to push along book sales was the promotional blitz accompanying the director Douglas Sirk's remake of Imitation of Life, which Universal released in April 1959. Unlike the producers of the remakes of Back Street and Humoresque, Ross Hunter took Fannie to lunch in New York as early as 1956 to get her ideas for updating the story and then to make sure she was fully involved with its eventual promotional campaign. He even sent Fannie to meet the press with the young Sandra Dee, who starred in the film along with Lana Turner, Juanita Moore, John Gavin, and Susan Kohner. To suit audiences in the new era, there was no waffle or pancake business partnership between the Lana Turner and Juanita Moore characters, only the relationship of an actress (one of the few approved professions for a white woman in the 1950s) and the black homemaker (also approved) who looks after both of their daughters.

Ironically, Fannie barely mentions her 1933 novel in her memoirs, even though this second film version of it proved to be such a bouncy springboard for promoting Anatomy's publication. Imitation of Life rates only one impossibly worded sentence in Anatomy of Me—an apparent afterthought appended out of time sequence to a discussion of race relations in the post–World War II period.

Again, the picture had a smashing box-office success, and Hunter seemed truly grateful for Fannie's part in it all. "So many critics panned it," he wrote her after the release, "but, as I told the man at the New York Times, I make pictures for the public—warm, human beings who want to laugh or cry—who want to share that emotion with their fellowman—and not for 'the so-called critics.' Oh, thousands of letters keep coming in from all over the country, thanking me for the picture. And I, in turn, must thank you—for the inspiration and for the magnificent story. Also, thanks for your constant help—you were out of this world." In a 1995 poll conducted by the New York Daily News, the movie still ranked in the top-ten all-time favorite films.

Hunter then went to work on a new version of Fannie's Back Street, the third in thirty years. David Miller directed this one, in modern dress, featuring Susan Hayward, John Gavin, and Vera Miles.

Miller sent Fannie a copy of the treatment, which she found objectionable from start to finish. "Personally, at the risk of appearing egoistic and egotistic, I think that my novel *Back Street* is too entrenched in the American mind and heart to say nothing of European countries to find this 'hopped-up' version acceptable," she wrote Hunter in response. "Even the phrase 'Back Street' is now idiom both in America and France, as one commentator recently put it—the novel is entrenched as a small classic. Ray Schmidt is jazzed up to a degree where she is obscured by clouds of tinseled and unconvincing success," Fannie told him. "It is the same treatment employed in the case of Lana Turner in *Imitation of Life* where she was skyrocketed into stardom. To attempt to try to repeat in *Back Street* the technique and devices successfully used in *Imitation of Life* is in my opinion a mistake. My Ray Schmidt was no genius. She would have had no capacity for the sophistications, high powered successes and nightclub excesses indicated in her present characterization."

In Fannie's view the new version lost all of Ray's major characteristics—"the stark loneliness and selflessness, the sacrifices inherent in this study of a woman to whom life has one meaning. . . . The story becomes a conventional sophisticated yarn." Her *Back Street,* she said, was a period piece, set in the 1890s, "where I still think it belongs although I am by no means certain about my judgment in this particular matter." Perhaps, she ventured, the World War II era would be even more effective. Fannie told Louella Parsons of her complaints about the treatment, and Parsons printed them in her column.

Hunter read Fannie's letter over several times before responding but in the end held to his own convictions about what was needed to update the classic story for modern-day audiences. He reminded Fannie that neither of the earlier versions of the film had been financially successful—although his personal favorite was the first one, with John Boles and Irene Dunne. He read the book again, trying to analyze Fannie's story against the prevailing market for love stories. His conclusion? That Ray—he thought of her with the more modern spelling of Rae—had to be a "woman of the world, so to speak, who has pulled herself up by her own bootstraps, who perhaps has had many men—but when she meets Paul [Walter], no one—nothing matters, but her great love for him, her great need to be with him wherever he may be—whatever shame may come her way." The story, he said, had to resonate for the audiences of the day —"up to their standards of thinking and acceptability." If it were to be a period piece, he argued, Universal might as well rerelease the original.

Hunter wrote Fannie again when shooting was well under way, convinced, or at least trying to convince himself, that she was going to be pleased with the outcome. "We have attempted to dramatize what the other two pictures merely talked about—and thus far the results are very gratifying," he said.

> Rae Smith is such a warm, sensitive—yet exciting
> woman—and you understand her loneliness, her love and
> her heartbreak as though it were your own story she was
> a part of. Where at times, *Imitation of Life* strived for
> sensationalism, *Back Street* simply but deftly tells its

story and leaves the spectator, the eavesdropper,
completely drained. For the Rae Smith of *Back Street* is
the Rae Smith of so many women of today—and her
story will hit home. The good taste, the reasons why—
are ably set forth on the screen—and I can't wait for you
to see the finished product so you, too, will be proud of
our achievement. I ran forty-five minutes of cut film on
Tuesday and there wasn't a dry eye in the theater.

Whether or not Fannie liked these latter-day remakes, she certainly was not adverse to the renewed interest in her work they occasioned. A brand-new paperback edition of *Imitation of Life* came out, refreshed with Lana Turner and John Gavin on its cover. The book sold some half a million copies, and the royalties gave her a welcome eighty-five-hundred-dollar income boost in 1960.

Fannie's "remittance advice" on the paperback sale arrived from Harpers, eerily timed to the saddening news from Fort Pierce, Florida, that Zora Neale Hurston, who had been so present in Fannie's life at the time she was writing *Imitation*, had died in "obscurity and poverty," according to the Associated Press, after suffering a stroke almost a year earlier. She had been living in the county welfare home, and neither Fannie nor Carl Van Vechten had heard from her in a decade. Local friends had arranged for a burial on February 7, but in a grave left forlornly unmarked.

Van Vechten and Fannie commiserated, saddened over the tragic end of their old friend, who had deliberately removed herself from the "large group of us who felt puzzlement and still do. Where lurked her ultimate defeat, ending in retreat? Why and how?" Fannie wondered.

The words appeared in an appreciation of Zora that Fannie wrote for Yale University's *Library Gazette*. Actually, it was Van Vechten who had been asked to write the personality sketch, but he deferred to Fannie as the logical second choice. At eighty, he told her, he felt that his memory was too abominable to take on the task. Zora was someone whose friendship the two of them had shared since the very beginning, he reminded Fannie, "a common annoyance, a common love, something we will both remember with a great deal of pleasure." He urged Fannie to do "Princess Zora" full justice, describing both her "shortcomings as well as her vitality and charm."

In just over two weeks Fannie sent the piece to the *Gazette*'s editor, Donald Gallup. "Feel no obligation to use this opus," she told him in a brief note. "It was written in transit—during a lecture tour—and I fear shows it."

Actually, it is a charming and presumably heartfelt tribute to someone for whom Fannie's affection and professional regard are clear. "Zora had the gift of walking into hearts," Fannie wrote, "she herself was a gift to both her race and the human race." Irresponsibility, Fannie said, was one of her endearing qualities. "Zora late, Zora sleeping through an appointment, Zora failing to meet an obligation, were actually part of a charm you dared not douse. . . . She lived carelessly, at least at the time I knew her, and her zest for life was cruelly at odds with her lonely death."

The only curious aspect of the tribute is Fannie's fractured reconstruction of the circumstances that brought the two women together, which varies markedly from the actual facts. There may be a simple explanation: Fannie was seventy-five at the time of the writing, working from her aging memory, made all the more suspect by a lifetime habit of tailoring real-life episodes to the needs of a story line. In this instance she was recalling events and circumstances that not only occurred as much as thirty-five years earlier but involved a protégée with whom she had lost contact and whom, for whatever reason, she had elected to leave out of *Anatomy of Me*.

In the article Fannie said Zora "swung into my orbit" not as the Barnard undergraduate she was but as a new graduate of the college seeking the position of live-in secretary even though she could barely type. Omitting mention of their earlier meeting at the *Opportunity* magazine literary competition, Fannie said that Zora had "only vaguely mentioned her writing intention and ambitions." This explanation set up the next part of Fannie's scenario: that when Zora did not work out as a secretary—when her "gay unpredictability got out of hand"—she allowed her to stay on. Here Fannie offers a bit of supposed dialogue: "Zora, consider yourself fired. You are my idea of the world's worst secretary. As a matter of fact, I think I should be your secretary. But you are welcome to live on here until you are settled elsewhere." Fannie then adds that Zora "remained on for about a year, still in my employ, but now in the capacity of chauffeur," driving with a "sure relaxed skill on the frequent trips north, east, south, and west that we took together."

In this paragraph, for reasons that can only be speculated about, Fannie has telescoped Zora's very brief tenure as her live-in, part-time student-secretary with the car trips the two women made a full six and then nine years later, when Zora was an established anthropologist, producer, and fellow writer with a growing following of her own.

Though Fannie's version reads differently on the cusp of the millennium, in the context of 1925, or even of 1960, there was nothing inherently demeaning about a brilliant young woman with literary aspirations fresh out of college taking a job as live-in assistant to a famous writer. Entry-level positions in the workforce rarely promised much more than this for women in either day, even for those with undergraduate degrees from the most prestigious schools. Compared with most other possible jobs, this one at least had some glamour.

By choosing to remember that she was only vaguely aware of any writing ambition of Zora's, Fannie found an economical way to establish how she and Zora came to know each other and why Zora ended up driving her around. Remember that Zora had already written about the car trips in both her *Saturday Review* article in 1937, where she omitted any time frame, and *Dust Tracks on a*

Road in 1942, where she set her secretarial stint with "Miss Hurst" clearly in her undergraduate days but adds in the present tense: "She likes for me to drive her and we have made several tours." Fannie, by saying the driving occurred in the inconsequential year after Zora's graduation, avoided casting a poor reflection on herself by having to explain how she could reduce someone of Zora's stature to the role of chauffeur. What Fannie could not have anticipated was how strange and demeaning her skewed telling of the story would seem anyway to readers in a time when Zora's literary legacy had so soundly outclassed her own.

"To life, to her people, she left a bequest of good writing and the memory of an iridescent personality of many colors," Fannie wrote in conclusion. "Her short shelf of writings deserves to endure. Undoubtedly, her memory will in the minds and hearts of her friends. We rejoice that she passed this way so brightly but alas, too briefly."

Van Vechten was so moved by the piece, he cried. "You make all the girl's faults seem to be her virtues," he told Fannie in a letter. "As a matter of fact, they were NOT faults, they were characteristics and there's quite a difference. What it comes down to is the fact that Zora was put together entirely differently from the rest of mankind. Her reactions were always original because they were always her OWN."

Chapter *37*

"No finer epitaph"

Fannie wasn't exactly "the First Lady of Television," though this is what New York Mayor Robert Wagner dubbed her at a party on behalf of the Federation of Women's Clubs in 1958. But for a woman of a certain age Fannie certainly had gotten, and continued to get, an impressive amount of small screen exposure. The NBC *Matinee Hour* dramatized two more of her old short stories, "At Mrs. Leland's" and "Forty-Five." She sashayed through a *Person-to-Person* interview with Edward R. Murrow and triumphed in a head-on collision with the young, brash Mike Wallace on the confrontational local CBS late-night program called *Night Beat. The 20th Century* featured her prominently in the biography it aired of Fiorello La Guardia. And in 1959 Fannie signed with the public broadcasting affiliate in New York to host her own show, *The Fannie Hurst Showcase.* Five days a week the program featured Fannie and a panel of experts in unrehearsed conversation on any number of controversial topics.

"How do you do, Mr. Murrow. Welcome to my house."

Fannie greeted the cameramen from *Person-to-Person* on the evening of June 18, 1954, perched regally on a seat in her study, her "chamber of horrors . . . at its most horrific," she called it. She had moved her work space from the third-floor chapel to the second floor of the eight-room triplex after Jack's death. Murrow conducted the interview from the CBS studios farther downtown, seated in an armchair beneath a haze of smoke emanating from his ever-smoldering cigarette. He saw Fannie at the moment his viewers did, through a large screen, having first introduced her with a quotation from a newspaper editorial: That America's cultural history would be different if writers such as Eugene O'Neill, Fannie Hurst, and John La Farge had not lived and worked.

Fannie had dressed carefully for the appearance. Her black cocktail dress was sexy, sleeveless, off-the-shoulder. Its full tea-length skirt accentuated her tiny waist. For back-shot interest, the dress dipped to a low V with two large black bows on which to focus as she descended the staircase. She never stopped petting her Yorkshire terrier, making sure the camera had a chance to catch her signature jewelry in the process—the gigantic calla lily brooch, the uncut faux emerald ring, and the oversized gold cuff on her wrist. Her hair was jet-black, no doubt with the help of dye at this point, but still pulled tightly off the face in her signature bun. Her makeup was soft and natural. Fannie was nearly seventy at the time, but there is not a trace of matronliness. She is a striking, elegant presence.

There were no great revelations, no surprises in her answers to the predetermined questions, but the format left just enough room for a measure of spontaneity, enough to warrant the bother of broadcasting the segment live. Even so, a version of truth comes across. The viewer sees a vital presence. Fannie's vocal and facial animation and the inflection of her speech are unmistakable. She has a poised but provocative style. She seems candid but actually reveals little of consequence. She gives off light but no heat. She is not someone to hug.

"Of all the writing you have done," Murrow asked, "what book has given you the most complete personal satisfaction?"

Fannie loved the way he put the question and quickly answered, *"Lummox,"* feeling the need to explain that it was "an earlier book that nobody knows very much about. And I like it," she said. "I don't know if anybody else likes it . . . and I had a good time doing it."

Murrow said the critics had classified her as a writer who wrote for and about women but that her works seemed also to have an underlying theme of concern for social justice, a feeling for the underdog. Did she agree?

"I don't read my notices, believe it or not," she said. "Why suffer?" But she went on to answer his direct question about women. "It may be true," she said, "but it isn't because I'm particularly interested in women, although I like women. I think it's because I'm interested in minorities, Mr. Murrow. I'm interested in the people who have to contend with the pressure of larger groups and I'm interested in women also because a great deal of what's happened to us makes us more interesting in our evolving processes than you mere men. Don't forget that in the last hundred years or so, nothing so much has happened to you in the way of change or your social status." Women, on the contrary, she said, were still evolving socially, politically, and emotionally and therefore were more interesting to write about.

She spoke of her two-hour walks in the park each morning and how her two terriers, Lilliputian and Calla Lily, had better sense than to join her. She liked small, portable dogs, she said, because their size enabled her to do sly and tricky things with them, such as taking them to places where they were not entirely welcome.

She led the camera on a tour of the first two floors of the triplex, peering through a second-floor interior window onto her sixty-foot-long gallery— "what we in the Midwest call 'the sittin' room,' " she quipped, lapsing for just that phrase into the twang that evoked the memory of Rose and Sam. She elucidated on her passion for all things Gothic—her love for old, well-worn wood, her disinterest in the "chromium and plate glass" fashion of the day. The tour moved through her paneled library into the relatively small dining room with its curious L-shaped table layout, Gothic-arched wooden chairs, and handsome old paneling. She had brought it piece by piece from a palace in Florence that was being torn down while she was visiting once.

Morrow asked if she had a hobby.

"Now I'm going to say something that is going to be rather unpopular," she said.

"Good," he replied, and she went on to say that nothing bored her more than the notion of a self-conscious hobby. "I don't quite understand this dedication to the idea of preparing ourselves for that ultimate hobby, that time when the curtain drops, so to speak, and we have nothing more to do or say but to collect green glass with worts."

She expounded further on the subject, then Morrow thanked her and said good night. "Good night, Mr. Murrow," Fannie said, and the camera cut to a word from the show's sponsor, Amoco.

Forty years after his interview with Fannie, Mike Wallace could still recall the details. "At the time, *Night Beat* had just been on the air a short time," he said, "one of those phenomena that sometimes hits in New York and suddenly everybody is watching." Even at that point in her life, Fannie was just the sort of guest everyone wanted to see on the show. "She was a player," he said, "still a player at that point . . . luminous dark brown eyes . . . black hair . . . big calla lily . . . very impressive. She was the kind of open, interesting, provocative person that people tuned in to see."

On a totally darkened set, the host and his guest each sat at a small square table with only a spotlight and a bulbous microphone to adorn it. Wallace, in his abrasive, insistent way, recalled asking "the kinds of questions that everyone wanted asked"—shocking at the time but tame by later standards. He pressed Fannie for details of her personal life, but she held him off, clearly reluctant to discuss what she considered private. From there he segued into questions about *Back Street,* which gave her an opening to fire her own shot: "Well, you keep asking questions of this nature, when did you read *Back Street*?" was how Wallace remembered the retort. This forced him to admit on the air that he had not reread the book anytime recently, confessing, in effect, that he had come to the interview improperly prepared. "And she made that quite apparent to me," he said good-naturedly.

"We enjoyed your 'battle' with Mike Wallace ever so much," wrote a couple of fans from Great Neck, Long Island. "Perhaps Mr. Wallace will be a little more cautious from now on. You were wonderful!"

Three years later, in 1959, under the title "Powerhouse," *The New Yorker* declared her "one of the great natural wonders of our time," who had been "generating and dispensing as much energy hereabouts as Consolidated Edison." At the time Fannie was also telling stories to crowds of children in Central Park near the statue of Hans Christian Andersen. In 1956 she had gone to battle with New York City Parks Commissioner Robert Moses over plans to eliminate a Central Park playground in favor of a parking lot. She also never stopped badgering America's women to take their place outside the home. She was a vocal, consistent, and pioneering crusader for women's advancement, on the soapbox for years before it was fashionable. It is an achievement for which she has never been given credit.

∞

Doubleday published three more of Fannie's novels, *Family!* in 1960, *God Must Be Sad* in 1961, and *Fool—Be Still* in 1964. Her sales for each of these novels stood at somewhere between ten and thirteen thousand copies. This may have been less than in the past, but her audience was solid and loyal enough for Doubleday to continue to take her seriously. Ken McCormick summed up the work of these later years best: "She had pretty well exhausted her subjects, but the will to go on writing was there."

In fact, the will to go on doing just about everything was there. Also in 1964, at the age of seventy-nine, Fannie began hosting another public television program, *Pleased to Meet You*. This was a weekly fifteen-minute interview show in which the "baubled and bangled author," according to the reviewer John Horn in the *New York Herald Tribune,* showed promise of providing a "friendly and disarming approach" to television. But two months into the program, Horn changed his mind. "The guests are promising still," he reported, "but they are never—at least in my experience—drawn out. They remain shadows, on guarded company behavior, as did a polite young delicatessen owner last night as he listened to Miss Hurst talk too much about her attitudes, thoughts, opinions. . . . A good interviewer is curious, self-effacing, listens acutely, explores, leads, never talks unless he has to. Miss Hurst violates all these common rules, but not without impunity." The producer moved hastily to give Fannie his vote of confidence, but the show was canceled anyway after its first twenty-one-week season.

∞

There were honors yet to collect. The Albert Einstein College of Medicine staged a testimonial dinner for her with Eleanor Roosevelt and Dr. Benjamin A. Cohen, undersecretary-general of the United Nations, as principal speakers. President Harry S Truman appointed her to the board of the World Health Organization. Her birthplace, Hamilton, Ohio, invited her "home" in 1966 to celebrate what Mayor Thomas Kindness and Governor James A. Rhodes declared "The Fannie Hurst Days." And the Institute for Human-Animal Relationship also honored her with a dinner. Now that the years of unpleasantness with Washington University were behind her, Fannie might have jumped at the chance to attend her fifty-seventh class reunion in 1966, also held largely in her honor, but this one she skipped. "My reason for absenting myself, weakly human," she confessed to Lois. "You have stature and dignity—I dodge—or at least try to dodge, as if one can, the 1776-elder department by ignoring the calendar." Aware that she had been a celebrity long enough for the arithmetic of her life to be obvious to just about anyone, Fannie said she still felt entitled to "an Achilles heel or two." She told Lois that when a doctor once asked her how old she was, she had to reply, "I've lied about it for so long that I actually don't know—"

There was even the desire to prepare for an orderly end. Fannie had sent her personal papers to the Harry Ransom Humanities Research Center at the University of Texas and wrote a will which she signed in a clear and steady hand on February 5, 1968. She even had written two more novels in those last four years, one which she relegated, untitled, to the "deep freeze" (as she told Lois, William Faulkner was said to have eight novels in the deep freeze, "which reassures me a bit"). The other, "Lonely Is Only a Word," ended up with Perry Knowlton at Curtis Brown, the agency that handled all the international rights to her many books. Over the years Fannie's work had been translated into dozens of languages.

Fannie directed her executors to have her body cremated, just as Jack's had been, but to deposit her ashes under a small stone monument adjoining her parents' burial site in St. Louis, inscribed as follows: FANNIE HURST, DAUGHTER OF SAMUEL AND ROSE HURST, WIFE OF JACQUES DANIELSON—GRATITUDE TO THEM AND THE WORLD. Jacques's ashes she dispersed on her own.

To the Museum of the City of New York went her most signature pieces of jewelry, the Indian emerald cabochon ring and matching bracelet that she continually wore along with the green-gold life-sized calla lily set in diamonds and topaz. The calla, she variously had said, was her symbol of peace and serenity, her individuality, or Jacques's love. To Washington University she gave half the books she had written housed in her personal library. The other half went to Brandeis. Two hundred dollars each went to her houseman and a seven-year-old girl in Larchmont, and Sally Maguire, her aide and companion in these later years, had the pick of her jewelry and furs. She also got instructions to keep her dogs and lavish the care on them that Fannie always had.

Albert Einstein College of Medicine received the residue of Samuel Hurst's estate to add to the trust Fannie already had established for the maintenance of the laboratory she had donated in Jacques's memory. Now she asked further that the name be changed to the Jacques Danielson and Fannie Hurst Laboratory Unit. Rights to her literary estate went jointly to Washington University and Brandeis. The two universities also got the rest of her property, with which to establish important literary professorships in her name. The schools actually received just shy of a million dollars each.

Eighteen days after Fannie signed her will, she died at home in bed at 1:30 in the afternoon at age eighty-two. Her physician, Dr. William Hitzig, had visited her just a few hours earlier. Her death certificate does not record the cause of her death, but Perry Knowlton, the agent called in to evaluate her literary estate, remembered being told that she had cancer. Her cemetery record in St.

Louis gives the same information. Two hundred invited guests attended her private memorial service a few days after her death, conducted by Dr. Algernon Black of the Ethical Culture Society of New York. Outside the Frank E. Campbell Funeral Home, a cluster of fifty fans held vigil in the rain.

Fannie rated the honor of a front-page obituary. In *The New York Times* that year, of some forty-seven hundred death notices listed in the obituary index, only twenty-eight merited front-page handling, and of those, only five others were women. Lurleen Wallace, the first woman governor of Alabama, who ran as a surrogate for her husband, George, when he could not succeed himself; Lise Meitner, the Austrian-born physicist credited with discoveries that led to the creation of the first atom bomb; the actress Tallulah Bankhead; the dancer Ruth St. Denis; and that other Midwest-born writer who liked to focus on the little people, the one born the same year as Fannie, her old nemesis, Edna Ferber.

But of that select group only Fannie warranted a special "appreciation," a warm remembrance that appeared on the editorial page of the *Times* to mark her passing. "Fannie Hurst's great talent as short-story writer and novelist was an ability to infuse her romances with the pulse of life," it began. "Her people were recognizable; their emotional crises were real. Critics might disdain her for lack of literary qualities, but millions found Miss Hurst's heartthrob stories unforgettable. One reason was her empathy for the problems of others."

Herbert Mayes, then editor of the *Saturday Review,* had always had a slightly strained relationship with Fannie, stemming from a disagreement years back over the way he changed the title of one of her stories. Deliberately she referred to him as "Mr. Mapes" for years to come. Even so, she was so much a part of his "personal nostalgia" that he was moved to comment on the loss of her as "a longtime almost friend."

"Fannie Hurst, was I suppose the expression is, a good soul. Thoughtful. Always ready to do a good turn and not fussy about where it had to be done or how much of her time it took. Always ready to encourage a new writer. A dedicated citizen. Active on many committees in many civic causes. A little pretentious, as with her lily affectation and her imposing apartment on West Sixty-seventh Street. Most people who knew her liked her," Mayes wrote.

In Mayes's view nothing Fannie wrote was of much consequence. She achieved her enormous popularity as an author because she could "build a grand plot (itself no mean achievement) and dress it down with sloppy sentimentality".

"Her stature as a storyteller was high; as a writer, low," he said, a thought put in better perspective by her editor at Doubleday, Ken McCormick. Fannie may have been "basically a fairly corny artist," as he put it, but what is the value of someone who writes beautifully but "can't tell a story worth a damn?"

She herself had reflected on her writing career at several points in *Anatomy of Me.* She said she never wrote her stories with "editors, masses or classes" in mind because "I had not the skill to tailor them to fashion." They came out the way they did "because I felt them and saw them and lived them that way, and that was how it had to be."

She saw herself as one who reached always with an arm too short to touch her objectives. Her metaphor: going through life in a state of chronic labor pains, for which there is no anesthetic. She would liked to have been able to say with William Saroyan: "I am proud to be the writer I am," but never could. Instead, for Fannie, it was "But I am proud to be the writer who still aspires to be the writer I am not and is ready to struggle on and on."

"To few is given to walk the literary heights," she reasoned. "But even valley folk can keep their sites [sic] high." She chided herself as "an avowed member of the 'less' group," "a goof," someone who always just followed her own literary nose, for better or worse.

Fannie Hurst could always tell a story. In the words of that unnamed *Times* editorialist, she knew how to speak "unabashedly to the human heart." And for a writer or a storyteller, he added, there is no finer epitaph.

ACKNOWLEDGMENTS

A listing such as this cannot really convey the extent or depth of my gratitude to all of the following for

their collections and staff,

The Harry Ransom Humanities Research Center at the University of Texas at Austin houses the bulk of Fannie Hurst's papers, the Harper & Bros. Collection, and the Alfred A. Knopf Collection, and awarded me a three-month Mellon Fellowship in 1995 to study them. Special thanks to Rich Oram, Cathy Henderson, Elizabeth Dunn, and the HRC's extremely able staff. My gratitude extends also to Donna Elkins, an independent researcher who became an extra set of eyes and arms in Austin for the duration of the project.

Brandeis University and Washington University, whose libraries house the rest of Hurst's papers, are joint trustees of her literary estate. Special thanks to Charles Cutter at Brandeis and Carol Prietto and Allison Carrick at Washington University for their kindnesses during my stays.

Dartmouth College Library, Special Collections, houses the Vilhjalmur Stefansson Papers. Special thanks to Philip Cronenwett for his generous assistance. In this connection, thanks also to Evelyn Stefansson Nef, to whom I am very indebted.

In St. Louis, the St. Louis Public Schools Record Center and Archives has Hurst's school records. Special thanks to Sharon Huffman, who took on the mining as a personal crusade and hosted a tour of Hurst's many St. Louis residences, and to Anna Marie Cole. The St. Louis Mercantile Library has some important material—my thanks to Charles Brown. So does the St. Louis Public Library, the private Central High School collection of Gus and Sheila Pavlakis, and the Missouri Historical Society.

The New York Public Library contained a multitude of resources, especially in the following departments: Manuscripts and Archives, the A. A. Berg Collection, the Schomburg Center for Research in Black Culture, and The Billy Rose Theater Collection of the Library for the Performing Arts at Lincoln Center. Also in New York, the Theater Collection, Museum of the City of New York, was important, as was the New York City Municipal Archives and the Fales Library of New York University. The Society Library of New York City and the New-York Historical Society were frequent destinations and provided numerous courtesies.

Columbia University Library, Rare Books and Manuscripts, has numerous collections of importance to this research, indexed under Hurst's name. Columbia University Archives was consulted, as was the Barnard College Archives for Zora Neale Hurston material.

In Philadelphia, the Van Pelt–Dietrich Library at the University of Pennsylvania was helpful with Hurst's correspondence with Theodore Dreiser and several other collections that contained her letters (special thanks to Dr. Nancy Shawcross), and the Urban Archives of Temple University Libraries provided important material from *The Philadelphia Bulletin* newspaper morgue (special thanks to Karen Wright). The CIBARS research service also helped.

The Yale Collection of American Literature, Beinecke Rare Book and Manuscript Library, has Hurst material in several of its collections, including the James Weldon Johnson Papers and Carl Van Vechten Papers. The Sterling Memorial Library at Yale houses the papers of Colonel Edward M. House.

Princeton University Libraries, Department of Rare Books and Special Collections, had several collections of interest indexed under Hurst's name, as did the Arthur and Elizabeth Schlesinger Library on the History of Women in America at Radcliffe College, and the Houghton Library at Harvard University.

The University of Florida, George A. Smathers Library, Department of Special Collections, and the University of Florida at Gainesville Library, Manuscripts Department, both sent Zora Neale Hurston material, as did the the American Jewish Archives at Hebrew Union College from its Annie Nathan Meyer Collection (special thanks to Kevin Profitt and Kathy Spray and to Robert Hemenway for telling me about it).

The American Jewish Historical Society provided correspondence with Hurst from Rabbi Stephen Wise.

The Library of Congress, Manuscripts Department; The National Archives; and the Department of Justice, Federal Bureau of Investigation, all provided Hurst material and had other collections of interest.

Bancroft Library, University of California at Berkeley, houses the Charles and Kathleen Norris Papers and the Gertrude Atherton Papers, which were of interest.

CBS Archives provided the tape of Hurst's *Person-to-Person* interview with Edward R. Murrow (special thanks to Neil Waldman).

Cosmopolitan magazine opened its author index-card file, which was indispensable in determining how much Hurst actually earned and when various stories appeared in the magazine.

And numerous other libraries provided useful material or information: The Franklin Delano Roosevelt Library (special thanks to Bob Parks); the National Library of Canada; the Huntington Library, Department of Manuscripts (special thanks to Sue Hodson); Rollins College Library (special thanks to Kay Reich); Harper & Bros. Archives (special thanks to Donna Slawsky); the Wisconsin State Historical

Society and the Milwaukee Urban Archives; the John S. Guggenheim Foundation Archives (special thanks to Thomas Tanselle); New Mt. Sinai Cemetery (special thanks to Mary Pool); Butler County (Ohio) Records Center & Archives (special thanks to Maxine Young); and the *St. Louis Post-Dispatch.*

Various historical societies and public libraries across the country also provided material, most notably those in Mt. Clemens, Michigan; Port Washington, New York; Lakewood, New Jersey; Huntington, West Virginia; Asheville, North Carolina; and Hamilton, Ohio.

their film research resources,

The Center for Motion Picture Study, Margaret Herrick Library, Academy of Motion Picture Arts and Sciences Academy Foundation; Library of Congress (special thanks to Madeline Matz); Turner Entertainment Company (special thanks to Kathy Lendech); the University of California at Los Angeles Film Library; the Wisconsin Center for Film and Theater Research; and the University of Southern California Film Library.

their research assistance,

Marilynn Abrams, Michael Bouthillier, Anna Valeria Cannillo, Marsha Saron Dennis, Donna Elkins, Leslie Falk, Marjorie Feld, Selina Goren, Enid Klass, Jill Krauss, Jane Manners, Catherine Robe, Adam Vine, Ricki Weiss, and Nora Zimmett. For help with collecting Hurst's out-of-print books, special thanks also to Barbara Cohen, Grace Heckinger, Judith Stonehill, and Ian Wright.

their shared recollections,

Ethel Rabinowitz Amatneek, Rudd Brown, Joan Feinberg Futter, Elizabeth Jaffe, Ken McCormick, Jeanne Brownstein Silverberg, and Mike Wallace.

their expertise,

Joyce Antler, Cari Beauchamp, Temma Berg, Ed Bleier, Valerie Boyd, Blanche Wiesen Cook, Louise DeSalvo, Joan Feinberg Futter, Manuela Cerri Goren, Robert Hemenway, Peter C. Jones, Carla Kaplan, Bruce Kellner, Susan Koppelman, Anne McCormick, Joan Mellen, Luke Pontifell, Arnold Rampersad, Abe Ravitz, Victoria Sanders, Michele Slung, and Cheryl Wall.

reading parts or all of the manuscript in draft,

Cari Beauchamp, Ted Bishop, Donna Elkins, Alex Goren, Gail Gregg, Carla Kaplan, Arnold Rampersad, Daniel Selznick, and Ellen Walterscheid.

seeing the book to publication,

Peter Bernstein, Lee Boudreaux, Nicki Britton, Philippa Brophy, Susan M.S. Brown, Benjamin Dreyer, Carie Freimuth, Deb Futter, Kate Larkin, Heidi North, Naomi

Osnos. Thanks also in this connection to the idea's earliest proponents, Peter Osnos and Steve Wasserman.

wise and patient listening,

Geraldine Baum, Cari Beauchamp, Bettina Bosé, Philippa Brophy, Janet Cawley, Rick Davies, Sue Davies, Ernest DeSalvo, Louise DeSalvo, Charlotte Frieze, Alex Goren, Andrea Goren, Dolphy Goren, Manuela Cerri Goren, Selina Goren, Gail Gregg, Peter C. Jones, Viviana Kasam, Brett Kroeger, Malka Margolies, Marta Martin, Marsha Pinson, Luke Pontifell, Savine Pontifell, Paula Span, Rusty Unger, Ellen Walterscheid, Avi Weinstein, David Weinstein, Helen Weinstein, and Randy Weinstein.

forbearance,

Alex Goren.

Brooke Kroeger

Published Works by Fannie Hurst

(Publisher is Harper & Bros., except when otherwise indicated)

SHORT-STORY COLLECTIONS

1914	*Just Around the Corner*
1916	*Every Soul Hath Its Song*
1918	*Gaslight Sonatas*
1919	*Humoresque*
1922	*The Vertical City*
1927	*Song of Life* (Alfred A. Knopf)
1929	*Procession*
1937	*We Are Ten*

NOVELS

1921	*Star-Dust: The Story of an American Girl*
1923	*Lummox*
1926	*Mannequin* (Alfred A. Knopf)
1926	*Appassionata* (Alfred A. Knopf)
1928	*A President Is Born*
1929	*Five and Ten*
1931	*Back Street*
1933	*Imitation of Life*
1934	*Anitra's Dance*
1936	*Great Laughter*
1942	*Lonely Parade*
1944	*Hallelujah*
1947	*The Hands of Veronica*
1950	*Anywoman*
1951	*The Man with One Head* (London: Jonathan Cape Ltd.)
1960	*Family! A Novel* (Doubleday & Co.)
1961	*God Must Be Sad* (Doubleday & Co.)
1964	*Fool—Be Still* (Doubleday & Co.)

NONFICTION

1958	*Anatomy of Me* (Doubleday & Co.)

MISCELLANY

1935	*No Food with My Meals*
1942	*White Christmas* (Doubleday, Doran & Co.)

CHRONOLOGICAL INDEX OF SELECTED SHORT STORIES BY FANNIE HURST

(List does not include short-short fiction Hurst often wrote while under contract to the McClure's newspaper syndicate from 1924–1930.)

1904

"An Episode" [Central] *High School News* (St. Louis, Mo.) Dec. 1904, Christmas issue

1906

"The Blasé Junior Soliloquizes" *Student Life* (Washington U.), Nov. 28, 1906

1907

"A Mood" *Student Life,* Apr. 24, 1907

"The Girl and the Woman" *Student Life,* Oct. 9, 1907

"Say, Said the College Man" *Student Life,* Oct. 23, 1907

"Her Decision" *Student Life,* Oct. 23, 1907

"Druscilla's Proposal" *Student Life,* Nov. 13, 1907

"Vengeance" *Student Life,* Nov. 20, 1907

"The GodHead" *Student Life,* Nov. 27, 1907

"The Fear" *Student Life,* Dec. 4, 1907

1908

"The Fear" *Student Life,* Feb. 5, 1908

"To a Skull" *Student Life,* Feb. 19, 1908

"Love Came Over One Night" *Student Life,* May 20, 1908

"The Professor's Conversion" *Student Life,* May 20, 1908

"A Choice Finds" *Student Life,* May 27, 1908

"Twilight" *Student Life,* Oct. 7, 1908

"The Vigil" *Student Life,* Nov. 11, 1908

1909

"1909" *Student Life,* Oct. 7, 1909

"His Commencement" *The Hatchet,* Spring 1909

1910

"The Dominant Force" *Reedy's Mirror,* Feb. 3, 1910, p. 8

"The Gropers" *Reedy's Mirror,* May 26, 1910, pp. 6–7

"Prose" *Reedy's Mirror,* Dec. 22, 1910, pp. 39, 41

1912

"The Seventh Day" *Smith's Magazine,* Vol. 14, No. 4, Jan. 1912, pp. 631–636

"Dead Sea Fruit" *Cavalier,* Vol. 12, No. 1, Feb. 3, 1912, pp. 85–88

"The Nth Commandment" *Saturday Evening Post,* Vol. 187, No. 23, Dec. 5, 1914, pp. 12–14, 44–46. Also *Every Soul Hath Its Song*

"Mind-Cat!" *Saturday Evening Post,* Vol. 187, No. 26, Dec. 26, 1914, pp. 13–16, 32–33

1915

"T.B." *Saturday Evening Post,* Vol. 187, No. 28, Jan. 9, 1915, pp. 8–11, 32–34. Also *Every Soul Hath Its Song*

"Hochenheimer of Cincinnati" *Saturday Evening Post,* Vol. 187, No. 33, Feb. 15, 1915, pp. 6–8, 57–59, 61–62, 65. Also *Every Soul Hath Its Song*

"Ever Ever Green" *Metropolitan,* Vol. 41, No. 5, Mar. 1915, pp. 15–18, 64–70

"White Goods" *Metropolitan,* Vol. 42, No. 3, July 1915, pp. 19–22, 53–54, 56–58. Also *Humoresque*

"The Good Provider" *Saturday Evening Post,* Vol. 187, No. 7, Aug. 14, 1915, pp. 12–16, 34–35. Also *Just Around the Corner*

"Rolling Stock" *Metropolitan,* Vol. 42, No. 5, Sept. 1915, pp. 18, 20, 67–72. Also *Every Soul Hath Its Song*

"Sea Gullibles" *Saturday Evening Post,* Vol. 188, No. 23, Dec. 4, 1915, pp. 17–20, 56–58, 61–62. Also *Every Soul Hath Its Song*

"The Name and the Game" *Metropolitan,* Vol. 43, No. 2, Dec. 1915, pp. 25–28, 60, 63. Also *Every Soul Hath Its Song*

1916

"Through a Glass Darkly" *Metropolitan,* Vol. 43, No. 3, Jan. 1916, pp. 19–22, 58, 60, 62–63

"Sob Sister" *Metropolitan,* Vol. 43, No. 4, Feb. 1916, pp. 27–29, 34, 40, 42–43. Also *Every Soul Hath Its Song*

"In Memoriam" *Saturday Evening Post,* Vol. 188, No. 38, Mar. 18, 1916, pp. 20–23, 61–62, 65–66. Also *Every Soul Hath Its Song*

"A Birdie in the House" *Metropolitan,* Vol. 43, No. 5, Mar. 1916, pp. 21–24, 53–57

"Thine Is Not Mine" *Metropolitan,* Vol. 43, No. 6, May 1916, pp. 19–21, 59–65, 70–72

"Brunt" *Metropolitan,* Vol. 44, No. 1, June 1916, pp. 22–24, 57–62

"Ice Water, Pl——" *Collier's,* Oct. 21, 1916, pp. 5–7. Also *Gaslight Sonatas*

1917

"The Wrong Pew" *Saturday Evening Post,* Vol. 189, No. 38, Jan. 6, 1917, pp. 5–7, 41, 43, 45. Also *Humoresque*

"Hers Not to Reason Why" *Cosmopolitan,* Vol. 62, No. 4, Mar. 1917, pp. 17–23, 106–108. Also *Gaslight Sonatas*

"Solitary Reaper" *Cosmopolitan,* Vol. 62, No. 6, Mar. 1917, pp. 34–41, 104–110

"Would You?" *Metropolitan,* Vol. 45, No. 6, May 1917, pp. 11–13, 54–61

"Oats for the Woman" *Cosmopolitan,* Vol. 63, No. 1, June 1917, pp. 20–27, 119–125. Also *Humoresque*

"Golden Fleece" *Cosmopolitan,* Vol. 63, No. 2, July 1917, pp. 38–45, 126–131. Also *Gaslight Sonatas*

"Get Ready the Wreaths" *Cosmopolitan,* Vol. 63, No. 4, Sept. 1917, pp. 57–64, 100–106. Also *Gaslight Sonatas*

"Sieve of Fulfillment" *Cosmopolitan,* Vol. 63, No. 5, Oct. 1917, pp. 53–59, 110–116. Also *Gaslight Sonatas*

"On the Heights" *Cosmopolitan,* Vol. 64, No. 1, Dec. 1917, pp. 16–23, 112–116

1918

"Nightshade" *Cosmopolitan,* Vol. 64, No. 2, Jan. 1918, pp. 20–27, 107–111. Also *Gaslight Sonatas*

"Bitter Sweet" *Cosmopolitan,* Vol. 64, No. 4, Mar. 1918, pp. 14–21, 109–116. Also *Gaslight Sonatas*

"A Boob Spelled Backwards" *Cosmopolitan,* Vol. 64, No. 5, Apr. 1918, pp. 28–35, 113–118. Also *Humoresque*

"A Petal on the Current" *Cosmopolitan,* Vol. 65, No. 1, June 1918, pp. 42–48, 138–141, 144. Also *Humoresque*

"She Also Serves" *Cosmopolitan,* Vol. 65, No. 5, Oct. 1918, pp. 60–63, 100

"Heads" *Cosmopolitan,* Vol. 65, No. 6, Nov. 1919, pp. 22–29, 18–136. Also *Humoresque*

1919

"The Comeback" *Cosmopolitan,* Vol. 66, No. 3, Feb. 1919, pp. 14–21, 84–88

"Humoresque" *Cosmopolitan,* Vol. 66, No. 4, Mar. 1919, pp. 32–39, 94–100. Also *Humoresque*

"Even As You and I" *Cosmopolitan,* Vol. 66, No. 5, Apr. 1919, pp. 22–29, 134–138. Also *Humoresque*

"Back Pay" *Cosmopolitan,* Vol. 67, No. 6, Nov. 1919, pp. 35–40, 129–140. Also *Vertical City*

1920

"Star-Dust" (*Star-Dust*) *Cosmopolitan,* serial, Vol. 68, Nos. 3–6, Mar.–May 1920; Vol. 69, 1–6, June–Dec. 1920

1921

"Guilty" *Cosmopolitan,* Vol. 70, No. 2, Feb. 1921, pp. 14–19, 103–109. Also *Vertical City*

"Roulette" *Cosmopolitan,* Vol. 70, No. 5, May 1921, pp. 18–25, 128–138. Also *Vertical City*

"She Walks in Beauty" *Cosmopolitan,* Vol. 71, No. 2, Aug. 1921, pp. 28–34, 152–158. Also *Vertical City*

"The Vertical City" *Cosmopolitan,* Vol. 71, No. 5, Nov. 1921, pp. 35–41, 130–134. Also *Vertical City*

1922

"The Smudge" *Cosmopolitan,* Vol. 72, No. 3, Mar. 1922, pp. 36–42, 90–92. Also *Vertical City*

"Forty-Five" *Cosmopolitan,* Vol. 73, No. 5, Dec. 1922, pp. 14–21, 102–116. Also *Song of Life*

1923

"The Brinkerhoff Brothers" *Cosmopolitan,* Vol. 74, No. 4, Apr. 1923, pp. 74–79, 144–152. Also *Song of Life*

"Seven Candles" *Cosmopolitan,* Vol. 75, No. 3, Sept. 1923, pp. 36–41, 164–171. (From *Lummox*)

"The Spangle That Could Be a Tear" *Bookman,* No. 58, Dec. 1923, pp. 373–377

1925

"The Gold in Fish" *Cosmopolitan,* Vol. 79, No. 2, Aug. 1925, pp. 28–31, 185–194. Also *Song of Life*

"Mannequin" (*Mannequin*) *Liberty Weekly,* serial, Vol. 2, Nos. 31–34, Dec. 5, 12, 19, 26, 1925; Vol. 3, Nos. 4–8, Jan. 16, 23, 30, Feb. 6, 13, 20, 1926

"A House of Men" *Cosmopolitan,* Vol. 79, No. 3, Sept. 1925

1926

"The Smirk" *Harper's Bazar,* Vol. 61, No. 2559, Jan. 1926, pp. 78–79, 122

"Who ARE You?" *Cosmopolitan,* Vol. 80, No. 1, Jan. 1926, pp. 44–47, 131–136. Also *Song of Life*

"Gold Does Glitter" *Harper's Bazar,* Vol. 61, No. 2561, Mar. 1926, pp. 96–97, 126

"Madagascar Ho!" *Cosmopolitan,* Vol. 80, No. 3, Mar. 1926, pp. 48–51, 144–148. Also *Song of Life*

"Here Comes the Bride" *Cosmopolitan,* Vol. 80, No. 4, Apr. 1926, pp. 38–41, 184–198. Also *Song of Life*

"Song of Life" *Cosmopolitan,* Vol. 81, No. 3, Sept. 1926, pp. 36–39, 185–190. Also *Song of Life*

1927

"Wrath" *Song of Life*

"The Left Hand of God" *Cosmopolitan,* Vol. 83, No. 6, Dec. 1927, pp. 26–29, 173–181

1928

"Give This Little Girl a Hand" *Cosmopolitan,* Vol. 84, No. 2, Feb. 1928, pp. 30–35, 124–132. Also *Procession*

"The Hossie-Frossie" *Cosmopolitan,* Vol. 85, No. 3, Sept. 1928, pp. 38–41, 124–132. Also *Procession*

"Sissy" ("The Young Prince") *Cosmopolitan,* Vol. 85, No. 4, Oct. 1928, pp. 32–35, 196–209. Also *Procession*

"The Third Husband" *Cosmopolitan,* Vol. 85, No. 6, Dec. 1928, pp. 44–47, 175–182. Also *Procession*

1929

"Five and Ten" (*Five and Ten*) *Cosmopolitan,* serial, Vol. 86, Nos. 4–6, Apr.–June 1929; Vol. 87, Nos. 1–3, July–Sept. 1929

1930

"Carrousel" *Cosmopolitan,* Vol. 88, No. 1, Jan. 1930, pp. 20–25, 163–165. Also *We Are Ten*

1939

"Mamma and Her First National Bank" *Saturday Evening Post,* Vol. 211, No. 38, Mar. 18, 1939, pp. 16–17 ffl

"Play That Thing" *Pictorial Review,* Vol. 40, No. 6, Mar. 1939, pp. 7–9, 32 ffl

"Lora Made a Little Mistake" New York *Daily News,* Aug. 13, 1939

1940

"Rosemary for Remembrance" *Good Housekeeping,* Vol. 111, No. 2, Aug. 1940, pp. 28–29, 128–133

"Rhinestones Preferred" *Cosmopolitan,* Vol. 109, No. 6, Dec. 1940, pp. 32–35, 97–102

1941

"Exempted" *Liberty Weekly,* Vol. 18, No. 45, Nov. 8, 1941, pp. 12–15, 56–59

1942

"What Does Miss Firper Think About?" *Good Housekeeping,* Vol. 114, No. 1, Jan. 1942, pp. 30–31, 78–82

"Who Is Sylvia?" *Good Housekeeping,* Vol. 115, No. 1, July 1942, pp. 20–21, 151–156

1945

"Something to Write Home About" *Canadian Home Journal,* Vol. 42, No. 5, Sept. 1945, pp. 14–15, 22–25, 50

1947

"The Name is Mary" *American Magazine,* Vol. 143, Jan. 1947, pp. 52–56, 61–83

1952

"Something Thicker Than Water" ("Abe Adolphus") *Canadian Home Journal,* Mar. 1952, pp. 10–11, 57–66

FANNIE HURST FILMOGRAPHY

1918

Her Great Chance U.S. bw silent Select *wd* Charles Maigne. Starring Alice Brady, David Powell, Nellie Parker Spaulding, Gloria Goodwin, Gertrude Barry, Hardee Kirkland From FH story "Golden Fleece"

1919

The Day She Paid U.S. bw silent Universal *d* Rex Ingram. *w* Walemar Young. Starring Francelia Billington, Charles Clay, Harry von Meter From FH story "Oats for the Woman"

The Petal on the Current US bw silent Universal *d* Tod Browning. Starring Robert Anderson, Gertrude Claire, Mary MacLaren From FH story

1920

Humoresque U.S. bw silent Famous Players–Lasky/Cosmopolitan *d* Frank Borzage. *w* Frances Marion. Starring Gaston Glass, Vera Gordon, Alma Rubens, Dore Davidson From FH story

1921

Just Around the Corner U.S. bw silent Paramount/Cosmopolitan *wd* Frances Marion. Starring Margaret Seddon, Lewis Sargent, Sigrid Holmquist, Eddie Phillips From FH story "Superman"

Star-Dust U.S. bw silent Associated First National/Hobart Henley *d* Hobart Henley. *w* Anthony Paul Kelly. Starring Hope Hampton, Edna Ross, Tom Maguire, Mary Foy, Charles Mussett, Vivia Ogden From FH novel

1922

The Good Provider U.S. bw silent Paramount/Cosmopolitan *d* Frank Borzage. *w* John Lynch. Starring Vera Gordon, Dore Davidson, Miriam Battista, Vivienne Osborne From FH story

Back Pay U.S. bw silent Paramount/Cosmopolitan *d* Frank Borzage. *w* Frances Marion. Starring Seena Owen, Matt Moore, J. Barney Sherry, Ethel Duray From FH story

1923

The Nth Commandment U.S. bw silent Paramount/Cosmopolitan (Frank Borzage, Frances Marion) *d* Borzage. *w* Marion. Starring Colleen Moore, James Morrison, Eddie Phillips, Charlotte Merriam From FH story

1926

The Untamed Lady U.S. bw silent Paramount/Famous Players–Lasky *d* Frank Tuttle. *w* James Ashmore Creelman, FH. Starring Gloria Swanson,

Lawrence Gray, Joseph W. Smiley, Charles Graham   From FH scenario "The Taming of Gloria"

Mannequin   U.S.   bw   silent   Paramount/Famous Players–Lasky (James Cruze)   *d* Cruze. *w* Frances Agnew, Walter Woods. Starring Alice Joyce, Warner Baxter, Dolores Costello, ZaSu Pitts, Walter Pidgeon   From FH scenario, later published as a novel

1928

Wheel of Chance   U.S.   bw   silent   First National   *d* Alfred Santell. *w* Gerald C. Duffy. Starring Richard Barthelmess, Lina Basquette, Warner Oland, Margaret Livingston, Sidney Franklin, Martha Franklin, and Ann Schaefer   From FH novelette "Roulette"

1929

The Younger Generation   U.S.   75m   bw   mono   Columbia (Jack Cohn, Joe Cooke)   *d* Frank Capra. *w* Howard J. Green, Sonya Levien. Starring Jean Hersholt, Lina Basquette, Ricardo Cortez, Syd Crossley, Martha Franklin, Rosa Rosanova   From FH play *It Is to Laugh* and story "The Gold in Fish"

1930

Lummox   U.S.   bw   United Artists/Feature   *d* Herbert Brenon. *w* Elizabeth Meehan, FH. Starring Winifred Westover, Dorothy Janis, Lydia Yeamans Titus, Ida Darling, Ben Lyon, Louise Beavers   From FH novel

The Painted Angel   (musical; aka *The Broadway Hostess*)   U.S.   68m   bw   silent/Vitaphone   Warner Bros.   *d* Millard Webb. *w* Forrest Halsey. Starring Billie Dove, Edmund Lowe, George MacFarlane, Cissy Fitzgerald, J. Farrell MacDonald, Peter Higgins   From the FH story "Give This Little Girl a Hand"

Back Pay (remake of 1922 original)   U.S.   bw   mono   First National (Walter Morosco)   *d* William A. Seiter. *w* Francis Edward Faragoh. Starring Corinne Griffith, Grant Withers, Montague Love, Hallam Cooley, Louise Beavers, Louise Cooley   From FH story

1931

Five and Ten (aka *Daughter of Luxury*)   U.S.   88m   bw   mono Metro-Goldwyn-Mayer (Marion Davies, Robert Z. Leonard)   *d* Leonard. *w* Edith Fitzgerald, A. P. Younger. Starring Marion Davies, Leslie Howard, Richard Bennett, Irene Rich, Mary Duncan   From FH novel

1932

Back Street   U.S.   93m   bw   mono   Universal (Carl Laemmle, Jr.)   *d* John M. Stahl. *w* Gladys Lehman, Lynn Starling, Ben Hecht. Starring Irene Dunne, John Boles, June Clyde, George Meeker, ZaSu Pitts, Shirley Grey, Doris Lloyd   From FH novel

Symphony of Six Million (aka *Melody of Life*)   U.S.   94m   bw   mono   RKO Radio (David O. Selznick)   *d* Gregory La Cava. *w* J. Walter Ruben, Bernard Schubert, James Seymour. Starring Irene Dunne, Ricardo Cortez, Gregory Ratoff, Anna Appel, Lita Chevret   Based on original FH scenario

1933

East of Fifth Avenue U.S. 74m bw mono Columbia *d* Albert S. Rogell. *w* Jo Swerling. Starring Walter Byron, Mary Carlisle, Louise Carter, Walter Connolly, Maude Eburne Initial scenario was FH's "Park Avenue"

Hello, Everybody! (musical; aka *Getting Acquainted*) U.S. bw mono Paramount *d* William A. Seiter. *w* Lawrence Hazard, Dorothy Yost. Starring Kate Smith, Randolph Scott, Irving Bacon, George Bancroft, George Barbier, Sally Blane, Marguerite Campbell Based on original FH scenario

1934

Imitation of Life U.S. 106m bw mono Universal (Carl Laemmle, Jr.) *d* John M. Stahl. *w* William Hurlbut, Preston Sturges. Starring Claudette Colbert, Warren William, Louise Beavers, Ned Sparks, Fredi Washington, Rochelle Hudson From FH novel AAN Best Picture; Best Assistant Director Scott R. Beal; Best Sound, Recording Gilbert Kurland

1938

Four Daughters U.S. 90m bw mono Warner Bros. (Hal B. Wallis) *d* Michael Curtiz. *w* Lenore J. Coffee, Julius J. Epstein. Starring Claude Rains, May Robson, John Garfield, Lola Lane, Priscilla Lane, Rosemary Lane, Dick Foran, Jeffrey Lynn, Frank McHugh, Vera Lewis, Gale Page From FH story "Sister Act" AAN Best Picture; Script; Curtiz; Garfield

1939

Daughters Courageous (aka *American Family, A Family Affair, Family Reunion*) U.S. 107m bw mono Warner Bros. (Hal B. Wallis) *d* Michael Curtiz. *w* Julius J. Epstein, Philip G. Epstein, Dorothy Bennett, Irving White. Starring Gale Page, Frank McHugh, John Garfield, Jeffrey Lynn, Claude Rains, May Robson, Priscilla Lane, Rosemary Lane, Lola Lane, Dick Foran, George Humbert Based on FH idea

Four Wives U.S. 110m bw mono Warner Bros. (Hal B. Wallis) *d* Michael Curtiz. *w* Julius J. Epstein, Philip G. Epstein, Maurice Hanline. Starring Claude Rains, Priscilla Lane, Rosemary Lane, Lola Lane, Gale Page Based on FH characters

1941

Four Mothers U.S. 86m bw mono Warner Bros. (Henry Blanke) *d* William Keighley *w* Stephen Morehouse Avery. Starring Priscilla Lane, Rosemary Lane, Lola Lane, Gale Page, Claude Rains Based on FH characters

Back Street (remake of 1932 original) U.S. 89m bw mono Universal (Bruce Manning) *d* Robert Stevenson. *w* Felix Jackson, Manning. Starring Charles Boyer, Margaret Sullavan, Richard Carlson, Frank McHugh, Tim Holt, Frank Jenks, Esther Dale Based on FH novel AAN Best Music, Frank Skinner

1946

Humoresque (remake of 1920 original) U.S. 125m bw mono Warner Bros. (Jerry Wald) *d* Jean Negulesco. *w* Zachary Gold, Clifford Odets. Starring Joan Crawford, John Garfield, Oscar Levant, J. Carrol Naish, Joan Chandler, Peggy Knudsen Based on FH story. AAN Best Music, Franz Waxman

1948

Angelitos negros Mex. 100m bw mono Rodríguez Hermanos (Ramón Peón)
d Joselito Rodríguez. *w* Félix B. Caignet, Rogelio A. González, J. Rodríguez. Starring Pedro Infante, Emilia Guiú, Rita Montaner, Titina Romay, Chela Castro
From FH novel *Imitation of Life*

1954

Young at Heart (remake of 1938 *Four Daughters*) U.S. 117m color Warner
Bros. (Henry Blanke) *d* Gordon Douglas. *w* Lenore J. Coffee, Julius J. Epstein,
Liam O'Brien. Starring Doris Day, Frank Sinatra, Ethel Barrymore, Marjorie Bennett, Ivan Browning, Gig Young, Dorothy Malone, Robert Keith From FH novelette

1959

Imitation of Life (remake of 1934 original) U.S. 124m color Universal (Ross
Hunter) *d* Douglas Sirk. *w* Eleanore Griffin, Allan Scott. Starring Lana Turner,
John Gavin, Sandra Dee, Troy Donahue, Susan Kohner, Juanita Moore, Mahalia
Jackson From FH novel AAN Moore; Kohner

1961

Back Street (second remake of 1932 original) U.S. 107m color Universal
(Ross Hunter) *d* David Miller. *w* Eleanore Griffin. Starring Susan Hayward,
John Gavin, Vera Miles, Charles Drake, Virginia Grey From FH novel AAN
Best Costume Design, Jean Louis

SELECTED BIBLIOGRAPHY

Acker, Ally. *Reel Women: Pioneers of the Cinema, 1896 to the Present*. New York: Continuum, 1993.

Austin, Mary. *Everyman's Genius*. Indianapolis: Bobbs-Merrill, 1925.

Baker, Harry T. *The Contemporary Short Story*. Boston: Heath, 1916.

Basinger, Jeanine. *A Woman's View: How Hollywood Spoke to Women, 1930–1960*. New York: Knopf, 1993.

Beard, Mary Ritter. *On Understanding Women*. New York: Longmans, Green, 1931.

———. *Woman as Force in History*. New York: Macmillan, 1946.

Blackmar, Elizabeth, and Ron Rosenzweig. *The Park and the People: A History of Central Park*. Ithaca: Cornell University Press, 1992.

Bodner, Allen. *When Boxing Was a Jewish Sport*. Westport, Conn.: Praeger, 1997.

Boris, Joseph J. ed. *Who's Who in Colored America*. New York: Who's Who in Colored America Corp., 1928–29.

Brandimarte, Cynthia Ann. "Fannie Hurst and Her Fiction: Prescriptions for America's Working Women." Thesis, Graduate School of the University of Texas at Austin, 1980.

Brown, Julie, ed. *American Women Short Story Writers*. New York: Garland Reference Library, 1995.

Brown, Sterling. *The Negro in American Fiction*. Washington, D.C.: Associates in Negro Folk Education, 1937. Also, New York: Atheneum, 1969.

Brownlow, Kevin. *Behind the Mask of Innocence*. New York: Knopf, 1990.

———. *The Parade's Gone By*. New York: Knopf, 1968.

Burgess, Gelett, et al. *My Maiden Effort: Being the Personal Confessions of Well-Known American Authors as to Their Literary Beginnings*. New York: Doubleday, Page, 1921.

Burke, James Henry, and Alice Payne Hackett. *Eighty Years of Best Sellers, 1895–1975*. New York: Bowker, 1977.

Burton, Harry Payne, ed. *Favorite Stories by Famous Writers*. New York: Cosmopolitan Corp., 1932.

Byars, Jackie. *All That Hollywood Allows*. Chapel Hill, N.C.: University of North Carolina Press, 1991.

Capra, Frank. *The Name Above the Title*. 1971. Reprint, New York: Da Capo Press, 1997.

Caputi, Jane. "Specifying Fannie Hurst: Langston Hughes' *Limitations of Life,* Zora Neale Hurston's *Their Eyes Were Watching God,* and Toni Morrison's *The Bluest Eye* as 'Answers' to Hurst's *Imitation of Life*." *Black American Literature Forum,* Vol. 24, No. 4, Winter 1990, pp. 697–716.

Carson, Diane, Linda Dittmar, and Janice R. Welsch, eds. *Feminist Film Criticism*. Minneapolis: University of Minnesota Press, 1994.

Case, Frank. *Tales of a Wayward Inn*. New York: Lippincott, 1938.

Collins, Joseph. *Taking the Literary Pulse: Psychological Studies of Life and Letters*. New York: Doran, 1924.

Congdon, Don, ed. *The Thirties: A Time to Remember*. New York: Simon & Schuster, 1962.

Costello, Bonnie, gen. ed., Celeste Goodridge, and Cristanne Miller. *The Selected Letters of Marianne Moore*. New York: Knopf, 1997.

Cranmer, Catharine. "Little Visits with Literary Missourians." *Missouri Historical Review,* Apr. 1925, pp. 389–396.

———. "Fannie Hurst Is Interviewed." *Writer's Monthly,* Vol. 26, Sept. 1925, pp. 200–205.

Cripps, Thomas. *Making Movies Black: The Hollywood Message from World War II to the Civil Rights Era*. New York: Oxford University Press, 1993.

Dague, Elizabeth. "Images of Work, Glimpses of Professionalism in Selected Nineteenth- and Twentieth-Century Novels." *Frontiers,* Vol. 5, No. 1, 1980, pp. 50–55.

Davis, Robert H., and Arthur B. Maurice. *The Caliph of Bagdad: Being Arabian Nights Flashes of the Life, Letters and World of O. Henry*. New York: Appleton, 1931.

Dearborn, Mary V. *Queen of Bohemia: The Life of Louise Bryant*. Boston: Houghton Mifflin, 1996.

Derleth, August. *Still Small Voice: The Biography of Zona Gale*. New York: Appleton-Century, 1940.

Douglas, Ann. *Terrible Honesty: Mongrel Manhattan in the 1920s*. New York: Farrar, Straus & Giroux, 1995.

Dressler, Marie. *My Own Story as Told to Mildred Harrington*. Boston: Little, Brown, 1934.

Egan, Maurice Francis. "American Family Life in Fiction." *Catholic World,* Vol. 110, Dec. 1919, pp. 289–304.

Findling, John E. *Dictionary of American Diplomatic History*. New York: Greenwood, 1989.

Fischer, Lucy, ed. *Imitation of Life: Douglas Sirk, Director*. New Brunswick, N.J.: Rutgers University Press, 1991.

Friedman, Lester D. *Jewish Image in American Film*. Secaucus, N.J.: Citadel, 1987.

Frohman, Daniel. *Daniel Frohman Presents: An Autobiography*. New York: Claude Kendall & Willoughby Sharp, 1935.

Gabler, Neal. *An Empire of Their Own: How the Jews Invented Hollywood*. New York: Crown, 1988.

Glendinning, Victoria. *Rebecca West: A Life*. New York: Knopf, 1987.

Goodman, Henry, ed. *Creating the Short Story*. New York: Harcourt Brace, 1929.

Harriman, Margaret Case. *The Vicious Circle: The Story of the Algonquin Round Table*. New York: Rinehart, 1951.

Hemenway, Robert. *Zora Neale Hurston: A Literary Biography*. Urbana and Chicago: University of Illinois Press, 1980.

Hill, Lynda Marion. *Social Rituals and the Verbal Art of Zora Neale Hurston*. Washington, D.C.: Howard University Press, 1996.

Hoffman, Frederick J. *The Twenties: American Writing in the Postwar Decade*. New York: Viking, 1955.

Hubbell, Jay B. *Who Are the Major American Writers?* Durham, N.C.: Duke University Press, 1972.

Huggins, Nathan Irvin. *Harlem Renaissance.* New York: Oxford University Press, 1971.

Hurston, Zora Neale. *Dust Tracks on a Road.* 1942. Reprint, New York: HarperPerennial, 1996.

———. *Hurston: Folklore, Memoirs, and Other Writings.* New York: Library of America, 1995.

———. *Jonah's Gourd Vine.* Philadelphia: J.B. Lippincott, 1934.

Hutchinson, George. *The Harlem Renaissance in Black and White.* Cambridge, Mass.: Harvard University Press, 1995.

Johns, Orrick. *Time of Our Lives: The Story of My Father and Myself.* New York: Stackpole, 1937.

Kessner, Thomas. *Fiorello H. La Guardia and the Making of Modern New York.* New York: McGraw-Hill 1989.

Kilmer, Joyce. *Literature in the Making by Some of Its Makers.* New York: Harper, 1917.

Kisseloff, Jeff. *The Box: An Oral History of Television, 1920–1961.* New York: Viking, 1995.

Koppelman, Susan. "The Educations of Fannie Hurst." *Women's Studies International Forum,* Vol. 10, No. 5, 1987, pp. 503–516.

Koppelman, Susan, ed. *"May Your Days Be Merry and Bright" and Other Christmas Stories by Women.* Detroit: Wayne State University Press, 1988.

Kuehl, John, and Jackson Bryer, eds. *Dear Scott, Dear Max: The Fitzgerald-Perkins Correspondence.* New York: Scribner's, 1971, p. 25.

Lash, Joseph P. *A World of Love: Eleanor Roosevelt and Her Friends, 1943 to 1962.* New York: Doubleday, 1984.

Laurel, Jeanne Phoenix. "Double Veil: Cross-Racial Characterizations in Six American Women's Novels, 1909–1948." Thesis, Indiana University, 1990.

Lewis, David Levering. *When Harlem Was in Vogue.* New York: Oxford University Press, 1979.

Lawrence, Margaret. *The School of Femininity: A Book for and About Women as They Are Interpreted Through Feminine Writers of Yesterday and Today.* New York: Stokes, 1936.

Lichtenstein, Diane. "Fannie Hurst and Her Nineteenth Century Predecessors." *Studies in American Jewish Literature,* Vol. 7, No. 1, 1988, pp. 25–39.

———. *On Whose Native Ground? Nineteenth-Century Myths of American Womanhood and Jewish Women Writers.* Ph.D. diss., University of Pennsylvania, 1985, UMI Dissertation Service.

Loggins, Vernon. *I Hear America: Literature in the United States Since 1900.* 1937. Reprint, New York: Biblo & Tannen, 1967.

Long, Ray. *Twenty Best Short Stories in Ray Long's Twenty Years as an Editor.* New York: Ray Long and Richard R. Smith, 1932.

Long, Ray, et al. *My Favorite Story.* New York: International Magazine, 1928.

Lotz, Philip Henry, ed. *Distinguished American Jews.* 1945. Reprint, Freeport, N.Y.: Books for Libraries Press, 1970.

Luccock, Halford Edward. *Contemporary American Literature and Religion.* New York: Willet Clark, 1934.

McBride, Joseph. *Frank Capra: The Catastrophe of Success.* New York: Touchstone, 1992.

McNeil, Alex. *Total Television,* 4th ed. New York: Penguin, 1996.

368

Mann, Arthur. *La Guardia: A Fighter Against His Times, 1882–1933*. Philadelphia: Lippincott, 1959.

Marbury, Elisabeth. *My Crystal Ball: Reminiscences*. New York: Boni & Liveright, 1923.

Mitchell, Joseph. *Up in the Old Hotel*. New York: Vintage, 1993.

Monteux, Fifi (Pierre). *Everyone Is Someone*. New York: Farrar, Straus & Cudaway, 1962.

Morris, Lloyd. *Incredible New York: High Life and Low Life from 1850 to 1950*. 1951. Reprint, Syracuse: Syracuse University Press, 1966, pp. 301–315.

Mott, Frank Luther. *History of American Magazines*, Cambridge, Mass.: Harvard University Press, 1938–1968.

Nash, Jay Robert, and Stanley Ralph Ross. *The Motion Picture Guide*. All volumes. Chicago: Cinebooks, 1986.

Nowlan, Robert A., and Gwendolyn Wright Nolan. *Cinema Sequels and Remakes, 1903–1987*. Chicago: Prism, 1989.

O'Brien, Edward J., ed. *The Best Short Stories of 1915*. Boston: Small, Maynard & Co., 1916.

———. *The Best Short Stories of 1916*. Boston: Small, Maynard, 1917.

———. *The Best Short Stories of 1918*. Boston: Small, Maynard, 1919.

———. *The Best Short Stories of 1920*. Boston: Small, Maynard, 1921.

———. *The Best Short Stories of 1921*. Boston: Small, Maynard, 1922.

———. *The Best Short Stories of 1922*. Boston: Small, Maynard, 1923.

———. *The Best Short Stories of 1923*. Boston: Small, Maynard, 1924.

———. *The Best Short Stories of 1924*. Boston: Small, Maynard, 1925.

———. *The Best Short Stories of 1925*. Boston: Small, Maynard, 1926.

———. *The Best Short Stories of 1926*. New York: Dodd, Mead, 1927.

———. *The Best Short Stories of 1927*. New York: Dodd, Mead, 1928.

———. *The Best Short Stories of 1929*. New York: Dodd, Mead, 1930.

———. *The Best Short Stories of 1930*. New York: Dodd, Mead, 1931.

O'Brien, Sharon. *Willa Cather: The Emerging Voice*. New York: Oxford University Press, 1987.

Overton, Grant. *The Women Who Make Our Novels*, rev. ed. Freeport, N.Y.: Books for Libraries Press, 1967.

Overton, Grant, ed. *Mirrors of the Year: A National Review of the Outstanding Figures, Trends and Events of 1926–1927*. New York: Stokes, 1927.

Overton, Grant, et al. *Fannie Hurst, A Critical Appreciation*. New York: Harper, 1928.

Pearce, T. M., ed. *Literary America, 1903–1934: The Mary Austin Letters*. Westport, Conn.: Greenwood, 1979.

Poague, Leland. *Another Frank Capra*. New York: Press Syndicate of the University of Cambridge, 1994.

Pollock, Channing. *Harvest of My Years: An Autobiography*. Indianapolis: Bobbs-Merrill, 1943.

Pruett, Lorine, and Iva Lowther Peters. *Women Workers Through the Depression*. New York: Macmillan, 1934.

Queen, Ellery, ed. *The Literature of Crime: Stories by World-Famous Authors*. Boston: Little, Brown, 1950, pp. 380–405.

Radway, Janice A. *A Feeling for Books: The Book-of-the-Month Club, Literary Taste, and Middle-Class Desire*. Chapel Hill, N.C.: University of North Carolina Press, 1997.

Rampersad, Arnold. *The Life of Langston Hughes, Vol. 1, 1902–41.* New York: Oxford University Press, 1986.

Ray, Gordon N. *H. G. Wells and Rebecca West.* New Haven: Yale University Press, 1974.

Riggio, Thomas P., ed. *Theodore Dreiser: The American Diaries, 1902–1926.* Philadelphia: University of Pennsylvania Press, 1982.

Robinson, Kenneth Allan, ed. *Contemporary Short Stories.* Boston: Houghton Mifflin, 1924.

Rollyson, Carl. *Rebecca West: A Life.* New York: Scribner, 1996.

Rose, Blanche Waltrip. "Fannie Hurst Talks to Writers." *Writer's Monthly,* Vol. 30, Nov. 1927, pp. 400–403.

Rubin, Joan Shelley. *The Making of Middle Brow Culture.* Chapel Hill, N.C.: University of North Carolina Press, 1992.

Sara, Dorothy. *Tales for Frails.* New York: Cadillac, 1946.

Sardi, Vincent, and Richard Gehman. *Sardi's: The Story of a Famous Restaurant.* New York: Henry Holt, 1953.

Schatz, Thomas. *The Genius of the System: Hollywood Filmmaking in the Studio Era.* New York: Metropolitan Books, 1988.

Schulberg, Budd. *Sparring with Hemingway.* Chicago: Dee, 1995, pp. 53–63.

Schwarz, Judith. *The Radical Feminists of Heterodoxy: Greenwich Village, 1912–1940,* rev. ed. Norwich, Vt.: New Victoria, 1986.

Schweikert, H. C., ed. *Short Stories.* New York: Harcourt, Brace, 1937.

Shaughnessy, Mary Rose. *Myths About Love and Woman.* New York: Gordon Press, 1980.

Shipman, David. *The Great Movie Stars: The Golden Years.* New York: Little, Brown, 1989.

Shockley, Ann Allen and Sue P. Chandler, eds., *Living Black American Authors.* New York: Bowker, 1973.

Sibley, Carroll. *Barrie and His Contemporaries.* Webster Groves, Mo.: International Mark Twain Society, 1936.

Sobol, Louis. *The Longest Street: A Memoir.* New York: Crown, 1968.

Stefansson, Vilhjalmur. *Discovery: The Autobiography of Vilhjalmur Stefansson.* New York: McGraw-Hill, 1964.

Stiles, Lela. *The Man Behind Roosevelt: The Story of Louis McHenry Howe.* Cleveland: World, 1954.

Stokes, Horace Winston, ed. *Mirrors of the Year: A National Revue of the Outstanding Figures, Trends and Events of 1927–28.* New York: Stokes, 1928.

Tebbel, John. *George Horace Lorimer and the Saturday Evening Post.* Garden City, N.Y.: Country Life Press, 1948.

Tebbel, John, and Mary Ellen Zuckerman. *The Magazine in America, 1741–1990.* New York: Oxford University Press, 1991.

Towne, Charles Hanson. *This New York of Mine.* New York: Cosmopolitan Book Corp., 1931.

Uffen, Ellen Serlen. "The Novels of Fannie Hurst: Notes Toward a Definition of Popular Fiction." *Journal of American Culture,* Vol. 1, 1978, pp. 574–583.

———. *Strands of the Cable: The Place of the Past in Jewish American Women's Writing.* New York: Lang, 1992.

Van Voris, Jacqueline. *Carrie Chapman Catt: A Public Life.* New York: Feminist Press, 1987.

Vickers, Sarah P. "The Life of Ruth Bryan Owen: Florida's First Congresswoman and America's First Woman Diplomat." Diss., Florida State University, 1994.

Wall, Cheryl A. *Women of the Harlem Renaissance*. Bloomington: University of Indiana Press, 1995.

Ward, Christopher. "Stummox by Fannie Wurst." In *Twisted Tales*. New York: Henry Holt, 1924, pp. 1–7.

Weber, Ronald. *Hired Pens: Professional Writers in America's Golden Age of Print*. Athens: Ohio University Press, 1997.

Wentworth, Harold, and Stuart Berg Flexner, eds. *Dictionary of American Slang*, 2d supp'd. ed. New York: Crowell, 1975.

Williams, Blanche Colton. *The O. Henry Memorial Award Prize Stories, 1919*. Garden City, N.Y.: Doubleday, Page, 1920.

Wittenstein, Kate E. "The Heterodoxy Club and American Feminism, 1912–1930." Thesis, Boston University, 1989.

Woodward, W. E. *The Gift of Life*. New York: Dutton, 1947.

NOTES

KEY TO ENDNOTE ABBREVIATIONS

Word and Name Abbreviations
appt-bk = appointment book
appt-cal = appointment calendar
c. = circa
cbl = cable
int = interview
ltr = letter
undtd = undated
unid = unidentified
FH = Fannie Hurst
JSD = Jacques S. Danielson
Stef = Vilhjalmur Stefansson

Abbreviations for Publishers and Publications
Anat = FH, *Anatomy of Life*
SEP = *Saturday Evening Post*
MET = *Metropolitan Magazine*
Cosmo = *Cosmopolitan*
Hearst = Hearst Corp.
NYT = *The New York Times*
StLP-D = *St. Louis Post-Dispatch*

Abbreviations for Libraries, Archives, and Specific Files
AmJwshArch = Jacob Rader Marcus Center of the American Jewish Archives, Cincinnati, Ohio, Annie Nathan Meyers Papers, Manuscript Collection, No. 7
AmJwshHist = American Jewish Historical Society
Bran = Brandeis University Library, Special Collections, Fannie Hurst Collection
CBS = Columbia Broadcasting Company News Archives
Colum = Rare Books and Manuscripts Library, Columbia University Libraries
Dart = Dartmouth College Library, Rare Books and Manuscripts
FDR = Franklin Delano Roosevelt Memorial Library, Hyde Park, N.Y.
Film = Center for Motion Picture Study, Margaret Herrick Library of the Academy of Motion Picture Arts and Sciences Academy Foundation
Fla = University of Florida, George A. Smathers Libraries, Department of Special Collections, Zora Neale Hurston Collection
Hough = Houghton Library, Harvard University

HRC = Harry Ransom Humanities Research Center, University of Texas at Austin

Hunt = Henry E. Huntington Library

KCPL = Kansas City (Mo.) Public Library, Special Collections

LOC = Library of Congress, Manuscripts

MHS = Missouri Historical Society

MusCNY = Theatre Collection of the Museum of the City of New York

NatlArch = U.S. National Archives

NYPL-Berg = New York Public Library, A. A. Berg Collection

NYPL-BR = New York Public Library, Library for the Performing Arts, Billy Rose Theater Collection

NYPL-Rare = New York Public Library, Manuscripts and Archives Division (Rare Books and Manuscripts)

NYPL-Schomburg = New York Public Library, Schomburg Center for Research in Black Culture

NYUArch = New York University Office of University Archives

NYU-Fales = New York University, Fales Library and Special Collections

Penn = University of Pennsylvania, University Libraries, Special Collections Department, Van Pelt Library

Prin = Princeton University Library, Department of Rare Books and Special Collections

Rad = Arthur and Elizabeth Schlesinger Library on the History of Women in America at Radcliffe College, Harvard University

StLCC = St. Louis Civil Court, Circuit Court, City of St. Louis Records

StLMerc = St. Louis Mercantile Library

StLPubLib = St. Louis Public Library Newspaper Collection

StLPubSch = St. Louis Public School Records and Archives

Temp = Temple University Libraries, Urban Archives

UC-Berk = Bancroft Library, University of California, Berkeley

WashArch = Washington University, Olin Library, University Archives

WashSpc = Washington University, Olin Library, Special Collections

Wis = Wisconsin State Historical Society

Yale = Yale University, Beinecke Rare Book and Manuscript Library, or the Sterling Memorial Library

INTRODUCTION

PAGE

xiii   "WRITE A BOOK . . ." HRC, FH/151/2. FH to Joseph Levy, undtd 1923.

xiii   O'BRIEN WHO PREDICTED Edward J. O'Brien, ed., *The Best Short Stories of 1916* (Boston: Small, Maynard, 1917), p. 377. *Golden Book,* Vol. 9, No. 50, Feb. 1929, p. 8.

xiii   "PENETRATING . . ." W. D. Howells, "Editor's Easy Chair," *Harper's Monthly,* Vol. 130, May 1915, pp. 958–961.

xiv   STAR-DUST, NETTED Hearst, *Cosmo,* FH files. *Star-Dust* bought Nov. 15, 1919. Paid in ten monthly installments of $1,750 between March and December 1920. Also, HRC. FH/255/2. Contracts. Alice Kauser to JSD, Jan. 8, 1921.

xiv   STEADY AT THAT PRICE Hearst, *Cosmo,* FH files.

xiv   "I WOULD RATHER . . . CLASSIC FAILURE . . ." *Anat,* p. 92.

xiv   "*ARTISTIC* ACCLAIM . . ." HRC, FH/151/2. FH to Joseph Levy, undtd 1923.

xiv   "I WOULD RATHER . . . CLASSICAL FAILURE" WashArch *Alumni Bulletin,* Feb. 1950. Also HRC. FH/240/2. Edna Wahlert McCourt to FH, Mar. 25, 1950. In the *Bulletin* piece, FH wrote, "Edna Wahlert, who headed a local literary group, and who is alleged to have said that I was alleged to have said: 'I would rather be a popular success than a classical failure.' " After the *Bulletin* piece appeared, Wahlert wrote FH immediately, charging that there was no "alleged" about it: FH had made the remark to a St. Louis newspaper reporter, who printed it in a prophecy of Wahlert. Wahlert's monograph *Completion of Coleridge's Christabel: A Story of Destiny and Peace* was published the year FH graduated from Washington University, 1909.

xvi   "HOUSE WITHIN AN APARTMENT HOUSE" CBS. Int., Edward R. Murrow with FH, *Person-to-Person,* live telecast, June 18, 1954.

xvi   "MOST FAMOUS STUDIO . . ." Tracie Rozhon, "Habitats/Hotel des Artistes: Rare Sale for Tall Triplex," *NYT,* Sept. 12, 1993, 10:6:1.

CHAPTER ONE

PAGE

3   FIRST KNOWN PUBLISHED WORK StLPubSch, FH's registration and commencement records make clear that Central High School had September and January entrance and graduation in these years.

3   "THEN HE ROSE . . ." WashSpc, Arthur Proetz Papers 1/7, *High School News,* Christmas No., 1904, pp. 3–4.

3   SHE LIKED TO CLAIM FH, "I Come Across," *American Magazine,* Vol. 87, No. 3, Mar. 1919, p. 39. The information is also repeated in numerous other FH profiles.

3   "AN OLD-MAID SCHOOLTEACHER . . ." *Anat,* p. 75.

3   ENTERED WASHINGTON UNIVERSITY WashArch, Registrar, FH official transcript, 1905–1909.

3   "THE KNEES OF NEWBORN CALVES" FH, "How a City Looks to Miss Hurst after Ten Years," *StLP-D,* Feb. 25, 1929, 1:1, 4:1–4.

3   SUITCASE U. Mrs. Carl G. Campbell, "Huntington Woman Pens a Close Up of Fannie Hurst," *Sunday Advertiser,* Jan. 17, 1926.

4   FRIENDS OFTEN SAW THE LIGHTS WashArch, *Student Life,* Nov. 25, 1908, p. 11.

4   AIR OF A SERIOUS SCHOLAR Campbell, "Huntington Woman Pens."

4   HER A'S IN SUBJECTS WashArch, Registrar, FH official transcript.

4   "MORE CONSPICUOUS THAN DISTINGUISHED" *Anat,* p. 85.

4   "ENJOYED LIVING . . ." Campbell, "Huntington Woman Pens."

4   "SLASHING AROUND . . ." *Anat,* pp. 83–84.

4   AMONG A NUMBER OF STUDENTS Of the men among Fannie's St. Louis classmates and peers, Melville Burke became a respected theatrical director; Orrick Johns, a gifted and recognized poet; and Hugh Ferris, an architect of international renown. Ferris and Burke were at Washington University with her; Johns attended the University of Missouri at Columbia.

4   AKINS'S WORK WAS APPEARING WashArch, issues of the *Mirror,* 1905.

4 THE LEGENDARY WILLIAM MARION REEDY MHS, Love letters housed at the Missouri Historical Society unsealed after Akins's death in 1958 show that Reedy, twice married previously and in his forties, was in love with Akins and proposed marriage. See also *StLP-D*, Clarissa Start, "Love Letters Zoe Akins Sealed till Death," *StLP-D*, Nov. 25, 1958.

4 FANNIE ODDLY REMEMBERED In a self-mocking 1921 essay on the pretentiousness of her early work, FH claimed to have completed *Cristabel* herself at the age of sixteen. No such document survives. See Gelett, Burgess, intro. to *My Maiden Effort: Being the Personal Confessions of Well-Known American Authors as to their Literary Beginnings* (New York: Doubleday, Page, 1921), p. 116. See also Edna Wahlert, *Completion of Coleridge's Cristabel . . . a story of Destiny and Peace* (New York: Cochrance, 1909).

5 COULTER HAD LITTLE TIME WashArch, *Alumni Bulletin*, Feb. 1950, p. 7.

5 "TRANSPARENT . . ." *Anat*, p. 92.

5 OF THE 109 STUDENTS WashArch, General Catalogue, 1905–6, Washington *University Record*, Vol. 1, No. 3, Nov. 1905.

5 THE BEST-KNOWN GIRL *Anat*, p. 85.

5 "WILL FANNIE HURST BECOME FAMOUS?" HRC, FH/100/2. Robert L. Bienstok to FH, Feb. 19, 1949.

5 "EVEN AWAY . . ." WashSpc, FH/207/5, Florine Shapleigh Maule to FH, Aug. 30, 1926.

5 "CAME TOGETHER AS A MATTER . . ." Edna Wahlert, signing herself "Ned," Wahlert, *StLP-D*, Letter to the Editor, Nov. 21, 1958, 2E:1.

5 THEY WELCOMED EDNA See "Missouri Women in History: Sara Teasdale." *Missouri Historical Review*, Vol. 62, No. 3, Apr. 1968, back cover.

5 COLLEGE SORORITIES FH, in response to an offer of honorary membership from the Jewish sorority Alpha Epsilon Phi, replied, "Unfortunately, ever since my own personal experience in college, I have been opposed to the kind of segregation that our present system of fraternal organizations almost automatically imposes upon American life. . . . My acceptance of the fine honor you would confer upon me would however be a refutation of my strong conviction that so long as the fraternity creates, for one reason or another, emphasis on religious differences, its climate is not healthy." HRC, FH/89/5, FH to Mrs. Stanley Baach, Alpha Epsilon Phi, Jan. 17, 1950.

5 SHE HAD THE PANACHE WashArch, Issues of *Student Life*, 1904–1909. Fannie's other college roles: Babble in *High Life Below Stairs*, Miss Blackwell in Winston Churchill's *Title Mart*, Mrs. Croaker in *The Good-Natured Man*, Lady Gay Spanker in Dion Bauciacault's *London Assurance*, and Louise de Glaciere in J. Palgrave Simpson's *Scrap of Paper*. By her junior year, as vice president of the drama club, the name of which changed to Thyrsus, Fannie began to assert some influence over the choice of material, urging less reliance on traditional farces.

5 "THE OTHERS APPEARED AMATEURISH" WashArch, *Student Life*, Jan. 13, 1909, p. 3.

5 THE CAST DEMANDED StLPubLib, *StLP-D*, Sunday Magazine, Apr. 22, 1934, p. 4.

6 "A TRIUMPH OF REALISM . . ." StLPubLib, Marguerite Martyn, " 'The Official Chaperone' by Washington University Student Embodies Varsity Spirit," *StLP-D*, June 17, 1909, 13:2–5.

6 FANNIE FASHIONED HER OWN KNOT Campbell, "Huntington Woman Pens."

6 "BEAUTIFUL, GIFTED, CARELESS CREATURE" WashArch, *The Alumni Bulletin,* Feb. 1950, p. 7.

6 "HOW ALL THE GIRLS ENVIED YOU!" HRC, FH/126/1, Olna Hudler Fant to FH, undtd [c. 1953].

6 OTHER FRIENDS Campbell, "Huntington Woman Pens."

6 "WHAT AN IMAGINATION! . . ." HRC, FH 126/1, Olna Hudler Fant to FH, Jan. 3, 1956.

6 RARELY HAD THERE BEEN A STUDENT Campbell, "Huntington Woman Pens."

7 ONE OF FANNIE HURST'S PROFESSORS Adele Starbird, "Fannie Hurst Success Story," *StLP-D,* Oct. 14, 1952, p. 2D.

7 "PREMARITAL IRREGULARITIES . . ." *Anat,* p. 87.

7 "SEXUAL AND OTHERWISE" HRC, FH/136/4, Meta Gruner to FH, Aug. 31, 1963, quoting Frederick Lewis Allen.

7 "LIKE SANDPAPER . . ." *Anat,* pp. 90–91.

7 "RINGING, MIRTHFUL LAUGHTER . . ." HRC, FH/126/1, Olna Hudler Fant to FH, undtd [c. 1953].

7 IT WAS SURELY AKINS WashArch, *Washington University Record, 1906–07,* lists Akins as a special student for this year. Her father, Thomas J. Akins, was at the time not a senator but the U.S. postmaster in St. Louis. It was several years later, in 1913, that he ran for the U.S. Senate, but he lost that election. See also *Anat,* pp. 84–87.

7 "WE DID NOT KNOW ANYBODY . . ." *Anat,* pp. 86–87.

8 FANNIE SUSPECTED EVEN REEDY *Anat,* p. 100.

8 "WHAT DID MEN SEE . . ." *Anat,* pp. 86–87.

8 "TALL PLUSH HAT . . ." HRC, FH/126/1, Olna Hudler Fant to FH, undtd [c. 1953].

8 "MORE INTIMATE WITH THE ANONYMOUS PUBLIC . . ." *Anat,* p. 88.

8 "THE BLASÉ JUNIOR SOLILOQUIZES." WashArch, *Student Life,* Nov. 28, 1906, p. 7.

8 "CAPTURE THE WINGED WORDS . . ." *Anat,* p. 83.

8–9 "A MOOD," "THE GIRL AND THE WOMAN" . . . / "NEAR THE CENTER . . ." WashArch, see all issues *Student Life,* 1906–1909. Specific references Oct. 9, 1907, p. 11; Oct. 23, 1907, p. 10; Nov. 13, 1907, p. 10; Nov. 27, 1907.

9 "NO FOREIGNER ARRIVING . . ." HRC, FH/171/3, FH for Leonard Lyon column, Sept. 18, 1941.

9 FANNIE ORIGINALLY WROTE WashArch, *Student Life,* Apr. 18, 1912, p. 6.

9 TALE OF A POOR COUPLE'S SIMPLE DELIGHTS FH, "The Joy of Living," *Mirror,* May 27, 1909, p. 4.

9 "FOR HER . . ." WashArch, *Student Life,* Apr. 18, 1912, p. 6.

9 "NOTES AND JOTTINGS . . ." FH, "I Come Across," *American Magazine,* Vol. 87, No. 3, Mar. 1919, pp. 39, 126.

CHAPTER TWO

PAGE

10 "THE HEARTACHES . . ." FH, "I Come Across," *American Magazine,* Mar. 1919, Vol. 87, No. 3, pp. 39, 126–130.

10 AT LEAST ONE LOCAL PROPOSAL OF MARRIAGE *Anat,* pp. 94–105.

10 "LIGHT," UNSIGNED WORK MHS, William Marion Reedy to Albert Bloch, Aug. 2, 1909.

10 NEVER FELT . . . THOUGH SHE BEGGED StLPubLib, "How City Looks to Miss Hurst After Ten Years," *StLP-D,* Feb. 25, 1929, 1:1, 4:1–4.

10 NEW MANUSCRIPTS . . . NONE APPEARED FH claims in *Anat* that Reedy published her story "Ain't Life Wonderful" when she was a junior in college. No such story appears then or later in *Reedy's Mirror.*

11 "A SAGE WHO LIVED . . ." *Anat,* p. 93.

11 "RACY RABELAISIAN QUALITY" HRC, FH/244/1, FH to Fred W. Wolf, June 29, 1939.

11 "HIS VAST BODY . . ." *Anat,* p. 100.

11 "KING OF GREATNESS . . ." HRC, FH/244/1, FH to Fred W. Wolf, June 29, 1939.

11 BEULAH/ "BOMBED OUT OF HER VIRGINITY . . ." *Anat,* pp. 101–102.

11 "FAT AND PLEASANT . . ." MHS, William Marion Reedy to Albert Bloch, Aug. 2, 1909. See also HRC, FH/180/6, Charles Van Ravenswaay to FH, with which Van Ravenswaay also sent a typed copy of Reedy's letter that omits references to weight and ambition.

12 SHE VOLUNTEERED . . . THE JEWISH EDUCATIONAL ALLIANCE HRC, FH/156/2, Philip L. Seman to FH, July 18, 1942.

12 "HEELS, COUNTERS AND TOP LIFTS" StLCC, Apr. 9, 1904, letterhead in court records indexed under Samuel H. Hurst.

12 YOUNG POLISH GIRLS *Anat,* p. 116.

12 INTRIGUING BILLBOARD WashArch, item, *Student Life,* Dec. 16, 1908, p. 8. See also HRC, FH/229/1, FH to Dorothy Thomas, Apr. 17, 1942, in which FH says she made the trip with both parents, a four-week graduation tour of her own choosing.

12 DETOURED TO MT. CLEMENS, MICHIGAN HRC, FH/176/3, J. W. Martin to FH, Feb. 22, 1911.

12 "LOVE BEFORE FIRST FULL SIGHT" HRC, FH/229/1, FH to Dorothy Thomas, Apr. 17, 1942. See also *Anat,* pp. 132–138.

12 "IN WHAT MIGHT HAVE BEEN . . ." *Anat,* pp. 132–141.

14 "THE DOMINANT FORCE" FH, "The Dominant Force," *Reedy's Mirror,* Feb. 3, 1910, p. 8.

14 "THE GROPERS" FH, "The Gropers," *Reedy's Mirror,* May 26, 1910, pp. 6–7.

14 "BLEEDING . . ." WashSpc, FH to Mrs. P. D. Cottle, Nov. 9, 1915.

14 STORIES . . . ATTRACTED AN ENORMOUS READERSHIP Harry Salpeter, "Fannie Hurst: Sob-Sister of American Fiction," *Bookman,* Vol. 23, Aug. 1931, p. 612. "The over-painted little shopgirl may not know Glenway Wescott from a Pullman car or Elizabeth Madox Roberts from a peak in the Sierra Nevada, but she will know that Fannie Hurst is an author."

15 "WITH ONE OF THOSE TERRIBLE CHINESE WALLS . . ."/ "ALL MY LIFE . . ." NYPL-Rare, Robert Hobart Davies Papers, FH, *Fannie Hurst by Fannie Hurst,* No. 7. "Slip-me-in-your-pocket Series" published by *Cosmo* advertising department. New York: International Magazine Co., 1919.

15 CLAIMED TO HAVE ENROLLED . . . AT COLUMBIA No records of any FH registration at Columbia University, Columbia University Division of General Education,

Barnard College, or Columbia Teachers' College survive. Registrars' examination of records, Nov. 1996.

15 SHE LIKED TO WALK See Joseph Mitchell, *Up in the Old Hotel*, New York: Vintage 1993, pp. 34–35. Mitchell, in 1940, writes of FH's relationship with Bowery Mazie, who had known FH at the time for eleven years.

15 "THE NOBILITY OF THE PEN" HRC, FH/134/3, Simon Goldstein to FH, Oct. 8, 1914.

15 THOUGH HER PARENTS OPPOSED HER MOVE FH, "Teddy Roosevelt and I," *Pageant*, June 1946, p. 18.

15 "WHEN HER GLASSES SEEMED TO BE MISPLACED . . ." HRC, FH/218/4, Mrs. G. Garnett Hedges to FH, Oct. 24, 1958.

15 "BARE TO AUSTERITY . . ." *Anat*, p. 147.

16 "STEP LIVELY" FH, "Teddy Roosevelt and I," p. 18.

16 "NOT TO HEAR THE SOUND . . ." FH, *Fannie Hurst by Fannie Hurst*.

16 "VARIOUS STAGES . . ." FH, "I Come Across," p. 126.

16 SHE MAILED HOME UNSIGNED CLIPPINGS *Anat*, p. 149.

16 ONE SMALL SUCCESS FH, "Prose," *Reedy's Mirror*, Dec. 22, 1910, 39:1–3.

16 "GRIM-KIND VIEW OF LIFE . . ." HRC, FH/201/1, William Marion Reedy to FH, Nov. 29, 1910.

16 "HIS PROFESSIONAL PROSPECTS . . ." HRC, FH/195/7, Henry Carter Patterson to FH, Feb. 18, 1935. See also *St. Louis Times, Star, Globe-Democrat, Post-Dispatch*, Feb. 19–21, 1911.

16 "IT IS NOT MISS HURST'S INTENTION . . ." StLPubLib, "Grace George and Della Fox Stars of the Week," *StLP-D*, Feb. 19, 1911, 7:2–5.

17 "BOTH THE SKETCH . . ." StLPubLib, "Columbia's New Bill," *St. Louis Star*, Feb. 21, 1911, 12:3.

17 "LACKED VITALITY . . ." StLPubLib, "Behan Gives Pathetic Italian Impersonation," *St. Louis Republic*, Feb. 21, 1911, 5:5.

17 "SINCERELY WORTHY" StLPubLib, " 'Sauce for the Goose' Is Very Clever Comedy," *StLP-D*, Feb. 21, 1911, 6:2.

17 "I HAVE OFTEN WONDERED . . ." HRC, FH/176/3, J. W. Martin to FH, Feb. 22, 1911.

17 "TERRIBLE" *Anat*, p. 111.

17 "MISERY AND COMPANY" FH, "Misery and Company," *NYT Sunday Magazine*, Mar. 19, 1911, p. 3.

17 "NO DISRESPECT . . ." HRC, FH/201/1, William Marion Reedy to FH, undtd. Accompanying lone envelope in file dated Mar. 9, 1911, which would correspond.

17 REJECTED AT THE DELINEATOR HRC, FH/117/2, J. H. Cosgrove, *Delineator*, to FH, Apr. 1, 1911.

17 THE AMERICAN MAGAZINE HRC, FH/92/1, John S. Phillips, *American Magazine*, to FH, May 2, 1911.

17 MUNSEY'S . . . STILL TURNED IT DOWN HRC, FH/116/1, Robert H. Davis to FH, Apr. 1, 1911.

17–18 BIT PART . . . TO PASS THE TIME FH, "I Come Across," p. 128.

18 "TOO CRUDE IN WORKMANSHIP" HRC, FH/182/2, H. E. Coffin, *Munsey's*, to FH, May 25, 1911.

18 HAMPTON'S MAGAZINE DID LIKEWISE HRC, FH/141/3, E. M. Kelly, *Hampton's* Magazine, to FH, June 2, 1911.

18 "UNUSUALLY GOOD" HRC, FH/92/1, John Phillips, *American Magazine,* to FH, June 7, 1911.

18 *SMITH'S* ACCEPTED IT HRC, FH/201/8, Charles Agnew MacGraw, *Smith's Magazine,* to FH, June 20, 1911.

18 TURNED DOWN THE BELASCO OFFER . . . KEEP IN TOUCH HRC, FH/99/1, William J. Dean, Belasco Theater, to FH, Aug. 4, 1911.

18 MOST REPEATED ANECDOTE HRC, FH/210/2, *SEP,* FH to Richard Thruelsen, Feb. 7, 1939. "It is true that I accumulated a considerable acreage of rejection slips from your distinguished journal before my first acceptance. In fact, they numbered thirty-five."

18 SUCCESSFUL WRITERS HRC, FH/116/1, Robert H. Davis to FH, Dec. 23, 1941.

18 "ONENESS OF PURPOSE"/ "UNFAILING MENTAL SEARCHLIGHT . . ." FH, "I Come Across," p. 130.

19 TWO OTHER MAGAZINES HAD TURNED DOWN HRC, FH/89/1, Robert Whiting, *Ainslee's,* to FH, Dec. 1, 1911. See also HRC, FH/172/3, George Turner, *McClure's,* to FH, Nov. 21, 1911.

19 BOUGHT IT ANYWAY FOR *CAVALIER* HRC, FH/116/1, Robert H. Davis to FH, Nov. 20, 1911.

19 "THE BEST THING YOU HAVE EVER SUBMITTED" HRC, FH/116/1, Robert H. Davis to FH, Jan. 22, 1912.

19 "LOCATED IN THE SAME WALK . . ." Ibid.

19 PHILLIPS/ "DOESN'T QUITE GET ACROSS . . ." HRC, FH/92/1, John S. Phillips, *American Magazine,* to FH, Feb. 19, 1912; FH/210/2, Churchill Williams, *SEP,* to FH, Feb. 8, 1912.

20 "VERY FAVORABLE IMPRESSION" HRC, FH/172/3, George Turner, *McClure's,* to FH, Apr. 30, 1912; FH/125/4, W. E. Prickett, *Everybody's,* to FH, Apr. 12, 1912.

20 "YOU WILL YET GIVE US THE PLEASURE . . ." HRC, FH/210/2, Churchill Williams, *SEP,* to FH, May 12, 1912.

20 "I AM SURE . . ." HRC, FH/210/2, George Lorimer, *SEP,* to FH, May 17, 1912.

20 "BULLY FOR YOU!" HRC, FH/210/2, Churchill Williams, *SEP,* to FH, May 17, 1912.

20 SHE EXPECTED A HUNDRED-DOLLAR PAYMENT Penn, FH to Albert Mordell, Nov. 12, 1916. See also Mordell's manuscript of int, similar time frame.

20 BOB DAVIS ATTEMPTED TO LOCK UP HRC, FH/116/1, Robert H. Davis to FH, May 21, 1912.

20 LORIMER . . . WROTE FANNIE HRC, FH/210/2, George Lorimer, *SEP,* to FH, May 31, 1912.

20 "THEM THERE HEBREW STORIES" HRC, FH/116/1, Robert H. Davis to FH, Sept. 15, 1914.

21 "TALK BOOK" HRC, FH/122/1, Harry Perton Steger, Doubleday, to FH, July 16, 1912; July 18, 1912.

21 "THERE IS ANOTHER KIND OF CHRISTMAS . . ." HRC, FH/116/1, Robert H. Davis to FH, Dec. 27, 1912.

21 "YOU ARE COMING . . ." HRC, FH/92/1, John Phillips, *American Magazine,* to FH, Nov. 6, 1912.

22 "WHAT I HAVE HITHERTO ADMIRED . . ." HRC, FH/211/1, William Schuyler to FH, Dec. 24, 1912.

CHAPTER THREE

PAGE

23   EARLY JANUARY 1913 HRC, FH/155/1 Amy Stein to FH, Dec. 24, 1913. See also FH/169/1, Carolyn Aronsohn Lisberger to FH, Oct. 29, 1958, and *Anat,* pp. 194–195.

23   "OVERHUNG THE NEW YORK CENTRAL . . ." *Anat,* p. 193.

23   SIX MONTHS LATER HRC, FH/116/1, see addressee notations in 1912–1914 letters from Robert H. Davis to FH.

23   "WELL-PLACED FAMILIES" *Anat,* p. 194. See also HRC, FH/155/1, Amy Stein to FH, Dec. 24, 1949.

23   "EVER BUBBLING, EFFERVESCENT HUMOR . . ." HRC, FH/169/1, Carolyn Aronsohn Lisberger to FH, Oct. 29, 1958.

23   "THEIR MANNER . . ." *Anat,* pp. 194–201.

25   "A SQUAT, BLACK-HAIRED . . . LITTLE FELLOW" *Anat,* p. 5.

25   "SUDDENLY HE HAD LESS TO EXPLAIN . . ." *Anat,* p. 174.

25   THE ENGAGEMENT WAS NOT TO BE/ "LIKE A BIT OF DRAGGING SEAWEED" *Anat,* p. 174.

25   METROPOLITAN ACCEPTED HRC, FH/241/2, Galbraith Welch to FH, Nov. 14, 1913.

26   "OTHERWISE, I'LL BE IN RATHER BAD . . ." HRC, FH/241/2, Galbraith Welch to FH, Aug. 15, 1913.

26   "SOMETHING TO SAY TO YOU . . ." HRC, FH/201/8, Paul R. Reynolds to FH, Jan. 29, 1914.

26   "OFFER THE BEST RETURNS" HRC, FH/241/2, Galbraith Welch to FH, Dec. 15, 1913; Dec. 16, 1913. See also HRC, FH/116/1, Robert H. Davis to FH, Dec. 17, 1913.

26   "A CRIMP IN HUMAN HAIR" DIDN'T SELL HRC, FH/241/2, Galbraith Welch to FH, Nov. 19, 1913; Dec. 11, 1913; Dec. 16, 1913; Jan. 4, 1914; May 13, 1914; May 29, 1914; June 9, 1914.

26   BOB DAVIS HAD ANALYZED HRC, FH/116/1, Robert H. Davis to FH, Sept. 25, 1912.

26   PUTTING IT OUT FOR SALE HRC, FH/241/2, Galbraith Welch to FH Jan. 14, 1914, with penciled note on back saying, "This is a two or three year old story that would not sell."

26–27   "NOT QUITE COMMERCIALLY . . ."/ WELCH PROMISED/ "FALL IN INCONSPICUOUSLY"/ "IT WON'T MAKE THE DENT . . ."/ "ATTENTION OF THE VERY BEST KIND"/THE MAGAZINE PROMISED/ THE CHECK ARRIVED HRC, FH/241/2, Galbraith Welch to FH, Dec. 16, 1913; Jan. 4, 1914; Jan. 29, 1914; Jan. 31, 1914; Feb. 9, 1914.

27   WELCH MANAGED TO SELL HRC, FH/241/2, Galbraith Welch to FH, May 12, 13, 14, 1914, recording $800 payment for "A Crimp in Human Hair."

27   FANNIE'S FIRST BOOK CONTRACT HRC, FH/241/2, Galbraith Welch to FH, Apr. 8, 17, 24, 1914.

27   "BREAKERS AHEAD!" RAN "Breakers Ahead!" *Cosmo,* June 1914, pp. 19–34.

27   THE EDITOR WAS VERY APOLOGETIC HRC, FH/241/2, Galbraith Welch to FH, May 12, 1914.

27   BETWEEN FEBRUARY AND JUNE HRC, FH/241/1, Galbraith Welch to FH, June 9, 1914, note is FH's in pencil in the margin with an arrow pointing to the words "A Crimp in Human Hair."

27 "I AM SO BUSY!" WashArch, FH Collection, Ser. 1: General Correspondence, 1913–1929, Folders 1–4, FH to Lois Toensfeldt, May 28, 1914.

28 "MAMA IS NOT INCLINED . . ." HRC, FH/151/2, Sam Hurst to FH, July 24, 1914.

28 "THE ARRANGEMENT LEAVES YOU . . ." HRC, FH/179/2, Carl Hovey, *Met,* to FH, June 23, 1914.

28 "FANNY [SIC] HURST IS NOW . . ." HRC, FH/116/1, Robert H. Davis to FH, June 23, 1914.

28 "ONE HUNDRED DOLLARS . . ."/ AMERICAN FILM SCOFFED HRC, FH/91/1, FH's hand-written explanation on a letter from the American Film Co., to FH, July 2, 1914.

28–29 THOUGH SHE HAD GIVEN HIM HRC, FH/201/8, Paul Revere Reynolds to FH, Aug. 14, 1914.

29 WELCH SENT HER A NOTE HRC, FH/241/2, Galbraith Welch to FH, Aug. 17, 1914.

29 THE THEATRICAL AGENTS HRC, FH/207/5, Frank W. Sanger and Walter C. Jordan, theatrical representatives, G. F. Bacon, to FH, Aug. 4 and 21, 1914.

29 "WHAT DO YOU KNOW ABOUT THIS WAR?" HRC, FH/116/1, Robert H. Davis to FH, Aug. 13 and 19, 1914.

29 WHAT FANNIE KNEW/ "ISN'T IT ALL TOO HARROWING . . ." WashArch, FH Collection, Ser. 1: General Correspondence 1913–1929, Folders 1–4, FH to Lois Toensfeldt, undtd, Sept. [1914].

29 *JUST AROUND THE CORNER* HRC, FH/139/2, Harper & Bros. to FH, Mar. 20, 1940.

29 ONE STOCK PRINTER'S ORNAMENT HRC, FH/138/1, Harper & Bros. Argosy Book-store Catalog 75 for Mar. 1935, Item 361.

29 "THE WORKMANSHIP IS UNEVEN . . ." "Just Around the Corner" [book review], *NYT,* Oct. 25, 1914, 19:462.

29 "BREVITY WOULD HAVE MADE . . ." "Just Around the Corner" [book review], *Independent,* Nov. 2, 1914, 80:174.

29 "THERE'S A CORE . . ." "Fannie Hurst's Stories," *Reedy's Mirror,* Oct. 16, 1914, 9:1.

30 THE BOOK SOLD HRC, FH/241/2, Galbraith Welch to FH, Feb. 25, 1915.

30 "THE WAR, AS YOU KNOW . . ." HRC, FH/241/2, Frederick A. Duneka, Harpers, to Galbraith Welch, Feb. 25, 1915.

30 "IN PRACTICALLY EVERY CASE . . ."/ DUNEKA OF HARPERS/ WELCH PESTERED HRC, FH/241/2, Galbraith Welch to FH, Feb. 25, 1915; Oct. 16, 1914.

30 PAUL REVERE REYNOLDS WROTE AGAIN HRC FH/201/8, Paul Revere Reynolds to FH, Sept. 22, 1914.

30 "INTEREST AND FLATTER" HRC, FH/241/2, Galbraith Welch to FH, Oct. 1, 1914.

30 "YOU SAY EDITORS . . ." HRC, FH/201/8, Paul R. Reynolds to FH, Oct. 2, 1914.

30 HOVEY GOT MIFFED HRC, FH/179/2, Carl Hovey and Sonia Levien to FH, June 23, July 2, July 8, Aug. 1, Oct. 12, 1914.

30 FURTHER, *METROPOLITAN* OFFERED HRC, FH/179/2, H. J. Whigham, *Met* editor, to FH, Dec. 17, 1914.

31 "SORRY AS THEY CAN BE . . ." HRC, FH/116/1, Robert H. Davis to FH, Jan. 6, 1915.

CHAPTER FOUR

PAGE

32 "ON THE RIM OF IT" HRC, FH/227/4, FH to Mittledorfer Straus, Dec. 15, 1914.

32 DYNAMIC SUFFRAGIST ORGANIZER *Anat,* pp. 244–245.

32 WHEN A FRIENDLESS PRISONER HRC, FH/147/1, Robert Hill, Montana State Prison, to FH, Jan.–June 1914.

32 "NOT EVEN THE SHANTIED SEGREGATION . . ." *Anat,* p. 279.

32–33 "SOCIALLY SOMNOLENT"/IT WOULD BE 1966 WashArch, FH Collection, Ser. 1: General Correspondence 1913–1929, Folder 1–4, FH to Lois Meier Toensfeldt, undtd, 1966.

33 "THE HURTING WAY . . ." *Anat,* pp. 278–279.

33 "DESPITE THE BACKWASH . . ." *Anat,* p. 249.

33 "MANY LOVEABLE TRAITS" Penn, Albert Mordell manuscript of int with FH, c. Nov. 1916.

33 NOR COULD FANNIE'S MOTHER RELATE *Anat,* p. 234.

33 "JUST A MATTER . . ." HRC, FH, Scrapbook 1, "FH, Noted Young Short Story Writer, Declares Feminism Has Arrived," *Tucson* (Ariz.) *Citizen,* Jan. 20, 1915.

33 EMBOLDENED WITH THE AUTHORITY *Anat,* p. 215.

33 SHE HAD LECTURED WashSpec, FH Collection, Ser. 1: General Correspondence, 1913–1929, Folders 1–4, FH to Lois Toensfeldt, Dec. 2, 1914.

34 "THE SILK AND SATIN CLASS . . ." "FH, Noted Young Short Story Writer."

34 SHE AND MITTIE LIKED TO SNOOP HRC, FH/227/4, FH to Mitteldorfer Straus, Dec. 15, 1944.

34 "THE LARGEST PRIVATE MENAGERIE . . ." "We Nominate for the Hall of Fame," *Vanity Fair,* Vol. 4, No. 3, May 1915, p. 36.

34 SHE MOVED/ "THE GRAND SHADE . . ." HRC, FH/197/4, FH to Jessie Wiley Voils, *Pictorial Review,* Oct. 5, 1937.

34 MAMA VISITED HRC, FH/227/4, FH to Mitteldorfer Straus, Dec. 15, 1944.

34 TENTATIVE FIRST VISIT OF JACQUES NYUArch, New York College of Music Bulletins, 1899–1900, 1904–5, 1909–10, 1910–11, all contain J. S. Danielson's name (actually Jacob, then J. S., then Jacques in artistic progression).

34 "STANDING IN THE DOORWAY . . ." HRC, FH/169/1, Carolyn Aronsohn Lisberger to FH, Oct. 29, 1958.

34 NEW YORK SUFFRAGE PARADE Jacqueline Van Voris, *Carrie Chapman Catt: A Public Life* (New York: Feminist Press, 1987), p. 128, citing a letter from Francis Sheehy Skeffington to Hanna Sheehy Skeffington, Oct. 23, 1915 (Personal Collection of Andee Sheehy Skeffington, Dublin, Ireland). See also "25,340 March in Suffrage Parade to the Applause of 250,000 Admirers; Spectacle Runs on in the Moonlight," *NYT,* Oct. 24, 1918, 1:6–8, 2:1–8, anecdote is *Anat,* p. 246, but *NYT* story confirms weather, crowd estimates, and presence of Frederic Howe among the male marchers.

34 "FIRM-FACED DOWAGERS . . ." *Anat,* p. 246.

34 HER HUSBAND, FREDERIC NatArch, *Official Register of the United States,* 1915 and 1917 ed., lists Frederic C. Howe as commissioner of immigration at the Port of New York, as does *NYT,* Oct. 24, 1918, 1:6–8, 2:1–8.

35 PAIR OF FIERY LIBERALS *Anat,* p. 246.

35 HETERODOXY WAS AN EARLY BASTION See Judith Schwarz, *The Radical Feminists of Heterodoxy: Greenwich Village, 1912–1940* (Lebanon, N.H.: New Victoria, 1982). See also Kate E. Wittenstein, "The Heterodoxy Club and American Feminism, 1912–1930" (Thesis, Boston University, 1989. Ann Arbor, Mich.: University Microfilms International).

35 FANNIE WAS NEVER PARTICULARLY ACTIVE HRC, FH/145/2, Frances Maule to FH, Dec. 6, 1934, FH to Frances Maule, Dec. 19, 1934.

35 "MY NAME IS THE SYMBOL . . ." Wittenstein, "Heterodoxy Club," p. 48.

35 NO ONE ELSE WOULD BE PRESENT HRC, FH/113/3, Willa S. Cather to FH, undtd.

35 "A BLEEDER UNDER CRITICISM . . ." *Anat,* pp. 259–260.

35 METROPOLITAN MAGAZINE HAD OFFERED "We Nominate for the Hall of Fame," p. 36.

35 NELLIE BLY'S . . . REPORTS The Nellie Bly reports appeared in the *New York Evening Journal* between Dec. 4, 1914, and Feb. 19, 1915. See also Brooke Kroeger, *Nellie Bly: Daredevil, Reporter, Feminist* (New York: Times Books, 1994), pp. 398–410.

35 REED GAVE FANNIE ELABORATE INSTRUCTIONS HRC, FH/201/1, John Reed to FH, Mar. 10, 1915.

36 WHEN THE STORY RAN HRC, FH, Scrapbook 1, undtd advertisement [c. Aug. 1915], "Covering the Big War," photo and ad copy about John Reed, FH, and Boardman Robinson, before plan to set sail for Russia.

36 " 'EVER EVER GREEN' IS GREAT! . . ." / "NO WRITER . . ." HRC, FH/179/2, Carl Hovey, *Met,* to FH, Jan. 6, 9, 1915.

37 THE STORY RATED Three-star ratings in *The Best Short Stories of 1915* also went to "T.B.," which was among the twenty stories O'Brien reprinted in the book, along with "Ever Ever Green" and "Rolling Stock." O'Brien also gave two stars to "Superman," "The Good Provider," "The Name and the Game," and "White Goods," and one star each to "Mind-Cat," "Sea-Gullibles," and "The Spring Song."

37 "I MUST AFFIRM . . ." Edward J. O'Brien, ed. *The Best Short Stories of 1915* (Boston: Small, Maynard, 1916), p. 10.

38 ANOTHER REVIEWER HRC, FH/192/1, Edward J. O'Brien to FH, May 23, 1916.

38 "AGAINST RETURN" . . . *Anat,* pp. 206–207.

38 "IT SEEMS TO ME . . ." WashSpc, FH Collection, Ser. 1: General Correspondence, 1913–1929, Folders 1–4, FH to Lois Toensfeldt, Dec. 2, 1914.

39 "WERE NOT SO GOOD . . ." HRC, FH/179/2, Carl Hovey, *Met,* to FH, Jan. 6, 1915.

39 ELIZABETH GARVER JORDAN HRC, FH/157/2, Elizabeth Garver Jordan to FH, Mar. 18, 1915.

39 "BECAUSE SHE HAS SHOWN US . . ." "We Nominate for the Hall of Fame," p. 36.

39 "THE SAME ARTISTIC QUALITIES . . ." W. D. Howells, "Editor's Easy Chair," *Harper's Monthly,* Vol. 130, May 1915, pp. 958–961, esp. 959.

39 THREE MONTHS LATER Anne O'Hagan, "New York Women Who Earn $50,000 a Year," *Vanity Fair,* Aug. 1915, p. 25.

39 HER ACTUAL EARNINGS HRC, FH/274/6, "Miscellaneous 1911–1925," undtd income tax report on FH for 1925.

39 "I PAY THIS TAX . . ." O'Hagan, "New York Women Who Earn," p. 25.

40 SHE SPENT $400 HRC, FH/274/6, "Miscellaneous 1911–1925," undtd income tax report on FH for 1925.

40 SHE HAD MOVED OUT Joyce Kilmer, "Fannie Hurst Decries 'Chocolate Fudge' Tales," *NYT Magazine,* Aug. 6, 1916, p. 15.

40 "DISTRACTINGLY ATTRACTIVE . . ." Kathleen Norris, "A Genius of the Short Story," *Cosmo,* Sept. 1918, p. 93.

40 ONLY TWO STORIES HIGH Description courtesy of Christopher Gray, Metropolitan History, New York City.

40 "A REGULAR PRE-DREADNOUGHT EFFECT" HRC, FH/179/2, Carl Hovey to FH, June 29, 1915.

40 HIS BOSS . . . WROTE FANNIE HRC, FH/179/2, H. J. Whigham, *Met,* to FH, July 7, 1915.

40 *METROPOLITAN* HAD A BACKLOG HRC, FH/172/3, Charles Hanson Towne, *McClure's,* to FH, Sept. 6, 1915.

40 MORE OF A DIRECT COMPETITOR HRC, FH/179/2, H. J. Whigham, *Met,* to FH, Oct. 19, 1915.

40 TOWNE HAD BEEN UNABLE TO OFFER HRC, FH/172/3, Charles Hanson Towne, *McClure's,* to FH, Sept. 6, 1915.

41 PEOPLE FROM THE STAGE SOCIETY HRC, FH/179/2, H. J. Whigham, *Met,* to FH, July 7, 1915.

41 PROSPECT CLEARLY ENTICED HER HRC, FH/255/2, contract between FH and Harriet Ford, Dec. 16, 1915.

CHAPTER FIVE

PAGE

42 "A BIG GERMAN PRETZEL . . ." HRC, FH/116/1, Robert H. Davis to FH, Jan. 10, 1916.

42 SHE IMMEDIATELY WROTE HRC, FH/179/2, J. B. Kelly, *Met,* to FH, Jan. 14 and 19, 1916.

42 PAUL REVERE REYNOLDS SURFACED HRC, FH/201/8, Paul Revere Reynolds to FH, Jan. 12, 1916.

42 "BELIEVE ME . . ." HRC, FH/116/1, Robert H. Davis to FH, Jan. 10, 1916.

43 THE AUTHORS' LEAGUE'S INVITATION HRC, FH/95/3, Authors' League of America to FH, June 28, 1916.

43 "BE AT THE TRULY . . ." HRC, FH/188/4, Ida Blair to FH, May 27, 1916. See also June 1, 1916, and others in this file.

43 AUSTIN CONTRIBUTED A CHAPTER Elizabeth Garver Jordan, ed., *The Sturdy Oak: A Composite Novel of American Politics by Fourteen American Authors* (New York: Henry Holt, 1917).

43 "SURPRISINGLY SATISFACTORY" *Reedy's Mirror,* Dec. 21, 1917, pp. 888–889.

44 "IRRESISTIBLY MELTING . . ." HRC, FH/151/1, Rupert Hughes to FH, Oct. 18, 1916.

44 "GAINS TREMENDOUS EMOTIONAL VALUES . . ." Edward J. O'Brien, ed., *The Best Short Stories of 1916* (Boston: Small, Maynard, 1917), p. 384.

44 "BRUTAL, BUT IT IS ALSO STRONG . . ." Review, *Every Soul Hath Its Song, NYT,* 4:483:2, Nov. 12, 1916.

44 "QUITE THE BIGGEST SHORT STORY . . ." HRC, FH/191/4, Kathleen Norris to FH Nov. [undtd], 1916.

44 "MAY PROVE TO BE THE MOST ESSENTIAL . . ." O'Brien, *Best Short Stories of 1916,* p. 377. He awarded two stars each to "In Memoriam," "Brunt," and "Through a Glass Darkly."

45 "I PRESUME IT MAY BE WORTH . . ." "Lay Your Servant Girl Troubles to Eight-Hour Day," *St. Louis Star,* Oct. 3, 1916, 2:5–6.

45 "ALMOST THE MOST DESTRUCTIVE REQUIREMENT . . ." HRC, FH, Scrapbook 1, John Nicholas Beffel, "Books and Builders of Books," unid, undtd.

45   "A MISTRESS OF THE POST-HENRY TRICKS . . ." Unsigned, "Interpretations in Little," *Nation,* Vol. 106, No. 2759, May 18, 1918, pp. 597–598.

45   JOYCE KILMER . . . ASKED Joyce Kilmer, *Literature in the Making by Some of Its Makers* (New York: Harper & Bros., 1917).

46   "CHOCOLATE FUDGE" FICTION . . . Joyce Kilmer, "Fannie Hurst Decries 'Chocolate Fudge' Tales," *NYT Magazine,* Aug. 6, 1916, p. 15.

46   "LIKE PUBLIC DANCERS . . ." Unsigned, "Tales Well-Made," *Nation,* Vol. 108, No. 2812, May 24, 1919, pp. 829–840.

46   "LAY ASIDE HIS PEN . . ."/ "PICTURIZED FICTION . . ." Kilmer, "Hurst Decries 'Chocolate Fudge' Tales," p. 15.

46   SHE VENTURED NO COMMENT See Neal Gabler, *An Empire of Their Own: How the Jews Invented Hollywood* (New York: Crown, 1988), pp. 90–91. Also Kevin Brownlow, *The Parade's Gone By* (New York: Knopf, 1968); Gene Brown, *Movie Time* (New York: Macmillan, 1995), pp. 29–36.

46   FANNIE DID LET DROP *Little Lord Fauntleroy,* reviews, *Variety,* June 26, 1914.

46   "LAW OF COMPOSITION . . ." Kilmer, "Hurst Decries 'Chocolate Fudge' Tales," p. 15.

47   "WITH FINE DEMOCRATIC HEART . . ." O'Brien, *Best Short Stories of 1916,* pp. 4–5.

47   "THE LORD KNOWS WHERE . . ." HRC, FH/116/1, Robert H. Davis to FH, Jan. 25, 1916.

47   "AMONG THE FOUR OR FIVE . . ." HRC, FH/192/1, Edward J. O'Brien to FH Oct. 25, 1916.

47   "I NEVER MADE A SINGLE PROPHESY . . ." HRC, FH/116/1, Robert H. Davis to FH, Oct. 20, 1916.

47   "THERE IS NO OTHER WRITER . . ." HRC, FH, Scrapbook 1, Sidney Baldwin, "Fanny Hurst," unid, July 16, 1916.

47   "WE ARE ALL LOOKING . . ." HRC, FH, Scrapbook 1, Charles Hanson Towne, "The Managing Editor Speaks," *McClure's,* Aug. 1916.

47   "THE YIDDISH DESCENDENTS . . ." John Kuehl and Jackson Bryer, eds., *Dear Scott, Dear Max: The Fitzgerald-Perkins Correspondence* (New York: Scribner's, 1971), p. 25.

47   "NOT PRODUCED AMONG 'EM . . ." F. Scott Fitzgerald, *This Side of Paradise* (1920; reprint, New York: Modern Library, 1996), p. 246.

48   "THE OLD MYSTERY . . ." Kathleen Norris, "A Genius of the Short Story," *Cosmo,* Sept. 1918, pp. 92–93, 134. See FH, "About the Author of Mother," *Good Housekeeping,* Nov. 1917, 65:24–25.

48   CHARLES WROTE FANNIE FH, "About the Author of Mother," pp. 24–25.

48   "IT'S NOT FULSOME PRAISE . . ." HRC, FH/112/3, Douglas Z. Doty to FH, May 9, 1918.

48   "HERE YOU ARE . . ." HRC, FH/191/4, Kathleen Norris to FH, May [undtd], 1918.

48   "THE APPARENTLY RAMBLING CONVERSATIONS . . ." Norris, "Genius of the Short Story," pp. 92–93, 134.

48   "THE TRENCHANT WORD . . ."/ O. HENRY, BY CONTRAST H. C. Schweikert, ed. *Short Stories* (New York: Harcourt, Brace, 1937), pp. 92–93.

49   "UNCOMMON STORYTELLING POWERS" Unsigned, "Tales Well-Made," *Nation,* Vol. 108, No. 2812, May 24, 1919, pp. 829–840.

49 "CLEAVAGE . . ." Grant Overton, *The Women Who Make Our Novels*, rev. ed. (Freeport, NY: Books for Libraries Press, 1967), pp. 180–186.

49 "FEMININE O. HENRY . . ." Unsigned, "Tales Well-Made," pp. 829–840.

49 "SOMETHING PLEASANT"/ A REAL FRIENDSHIP HRC, FH/128/1, Edna Ferber to FH, Nov. 7, 14, 1916; Oct. 12, 1926; Oct. 5, Dec. 2, 1927; May 7, 1930.

49 COSMOPOLITAN HAD BEEN PAYING Hearst, *Cosmo*, index-card file card on Booth Tarkington shows, for example, payments of $1,750 for "His Reward Merit," bought Mar. 1, 1915, published July 1915; and $2,000 for "Penrod Jashber," bought Jan. 2, 1917. Edward J. O'Brien at the time thought as highly of FH's stories as the magazine did. His *Best Short Stories* volumes for 1917 through 1920 gave three stars to "Hers Not to Reason Why" and two stars to "Oats for the Woman," "Nightshade," "Even as You and I," "White Goods," "A Boob Spelled Backwards," and "A Petal on the Current." One star went to "Bittersweet," "She Also Serves," "Heads," and "The Wrong Pew."

49 "BREATHLESS PERIOD . . ." WashArch, FH Collection, Ser. 1, General Correspondence, 1913–1929, Folders 1–4, FH to Lois Meier Toensfeldt, Feb. 18, 1917.

50 SISSON TOOK A LEAVE HRC, FH/222/1, Edgar Sisson to FH, June 7, 1917.

50 "I DO NOT THINK . . ." HRC, FH/119/3, Dorothy Dix to FH, Oct. 25, 1917.

50 LAND OF THE FREE, HAD ITS OUT-OF-TOWN TRYOUT HRC, FH, Scrapbook 1, Program, Savoy Theatre, Asbury Park, N.J., July 16, 17, 18, 1917.

50 "THIS IS MY GAME . . ." HRC, FH/102/2, William A. Brady to FH, Sept. 11, 1917.

50 "SEEMED LIMITED ONLY BY THE INADEQUACY . . ." HRC, FH, Scrapbook 1. See also "Florence Nash in Immigrant Drama," *NYT*, Oct. 3, 1917, 11:1.

50 ASCENDANCY OF THE WOMAN PLAYWRIGHT Anna Steese Richardson, "Lady Broadway," *McClure's*, Dec. 1917.

50 THE SHOW RAN *Best Plays of 1909–1919*, p. 609.

51 UNDER CONTRACT SINCE AUGUST 1916 HRC, FH/255/2, Contract, Klaw and Erlanger with FH and Harriet Ford, Aug. 17, 1916, providing $1,000 advance. See also HRC, FH, Scrapbook 1, Mar. 4, 1917, "Another Hurst-Ford play . . ."

51 PRODUCERS SOUGHT THE RIGHTS "Golden Fleece" rated one star in Edward J. O'Brien's *Best Short Stories*; "A Petal on the Current" got two.

51 "GOLDEN FLEECE" WENT TO SELECT HRC, FH/201/8, Paul R. Reynolds to FH, June 17, 20, 27, July 8, and Sept. 12, 1918, all concern negotiations for "Golden Fleece" and name change to *Her Great Chance*.

51 CHARLES MAIGNE ADAPTED THE STORY Review, *Variety*, Oct. 18, 1918.

51 THE PLOT INVOLVES Film, Universal Pictures Co., Library Properties, Synopses and Descriptive Data, Vol. 6, File 6556, "Golden Fleece."

51 FANNIE ULTIMATELY RECEIVED A $1,750 HRC, FH/255/2, Contract, Robertson-Cole (Harry F. Robertson and Rufus Sidman Cole) to FH, re: bill of sale for story "Oats for the Woman," Mar. 19, 1919.

51 SHE POSED A CONUNDRUM FH, *Humoresque*, "Oats for the Woman" (New York: Harper & Bros., 1919), pp. 45–84.

51 "COME OUT RIGHT" Unsigned, "Movie Morals," *New Republic*, Aug. 25, 1917, pp. 100–101.

51 "TO SAY THAT THE SCREEN VERSION . . ." Review, *Variety*, Aug. 8, 1919.

52 "MISS HURST IS AN UNUSUAL PERSON . . ." Unsigned, "The Petal on the Current," *Variety,* Aug. 8, 1919.

52 REPRINTED A STORY OF HERS HRC, FH/192/1, Edward J. O'Brien to FH, Dec. 3, 1917. "Get Ready the Wreaths" appeared in the 1917 *Best Short Stories* volume.

52 "HERS NOT TO REASON WHY" HRC, FH/112/3, Douglas Doty to FH, Aug. 17, 1918.

52 THE BEST STORY/ "THE VERY FEW . . ." Edward J. O'Brien, ed., *Best Short Stories of 1918* (Boston: Small, Maynard, 1919), p. 378.

52 "GRIPPING LITTLE TALE . . ." / "HUMANITY AND LACK . . ." Review, *Gaslight Sonatas, NYT,* Apr. 28, 1918, 193:2.

52 FANNIE STILL HAD RELATIVES HRC, FH/112/3, Douglas Doty to FH, Aug. 17, 1918.

52 TO LOOK INTO THE STATE OF SOCIAL HYGIENE NatArch, Records of War Department, General and Special Staffs, Records Group 65, wire to and letter from FH, Aug. 1–2, 1918, and letter to FH, Aug. 4, 1918.

52 "GOVERNMENT JOB" / "STEALTHY TRIPS . . ." WashArch, FH Collection, Ser. 1: General Correspondence 1913–1929, FH to Lois Meier Toensfeldt, undtd [1918].

53 "WHEN THEY FOUND HIM . . ." NatArch, Records of War Department, General and Special Staffs, Records Group 65, wire to and letter from FH, Aug. 1–2, 1918, and letter to FH, Aug. 4, 1918.

53 "A DAY OR TWO . . ." WashArch, FH Collection, Ser. 1: General Correspondence 1913–1929, FH to Lois Meier Toensfeldt, undtd [1929].

53 "A HOT DAY IN THE HOT SLUMS" NatArch, Records of War Department, General and Special Staffs, Records Group 65, wire to and letter from FH, Aug. 1–2, 1918, and letter to FH, Aug. 4, 1918.

53 "I SHALL CONTINUE . . ." HRC, FH/201/1, William Marion Reedy to FH, Oct. 31, 1918.

53 "HE HAD THE HONOR . . ." FH, "Samuel Merwin, Romantic Realist," *Cosmo,* Vol. 61, No. 6, Nov. 1918, pp. 60–61.

53 "THERE MUST HAVE BEEN . . ." HRC, FH/178/3, Samuel Merwin to FH, Oct. 16, 1918.

CHAPTER SIX

PAGE

54 SIDDALL . . . KEPT PRESSING HRC, FH/92/1, John M. Siddall, *American Magazine,* to FH, Nov. 30, Dec. 17, 1917; and Jan. 2, Feb. 11, Feb. 23, Feb. 25, Mar. 29, Apr. 5, Apr. 29, June 21, 1918.

54 "LET YOURSELF GO . . ." HRC, FH/92/1, John M. Siddall, *American Magazine,* to FH, Dec. 17, 1917.

54 "YOU HAVE AN ABSOLUTE . . . STORY TO TELL . . ." HRC, FH/92/1, John M. Siddall, *American Magazine,* to FH, Feb. 11, 1918.

54 "JUST SIT DOWN . . ." HRC, FH/92/1, John M. Siddall, *American Magazine,* to FH, Apr. 5, 1918.

54 FANNIE HURST—HERSELF NYPL-BR, Marion Golde, "Fannie Hurst—Herself," *Jewish News,* Mar. 22, 1918, pp. 1–2.

54 ADDING A YEAR TO HER OSTENSIBLE AGE FH, "I Come Across," *American Magazine,* Vol. 87, No. 3, Mar. 1919, pp. 38–39, 126–130.

54–55 CALLING ATTENTION TO THE FACT/ "YOU ARE A PUBLIC CHARACTER . . ." HRC, FH/92/1, John M. Siddall, *American Magazine,* to FH, May 17 and 23, 1919.

55 "MY PRINTED REJECTION SLIPS . . ." FH, "I Come Across," p. 130.

55 BELL SYNDICATE STARTED NEGOTIATIONS HRC, FH/242/1, Wheeler and Bell Syndicates to FH, Mar. 22, 1918, June 6, 1918, and Sept. 23, 1919.

55 MOTION-PICTURE PLOT HRC, FH/134/3, Elizabeth Jordan, Samuel Goldwyn, to FH, Feb. 12, 1918.

55 HIS FIRST LETTER TO FANNIE HRC, FH/201/1, Ray Long, *Redbook,* to FH, Nov. 25, Nov. 30, Dec. 5, Dec. 10, 1918.

55 "TO GIVE THE CLOSE SORT . . ."/ "VERY VIVID POWER"/ "I SINCERELY BELIEVE . . ."/ Ray Long, *Redbook,* to FH, Nov. 25, 1918.

56 "A TERRIFIC WALLOP . . ." Ray Long, *Redbook,* to FH, Nov. 30, 1918.

56 "I HAVE ALWAYS CONTENDED . . ." Ray Long, *Redbook,* to FH, Dec. 5, 1918.

56 FIVE DAYS AFTER THAT Ray Long, *Redbook,* to FH, Dec. 10, 1918.

57 EDNA FERBER PRODUCED Blanche Colton Williams, ed., *O. Henry Memorial Award Prize Stories of 1919* (Garden City NY.: Doubleday, Page, 1920), pp. vii–xvii, 148–149.

57 O'BRIEN GAVE IT HIS HIGHEST Edward J. O'Brien, ed., *The Best Short Stories of 1920* (Boston: Small, Maynard, 1921), p. 439.

57 "AN ECONOMY OF DETAIL . . ." O'Brien, *Best Short Stories of 1920,* p. 398.

58 DID HE DIE HRC, FH/130/2, Beverly Cramer and Shirley Boers to FH, Oct. 28, 1947.

58 "MY FEELING WHEN I WROTE . . ." HRC, FH/130/2, FH to Beverly Cramer and Shirley Boers, Oct. 29, 1947.

58 "EXPECTANT, MUSIC-HUNGRY, POPULAR-PRICED AUDIENCE . . ." FH, *My Favorite Story* (New York: International Magazine Co., 1928), p. 1.

59 "A NEW AND A SEER'S LOOK . . ." FH, "Pleased to Meet You!" *McClure's,* Vol. 61, No. 4, July 1919, pp. 15, 68.

59 "THE OPTIMISM OF HOPE" Frances Marion, "Why Do They Change the Stories on Screen?" *Photoplay,* Mar. 1926, p. 30 ff., courtesy of Cari Beauchamp.

59 HUMORESQUE WAS A THUNDEROUS SUCCESS " 'Humoresque' Huge Triumph," *Motion Picture News,* June 19, 1920, courtesy of Cari Beauchamp. See also Kevin Brownlow, *Behind the Mask of Innocence* (New York: Knopf, 1990), pp. 385–392.

59 "BIGGEST SCREEN OFFERING . . ." " 'Humoresque' Huge Triumph," *Motion Picture News,* June 19, 1920.

59 "AN IMPERTINENT FABLE . . ." See Lester D. Friedman, *Jewish Image in American Film* (Secaucus, N.J.: Citadel 1987), p. 28.

60 "THE FACT THAT ITS CHIEF CHARACTERS . . ." "The Winner of the *Photoplay* Medal of Honor," *Photoplay,* Dec. 1921, p. 56.

60 THE NEXT FOUR YEARS' WINNERS Marion, "Why Do They Change the Stories?" p. 56.

60 FANNIE INITIALLY OBJECTED See Cari Beauchamp, *Without Lying Down: Frances Marion and the Powerful Women of Early Hollywood* (New York: Scribner, 1997), p. 118.

60 "HAVING COME IN . . ." HRC, FH/144/1, FH, probably not sent, to William Randolph Hearst, undtd, c. early 1921.

60 FANNIE'S TOTAL EARNINGS Hearst Corp., *Cosmo* files, FH, author index-card files. *Star-Dust,* bought Nov. 15, 1919, for $17,500, paid in ten monthly installments

of $1,750 between Mar. and Dec. of 1920. See also HRC, FH/255/2, Contracts, Alice Krauser to JSD, Jan. 8, 1921, agreement of Hope Hampton to buy film rights to *Star-Dust* for $30,000. Agreement with Harper & Bros. unavailable but certainly in the range of a few thousand dollars, bringing the total to at least $50,000.

60 COVER THE REPUBLICAN CONVENTION HRC, FH/242/1, agreement between FH and Wheeler Syndicate, Mar. 16, 1920.

60 GET FANNIE TO RELEASE HER EARLY "UNFIT" WORKS HRC, FH/242/1, Mildred Barbour to FH, Wheeler Syndicate, Oct. 4, 1920.

60 A STAGE PLAY ONCE AND A FILM TWICE HRC, FH/153/1, William LeBaron, International Film Corp., to FH, Oct. 31, 1919.

60 NEW YORK PREMIERE OF . . . *HUMORESQUE* Film, Adolph Zukor Collection, Folder 31.

CHAPTER SEVEN

PAGE

61 RATHER BE WITH JACK *Anat*, pp. 222–223.

61 THE BOHEMIANS NYPL, Lincoln Center, Music Library. The Bohemians, New York Musicians' Club. List of members issued Sept. 1977. Musicians Foundation, Nov. 14, 1914.

61 THEIR IMPORTANCE IN EACH OTHER'S LIVES *Anat*, p. 224.

62 "THE WILDS OF ASIA" *Anat*, p. 249.

62 "EACH PEARL A TEAR"/ LEFT FOR GOOD *Anat*, p. 268.

63 "THE EMOTIONAL LABYRINTH" *Anat*, p. 269.

63 LAKEWOOD, NEW JERSEY Description of Lakewood, N.J., c. 1915, courtesy of Judith Robinson, reference librarian, Lakewood Public Library, July 10, 1998.

63 THE CEREMONY TOOK PLACE State of New Jersey, Bureau of Vital Statistics, Certificate and Record of Marriage 698, Jacob S. Danielson and Fanny [sic] Hurst, May 5, 1915. The Lakewood City Directory of 1908 lists Justice of the Peace Andrew J. Searing and his wife, Ellen E. C. Searing, both signatories on the license. (City directory record courtesy of Judith Robinson, Lakewood Public Library.)

63 THE NEWS FINALLY BROKE *Anat*, p. 285.

63 FANNIE HURST WED *NYT*, May 4, 1920, 1:4, 5:2.

64 FIVE YEARS OF SECRECY . . . NOT . . . BY DESIGN *Anat*, p. 268.

64 "I HAD EVERYTHING . . ." *Anat*, p. 271.

64 "LESSEN MY CAPACITY . . ." "FH Wed, etc." *NYT*, May 4, 1920, 1:4, 5:2.

65 "IT IS FREEDOM! . . ." "Husband Approves FH's Idea," *NYT*, May 5, 1920.

65 "SHE HAS FOUND THAT WHICH IS RARER . . ." Ibid.

65 BRISBANE DEVOTED THE FIRST HALF Arthur Brisbane, "Two Breakfasts a Week, Fewer Later, Don't Mix the Johnsons, Spare Your Heart," *New York Journal-American*, May 5, 1920, 1:1.

66 "MANY PROFESSIONAL WOMEN . . ." HRC, FH/228/4, G. Bernard Shaw, London, to Orton Tewson, Cross Atlantic Newspaper Service, postcard, May 6, 1920.

66 "EVERYBODY AGREES THAT A LITTLE SEPARATION . . ." "Miss Hurst's Marriage," *Reedy's Mirror*, May 13, 1920, 385:2.

66 "IT DOES NOT MEAN A SERIES . . ." NYPL-BR, FH Clippings, "FH Is Wrong, Says a Woman Lawyer," *New York Evening Mail,* May 5, 1920.

66 "THIS IS A GOOD TRICK . . ." / "I DO NOT THINK MANY WOMEN . . ." "FH's Hubby Says Union Is Ideal," *St. Louis Globe-Democrat,* May 5, 1920, 3:4–5.

66 "AVOID GROWING MISCONCEPTIONS . . ." "Living Apart Cheap, Danielson Says," *NYT,* May 7, 1920, 12:1.

67 JACQUES HAD APPLIED U.S. District Court, Southern District, Records, U.S. Department of Labor Naturalization Service, No. 65366. U.S. Declaration of Intention, Sept. 10, 1917. And Petition for Naturalization, Jacques Danielson, No. 32988, Approved, Dec. 14, 1920.

67 "SIMPLY NAUSEATING" "FH Here Without Husband Says 'No More Publicity,' " *St. Louis Globe-Democrat,* June 2, 1920, 1:4–5.

CHAPTER EIGHT

PAGE

71 COUÉ/CHAPERONES/THE LENDING LIBRARIES/ "NECKED AND SMOKED . . ." *Anat,* pp. 233–234.

71 "SEX IS A DISCOVERY . . ."/ "FABLED MINORITY" *Anat,* p. 257–258.

71 SCOTT FITZGERALD *Anat,* p. 218. See also HRC, FH/128/5, Mrs. F. Scott Fitzgerald to FH, accepting a dinner invitation for Jan. 1923 or 1924 for her and Fitzgerald.

71 "ONE OF THE MILLIONS . . ."/ "I WOULD HAVE BEEN TONGUE-TIED . . ." *Anat,* pp. 258–259.

71 "A LOOSELY ASSEMBLED GROUP . . ." *Anat,* p. 225.

72 "A POPULAR WRITER . . ." Margaret Case Harriman, *The Vicious Circle: The Story of the Algonquin Round Table* (New York: Rinehart, 1951), p. 47.

72 "THIS WAS THE GLIB . . ." *Anat,* p. 225.

72 "SOME OF THEM WERE MORE . . ." *Anat,* p. 217.

72 AS DOROTHY PARKER WOULD HRC, FH/195/3, Dorothy Parker to FH, Apr. 26 and May 5, 1939; Feb. 17, 1942; Nov. 10 and Dec. 26, 1944; Feb. 9, 1945; Dec. 15, 1947; Feb. 29, 1948.

72 IF NEW YORK LITERARY LIFE HAD A CENTER *Anat,* p. 224.

72 LUNCH AND DINNER PARTNERS HRC, FH/255/1, FH appt-cal, 1925.

72 FANNIE GOT TO KNOW *Anat,* p. 224.

72 THEODORE DREISER STRUCK UP AN ACQUAINTANCESHIP Thomas P. Riggio, ed., *Theodore Dreiser: The American Diaries, 1902–1926* (Philadelphia: University of Pennsylvania Press, 1982), p. 177.

72 FAVORITE DREISER ANECDOTE *Anat,* pp. 362–363. FH's anecdote has Dreiser joining her on "the plane" for St. Louis, where she was going to see her parents. Since it involves both her parents, it would have had to have taken place before 1925, the year her father died, except FH traveled exclusively by train in that period. In that same telling FH has Dreiser saying, "I lived all of my life without God and I might have had Him always . . . . He died a few months later." Actually, Dreiser died in 1945; he and FH had not been on speaking terms since 1932. FH may have used the airport/plane detail to make the story sound more current, or to

make the number of hours she and Dreiser were alone together less eyebrow-raising. Perhaps the train ride wasn't to St. Louis at all.

73 SOME OF THE CHARACTERIZATIONS HRC, FH/49/8, FH, "One Dramatic Moment," written for *Reader's Digest,* concerned observations of FH about a boardinghouse matron and her grandson, very much like an episode in *Star-Dust.* The novel is also peopled with Wempners and Calverts, both names taken from families who boarded along with the Hursts in FH's childhood years.

73 "A MORE OR LESS BREATHTAKING EXPERIMENT . . ." "Star-Dust," *NYT,* Apr. 10, 1921, 3:18–19.

73 "FULL OF OBSERVATION . . ." "Star-Dust," *Literary Review,* May 14, 1921, p. 3.

73 " 'PULSE BEATS OF LIFE' . . ." "Star-Dust" *Bookman,* July 1921, 53:460.

74 PAYING FANNIE . . . $17,500 *Cosmo, Star-Dust* payments from the magazine began on Nov. 28, 1920, indicating the acceptance date of the work some weeks earlier. Ray Long first broached the idea with her in his letter of Nov. 15, 1919. (HRC, FH/201/1, Ray Long, *Redbook,* to FH, Nov. 15, 1919, and subsequent.)

74 FANNIE'S NOVEL HAD COMMANDED HRC, FH/255/2, R. L. Giffen to JSD, Jan. 8, 1921, with $22,000 check for balance of payment due on *Star-Dust.*

74 JACQUES THOUGHT HRC, FH/255/2, R. L. Giffen to JSD, Oct. 19, 1923.

74 THE BOOK VERSION HRC, FH/257/13 Harper & Bros. royalty statement for June 30, 1921, shows a debit balance of $1,995.57. Three months after publication it had sold only 3,894 copies. Of course, many of her readers had already seen the work in *Cosmo,* which claimed a circulation of 1.25 million at the time.

74 APARTMENT BUILDING *Real Estate Record,* New York: Real Estate Board of New York, Vol. Jan.–June 1921, Jan. 29, 1921.

74 HIGHLY SENTIMENTALIZED SCREENPLAY "Star-Dust," *Variety,* Feb. 10, 1922.

74 NO ONE BEFORE THIS StLPubLib, FH, "FH Tells Why She Repudiated Film of Her Story," *StLP-D,* Dec. 18, 1921, 6:1–4.

74–75 "ADAPTED FROM THE NOVEL . . ."/ "GARBLED AND MANGLED . . ." Colum, Curtis Brown Manuscript Collection, Stern and Rubens, Benjamin Stern to FH, Dec. 16, 1921.

75 HOPE HAMPTON PRODUCTIONS HRC, FH, Scrapbook 1, "Miss Hurst Faces a $250,000 Suit: Author of *Star-Dust* libeled film version of her story, asserts J. A. Brulator, head of Hope Hampton Productions." Clipping, unid, Dec. 18, 1921. See also Colum, Curtis Brown Manuscript Collection, Stern and Rubens, FH–Benjamin Stern correspondence, Dec. 1921–Dec. 1924.

75 "IN VIEW OF THESE FACTS . . ." "Fannie Hurst Retracts," *NYT,* Jan. 11, 1925, 31:4.

75 TOO EMBARRASSING TO DEFEND FH often would deliberately leave both *Star-Dust* and *Mannequin* off compilation lists of her complete works.

75 "FIVE-BY-FIVE" HRC, FH/201/2, *Reader's Digest,* unpublished manuscript, undtd, c. Oct. 16, 1951 (see Grace Naismith to FH of that date).

76 "WHO SPEAKS FOR HERSELF" FH, "Women Having Lot to Say, FH Finds," *NY American,* June 27, 1920, 3:2–3.

76 "I LIKE YOU"/ "WERE ASTUTELY TIED . . ."/ "I CREATE THE COMPULSION . . ." HRC, FH/201/2, unpublished, undtd manuscript, intended for *Reader's Digest* (see accompanying letter, FH/201/2, Grace Naismith to FH, Oct. 16, 1951. FH erroneously sets the meeting in Chicago, but Marbury was a Democrat and FH's June 27, 1920, story from San Francisco indicates the meeting was there).

76 ELISABETH MARBURY'S AGENCY/MARBURY ADVISED HRC, FH/175/5, Elisabeth Marbury to FH, Jan. 12, 1921, and subsequent.

76 MARBURY HAD SOLD THE STAGE RIGHTS HRC, FH/256/1, Contract, A. H. Woods and FH for "Back Bay," dramatic rights, Jan. 29, 1921.

76 NEGOTIATED A SECOND DEAL NYPL-Berg, FH, American Play Co., Contract 493, between FH and Sam H. Harris for "Roulette," Feb. 14, 1921.

76 DRAMATIC RIGHTS TO "ROULETTE" HRC, FH/255/2, Contract, Sam. H. Harris and FH for "Roulette." See also NYPL-Berg, FH, American Play Co., Contract 493, between FH and Sam H. Harris for "Roulette," Feb. 14, 1921.

76 EIGHTEEN-THOUSAND-WORD NOVELETTE "Roulette" rated two stars in *Best Short Stories.*

76 WHAT *THE NEW YORK TIMES* CONSIDERED Review, *The Vertical City, NYT,* Apr. 30, 1922, 3:14:4.

77 DECIDED TO RUN THE WHOLE STORY HRC, FH/112/3, Verne Porter, *Cosmo,* to FH, Apr. 1, 1921.

77 WE ENLARGED THIS MAGAZINE . . . / THE LONGEST SHORT STORY FH, "Roulette," *Cosmo,* May 1921, pp. 18–19 ff.

77 "COOL FOREST MIND . . ." Inez Haynes Irwin, "FH's Hurst," *Bookman,* June 21, 1921, 53:335.

77 "A GREAT MASTERPIECE . . ." FH, "She Walks in Beauty," *Cosmo,* Vol. 71, No. 2, Aug. 1921, pp. 152–158. More objectively, Edward J. O'Brien gave it three stars in *Best Short Stories of 1921.*

77 "GUILTY" Edward J. O'Brien gave "Guilty" two stars in *Best Short Stories.*

77 MANY ELEMENTS VERBOTEN/ HOW OBJECTIONABLE HER STORY/"CONTAINED FRANKNESS . . ." Ray Long, *Twenty Best Short Stories in Ray Long's Twenty Years as an Editor* (New York: Ray Long and Richard R. Smith, 1932).

77 "CLEAR UP IN THE AIR . . ."/ THEY LIKED IT TOO MUCH/ "YOU ARE THE ONLY WRITER . . ." HRC, FH/255/2, Contracts, Ray Long to FH, Nov. 6, 1920.

77 "THE HELL THAT WE BOTH GOT . . ." Bran, Box 2B, Ray Long to FH, Dec. 28, 1926.

78 "THE MOST DARING PIECE . . ." Hearst, *Cosmo,* Jan. 1921 promotion, table of contents page.

78 SUBSCRIPTION CANCELLATIONS HRC, FH/112/3, see letters of J. Mitchell Thorsen, Feb. 25 and Mar. 7, 1921. See also Long, *Twenty Best Short Stories.*

78 "THIS FISHY THING . . ." HRC, FH/110/6. Also Colum, Blanche Colton Williams to FH, Oct. 15, 1920.

78 "SENDS A REAL CHILL . . ." *NYT,* Book Review, Apr. 30, 1922, 14:4. See also, HRC, FH/112/3, J. Mitchell Thorsen to H. F. Jones, *Cosmo,* Feb. 25, 1921.

78 HER STORIES WERE NOW COMMANDING Hearst, *Cosmo,* author index-card file, price went from $1,750 for each of ten installments for *Star-Dust* to $2,000 starting with the sale of "Guilty," Nov. 11, 1920.

78 HAD REPEATEDLY REFUSED TO RESELL/ "IN THESE HEYDAY YEARS . . ."/ BROADWAY THEATER MANAGERS/ SHE URGED HIM TO DELAY FH to William Randolph Hearst, undtd, probably unsent, c. Jan. 1921.

78 MARBURY OFFERED TO INTERCEDE HRC, FH/175/5, Elisabeth Marbury to FH, Jan. 12, 1921.

78 IN HEARST'S VIEW HRC, FH/144/1, FH to William Randolph Hearst, undtd, probably unsent, c. Jan. 1921.

79   ON TOP OF THE TWENTY-FIVE HUNDRED DOLLARS HRC, FH/170/2, Ray Long to FH, Nov. 4, 1921.

79   "OLD OAKEN BUCKET STORY . . ." "Back Pay," *Variety,* Feb. 17, 1922.

79   "SPECIAL" "Just Around the Corner," *Variety,* Jan. 6, 1922.

79   NEW GOLDWYN PRODUCTION/ "WE ARE USING YOUR 'LINGO' . . ."/ "CORKING . . . SUCCESS" HRC, FH/112/3, William LeBaron, Cosmopolitan Productions, to FH, Apr. 3, 1922.

79   *VARIETY* GAVE IT "The Good Provider," *Variety,* Apr. 14, 1922.

79   FANNIE, WHO HAD CAUSED "Fannie Hurst Sails Pleased over Film," *NY American,* Feb. 19, 1922.

79   AS FOR THE PLAY *Best Plays of 1920–21* reports it had seventy-nine performances, pp. 405–406.

80   "THE PROLIFIC FANNIE HURST" Alexander Woollcott, "Fannie's First Play," *NYT,* Aug. 31, 1921, 8:2.

80   "DURING ONE OF THE INTERMISSIONS . . ." "Back Pay Starts," *NY Sun,* Aug. 31, 1921. See also, same date, *NY Telegram, NY Herald, NY World, NY Mail, NY Tribune, NY American.* Only the *American,* Hearst's paper, expressed unqualified enthusiasm for the play.

80   SAM HARRIS LET THE THEATRICAL NIGHTS NYPL-Berg, FH, American Play Co., registered letter of contract abrogation from Sam H. Harris to Richard J. Madden, Dec. 24, 1921.

80   A. H. WOODS PICKED UP THE OPTION NYPL-Berg, FH, American Play Co., contract dated Nov. 22, 1922. One-thousand-dollar advance to FH and JSD from A. H. Woods (minus 10 percent commission.)

80   HER PRICE PER STORY Hearst, *Cosmo,* author index-card file, FH.

80   SHE HELD VERY TIGHT Colum, Curtis Brown Collection, Stern and Rubens files, FH, Nov. 18, [1921].

CHAPTER NINE

PAGE

81   FOURTH COLLECTION OF HER STORIES The book included all of FH's stories for *Cosmo* for 1921.

81   "THE SMUDGE" "The Smudge" got three stars in *Best Short Stories of 1922.*

81   A CHARACTER ALWAYS SUGGESTED/ "LITTLE UNKNOWN PEOPLE . . ." FH, "The Character Genesis," *Editor,* May 6, 1922, pp. 34–35.

81   O'BRIEN WAS HIGHLY COMPLIMENTARY "Back Pay" and "She Walks in Beauty" both rated three stars from Edward J. O'Brien in *Best Short Stories of 1921.* "Roulette," "Guilty," and "The Vertical City" each rated two. "The Smudge" got three stars in *Best Short Stories of 1922.*

82   "MISS HURST'S WORST VICE . . ." "The Vertical City," *NYT,* Apr. 30, 1922, 3:14:4.

82   "CRUDE AND CHAOTIC . . ." E.F.E., "Vertical City," *Boston Transcript,* Mar. 22, 1922, p. 4.

82   "IS AS LIVELY AND HARDHITTING . . ." N. P. Dawson, "Vertical City," *Literary Review,* Apr. 15, 1922, p. 579.

82   RUTH RAPHAEL . . . WROTE FANNIE/ "TWO-BREAKFASTS-A-WEEK-STUFF . . ."/ "YOU GET ACROSS . . ." HRC, FH/200/6, Ruth Raphael to FH, May 9, 1922.

83 OLYMPIC CARRIED FANNIE AND JACQUES "Fannie Hurst Sails, Pleased over Film," *New York Journal-American,* Feb. 19, 1922.

83 FANNIE'S ITINERARY HRC, FH/255/1, 1922 appt-cal entry for Feb. 18, 1922.

83 CHILDREN ARE CRYING . . . HRC, FH/170/2, cbl, Ray Long to FH, June 30, 1922.

83 A YEAR LATE WITH THE PLAY HRC, FH/99/1, cbl, David Belasco to FH, Feb. 18, 1922; ltr, May 3, 1922. See also NYPL-Berg, American Play Co., contract, ltr of Feb. 20, 1922, extending play deadline by one year to Mar. 9, 1922 (originally due Mar. 9, 1921).

83 HE OFFERED A THOUSAND DOLLARS HRC, FH/238/1, cbl, Ida Vernon to FH in St. Louis, Aug. 14, 1922.

83 "MY KNEE IN THE DUST . . ." HRC, FH/191/4, Charles Norris to FH, Nov. 20, 1922.

83 "THERE IS THE PARIS . . ." FH, *Song of Life* (New York: Harper & Bros., 1922), pp. 199–238. See also FH, "Forty-Five," *Cosmo,* Dec. 1922.

85 "HUNG LIKE A CRAG . . ." *Anat,* pp. 252–253. In *Anat* FH places this visit in 1913. She actually may have visited Ravello on that occasion, but this was not the point at which she met Stef. It is an intentional obfuscation.

85 "NEVER BEFORE, I MAY EVEN SAY . . ." *Anat,* p. 254.

85 "I HOPE THAT THE SPELL . . ." HRC, FH/99/1, David Belasco to FH, May 3, 1922.

85 ENCLOSED A PHOTOGRAPH HRC, FH/99/1, David Belasco to FH, May 3, 1922. See also FH/227/4, Mitteldorfer Straus to FH, May 17, 1922.

85 LONDON, THIS VISIT/ FLOWERED INTO A FRIENDSHIP HRC, FH/255/1, 1922 appt-cal entries for May 22, 26, and 28, 1922.

85 BREAKUP OF HER LONG AFFAIR Carl Rollyson, *Rebecca West: A Life* (New York: Scribner, 1996), p. 87.

85 "A JEWESS OF THE MOST OPULENT . . ." As quoted in Rollyson, *Rebecca West,* p. 98, and Victoria Glendinning, *Rebecca West: A Life* (New York: Knopf, 1987), p. 98, citing R. West ltr to Lettie, Feb. 8, 1924.

85–86 HER PARENTS . . . COMPLAINED BITTERLY NYPL-Rare, Robert Hobart Davis Papers, FH, Box 17, FH to RHD, July 15, 1922.

86 "THE PINNACLES NOT YET SIGHTED . . ." "Fannie Hurst Home for Rest, Tells Why She Is Not Success," *St. Louis Globe-Democrat,* Aug. 13, 1922.

CHAPTER TEN

PAGE

87 DELINEATOR . . . SHORT STORIES HRC, FH/117/2, Mary Derieux, fiction editor, *Delineator,* Aug. 13, 1922.

87 WHEELER SYNDICATE BOUGHT THIRTEEN HRC, FH/257/13, Wheeler Syndicate to FH, Aug. 31, 1922, with payment.

87 "PARODY OUTLINE OF LITERATURE" HR, FH/120/2, John Farrar, George B. Doran Co., Sept. 8, 1922.

87 MCCALL'S . . . BEGAN COURTING/ "CHRISTMAS TREE OF STARS"/ REQUEST FOR A PIECE COMPARING/ SPRING SYMPOSIUM HR, FH/172/2, Adele Miller, *McCall's,* to FH, Sept. 12, 26, Oct. 28, Nov. 3, 1922.

87 AUTHORS' GUILD NOMINATED HRC, FH/95/3, Authors' Guild to FH, Oct. 7 and 11, 1922.

87 CONGRATULATIONS . . . HRC, FH/151/2, Sam and Rose Hurst to FH, cbl, Oct. 18, 1922.

88 STRONGER "WAR NOTE" . . . WAR MOTIF/"SHE HAS A COLD . . ." NYPL-Rare, Robert Hobart Davis Papers, Box 17, FH to RHD, Dec. 30, 1922.

88 "THE TYPES FLOURISH . . ." HRC, FH/117/2, FH, hand-draft ltr to George Tyler, undtd [draft on back of letter from *The Delineator*].

88 RELATIONSHIP BETWEEN CALORIE INTAKE See Ann Douglas, *Terrible Honesty: Mongrel Manhattan in the 1920s* (New York: Farrar, Straus & Giroux, 1995), p. 52. According to Douglas, the early 1920s brought in the discovery of vitamins and the Detecto bathroom scale. Though the measurement of food's energy had been established in the 1890s, calories were not widely understood until the late 1910s and 1920s.

88–89 "PERFORMANCE OF MOVING BEAUTY . . ." MusCNY, Alexander Woollcott, "Shouts and Murmurs," *New York Herald*, Feb. 28, 1923.

89 "INCOMPARABLY SUBTLE AND BEAUTIFUL" MusCNY, John Corbin, "The Play," *NYT*, Feb. 28, 1923.

89 "LIMITED BY AN AUTHOR'S LINES"/THE TAYLOR TOUCH/DECLINED TO TAKE THE STAGE HR, Scrapbooks, *Humoresque*, Percy Hammond, "Fannie Hurst's Comedy Was Not to Her Liking," *Philadelphia Record*, Mar. 11, 1923.

89 "NOT PROSPERING . . ." HR, Scrapbooks, *Humoresque*, Heywood Broun, *Philadelphia American*, Mar. 11, 1923.

89 THE PLAY CLOSED/ "LACK OF PUBLIC SUPPORT" "*Humoresque*, a Flop," *Clipper*, Mar. 21, 1923. See also *Best Plays of 1922–23*, p. 14.

89 "SHOULD IT BE MERELY THE PLAY . . ."/ "ONLY AN EPISODE . . ." HR, FH/224/4, Stef to FH, Jan. 17 and 22, 1923.

90 "BOOK OF THE YEAR" HR, Fulton Oursler, MacFadden Publications, to FH, Mar. 26, 1923.

90 "RISE ABOVE TEMPORARY MARKETABILITY" HR, FH/244/4, Stef to FH, May 14, 1923.

90 "IF YOU VALUE YOUR PLACE . . ." HR, FH/244/4, Stef to FH, June 10, 1923.

90 "THE ONLY AMERICAN WRITER . . ." HR, Ray Long, International Magazines Co., to FH, Jan. 12, 1923.

90 DECLINED TO SIGN A NEW CONTRACT HR, Ray Long, International Magazines Co., to FH, Mar. 7, 1923.

90 HIGHEST RANKING IN *BEST SHORT STORIES* O'Brien also gave three stars to "Seven Candles," the excerpt from *Lummox*. "Forty-Five" got two.

90–91 "WHAT YOU WANT IS SALES . . ."/ "IT SEEMS TO ME . . ." HR, FH/191/4, Charles Norris to FH, May 19, 1923, and Dec. 18, 1922.

91 ALL QUICKLY OFFERED CONTRACTS HRC, see 1923 ltrs FH/160/1, Knopf; FH/174/2, Macmillan; FH/141/4 Harcourt; FH/101/2 Bobbs-Merrill.

91 MOVIE RIGHTS . . . WENT NOWHERE/"WHILE I AM SURE . . ." HR, FH/158/3, R. L. Giffen, Alice Kauser agency, to FH, Oct. 19, 1923.

91 RELIED ON HIM TO CLEAN UP Ethel Rabinowitz Amatneek, FH's secretary, 1932–1936, on videotape of lecture by Susan Koppelman, Brandeis University Library, 1993, entitled "FH: The Woman, Writer, and Social Activist." Also various personal ints with author, 1998.

91 "SUMMER OF ANXIETY"/ "FINALLY SHE IS RESPONDING . . ." WashSpc, FH Collection, Ser. I, General Correspondence 1913–1929, FH to Lois Toensfeldt, Aug. 29, 1923.

91 "CHILDREN, AFTER ALL . . ." HR, FH/221/2, Sam "Shippie" Shipman to FH, Aug. 2, 1923.

91 "HOWEVER DO YOU MANAGE . . ." HR, FH/224/4, Stef to FH, Aug. 21, 1923.

91 THE NEW YORK NEWSPAPERS . . . INTEGRITY HR, Scrapbooks 31, *NY Tribune,* Oct. 7, 1923; *NY World,* Oct. 7, 1923.

92 "SHORN OF MANY POUNDS" HR, Scrapbooks, *Lummox-Humoresque,* "Fannie Hurst Shorn of Many Pounds," Cleveland *Plain Dealer,* Dec. 2, 1923.

92 "MRS. WHARTON'S PREFACE . . ." Charles Prin, Scribner's Sons (CO101) Records * Series: Author Files 1, 70/H Misc., Maxwell Perkins to FH, Feb. 25, 1924.

92 "THE DEEPEST WELLS . . ." "Fannie Hurst Portrays a New York Lummox," *NYT Book Review,* Oct. 14, 1923, p. 5.

92 "SO MUCH BAD . . ." J. W. Krutch, *Literary Review,* Oct. 20, 1923, p. 145.

92 "MAKE AN EMOTION RISE . . ." Heywood Broun, "It Seems to Me," *NY World,* Oct. 30, 1923, p. 1.

92 "IT WAS GOOD TO SET OUT . . ." FH, *Lummox* (New York: Harper & Bros., 1923), p. 7.

92 "ANNOYING, OFFENSIVE, PUZZLING" John Farrar, "Epic of Maternity," *NY Tribune,* Oct. 14, 1923, p. 24.

93 MORE LIKE A BLURB *International Book Review,* Vol. 1, Oct. 23, 1923, p. 24.

93 "EXUBERANCE . . ." HR, Scrapbooks, *Lummox-Humoresque,* Rebecca West, *Columbus* (Ohio) *Journal,* Dec. 16, 1923.

93 "GREAT ART . . ."/"THE BEST NOVEL . . ." Advertisement, *NYT Book Review,* Apr. 27, 1924, p. 19.

93 "IT DOES SEEM REMARKABLE . . ." HR, FH/149/3, Marie Jenny Howe to FH, Oct. 28, 1923.

93 "SOUL AND SELF . . ." HR, FH/142/2, Rabbi Leon Harrison to FH, Nov. 28, 1923.

93 "ALL THE IMMENSE POWER . . ." HR, FH/132/1, Stanley F. Babb, *Galveston News,* to FH, Oct. 22, 1923.

93 "SKILL AND DEXTERITY . . ." Joseph Collins, *Taking the Literary Pulse: Psychological Studies of Life and Letters* (New York: Doran, 1924), pp. 122–125.

93 CHRISTOPHER WARD'S SERIES OF PARODIES Christopher Ward, *Twisted Tales* (New York: Henry Holt, 1924), pp. 1–7.

93 "I AM SO HAPPY . . ." HR, FH/151/2, FH to Joe Koppel, Cincinnati, undtd [1923].

94 "ONE DAY YOU SAID . . ." Author's collection. Inscription, "To R.H.D.," signed by FH in first edition of *Lummox.*

CHAPTER ELEVEN

PAGE

95 "*ARTISTIC* SUCCESSES . . ." HRC, FH/151/2, FH to Joe Koppel, Cincinnati, undtd [1923].

95 "APARTMENT OF LAUGHTER"/"HAPPINESS DWELT HERE," *Anat,* p. 274.

95 ENDED UP PAYING RENT HRC, FH/151/2, FH to Joe Koppel, Cincinnati, undtd [1923].

95 *NEW YORK TIMES MAGAZINE* REPORTER INTERVIEWED FANNIE HRC, FH/128/1, Rose Feld, *NYT,* to FH, Dec. 6, 1923.

95–96 BUT THE WRITER POINTED OUT . . . / "INSTINCTS OF THE HUMAN RACE" Rose C. Feld, "Eight Years After a Novel Marriage," *NYT Magazine,* Dec. 9, 1923, p. 1.

96 "PROPINQUITY" FH, "Propinquity," *Liberty,* Vol. 1, No. 2, pp. 3, 5.

96 PARALLEL LOVE AFFAIR Author int with Evelyn Stefansson Nef, Jan. 22, 1996.

96 AMONG HER PAPERS . . . HRC, FH/93/5, Maxwell Anderson to FH, May 23, 1927.

97 "I AM BULGING . . ." *Anat,* pp. 255–256.

97 "DID NOT COME"/ THE CREATIVE ASPECTS *Anat,* p. 273.

97 HER ATTITUDE TOWARD STEF *Anat,* p. 254.

97 LETTERS OF REBECCA WEST HRC, FH/241/6, 1922–1935, R. West correspondence with FH.

97 "MANUFACTURED GRAND RAPIDS STUFF"/ "TWO GLORIOUS SPANISH BEDS . . ." HRC, FH/151/2, FH to Joe Koppel, Cincinnati, undtd [1923].

98 "THE SPANGLE THAT COULD BE A TEAR" FH, "Every Spangle a Tear," *Bookman,* Dec. 1923, 58:373–377; "WHITE APES" FH, "White Apes," *Forum,* Mar. 1924, 71:290–303 and Apr. 1924, 71:459–478.

98 HENRY GODDARD LEACH . . . REPPLIER AND ANNE DOUGLAS SEDGWICK HRC, FH/129/3, *Forum,* to FH, Dec. 19, 1923.

98 "MORE MAGAZINEABLE" HRC, FH/172/2, Harry Burton, *McCall's,* to FH, Feb. 1, 1924.

98 LUCRATIVE WEEKLY COLUMN HRC, FH/172/3, Edith O'Dell, McClure's Syndicate, to FH, Dec. 1923.

98 THIRTY-FOUR PAPERS HAD SIGNED HRC, FH/172/3, Edith O'Dell, McClure's Syndicate, to FH, June 10, 1923.

98 "BREAKING A SHORT STORY . . ." Dart, Stef correspondence, Box 111 (Addendum, Box 2), Stef Correspondence, Gretchen-Wright, FH to Stef, c. Mar. 1, 1924.

98 ONLY TWENTY DAYS HRC, FH/255/1, appt-bk, 1924, note says "started novel" on Jan. 21, 1924.

98 MET HER ASKING PRICE/ "ROCKING CHAIR POSITION . . ." HRC, FH/172/2, Harry Burton, *McCall's,* to FH, Feb. 1, 1924. Re Burton's wife, see obituary, Katherine Kurz Burton, *NYT,* Sept. 24, 1969, 47:1.

98 FANNIE CONFIDED Dart, Stef correspondence, Box 111 (addendum Box 2), Gretchen-Wright, FH correspondence, FH to Stef, c. Jan. 31, 1924.

99 THE BOOKMAN, AFTER ALL "Literary Spotlight," *Bookman,* Jan. 1924, 58:552–556.

99 WHEN REBECCA WEST/ "THINGS MARVELOUS TO RECALL" Gordon N. Ray, *H. G. Wells and Rebecca West* (New Haven: Yale University Press, 1977), p. 155.

99 SHE WAS SUFFERING See Ray, *H. G. Wells and Rebecca West,* pp. 153–157, 203 (R. West ltr to S. K. Ratcliffe, Mar. 21, 1923). Also Victoria Glendinning, *Rebecca West: A Life* (New York: Knopf, 1987), p. 95; and Carl Rollyson, *Rebecca West: A Life* (New York: Scribner, 1996) pp. 95–100.

99 TO FANNIE SHE CONFIDED HRC, FH/241/6, Rebecca West to FH, various undated c. 1924–29; also, June 12, 1924; Aug. 27, 1928; and Oct. 31, 1929. Also, see Ray, *H.G. Wells and Rebecca West,* ltr to S. K. Ratcliffe, Mar. 21, 1923, and Rollyson, *Rebecca West,* pp. 95–100.

99 "THINGS ARE DIFFICULT . . ." Dart, Stef correspondence, Box 111 (addendum Box 2), Gretchen-Wright, FH to Stef, Jan. 16, 1924.

100 ZONA GALE . . . ANITA LOOS AND JOHN EMERSON HRC, FH/170/4, Anita Loos to FH, Jan. 2, 1924.

100 BOB AND MADGE DAVIS HRC, FH/116/1, Robert Hobart Davis to FH, Jan. 5, 1924.

100 CARL HOVEY AND SONYA LEVIEN/ LEVIEN TOLD FANNIE HRC, FH/149/2, Sonya Levien to FH, Jan. 6, 1924.

100 GLORIA SWANSON HRC, FH/255/1, appt-bk, 1924, Jan. 14, 1924.

100 DINNER WITH ZONA GALE AND REBECCA HRC, FH/255/1, appt-bk, 1924. Jan. 18, 1924. Also Dart, Stef correspondence, Box 111 (addendum Box 2), Gretchen-Wright, FH correspondence, FH to Stef, c. Jan. 17, 1924.

100 FANNIE LIKED WRITING STEF Dart, Stef correspondence, Box 111 (addendum Box 2), Gretchen-Wright, FH correspondence, FH to Stef, c. Jan. 31, 1924.

100 F. SCOTT FITZGERALD HRC, FH/255/1, appt-bk, 1924, Feb. 10, 1924.

100 "I LOATHE AGENTS" Dart, Stef correspondence, Box 111 (addendum Box 2), Gretchen-Wright, FH correspondence, FH to Stef, c. Jan. 30 or Feb. 5, 1924.

101 AS SHE LATER EXPLAINED Dart, Stef correspondence, Box 111 (addendum Box 2), Gretchen-Wright, FH correspondence, Elisabeth Marbury to FH, Jan. 29, 1924.

101 "LUMMOX THE SENSATIONAL BEST SELLER . . ." Dart, Stef correspondence, Box 111 (addendum Box 2), Gretchen-Wright, FH correspondence, notice of R. L. Giffen, c. Jan. 24, 1924.

101 MARBURY SAW THE NOTICE Dart, Stef correspondence, Box 111 (addendum Box 2), Gretchen-Wright, FH correspondence, Elisabeth Marbury to FH, Jan. 25, 1924.

101 MARBURY'S "BRILLIANT" ASSISTANT Elisabeth Marbury, *My Crystal Ball: Reminiscences* (New York: Boni & Liveright, 1923), pp. 136–137.

101–102 "OF COURSE, IT IS QUITE ALRIGHT [SIC] . . ."/ "SOONER THAN DISAPPOINT . . ."/ "I KNOW IT ISN'T THE IMMEDIATE MONEY . . ."/ "IF YOU FEEL . . ."/ "IN ALL SINCERITY" Dart, Stef correspondence, Box 111 (addendum Box 2), Gretchen-Wright, FH correspondence, Elisabeth Marbury to FH, FH to Stef, Jan. 29, 1924.

CHAPTER TWELVE

PAGE

103–104 "UNEXPECTED BAD PLACES . . ."/ "THE DAILY STINT" Dart, Stef correspondence, Box 111 (addendum Box 2), Gretchen-Wright, FH correspondence, FH to Stef, c. Jan. 14, 15, 16, 17, 31, 1924.

104 "LOVELY . . . BUT IT'S WORTH IT!" Dart, Stef correspondence, Box 111 (addendum Box 2), Gretchen-Wright, FH correspondence, FH to Stef, c. Jan. 16, 1924.

104 FANNIE COULD NOT REARRANGE . . . / "I SHALL INSTRUCT YOU" Dart, Stef correspondence, Box 111 (addendum Box 2), Gretchen-Wright, FH correspondence, FH to Stef, c. Jan. 31, 1924.

105 "PRACTICALLY EVERY OCCUPANT . . ." "Does a Moment of Revolt Come to Every Married Man?" *McCall's*, Vol. 51, No. 6, Mar. 1924, p. 36.

105 THE SCREEN PLOT VARIED HRC, Scrapbooks, 1924, review, undocumented, Cresco (Iowa) Theater playing *The Nth Commandment*.

105 FANNIE ADDRESSED THE CHAMBER Dart, Stef correspondence, Box 111 (addendum box 2), Gretchen-Wright, FH correspondence, Apr. 3, 1924.

105 A GRADUATE SCHOOL PROFESSOR HRC, FH/240/2, Professor Heller, Washington University, to FH, Apr. 4, 1924.

106 "THE CROSS OF GOLD" *Anat,* p. 37.

106 RUTH WAS UPSETTING HER PARENTS Sarah P. Vickers, "The Life of Ruth Bryan Owen: Florida's First Congresswoman and America's First Woman Diplomat" (Diss., Florida State University, 1994), p. 25.

106 "HAD THE SMALL GIRLS . . ." *Anat*, p. 37.

106 THE WOOLWICH GIRLS CLUB/ ENTERTAINING THE TROOPS HRC, FH/194/1, 1935 bio, Ruth Bryan Owen file.

106 A LATER ATTACK Dissertation, Vickers, "Life of Ruth Bryan Owen," p. 50.

106 PHENOMENAL PUBLIC SPEAKER HRC, FH/194/1, 1935 bio, Ruth Bryan Owen file.

106 "FELL IN LOVE . . ." HRC, FH/Misc "R," Ruth Bryan Owen to Stef, May 21, 1924.

107 "PERHAPS IF I WERE . . ." Hunt, AU 3206-3213, FH to Mary Austin, undtd [May 1924].

107 ANNE NICHOLS MusCNY, Theater Collection, Jean Meegan, untitled, undtd int with Anne Nichols.

107 "NO WORSE THAN A BAD COLD" MusCNY, Theater Collection, Alexander Woollcott, "The Stage," undtd, undocumented, c. 1927.

107 ORIGINAL PRODUCTION Walter Rigdon, ed., *Notable Names in the American Theater* (Clifton, N. J.: J. T. White, 1976).

107 "THAT DOES NOT MEAN . . ." HRC, FH/95/2, Mary Austin to FH, undtd [May 1924].

108 "THERE USUALLY ARISES . . ." Hunt, AU 3206-3213, FH to Mary Austin, Feb. 9, 1925.

108 "YOU ARE SO INNOCENT . . ." Hunt, AU 3206-3213, Mary Austin to FH, Apr. 27, 1925.

CHAPTER THIRTEEN

PAGE

109 RAY LONG HAD OFFERED HRC, FH/153/4, Ray Long, International Magazine Co., to FH, May 18, 1922.

109 THE SAME THING HAPPENED HRC, FH/105/2, Harry Burton to FH, June 23, 1922. See also FH/172/2, Harry Burton, *McCall's*, to FH, July 11, 1922.

109 ACCORDING TO SEVERAL PROFILES According to the passenger ship manifesto of the SS *August Victoria* on its arrival at the Port of New York on July 20, 1891, Jacob Danielson, age seventeen, arrived in the United States along with Hillel Danielson, age thirty-four, and Rubin Danielson, age twenty-four, presumably his brothers. Each was identified as a "music man." They left from Moscow with one piece of luggage each and occupied space in steerage A. The 1905 New York State census shows the Danielson household consisting of siblings Jacob, Henry, and Anna, and their father, Samuel. Again, all, including the father, are listed as musicians. (Actually, Jacob is listed as seventy-three years old and head of household and Samuel as thirty, but this is clearly a transcription error.) Grateful acknowledgment to Marsha Saron Dennis, who conducted the research.

109 FANNIE SEEMED DELIGHTED Hunt, AP 841-848, FH to A. B. Paine, June–July 1924.

109 "FALLING CIVILIZATION" HRC, FH/105/2, Harry Burton to FH, June 23, 1922. See also FH/172/2, Harry Burton, *McCall's*, to FH, July 11, 1922.

109 "TO SEE WHAT HAS HAPPENED . . ." "Fannie Hurst Home for Rest, Tells Why She Is Not Success," *St. Louis Globe-Democrat,* Aug. 13, 1922.

110 "THERE IS ALL OF YOUTH'S CRUDITY . . ." Walter Duranty, "Fanny [*sic*] Hurst Finds
     Youth Rule Russia," *NYT,* Aug. 19, 1922, 26:6.

110 "A GREAT BEAST . . ."/ "A WOMAN MUCH MORE RED . . ."/ "HIGHLY LAUDABLE RE-
     FORM . . ." "One Woman Changes Her Mind," *NYT,* Aug. 27, 1924, 16:5–6.

110 LATER THE EDITOR EXPLAINED/ "GROTESQUE . . ." FH, "What Fannie Hurst Really
     Thinks," *Nation,* Vol. 119, No. 3090, Sept. 24, 1924, p. 313.

110 "IN A WAY THAT GIVES AN INSIGHT . . ." FH, "Fannie Hurst Tells the Human Side of
     Russia's Drama," *NY World,* Mar. 15, 1925, 2:1:1–8.

111 "I HAVE BEEN TO RUSSIA . . ." FH, "Fannie Hurst Tells the Human Side of Russia's
     Drama," II 1:1–8. See also, FH, "Main Street—Russia," *McCall's,* Vol. 52, No. 4,
     Jan. 1925, pp. 10ff; No. 5, Feb. 1925, pp. 8ff; No. 6, Mar. 1925, pp. 10ff.

111 "A GRILLING MILE . . ."/ ONE OF HIS FAVORITES/ THEY MET AGAIN *Anat,* pp. 296–297.

111 LIVING OUT HIS LAST MONTHS *Anat,* p. 296–297. See also, verifying time frame,
     Colum, James O. Brown Collection, cbl, George Bye to FH, Aug. 18, 1938, et al.

111 LEONE MOATS ARRANGED HRC, FH/181/1, Leone Moats to FH undtd. See also *Anat,*
     pp. 296–297.

111 "TO THE LAST BREATH . . ." FH, "Main Street—Russia," pp. 60–61.

112 "NOT SINCE I HAVE BEEN EDITOR HERE . . ." HRC, FH/172/2, Harry Burton, *McCall's,*
     to FH, Oct. 16, 1923.

112 STEF'S . . . TO TROTSKY Dart, Stef correspondence, Box 111 (addendum Box 2),
     Gretchen-Wright, FH correspondence, Stef to FH, Oct. 24, 1924.

112 INSTEAD, THE EDITORS CLAIMED HRC, FH/172/2, Adele Miller, *McCall's,* to FH, Apr.
     6, 1925.

112 "REDUCING MY SCRIPT TO PULP" Colum, Curtis Brown Manuscript Collection, FH
     to Benjamin Stern, Stern and Reubens, undtd [1925].

112 IN THE END SHE WALKED AWAY Colum, Curtis Brown Manuscript Collection, Ben-
     jamin Stern, Stern and Reubens, to FH, Apr. 18 and Apr. 21, 1927.

112 "I KNOW YOU ARE IN RATHER A FINANCIAL JAM . . ." Dart, Stef correspondence, Box
     13, Stef to FH, and FH to Stef, Jan. 13, 1925.

112 IT COULD NOT HAVE ESCAPED HER James Henry Burke and Alice Payne Hackett,
     Eighty Years of Best Sellers, 1895–1975 (New York: Bowker, 1977), pp. 95–97.
     Lists compiled by *Publishers Weekly.*

113 FANNIE ACCEPTED AN ADVANCE HRC, FH/255/2, Contracts, FH and Alfred A.
     Knopf, for *Appassionata,* Mar. 2, 1925.

113 "HELL . . . LIFE'S MUCH TOO SHORT . . ." HRC, FH/101/3, Horace Liveright to FH,
     Apr. 18, 1925.

113 FANNIE LOATHED PUBLIC SPEAKING HRC, FH/172/3, Edith O'Dell, McClure's Syndi-
     cate, to FH, Dec. 22, 1924.

113 "THE AWFULNESS" Dart, Stef correspondence, Box 111 (addendum Box 2),
     Gretchen-Wright, FH correspondence, FH to Stef, Mar. 28, 1925.

113 FOUR TO FIVE HUNDRED DOLLARS HRC, FH/89/2, Louis J. Alber to FH, Nov. 16,
     1923; Mar. 20, 1924.

113 FANNIE'S DECISION TO OVERCOME HER DREAD HRC, FH/172/3, Edith O'Dell,
     McClure's Syndicate, to FH, Dec. 22, 1924.

113 "SHAMED ME INTO SUCCESS . . ." NYPL-Rare, Robert Hobart Davis Papers, FH post-
     card to Bob Davis, Mar. 9, 1925.

114 HUMOR HER MOTHER *Anat,* p. 313.

114 AN ESTATE WORTH SOME ONE HUNDRED THOUSAND DOLLARS HRC, FH/103/5, Samuel Hurst estate documents, Leahy, Saunders and Walther, Apr.–Sept. 1925.

114 "HER LIFE LINE WAS TOO FUSED . . ." *Anat,* p. 313.

114 "DEAR BOB . . ." NYPL-Rare, Robert Hobart Davis Papers, FH to Bob Davis, Mar. 13, 1925.

114 "MOURNFUL NOTE . . ." HRC, FH/142/2, the Rev. Leon Harrison to FH, Apr. 8, 1925.

114 AWFULLY SORRY . . . Dart, Stef correspondence, Box 111 (addendum Box 2), Gretchen-Wright, cbl, Stef to FH, Mar. 13, 1925.

114 SHE HEADED WEST HRC, FH/255/1, appt-cal, 1925 entries, Mar. 16, 1925.

114 LACK OF POSITIVE FEEDBACK/ "AWFULNESS"/ "SPINACH IS JUSTIFIED" Dart, Stef correspondence, Box 111 (addendum Box 2), Gretchen-Wright, FH correspondence, FH to Stef, Mar. 22 and Mar. 28, 1925, clipping enclosed, *Houston Chronicle,* Mar. 28, 1925.

115 "I AM ANXIOUS . . ." HRC, FH/161.1, JSD to Blanche Knopf, Apr. 3, 1925.

115 FANNIE AND JACK WENT BACK "Fannie Hurst Takes Holiday with Husband," *NYT,* May 6, 1925, 3:3.

115 "ART IN ITSELF . . ." HRC, FH/106/2, Sarah Cantor, *The Day,* to FH, July 24, 1926, with copy of translation of B. Z. Goldberg, "One of the Four Million," *The Day,* undtd [c. July 1925].

115 $3,250 PER STORY Colum, Curtis Brown Manuscript Collection, Arthur McKeogh and Ray Long to FH, Nov. 17, Dec. 8, 1924; B. H. Stern to FH, Dec. 10, 1924; and FH to International Magazine Co., Dec. 10, 1924.

115 THE TWO THAT APPEARED IN 1925 "A House of Men" rated two stars in *Best Short Stories* and "The Gold in Fish," only one.

116 FANNIE FELT SHE HAD THE LEVERAGE HRC, FH/200/6, Ruth Raphael to FH, Aug. 6, 1925.

116 "ONCE I HAVE USED THE GERM OF AN IDEA . . ." HRC, FH/172/3, FH to Clinton Brainard, McClure's Syndicate, to FH, Oct. 6, 1925.

116 WHOLE YEAR'S CONTRACT FROM MCCLURE'S HRC, FH/255/2, Contracts, Edith O'Dell, McClure's Syndicate, to FH, Feb. 6, 1925.

116 "ARE A WOMAN'S SECRETS HER OWN?" . . . *Liberty,* Vol. 1, No. 17, Aug. 30, 1924, pp. 7 ff.; Vol. 1, No. 28, Nov. 15, 1924, pp. 5 ff.; Vol. 1, No. 48, Apr. 4, 1925, pp. 5 ff.; Vol. 2, No. 11, July 18, 1925, p. 12.

116 "LIBERTY'S GREATEST CONTEST" FH, "Fannie Hurst Urges You to Enter *Liberty's* Greatest Contest," Vol. 1, No. 52, May 2, 1925, p. 41.

117 IMAGINE THEN THE CYNICISM HRC, FH Scrapbooks, *Mannequin, Liberty* announcement of Aug. 22, 1925.

117 FANNIE TOOK UP RESIDENCE HRC, FH/168/2, FH to John Wheeler, executive editor, *Liberty,* July 11, 1925.

117 "WOULD YOU OBJECT . . ." HRC, FH/168/2, John Wheeler, *Liberty,* to FH, June 25, 1925.

117 "THE MOVING FINGER WRITES"/ "ORCHID"/ "SONG WITHOUT WORDS" HRC, FH/168/2, FH to John Wheeler, *Liberty,* July 4, 1925.

117 "THAT ELEGANT FLOWER"/ "GIRDLES OF GARLANDS" HRC, FH/168/2, FH to John Wheeler, *Liberty,* July 11 and July 20, 1925.

117　CONSENSUS FORMED AROUND "MANNEQUIN"　HRC, FH/168/2, to John Wheeler, executive editor, *Liberty,* Aug. 6, 1925.

117–118　"THE CINEMA WAY OF DOING THINGS . . . GORGEOUSNESS"　HRC, FH/175/5, FH to Elisabeth Marbury, July 12, July 25, and Aug. 9, 1925.

118　GOT FANNIE A TWENTY-FIVE-THOUSAND-DOLLAR DEAL　HRC, FH/255/2, Contracts, FH and Famous Players–Lasky Corp., agreement for original story provisionally titled "The Taming of Gloria," signed by Jesse Lasky and FH, Sept. 24, 1925.

118　SHE ALSO HAND-DELIVERED/ "THE ROLE REQUIRES"　HRC, FH/197/3, FH to Mary Pickford, July 15 and July 16, 1925.

118　PICKFORD WAS POLITE　HRC, FH/255/1, appt-bks, entry, July 25, 1925, dinner at Mary Pickford's with Lillian Gish.

118　FANNIE HAD APPROACHED GISH　HRC, FH/133/4, cbl, FH to Lillian Gish, May 25, 1925.

118　OVER A CASUAL LUNCH . . . A JEWISH ROLE　HRC, FH/241/1, cbl, Lois Weber to FH, Aug. 20, 1925.

118　FANNIE'S APPOINTMENT CALENDAR　HRC, FH/255/1, appt-bk, 1925, Aug. entries.

118　"A MERRY SORT . . . MY MERCILESS SPEED"　HRC, FH/200/6, FH to Ruth Raphael, July 17, 1925.

118　SHE POLISHED THE MANUSCRIPT OF *APPASSIONATA*　HRC, FH/161/1, FH to Blanche Knopf, July 9 and Aug. 20, 1925.

118　SHE OFFERED *COSMOPOLITAN* A SHORT STORY　HRC, FH/170/2, FH to Ray Long, *Cosmo,* July 13, 1925, and cbls, FH to Long, Aug. 18, 1925; and Long to FH, Aug. 18, 1925.

118　"I HAVE BEEN TO HOLLYWOOD"　HRC, FH/168/2, FH to John Wheeler, *Liberty,* July 17, 1925; Wheeler to FH, Sept. 17, 1925. See also FH, "I Have Been to Hollywood," *Liberty,* Nov. 14, 1925.

119　A STAGE VERSION OF *LUMMOX* / TELLING DAVID BELASCO　HRC, FH/158/3, FH to R. L. Giffen, Alice Kauser agency, Aug. 11, 1925; HRC, FH/99/1, FH to David Belasco, July 11, 1925.

119　"BE OF GOOD CHEER . . ."/ "MUSICAL COMEDY FARCE . . ."　HRC, FH/161/1, FH to Blanche Knopf, July 9, 1925.

119　THERE WAS NO NEED　HRC, FH/200/6, FH to Ruth Raphael, Aug. 1, 1925, "Contrary to all my fears, my publishers are ecstatic over everything. Incredibly so."

119　FANNIE WANTED RUTH TO EMPHASIZE　HRC, FH/200/6, FH to Ruth Raphael, Aug. 9, 1925.

119　"YOUR LETTER FINDS ME . . ."　HRC, FH/241/6, FH to Rebecca West, July 11, 1925.

119　"IN A BUNGALOW FACING . . ."　HRC, FH/241/6, Rebecca West to FH, undtd.

119　"MOVIE QUEEN OF GRADE X . . ."　HRC, FH/175/5, FH to Elisabeth Marbury, Aug. 9, 1925.

119　"NEGLECTED HIM . . ."　HRC, FH/175/5, FH to Elisabeth Marbury, July 25, 1925.

120　"FROM THE STATE . . ."　HRC, FH/224/4, FH to Stef, July 26, 1925.

120　"BECAUSE I HAD HEARD . . ."　HRC, FH/224/4, Stef to FH, Aug. 16, 1925.

120　I AM SCARED . . .　HRC, FH/115/2, FH/74/5, cbl, FH to JSD, July 30, 1925.

120　JACQUES CABLED BACK　HRC, FH/115/2, FH/74/5, cbl, FH to JSD, Aug. 3, 1925.

120　THINKING OF YOU . . .　HRC, FH/115/2, FH/74/5, cbl, FH to JSD, Aug. 3, 1925.

120　HAVE NO MAILING ADDRESS . . .　Dart, Stef correspondence, Box 111 (addendum Box 2), Gretchen-Wright, cbl, Aug. 24, 1925.

CHAPTER FOURTEEN

PAGE

121 "NEGRO MATTERS" HRC, Fannie's files on subjects and organizations devoted to African-American causes appear under this heading.

121 MORE THAN SEVEN HUNDRED ENTRANTS NYPL-Schomburg, "May *Opportunity* Magazine to Announce Literary Contest Winners," *NY Amsterdam News,* Apr. 29, 1925.

121 "THAT THE AMERICAN NEGRO . . ." NYPL, "A Negro Renaissance," *NY Amsterdam News,* May 13, 1925.

121 FIRST PRIZE FOR POETRY "Prizes to Negro Writers," *NYT,* May 2, 1925, 17:4.

122 "SPUNK" HRC, FH/152/2, Annie Nathan Meyer to FH, Jan. 13, 1935.

122 COLOR STRUCK "Contest Awards," *Opportunity,* Vol. 3, No. 29, May 1925, p. 142, Hurston shared second prize in the play category with an aspiring Philadelphia playwright named Warren A. MacDonald.

122 JOHNSON ALREADY HAD PUBLISHED Cheryl A. Wall, *Women of the Harlem Renaissance* (Bloomington: University of Indiana Press, 1995), p. 146.

122 "CULLAH STRUUUUUK" Robert Hemenway, *Zora Neale Hurston: A Literary Biography* (Urbana and Chicago: University of Illinois Press, 1980), p. 60, Hemenway quoting the playwright May Miller, who was present.

122 "LIVED LAUGHINGLY . . ."/ FANNIE'S OWN DESIRE FH, "Zora Hurston: A Personality Sketch," *Library Gazette,* Yale University, No. 35, 1961, p. 19.

122 "A STUNNING WENCH . . ." Zora Neale Hurston, "FH by Her Ex-Amanuensis," *Saturday Review of Literature,* Oct. 3, 1937, p. 15.

122 CHANCE TO GO TO BARNARD HRC, FH/152/2, Annie Nathan Meyer to FH, Jan. 13, 1935.

122 "DISTINCTLY PROMISING" AmJwshArch, Annie Nathan Meyer Papers, Manuscript Collection 7, Folder 7/3, Virginia Gildersleeve, Barnard dean, to Meyer, June 9, 1925.

123 ZORA REGISTERED Barnard College, Registrar. Registration record of Zora Neale Hurston shows entrance Sept. 1925–26, not at school 1927; degree granted Feb. 1928.

123 "BARNARD'S SACRED BLACK COW" Zora Neale Hurston, *Dust Tracks on a Road* (1942; reprint, New York: HarperPerennial, 1996), p. 193.

123 SHE STILL NEEDED $117/ NOTHING NEW FOR ZORA AmJwshArch, Annie Nathan Meyer Papers, Manuscript Collection 7, Folder 7/3, Virginia Gildersleeve, Barnard dean, to Meyer, Oct. 2, Oct. 17, 1925.

123 WHILE IN WASHINGTON Wall, *Women of the Harlem Renaissance,* See also Hemenway, *Zora Neale Hurston.*

123 FANNIE WROTE VAN VECHTEN Yale, Za Van Vechten 63, FH to Carl Van Vechten, Sept. 24, 1925.

123 "I AM SURE . . ." AmJwshArch, Annie Nathan Meyer Papers, Manuscript Collection 7, Folder 7/3, Zora Neale Hurston to Meyer, Oct. 17, 1925.

123 "I WAS TICKLED . . ." HRC, FH/179/3, Annie Nathan Meyer, Nov. 2, 1925.

123 STUDENT LOAN FUND/ ZORA'S FELLOW STUDENTS/ ZORA WAS AT WORK AmJwshArch, Annie Nathan Meyer Papers, Manuscript Collection 7, Folder 7/3, Zora Neale Hurston to Meyer, Nov. 5, Dec. 13, Nov. 10, 1925.

123–124 "THE SHINE"/ "HER SHORTHAND . . ." FH, "Zora Hurston."

124 "FH/ZH" HRC, FH/97/4, ltr filed under Barnwell, dated Nov. 10, 1925.

124 ZORA TOOK A ROOM AmJwshArch, Annie Nathan Meyer Papers, Manuscript Collection 7, Folder 7/3, Zora Neale Hurston to Meyer, Dec. 6, 1925, with return address of 108 West 131st St., also appears on ltr of same date, Yale, Carl Van Vechten Papers. Zora Neale Hurston to Van Vechten, Dec. 6, 1925.

124 FOUND A WAY TO EARN/ "ON THE WHOLE . . ."/ SOME PART-TIME WORK AmJwshArch, Annie Nathan Meyer Papers, Manuscript Collection 7, Folder 7/3, Zora Neale Hurston to Meyer, Dec. 6, 1925.

124 WORK-STUDY ARRANGEMENT A couple of significant inaccuracies published with Zora's 1937 profile of Fannie in the *Saturday Review* and in Fannie's 1961 profile of Zora in the Yale *Library Gazette* account for confusion over the specifics of the early days of their relationship.

124 TWO OF ZORA'S ARTICLES Yale, Carl Van Vechten Papers, Zora Neale Hurston to Van Vechten, Jan. 5, 1926.

124 "I DO NOT WISH TO BECOME HURSTIZED . . ." AmJwshArch, Annie Nathan Meyer Papers, Manuscript Collection 7, Folder 7/3, Zora Neale Hurston to Meyer, Dec. 13, 1925.

124 ZORA WROTE TO HER PROSPECTIVE SISTER-IN-LAW Fla, No. 72, Box 2, Zora Neale Hurston to Constance Sheen, Jan. 5, 1926.

124 IMPRESSIVE ARRAY OF HOUSEHOLD NAMES Fla, No. 71, Box 2, Zora Neale Hurston to Constance Sheen, Feb. 2, 1926, and No. 72, Box 2, Jan. 5, 1926.

125 PROBLEMS COMPLETING REGISTRATION/ "I WONDER WHETHER . . ." AmJwshArch, Annie Nathan Meyer Papers, Manuscript Collection 7, Folder 7/3, Zora Neale Hurston to Meyer, undtd [Jan. 1926], Jan, 31, 1926, Feb. 5, 1926. Also, Virginia Gildersleeve to Meyer, Feb. 9, 1926.

125 "I GOT A CALL . . ." HRC, FH/152/2, Zora Neale Hurston to FH, Mar. 16, [1926].

125 "ZORA—108 WEST . . ." HRC, FH/255/1, appt-bk for 1926, entry of Mar. 25, 1926.

125 BARNARD WAS CLOSED/ "SHE WAS CASUAL . . ." FH, "Zora Hurston," pp. 19–20.

125 "ZORA—NOON" appt-bk for 1926, entry of Apr. 1, 1926.

126 PERPETUATED THE FICTION FH, "Zora Hurston," p. 17.

126 A TENTH OF THAT AMOUNT Chronology by Cheryl A. Wall, contained in *Hurston: Folklore, Memoirs, and Other Writings* (New York: Library of America, 1995), pp. 969, 973, references to publisher advances in 1933 ($200) and 1939 ($500).

126 NO OTHER SUCH RELATIONSHIP See various correspondence of FH with protéges and would-be protéges: Bran, Box 3a, FH–John Bryan, son of Ruth Bryan Owen; HRC, FH/169/4, FH–Dorothy Loeb correspondence; FH/190/4, FH–John Newberry correspondence; FH/204/2, FH–Murrey Rosen correspondence; FH/200/4, FH–William Raney correspondence; FH/210/6 FH–Gertrude Schleier correspondence; FH/246/1, FH–Laura Emily Wood correspondence.

126–127 MOVED TO THE FAMILIAR FORM Zora–Carl Van Vechten information and subsequent insight enabled by Valerie Boyd, June 9, 1998.

127 "AWASH IN SPLENDOR" FH, "Zora Hurston," p. 19.

CHAPTER FIFTEEN

PAGE

128   FIVE NEW STORIES The stories were "Who Are You?" "The Smirk," "Here Comes the Bride," "Gold Does Glitter," and "Madagascar, Ho!"

128   "WHOSE AIM IS TO WRITE . . ." Virginia Woolf, "American Fiction," *Saturday Review of Literature,* Aug. 1, 1925, Vol. 2, No. 1, p. 2:1.

128   EVERYONE WAS PLEASED HRC, FH/153/4, International Magazine Co., Ray Long and Arthur McKeogh to FH, Nov. 4, 10, 23, 25, and Dec. 4 and 15, 1925.

128   INCLUDING EDWARD O'BRIEN O'Brien also gave three stars to "Who Are You?" and "Madagascar, Ho!" One star each went to "Gold Does Glitter" and "Here Comes the Bride."

128   "A SMART BIT" Editor's note, *Harper's Bazar,* Vol. 61, No. 2559, Jan. 1926, p. 63.

128   MADELINE BORG . . . CONVINCED HER "Pageant by Fannie Hurst," *NYT,* Oct. 29, 1925, 29:1.

128   FANNIE ADDRESSED THE WOMEN'S DIVISION "Women's Total is 250,000," *NYT,* Apr. 26, 1926, 10:5; also "Jews Pick Leaders in $6,000,000 Drive," *NYT,* Apr. 22, 1926, 16:3.

129   WRITE ABOUT THE JEWS Colum, Special Manuscript Collection, Marie (Missy, Mrs. William Brown) Maloney to FH and reply, Apr. 22, 1927.

129   LACK OF SYMPATHY WITH THE ZIONIST MOVEMENT HRC, FH/117/2, FH to Oliver Degelman, Jan. 23, 1931. See also, HRC, scrapbooks, *Five and Ten* and *A President Is Born,* undtd and unidentified publication, int with Maurice A. Bergman [c. 1928].

129   KNOPF HAD NOT YET PUBLISHED HRC, FH/161/1, Blanche Knopf to FH, Dec. 8, 1925.

129   "NERVOUS INDIGESTION" Dart, Stef correspondence Box 111 (addendum Box 2), Gretchen-Wright, FH to Stef, Oct. 30, 1925.

129   MARBURY'S AMERICAN PLAY COMPANY HRC, FH/92/1, John Rumsey, American Play Co., to FH, Dec. 23, 1925.

129   "I HAVE BEEN GOING . . ."/ "GIVING IN BETWEEN PEOPLE . . ." Dart, Stef correspondence, Box 111 (addendum Box 2), Gretchen-Wright, Stef to FH, Dec. 29, 1925; FH to Stef, c. Dec. 30, 1925.

130   "ABUNDANT FAULTS . . ." "Fannie Hurst Writes of Squalor and Luxury," *NYT Book Review,* Aug. 8, 1926, 6:1.

130   THIRTY THOUSAND COPIES HRC, FH/161/1, Blanche Knopf to FH, Mar. 2, 1926.

130   "LOVE OF HER OWN INTACT LOVELINESS" "Fannie Hurst Writes of Squalor and Luxury," 6:1.

130   "UNITES THE MYSTICAL . . ." Grant Overton, *The Women Who Make Our Novels,* rev. ed. (Freeport: N.Y.: Books for Libraries Press, 1967), pp. 180–186.

130   "A SHEER TRIUMPH . . ." Henry Longan Stuart, "Matter Wins over Form in *Appassionata,*" *NYT Book Review,* Jan. 24, 1926, 5:1–5.

130   "NOT OF OUR FAITH . . ." Colum, Curtis Brown Manuscript Collection, B. H. Stern file for FH, Rev. William B. Martin, Holy Family Rectory, New Rochelle, N.Y., to FH, Oct. 22, 1925.

130   "INFINITELY GREATER DELICACY" Review, *Catholic World,* Apr. 1926, 123:128.

130   "POIGNANTLY BEAUTIFUL AND TRUE . . ." HRC, FH/259/3, Frances Stirling Clarke to FH, Apr. 16, 1926.

130 "ESSENTIAL SECRET" HRC, FH/94/1, S. Baldwin to FH, [1926].

130 "INNER INTIMATE KNOWLEDGE . . ." HRC, FH/94/1, Fr. Daniel S. Rankin, S.J., Marist College, to FH, Feb. 20, 1926.

130 "BEAUTIFUL, REVERENT . . ." HRC, FH/94/1, Edward S. Murphy, S.S.J., Epiphany Apostolic, Newburgh, N.Y., to FH, Feb. 10, 1926.

130 AT LEAST TWO READERS HRC, FH/259/3, Esther Miller, Donora, Pa., to FH, Feb. 1, 1926; and HRC, FH/157/1, Georgia Douglas Johnson, Dept. of Labor, Office of the Secretary, to FH, undtd.

130 "HOW CONFUSING . . ." ltr to BWK from Nancy Schorgl, May 13, 1996, and special thanks.

131 CANBY APOLOGIZED HRC, FH/210/1, Henry S. Canby, ed., *Saturday Review,* to FH, Feb. 9, 1926.

131 "A SERIOUS INSULT . . ." Morris, Lloyd, Review, *Saturday Review of Literature,* Feb. 6, 1926, 2:540.

131 "DECIDEDLY AND CHARACTERISTICALLY SECONDHAND . . ." HRC, FH Scrapbooks, clipping, *Appassionata,* c. Jan.–Feb. 1926.

131 "BREATHLESS WITH HER ROARING POWER . . ." Robert Littell, Review, *New Republic,* Feb. 3, 1926, 45:302–303.

131 "IT'S A BAD PICTURE . . ." Review, *The Untamed Lady, Variety,* Mar. 17, 1926.

131 LETTERS FLOODED HER MAILBOX "FH Wins Liberty," etc., *St. Louis Globe-Democrat,* Aug. 17, 1925, 3:1.

131 FENDED OFF THE LAWSUIT HRC, FH/126/1, Louis E. Swarts, Famous Players–Lasky Legal Dept., to FH, Sept. 14, 1925.

131 "THERE HAVE BEEN MANY INSTANCES . . ." HRC, FH/142/2, FH as secretary to Lillian Hartwell, Sept. 17, 1926.

132 "LARGE NUMBER OF UNFORTUNATE ASPIRANTS . . ." HRC, FH/142/2, Lillian Hartwell to FH, Sept. 17, 1926.

132 "POOR, DISTURBED SOULS . . ." "Sues Fannie Hurst over $50,000 Story," *NYT,* Aug. 20, 1926.

132 "WHEN I TELL YOU . . ." HRC, FH/207/6, FH to Margaret Sanger, Aug. 25, 1925.

132 "VAST, IMPERSONAL MIEN . . ." HRC, FH/136/4, FH to Gladys Gruner, Oct. 6 and 7, 1925.

132 SHE TITHED 10 PERCENT HRC, FH/95/1, FH cbl to George Creel, Authors' League, Aug. 25, 1925.

132 "MANNEQUIN: IN WHICH . . ." HRC, FH/161/1, FH to Blanche Knopf, July 2, 1925.

133 IGNORE HER PROTEST . . . HRC, FH t/1168/2, Harvey Duell, *Liberty,* Dec. 28, 1925.

133 WHEELER TOLD FANNIE/ THE MOVIE APPEARS HRC, FH/99/2, John N. Wheeler, Bell Syndicate, to FH, Mar. 16, 1926.

133 "FANNY [SIC] HURST HASN'T ANYTHING . . ."/ RATED THE PICTURE AVERAGE *Mannequin, Variety,* Jan. 13, 1926. See also HRC, FH/99/2, John N. Wheeler, Bell Syndicate, to FH, Mar. 16, 1926.

133 UNIVERSAL IN THEIR DISDAIN Only Dorothea Mann in the *Boston Transcript* (Aug. 7, 1926) was positive about *Mannequin,* but FH files at HRC indicate they were warm acquaintances. See also *NYT Book Review,* Aug. 8, 1926, 6:1; *Jewish American Writers Bibliography; Book Review Digest.*

133 "THE DARK AGES OF MY WORK" HRC, FH/142/1, FH to Harper Bros., Mar. 14, 1930.

133 SHE TOLD *MCCLURE'S* HRC, FH/172/3, FH to *McClure's,* June 25, 1927.

133 "IT IS REALLY A SCENARIO . . ." HRC, FH/157/1, Merle Johnson, *America's First Editions,* to FH, Oct. 6, 1930; FH to Johnson, Oct. 9, 1930.

133 "A TRAP . . ." Overton, *Women Who Make Our Novels,* pp. 184–185.

134 "AN ANTIDOTE THAT MATTERS . . ."/ "SUDDENLY, THE ENTIRE IDEA . . ." HRC, Knopf Collection, FH to Blanche Knopf, undtd [before June 30, 1926].

CHAPTER SIXTEEN

PAGE

135 "KEEP FIT THROUGH FIT . . ." FH, "No Food with My Meals," *Liberty,* June 5, 1926, p. 12.

136 NO ILL EFFECT Robert Louis Taylor, "Klondike Stef," in *Doctor, Lawyer, Merchant, Chief* (New York: Doubleday, 1948), pp. 112–117.

136 "I BATHE ME . . ." HRC, FH/230/1, Lois Toensfeldt to FH, Aug. 8, 1925.

137 DAILY TRIP TO A GYMNASIUM HRC, FH/255/1, appt-bk, 1928, see Nov. and Dec. entries.

137 TAKE MY ADVICE . . . HRC, FH/151/2, Rose Hurst cbl to FH, Nov. 4, 1928.

137 SLENDER . . . REFLECTED THE SPIRIT HRC, FH/196/3, Ethel Peyser to FH, Nov. 21, 1928; FH to Peyser, Nov. 30, 1928.

137 "MY LEAN AND MEAGER DIET . . ." WashSpc, FH Collection, Ser. I: General Correspondence, Folders 1–4, FH to Lois Meier Toensfeldt, Dec. 12, 1928.

137 "TO GYRATE SEMI-OCCASIONALLY . . ." HRC, FH/241/6, FH to Rebecca West, Jan. 5, 1928.

138 VERY BUSY CULTIVATING JUST ABOUT ANYONE HRC, FH/255/2, see appt-bks, 1926–1928.

138 INTERSPERSED ARE *Anat,* p. 219.

138 FANNIE KEPT TRYING Dart, Stef correspondence, Frazier Hunt, International Magazine Co., to FH, May 4, 1926.

138 "HAS BEEN A SUCCESS . . ."/ PLAN TO GO TO OXFORD "Liner for Italy Crowded," *NYT,* May 13, 1926, 23:1.

138 "GO IN FOR STUDY . . ." Miriam Teichner, "What Fannie Means to *Me!* Fannie Hurst Tells!" *Success,* Vol. 10, No. 12, Dec. 1926, pp. 32–34, 73.

138 HER DREAM PROJECT Harry Salpeter, "Fannie Hurst, Sob-Sister of American Fiction," *Bookman,* Aug. 1931, p. 612.

139 "THAT'S WHAT FAME MEANS . . ." Teichner, "What Fannie Means to *Me!*" pp. 32–34, 73.

139 "WILL NEVER BE JAILED . . ." Zora Neale Hurston, *Folklore, Memoirs, and Other Writings* (New York: Library of America, 1995), p. 738.

139 RENEWED HER ACQUAINTANCE HRC, FH/122/4, see correspondence 1928, 1929, FH and Theodore Dreiser.

139 CALLED ON TO SPEAK "City Character Bad, Walker Agrees," *NYT,* Apr. 21, 1926, 20:5.

139 "ONE OF AMERICA'S KEENEST MINDS" *Redbook,* Vol. 49, No. 4, Aug. 1927, Table of Contents, "One of America's Keenest Minds Appraises Women's Freedom."

139 WILLINGLY DRAFTED HRC, FH/189/3, see correspondence, FH and Belle Davis, from 1926 on.

140   "I AM DEEP IN THE THROES . . ." WashSpc, FH Collection, Ser. I: General Correspondence, Folders 1–4, FH to Lois Meier Toensfeldt, Jan. 7, 1927.

140   "THE MOST AMERICAN THING . . ." Teichner, "What Fannie Means to *Me*!" pp. 32–34, 73.

140   RODEO WEST Of this group of stories, "Song of Life," rated two stars in *Best Short Stories of 1928,* as did "Give This Little Girl a Hand"; the third story was titled "The Left Hand of God."

140   "I CONFESS . . ." H. W. Boynton, Review, *Song of Life, NY Sun,* Mar. 5, 1927.

140   DECEMBER 26, 1927, PREMIERE WashSpc, FH Collection, Ser. 1: General Correspondence, Folders 1–4, FH to Lois Meier Toensfeldt, Jan. 7, 1927, saying in play rehearsal; HRC, FH/180/4, FH to Robert Milton, Nov. 30, 1927, cites rehearsals starting that day. Premiere at Eltinge Theatre was Dec. 26, 1927.

141   "MAULED AND RESHAPED . . ." FH, "When the Novelist Turns Playwright," *Theatre* magazine, Vol. 45, Apr. 1927, pp. 7, 66.

141   BELASCO REJECTED THE IDEA/ "IT IS EXTREMELY UNCOMFORTABLE . . ." HRC, FH/92/1, FH to John Rumsey, American Play Co., Jan 30, 1929.

141   "NONE TOO LUSTROUS"/ "LEISURE GIVES ME . . ." Yale, Beinecke, Rebecca West Papers, Ser. 1, Box 10, FH to Rebecca West, undtd [c. Nov. 1927].

141   "WHY IN THE WIDE WORLD . . ." HRC, FH/241/6, Beinecke, Rebecca West to FH, undtd [from 1 Raymond Building, Gray's Inn, W.E.]

141   "WIELDED HER PEN DEFTLY . . ." MusCNY, undtd, unidentified clipping filed under *It Is to Laugh.*

142   "AUTHOR! AUTHOR!" HRC, FH/162/3, Alexander Barbour, Lambert Theater Corp., to FH, Dec. 27, 1927.

142   "AN ABORTION" HRC, FH/96/2, FH to Constance Ballard, Feb. 7, 1928.

142   "I'LL MAKE THE GRADE YET!" HRC, FH/241/6, FH to Rebecca West, Jan. 5, 1928.

CHAPTER SEVENTEEN

PAGE

143   THE PIECE DULY APPEARED "Fannie Hurst Paints Great Human Drama of Poor in Armory," *NY American,* Dec. 25, 1925, 1:7–8.

143   TRAVEL QUOTAS "Al Jolson Returns; No Divorce, He Says," *NYT,* Aug. 17, 1926, 22:2.

143   SIMILAR LEGISLATION "Americans Differ on Divorce News," *NYT,* Dec. 12, 1926, 28:3.

143   "IT SAVES THEM FROM EARLY MARRIAGE . . ."/ "INSIDE OF ME . . ." "Fannie Hurst Suggests Divorce Cure," *NY American,* Mar. 15, 1927, 1:1–8.

144   "SUPPOSE MRS. SNYDER . . ." "Ruth's Soul Died on Murder Night, Says Fannie Hurst," *NY Journal-American,* May 3, 1927.

144   "BASEBALL, GOLF . . ." "Raps 'Tired' Business Man," *NYT,* Jan. 12, 1927.

144   REPEATED THIS THEME "Tells Clubwomen to Uplift Husbands," *NYT,* Feb. 8, 1930.

144   REDBOOK DEVOTED SOME FOUR THOUSAND WORDS FH, "What of It? Have We Women Freed Ourselves from Men or Do They Own Us More Than Ever Before?" *Redbook,* Aug. 1927, pp. 60–62, 106, 108.

145 FANNIE'S PROTEST "Future of Fall Fashions," *NYT*, Oct. 11, 1927, 30:6.

145 "COMPETITION IN THE MAGAZINE FIELD . . ." HRC, FH/170/2, Ray Long to FH, Sept. 15, 1927.

145 "FAIR AND FRANK" HRC, FH/201/1, Edwin Balmer, *Redbook*, to FH, Sept. 21, 1927.

145 TEN THOUSAND OFFICE WORKERS "Back Clerical Union's Aim," *NYT*, Oct. 19, 1927, 27:4.

145 SHE PAID HER OWN SECRETARY Ethel Rabinowitz Amatneek, FH's secretary from 1932 to 1936, was hired at a salary of ten dollars a week (int with Author, Sept. 30, 1997).

145 "VASTLY MORE INTERESTING . . ." "Hold That World Still Is Romantic," *NYT*, Jan. 23, 1928, 44:5.

145 "WITH A FRESH EYE . . ." " 'Uncivilized Spectacle,' Fannie Hurst Says," *Pittsburgh Sun Telegraph*, Jan. 26, 1928, 1:2 ff.

146 "UNEARTH THE FORCES . . ." FH, "Don't Force Labor to Its Knees, Capital Is Warned," *Pittsburgh Sun Telegraph*, Jan. 26, 1928, 1:2 ff.

146 URGING AN IMMEDIATE TRUCE FH, "Fannie Hurst Urges Truce Pending U.S. Strike Probe," *Pittsburgh Sun Telegraph*, Feb. 2, 1928, 1:5–6. See also "Both Sides in Mine Strike May Lose—Fannie Hurst," Jan. 31, 1928, 1:5–6.

146 "NO ONE CAN LOOK . . ." HRC, FH/197/3, FH to H. M. Bittner, Jan. 31, 1928.

146 THE DESOLATION SHE HAD WITNESSED HRC, FH/112/3, FH to Ida Verdon, *Cosmo*, Feb. 1, 1928.

146 THE SUFFERING WAS MORE DESPERATE "Fannie Hurst Calls Coal Fields Condition 'Cancer,' " *NY American*, Mar. 21, 1928, 2:6–7.

146 "AS A MATTER OF FACT . . ." HRC FH/197/3, H. M. Bittner, *Pittsburgh Sun Telegraph*, to FH, Mar. 23, 1928.

146 PREDICTED A PULITZER HRC, FH/199/3, Robert H. Davis cbl to FH, Dec. 14, 1927.

146 SO DID . . . INEZ HAYNES IRWIN HRC, FH/154/1, Inez Haynes Irwin to FH, Dec. 14, 1927.

146 "I WONDER . . ." HRC, FH/241/6, FH to Rebecca West, Jan. 5, 1928.

146 "PRAIRIE FEELING . . ." HRC, FH/241/6, Rebecca West to FH, undtd [c. Feb. 1928].

146 THIS DEVICE ALLOWED "Born and Made," *Nation*, Mar. 21, 1928, pp. 323–324.

147 THE ANSWER WAS NO HRC, FH/199/3, Margaretta Van Rensselaer Schuyler to FH, May 21, 1928.

147 "THE FACT THAT . . ." HRC, FH/199/3, *A President Is Born*, FH to Harry Hansen, *NY World*, Apr. 2, 1930.

147 "DISTRESSING FONDNESS" H. W. Boynton, "A Future President: A Fine Group Portrait by Fannie Hurst," *NY Sun*, Jan. 7, 1928.

147 "A CONSIDERABLE STORY . . ." Henry S. Canby, "How to Make a President," *Saturday Review of Literature*, Jan. 28, 1928, pp. 545–547.

147 "I CAN FIND . . ." Dorothy Parker, "Re-Enter Miss Hurst, Followed by Mr. Tarkington," *New Yorker*, Jan. 28, 1928. Also in *The Portable Dorothy Parker* (New York: Viking, 1973), pp. 483–486.

147 BY THE FOURTH WEEK HRC, FH/96/2, FH to Constance Ballard, Feb, 7, 1928.

147 THE PUBLISHER HAD WRESTED HER BACK HRC, FH/199/3, JSD to William Briggs, Harper and Bros., Jan. 7, 1928.

147 "OUR FANNIE HURST . . ." Tess Slesinger, "The President's Father and Son," *NY Evening Post*, Jan. 14, 1928, p. 13.

148 "KNOWS AS WELL AS I DO . . ." "E. S.," Review, *Procession, New Statesman*, July 27, 1929, 33:500.

CHAPTER EIGHTEEN

PAGE

149 "RECREATE THE DEADLY, MADDENING MONOTONY . . ." Review, *Procession, NY Herald Tribune*, Feb. 24, 1929. Edward J. O'Brien gave "Hossie Frossie" one star in *Best Short Stories*.

149 "BEARCAT" HRC, FH/170/2, Ray Long to FH, Apr. 13, 1928.

149 "A LITTLE REFINING AND RESTRAINING ARTISTRY" Review, *Procession, NYT*, Jan. 27, 1929, 4:8:4, 16:2.

149 "SISSY" Hearst, *Cosmo* index-card files for FH, published Oct. 1928.

149–150 NAMED BERNARD HRC, FH/160/1, Bernard Knudsen to FH, Sept. 16, 1928. Also HRC, FH/177/1, Wilfred Mawson to FH, Feb. 8, 1929.

150 UPPED HER PRICE PER STORY Hearst, *Cosmo*, author index-card file, no. 1411.

150 GOOD STORY GONE WRONG Review, *Procession, NY Herald Tribune*, Feb. 24, 1929. The story, however, got two stars in *Best Short Stories*.

150 SILENT FILM RIGHTS TO "ROULETTE" HRC, FH/255/2, Larry Giffen of Alice Kauser agency to FH, Dec. 24, 1927.

150 EXCELLENT REVIEWS Film, scrapbook collection, Manuscript Collection 124, Richard Barthelmess Collection, Scrapbook 29 of 50, *The Wheel of Chance*, reviews of June and July 1928.

150 COLUMBIA PICTURES BOUGHT THE RIGHTS HRC, FH/100/2, Joseph P. Bickerton to FH, Mar. 16, 1928.

150 COLUMBIA HIRED FRANK CAPRA . . . QUIET ON THE SET Frank Capra, *The Name Above the Title* (1971; reprint, New York: Da Capo Press, 1997), pp. 450, 101.

150 SOUND ENGINEERS RECORDED THE TRACK Joseph McBride, *Frank Capra: The Catastrophe of Success* (New York: Touchstone, 1992), pp. 201–202.

150 THE NEW YORK OPENING Review, *The Younger Generation, Variety*, Mar. 20, 1929. See also McBride, *Frank Capra*, pp. 201–203.

150 LOIS WEBER OFFERED A HOLLOW APOLOGY HRC, FH/132/2, Lois Weber to FH, Apr. 22, 1929.

150 "SENTIMENTAL OIL . . ." Review, *Younger Generation, Variety*, Mar. 20, 1929.

151 "A PRETTY DULL EFFORT . . ." Review, *The Younger Generation, NY Post*, Mar. 12, 1929. See also Film, Manuscript Collection U-50, Jean Hersholt Collection, Scrapbook 8 of 25, reviews 1928–1931, *The Younger Generation*, pp. 97–124.

151 "ANOTHER ONE OF THOSE ULTRA SENTIMENTAL . . ." Review, *The Younger Generation, NY Evening Journal*, Mar. 12, 1929. See also Film, Manuscript Collection U-50, Jean Hersholt Collection, Scrapbook 8 of 25, reviews 1928–1931, *The Younger Generation*, pp. 97–124.

151 YET CAPRA'S BIOGRAPHER THOUGHT THE PICTURE McBride, *Frank Capra*, pp. 202–203.

151 "INJUDICIOUSLY AND SO WILLFULLY" HRC, FH Scrapbooks, review, *The Younger Generation, Boston Herald*, Apr. 22, 1929.

151 FANNIE WAS ECSTATIC See HRC, FH/102/4, Herbert Brenon–FH correspondence 1928–1930, all. Also HRC, FH/177/3, Elizabeth (Betty) Meehan–FH correspondence, 1928–1930.

151 "HIS INTELLECTUAL CURIOSITY . . ." FH, "An Author Is the Person That Wrote the Story," *Theatre* magazine, Aug. 1929, pp. 14, 66.

151 LOSE A DRAMATIC AMOUNT OF WEIGHT . . . BY PARTY NIGHT HRC, FH/177/3, Elizabeth Meehan to FH, June 10, 1929.

151 JULIA SAID ROSE WAS CONTRITE HRC, FH/104/2, Julia Brown to FH, undtd, 1929.

152 "I WORK ALL MORNING . . ." HRC, FH/104/2, FH to Julia Browne, May 8, 1929.

152 "A SERIES OF EXCLAMATION POINTS . . ."/ "WHAT COULD YOU DO . . ." HRC, FH/175/5, FH to Elisabeth Marbury, May 6, 1929.

152 "HOLLYWOOD, HOLLYWOODN'T" FH, "Hollywood, Hollywoodn't," *Redbook,* Oct. 1929, pp. 43–45, 161–163.

152 TEN BROADWAY FUGITIVES HRC, FH/175/5, FH to Elisabeth Marbury, May 1, 1929.

152 THE TALKIES, SHE PREDICTED FH, "Hollywood, Hollywoodn't," pp. 43–45, 161–163.

152 "BALM ON OLD WOUNDS"/ THE AUTHOR'S FUNDAMENTAL IDEA FH, "Author Is the Person," pp. 14, 66.

153 "SINGULARLY CONVINCING" Film, Scrapbook Collection, Audrey Chamberlin Scrapbook, No. 32 or 46, *Lummox,* pp. 34–37.

153 "NO PROMISE OF CUSTOMARY ENTERTAINMENT" Film, Scrapbook Collection, Audrey Chamberlin Scrapbook, No. 32 or 46, *Lummox,* pp. 34–37.

153 "A STEPCHILD"/ "I DON'T THINK I'VE EVER READ . . ." HRC, FH/177/3, Elizabeth Meehan to FH, Mar. 4, 1930; FH to Meehan, Mar. 8, 1930.

153 THE STORY PROMPTLY SOLD HRC, FH/255/2, contract between FH and First National Pictures Corp., dated June 4, 1928.

153 *THE PAINTED ANGEL* HRC, FH/176/1, Ned Marin, First National Studios, to FH, June 21, July 5 and 13, [1929].

153 THE FILM, RELEASED IN JANUARY 1930 HRC, FH/255/2, Contracts. See Mar. 2, 1928, FH with Tiffany-Stahl Productions and also June 4, 1929, with First National Productions. See also Review, *The Painted Angel, Variety,* Jan. 8, 1930.

153 *VARIETY* THOUGHT THE MOVIE Review, *The Painted Angel, Variety,* Jan. 8, 1930.

153 THE SOUND RIGHTS TO "HUMORESQUE" HRC, FH/112/3, via Ray Long, *Cosmo,* to FH, Jan. 23 and Feb. 8, 1929.

153 "MISS HURST . . . WROTE THIS ONE . . ." Review, *Back Pay, Variety,* Jan. 8, 1930.

153 "BY NO STRETCH OF THE IMAGINATION . . ." FH, "Author Is the Person," 1929, pp. 14, 66.

154 THE STUDIO RESPONDED HRC, FH/233/2, FH to John Considine, United Artists, Apr. 29, 1929.

154 FANNIE TURNED DOWN A MILLION DOLLARS HRC, FH/116/1, Robert H. Davis to FH, May 31, 1929.

154 "I CAN'T TELL . . ." HRC, FH/112/3, *Cosmo,* Ray Long, to FH, Mar. 25, 1929.

154 "HER USUAL DEEP PERCEPTION . . ." Isadora Bennett, Review, *Five and Ten, Bookman,* Dec. 1929, pp. 450–451.

154 "HERE IS EMOTION . . ." Alice Parsons Beal, Review, *Five and Ten, Nation,* Oct. 2, 1929, p. 358.

154 "PAGES OF IMPRESSIVE NARRATIVE . . ." Review, *Five and Ten, Saturday Review of Literature,* Dec. 28, 1929, p. 608.

155 "GRIM AS FATE . . ." HRC, FH/112/3, *Cosmo,* Ray Long, to FH, Aug. 19, 1929.

155 "IN A TRAGIC . . ." *Anat,* p. 315.

155 IN FANNIE'S WORDS, AN EMPTY COCOON *Anat,* p. 314.

155   "THE SERIES OF HIDEOUS EXPERIENCES" . . . PAMPERING HER MOTHER/ "I HAVE LIVED AROUND YOU . . ." RHC, FH/104/2, Julia Browne to FH, undtd, 1929; FH to Browne, Apr. 12, May 8, May 9, 1929.

156   "I AM REALLY HOPEFUL . . ." HRC, FH/104/2, FH to Julia Browne, May 14, 1929.

156   "HIGH-VOLTAGE TEMPERAMENT"/ "NO DOUBT PSYCHIATRY COULD DETECT . . ." *Anat,* p. 316.

156   "THESE RIDICULOUS MOMENTS . . ." *Anat,* p. 89.

157   FANNIE OFTEN WONDERED IF HER SUCCESS *Anat,* p. 316.

157   SHE DIED OF A CEREBRAL HEMORRHAGE Bran, Box 11C, Life Extension Institute health summaries, No. 1, FH reports in medical examination form that her mother died of a cerebral hemorrhage at age sixty-eight and her father of a kidney tumor at age seventy-two. New Mt. Sinai Cemetery records list father's cause of death as "hypernathonia"[*sic*] and mother's as myocarditis.

157   LOIS TOENSFELDT THOUGHT FANNIE HAD RISEN NOBLY HRC, FH/230/1, Lois Toensfeldt to FH, Oct. 7, 1929.

157   GRIEVING, FANNIE TOLD LOIS HRC, FH/230/1, FH to Lois Toensfeldt, Jan. 15, 1930.

157   TO BOB DAVIS, SHE SAID THAT LIFE HRC, FH/116/1, FH to Robert H. Davis, Nov. 1, 1929.

157   "THE CELESTIAL CHOIR . . ." HRC, FH/120/1, Robert H. Davis to FH [misfiled under Norman Douglas], Nov. 18, 1929.

157   GRANT OVERTON GOT HER TO AGREE HRC, FH/255/2, Contracts, FH and Crowell Publishing Co., *The Country Home,* Nov. 11, 1929.

157   PAUL PALMER . . . ENGAGED HER HRC, FH/246/2, Paul Palmer, Sunday editor, *NY World,* to FH, Sept. 18, 1929.

157   OTHER CONTRIBUTIONS Bertrand Russell et al., *Divorce* (New York: John Day, [1930?]).

158   YOUNG DOROTHY WEST "Contest Awards," *Opportunity,* Vol. 4, No. 41, May 1926, pp. 156–157. Fannie attended the 1926 awards dinner but did not judge the competition.

158   WEST WAS STAYING AT ZORA'S HRC, FH/241/5, Dorothy West to FH, Nov. 16, 1929.

158   THE CONTRACT PROHIBITED HER HRC, FH/172/3, see 1929–1930 entries in McClure's Syndicate file.

158   "A CHICKEN-HEARTED JELLY FISH" HRC, FH/99/2, FH to John Wheeler, Bell Syndicate, Nov. 4, 1929.

158   A LUCRATIVE CONTRACT HRC, FH/255/2, Contracts, FH with King Features Syndicate, Nov. 15, 1929.

158   "YOU WILL BE FORTY . . ." HRC, FH/244/4, Stef to FH, May 23, 1929.

CHAPTER NINETEEN

PAGE

161   "OH BETTY . . ." HRC, FH/177/3, FH to Betty Meehan, Feb. 21, 1931.

161   "THIRST FOR THE SVELTE LINE . . ."/ "GOOD LORD HOW . . ."/ "CROSS THE SUNLIGHT TWICE . . ." HRC, FH/116/1, Robert H. Davis to FH, Jan. 15, 1931, June 5, 1930, Sept. 23, 1932.

161   WHEN SHE REALIZED HOW CLOSE HRC, FH/207/1, to Emanie Sachs, Jan. 23, 1930; Walter Sachs to FH, Feb. 10, 1930; FH to Sachs, Feb. 13, 1930.

162 SCHMIDT HAPPENED TO BE HRC, FH/224/1, Dr. Henry James Spencer to FH, Aug. 11, 1930.

162 "MISER LOVER" HRC, Scrapbooks, *Back Streets,* 1931–32, Rebecca West, Review, *Back Street, London Daily Telegraph,* Feb. 20, 1931.

163 "GORGEOUS" HRC, FH/112/3, Ray Long, *Cosmo,* to FH, Aug. 11, 1930.

163 BACK STREETS—PLURAL HRC, FH/170/2, Ray Long to FH, May and June letters, 1930.

163 "AS A PICKER OF SERIALS . . ." HRC, FH/112/3, FH to Ray Long, Feb. 18, 1931.

163 LURED FANNIE TO SIGN ON HRC, FH/202/5, Farrar Rinehart Publishers, copy of original agreement for publication on *Back Street* dated Sept. 23, 1930, between Cosmopolitan Book Corp. and FH.

163 "PUBLICATION ON A SCALE . . ." HRC, FH/112/3, FH to Sam Smith, Cosmopolitan Books, Mar. 7, 1931.

163 "LOCAL GIRL" HRC, FH/113/1, FH to *Country Home,* Oct. 23, 1930.

163 BEST-SELLER FIGURES James Henry Burke and Alice Payne Hackett, *Eighty Years of Best Sellers, 1895–1975* (New York: Bowker, 1977), p. 111.

163 FORTY-FIVE THOUSAND BOOKS HRC, FH/112/3, Sam Smith to FH, Mar. 11, 1931.

164 "NIGHTMARE . . ." "Priestley Arrives, City a 'Nightmare,' " *NYT,* Feb. 19, 1931, 20:1.

164 "COURT-MARTIALED BY LAUGHTER . . ." "Court-Martial by Laughter of J. B. Priestley for 'Half-Baked' Gibes Urged by Miss Hurst," *NYT,* Feb. 21, 1931, 13:3.

164 "FEW LITTLE JOKES . . ." HRC, FH/199/4, FH to J. B. Priestley, Oct. 19, 1942; Priestley to FH, Nov. 28, 1942.

164 "ALL TOO THRILLING . . ." HRC, FH/177/3, FH to Betty Meehan, Feb. 21, 1931.

164 "SHE IS NAIVELY UNAWARE . . ." HRC, Scrapbooks, *Back Street,* 1931, Rebecca West, Review, *Back Street, London Daily Telegraph,* Feb. 20, 1931.

164 WEST'S WILLINGNESS TO WRAP HER COMPLIMENTS NYPL-Berg, FH to Carl Van Vechten, Feb. 3, 1937.

164 "*BACK STREET* HAS LEFT ME . . ." HRC, FH/97/1, *Back Street,* Helen L. Bestercey to FH, Feb. 18, 1931.

164 "I WAS WRUNG . . ." HRC, FH/97/1, *Back Street,* Lisa Liven [Given?] to FH, Feb. 18, 1931.

164 "I HAVE EATEN . . ." HRC, FH/97/1, *Back Street,* Sheila Doriesthorpe to FH, Mar. 30, 1931.

164 "FANNIE HURST, GENIUS" HRC, FH/97/1, *Back Street,* Honore Barnett to FH, Mar. 10, 1931.

164 ON VALENTINE'S DAY, 1931 Film, Universal Pictures, Inc., Library Properties, Vol. 3, Files 5800–5999, 5987, *Back Street,* purchased Feb. 14, 1931, price: $35,000.

165 SHE SIGNED THAT CONTRACT HRC, FH/200/3, Contract, FH and RKO, Apr. 17, 1931.

165 "WITH UNABATED ZEAL"/ THE FIRST DRAFT HRC, FH/200/3, RKO Pictures, correspondence, William LeBaron and FH, Apr. 17 to May 12, 1931.

165 SINCE FANNIE ANNOUNCED FH, "An Author Is the Person That Wrote the Story," *Theatre* magazine, Aug. 1929, pp. 14, 66.

165 "HIGHLY SPECIAL TECHNIQUE . . ." HRC, FH/128/2, FH to William Beaton, *Film Spectator,* May 2, 1931.

165 DASH INTO THE BUSHES Int, Author with Ethel Rabinowitz Amatneek (FH's secretary, 1932–1936), Sept. 27, 1997.

166 "I WAS JEALOUS OF HIM . . ." *Anat,* p. 254.

166 RETREAT IN PRIVACY Dart, Stef correspondence, Box 111, Addendum Box, Gretchen-Wright, FH correspondence, see file, June 4–20, 1931.

166 THE PLAN FELL APART HRC, FH/112/3, FH to Ray Long, *Cosmo,* May 20, 1931.

166 DESTROY Dart, Stef correspondence, Box 111, Addendum Box, Gretchen-Wright, FH correspondence, see file, June 4–20, 1931.

166 KEEP THEM SEPARATE The box containing these secret letters from Fannie did not accompany his personal papers when he gave them to Dartmouth College. They were found in an attic in the Vermont farm he eventually bought with the woman he married in 1939. A subsequent owner offered the box for sale, and Dartmouth bought it.

166 "DEAREST, DEAR . . ." / "MY UNIVERSE IS SHOT . . ." Dart, Stef correspondence, Box 111, Addendum Box, Gretchen-Wright, FH correspondence, FH to Stef, June 1, 1931.

167 TO VISIT ELISABETH MARBURY Zora Neale Hurston, *Hurston: Folklore, Memoirs, and Other Writings* (New York: Library of America, 1995), p. 968.

167 UNDERSTAND YOU WILL BE MOTORING . . . Dart, Stef correspondence, Box 111, Addendum Box, Gretchen-Wright, FH correspondence, Nola Erikson to FH, June 6, 1931.

167 SHOULD KEEP HIM IN MIND Dart, Stef correspondence, Box 111, Addendum Box, Gretchen-Wright, FH correspondence, Stef to FH, June 6, 1931.

167 "ONE OF HER BIZARRE FROCKS . . ." FH, "Zora Hurston: A Personality Sketch," *Library Gazette,* Yale University, No. 35, 1961, p. 20.

167 BY TUESDAY AFTERNOON Dart, Stef correspondence, Box 111, Addendum Box, Gretchen-Wright, FH correspondence, cb1, FH to Stef, June 9, 1931.

167 ZORA ALSO MEMORIALIZED THAT TRIP Zora Neale Hurston, "Fannie Hurst by Her Ex-Amanuensis," *Saturday Review,* Oct. 9, 1937, pp. 15–16.

168 WHAT ZORA REMEMBERED Dart, Stef correspondence, Box 111, Addendum Box, Gretchen-Wright, FH correspondence, FH to Stef, June 7–16, 1931.

169 ZORA'S REPETITION OF THE STORY Zora Neale Hurston, *Dust Tracks on a Road* (New York: J. B. Lippincott, 1942), pp. 193–197.

169 "HAVE SEEN NO ONE . . ."/ "TRY DRAINING . . ."/ "DEPENDING ON THE OUTCOME . . ." Dart, Stef correspondence, Box 111, Addendum Box, Gretchen-Wright, FH correspondence, FH to Stef, June 16, 19, 1931.

169 EIGHT-WEEK CAMPER TRIP HRC, FH/194/1, Ruth Bryan Owen–FH correspondence, Feb.–June 1931.

169 "AN INNOCUOUS LITTLE VISIT . . ." HRC, FH/194/1, FH to Minne Oppenheimer, Oct. 6, 1931.

169 HOW SYMBOLIC "FH in Escape," *NYT,* July 27, 1931, 18:2.

169 "THE WHOLE WORLD SEEMS . . ." HRC, FH/194/1, Ruth Bryan Owen to FH, Oct. 19, 1931.

169–170 "STRENUOUS . . . INVASION . . ." HRC, FH/194/1, FH to Minne Oppenheimer, Oct. 6, 1931.

170 "MUCH SQUALOR . . ." "FH Finds Youth Rules in Russia," *NYT,* Aug. 27, 1931, 9:3.

170 TWO-THOUSAND-DOLLAR FEE HRC, FH/255/2, Contracts, FH with Curtis Publishing Co., Philadelphia, Sept. 22, 1931. See also FH, "Russian Goose Hangs High," *Saturday Evening Post,* Nov. 7, 1931, pp. 25 ff.

170 A THOUSAND EMPTY STOMACHS FH, "Russian Goose Hangs High."

170 RETURN JOURNEY TO HIS BIRTHPLACE NatArch, State Dept. Files, Decimal File 861.5017, Division of Western European Affairs, Despatch No. 940, John Ball Osborne, U.S. Consul General, Stockholm, "Conditions in Soviet Russia," Aug. 22, 1931, filed Sept. 5, 1931.

170 JACK DEMANDED A MILLION DOLLARS Int, Author with Evelyn Nef, Jan. 16, 1996.

170 "ALIMONY LEECHES" FH, "Alimony Leeches," *American Magazine,* Mar. 21, 1932.

170 "ONLY THE MOST SUBTLE . . ." *Anat,* pp. 271, 264.

171 "SYMPHONY OF SEVEN MILLION" HRC, FH/200/3, FH–RKO correspondence, David O. Selznick and various, Dec. 1931–Mar. 1932.

171 "AS A STORY-TELLER . . ." Harry Salpeter, "Fannie Hurst: Sob-Sister of American Fiction." *Bookman,* Aug. 1931, p. 613.

CHAPTER TWENTY

PAGE

172 KING FEATURES HAD LET HER CONTRACT LAPSE HRC, FH/159/3, FH to J. V. Connolly, King Features, Oct. 31, 1932, contract covered the calendar years 1930–1932.

172 "FANNIE HURST OPENS DRIVE . . ." "Women Ask Disarmament," *NYT,* Nov. 5, 1931, 23:4.

172 "STAGE CENSOR FAILS . . ." Mar. 2, 1931, 21:1.

172 "AIDED BY FANNIE HURST" Feb. 23, 1931, 20:2.

172 "MISS HURST AIDS PACIFISTS" Apr. 22, 1930, 12:3.

172 "NOTED WRITERS AID TEXTILE STRIKERS" Aug. 19, 1929, 39:1.

172 "MOST PUBLICIZED . . ." Harry Salpeter, "Fannie Hurst: Sob-Sister of American Fiction," *Bookman,* Aug. 1931, pp. 613–614.

173 DISCREET BUT GENEROUS LOANS HRC, friends often called on FH for loans, though many of these requests came after the Depression. Among the recipients of funds were Stef, John and Helen Erskine, Murray Levin, Albert Richter-Rothschild, Charles Hanson Towne, Edward Jackson, Mabel Search, Louis Mann, and Zora Neale Hurston.

173 "MOST OF THE TIME . . ." HRC, FH/161/1, FH to Blanche Knopf, Nov. 29, 1930.

173 "YOU DIDN'T MENTION THE DEPRESSION . . ." HRC, FH/230/1, Lois Toensfeldt to FH, Nov. 20, 1932.

173 SAMUEL SEABURY HEARINGS See Don Congdon, ed. *The Thirties: A Time to Remember* (New York: Simon & Schuster, 1962), pp. 189–201.

173 HER OWN NEWSPAPER HEADLINES "Fannie Hurst, Spectator at Probe Hearings, Indicts Public Indifference," *NY Journal-American,* Apr. 1, 1932; "Fannie Hurst . . ." *NY Telegram,* Mar. 31, 1932.

173 ALTERING A TRIAL TRANSCRIPT Editorial, "The Case of Magistrate Norris," *NYT,* June 26, 1931, 22:3–4; case details: May 20, 1931, 1:3; June 24, 1931, 1:6; June 25, 1931, 1:4.

173 "IF AT ANY TIME . . ."/ SHE POURED TEA/ LETTER OF SUPPORT HRC, FH/191/3, FH to Judge Jean Norris, Feb. 22, 1928; Mar. 25, Dec. 12, Dec. 13, 1930; Jan. 6, Mar. 10, Nov. 28, 1931.

173 FANNIE'S EDITOR AT THE TIME HRC, FH/138/1, William Briggs, Harper & Bros., to FH, Mar. 17, 1932; FH/191/3, FH to Judge Jean Norris, Mar. 18, 1932.

173 SO DID THE RELATIONSHIP HRC, FH/138/1, nothing in file after 1932 except two polite refusals in July and August 1936.

174 WHEN THEODORE DREISER ASKED HER/ "I FEAR . . ." Penn, Theodore Dreiser Collection, Dreiser to FH, Jan. 28 and Feb. 4, 1932; FH to Dreiser, Feb. 8, 1932.

175 RUTH'S AMBITION HRC, FH/194/1, FH to Ruth Bryan Owen, May 11, 1932.

175 "WITH ALL THAT IMPLIES . . ."/ "I WOULD BE SO GRATEFUL . . ."/ "I WANT YOUR MIGHTY ARM . . ."/ "THE PLACING TOGETHER . . ." HRC, FH/194/1, Ruth Bryan Owen to FH, Jan. 13, May 12, Sept. 22, 1928.

175 WOMEN IN THE SEVENTY-FIRST CONGRESS The other women representatives were Florence Prag Kahn (R.-Calif.), Mary Teresa Norton (D.-N.J.), Edith Nourse Rogers (R.-Mass.), Katherine Langley (R.-Ky.), Pearl Peden Oldfield (D.-Ark.), Ruth Hanna McCormick (R.-Ill.), and Ruth Baker Pratt (R.-N.Y.).

175 HAD REVOKED RUTH'S CITIZENSHIP Sarah P. Vickers, "The Life of Ruth Bryan Owen: Florida's First Congresswoman and America's First Woman Diplomat" (Diss., Florida State University, 1994), pp. 95–99.

175 "FIRST THE GOVERNMENT TAKES AWAY . . ." HRC, FH/194/1, Ruth Bryan Owen to FH, Dec. 11, 1928.

176 "TO LIFT A LOUD VOICE . . ." HRC, FH to Ruth Bryan Owen, Nov. 30, 1928.

176 "STIR UP . . ."/ "ARM THEM . . ."/ "AT WHICH TIME . . ." HRC, FH/194/1, Ruth Bryan Owen to FH, Jan. 6, Mar. 2, July 19, 1929.

176 A FEW VERY SMALL FAVORS HRC, FH/194/1, Ruth Bryan Owen–FH correspondence, May 16, July 19, Sept. 6, 1929; Mar. 4, Mar. 5, 1930.

176 "COOK UP SOME KIND OF SYNCHRONIZATION . . ." HRC, FH/194/1, Ruth Bryan Owen–FH correspondence, Sept. 22–23, 1930.

176 IN LONDON IN THE SUMMER OF 1930 Bran, FH appt-bks, Box 1, 1930. Also, Stef, *Discovery: The Autobiography of Vilhjalmur Stefansson* (New York: McGraw-Hill, 1964), p. 272.

176 "WHICH ARE THE 5 PER CENT VEGETABLES . . ." HRC, FH/194/1, Ruth Bryan Owen to FH, May 9, 1931.

176 "INDISCREET DIET UNDERMINES HEALTH" HRC, FH/194/1, FH to Ruth Bryan Owen, May 15, 1931.

176 "FOR ANY CLARION CALLS . . ." HRC, FH/194/1, Ruth Bryan Owen to FH, Oct. 3, 1931.

176 "I'VE JUST BEEN WALLOWING . . ." HRC, FH/194/1, FH to Ruth Bryan Owen, Nov. 9, 1931.

177 "I THINK YOU CAN PROBABLY GIVE ME . . ." HRC, FH/105/1, Eleanor Roosevelt to FH, Apr. 23, 1931.

177 LUNCH WITH MRS. ROOSEVELT/ "HOME FOR DINNER . . ." HRC, FH/205/1, Eleanor Roosevelt to FH, Sept. 1, 1931, invitation to lunch Sept. 17, 1931, at 39 East Sixty-fifth St.

177 ROOSEVELT HIMSELF HRC, FH/205/5, Marguerite LeHand to FH, Nov. 18, 1931.

177 THEY STOPPED FOR LUNCH HRC, FH/205/1, FH to Eleanor Roosevelt, Nov. 9, 1931.

177 "WHY NOT GO LOOK AGAIN?"/ JACQUES'S EMERGENCY APPENDECTOMY HRC, FH/205/5, FDR to FH, Nov. 16, Dec. 18, 1931.

177 FANNIE INVITED HRC, FH/205/1, Eleanor Roosevelt's secretary to FH, Dec. 4, 1931, accepting invitation for Dec. 10, 1931. See also HRC, FH/131/1–5, Daniel

Frohman to FH, Dec. 21, 1931, and Bran, Box 1, Ledgers, etc., appt-bk of 1931, entries for Dec. 10, 21, 1931.

177   "COULD HAVE HEARD . . ." HRC, FH/131/1–5, Daniel Frohman to FH, Dec. 21, 1931.

177   FANNIE'S UNFAILING FRIENDSHIP Channing Pollock, *Harvest of My Years: An Autobiography* (Indianapolis, New York: Bobbs-Merrill, 1943), pp. 356–359.

177   "THIS IS JUST TO SAY . . ." HRC, FH/205/5, FH to FDR, July 1, 1932.

177   BOTH THE GOVERNOR AND MRS. ROOSEVELT HRC, FH/205/1, Eleanor Roosevelt to FH, July 15, 1932. See also FH/205/5, FDR to FH, Aug. 8, 1932.

178   "TOO IMPORTANT, TOO PRECIOUS . . ." HRC, FH/194/1, FH to Ruth Bryan Owen, undtd, 1932.

178   "ROOSEVELT HAS INTIMATED . . ." HRC, FH/194/1, Ruth Bryan Owen to FH, July 3, 1932.

178   "I WONDER IF YOU WILL DO . . ." HRC, FH/205/1, Eleanor Roosevelt to FH, Sept. 10, 1932.

178   IT ELICITED LAVISH GRATITUDE HRC, FH/205/1, Eleanor Roosevelt to FH, Nov. 25, 1932. See also FH/205/5, FDR to FH, Nov. 18, 1932.

178   FANNIE ALSO GOT WIDE COVERAGE "Roosevelt's Lead in Polls Analyzed," *NYT,* Oct. 17, 1932, 2:2.

178   " 'JUST PEOPLE' . . ." HRC, NY Journal-American morgue, "Roosevelts Free of Formality or Sham," Says Fannie Hurst, *NY Journal-American,* Oct. 3, 1932.

178   MOORE ROLLED HER EYES Bonnie Costello et al., *The Selected Letters of Marianne Moore* (New York: Knopf, 1997), p. 283, citing letter to Kenneth Burke, philosopher and critic, Nov. 30, 1932.

178–179   "TEMPORARY MAKESHIFT . . ."/ THE WEEK'S FOOD AND RENT "Idle Women See Their Relics Sold," *NYT,* Nov. 30, 1932, 21:6.

179   "COUPLED WITH THE NAME R.B.O."/ "GOING TO TAKE SOMETHING . . ."/ RUTH WAS AT THE HEARST ESTATE/ ASKED FANNIE TO EASE HER APPROACH HRC, FH/194/1, Ruth Bryan Owen to FH, Oct. 31, Nov. 19, 1932.

179   LUNCH THE NEXT WEEK Bran, Box 1, Ledgers, appt-bks, etc., 1932, entry for Dec. 6, 1932.

179   "ENCOURAGING INDICATIONS . . ."/ "HURRAH . . ." HRC, FH/194/1, Ruth Bryan Owen to FH, Dec. 9, 1932.

179   "INDISPUTABLY ACCURATE . . ." HRC, FH/246/1, William E. Woodward to FH, Dec. 18, 1932.

180   GOOD PORTENT . . . HRC, FH/194/1, cbl, FH to Ruth Bryan Owen, Jan. 17, 1933.

180   HE ADVISED FANNIE TO PUT TOGETHER HRC, FH/118/1, Democratic Party, James A. Farley to FH, Jan. 12, 1933; FH to Farley, Jan. 10, 1933.

180   TRIBUTE DINNER/ "THIS SHIFTING WORLD" FH to Mrs. Frank A. Vanderlip, Jan. 26 and 31, 1933, private collection.

180   VERY SELECT GUEST LIST Bran, Box 1, Ledgers, appt-bks, 1933, entry for Jan. 6, 1933.

180   "POSSIBLY HELP A LITTLE" Dart, Stef correspondence, Box 111, Addendum Box, Gretchen-Wright, FH correspondence, cbl, Stef to Ruth Bryan Owen, Feb. 9, 1933.

180   "REST ROOMS" . . . FOR UNEMPLOYED GIRLS HRC, FH/93/5, Ann Anderson to FH, Jan. 8, 1932.

180–181 "YOU WILL NOT BE ASKED . . ."/ "YOU HAVE BEEN A VERY DEAR FRIEND . . ." HRC, FH/205/1, Eleanor Roosevelt to FH, Dec. 29, 1932, and June 19, 1933.

181 FANNIE DID LITTLE FOR THE PROJECT HRC, FH/205/3, Eleanor Roosevelt Committee for Rest Rooms for Unemployed Girls, Jan.–May 1933.

181 "FINANCIALLY NOT IN THE RUNNING" HRC, FH/205/3, Eleanor Roosevelt Committee for Rest Rooms for Unemployed Girls, FH to Virginia Potter, Dec. 28, 1933.

181 YEZIERSKA, SADLY, HAD FALLEN VICTIM HRC, FH/248/1, Anzia Yezierska–FH correspondence, Jan. 9, 11, 13, 1933.

181 FANNIE WROTE LETTERS . . . ON YEZIERSKA'S BEHALF Yale, Za, William Lyon Phelps correspondence, FH to Dr. William Lyon Phelps, Yale University, Jan. 19, 1933.

181 "PLEASE BURN ALL THE CANDLES . . ." HRC, FH/194/1, Ruth Bryan Owen to FH, Mar. 21, 1933.

181 SHE APPEALED TO HIM ONCE AGAIN HRC, FH/118/1, Democratic Party, FH to James A. Farley, Feb. 23, 1933.

181 "BUT I KNOW THAT THE GOVERNOR . . ." HRC, FH/118/1, Democratic Party, James A. Farley to FH, Feb. 17, 1933.

181 RUTH GOT FANNIE AN EXTRA TICKET HRC, FH/194/1, Ruth Bryan Owen to FH, Feb. 16, 1933.

181 "TO PERFORM ANY SERVICES . . ." HRC, FH/205/1, FH to Eleanor Roosevelt, Mar. 8, 1933.

181 LUNCH WITH THE FIRST LADY Bran, Box 1, Ledgers, appt-bks, 1933, entry for Mar. 15, 1933.

181 MARGINALLY INVOLVED WITH THE TRIBUTE DINNER HRC, FH/196/3, FH to Frances Perkins, Mar. 21, 1933.

182 "I DO NOT KNOW THE TECHNIQUE . . ." HRC, FH/194/1, FH to Ruth Bryan Owen, Apr. 11, 1933.

182 URGE RECONSIDERATION . . . Dart, Stef correspondence, Box 111, Addendum Box, Gretchen-Wright, FH correspondence, FH to Stef, May 3, 1933.

182 YOUR TELEGRAM HAS WESTERN UNION'S LABEL . . . Dart, Stef correspondence, Box 111, Addendum Box, Gretchen-Wright, FH correspondence, FH to Stef, May 3, 1933.

182 A SUSPICIOUSLY WELL-TIMED ARTICLE Col. Edward Mandell House, "Women in Washington?" *Cosmo,* Vol. 94, No. 5, May 1933, pp. 34–35, 122.

182 "SHE IS AN OUTSTANDING FIGURE . . ." WashArch, "Col. E. M. House Calls FH '09 Outstanding Figure in United States," *Alumni Bulletin,* June 1933, p. 6.

182 "YOU ARE THE GODMOTHER . . ." Yale, Sterling, Col. E. M. House Papers, Box 63A, Folder 2041; FH to House, Apr. 8, 1933; House to FH, Apr. 10, 1933.

182 THE FIRST LADY INVITED HER TO LUNCH HRC, FH/205/5, Eleanor Roosevelt to FH, May 14, 1933.

182–183 FANNIE SENT OCCASIONAL NOTES/ A RETURN VISIT TO HYDE PARK HRC, FH/205/1, FH to Eleanor Roosevelt, Eleanor Roosevelt to FH, June 17 and Oct. 17, 1933.

183 "HIGH-WATER EXPERIENCE" HRC, FH/205/5, FH to Eleanor Roosevelt, Dec. 7, 1933.

183 "I AM MORE THAN EVER CONVINCED . . ." HRC, FH/132/3, FH to Rosamond Pinchot Gaston, Dec. 7, 1933.

183 THE PET NAME CIRCE HRC, FH/149/4, FH–Louis McHenry Howe correspondence.

CHAPTER TWENTY-ONE

PAGE

184 EXPRESSLY FOR THE SCREEN HRC, FH/200/3, William LeBaron–FH correspondence, Apr.–Sept. 1931.

184 "CHEAP POPPYCOCK" HRC, FH/200/3, FH to David O. Selznick, Dec. 29, 1931.

184 WHEN VERA GORDON HRC, FH/134/4, Vera Gordon to FH, Jan. 3, 1932; FH to Gordon, Jan. 5, 1932.

184 "A STORY OF HUMAN BEINGS . . ." HRC, FH/200/3, FH to David O. Selznick, Dec. 29, 1932.

184 AVOID THOSE PITFALLS HRC, FH/200/3, David O. Selznick to FH, Jan. 16, 1932.

184 "IT HAS PRECISELY THE SAME PATTERN . . ." Review, *Symphony of Six Million, Variety,* Apr. 19, 1932.

185 IN THE OPINION OF RKO'S SALES PROMOTION MANAGER HRC, FH/200/3, Kenneth Hallam, Sales Promotion Manager, RKO, to FH, Mar. 29, 1932.

185 "DO YOU AGREE . . ." HRC, FH/235/1, FH to Charles Beahan, Universal Studios, July 25, 1932.

185 JOHN ADAMS HRC, FH/200/3, FH–RKO correspondence, June 11, 1932, and subsequent. See also, FH/126/1, John Fall, *Contemporary American Authors,* to FH, June 18, 1939; FH to J. Fall, June 20, 1939.

185 MUCH TO HER DISTRESS HRC, FH/138/1, FH to William Briggs, Harper & Bros., June 11, 1932.

185 BORE SO LITTLE SEMBLANCE HRC, FH/110/4, FH to Walter Wanger, Columbia Pictures, June 7, 1932.

185 "LADYSHIP" HRC, FH/110/4, FH to Walter Wanger, June 1, 3, 4, 14, 1932.

185 PARAMOUNT HIRED HER Colum, Curtis Brown Collection, J. H. Karp, Paramount Publix Corp., to FH, contract, Sept. 12, 1932.

185 AMERICA'S MOST POPULAR SONGSTRESS Film, Paramount Script files, *Hello, Everybody!*

185 POOREST BOX-OFFICE SHOWING Jay Robert Nash and Stanley Ralph Ross, *The Motion Picture Guide* (Chicago: Cinebooks, 1986), Vol. H–K, 1927–1983, p. 1196.

185 "WHILE COMMERCE HAD . . ." Review, *Hello, Everybody! Variety,* Jan. 31, 1933.

186 "A TEAR-JERKER . . ."/ "ALL THE VARIEGATED HIGHLIGHTS . . ." Review, *Back Street, Variety,* Aug. 30, 1932.

186 "PRIDE AND GRATIFICATION . . ." HRC, FH/235/1, FH to Charles Beahan, Universal Studios, July 25, 1932.

186 THEODORE DREISER BECAME CONVINCED See W. A. Swanberg, *Dreiser* (New York: Scriber's, 1965), pp. 433–434, citing Theodore Dreiser to Carl Laemmle, Jr., Aug. 23, 1935.

186 NOT BECAUSE DREISER WAS ACCUSING HER Colum, Curtis Brown Collection, Benjamin Stern, Stern and Rubens, to FH, Jan. 17, 1935.

186 FIRING OFF AN ANGRY LETTER Penn, Theodore Dreiser Collection, Dreiser to Carl Laemmle, Jr., Aug. 23, 1935.

186 "ATTEMPT AT NONCHALANCE . . ." Penn, Theodore Dreiser Collection, Dreiser to Mr. Cochrane, Universal, Oct. 1, 1935.

187 "THE WHITE HOPE . . ."/ "THAT HATEFUL HYENA" Penn, FH to Theodore Dreiser, undtd [1917]; Bran, Box 8A, Folder 3, diaries, 1937, entry for Jan. 3, 1937.

187 "CREED, RACE MEAN NOTHING . . ." HRC, FH, Scrapbooks, 1931, undtd, undocumented article, c. 1931.

187 "YOU HAVE BEEN SUCH . . ." HRC, FH/192/4, Charles S. Johnson, ed., *Opportunity,* to
FH, Jan. 18, 1928.

187 "YOU HAVE INSPIRED . . ." HRC, FH/199/5, Ivy Bailey, *The American Public Opinion,*
to FH, Feb. 14, 1940.

187 "YOU, MISS HURST . . ." HRC, FH/189/1, James Hubert, National Urban League, to
FH, May 11, 1942.

187 "TABOO-TEA . . ." Yale, Za, FH to Carl Van Vechten, May 7, 1926.

187 FBI HAD BEEN KEEPING TABS U.S. Dept. of Justice, FBI, File 77-52888, FH, with cross
reference to the file of JSD. Though numerous committee- and dinner-committee
lists on which the name of FH appears are cited as Communist fronts, these did
not appear to be the cause for particular alarm. FH passed the FBI investigation
leading to her confirmation as an official U.S. delegate to the Fifth World Health
Assembly in Geneva in 1952, while the House Committee on Un-American Activities, cited repeatedly in the file, was highly active.

187–188 "SOMETHING I DON'T PARTICULARLY THINK ABOUT" Floyd Calvin, "No Racial
Likes or Dislikes," unidentified publication, Mar. 16 [no year but FH mentions
having just read Claude McKay's *Home to Harlem,* which was released in 1928]
HRC, FH, Scrapbooks, *Five and Ten* and *A President Is Born* [1928–29].

188 "NEEDS YOU SO! . . ." HRC, FH/189/3, FH Holiday Season 1927 appeal letter for Na-
tional Health Circle for Colored People. For a brief bio of Belle Davis, see Joseph
J. Boris, ed., *Who's Who in Colored America* (New York: Who's Who in Colored
America Corp., 1928–29), p. 191.

188 "LANGUID-MINDED" HRC, FH/246/2, Devere Allen to FH, Apr. 25, 1927.

188 EVERY BIT AS ILL-CONSIDERED HRC, FH/189/3, FH Holiday Season 1927 appeal letter for National Health Circle for Colored People.

188 "UNSUSPECTED QUALITIES . . ." HRC, FH/246/2, Devere Allen to FH, Apr. 25, 1927.

188–189 "EXAGGERATED RACE CONSCIOUSNESS . . ." HRC, FH/246/2, FH to Devere
Allen, June 13, 1927.

189 THE EXECUTIVE AND LITERARY EDITOR Zora Neale Hurston, *Hurston: Folklore, Memoirs, and Other Writings* (New York: Library of America, 1995), pp. 826–829.
"How It Feels to Be Colored Me" was published in 1928.

189 A PUBLIC STATEMENT ON BEHALF HRC, FH/211/2, Langston Hughes to FH, Oct. 31,
1933.

189 "I FEEL THAT NOT ONLY . . ." HRC, FH/211/2, FH to Langston Hughes, Nov. 17,
1933.

189 "FULL AND FRANK"/ THE LIST OF REFERENCES/ "TALENTED AND PECULIARLY CAPA-
BLE . . ." HRC, FH/152/2, Henry Allen Moe, John Simon Guggenheim Memorial
Foundation, to FH, Nov. 29, 1933; FH to Moe, Dec. 2, 1933 (J. S. Guggenheim
Memorial Foundation Archives).

189 ZORA TOLD FANNIE Bran, Box 3B, Personal Correspondence, Zora Neale Hurston,
Sanford, FL to FH, undtd [Dec. 1933 or Jan. 1934]: "Thanks for even consider-
ing writing the introduction [to *Jonah's Gourd Vine*] and the fine letter to the
Guggenheim Foundation. I loved it."

189 ZORA WAS NOT AWARDED John Simon Guggenheim Memorial Foundation, see Zora
Neale Hurston application file, 1933–34, including reference letters of Drs. Ruth

Benedict and Franz Boas, Fannie Hurst, Max Eastman, and Carl Van Vechten. Benedict (Nov. 15, 1933) said she did not think Zora could present conclusions on the origin of black culture, which she had set out as her objective; she also thought Zora would be able to find more appropriate support than the Guggenheim Foundation. Boas said he did not think Zora was of the right caliber for such a fellowship, nor did he think she could come back with significant enough results in West Africa to warrant the financial outlay.

190 "WITH GUSTO AND PLEASURE" Bran, Personal Correspondence, Box 3B, Zora Neale Hurston to FH, Dec. 7, 1933.

190 FANNIE WROTE TO LIPPINCOTT Bran, Correspondence with Publishers, see full file, FH–J. B. Lippincott, Jan. 9–Oct. 19, 1934.

190 "HERE IN THIS WORK . . ."/ ON THE ROAD TOGETHER AGAIN Bran, Personal Correspondence, Box 3B, FH to Zora Neale Hurston, Feb. 14, 1934.

190 "BRILLIANTLY FACILE SPADE" The word *spade* entered the language in 1931 as a derogatory slang for "a Negro, especially a very dark-skinned Negro." Harold Wentworth and Stuart Berg Flexner, eds., *Dictionary of American Slang,* 2d suppl. ed. (New York: Thomas Y. Crowell, 1975), p. 505.

190 NAACP'S TWENTY-FIFTH ANNIVERSARY DINNER HRC, FH/189/1, William Pickens, NAACP to FH, Mar. 15, 19, 1934; Jan. 11, 1935.

190 "IT BECOMES GROTESQUE . . ." HRC, FH/247/1, Writers League Against Lynching, FH for *The Crisis* magazine, Nov. 27, 1934. Also, FH/211/2, Anti-lynching telegram to Gov. James Rolph, Jr., of California signed by eighty authors.

191 "SEGREGATES US . . ." Freida Friedman, "Fannie Hurst's Success," *Jewish Tribune,* Vol. 86, No. 2, July 10, 1925, p. 4.

191 "SHE SPEAKS DECISIVELY . . ." HRC, FH, Scrapbooks, *A President Is Born* and *Five and Ten;* Maurice A. Bergman, "FH on Contemporary Problems—The Author of a Pulitzer Prize possibility speaks on Companionate Marriage, the Coal Fields and Zionism," undtd, undocumented.

191 "DEATHLESS QUALITY . . ." HRC, FH/117/2, FH to Oliver Degelman, Jan. 23, 1931, "I am not in sympathy with the group movement of Zionism."

191 "THE LAST CARBON COPY . . ." HRC, FH, Scrapbooks, *Back Street,* undtd, undocumented article c. 1931 [possibly int with Meyer Leven in the *Canadian Jewish Chronicle* entitled "Inhibitions and Intermarriage"].

191 "TRUE, HE IS BREAKING AWAY . . ." Friedman, "Fannie Hurst's Success," p. 4.

191 "A WHOLE LINE OF INVISIBLE ANCESTORS . . ." HRC, FH, Scrapbooks, *Back Street,* undtd, undocumented article c. 1931.

191 "WITHOUT DISTINCTION . . ." HRC, FH/222/10, appeal letter [1923] from the American Committee for the Relief of Victimized German Children, operating under the auspices of the American Committee against Fascist Oppression in Germany.

191 SUPPORTED BY A GROUP Yale, James Weldon Johnson Collection, Box 222, Folder 10, Ser. 1, Correspondence Hu–Iz, FH, appeal letter [1923] from the American Committee for the Relief of Victimized German Children, operating under the auspices of the American Committee against Fascist Oppression in Germany. Its members included Roger Baldwin, A. A. Brill, Heywood Broun, Walter Damrosch, John Dos Passos, Suzanne La Follete, Oswald Garrison Villard, and William Allen White.

191–192 EXPRESSED ALARM OVER THE TORTURE/ "I HAVE BEEN IN GERMANY . . ." HRC, FH/238/1, George Sylvester Viereck to FH, Nov. 21, 1933.

192 NOT AN ISOLATED ONE For a fuller treatment see Howard Sachar, *History of the Jews in America* (New York: Knopf, 1994), pp. 468–472.

192 "INTOLERANCE, AS INDICATED . . ." HRC, FH/238/1, FH–George Sylvester Viereck correspondence, Nov. 21, Dec. 11, Dec. 12, 1933.

192 "USE AND ABUSE" HRC, FH/249/4, Anne (Mrs. Henry) Zuckerman to FH, Jan. 24, 1934.

192 HER ANTI-HITLER STATEMENTS See *Hitler's Reign of Terror, Variety,* May 1, 1934. See also Film, MPAA Production Code Files, *Hitler's Reign of Terror.* Film opened Apr. 30, 1934. This anti-Nazi propagation film was largely based on filmed reenactments of interviews Cornelius Vanderbilt, Jr., conducted in Germany in 1932 with high-level Nazi officials.

192 "THERE IS MUCH TO BE SAID . . ." Walter Duranty, Vincent Sheean, FH, and Morris Markey, "John Doe in Today's World as He Fares Under Communism, as He Fares Under Fascism, as He Fares Under Nazism, as He Fares Under New Dealism," *Cosmo,* Vol. 98, No. 3, Mar. 1935, pp. 27, 169–171.

193 WALTER LIPPMANN . . . OPPOSED See Sachar, *History of the Jews,* pp. 470–472.

193 "TO TAKE UP THE QUESTION . . ."/ "I HAVE BITTER REASON . . ." HRC, FH/156/3, Jewish Matters, Louise W. (Mrs. Stephen) Wise to FH, Apr. 9, 1935; FH to Mrs. Wise, Apr. 9, 1935.

CHAPTER TWENTY-TWO

PAGE

194 "AN ACUTE CASE . . ." NYPL, Robert Harris Davis Papers, FH to Davis, undtd [Sept. 1932].

194 TO CLOSE FRIENDS HRC, FH/154/4, *Imitation of Life,* David McCord to FH undtd [1931]. Also FH/230/1, Lois Toensfeldt to FH undtd [1931/32] and NYPL, Robert Harris Davis Papers, Box 17, FH to Davis, undtd [Sept. 1932].

194 "I HATED IT . . ." Ada Patterson, "A Woman for President? Fannie Hurst Says It's Possible," *Psychology,* Vol. 20, No. 7, May 1934, p. 15.

194 THE NOVEL STARTED TO FORM HRC, FH/112/3, Saul Flaumm, Cosmo Books, to FH, May 28, 1931.

194 "TIME WAS IN NO SENSE [HER] OWN" HRC, FH/195/8, FH to Ada Patterson, Oct. 16, 1931. See also FH/166/1, FH to William Lengel, *Cosmo,* Oct. 21, 1931.

194 THE CONSTANT DISRUPTION "Women Ask Disarmament," *NYT,* Nov. 5, 1931, 23:4; "Fannie Hurst Finds Puritanism Waning," *NYT,* Dec. 3, 1931; "Asks Salvation Army Aid," *NYT,* May 26, 1932.

194 ONE OF BERLIN'S FIRST ACTS See John Tebbel and Mary Zuckerman, *The Magazine in America: 1741–1990* (New York: Oxford University Press, 1991), p. 153.

194 HARRY BURTON OF *MCCALL'S* HRC, FH/112/3, William Lengel, Oct. 13, 1931.

194 THIS WAS BEFORE HRC, FH/142/1, FH to William Briggs, Harper & Bros., Oct. 15, 1931. Also HRC, FH/138/1, Harper & Bros., agreement to FH, Oct. 21, 1931, and Feb. 2, 1933.

194–195 SHE SOLD HER STORY Hearst, *Cosmo* magazine index-card files, $4,000, Apr. 1, 1932.

195 MANAGED TO RESELL IT HRC, FH/143/2, Leland Hayward's office to FH, Nov. 25 and Dec. 10, 1932.

195 PICTORIAL PAID HER HRC, FH/255/2, Contract, Pictorial Review Co., FH and T. Von
     Ziekursch, ed., $4,000 for *Soiled Dove,* May 25, 1932. (Published as "One in
     Three Thousand.")

195 THE MOST FANNIE WOULD EVER RECEIVE HRC, FH/255/2, *Pictorial Review* to FH,
     Contract, June 2, 1932. Also HRC, FH/154/4, FH to T. Von Ziekursch, *Pictorial
     Review,* May 31, 1932.

195 ONCE-SUCCESSFUL BUSINESSWOMEN ADMITTED "Idle Women See Their Relics Sold,"
     NYT, Nov. 30, 1932, 21:6.

195 NEED OF WISE COUNSEL HRC, FH/230/1, FH to Lois Toensfeldt, June 8, 1933. Also
     FH/198/1, Channing Pollack to FH, Jan. 26, 1933, and FH/154/4, David McCord
     to FH, undtd [1932–33].

195 "WITH A ROUND BLACK MOON . . ." FH, *Imitation of Life,* p. 91.

196 "NATURALLY, I WANT TO THINK . . ." NYPL, Robert Hobart Davis Papers, Box 17, FH
     to Davis, undtd [Sept. 1932].

196 NO. DAVIS/DO YOU MEAN . . . /NOT PUBLISH. BOB HRC, FH/116/1, Robert H. Davis to
     FH, Oct. 17, 1932.

196 FANNIE THANKED HIM NYPL, Davis Papers, Box 17, FH to Davis, Nov. 3, 1932.

196 "IN NO PARTICULAR RISES . . ." HRC, FH/116/1, Robert H. Davis to FH, Oct. 17, 1932.

197 ITS EIGHTH PRINTING *Publishers Weekly,* Vol. 123, No. 10, Mar. 11, 1933, p. 946.

197 A CREDIBLE SHOWING See *Publishers Weekly,* best-sellers compilations, Feb. 13, Mar.
     19, Apr. 9, 16, 23, 30, 1932, [Vol. 121, Nos. 7, 12, 15, 16, 17, 18]. See also Bran,
     Box 2Q, Correspondence with Publishers, Royalty Settlement, *Imitation of Life,*
     Feb. 1–June 30, 1933, 15,910 plus assorted other copies resulting in royalty of
     $6,145.72 minus $5,000 advance and sundry for net royalty to FH of $1,125.36.

197 SOLD THE MOVIE RIGHTS HRC, FH/154/4, *Imitation of Life,* Universal to FH, May
     11, 1933.

197 BEA AND DELILAH For fuller discussion of the novel and other provocative interpre-
     tations, see Jeanne Phoenix Laurel, "Double Veil: Cross-Racial Characterizations
     in Six American Women's Novels, 1909–1948" (Thesis, Indiana University,
     1990), pp. 122–149; Cynthia Ann Brandimarte, "Fannie Hurst and Her Fiction:
     Prescriptions for America's Working Women" (Thesis, University of Texas,
     1980), pp. 261–270.

197 "THE ROMANCE OF THE AMERICAN WOMAN'S . . ." HRC, FH/154/4, Promotion in
     Oct. 1932 issue of *Pictorial Review* for "Sugar House."

197 "ENORMOUSLY READ . . ." "Business Woman," *NYT Book Review,* Feb. 5, 1933, 7:4,
     14:1.

197 "SLOPPY, VERBLESS PROSE . . ." Archer Winston, Review, *Booklist,* No. 22, Apr. 1933,
     p. 241.

198 "GONE ARE THE DAYS . . ." Mary Carroll, "This Freedom," *Independent Woman,* Vol.
     10, Apr. 1931, pp. 149, 192.

198 "OVERCOLORED" *Christian Science Monitor,* Feb. 25, 1933, p. 10.

198 "A TRIUMPH . . ." Mary Ross, *Books,* Feb. 5, 1933, p. 4.

198 "ONE OF THE MOST MAGNIFICENTLY DRAWN . . ." "Of Women," *Cincinnati Enquirer,*
     Feb. 11, 1933.

198 "LET ME PASS!" Helen Wolff, "The Negro Question," *San Francisco Chronicle,* Feb.
     12, 1933.

199 "ONE OF THE MOST HUMAN DOCUMENTS . . ." Robert H. Wilson, "Speaking of Books," Chicago *Herald Examiner,* Feb. 28, 1933.

199 THE ORIGINS OF FANNIE'S BLACK CHARACTERS See Jane Caputi, "Specifying Fannie Hurst: Langston Hughes' *Limitations of Life,* Zora Neale Hurston's *Their Eyes Were Watching God,* and Toni Morrison's *The Bluest Eye* as 'Answers' to Hurst's *Imitation of Life,*" *Black American Literature Forum,* Vol. 24, No. 4, Winter 1990.

199 "LIGHT OF FULL MOON . . ." FH, *Imitation of Life,* p. 104.

199 TO TEMPT HER TO TRAVEL See, for example, HR, FH/152/2, Zora Neale Hurston to FH, July 3, 1936.

199 "THE OGRE OF DISCRIMINATION"/ " 'IF YOU ARE GOING . . .' " FH, "Zora Hurston: A Personality Sketch," *Library Gazette,* Yale University, 1961, p. 20.

199 NEITHER DELILAH NOR PEOLA See Caputi, "Specifying Fannie Hurst."

199 "THAT RECURRING AND PUZZLING TRAIT . . ." FH, "Zora Hurston," 1960, p. 20.

199 "AUNT JEMIMA" See Caputi, "Specifying Fannie Hurst."

199 "MISS FANNIE" WAS A NAME HRC. There were several letters addressed to "Miss Fannie" in connection with the settling of FH's father's estate in St. Louis.

200 FANNIE CLAIMED NOT TO RECALL HRC, FH/197/3, Mrs. LeRoy Pinkusohn to FH, June 15, 1935.

200 "IN THE SUBLIME DEMOCRACY OF CHILDHOOD" FH, *Imitation of Life,* p. 111.

201 FANNIE WAS PAYING Ints with Ethel Rabinowitz Amatneek, FH's secretary 1932–1936, Summer 1998.

201 "WHAT'S JES' NAUGHTY . . ." FH, *Imitation of Life,* p. 119.

201 "AIN'T YOU GOT NO WAY . . ." FH, *Imitation of Life,* p. 121.

202 SHE HAS TRAINED Actually a reader pointed out a mistake in Fannie's depiction: a librarian required a university degree. Fannie has Peola only as a high school graduate at the point at which she pursues this career.

202–203 "YAS'M"/ BEA HAS DELILAH POSE/ SHE GIVES COMFORT/ "NATURAL AS TIDES" FH, *Imitation of Life,* pp. 141, 104–105, 179–181, 180–181.

203 HOW PERILOUS PEOLA'S FUTURE Insight of Marsha Pinson, Nov. 8, 1997.

203–204 "I KNOW PEOLA . . ." HRC, see Files FH/75/1, FH/154/4, and FH/263/1,2,3 for fan mail from the novel; HRC, FH/75/1, Indianapolis woman to FH, Dec. 18, 1934.

204 "LIVING CONTENT TO DO ONE'S BEST . . ." HRC, FH/75/1, Fan letter [signature illegible from the Bolivar, 230 Central Park West, NYC] to FH, Dec. 15, 1934.

204 "YOUR VIVID PAGES . . ."/ "IN ITS SMALL WAY . . ." HRC, FH/189/1, Folder 2, Edward F. Murphy, S.S.J., to FH, Mar. 14, 1934; FH to Murphy, Mar. 22, 1934.

CHAPTER TWENTY-THREE

PAGE

205 "STENTORIAN SOBBING . . ." Andre Sennwald, "The Screen," *NYT,* Nov. 24, 1934, 19:1.

205 "INSIGHT, SYMPATHETIC UNDERSTANDING . . ." HRC, FH/235/1, FH to John Stahl, Universal Studios, Nov. 21, 1934.

205 THE LEVEL OF HER SINCERITY HRC, FH/235/1, FH to John Stahl, Universal Studios, Nov. 21, 1934.

205 "ITS RECEPTION IN THE SOUTH . . ." Review, *Imitation of Life, Variety,* Nov. 27, 1934.

205 DOLPH FRANTZ . . . WROTE Film, MPAA Production Code Administrative files, ltr, Dolph Frantz, *Shreveport Journal,* to Adolph Zukor, Aug. 25, 1937.

205 NUMBER ONE OR TWO SLOT Film, MPAA Production Code Administrative files, Carl Laemmle, Jr., Universal Studios production figures provided to Joseph I. Breen, Jan. 24, 1935.

206 BREEN EXPLAINED Film, MPAA Production Code Administrative files, correspondence Jan. 1935 between Robert Gaylor, Grand Encampment, Knights Templar, San Francisco, and Joseph I. Breen.

206 "THE MOST SHAMELESS TEARJERKER . . ." Sennwald, "The Screen."

206 DISAPPOINTED IN THE FILM'S TREATMENT Richard Watts, Jr., "On the Screen," *NY Herald Tribune,* Nov. 24, 1934.

206 TIMID ON THE TRAGIC THEME William Boehnel, "Film Deals Timidly with Social Issues," undtd, unidentified, HRC, FH/Scrapbook 40.

206 "HAD A WAY OF FORCING HERSELF . . ." "On the Current Screen," *Literary Digest,* Dec. 8, 1934.

207 "A SENSATION IN HARLEM" "A Sensation in Harlem," *NY Amsterdam News,* Jan. 26, 1935, p. 10.

207 "BUT OF COURSE . . ." "Color Bars Louise Beavers from Award," *NY Amsterdam News,* Mar. 2, 1935, 15:7.

207 "THE GREATEST CONDEMNATION . . ." E. Washington Rhodes, "Greatest Condemnation of Prejudice in America Seen in *Imitation of Life,*" *Philadelphia Tribune,* Feb. 14, 1935.

207 "OLD STEREOTYPE . . ." Sterling Brown, "Once a Pancake," *Opportunity,* Vol. 13, No. 3, Mar. 1935, pp. 87–88.

207 "POLITE SINCERE ATTACHMENT . . ."/ TRIBUTE TO BLACK MOTHERHOOD F. A. Cone, "Imitation of Life," "Letter Box," *NY Amsterdam News,* Jan. 19, 1935, p. 8.

207 "SHOWED THE TENDENCIES . . ." Paul S. Locker, "Calls Picture Insult," *NY Amsterdam News,* Jan. 26, 1935, p. 8.

207–208 WEST INDIAN AND AFRICAN-AMERICAN BLACKS/ "WE HAVE OUR DELILAHS . . ." S. T. Simmons "Home and Abroad," *NY Amsterdam News,* Feb. 2, 1935, p. 8.

208 A JUSTIFIED AND FLATTERING PROFILE Chauncey Townsend, "Out of the Kitchen," *Crisis,* Vol. 42, No. 1, Jan. 1935, pp. 15, 29.

208 "SO FULL OF VICIOUS ANTI-NEGRO PROPAGANDA . . ." Pauline Flora Byrd, "Imitation of Life," *Crisis,* Vol. 42, No. 3, Mar. 1935, pp. 91–92.

208 "THE DOCILE TYPE . . ." Frank T. Wood, Jr., "Imitation of Life Again," *Crisis,* Vol. 42, No. 9, Sept. 1935, p. 283.

208 "WHY NOT REGARD THE PICTURE . . ." "Why Not Consider Imitation of Life Merely a Story, Louise Beavers Asks." *NY Amsterdam News,* Feb. 16, 1925, 3:2–5.

209 PROPAGANDA FAVORING THE AMERICAN BLACK Mercer Cook, "Imitation of Life in Paris." *Crisis,* Vol. 42, No. 5, June 1935, pp. 182, 188. Biographical material on Cook is from Ann Allen Shockley and Sue P. Chandler, eds., *Living Black American Authors* (New York: Bowker, 1973), p. 34.

209 "THE PLAY SHOWS . . ." Rhodes, "Greatest Condemnation."

210 "FOR ME UNDER ANY FINANCIAL TERMS . . ." FH, *Imitation of Life,* p. 263.

210 "WE'S PARTNERS . . ." FH, *Imitation of Life,* p. 96.

210 "TRUE FOLKELOQUENCE . . ." Brown, "Once a Pancake," pp. 87–88. Biographical

details of Brown are from Robert Bone's preface to Brown's *Negro Poetry and Drama,* and *The Negro in American Fiction* (New York: Atheneum, 1969).

211　IN PRIVATE LETTERS　HRC, FH/189/1, Thomas Wallace Swann to FH, Apr. 11, 1935; FH to Swann, Mar. [*sic*] 13, 1935. See also HRC, FH/189/1, NAACP, Ann Sawyer to FH, Jan. 24, 1935; FH to Sawyer, Mar. 13, 1935.

211　"FALL SHORT OR DEVIATE . . ."　FH, "Miss Fannie Hurst," *Opportunity,* Vol. 13, No. 4, Apr. 1935, p. 121.

211　"BUT I DO NOT CONSIDER . . ."　Sterling Brown, "Mr. Sterling A. Brown," *Opportunity,* Vol. 13, No. 4, Apr. 1935, p. 121.

212　"MY CAFE AU LAIT . . ."　Colum, Helen Worden Erskine Collection, undtd [c. Feb. 1934].

212　FANNIE ENCOURAGED WORDEN'S INTEREST　HRC, FH/152/2, Zora Neale Hurston to FH, Mar. 8, 1934.

212　THE WOMEN MEANDERED　Bran, Box 3B, FH to Zora Neale Hurston, Feb. 14, 1934. Fannie arrived in Palm Beach on Feb. 17, 1934, spoke at Rollins on Feb. 25, and was back in NY on Feb. 27. See also Yale, FH, "Zora Neale Hurston: A Personality Sketch," *Library Gazette,* Yale University, 1961, p. 17.

213　"THAT WHICH I KNOW YOU VALUE . . ."　HRC, FH/152/2, Zora Neale Hurston to FH, Mar. 8, 1934.

213　FANNIE MADE BRIEF REMARKS　HRC, FH/152/2, Annie Nathan Meyer to FH, Jan. 13, May 1, 7, 1935; FH to Meyer, Jan. 14, May 6, 1935.

213　BROWN'S FIRST ARTICLE APPEARED　HRC, FH/152/2, Annie Nathan Meyer to FH, May 1 and 7, 1935; FH to Meyer, May 6 and 7, 1935.

213　SUPPORT FOR ZORA'S APPLICATION　John Simon Guggenheim Memorial Foundation, Zora Neale Hurston application for fellowship, Nov. 15, 1935. FH letter of recommendation dated Dec. 11, 1935, is free from her customary faux pas. Hurston asked neither Franz Boas nor Ruth Benedict to write academic reference letters for her this time. Instead, she asked Edwin O. Grover of Rollins College and Melville Herskovits, who had been a part of the Columbia group but was teaching at Northwestern University at the time of her request. Both gave her ringing endorsements.

213　"DO YOU KNOW . . ."　HRC, FH/152/2, Zora Neale Hurston to FH, July 3, 1936.

213　"A GRAND SET OF ADMIRERS . . ."　HRC, FH/152/2, Zora Neale Hurston to FH, Jan. 30 and Feb. 6, 1940.

213　FANNIE'S FEEBLE ATTEMPT　See Jane Caputi, "Specifying Fannie Hurst: Langston Hughes' *Limitations of Life,* Zora Neale Hurston's *Their Eyes Were Watching God,* and Toni Morrison's *The Bluest Eye* as 'Answers' to Hurst's *Imitation of Life,*" *Black American Literature Forum,* Vol. 24, No. 4, Winter 1990, pp. 697–716.

214　"AS A NEGRO . . ."　HRC, FH/151/1, Langston Hughes to FH, July 13, 1937.

214　A BITING PARODY　Re: "Limitations of Life," see Arnold Rampersad, *The Life of Langston Hughes, Vol. I: 1902–1941* (New York: Oxford University Press, 1986), pp. 364–365.

214　"SENSATION OF THE EVENING . . ."　"Suitcase in Second Season," *NY Amsterdam News,* Nov. 5, 1938, p. 20.

214　WHO HAD WRITTEN BLURBS　Yale, James Weldon Johnson Collection, General Correspondence, Box 76, Restricted, FH to Langston Hughes, blurb for *Not Without Laughter,* Sept. 12, 1930.

214 SUPPORTED HIS CAUSES HRC, FH/151/1, Langston Hughes to FH, July 13, 1937; FH to Hughes, July 13, 1937. Also HRC FH/211/2, Langston Hughes to FH, Oct. 31, 1933; FH to Hughes, Nov. 17, 1933. See also Arnold Rampersad, *The Life of Langston Hughes, Vol. II: 1941–1967* (New York: Oxford University Press, 1988), p. 282. Fannie introduced Hughes at an evening concert made up exclusively of his songs in 1958.

214 GLADLY OFFERED COMMENT Arnold Rampersad, *The Life of Langston Hughes, Vol. I,* p. 388.

214 HOW NICE TO HEAR . . . HRC, FH/151/1, Langston Hughes to FH, July 25, 1949. See also Caputi, "Specifying Fannie Hurst."

214 "HOW LOVELY OF YOU!" Yale, Langston Hughes, James Weldon Johnson Collection, Box 76, Restricted, FH to Hughes, July 29, 1949.

CHAPTER TWENTY-FOUR

PAGE

215 "A MAGNIFICENT UNREST . . ." Int, Arthur Mann with FH, Nov. 12, 1956, cited in Arthur Mann, *La Guardia: A Fighter Against His Times, 1882–1933* (Philadelphia: Lippincott, 1959), p. 49.

215 "BLAZING REBEL . . ." FH, "Sees La Guardia a Blazing Rebel," *NY World,* Women's Section, Oct. 13, 1929, p. 1.

215 THANKS FOR YOUR LETTER . . . HRC, FH/163/1, cbl, Fiorello La Guardia to FH, Nov. 26, 1932.

215 "I HOPE YOUR LIVER . . ." HRC, FH/163/1–4, Fiorello La Guardia to FH, undtd.

216 "I FEEL SO STRONGLY . . ."/ "I WOULD NOT FOR WORLDS . . ."/ CYD'S HEART WAS TOO BIG Bran, Box 3C, FH to Fiorello La Guardia, Sept. 28, Oct. 28, Dec. 1, 1933; Fiorello La Guardia to FH, Dec. 4, 1933.

216 COLDEST DAY ON RECORD/ "THE NAPOLEONIC LITTLE DYNAMO . . ." HRC, FH/194/2, FH to Ruth Bryan Owen, Feb. 9, 1934. Also, "Mercury 14.3 Below Zero on NY's Coldest Day, *NYT,* Feb. 10, 1934, 31:8, also 1:1:4–5.

216 "FANTASTIC BARGAIN" HRC, FH/194/1, Ruth Bryan Owen to FH, July 10, 1933.

216 "PANGS OF CONSCIENCE" HRC, FH/194/2, Ruth Bryan Owen to FH, Aug. 2 and 3, 1933.

216 DUTIFULLY CARRIED THE EMBARRASSING IDEA HRC, FH/144/1, FH to Millicent Hearst, Aug. 3, 1933.

216 SHE LOVED THE DECISION Bran, Box 3C, FH to Fiorello La Guardia, Mar. 10 and June 8, 1934.

216 TAVERN ON THE GREEN Elizabeth Blackmar and Ron Rosenzweig, *The Park and the People: A History of Central Park* (Ithaca Cornell University Press, 1992), p. 454.

217 "TO ANTAGONIZE . . ." Bran, Box 3C, FH to Fiorello La Guardia, June 21, 1934.

217 "WOMEN IN TENEMENT KITCHENS . . ." HRC, FH/163/1, FH to Fiorello La Guardia, Jan. 23, 1936.

217 ONLY A FORM LETTER HRC, FH/163/1, Mayor's Office to FH, Jan. 24, 1936.

217 "IN THE TREMENDOUSLY IMPORTANT UNDERTAKING . . ."/ "AS I'VE TOLD YOU . . ." Bran, Box 3C, Fiorello La Guardia to FH, Sept. 13, 1934; FH to La Guardia, Sept. 18, 1934.

217 A SPOT ON THE NEW YORK CITY COMMISSION FOR THE WORLD'S FAIR HRC, FH/188/1, NYC World's Fair Commission, Fiorello La Guardia to FH, Sept. 18, 22, 1936. See also NYPL-Rare, World's Fair Commission 1939–40.C3.84–Cr.106, Box 73, Folder 34.100.

217 FANNIE CONSIDERED THE FAIR HRC, FH/155/2, FH to Alfredo Janni, Oct. 10, 1936. See also full file, HRC, FH/188/1, NYC World's Fair Commission.

217 "THE EVILS"/ HE MADE HER A CONSULTANT HRC, FH/163/1, Fiorello La Guardia to FH, Sept. 1, 1938, Nov. 4, 1939; FH to La Guardia, Sept. 3, 1938, Nov. 6, 1939.

218 "FULL OF RIBS . . ." HRC, FH/240/3, FH to Eddie Wasserman, Dec. 8, 1930.

218 "THE JEAN HARLOW ANGLE . . ." FH, "No Food with My Meals," pt. 2, *Liberty,* Mar. 2, 1935, p. 26.

218 "WHAT ARE THE PLANS . . ." HRC, FH/116/1, Robert H. Davis to FH, Dec. 27, 1932.

218 THE NEW SLEEKNESS HRC, FH/202/6, Anna Steese Richardson to FH, Apr. 24, 1931.

218 "A VISION . . ." HRC, FH/174/4, O. O. McIntyre, undtd [1933].

218 "NO, NO . . ." HRC, FH/130/3, FH exchange with W. Friedman, Sept. 25–27, 1947.

218 LA GUARDIA WAS EQUALLY IN THRALL/ "BE AS CONSERVATIVE . . ." HRC, FH/163/1, Fiorello La Guardia to FH, Aug. 23, 1935; FH to La Guardia, Aug. 29, 1935.

219 "GUESS HOW MUCH SHE WEIGHS . . ." FH, "No Food with My Meals," pt. 1, *Liberty,* Feb. 23, 1935, pp. 19–26.

220 "FLABBY MUSCULATURE"/ THOUGH SHE CONTINUED TO FEEL ROBUST Bran, Box 11C, Life Extension Institute report, Apr. 18, 1932, and June 16, 1933. Also HRC, FH/274/1, Life Extension Institute report, May 19, 1934.

220 BERNARR MACFADDEN/ "SUPPLY NUTRITIVE SUFFICIENCIES . . ." HRC, FH/173/5, Bernarr Macfadden to FH, June 29, 1934; FH to Bernarr Macfadden, June 30, 1934.

220 WHAT SHE ADDED HRC, FH/244/4, Vilhjalmur Steffanson to FH, Apr. 1, 1935.

220 "THE MIRACLE OF IT . . ." FH, "No Food with My Meals," pt. 2, p. 26.

221 "THAT'S THE WAY I'M BUILT . . ." HRC, FH/130/4, FH to William and Jenny Frieder, Aug. 26, 1937.

221 "THE MAE WEST ATAVISM . . ." FH, "No Food with My Meals," pt. 2, pp. 28–30.

221 WHEN HARPERS PRESENTED HRC, FH/138/1, FH to William Briggs, Jan. 10, 1935; Briggs to FH, Jan. 15, 1935. Briggs solved the problem by using only the woman's hands in the drawing.

221 "RIDICULOUS LIGHT . . ." HRC, FH/99/2, FH to John N. Wheeler, Bell Syndicate, Jan. 8, 1937.

221 FANNIE'S WEIGHT HAD EDGED HRC, FH/274/1, Life Extension Institute, 1936 examination shows weight of 150 pounds.

221–222 "DO NOT WORRY . . ."/ "I AM TWO POUNDS UP . . ."/ "THE VOLUBLE . . ." HRC, FH/212/3, Dr. Benjamin Shallett to FH, Aug. 10 and Nov. 7, 1940; FH to Dr. Benjamin Shallett, Nov. 6, 1940.

222 "HUMDINGER . . ." Bran, Box Q2, Correspondence with Publishers, FH to William Briggs, Harper & Bros., Mar. 11, 1933.

222 "THE NEW DAY . . ." Ada Patterson, "A Woman for President? Fannie Hurst Says It's Possible," *Psychology,* Vol. 20, No. 7, May 1934, p. 15.

222 "ONE STRIVES TO BELIEVE . . ." HRC, FH/132/1, FH to Zona Gale, Nov. 15, 1933.

222 THE WORK WENT SO WELL Bran, Box 2B, FH to William Lengel, *Cosmo,* June 7, 1933.

222   "WITH THE GREATEST FACILITY . . ." Patterson, "A Woman for President?" p. 15.

222   HARRY BURTON AT *COSMOPOLITAN*   HRC, FH/177/3, Elizabeth Meehan to FH [undtd, c. Nov. 1934].

222   FANNIE QUICKLY SENT OFF   See HRC, FH/129/4, FH–Ray Long, Fox Studios Correspondence (1933–34). Also FH/195/4, FH–Richard Halliday correspondence, Paramount Studios (1933–34).

222   FANNIE PICTURED KATHARINE HEPBURN   HRC, FH/144/3, FH to Katharine Hepburn, Dec. 18, 1933. Also FH/129/4, Ray Long, Fox Film Corp., to FH, Dec. 28, 1933, Jan. 2, Feb. 5, 1934; FH to Long, Mar. 31, 1934.

222   "WELL, YOU'VE DONE IT . . ."   Bran, Box 2Q, Correspondence with Publishers, Harry Burton, *Cosmo,* to FH, Nov. 20, 1933.

223   REMINDING HER SOON AFTER   Colum, Curtis Brown Collection, Stern and Reubens, Harry Payne Burton to FH, Jan. 22, 1934, referring to contract dated May 22, 1928.

223   THE GRAND GAY NINETIES PARTY   HRC, NY Journal-American morgue, *NY Journal* clipping, Nov. 28, 1933.

223   THE PUBLISHER ALSO AGREED   Colum, Curtis Brown Collection, Stern and Reubens, William Briggs to FH, Dec. 20, 1933. *American Symphony* was the working title for *Anitra's Dance.* Also Bran, Box 2Q, Correspondence with Publishers, Dec. 20, 1933, Jan. 30, 1934.

223   PRELIMINARY ORDER OF FOUR THOUSAND   Bran, Box 2Q, Correspondence with Publishers, Cass Canfield to FH, Mar. 19, 1934.

223   "PERHAPS THE BEST PRESENTATION . . ."   HRC, FH/116/1, Robert H. Davis to FH, Mar. 28, 1934.

223   "THE PRESIDENT CONTINUES TO ASTOUND . . ."   HRC, FH/194/1, FH to Ruth Bryan Owen, Jan. 5, 1934.

224   "NEW UNDER THE SUN . . ."   FH, "Here Comes Mrs. Roosevelt," Rollins College Library, Archives, Rollins College News Service, undtd release [Feb. 25, 1934].

224   FANNIE WAS BACK AT THE WHITE HOUSE   HRC, FH/205/1, FH to Malvina Thompson, Mar. 14, 1934; cbl, Eleanor Roosevelt to FH, Mar. 17, 1934.

224   THE WOMEN'S PRESS CLUB DINNER   HRC, FH/205/1, FH to Eleanor Roosevelt, Mar. 14, 1934; ER to FH Mar. 17, 1934; FH to ER, Mar. 21, 1934. Also HRC, Scrapbooks, 1934, *NY Evening Journal,* Mar. 20, 1934.

224   THE INTIMATE LUNCHEON FANNIE HAD SCHEDULED   Bran, Box 2Q, Correspondence with Publishers, FH secretary to Ramona Herdman, Harper & Bros., Mar. 21, 1934.

224   QUIETLY, FANNIE HAD APPROACHED COLONEL HOUSE   HRC, FH/149/1, FH to Colonel Edward M. House, Mar. 15, 1934.

224   HOUSE HAD FOLLOWED UP   Yale, Sterling, Edward M. House Papers, Box 63a, Folder 2041, FH–House Correspondence, Mar. 19, Apr. 3, 11, 16, 1934, including House to George Dern, Secretary of War, with endorsement of Stef's candidacy for some post.

224   JOIN THE BOARD OF THE VISITING NURSES' ASSOCIATION . . . HENRY STREET SETTLEMENT HOUSE   HRC, FH/205/6, Sara Delano Roosevelt to FH, Jan. 8, 1934; June 5, Nov. 5, 1935; FH to Sara Delano Roosevelt, June 6, 1935.

224   "I CAN'T SO WON'T . . ."   HRC, FH/205/1, FH to Eleanor Roosevelt, Mar. 21, 1934.

225 FANNIE'S PRIVATE HOPE HRC, FH/230/1, FH to Lois Toensfeldt, June 8, 1935.

225 "A LARGE-SCALE AND AMBITIOUS PIECE . . ." Louis Kronenberger, "Fannie Hurst's Portrait of a Genius," *NYT,* Mar. 25, 1934, 5: 9:2–4.

225 HER DECISION TO TAKE DRIVING LESSONS Bran, Box 2B, Columbus Circle Driving School, Mar. 30–Sept. 4, 1934.

225 HER APPEARANCE AT LEONEBEL JACOBS'S STUDIO PARTY HRC, Scrapbook, 1934, clipping, *NYT,* Apr. 9, 1934.

225 FANNIE BEGGED OFF WRITING ANY OTHERS FH, "Tomorrow's Bride," *Collier's,* Apr. 14, 1934, 93:17, and "Ticket to Life," *Collier's,* Dec. 8, 1934, 94:19. Earlier, FH, "Clean," *Collier's,* Apr. 1, 1933, 91:7. See also HRC, FH/110/4, FH correspondence with *Collier's,* 1933–34.

226 "THEY STAND OUT FROM THE CROWD" "They Stand Out from the Crowd," *Literary Digest,* Apr. 21, 1934, 117:14. Other notables on the page are Otto van Hapsburg, Charlotte E. Carr, Aaron Rabinowitz, William "Jack" Leather, and Wallace Beery.

226 A NEWSPAPER PHOTOGRAPHER CAUGHT A SHOT NYPL-Rare, George Hellman Papers, Selected Correspondence, Box 14, Hellman to FH, Clipping, *NY Evening Journal,* June 8, 1934. See also HRC, FH/125/2, John Erskine to FH [undtd].

226 TOOK LESSONS FROM HER GREENGROCER'S . . . SON HRC, FH/204/2.

226 NO SHORTAGE OF WILLING DANCE ESCORTS Bran, Box 8A, appt-bks, see entries throughout the 1940s. Escorts included Murray Rosen, Milton Traubman, and Albert Richter-Rothschild, among others.

CHAPTER TWENTY-FIVE

PAGE

227 ANOTHER REQUEST FROM THE FIRST LADY HRC, FH/205/1, Eleanor Roosevelt to FH, Apr. 30, 1934.

227 "BEAT-OF-THE-DRUM" HRC, FH/205/1, FH to Eleanor Roosevelt, May 18, 1934.

227 TO EXTOL THE FIRST LADY'S VIRTUES HRC, FH/205/1, Eleanor Roosevelt to FH, June 12, 1934.

227 "ALTHOUGH RADIO AND PRESS . . ." HRC, FH/194/1, FH to Ruth Bryan Owen, Mar. 11, 1936; FH/205/1, FH to Eleanor Roosevelt, May 18, 1934.

227 "A FREE HAND . . ." HRC, FH/205/1, Eleanor Roosevelt to FH, May 22, 1934.

227 "SOMEHOW, SOMEWAY" HRC, FH/205/1, FH to Eleanor Roosevelt, June 21, 1934.

227 SHE COULD FIND A WAY HRC, FH/183/4, FH to Martin Aylesworth, NBC, June 25, 1934.

227 AMONG THE OTHER LUMINARIES/ "RIDICULOUS AS IT IS . . ." *NY Post,* June 19, 1934, pp. 1–3.

227 BEING PHOTOGRAPHED SEWING *NY Evening Journal,* July 21, 1934, 25:5; *NY American,* July 24, 1934, 5:2.

228 "I WILL SAY THIS . . ." HRC, NY Journal-American Morgue, *NY Evening Journal,* Sept. 4, 1934.

228 ANOTHER WHITE HOUSE VISIT Bran, Box 1, Ledgers, appt-bks, diaries, see entry May 14, 1934, "White House Lunch, ER."

228 "NOT TO INDULGE . . ." HRC, FH/205/1, FH to Eleanor Roosevelt, Oct. 17, 1934; Roosevelt to FH, Oct. 19, 1934.

228 "MY DEAR WHITE HOUSE DARLING" HRC, FH/2131/1–5, Daniel Frohman to FH, Feb. 8, 1934.

228 "STRANGE AND EXCITING LITTLE MAN . . ." HRC, FH/277/1, FH to Lela Stiles, Louis M. Howe's biographer, Mar. 11, 1948.

229 "ANIMALS BEHAVE . . ."/ "DEAR CIRCE . . ." HRC, FH/149/4, Col. Louis McHenry Howe to FH, undtd.

229 "LET ME GIVE YOU . . ." HRC, FH/277/1, FH to Lela Stiles, Louis M. Howe's biographer, Mar. 11, 1948.

229 "THAT I DWELL TOO FAR OUTSIDE . . ." HRC, FH/149/1, FH to Louis McHenry Howe, Dec. 28, 1934.

229 "I AM A THICK-SKINNED BOOR . . ."/ "GRATEFUL AND CHASTENED" HRC, FH/277/1, FH to Lela Stiles, Louis M. Howe's biographer, Mar. 11, 1948.

229 "IN YOUR CHRISTMAS GIFT . . ." HRC, FH/149/1, Louis McHenry Howe to FH, undtd [Christmas 1934].

229 "FOR THE MOST PART . . ." HRC, FH/194/2, FH to Ruth Bryan Owen, Feb. 8, 1935.

229 HOWE'S HEALTH HRC, FH/149/1, Mary Howe Baker to FH, Apr. 2, 1935.

229 "ONE OF MY CLOSEST FRIENDS . . ." Bran, Box 3B, Personal Correspondence, FH to Zora Neale Hurston, Mar. 23, 1935.

230 "I GUESS YOU ARE READING . . ." HRC, FH/130/4, FH to Mr. and Mrs. William Frieder [Uncle Billy and Aunt Jenny], Mar. 23, 1935.

230 "SHOULD WOMEN BE ALLOWED TO WORK?" WashSpc, Ser. 1, Personal Correspondence, FH to Lois Toensfeldt, Feb. 6, 1936. The panelists included FH, Eleanor Roosevelt, Frances Perkins, the author George Creel, Civil Service Commissioner Lucille Foster McMillan, Hurston Thompson of the Federal Trade Commission, William S. Culbertson, former ambassador to Chile, and Assistant Treasury Secretary Josephine Roche (Bran, Box 8A, Folder 1, Diaries, 1936–37, Feb. 2, 1936).

230 "PLAYFUL, AMUSING . . ."/ "PLEASANT, CHATTY" Bran, Box 8A, Folder 1, Diaries, 1936–37.

230 "DO SOME RADIO WORK . . ." Bran, Box 8A, Folder 1, Diaries, 1936–37, Feb. 3, 1936.

230 TWO WEEKS LATER Bran, Box 8A, Folder 1, Diaries, 1936–37, Feb. 17, 1936.

230 "THE USUAL WHITE HOUSE THRILL" HRC, FH/194/2, FH to Ruth Bryan Owen, Feb. 14, 1936.

230 HER NEWSPAPER COLUMN WashSpc, Ser. 1, Personal Correspondence, Lois Toensfeldt File, ER, "My Day," *NY World-Telegram,* Feb. [4?], 1936.

230 "DRAW THE BUNNIES . . ." HRC, FH/149/1, FH to Louis McHenry Howe, Feb. 7, 1936.

231 CHOICES FOR THE OTHER "FIRST LADIES" HRC, FH/194/1, Ruth Bryan Owen to FH, Mar. 22, 1935.

231 "BUG TOWN WOMEN'S LEAGUE . . ." HRC, FH/149/1, Louis McHenry Howe to FH, Mar. 4, 1936.

231 "I HAVE BEEN THINKING . . ." HRC, FH/149/1, FH to Louis McHenry Howe, Mar. 20, 1936.

231 HOWE'S WHITE HOUSE FUNERAL HRC, FH/149/1, White House Telegram to FH, Apr. 20, 1936.

231 "FATHER OFTEN SPOKE . . ." HRC, FH/149/1, Mary Howe Baker to FH, May 4, 1936.

232 "PULSING WITH CHANGE . . ." Ada Patterson, "A Woman for President? Fannie Hurst Says Its Possible," *Psychology,* Vol. 20, No. 7, May 1934, p. 48.

232 "OUT OF [THEIR] SWADDLING CLOTHES" FH, "Are We Coming or Are We Going?" *Vital Speeches,* Dec. 3, 1934, 1:159–160.

232 "WHERE ARE THOSE DREAMS . . ." HRC, FH/154/1, FH to Inez Hayes Irwin, Feb. 17, 1931.

232 ENTERTAINING IN A PLACE HRC, FH/154/1, Inez Hayes Irwin to FH, Feb. 18, 1931.

232 "BEAUTIFUL BUT DUMB . . ." FH, "That Elusive Something," *Independent Woman,* 13:70, Mar. 1934, 13.

232 "CALAMITY OF 1929 . . ." FH, "Are We Coming or Are We Going?" pp. 159–160.

233 DOROTHY THOMPSON . . . REITERATED THIS CONCERN "Colleagues Honor 24 'Career Women,' " *NYT,* Mar. 19, 1936, 22:1.

233 "THE LANGUID PSYCHOLOGY . . ." FH, "Are We Coming or Are We Going?" pp. 159–160.

233 FANNIE IMMEDIATELY REPORTED HRC, FH/194/1, FH to Ruth Bryan Owen, Feb. 8, 1935; Owen to FH, Feb. 9, 1935.

233 BACK ON HOME SOIL FDR Library, James A. Farley to Ruth Bryan Owen, July 18, 1935, as cited in Sarah P. Vickers, "The life of Ruth Bryan Owen: Florida's First Congresswoman and America's First Woman Diplomat (Diss., Florida State University, 1994), p. 194.

233 "OF COURSE YOU AND I . . ." HRC, FH/194/1, Ruth Bryan Owen to FH, Oct. 11, 1935.

233 RUTH WAS CERTAINLY HIGH Patterson, "A Woman for President?" pp. 48 ff.

233 "NOT AS FAR AWAY . . ." HRC, FH/194/1, Ruth Bryan Owen to FH, Oct. 11, 1935.

234 "TO PLUNGE INTO THE FRAY . . ." HRC, FH/194/1, Ruth Bryan Owen to FH, Feb. 29, 1936.

234 "TO FIX OUR BROKEN . . . MACHINERY . . ." HRC, FH/194/1, FH to Ruth Bryan Owen, Mar. 11, 1936.

234 "THE EXTRAORDINARY STRIDES . . ." HRC, FH/194/1, FH to Ruth Bryan Owen's secretary, Mrs. Hill, May 21, 1935.

234 "ONE HAS THE FEELING . . ." HRC, FH/194/1, FH to Ruth Bryan Owen, Mar. 11, 1936.

234 "ONE OF THE STRIKING FIGURES . . ." "Sees Mrs. Roosevelt as Tradition Breaker," *NYT,* June 26, 1936, 12:2.

234–235 "THEY WERE HILARIOUS . . ." HRC, FH/165/5, FH to Kitty Owen [Meeker] Lehman, undtd [July 1936].

235 DEWSON, IN TURN, ASKED FDR, Mary W. Dewson Papers, Molly Dewson to Eleanor Roosevelt, July 18, 1936, as cited in Vickers, "Ruth Bryan Owen," p. 207.

235 RUTH BARRELED THROUGH NEW YORK STATE HRC, FH/194/1, Ruth Bryan Owen to FH, Sept. 13, 1936.

235 A MONTH WITH A BROKEN LEG HRC, FH/194/1 FH to Ruth Bryan Owen, Sept. 13 and 30, 1936.

235 ALMOST AS PROBLEMATIC Vickers, "Ruth Bryan Owen," pp. 208–209.

235 WENT ON TO COPENHAGEN HRC, FH/194/1, Ruth Bryan Owen, Jan. 4, 1937.

235 NEW THOUGHTS ABOUT HER FUTURE Ruth Bryan Owen to Bess Furman, June 3, 1936, as quoted in Vickers, "Ruth Bryan Owen," pp. 200–201.

235 "WITH EUROPEAN WAR CLOUDS . . ." HRC, FH/194/1, Ruth Bryan Owen to FH, Jan. 4, 1937.

236 SHE ALSO PROMISED TO SNOOP HRC, FH/194/1, FH to Ruth Bryan Owen, Jan. 16, 1937.

CHAPTER TWENTY-SIX

PAGE

237 INSPIRED BY THE BIRTH The quintuplets were born to Olivia and Elzire Dionne in North Bay, Ont., on May 28, 1934.

237 FANNIE ADVOCATED REARING EACH FH, "The Misses Dionne," Manuscript submitted to *Cosmo,* Apr. 18, 1936, see HRC, FH/47/4. Also HRC, FH/112/3, FH to Robert MacBride, *Cosmo,* Apr. 18, 1936.

237 "FIVE FATHERS" Hearst, *Cosmo,* magazine files, index-card file, "Five Fathers" was purchased June 8, 1934, and published in Dec. 1934 issue.

237 SHE PUT THE EMPHASIS See HRC, FH/112/3, FH to Harry Burton, *Cosmo,* Sept. 28, 1936, and draft not sent, undtd.

237 "HOME, JAMES" Hearst, *Cosmo,* index-card file, "Home, James" was purchased Apr. 1935 for $4,000 and published in June 1936.

238 RETURNED TO ST. LOUIS HRC, FH/230/1, Lois Toensfeldt to FH, May 10, 1934; FH/240/2, Washington University, Frank M. Debatin to FH, May 29, 1934; Philo Stevenson to FH, June 8, 1934. See also StLP-D morgue files, FH article, 2:3B, FH in St. Louis, first time in twelve years, June 10, 1934.

238 THE DAY HAUPTMANN'S WIFE TESTIFIED FH, "Loyalty of Wife Impresses Writer," *NYT,* Jan. 31, 1935, 13:1 (via North America Newspaper Alliance [NANA]).

238 "AN INSPIRED, IMPASSIONED . . ." HRC, FH/241/2 Alice Weber to FH, Feb. 6, 1935.

238 "VULGAR, SENSATIONAL . . ." FH et al., "Why They'll Never Forget the Trial of the Century," *Cosmo,* Vol. 98, No. 5, May 1935, pp. 34–36, 180–181.

238 PLEASURE TRAVEL Bran, Box 3B, FH to Zora Neale Hurston, May 7, 1935.

238 SIDNEY BOWMAN . . . HAD ARRANGED HRC, FH/143/3, Hawaii, see correspondence, Jan. 26–Aug. 17, 1935.

238 FANNIE PRODUCED/ "I HOPE YOU ARE NOT GOING . . ." HRC, FH/143/3, FH to Sidney Bowman, Sept. 17, 1935.

239 IGNORE HAWAII'S ACCOMPLISHMENTS . . . HRC, FH/143/4, Sidney Bowman, cbl to FH, Sept. 20, 1935.

239 "SOLELY ON ONE CLAUSE . . ." HRC, FH/143/2, FH to Sidney Bowman, Sept. 21, 1935.

239 BOWMAN THEN REVERSED HIMSELF HRC, FH/143/3, FH–Sidney Bowman correspondence, Sept. 25, 27, Oct. 15, 21, 1935.

239 "HAWAII, CRUCIBLE . . ." HRC, FH/143/3, Sidney Bowman to FH, Dec. 13, 1935.

239 HER MUSE HAD MOVED ON HRC, FH/143/3, Sidney Bowman–FH correspondence, Dec. 13, 1935; Jan. 4, Nov. 10, Nov. 18, 1936; Feb. 8, 1937.

239 THREE YEARS AFTER THE JUNKET FH, "Outpost of Paradise," *Cosmo,* July 1938.

239 DINNER FOR ALBERT EINSTEIN HRC, FH/181/3, FH to Henry Morgenthau, Sr., May 6 and Dec. 16, 1935.

239 "DO YOU KNOW . . ." HRC, FH/237/3, FH to Carl Van Vechten, Jan. 20, 1944.

239 IT EMBARRASSED FANNIE HRC, FH/160/2, FH to Rebecca Kohut, Sept. 4, 1935.

240 WROTE PERKINS A LETTER OF APOLOGY HRC, FH/196/3, FH to Frances Perkins, U.S. Secretary of Labor, Nov. 15, 1935.

240 THE SITUATION IN GERMANY WORSENED Howard Sachar, *History of the Jews in America* (New York: Knopf, 1994), pp. 471–473.

240 SWIFTLY DECLINED HRC, FH/156/3, Mrs. William Dick Sporborg to FH, Feb. 17, 1936; FH to Sporborg, Feb. 18, 1936.

240 "PUZZLED, BEWILDERED . . ." HRC, FH/156/3, FH to Nathan Strauss, United Palestine Appeal, Aug. 18, 1936.

240 "JEWS IN AMERICA" "Jews in America," *Fortune,* Feb. 1936, pp. 78–85, 128–136, 141–144.

240 "INSTEAD OF FIRST AND FOREMOST . . ." HRC, FH/156/3, FH to Jay Levenson, Philadelphia, Mar. 24, 1936.

240 "SAVE MY VOICE . . ." HRC, FH/156/3, FH to Morris Novick, Mar. 30, 1936.

240 "THIS IS SUCH A STRATEGIC MOMENT . . ." HRC, FH/156/3, FH to Rabbi Stephen Wise, Jan. 8, 1937.

241 "I DON'T THINK IT'S FAIR . . ."/ "UNUSED AND UNUSABLE MANUSCRIPTS . . ."/ "SISTER ACT" WAS NEXT/ "IT WOULD DO SOMETHING . . ." HRC, FH/112/3, FH to Harry Burton, *Cosmo,* Jan. 20, Feb. 25, July 18, 1936.

241 ANOTHER TRIBUTE TO THE FIRST LADY FH, "The First First Lady," *Democratic Digest,* Mar. 1935, p. 7 [FDR Library].

241 FANNIE'S ASSIGNMENT FDR, FH, "The Call to Arts," *The Democratic Convention 1936,* pp. 317–318. See also Bran, Box 8A, Diaries, 1936–37, Apr. 3, 1936.

241 "WHERE I SHOULD LIKE TO LIVE" FH, "Where I Should Like to Live," *Forum,* No. 95, May 1936, p. 310.

241 "QUITE A STARTLER" HRC, FH/194/2, FH to Ruth Bryan Owen, Apr. 7, 1936.

241 "HE'S A MOTHER'S BOY . . ." HRC, FH/47/8, FH, "He-Sez and She-Sez," manuscript, undtd [c. Apr. 1936] for Democratic Convention Book, but apparently not published.

242 "COLLOQUIAL SURVEY" HRC, FH/205/4, FH to Steve Early, May 29, 1936; Early to FH, June 6, 1936.

242 TO PLACE SOME MAGAZINE ARTICLES HRC, FH/205/4, Franklin Delano Roosevelt to FH, June 20, 1936.

242 FANNIE WAS AT HER DESK/ "STEF AND A NEWSREEL"/ "HAD DINNER WITH JACK AND STEF . . ."/ TO SIGNIFY NOTHING Bran, Box 8A, Diaries, 1936–37, Mar. 30, Apr. 3, 1936.

242 "THE ABSENTEE PRESIDENT" HRC, FH/95/3, FH to Hendrik Van Loon, Dec. 31, 1937.

242 SHE HAD GOTTEN FIRM ASSURANCE HRC, FH/150/4, Housing, FH to Helen Alfred, May 15, 1936; Alfred to FH, May 21, 1936.

242 "SUCH FANTASTIC TERMS" Bran, Box 8A, Diaries, 1936–37, Apr. 3, 1936.

242 "THE CRUELEST BUTCHERY . . ." HRC, FH/197/4, FH to Herbert Mapes [sic], *Pictorial Review,* July 21, 1936.

243 "BACKBONE OF AMERICAN *BELLES LETTRES* . . ." Tim Page, ed., *The Diaries of Dawn Powell 1931–1965* (South Royalton, Vt.: Steerforth Press, 1995), p. 117.

CHAPTER TWENTY-SEVEN

PAGE

244 FANNIE AGREED TO HAVE STEWART HRC, FH/225/2, Contracts, FH and Rosalie Stewart of H. E. Edington–F. W. Vincent Inc. Stewart to act as FH's motion-picture

representative for one year from date of agreement on basis of 10 percent commission, Aug. 14, 1935.

244–245 ALL FALL AND WINTER/ "AS OPPORTUNITIES . . ."/ METRO-GOLDWYN-MAYER INTERESTED . . . / YOUR STORY . . . / TWO DAYS BEFORE THE AGENT AGREEMENT RAN OUT HRC, FH/255/2, correspondence, FH–Rosalie Stewart, Aug. 14, 1935–Dec. 5, 1935; FH to Rosalie Stewart, not sent, Feb. 25, 1936; July 28–Aug. 12, 1936; Rosalie Stewart to FH, July 22, July 23, 1936; cbls, FH–Rosalie Stewart, July 24 and July 27, 1936; Rosalie Stewart to FH, July 22, 1936.

245 AS FOR THE FILM HRC, FH/179/1, William James Fadiman, MGM, to FH, Mar. 8, 1937.

245 "EXAGGERATED TENDENCY FOR REPETITIOUSNESS . . ." HRC, FH/96/2, FH to Vera Ballou, June 5, 1936.

245 IN THIS WAY, SHE IMPLIED HRC, FH/138/2, FH to William Briggs, June 13, 1936.

245 "IT WAS AND REMAINS MY UNHAPPY FACULTY . . ." *Anat,* pp. 302–303.

246 PERHAPS IT WAS A WAY Gratitude for this insight of Louise DeSalvo, Nov. 1997.

246 "A LITTLE SPECIALLY . . ."/ "EVERYTHING WE CAN . . ." HRC, FH/138/2, FH to Cass Canfield, July 7, 1936; Cass Canfield to FH, July 10, 1936.

246 "FLABBY"/ "MISERY" Bran, Box 8A, Folder 1, Diaries, 1936–37, June 3, 1936.

246 A DAY TRIP WITH STEF . . . / A JUNE LUNCH/ "BLISSFUL SOLITUDE" Bran, Box 8A, Diaries, 1936–37, May 30, June 28, Aug. 14, 1936.

246–247 STEWART ALSO USED THE OPPORTUNITY/ IF IT TURNED OUT TO BE TRUE HRC, FH/225/2, Rosalie Stewart to FH, Aug. 14, Aug. 18, 1936.

247 ADMITTING IN HER NOTE HRC, FH/110/4, Bill Lengel, Columbia Pictures, to FH, Aug. 6, 1936.

247 DAVID SELZNICK HRC, FH/212/1, David Selznick to FH, Aug. 13, 1936.

247 "QUITE EXTRAORDINARY" HRC, FH/225/2, FH to Rosalie Stewart, Aug. 20, 1936.

247 "ALL OF THE CHARACTERS . . ."/ PUSH THE BOOK AT MGM HRC, FH/179/1, William James Fadiman to FH, Aug. 20, 1936.

247 "VASTLY EXCITED" HRC, FH/135/1, *Great Laughter,* Charles Beahan, Universal, to FH, Aug. 26, 1936.

247–248 "THIRTY-FIVE THOUSAND?" . . . TO END THE CALL/ WEDNESDAY, THE TWENTY-SIXTH HRC, FH/235/1, Charles Beahan, Universal, to FH, Aug. 26, 1936. Also undtd, apparent transcription of FH–Beahan telephone conversation of Aug. 26, 1936.

248 "TERRIBLY ENTHUSIASTIC" HRC, FH/135/6, Rosalie Stewart to FH, Aug. 26, 1936.

248 KEEP THE DEAL OPEN . . . HRC, FH/135/6, *Great Laughter,* cbl, Bill Hawkins, United Artists, to FH, Aug. 26, 1936.

248 "PRACTICALLY BUY THEIR OWN STORIES" HRC, FH/135/6, *Great Laughter,* cbl, Rosalie Stewart to FH, Aug. 26, 1936.

248–250 "TWENTIETH CENTURY IS HYSTERICAL . . ."/ MISS RABIN SAID THE EPISODE/ "UNIVERSAL LEADS THE PACK . . ."/ "I'VE HAD EXPERIENCE . . ."/ "NOT ONLY THE IMMENSE DRAMATIC VALUES . . ."/ "I EXPECTED A WHOPPER . . ."/ STEALING HER PLOT/ "WHAT WOULD BE THE POINT . . ."/ "WITH BIDDERS . . ."/ "THAT HAS TO BE SEEN . . ."/ "FOUR-FOURTHS DEAD . . ."/ "WHEN THEY WEAR DOWN ROSALIE STEWART . . ."/ FANNIE WAS GLAD SHE HAD GOTTEN OUT/ "THE TELEGRAMS CONTINUE . . ."/ "JUST AS SLOW . . ." HRC, FH/200/2, Ethel Rabin[owitz] to FH, Wednesday early afternoon [Aug. 26, 1936], [Aug. 28, 1936]; FH to Ethel Rabin[owitz], Thursday,

[Aug. 27, 1936], [Aug. 28, 1936], [Aug. 29, 1936]. For *Gone with the Wind* purchase price, see David Thomson, *Showman: The Life of David O. Selznick* (New York: Alfred A. Knopf, 1992), pp. 212–215.

251 ANOTHER CABLE ARRIVED HRC, FH/225/2, cbl, Rosalie Stewart to FH, Aug. 30, 1936.

251 HAD ALREADY CLOSED WITH HER . . . / BY EVERY MEANS POSSIBLE . . . HRC, FH/235/1, cbls, Charles Beahan, Universal, to FH and Rosalie Stewart, Aug. 31, 1936.

251 SUGGEST YOU AND I . . . / BEAHAN HAD DEFAMED HER HRC, FH/255/2, Rosalie Stewart to FH, Aug. 31, 1936; FH to Rosalie Stewart, Sept. 2, 1936.

251 YOU ARE WRONG BOTH . . . HRC, FH/135/6, FH to Charlie Beahan, Universal, Sept. 1, 1936.

251–252 "UNTOLD MENTAL ANGUISH"/ "I HOPE THAT IS NOT TRUE . . ."/ STEWART, IN A LATER POSTMORTEM/ "VERBALLY REGISTER RESENTMENT"/ "I HAVE NO DESIRE . . ." HRC, FH/225/2, FH to Rosalie Stewart, Sept. 2, 1936; Rosalie Stewart to FH, Sept. 3, 1936.

252 THALBERG DIED Roland Flamini, *Thalberg: The Last Tycoon and the World of MGM* (New York: Crown, 1994), pp. 271–275.

252 FANNIE GOT ALL OF THE MONEY HRC, FH/221/1, Vivian Newcom, secretary to Norma Shearer, to FH, Nov. 10, 1936.

252 "ON THE DEBIT SIDE" HRC, FH/138/3, Bill Briggs, Harpers, to FH, Oct. 14, 1936.

252 "HARD TO FORGIVE . . ." Margaret Wallace, "Four Generations," *NYT Book Review*, Oct. 18, 1936, 7:1–3.

252 CANFIELD SENT FANNIE HRC, FH/138/3, Cass Canfield, Harpers, to FH, Dec. 1, 1936.

252 THE FIRST ROYALTY STATEMENT HRC, FH/138/3, Royalty Statement, July 1–Dec. 31, 1936, Harper and Brothers, Dec. 31, 1936.

252 THE WEEK OF DECEMBER 3 HRC, FH/138/3, FH–Bill Briggs correspondence, Dec. 1 and 3, 1936.

253 RAMONA HERDMAN DROPPED FANNIE A LINE HRC, FH/138/3, Ramona Herdman to FH, Jan. 7, 1937.

253 "I'M WORKING PRETTY GRAND NOW"/ "ODDS AND ENDS . . ." HRC, FH/138/3, FH to Bill Briggs, Harpers, Dec. 1, 1936.

253 "MY ONLY SECURITY . . ." HRC, FH/241/2, FH to Axel WennerGren, Oct. 31, 1934.

253 "NOW THAT THIS MATTER . . ." HRC, FH/244/4, FH (Ethel Rabinowitz) to Stef, Sept. 10, 1936.

253 ETHEL RABINOWITZ WAS A YOUNG TWENTY-ONE Int, Author with Ethel Rabinowitz Amatneek, Sept. 27, 1997.

255 "YOU WERE SIMPLY MARVELOUS . . ." HRC, FH/225/2, Rosalie Stewart to FH, Oct. 12, 1936.

255 WARNER BROS. PAID . . . SIXTY-FIVE THOUSAND DOLLARS HRC, FH/240/1, FH to Hal. B. Wallace, Oct. 8, 1936. See also FH/255/2, FH–Rosalie Stewart correspondence, Sept.–Oct. 1936.

255 HARRY BURTON PAID ANOTHER TEN THOUSAND HRC, FH/112/3, Harry Burton to FH, Oct. 29, 1936. Also HRC, FH/255/2, Contracts, *Cosmo* Corp. and FH for sole and exclusive first American serial rights to "Sister Act," $10,000, Nov. 9, 1936.

255 "ELAINE, DAUGHTER OF ELAINE" Hearst Corp., *Cosmo* files, index-card file, 5329, 5338, "Elaine, Daughter of Elaine" bought Nov. 1936, cost $4,000, published Oct. 1937. Also HRC, FH/255/2, cbl, Harry Burton to FH, Nov. 25, 1936.

255 AGA KHAN F. M. De Mello, "A Prophet Honored at Home," *NYT Magazine,* March 8, 1936, p. 21.

255 HE COMMITTED TO BUY THE STORY HRC, FH/112/3, Harry Burton, *Cosmo,* to FH, Dec. 4, 1936.

255 CONFIDENT MY VALUE LIES . . . / "CERTAIN IDEAS . . ."/ "THE IDEA HE BROUGHT ME . . ."/ "A PAGE OF HISTORY . . ." HRC, FH/225/2, FH to Rosalie Stewart, Nov. 6, [cbl] Nov. 7, Nov. 11, 1936.

256 "OF COURSE, LONG BEFORE THIS . . ."/ "TO FANNIE HURST . . ." Bran, Box 8A, Diaries, 1936–37, Nov. 3, Dec. 11, 1936.

257 PARAMOUNT ALREADY HAD PAID OUT/ "MASTER SCENE SCREENPLAY . . ." Film, Paramount Brief Sheets, Legal, summary of contract for "Show Business" with FH dated Nov. 20, 1936.

257 COME AT FIVE THOUSAND DOLLARS A WEEK HRC, FH/255/2, Contracts, FH and Paramount Public Corp., Nov. 13, 1936, FH for "Show Business." See also FH/255/2, Rosalie Stewart to FH, Nov. 18, 1936.

257 THIRTEEN-STORY DOWNTOWN HOTEL *Real Estate Record* (New York: Real Estate Board of New York, Vol. Jan.-June 1936), p. 45.

257 "THE FIRST 48 HOURS . . ." HRC, FH/138/3, FH to William Briggs, Harpers, Dec. 1, 1936.

257 CHRISTMAS EVE HRC, FH/225/2, FH to Rosalie Stewart, Dec. 24, 1936.

257 CHAMPAGNE-BATHED EGGS Bran, Box 8A, Diaries, 1936–37, Jan. 1, 1937.

257–258 "MORE SOLID STORY . . ."/ "WHIP THE STORY INTO SHAPE"/ "AN EPISODIC STORY . . ."/ DELIVERED THE REST OF THE INITIAL FORTY THOUSAND DOLLARS/ "THE FANNIE HURST WAY . . ." HRC, FH/225/2, Rosalie Stewart to FH, Jan. 6 and 7, 1937; FH to Rosalie Stewart, Jan. 7, Feb. 5, 1937.

258 "FROM THE GROUND UP"/ "PARAMOUNT IS AT FULL LIBERTY . . ." HRC, FH/225/2, FH to H. E. Edington, Mar. 12 and 13, 1937.

258 FIVE-MONTH JOURNEY HRC, FH/130/4, FH to William and Jennie Freighter, Sept. 2, 1937. Also FH/177/3, FH to Elizabeth Mahone, Sept. 22, 1937.

258 "WITH THE GLORIOUS SPEED . . ." HRC, FH/112/3, FH to Harry Payne Burton, Aug. 30, 1937.

258 "CRACKED THROUGH . . ." HRC, FH/116/1, FH to Robert Hobart Davis, Aug. 5, 1937.

258 HER AGA KHAN–LIKE YARN HRC, FH/112/3, *Cosmo,* FH–Harry Burton correspondence, Mar.–May 1938.

258–259 STEWART HAD NO LUCK/ "WHAT'S WHAT?"/ OF THE FOUR, ONLY "SISTER ACT" HRC, FH/225/2, FH to Rosalie Stewart, Aug. 5, 1937; Rosalie Stewart to FH, Aug. 10, 1937; FH–Rosalie Stewart correspondence, Jan.–July 1938.

259 FANNIE HAD TO THREATEN A LAWSUIT HRC, FH/225/2, FH to Rosalie Stewart, Mar. 16, 17 and Nov. 28, 1939. Also Robbie Coons, Hollywood column, *Richmond* (Va.) *News Leader,* Dec. 19, 1939, re: FH suit against Wagner for use of her characters.

259 AN ADDITIONAL $12,500 Colum, Curtis Brown Collection, Stern & Reuben, Benjamin Stern to FH, Wagner payment of $10,000 on Mar. 6, 1940. See also HRC, FH/255/2, second payment, $2,500, Dec. 16, 1940.

259 "SHOW BUSINESS" WOULD NEVER JELL Film, Memo of A. M. Botsford to Frank Freeman, re: "Show Business," July 26, 1940.

259 THE DEAL SHE STRUCK WITH GOLDWYN PICTURES HRC, FH/225/2, FH–Rosalie Stew-
     art correspondence, Oct. 25, 1937–Mar. 29, 1938. Also FH/134/3, Goldwyn–FH
     correspondence, Nov. 1937–Feb. 1938.

259 METEORIC STREAK THROUGH HOLLYWOOD WAS OVER HRC, FH/225/2, see Rosalie
     Stewart–FH correspondence, 1938 on.

CHAPTER TWENTY-EIGHT

PAGE

260 FIVE HUNDRED DOLLARS A MONTH HRC, FH/256/1, Lease, 1 West Sixty-seventh St.,
     dated Oct. 1, 1949. Also, FH/96/1, FH to Robert Backman, Mar. 29, 1951.

260 HER OVERALL PRODUCTION In the years between 1921 and 1929, Fannie published
     twenty-four short stories and six novels: *Lummox, Appassionata,* and *A President
     Is Born* as well as *Star-Dust, Mannequin,* and *Five and Ten,* which also appeared as
     magazine serials. There were three short-story collections in that period (*The
     Vertical City, Song of Life,* and *Procession*), which included twenty of the stories.
        After *Procession,* between 1929 and 1938, Fannie published *Back Street* and
     Imitation of Life, in both serial and novel format, and the novels *Anitra's Dance*
     and *Great Laughter. Sister Act* and *Bride of the Rajah* (1938) both ran as *Cosmo*
     serials—six novel-length works in all. The nonfiction *No Food with My Meals*
     was published along with fourteen short stories, ten of which were included in
     We Are Ten, her only collection published during the period. In the film arena,
     she also worked on *Hello, Everybody!, Symphony of Six Million,* "Once upon a
     Time," "Park Avenue," and "Show Business" during these years.

260 "STILLBORN" HRC, FH/138/4, FH to Ramona Herdman, undtd [c. Sept. 1937].

260 THE EFFORT NETTED ONLY ONE RESPONSE HRC, FH/200/6, Ruth Raphael to FH's sec-
     retary, Aug. 13, Oct. 4, 7, 8, 1937.

260 "SHEER BADNESS AND MAWKISHNESS . . ." [signed with initials E.H.W.] "Latest Works
     of Fiction," *NYT,* Sept. 26, 1937, 7:27:1–4.

260 "INDEED, FROM FIRST TO LAST . . ." Lucy Tomkins, "In the Florida Glades," *NYT,*
     Sept. 26, 1937, 7:29:1–2.

260 "SHOT THROUGH WITH THE LIGHTNING . . ." HRC, FH/169/1, FH to J. B. Lippincott,
     Aug. 25, 1937.

261 "THE NECESSARY PUMPING . . ." HRC, FH/138/4, FH to William Briggs, Harper &
     Bros., Oct. 7, 1937.

261 SERIOUS PROMOTIONAL ATTENTION HRC, FH/169/2, J. B. Lippincott–FH correspon-
     dence, Aug. 25, 30, 31, Sept. 1, 17, 21, and Oct. 11, 1937.

261 IDEA TO DOUBLE-SERVICE HRC, FH/169/1, J. B. Lippincott telephoned and met with
     FH several times in September about Hurston's new book and other matters.

261 "CURIOSITY ABOUT LIFE . . ." Isabel Wilder, "Novels in Outline," *Saturday Review,*
     Oct. 9, 1937, p. 16.

261 "ZORA NEALE HURSTON, FOR . . ." Zora Neale Hurston, "Fannie Hurst by Her Ex-
     Amanuensis," *Saturday Review,* Oct. 9, 1937, pp. 15–16.

261 TWENTY-FOUR YEARS LATER See FH, "Zora Neale Hurston: A Personality Sketch," *Li-
     brary Gazette,* Yale University, No. 35, 1961, p. 19.

261 "HOP FROM ONE EMOTION . . ." Hurston, "Fannie Hurst by Her Ex-Amanuensis," pp. 15–16.

262 MISS RABIN REMEMBERED Int, Author with Ethel Rabinowitz Amatneek, Sept. 28, 1997.

262 ARID IN PLACES . . . *Anat,* p. 254.

262 STEF EVEN TURNED OVER Dart, Stef, Box 13, FH, Stef to FH, Jan. 13, 1925.

263 "ABOUT AS OUT OF PLACE . . ."/ HIS NATURALIZATION/ "OUT OF THE MOOD FOR EITHER OF THEM"/ A BIRTHDAY PARTY/ "NICE TO HIM"/ "HEAVY AND DULL AND TIRED" Bran, Box 8A, Diaries 1936–37, June 4, 1936.

263 "TRUE, I HAVE BEEN EARNING . . ." HRC, FH/224/4, Stef to FH, Dec. 4, 1939.

263 STEF HAD BECOME DEEPLY INVOLVED Int, Author with Evelyn Stefansson Nef, Jan. 22, 1996.

263 "HE IS A KIND . . ." HRC, FH/160/4, FH to Alfred Kuttner, Apr. 20, 1942.

263 "TO STEF" FH sometimes favored a quotation on the dedication page and more often nothing at all. *Five and Ten* honored "New York, City of Cities" and *A President Is Born,* its fictional protagonist. The others that bore dedications were *Gaslight Sonatas,* to her parents; *Star-Dust,* to Bob Davis; *Humoresque,* to Daniel Frohman; and *Appassionata* to Pauline Rehbein, the aunt of Lois Meier Toensfeldt, who was an early mentor of Fannie's in St. Louis, "a beautiful woman with a wonderful, beautiful mind. She had a passionate hunger for things outside her natural sphere in life. She exerted great influence over me." (HR, Scrapbooks, St. Louis, p. 14. Undtd profile of FH by Madeline Wartell Lockwood.)

264 HIS PREDECESSOR, RAY LONG Long, born Mar. 23, 1878, died after a self-inflicted gunshot wound, July 9, 1935, four years after the Berlin coup in the Hearst empire. In that time he cofounded a publishing house that soon went bankrupt. On the verge of a nervous breakdown, he left for Tahiti, returning to work in Hollywood for a time, for *Photoplay* and the various Hollywood studios. His suicide took place in his Beverly Hills home.

264 "BEYOND EDITORIAL COMMENT . . ."/ "NOT ONLY DO I DISLIKE . . ."/ "EVEN WHEN THE GOING . . ." HRC, FH/112/3, FH to Harry Burton, *Cosmo,* Mar. 14, June 13, 15, 1938.

264 "RHINESTONES PREFERRED" HRC, FH/112/2, Burton's office sent it back for revisions, May 3, 1938.

265 "HOME, JAMES" HRC, FH/112/3, FH–Harry Burton correspondence, May 4, 5, 17, 1938. Hearst, *Cosmo,* index-card files, "Rhinestones Preferred," bought Apr. 3, 1939, published Dec. 1940.

265 "BUT DON'T RUN . . ." HRC, FH/112/3, Harry Burton to FH, May 20, 1938.

265 "COMEDY, TRAGEDY . . ." HRC, FH/112/3, FH to Harry Burton, *Cosmo,* May 23, 1938.

265 THE UNIQUE PERSPECTIVE HRC, FH/138/4, Cass Canfield, Harper & Bros, to FH, Dec. 2, 1937.

265 "THINK-OUT-LOUD STAGE . . ." HRC, FH/138/4, FH to Cass Canfield, Harper & Bros., Dec. 7, 1937.

265 SHE WAS QUITE CONTENT Bran, Box 1, Appt-bks, appt-bk for 1927 has Fannie's character index for the Miss Leland series. It includes a reference to "Mr. Mahler's Dance Class," which she actually had attended as a St. Louis teenager.

See also Robert Van Gelder, "An Interview with Miss Fannie Hurst," *NYT,* Jan. 25, 1942, 6:2:2.

266 "A HIGH LEVEL OF EXCELLENCE . . ."/ "DRAMATIC NEWSINESS . . ." HRC, FH/112/3, Harry Burton to FH, May 20, July 28, 1938.

266 "THE MIRACLE OF CHRISTMAS . . ." Adela Rogers St. Johns, "Unto Us," *Cosmo,* Jan. 1938, p. 20.

266 "I AM SUFFICIENTLY AHEAD . . ." HRC, FH/197/4, FH to Mabel Search, May 21, 1938.

266 "WHEN A STORY . . ."/ "I CHECKED WITH HARRY . . ." HRC, FH/197/4, Mabel Search, *Pictorial Review,* undtd [Dec. 1939].

266 HE STARTED INAUSPICIOUSLY HRC, FH/105/3, Bye got rejections for "Do Re Me Fah" from: the *Saturday Evening Post, American Magazine, McCall's, Collier's, This Week, Redbook,* the *Chicago Tribune, Scribner's,* and the *Atlantic Monthly.* All the editors of these magazines told Bye the story was too depressing.

267 THROUGH THE CASH-POOR DECADE *Cosmo* paid $4,000 for "The Third Husband" July 28, 1928 (published Dec. 1928), and the rate never went down. Hearst, *Cosmo,* index-card file, No. 1411 and thereafter.

267 BOUGHT UP THE OTHERS Colum, James O. Brown Collection, FH–George Bye correspondence, 1938–1940. See also HRC, FH/105/3 FH–George Bye correspondence, 1938–1940.

267 "ONE OF THE HIGHEST PAID . . ." Van Gelder, "Interview with Miss Fannie Hurst."

267 FANNIE HAD HER COUSIN WRITE HRC, FH/247/1, Sadie Hurst Wyman to the *NYT,* Mar. 5, 1939; to FH, Mar. 5, 1939; FH to Wyman, Mar. 8, 1939.

267 "THOSE PRESENT . . ." HRC, FH/228/1, FH to Arthur Hayes Sulzberger, Mar. 4, 1939.

267 FANNIE WAS ASSURED See *NYT,* Jan. 16, 1937, 15:5; Feb. 13, 1937, 11:8; Aug. 26, 1937, 24:4; Oct. 17, 1937, 6:6:5; Oct. 31, 1937, 5:3; Nov. 16, 1937, 24:2; Nov. 22, 1937, 5:1; Nov. 27, 1937, 15:4; Dec. 16, 1937, 10:4; Mar. 22, 1938, 15:2; Sept. 16, 1938, 44:2; Dec. 13, 1938.

267 "I WOULDN'T GO BACK . . ." FH, "I Wouldn't Go Back if I Could," *This Week,* Jan. 14, 1940, p. 2.

267 "THIS URGENT NOW" Colum, James O. Brown Collection, FH–George Bye correspondence, 1938–1940. See also HRC, FH/105/3, FH–George Bye correspondence, 1938–1940. See FH, "This Urgent Now," *Liberty,* Vol. 17, No. 45, Nov. 9, 1940, p. 17.

267 "FELT THE STATEMENTS . . ." HRC, FH/118/1, FH to Charles Michaelson, Democratic Party Headquarters, Oct. 9, 1940.

268 "HELP LIGHT THE WAY . . ." FH, "A Lamp in the Darkness," *Liberty,* May 14, 1940, p. 52.

268 "THE TERRIBLE MENTAL . . . SICKNESS . . ." "Miss Hurst Bewails 'Mental Sickness,' Speaks to Flatbush Council for Religious Goodwill," *NY World-Telegram,* Dec. 17, 1940.

268 TO GIVE READERS THE IMPRESSION FH, "Maturity," *Cosmo,* Vol. 110, No. 5, May 1941, pp. 15, 108–109. In this essay, clearly writing about her own experience, Fannie repeatedly contrasts the woman of nineteen and the woman of "twice nineteen." At fifty-five, she was closer to thrice.

268 "TODAY A WORLD . . ." FH, "I Wouldn't Go Back if I Could," p. 2.

269 "SWEET ARE THE USES . . ." Fannie had wanted to call it "Sweet Are the Uses of Ma-

turity," but *Cosmo* titled it "Maturity" (May 1941 issue); see HRC, FH/112/3, FH to B. J. Hawley, *Cosmo*, Mar. 6, 1941.

269   "COMPLETELY, ABSOLUTELY, FEARFULLY TRUTHFUL"   Van Gelder, "Interview with Miss Fannie Hurst."

269   EXPRESSIONS OF INTEREST   Van Gelder, "Interview with Miss Fannie Hurst." See also HRC, FH/179/1, William James Fadiman, MGM, to FH, Jan. 26, 1942; FH/112/3, Percy Waxman, *Cosmo*, to FH, Feb. 4, 1942; FH/105/3, George Bye to FH, Jan. 27, 1942, re: Wes Stout at *Saturday Evening Post*; FH/139/3, Bill Briggs, Harper & Bros., Apr. 28, 1942; FH/126/2, Bill Lengel, Fawcett Publications, Sept. 28, 1944.

269   "VULGARITIES . . ."   Van Gelder, "Interview with Miss Fannie Hurst."

CHAPTER TWENTY-NINE

PAGE

273   IN SPITE AND BECAUSE OF   See FH's "Mrs. Leland" series of short stories, including "Mamma and Papa," *Saturday Evening Post*, Nov. 19, 1938; "Mamma and the First National Bank" (*Saturday Evening Post*, Mar. 18, 1939, pp. 16–17 ff.); "At Mrs. Leland's": Episode Pertaining to Miss Haswell (HRC, FH/53/4 and FH/56/6); "The Cut Glass Bowl" (HRC, FH/53/40); "At Mrs. Leland's" (*Sunday News* [NY], Aug. 13, 1939); "Behind His Ears" (*Sunday News* [NY], Nov. 3, 1940; HRC, FH/53/3 and 5); "Sunday Afternoon" (*Woman's Home Companion*, July 1940); and "The Cluck Family" (HRC, FH/53/3 and 4).

273   MANY YEARS AFTER   Fannie began collecting material for an eventual autobiography around 1935. See Bran, Box 5B.

273   "BIG, DIGNIFIED, SILENT"   HRC, FH/106/1, Rosa Lee Calder to FH undtd.

273   "SO QUIET"   HRC, FH/106/1, Floyd Calvert to FH, July 21, 1959.

273   "SO GOOD TO MY BLIND HUSBAND . . ."   Bran, Box 5B, Autobiography research, ltr from Mrs. Janet Townshend undtd [1935].

273   "WARM-HEARTED . . ."   HRC, FH/126/1, Olna Hudler Fant to FH, undtd.

273   "HOW MANY WAYS . . ."   HRC, FH/106/1, Rosa Lee Calder to FH, undtd.

273   "SHE SAID SUCH FUNNY THINGS"   HRC, FH/106/1, Floyd Calvert to FH, July 21, 1959.

273   "SO INTERESTING . . ."   Bran, Box 5B, Autobiography research, ltr from Mrs. Janet Townshend undtd [1935].

273   "UNIQUE IN THE REAL SENSE . . ."   HRC, FH/126/1, Olna Hudler Fant to FH, Jan. 27, 1954.

273   "MAMA AND PAPA . . ."   *Anat,* p. 23.

274   "LIKE SO MANY CANDLES . . ."   *Anat,* pp. 3–4.

274   NEIGHBORS REMEMBERED HIM   HRC, FH/218/4, *Anat,* Mrs. G. Garnett Hedges to FH, Oct. 2, 1958.

274   "SOFT AS SILK . . ."   *Anat,* p. 4.

274   "AN EXTREMELY RETICENT MAN . . ."/ REFERRING TO HIS BOYHOOD   HRC, FH/151/2, FH to Henry Hurst, Oct. 17, 1938.

274   THE FUNERAL OF HER GRANDFATHER   Obituary, Samuel Hurst, *Memphis Scimitar,* Apr. 26, 1925.

274   "SMALL, DYNAMIC WOMAN . . ."   HRC, FH/151/2, FH to Henry Hurst, Oct. 17, 1938.

274   AS IF HE FOUND SHIRTSLEEVES/ "KNOWLEDGE IS POWER" *Anat,* p. 5.

274   "LIBERALS AND SOCIALISTS . . ." *Anat,* p. 22.

275   "PRETTY NEARLY EVERYBODY . . ." FH, "At Miss Leland's," *Sunday (NY Daily) News,* Aug. 13, 1939.

275   THE HURSTS FROM MEMPHIS U.S. Census, 1850, Simpson County, Miss., p. 299, lines 41–42, and p. 300, lines 1–3, household 168, household of Solomon Hurst. Samuel appears to have been born in 1849.

275   THEN NORTH HILLSBORO U.S. Census, 1860, North Hillsboro Scott County, Miss. p. 28, lines 19–26, household 171, household of Solomon Hurst.

275   HAD MUCH IN COMMON David Koppel, Rose's father, was a stock dealer, and Sam's father had been a merchant (1850 Census) and a farmer (1860 Census) before going into the grocery business, according to census records of 1850, 1860, and 1870, Shelby County, Memphis, Fifth Ward, p. 180, lines 30–37, dwelling 304, household 428.

275   BORN IN FRANCE FH, "At Miss Leland's" *Sunday (NY Daily) News,* Aug. 13, 1939; U.S. Census, 1860, North Hillsboro, Scott County, Miss. p. 28, lines 19–26, household 171, household of Solomon Hurst.

275   A WEDDING CEREMONY Butler County Records Center and Archives, Record of Issuing and Return of Marriage Licenses, Samuel Hurst and Rose Koppel, Jan. 11, 1885, p. 305.

275   "AN ELEGANT TRAVELING SUIT . . ." "From Monday's Daily," *Hamilton* (Ohio) *Telegraph,* Jan. 15, 1885.

275   THE ANGLICIZATION St.LPubSch, Elementary School Records, Stoddard School, 1892–93. Her name is listed on Annual Register as "Fannie Hurst" though the 1900 U.S. Census lists her as "Fanye."

275   VIRTUAL STRANGERS *Anat,* p. 40.

276   "A SPARE, MIRTHLESS WOMAN . . ."/ "ROARING, VULGAR . . ." *Anat,* p. 30.

276   KUTTY Information about Kaufman's nickname supplied by Jeanne Brownstein Silverberg, the daughter of Fannie's first cousin, Ruth Koppel Brownstein, daughter of Fannie's uncle Abraham Koppel and Rose Kahn Koppel.

276   IT WOULD FALL TO FANNIE Other than Fannie and Edna Hurst, the only other Koppel grandchild was Ruth, the daughter of Abraham and Rose Kahn Koppel. The date of her birth is not known, but Ruth's daughter, Jeanne Brownstein Silverberg, confirms that her mother graduated high school in 1910, indicating a probable birth year of 1892 or 1893.

276   "I MAY NOT HAVE BEEN WANTED . . ." *Anat,* p. 40.

276   "LIKE A BUTTERFLY . . ." *Anat,* p. 8.

276   "NOT ONLY LOVELY . . ." Bran, Box 5B, Miscellaneous Correspondence, relating to Autobiography, 1935, Lillian Becker to FH.

277   "MAMA ALWAYS CRIED . . ." *Anat,* pp. 8–10.

277   FOUND THE KITTEN DEAD . . . *Anat,* p. 67.

278   "THE SNAGS OF CIRCUMLOCATION . . ." *Anat,* p. 251.

278   "WITH NO NOTES TO GUIDE ME . . ." *Anat,* p. 12.

278   TO OMIT REFERENCE This insight is from Susan Koppelman, also a native St. Louisian, which she pointed out in a 1994 conversation with the author.

278   "GATEWAY TO THE WEST . . ." *Anat,* p. 13.

279 SHE ALMOST NEVER DREW HER CHARACTERS HRC, FH/159/1, Josie (née Daley) Kesl, to FH, Monday [undtd, c. Nov.–Dec.] 1931. See also, *Anat*, p. 33, FH writes, "Like most authors, I am repeatedly asked if I glean my characters from real life. Almost invariably no."

279 AUNT'S NAME REALLY WAS RAY *Anat*, pp. 126–127.

279 STEF'S WIDOW DID NOT RECOGNIZE Author telephone int. with Evelyn Stefansson Nef, Feb. 23, 1998.

279 "THREE QUIET AND MEMORABLE MEN . . ." *Anat*, p. 217.

279 THOUGH SHE WORKED HRC, FH/141/1, FH to Wilma Robi Hailpern, Mar. 9, Apr. 2, 1945.

280 "BARRING A FEW . . . UPS AND DOWNS . . ." *Anat*, p. 11.

280 NEVER OWNED ANY PLACE No Hurst ever owned the property on Cates Avenue, according to a title search generously conducted for this project by Sharon Huffman, St. Louis Public School Archivist.

280 "DURING THE PERIOD . . ." FH, "At Miss Leland's," *Sunday (NY Daily) News*, Aug. 13, 1939.

280 THE FAMILY'S FREQUENT MOVES From 1885 to 1901 Gould's St. Louis Directory shows residences for Samuel Hurst at the following addresses: 3144 School Street (1888–89); 2930 Locust (1890); 2702 Lucas (1891); 2839 Morgan (1892); 1215 Dolman (1893); 2930 Washington (1894); 3128 Laclede (1895); 4904 Fountain (1896); 5077 Page Blvd. (1897); 4478 West Belle Place (1898–99); and 4406 West Belle Place (1901–1906). The Hursts didn't move to the address at 5641 Cates Avenue until 1906, when Fannie was twenty-one and a sophomore in college.

281 THREE OF THOSE ADDRESSES WERE BOARDINGHOUSES According to Gould's St. Louis Directory entries, the boardinghouse of Mrs. Parker L. Cleveland was at 3128 Laclede, where the Hursts lived in 1894–95. The address at 4904 Fountain of 1895–96 was also shared by Charles Wempner and family, who boarded with the Hursts (see HRC, FH/241/2, Mrs. Charles Wempner to FH, Mar. 8, 1932). The Wempners and Calverts also shared the address at 4478 West Belle Place, where the Hursts are listed as living in the years 1896–97, 1897–98, and 1898–99.

281 SHE DOES NOT APPEAR FH returned to Stoddard in the fall of 1894, but her name does not appear on any other school registration in the district for the missing two years after Edna's death. In the 1894 directory, which would have been compiled in 1893, Samuel Hurst is not listed at all. A check of school registration in Hamilton, Ohio, for that period showed no registration for a Fannie Hurst. It is not clear where Fannie went to school those two years.

281 "FATTY SHOW-OFF" *Anat*, p. 61. See also HRC, FH/106/1, Floyd Calvert to FH, July 21, 1959.

281–282 "BOTH PAPA AND I REALIZED . . ."/ HER MOTHER DEMANDED/ "IT WAS IN MR. CLEVELAND'S DARK CAVE . . ." *Anat*, pp. 56–60.

282 "LOOK HERE, FRED . . ." FH, "Mamma and Her First National Bank," *Saturday Evening Post*, Mar. 18, 1939, pp. 17.

283 "WHAT A WOMAN . . ." *Anat*, p. 64.

283 THE HOUSE ON CATES AVENUE Mrs. Carl G. Campbell, "Huntington Woman Pens a Close Up of Fannie Hurst," *Saturday Advertiser* (Huntington, W.Va.), Jan. 17, 1926.

283 "QUITE THE FASHIONABLE THING TO DO" Bran, Box 5B, Misc. Correspondence re: Autobiography, 1935, Lillian Becker to FH, undtd.

283 "GLOOMY HALL" *Anat,* p. 56.

283 "OLD BLACK KATE" HRC, FH/106/1, Floyd Calvert to FH, July 21, 1959.

CHAPTER THIRTY

PAGE

284 "LITTLE ROLE-POLY SCHOOL GIRL . . ."/ AT THE CORNER OF HRC, FH/174/2, Edith Thorpe McMahon to FH, Dec. 19, 1927.

284 OVERCROWDED AND IMPERSONAL StLPubSch, St. Louis Public School District Annual Report, 1892–93, app. cxxxvi–cxxxvii. Listing for Stoddard School. See also StLPubSch, School Building Photographs, photo ID. FM261 with history/location status.

284 FANNIE WAS NOT AMONG THEM *Anat,* p. 23.

284 KAFFEEKLATSCHES *Anat,* pp. 34–35.

284 SHE USED TO SNEAK HRC, FH/110/1, FH to William C. Wolfe, *Columbus Dispatch,* Mar. 20, 1951.

284–285 SAM ALWAYS JOINED/ "PERSIFLAGE . . ." *Anat,* p. 34.

285 GRANDMA KOPPEL'S DEATH Record of Deaths, Probate Court, Butler County, Ohio, Records Center and Archives, Death Record 3 and 4, 1893–1908, p. 133. Carrie Koppel died Jan. 28, 1897.

285 AUNT JENNIE ALSO REMAINED U.S. Census records for 1880 and 1900 show the Koppel home was at 918 Central Avenue in Hamilton, Ohio.

285 "QUITE A BEAU . . ." *Anat,* pp. 31–34.

285 "JOLLY, GENIAL . . ." HRC, FH/106/1, Rosa Lee Calder to FH, undtd [c. 1940s].

285 "BASEBALL MASK . . ."/ ROSA LEE SAID Bran, Box 5B, Miscellaneous Correspondence, re: Autobiography, 1935, Rosa Lee Einhorn (Calder) to FH, undtd.

285 "FANNIE, PRACTICE!" Bran, Box 5B, Miscellaneous Correspondence, re: Autobiography, 1935, Mrs. Abraham Raphael to FH, undtd.

285 AS BACKHANDED A COMPLIMENT HRC, FH/158/1, Milton Kahn to FH, Oct. 7, 1931. Also *Anat,* pp. 28–30, 41.

285 "AUBREY BEARDSLEY SLENDERNESS . . ." *Anat,* p. 94.

286 "THERE WAS LITTLE TALK . . ." *Anat,* p. 38.

286 "INSTANTLY, THE LINE . . ." *Anat,* pp. 16–17.

286 HARPERLY HALL *Anat,* pp. 41–45.

286 NO SCHOOL BY THAT NAME Harperly Hall is the apartment building at 1 West Sixty-fourth, near all of Fannie's West Side residences since 1917. She also lived there briefly before she was permanently settled.

286 HOSMER HALL Bran, Box 5B, Miscellaneous Correspondence, re: Autobiography, 1935. Mrs. Frances (Windhorst) Lewis to FH. Enrollment records for the years in question for Hosmer Hall could not be located. The school was moved to Clayton, Mo., then closed down in 1936. Mary Institute, the other girls' school in St. Louis, shows no registration for FH in its records, nor do her college friends who went there give any indication that she ever studied there.

287 HOSMER CERTIFICATE GUARANTEED ADMISSION MHS, Archives, St. L 376 H 79, Annual Catalogue, Hosmer Hall, 1898–99. If FH did attend, it would have been between Sept. and Dec. 1900.

287 MARY INSTITUTE See Orrick Johns, *Time of Our Lives: The Story of My Father and Myself* (New York: Stackpole, 1937), p. 127.

287 "RELIGION," . . . "AS IF SHE WERE BITING OFF . . ." *Anat,* p. 42.

287 BUT STILL PAID THE SIXTY-FIVE DOLLARS MHS, Archives, St. L 376 H 79, Annual Catalogue, Hosmer Hall, 1898–99. This catalog, for the year before FH would have attended, lists a sixty-five-dollar tuition for the first college preparatory year, seventy dollars for the second year, and so on.

287 "IT PROVED A HEARTBREAKING EXPERIENCE . . ." *Anat,* p. 43.

287 "FEELING OUT OF THE HERD" *Anat,* p. 30.

288 "NO PEAKS AND NO DEPTHS . . ." See Johns, *Time of Our Lives,* pp. 127–128.

288 "A SLIGHTLY BUILT MAN . . ." *Anat,* pp. 51–53.

288 "RIGID AND ASHAMED SILENCE . . ." *Anat,* pp. 26, 53.

288 "DO YOU REMEMBER . . ." HRC, FH/211/1, William Schuyler to FH, Dec. 24, 1912.

289 "AS ANONYMOUS AS A PRISONER . . ." *Anat,* pp. 46, 47.

289 "INCOMPLETE" FOR HER SPANISH AND GEOMETRY StLPubSch, Central High School Record of Fannye Hurst, p. 66, 228, 194, 42, 10, Book 11, 10, 11, 12, 13. Graduate: Book 19, p. 178. Other references: Book and p. nos. 17:462; 18:383; 19:127; 19:407; 21:115; 21:429; 22:25. Graduate Record: *Vol.* Jan. 1901, p. 146.

289 COULD STILL PICTURE FANNIE/ "UNDERSTANDING OF AND KINDNESS TO THOSE . . ." Bran, Box 5B, Miscellaneous Correspondence, re: Autobiography, 1935, Mrs. Frances (Windhorst) Lewis to FH.

289 "A LOT OF OTHER SUPERB QUALITIES" HRC, FH/218/1–6, Olna Hudler Fant to FH, Nov. 17, 1958. Though Olna was Fannie's best friend at Washington University, she, like Frances Windhorst, was friendly with Fannie in high school and was in the same graduating class at Central High as Fannie, Jan. 1905.

289–290 FANNIE'S FAME/ "PROBABLY THE BEST FORWARD . . ."/ PRESIDENT OF THE GIRLS' ATHLETIC ASSOCIATION/ OFTEN PRACTICING/ THE CALLA LILY/ PULL PRANKS/ "WRITTEN BY FANNIE HURST" Bran, Box 5B, Miscellaneous Correspondence, re: Autobiography, 1935, Mrs. Frances (Windhorst) Lewis to FH.

290 A REFUSAL TO ALLOW HER *Anat,* pp. 77–78.

290 THIS SEEMS DOUBTFUL StLPubSch, Central High School record of Fannie Hurst, 1902–3 shows her failing chemistry reviews.

290 BOTH FRANK AND OLNA APPEAR Private collection of Gus and Sheila Pavlakis, Jan. 1905, Commencement Exercises program of Central High School.

290 "PAY THE PIPER" Bran, Box 5B, Miscellaneous Correspondence, re: Autobiography, 1935, Mrs. Frances (Windhorst) Lewis to FH.

290 SHARING HOT DOGS HRC, FH/225/1, Helen Warnhoff Stevens to FH, Jan. 3, 1936.

290 "FUNNY MAID . . ." HRC, FH/141/1, Wilma Robi Hailparn to FH, Apr. 13, 1945.

290 THE DOG NAMED FURY Bran, Box 5B, Miscellaneous Correspondence, re: Autobiography, 1935. Numerous of these letters refer to Fury.

290 "FURY MY LOVE" PULLING WILDLY HRC, FH/242/1, Lois Wilkes Whitaker to FH, Aug. 28, 1944.

290 HE BIT A MAN *Anat,* p. 70. Numerous of FH's friends remember the dog as being named Fury. Here FH refers to it as Annie.

290 "RELEASED SOMETHING HARD . . ." *Anat,* p. 69.

290 FAT, LONELY, AND JEWISH/ "BUT IT WAS ALWAYS . . ." HRC, FH/112/1, Olna Hudler Fant Cook to FH, Feb. 11, 1959.

291 "NEVER DID I DREAM . . ." HRC, FH/218/1–6, Olna Hudler Fant to FH, Nov. 17, 1958.

291 MILDRED HOYLE WAS MORE STRUCK HRC, FH/11/2, Mildred Hoyle Core to FH, July 2, 1942.

291 "TEASE MACHINE" HRC, FH/141/1, Wilma Robi Hailparn to FH, Apr. 13, 1945.

291 "JUST ANOTHER SQUIRMER . . ." *Anat,* p. 52.

291 "PSYCHIATRY HAS NEW NAMES . . ." *Anat,* p. 23.

291 "ALL KINDS OF NOSTALGIAS . . ." HRC, FH/141/1, FH to Wilma Robi Hailparn, Apr. 2, 1945.

CHAPTER THIRTY-ONE

PAGE

295 "I BARGED THROUGH . . ." *Anat,* p. 339.

295 FOUR MULTICITY TOURS HRC, FH/181/3, Henry Morgenthau, Jr., to FH, Jan. 8, 1942; FH to Morgenthau, May 25, 1942; FH/116/1, FH to Robert H. Davis, Jan. 23, 1942; FH/1401/1, FH to William Briggs, Harper & Bros., Sept. 30, 1943. Also *StLP-D,* Feb. 3, 1944, 3A:2. See also *Anat,* pp. 329–330, where there is the only mention of Ogden Nash.

295 HER VERY SMALL PART/ "CREATIVE ART DEMANDS . . ." "Miss Hurst Asks More of Women," *NYT,* Nov. 27, 1937, 15:4.

295 PRESTIGIOUS PANEL OF JUDGES Other judges were James Montgomery Flagg, H. L. Redman, John La Gatta, Brandshaw Crandall, and John Powers. Those setting the career-barring criteria also included Eddie Cantor, Lowell Thomas, Bruce Banton, Emily Post, Walter Pitkin, Neysa McMein, Mrs. Osa Johnson, Lillian Wald, George Ade, and Judge Jonah Goldstein.

295 THE CONTEST PARAMETERS "Ideal Girls Stir Fannie Hurst's Ire," *NYT,* Sept. 16, 1938, 44:2. (Early-edition story does not contain FH quotes.) See HRC, FH/90/3, the judges decided the winner should be "healthy and wholesome in appearance, rather than a glamour girl; that her interests should include intelligent understanding of current affairs and that her ambition after college should be marriage and a home rather than business and professional life."

296 SHE CALLED ON WOMEN "Miss Hurst Makes Plea for Defense," *NYT,* June 26, 1940, 26:4.

296 "I AM CONVINCED . . ." NYPL-BR, FH, Florence Wessels, "Peace Is a Woman's Job," *NY Journal-American,* Dec. 29, 1940.

296 GRINDING NUTS Colum, Helen Worden Erskine Papers, FH to Helen Worden, undtd [c. 1942].

296 "WHAT RINGING CHALLENGE . . ." HRC, FH/236/3, FH to Florence Kerr, National Advisory Committee of Community Service Projects, Jan. 6, 1941.

296 "IMPORTANT CREDENTIALS . . ." HRC, FH/123/1, FH to Steve Early, Mar. 10, 1941.

297 "EVEN THOSE WHO HAVE ALREADY DESERTED . . ."/ THE FIRST LADY CONCURRED HRC, FH/205/2, FH to Eleanor Roosevelt, May 3, 1941; Eleanor Roosevelt to FH, May 13, 1941.

297 "I DON'T KNOW WHAT TO SAY . . ." HRC, FH/211/5, FH to Mabel Search, Oct. 9,
1941. The Washington meetings on South America were on Oct. 10 and 12, 1941.

297 "FLEW TO WASHINGTON . . ." Bran, Box 8A, Diaries, 1941, Entry, Oct. 12, 1941.

297 FANNIE REVIVED HER OFFER HRC, FH/205/2, FH to Eleanor Roosevelt, Dec. 17,
1941; Roosevelt to FH, Dec. 29, 1941.

297 THE PRESIDENT ALREADY HAD DECIDED HRC. FH sent dozens of letters promoting
Ruth Bryan Owen Rohde for the position, e.g., FH/171/2, FH/246/1, FH/222/1,
FH/158/4, FH/145/1, Sept. 1941. In 1949 President Harry S Truman appointed
her an alternative representative to the Fourth UN General Assembly. Her term
expired in the mid-1950s. She also served as acting president of the Institute for
International Government before her death July 26, 1954, in Copenhagen.

297 "I HAVE NEITHER POLITICAL NOR . . . PERSONAL REASONS . . ." HRC, FH/163/2, FH to
Fiorello La Guardia, Jan. 13, Feb. 21, and Apr. 29, 1941.

297–298 LA GUARDIA URGED FANNIE/ "WOMEN IN LITERATURE COMMITTEE"/ "IDLE AND
USELESS . . ." HRC, FH/163/2, Fiorello La Guardia to FH, Oct. 2, 1941; FH to
Fiorello La Guardia, Oct. 2, 1941; June 11, 1942.

298 "I CAN UNDERSTAND YOUR POSSIBLE REASON . . ." HRC, FH/163/3, FH—unsent—to
Fiorello La Guardia, June 23 and 29, 1942. The letter she mailed on July 11,
1942 said only "This is the eleventh of July. On June 11 I wrote you a letter.
There has been no reply although I have made sure that you received it before
writing this one. Contents of above sent."

298 "WE WOMEN ARE NO LONGER . . ." "Fannie Hurst Sees Women Can Win," *NYT,* Jan.
22, 1942, 15:1.

298 "A NEW SPECIES . . ." "Fannie Hurst Sees Gains for Women," *NYT,* Feb. 6, 1942,
17:2.

298 "MY LIFE HAS CHANGED . . ." HRC, FH/104/2, FH to Julia Browne, Mar. 23, 1942.

298 ELEVEN OTHER WOMEN LEADERS "Twelve Women Leaders Agree World Cooperation
Is Vital," *NYT,* Apr. 8, 1943, 1:2–3, 16, 1–8. In addition to FH, participating
speakers were Margaret Culkin Banning, Mrs. Walter H. Beech, Pearl S. Buck,
Virginia Gildersleeve, Mrs. J. Borden Harriman, Judge Camille McGee Kelley,
Dorothy Kenyon, Dr. Margaret Mead, Edna St. Vincent Millay, Frieda S. Miller,
and U.S. Secretary of Labor Frances Perkins.

298 "DO WE, AS IN THE LAST WORLD WAR . . ." FH, "A Crisis in the History of Women:
Let Us Have Action Instead of Lip-Service" (Speech given Apr. 7, 1943), *Vital
Speeches,* May 15, 1943, 9:479–480.

298 "IT OCCURS TO ME . . ." HRC, FH/228/1, FH to Iphigene Sulzberger, Dec. 22, 1943.

299 "SERIOUSLY, FANNIE, DO WRITE . . ."/ "TRIVIALITIES . . ." Bran, Box 3C, Fiorello La
Guardia to FH, Mar. 15, 1943; FH to Fiorello La Guardia, Mar. 19, 1943.

299 OFFERING HER THE POSITION Bran, Box 8A, Diaries, 1943, Entry, Mar. 27, 1943.

299 HE EXTENDED THE TERM Bran, Box 3C, FH to Fiorello La Guardia, Apr. 2, 1943.

300 "YOUR SHADOW LOOMS . . ." HRC, FH/163/3, FH to Fiorello La Guardia, May 6,
1944.

300 SHE EXPLAINED HERSELF FURTHER HRC, FH/163/3, Fiorello La Guardia to FH, June
9, 1944, with typescript of FH letter to La Guardia, explaining the reasons for
her concurrence with the teachers' criticisms. Also "Denouncements of La
Guardia, etc." *NYT,* June 9, 1944.

300 "CUTE NEWS . . ." HRC, FH/190/1, FH, "Women Since Pearl Harbor," undtd manuscript in response to *NYT Book Review* request of Nov. 3, 1943.

300 "FOUR WALLS AND A MAN . . ." HRC, Journal-American Morgue, Gertrude Bailey, "Give a Gal a Home and a Man—And She'll Chuck Social Gains, Moans Fannie Hurst," *NY World-Telegram,* Dec. 22, 1943.

CHAPTER THIRTY-TWO

PAGE

301 MANNING OFFERED TO SEND/ "SO ESSENTIALLY MIDDLE WEST . . ." HRC, FH/235/1, Bruce Manning to FH, Jan. 15, 1941; FH to Bruce Manning, Jan. 21, 1941.

301 JOSEPH BREEN OF THE PRODUCTION CODE ADMINISTRATION See Thomas Schatz, *The Genius of the System: Hollywood Filmmaking in the Studio Era* (New York: Metropolitan Books, 1988), p. 167.

301 "NOT THE SLIGHTEST VALID OBJECTION . . ." Film, MPAA Production Code Administration Files Collection. Joseph Breen to Maurice Pivar, Universal, Mar. 29, 1940.

302 THE ONLY PROTEST ON FILE Film, MPAA Production Code Administration Files, *Back Street,* 1932/1940, Emmett F. Connely, President of the Investment Bankers of America, to MPA, Feb. 14, 1941.

302 "TERRIBLE . . ."/ "BOYER HAM ACTING" Bran, Box 8A, Diaries, 1941, Entry, Jan. 28, Feb. 16, 1941; June 21, 1943.

302 "BADLY STUCK" Robert Van Gelder, "An Interview with Miss Fannie Hurst," *NYT,* Jan. 25, 1942, 6:2:2.

302 SHE WROTE ONLY A FEW ARTICLES FH published stories and articles, 1940–1942: "A Lamp in the Darkness," *Liberty,* May 4, 1940, p. 52; "Sunday Afternoon," *Woman's Home Companion,* July 1940, 67:16–17; "Rosemary for Remembrance," *Good Housekeeping,* Aug. 1940, 111:28–29; "This Urgent Now," *Liberty,* Nov. 9, 1940, 17:45:17; [written earlier: "Rhinestones Preferred," *Cosmo,* Dec. 1940]; "Modern Magic for the Millions," *Opera News,* Dec. 30, 1940, Vol. 5, p. 5; "Cycle," *Good Housekeeping,* May 1941, 112:19; "Maturity" *Cosmo,* May 1941; "Exempted," *Liberty,* Nov. 8, 1942, Vol. 18, 45:12–15, 56–59; "What Does Miss Firper Think About," *Good Housekeeping,* Jan. 1940, 114:30–31; "Glamour as Usual?" *NYT Magazine,* Mar. 29, 1942, pp. 10–11; "Who Is Sylvia?" *Good Housekeeping,* July 1942, 115:20–21.

302 WHITE CHRISTMAS LOC, Manuscript Division, Ken McCormick Papers. Thomas B. Costain produced a small series of booklets about Christmas, of which this was one. See McCormick note, Aug. 7, 1991; correspondence, FH–Thomas B. Costain, Apr. 22 and May 6, 8, 12, 1942.

302 "I CAN'T EXPLAIN IT . . ." Van Gelder, "Interview with Miss Fannie Hurst."

302 SHE GOT HER INSPIRATION See HRC, FH/139/2, Alexander Lindley of Greenbaum, Wolff and Ernst, commenting on whether *Lonely Parade* exposes Harper & Bros. to a lawsuit because of possible identification between characters in the novel and living persons.

302 "TWO MOST IMPORTANT BOOKS" HRC, FH/139/2, FH to Henry Hoynes, Harper & Bros., Jan. 9, 1941. Hoynes reminded Fannie that Cosmopolitan Books had published *Back Street* when she blamed Harpers for its going out of print.

303 SIX-VOLUME REPRINT COLLECTION HRC, FH/139/2, Henry Hull to William Briggs, Apr. 9, 1941; Henry Hoyns to FH, Apr. 17, 1941.

303 "SKILLFUL FULLNESS . . ." HRC, FH/139/2, William Briggs to FH, Aug. 15, 1941.

303 FANNIE MUST HAVE ADMIRED HER FH's character even converts to Catholicism, as Marbury did in life. See FH/173/1, FH to McCosker of the McCosker-Hersfield Cardiac Foundation, Jan. 4, 1940, requesting a copy of Father Shean's speech at Heywood Broun's funeral, in which the priest summarized the psychological process by which Broun found his way to the church. "For about three years, I have been at work on a novel and one of my characters is confronted with groping his way toward the heaven of the church," FH wrote, also assuring McCosker there was no other similarity between the two characters.

303 "UNIQUE AND INTENSELY ORIGINAL NOVEL . . ." HRC, FH/179/1, William James Fadiman, MGM, to FH, Oct. 27, 1941.

303 A BOOK BY THE SAME NAME Bran, Box 8A, Diaries, 1940, Entry, Jan. 29, 1940, "Terribly depressed because my whole novel was planned around that title."

304 "DO MEN REALLY WANT . . ." HRC, FH/139/2, Ramona Herdman to FH, undtd, acknowledging FH suggestion list.

304 "A NEW MIND . . ." HRC, FH/139/2, draft of letter of FH to Cass Canfield, undtd [fall 1941].

304 HIRING AN OUTSIDE PUBLICIST HRC, FH/139/2, William Briggs to FH, Dec. 26, 1941.

304 "THERE IS NOTHING TO DO NOW . . ." HRC, FH/170/3, *Lonely Parade*, FH to Cass Canfield, Jan. 6, 1942.

304 NEXT CALL WAS TO CONSTANCE HOPE HRC, FH/150/2, Constance Hope bill to FH of $100 for a month's worth of publicity services, Apr. 1, 1942.

304 "INTERESTING CHARACTER DRAWING . . ." Catherine Van Dyne, *Library Journal*, Jan. 1, 1942, 67:40.

304 "SPICED WITH SHARP OBSERVATION . . ." Margaret Wallace, "Fannie Hurst's *Lonely Parade*," *NYT*, Jan. 11, 1942, 6:6:1.

304–305 "COULDN'T SHE HAVE BASED HER BOOK . . ."/ "COMPASSION AND CAPACITY . . ." HRC, FH/170/3, *Lonely Parade*, Albert M. Alexander to FH, Jan. 9, 1942; FH to Albert M. Alexander, Jan. 13, 1942.

305 "VERY HANDSOMELY" HRC, FH/139/3, see FH–Harpers correspondence (Henry Hoyns, Cass Canfield, Bill Briggs), Jan.–Mar. 1942.

305 "A STRANGE THING . . ." HRC, FH/139/1, FH to William Briggs, Apr. 30, 1942.

305 "A MORNING 'BATHROOM CURTAINS' . . ." HR, FH/105/3, FH to George Bye, Sept. 12, 1940.

305 "A WOMAN'S PLACE . . ." HRC, FH/110/5, CBS, FH to W. Smith, Nov. 28, 1939.

305 SHE BROADCAST FROM NEWARK HRC, FH Scrapbooks, 1922 period, Clipping, *Columbus* (Ohio) *Journal, Rochester Post-Express,* Nov. 5, 1922.

306 WOMEN'S RADIO REVIEW HRC, FH/183/4, NBC, Margaret Cuthbert to FH, Mar. 4 and 24, 1932; Claudine MacDonald to FH, undtd and June 19, 1933; Apr. 21, 1936, May 4, 1936.

306 LABOR ARBITRATION HRC, FH/249/1, Samuel Zack–FH correspondence, 1942–1949 re: *Labor Arbitration* (WMCA).

306 "UNUSUAL RADIO PERSONALITY"/ PRESENTATION HAD "SPLENDOR" HRC, FH/183/4, NBC, Margaret Cuthbert to FH, Mar. 24, 1932, and Nov. 2, 1939.

306   DOROTHY GORDON, FOR EXAMPLE HRC, FH/183/4, NBC, Dorothy Gordon to FH, Nov. 11, 1939, Nov. 17, 1939; FH to Gordon, Nov. 13, 1939 (show aired on Dec. 15, 1939).

306   "MADAGASCAR, HO!" HRC, FH/183/4, NBC, Stockton Helffrich to FH, Aug. 14, 1941, for Sept. 3, 1941, broadcast.

306   "DOLLY AND THE COLLEAGUES" HRC, FH/255/2, Contracts, the Biow Co. and FH to broadcast over the air on NBC an adaptation of "Dolly and the Colleagues." Single one-half-hour broadcast for $100 payment.

306   "FRANKLY AN ATTEMPT TO SEE . . ." NYPL-BR, FH Clipping File, *Variety,* June 3, 1942.

306   *SUNDAY EVENING AT FANNIE HURST'S* LOC, Motion Picture, Broadcasting, and Recorded Sound Division, "Sunday Evening at Fannie Hurst's," c. 1943, as cited in Joan Shelley Rubin, *The Making of Middle Brow Culture* (Chapel Hill: University of North Carolina Press, 1992), p. 267.

306   "ALIVE AND INTERESTING . . ." Bran, Box 8A, Diaries, 1943, Entry, Sept. 24, 1943.

306   POTENTIAL SPONSORS PROBABLY LIKED EVERYTHING HRC, FH/125/2, FH to John Erskine, Feb. 3, 1944.

307   *FANNIE HURST PRESENTS* HRC, FH/225/2, Thomas Stix to FH, June 20, 1944.

307   "MAIL-PULLER"/ STIX ADVISED AGAINST IT HRC, FH/225/2, Thomas Stix to FH, July 26, 1944. Also note FH/160/3, Anna Kross to Young & Rubicam, July 18, 1944.

307   HE TOLD HER NOT TO WORRY HRC, see FH/248/2, Contract, June 13, 1944; cbl, Erick Pinker, Young & Rubicam, to FH, July 12, 1944; FH/227/2, Thomas Stix–FH correspondence, Jan. 2, June 20, July 26, 1944.

307   "NOW THAT WE ARE ENTERING . . ." HRC, FH/227/2, FH to Thomas Stix, Jan. 14, 1946.

307   STIX MANAGED TO SIGN FANNIE/ "THE WEE SMALL HOURS"/ QUIT THE JOB HRC, FH/90/2, FH-ABC/WJZ, various correspondence, Oct. 10, 1946 to Mar. 17, 1947.

CHAPTER THIRTY-THREE

PAGE

308   "ARTIFICIAL SELF-STIMULATION"/ "I AM NEITHER DISAPPOINTED . . ."/ "THAT DARNED OLD HOME TOWN . . ." HRC, FH/104/2, FH to Julia Browne, Mar. 1, Apr. 6, 1939.

308   "GOOD BUT SOMEWHAT RESERVED PARENT" St.LP-D Morgue, "Fannie Hurst Surprised at Changes in Her Hometown," Apr. 23, 1940.

308   "EITHER MY HUMOR . . ."/ "EVERY TIME I OPEN MY MOUTH . . ." HRC, FH/230/1, FH to Lois Toensfeldt, Oct. 17, 1942.

309   REDISCOVER THE CITY Bran, 8A, Diaries, 1942, Entry, Oct. 9, 1942.

309   "URBANE TROGLODYTE . . ."/ "DO YOU THINK . . ." FN, *Hallelujah,* pp. 59, 62.

309   "YOU CAN'T EVALUATE IT CORRECTLY" StLMerc, Clippings, FH "Non-War Topics Now Trivial to Fannie Hurst, Here on War Tour," undtd [c. Oct. 8–9, 1942].

309   BRIGGS CALLED HIM OFF HRC, FH/139/3 and FH/140/1, Bill Briggs correspondence with Robert Ballou, Mabel Search, and Charles Hanson Towne, reported to FH, Feb.–Mar. 1943.

310   SHE REHIRED CONSTANCE HOPE HRC, FH/140/1, FH to Frank MacGregor, undtd [c. 1943].

310   "NEGRO CHILDREN AWAY . . ."/ ANOTHER WAR BOND DRIVE HRC, FH/150/2, FH's secretary to Constance Hope, Sept. 21, 1943.

310   NOT ONLY DID HOPE PLACE HRC, FH/150/2, Constance Hope to FH, Dec. 22, 1943.

310   THE FIRST WORD SKETCH "Fannie Hurst and Annie," *New Yorker,* Jan. 22, 1944, 16:3, 17:1–3.

310   THE GLOVE DESIGNER HRC, FH/150/2, Constance Hope to FH, Feb. 14, 1944.

310   "NOTHING WAS FURTHER . . ." HRC, FH/230/1, FH to Lois Toensfeldt, Jan. 24, 1944.

310   BURKE WAS LESS CONVINCED StLMerc, Clippings, FH, Harry R. Burke, "Vandeventer Place Ghost Walk Again," *St. Louis Globe-Democrat,* Jan. 9, 1944. Burke thought the Reedy character would be less inclined to involve himself with neurotics in the way that Fannie's Wooley did, and that he would have little patience with Lily Browne.

310   "IT IS AN EXTREMELY BAD NOVEL . . ." Katherine S. Rosin, "Lovely Innocent," *Saturday Review of Literature,* Feb. 5, 1944, p. 23.

311   "SUPERHEATED ATMOSPHERE . . ." "No. 22," *Time,* Vol. 43, Jan. 31, 1944, pp. 100–104.

311   "ON THOSE EARLY OCCASIONS . . ." FH, *Hallelujah,* p. 203.

311   "THE WEIRDEST ARRAY . . ." "Hallelujah, Another Hurst Book," *Newsweek,* Vol. 23, Jan. 17, 1944, p. 88.

311   "A MAGNUM OF SACCHARINE FERMENTATION . . ." Rose Feld, "Books and Things" (Lewis Gannett column), *NY Herald Tribune,* Jan. 8, 1944.

311   "IS IT LONG-SUFFERING VIRTUE . . ." HRC, FH Scrapbooks, *Hallelujah,* Orville Prescott, "Books of the Times," *NYT* [Jan? 1944.].

312   REPEATEDLY AND NEGATIVELY HRC, FH/228/1, FH to Arthur Hays Sulzberger, Jan. 4, 1944.

312   "THE SAME FLAMBOYANCE . . ." Edith Walton, "Perfect Pollyanna," *NYT,* Jan. 9, 1944, 7:5:3–5.

312   HE ALSO MADE A POINT/ "I AM TOLD . . ." HRC, FH/190/2, Arthur Hays Sulzberger to FH, Jan. 3, 1944.

312   "CONSIDERATE, FAIR . . ." HRC, FH/228/1, FH to Arthur Hays Sulzberger, Jan. 4, 1944.

313   "IT IS TOO BAD . . ." HRC, FH/190/2, Arthur Hays Sulzberger to FH, Jan. 3, 1944.

313   TOTAL DISTRIBUTION HRC, FH/140/2, Harper and Bros.–FH correspondence, Jan. 26, Feb. 29, 1944.

CHAPTER THIRTY-FOUR

PAGE

314   STOPPAGE . . . VERY MINOR REAR ARTERIES Bran, 3A, FH to Julia Browne, Feb. 3, 1943.

314   AMASSED FAR MORE MONEY For example, see Bran, Box IIC, Folder 29, stock report from Milton Traubner, July 28, 1937.

314   "VOLUME ONE" HRC, Harper Bros. Collection, FH to Frank MacGregor, Feb. 28, 1948.

315   BIT OF AN INFERIORITY COMPLEX HRC, FH/108/2, Jacques Chambrun to FH, June 28, 1942, citing ltr from her with the statement.

315 ALLOWED *MCCALL'S* TO TAKE TWO MONTHS HRC, FH/108/2, FH to Jacques Chambrun, Jan. 23, 1945; Chambrun to FH, Jan. 24, 1945.

315 EDITORS TOOK LIBERTIES HRC, FH/106/2, FH to Dawson, Sept. 20, 1945; Dawson to FH, Sept. 24, 1945. Also FH/108/2, FH to Chambrun, Sept. 20, 1945.

315 PROGRAMS TO HOLD DOWN DELINQUENCY "Famous Women Lend Talents to Help Youth," *NY Journal-American,* Nov. 18, 1943, 9:3–4.

315 PROBLEMS OF YOUTH COMMITTEE HRC, FH/163/2, Fiorello La Guardia to FH, May 16, 1944.

315 NO JOBS FOR WOMEN Margaret Pickel, "How Come No Jobs for Women," *NYT Magazine,* Jan. 27, 1946, pp. 20, 46–47.

315 "RECKLESS RECRIMINATION . . ." FH/197/3, FH to Margaret Pickel, Jan. 29, 1946.

315 "WILD ACCUSATIONS . . ." HRC, FH/197/3, Margaret B. Pickel to FH, Feb. 9, 1946.

315 "UNTIL WOMEN LEARN . . ." "Women Shirk Duty, Fannie Hurst Says," *StLP-D,* Oct. 18, 1946, 30:7.

316 URGING MEMBERS OF THE BLACK COMMUNITY NYPL-BR, FH Clippings, "Fannie Hurst Tells Way to Equality for Negroes," *NY Herald Tribune,* Jan. 14, 1938. Zora Neale Hurston introduced FH at the dinner.

316 "YOUR CONTRIBUTION . . ." HRC, FH/189/4, Negro Matters, National Urban League, Correspondence, 1939–1942.

316 RESIGN FOR GOOD HRC, FH/189/4, Negro Matters, National Urban League, Aug. 3, Sept. 26, Sept. 30, 1942.

316 "ALMOST DAILY THE BUSES . . ." Yale, Beinecke, Carl Van Vechten 63 ZA, FH to Van Vechten, Feb. 27, 1943.

316 SHE WROTE AN ARTICLE FH, "The Other and Unknown Harlem," *NYT Magazine,* Aug. 4, 1946, pp. 18–19, 38–39.

316 FANNIE OUTLINED HER CAUTIOUS STRATEGY . . . FH, "If I Were a Negro," *Negro Digest,* Feb. 26, 1946.

317 U.S. MILITARY HAD TREATED ITS BLACK SOLDIERS See also *Anat,* p. 338. "Outfits were black or white. Not black and white. Gold star mothers were sent abroad by the government in black and white contingents to visit the graves of their sons. How shocked St. Peter must have been when our colored heroes asked the way to the Negro pearly gates."

317 "FINE IN THEIR PLACE" *Anat,* pp. 22 (Sam), 231 (Rose).

318 THIRTY, BY HIS COUNT HRC, FH/116/1, Robert H. Davis to FH, Dec. 23, 1941; Jan. 1 and 14, 1942. The war made publication of such a volume an unattractive publishing prospect. Davis died Oct. 13, 1942.

318 "NOT AN EMOTION . . ." HRC, FH/119/2, Mary Dewson to FH, undtd.

318 PRESSURE MAYOR LA GUARDIA TO SPEAK HRC, FH/163/1, FH to Fiorello La Guardia, Sept. 24, 1940.

318 LOOKING AFTER HIS AILING SISTER NYPL-Berg, FH to A. A. Berg, various May 1948.

318 THE WAY AN AUTHOR . . . HRC, FH/204/2, FH correspondence, June 6, Aug. 19, 1944.

318 "IT IS RATHER IRONIC . . ." HRC, FH/204/2, FH correspondence, Aug. 24, 1944. See full correspondence, especially June–Nov. 1944.

319 "MY BUDGET . . ." HRC, FH/125/2, FH to Helen Worden Erskine, Oct. 3, 1947.

319 THEIR TEN-YEAR FRIENDSHIP HRC, FH/211/5, FH–Mabel Search correspondence, es-

pecially Search to FH, undtd [Sept. 1946]; FH to Search, Sept. 26, 1946; canceled FH check for $1,200, Sept. 30, 1946; undtd Search to FH expressing hope to repay; Search to attorneys Stern & Reubens, Feb. 25, 1949; FH to Stern & Reubens, Mar. 1, 1950; Search to FH regretting inability to repay, Oct. 25, 1950.

319   RELATIONSHIP WITH THE DIRECTOR ROBERT MILTON HRC, FH/180/4, FH–Robert Milton correspondence, especially FH to Milton, Nov. 5, Dec. 10, Dec. 16, 1937; Milton to FH, Nov. 14, 1937 and subsequent. FH does not respond to his numerous requests for help with Hollywood studios as she has in the past.

319   FANNIE ENTHUSIASTICALLY RECEIVED Bran, FH/8A/11, Diaries, 1942, Entry, Dec. 8, 1942.

319   FANNIE GENTLY THREATENED Bran, Box 11C, Folder 35, note dated Dec. 8, 1948, detailing loan of $2,500 to Albert Richter Rothschild to be repaid July 1, 1949, or sooner. Also, HRC, FH/202/4, FH to Rothschild, undtd.

319   "GOT TO GO HOME BLUES" Bran, Box 8A, Diaries, 1943, Entry, Oct. 29, 1943.

319   "TEASING CONFLICT . . ." *Anat*, p. 326.

320   "YOU ARE THE NEW . . ." HRC, FH/246/1, FH to Grant Wood, Jan. 23, Mar. 27, 1935; Wood to FH, Mar. 27, 1935.

320   "THE NEW HIGH WATER MARK . . ." HRC, FH/242/5, FH to Thorton Wilder, Feb. 7, 1938; Wilder to FH, Feb. 13, 1938.

320   THE COMMENTATOR CHARLES EDWARD RUSSELL LOC Manuscripts, Charles Edward Russell Collection, Vols. 20–23, FH Correspondence, 1938–1941.

320   AMONG THE FRIENDS SHE CONSIDERED *Anat*, p. 343. Her list of treasured friends includes "some broken off by death or circumstances": Julia Browne, Frances Windhorst, Lois Toensfeldt, Vilhjalmur Stefansson, Helen Worden, Milton Traubner, Dave and Uranie Davis, Elaine and Margaret Pogany, Benjamin Fine, Harry Herschfeld, Henrietta Additon, Madeline Borg, Carol Halpern, Anna Kross, Adele Nathan, Jil and David Stern, Robert Davis, Ruth Bryan Rohde, Lucille Tilles, Francine Larrimor, Fiorello La Guardia, Mischa Elman, Barbara Adler, Ethel Shanley, Constance Hope, George Hellman, John Erksine, Stella Karn, Mary Margaret McBride. And, p. 353, those who had died by her 1958 writing: Pauline Rehbein, Dean Snow, Marion Reedy, Robert Davis, Frank Crowninshield, Rutger Jewett, George Horace Lorimer, Elisabeth Marbury, Anne Morgan, Elsie de Wolfe, A. A. Berg, Fiorello La Guardia, Madeline Borg, Ruth Bryan Rohde, Willy Pogany, Ray Long, John Erskine.

320   "A DIE-HARD WHERE FRIENDS ARE CONCERNED" NYPL-Berg, FH to Carl Van Vechten, re: Rebecca West, Feb. 3, 1937.

320   LOST PATIENCE WITH REBECCA WEST See NYPL-Berg, FH to Carl Van Vechten with enclosure, Feb. 3, 1937, in which FH complains of a secretary's letter explaining why West is unable to see them on this visit. "The enclosed scarcely indicates the stuff of which warm human relationships are made. I feel no little mystification myself over the capacity of the lady to properly evaluate or appreciate the aforementioned human relations. However I am a die-hard where friends are concerned and I shall struggle a little longer to care about this mutual one of ours."

320   RELATIONSHIP WITH KATHLEEN NORRIS See HR, FH/191/4, FH–Charles and Kathleen Norris correspondence. Also UC-Berk, Bancroft Library, University of California, Berkeley, Norris Family Papers, MSS 70/100, Box 1, FH.

320 "HAPPIER IN THE SURGING SWARMS . . ."/ "I HAD CHOSEN MY JUNGLE . . ." *Anat,* p. 226.

321 THE YEAR AFTER THE TRIBUTE Zora Neale Hurston, *Dust Tracks on a Road* (New York: HarperPerennial, 1996), pp. 193–202. The chapter's title, "Two Women in Particular," refers to FH and Ethel Waters.

321 "FOR OLD TIME'S SAKE"/ DISTINGUISHED ALUMNA OF HOWARD UNIVERSITY Yale, Carl Van Vechten 63, Za, Zora Neale Hurston to FH, Feb. 15, 1943; award ceremony and banquet, Mar. 2, 1943.

321 "I DON'T THINK YOU WANT ME . . ." Bran, FH, Box 3D, Zora Neale Hurston, FH to Hurston, Feb. 19, 1943.

321 "PLEASE HELP ME . . ."/ "I KNOW THAT I AM INDEBTED . . ." HR, FH/152/2, Zora Neale Hurston to FH, Feb. 10, 1943.

321 FANNIE SENT ZORA MONEY/ "BY ANYTHING AND ALL THINGS . . ." HRC, FH/152/2, Zora Neale Hurston to FH, undated [1949].

321–322 "I SEE YOU ALWAYS SWIRLING . . ."/ "THE STABILITY OF FRIENDSHIP . . ." HRC, FH/152/2, Zora Neale Hurston to FH, Aug. 4, 1949; FH to Hurston, Aug. 19, 1949.

322 "NAUGHTY BUT NICE" Yale, Carl Van Vechten 63, Za, FH to Van Vechten, Apr. 19, 1950.

CHAPTER THIRTY-FIVE

PAGE

323 DIDN'T LIKE THE SUGGESTIONS HRC, FH/140/2, Frank MacGregor, Harper & Bros., to FH, Mar. 16, 1945.

323 "COLD STORAGE" HRC, Harper & Bros. Collection, FH, FH to Frank MacGregor, May 17, 1945.

323 MACGREGOR ACCEPTED HER DECISION HRC, FH/140/2, Frank MacGregor, Harper & Bros., to FH, Mar. 22, 1945.

323 "RUTHLESS JUDGMENT" HRC, Harper & Bros. Collection, FH, FH to Frank MacGregor, Dec. 12, 1945.

323 CAPE WAS ENTHUSIASTIC / GRUDGING RESPONSE HRC, Harper & Bros. Collection, FH, FH to Frank MacGregor, May 17, 1945. See also FH to Ramona Herdman, May 22, 1945; Herdman to FH, June 13, 1945, "Perhaps in these curious and uncertain days of paper shortages, you may be right to wait until the situation clears up a little." Also FH to Herdman, June 25, 1945.

323 "I REALIZE IT COULD HAVE BEEN . . ."/ MACGREGOR RESPONDED HRC, Harper & Bros. Collection, FH, FH to Frank MacGregor, Dec. 12 and 19, 1945.

324 POPULAR LIBRARY/ WORLD PUBLISHING COMPANY HRC, Harper & Bros. Collection, FH, Benjamin Stern, Stern & Reubens, to Harper Bros., Sept. 13, 1946; DBF to Stern, Sept. 25, 1946; William H. Rose to Frank MacGregor, Oct. 25, 1946.

324 COINCIDE WITH THE FILM'S DEBUT HRC, Harper & Bros. Collection, FH, Frank MacGregor to FH, Aug. 13, 1946.

324 NEW FILM STORY HAD LITTLE RESEMBLANCE Film, Victor Heerman Collection, Box 4/File 1. See also Heerman, Box 8/Miscellaneous, Bob Kane, Twentieth Century–Fox to Victor Heerman, Feb. 1, 1943.

324 STUDIO IGNORED HER OFFERS/ "LEGALLY, I MADE A STUPID CONTRACT . . ."/ "I THINK
     THE MANNER . . ." HRC, FH/159/3, FH to Dorothy Kilgallen, Jan. 15, 1947.

324 PROMPT WARNER TO PAY HER HRC, FH/256/1, Contracts, FH sells rights to "Hu-
     moresque" to Warner Bros., Jan. 20, 1947. Contract calls for right to four broad-
     casts of no more than sixty minutes in length with payment of $1,500 for first
     broadcast, nonrefundable, and a further $1,500 if any more were made, but not
     exceeding three.

324 PROMPTED POPULAR PIBRARY TO REQUEST HRC, Harper & Bros. Collection, Memo to
     FH, Jan. 11, 1946; Frank MacGregor to FH, Jan. 24, 1946; FH to MacGregor, Jan.
     29, 1946. The deal gave FH a share of a guaranteed royalty to Harpers of $3,500
     for "Humoresque" as well as a second contract with Harpers for 100,000 copies
     of *Five and Ten, Lummox, Imitation of Life,* and *A President Is Born.*

324 NOT EVEN THE MISSPELLING HRC, FH/140/3, FH to Frank MacGregor, Harper &
     Bros., Jan. 6, 1947.

325 "AS ALWAYS, HER SUCCESS . . ." Nona Balakian, "Miss Hurst's Streamlined Healer,"
     NYT Book Review, Jan. 26, 1947, 16:3–5.

325 SALES OF SIX HUNDRED COPIES/ "ON THE STILLBORN SIDE"/ "NOT DOING BADLY AT
     ALL . . ." HRC, Harper & Bros. Collection, FH, Frank MacGregor to FH, Feb. 5,
     6, and 28, 1947.

325 EFFORTS TO SECURE A VISA HRC, FH/206/5, Russia, Various, Jan. 13–June 10, 1947.

325 "VOLUME ONE" OVER TO MACGREGOR/ TOO MUCH OF A TEASE/ "I THINK I KNEW ALL
     THIS . . ."/ IANNIE TELEPHONED HIM TO COMPLAIN HRC, Harper & Bros. Collec-
     tion, FH, FH to Frank MacGregor, Feb. 28 and Mar. 30, 1948.

326 FANNIE'S OLD TITLES IN PAPERBACK HRC, Harper & Bros. Collection, FH, FH to
     Frank MacGregor, Oct. 27, 1948.

326 NORTH FOR A SUMMER NYPL-Berg, FH, FH to A. A. Berg, July 2, 1948.

326 MACGREGOR QUICKLY ACCEPTED THE BOOK/ "FULL-SIZED, COMPLETELY DEVEL-
     OPED . . ." HRC, FH/140/3, William Briggs to FH, Nov. 9, 1949.

326 "WOULD NOT BE BOOK PUBLICITY . . ." HRC, Harper & Bros. Collection, FH, FH to
     Frank MacGregor, undtd [Dec. 1949 or Jan. 1950].

326 HYMAN'S PLAN/ A THOUSAND-DOLLAR FEE HRC, Harper & Bros. Collection, FH, Dick
     Hyman to FH, Jan. 10, 1950.

326 MURDER TRIAL OF DR. HERMANN SANDER HRC, NY Journal-American Morgue, FH,
     coverage of murder trial of Dr. Hermann Sander as published in the *Journal-
     American,* Feb. 20–Mar. 10, 1950.

326 FANNIE HAD NO DIRECT COMPLAINTS HRC, Harper Bros. Collection, FH, FH to
     Frank MacGregor, Apr. 16, 1950.

326 "THE BROOKLYN SHARPIE . . ." Wilbur Watson, "Mr. Wrong," *NYT Book Review,* Apr.
     30, 1950, 32:4–5.

326 THAT LOYAL PUBLIC WAS DWINDLING HRC, Harper & Bros. Collection, FH, Frank
     MacGregor to FH, Apr. 25, 1950. Advance sale was 7,600 (compared with
     19,000 for *Hands of Veronica*), and first week sales were 219, against 600 for
     Veronica.

326 MACGREGOR GALLANTLY BLAMED/ "I DON'T WANT THE ADVANCE . . ." HRC, Harper &
     Bros. Collection, FH, FH to Frank MacGregor, Apr. 25 and Aug. 15, 1950.

327 EVENTUALLY HE ACCEPTED HRC, Harper & Bros. Collection, FH. See FH–Frank
     MacGregor exchanges of Apr. 27, 28, Aug. 15, Dec. 12, 20, and 27, 1950.

327 SENT IN HER CHECK HRC, Harper & Bros., FH, Frank MacGregor to FH, Jan. 4, 1951.

327 GIANT "Edna Ferber, Novelist, 82, Dies," *NYT*, Apr. 17, 1968, 1:2–4, 32:4–8.

327 "NOT UP TO THE AUTHOR'S USUAL STANDARD"/ "TOO MUCH OLD AGE IN IT"/ FOR FIVE HUNDRED DOLLARS AMERICAN HRC, FH/108/2, Jacques Chambrun to FH, Jan. 10 and Sept. 12, 1951.

327 A *READER'S DIGEST* EDITOR THOUGHT NOTHING HRC, FH/201/2, *Reader's Digest*, Grace Naismith to FH, Oct. 16, 1951; Feb. 7, 1952. FH appears to have ignored both the letter and the request to rewrite the story, or at least did not keep her replies among otherwise very complete records.

327 "GORGEOUS AND INDESTRUCTIBLE" Yale, Beinecke, George Doran, Za letter file, John Farrar to Norman Holmes Pearson, Mar. 22, 1949.

327 IT'S A PROBLEM HRC, FH/257/13, "It's a Problem," Dec. 3, 1951. The half-hour live program was broadcast live daily from Oct. 16, 1951 to Oct. 13, 1952. See also Alex McNeil, *Total Television*, 4th ed. (New York: Penguin, 1996), p. 416.

328 REGULAR APPEARANCES Bran, Appt-bks, Box 6, 1950–1952.

328 LIFE MAGAZINE WANTED FH, "Nourishing," *Life*, Aug. 24, 1953, Vol. 35, pp. 59, 62 ff.

328 TRYING TO REDUCE THEIR OVERHEAD HRC, FH/96/1, FH to Robert Bachman, Mar. 29, 1951; also, FH/256/1, Contracts, FH and 1 West Sixty-seventh Street, lease of Sept. 29, 1949.

328 NEW INCOME INFUSION/ "DID YOU CALL ME, JACK?" *Anat,* p. 364.

329 "MY DARLING LEFT ME . . ." Bran, FH, Box 6, Appt-bks, 1952, Mar. 1952, selected entries.

329 "THE 203RD MONDAY . . ."/ "YOU WERE MY ALL . . ." WashSpc, FH Collection, Ser. 2, Diaries, Box 3, 1956 yearbook.

329 "EVERY MONDAY MORNING . . ."/ "WHO PROVED THE GRANDEURS . . ." *Anat,* pp. 270–273.

329 THE TEMPO OF HIS LIFE WAS SLOWER HRC, NY Journal-American Morgue, Clippings, *NY Journal-American*, Mar. 4, 1952. Also StLP-D Morgue, Associated Press story of Mar. 4, 1952, 8B.

330 "MY DOMINATION OF HIM . . ." *Anat,* p. 288.

330 THIS I BELIEVE/ "NOW, PERSONALLY, I ASPIRE . . ." StLMerc, FH, Clipping, undocumented, "This I Believe," Feb. 23, 1953. Notes that the column also would be broadcast on the program presented by Edward R. Murrow over St. Louis radio station KMOX. Also, FH, "This I Believe," undoc., June 21, 1954.

330 "HE WAS ONE OF THE GREATEST INFLUENCES . . ." HRC, FH/241/2, Martha Ellen Wenz to FH, Mar. 23, 1952.

330 JACQUES'S ESTATE "Novelist Inherits $423,580," *NYT*, Mar. 1, 1956, 22:6.

330 "ME. ME. ME . . ." *Anat,* p. 271.

330 "FOR AWHILE SYMPATHY GLIDES . . ." HRC, FH/154/1, Inez Haynes Irwin to FH, Mar. 4, 1952.

331 ONE-WOMAN FUNERAL HRC, NY Journal-American Morgue, Clippings, *NY Journal-American*, Mar. 4, 1952. Also StLP-D Morgue, Associated Press story of Mar. 4, 1952, page 8B.

331 U.S. DELEGATE TO WORLD HEALTH ORGANIZATION CONFERENCE/ "SMALL IDENTIFICATION WITH W.H.O." . . . HRC, FH/246/2, FH to Dr. Leonard Scheele, U.S. Surgeon General, June 13, 1952. Also FH report on the assembly.

331   "DEARLY BELOVED . . ." WashSpc, FH Collection, Ser. 3, Diaries, Box 3, 1956, Entry, Mar. 12, 1956.
331   "IT WOULD SEEM THAT OUR SEA . . ." *Anat,* p. 273.

CHAPTER THIRTY-SIX

PAGE
332   "GRANITE SHOULDER" WashArch, FH, "Knock, Knock," *Alumni Bulletin,* Feb. 1950, pp. 6–8. Also HRC, FH/240/2, typescript with hand corrections.
332   "IN THE FOURTEEN YEARS . . ." HRC, FH/227/5, FH to Harry Thomson, May 31, 1923.
332   "NOT ONLY FROM THE ANGLE . . ." HRC, FH/227/5, FH to *Student Life,* Feb. 17, 1933.
332   THAT HER OWN SECRETARY . . . HRC, FH/240/2, Raymond Howes, Washington University, to FH, Feb. 22, 1933.
333   "APPLIED"/ "UNTRUE JUST ONE HUNDRED PERCENT" HRC, FH/230/1, Lois Meier Toensfeldt to FH, June 8, 1933.
333   FANNIE PETULANTLY DECLINED HRC, FH/230/1, Lois Meier Toensfeldt to FH, June 8, 1933. Also FH/240/2, FH to Raymond Howes, Washington University, June 22, 1933; Howes to FH, June 26, 1933.
333   "I HAVE NO HEART . . ." HRC, FH/195/7, Henry Carter Patterson to FH, Feb. 23, 1935.
333   "BEING ONLY TOO AWARE THAT WE QUAKERS . . ." HRC, FH/240/2. FH to Washington University with views on admission of qualified black students. Letter acknowledged, Aug. 26, 1948.
333   VERY LITTLE, VERY LATE Apparently forgetting about Patterson's letter of 1935 or her own of August 1948, questioning Washington University's policy of racial segregation, FH wrote to Lois Toensfeldt on May 27, 1967, as if this were brand-new information: "I realize with red face that all through college it never occurred to me that W. U. was segregated. That was the way things were. Of course for many years, I have been deep in the problem of our national disgrace." WashSpc, FH Collection, Ser. 1, General Correspondence, Folder 4, FH to Lois Toensfeldt, May 27, 1967. Washington University admitted its first black undergraduate in the fall of 1952. Various graduate programs desegregated between 1947 and 1952.
333   FOR HER TO RECEIVE THE HONORARY DEGREE HRC, FH/195/7, FH to Henry Carter Patterson, Dec. 19 and 21, 1944; Jan. 25, 1946.
333   TOOK PAINS TO DISTANCE HERSELF HRC, FH/240/2, FH to Washington University Chancellor George Throop, Jan. 26, 1944. Also FH/195/7, FH to Henry Carter Patterson, Dec. 19 and 21, 1944; Jan. 25, 1946.
333   COMPTON BEGAN MAKING PERIODIC REQUESTS HRC, FH/240/2, Washington University Chancellor Arthur Compton to FH, May 30, 1947.
333   "TIGHTER AND RIGHTER" RELATIONS FH, "Knock, Knock," pp. 6–8.
334   "I DON'T MIND TELLING YOU . . ." HRC, FH/240/2, letter to FH, Feb. 23, 1950.
334   A WILL SHE HAD PREPARED WashSpc, FH Collection, Unexecuted will and testament of FH, dated 1951, Fannie Hurst Danielson.
334   LONG-AWAITED INVITATION HRC, FH, 240/2, Washington University Chancellor Arthur Compton to FH, Feb. 27, 1953.

334 T. S. ELIOT, RETIRED JUDGE LEARNED HAND "Washington U. Honors Ten," *NYT,* June 11, 1953, 31:3. The other honorees were Mrs. Lillian Gilbreth, industrial engineer; Dr. Benjamin M. Duggar, discoverer of aureomycin; Charles Belknap, former president of Monsanto Chemical Co.; Archibald T. Davison, professor of music at Harvard University; Isidor Loeb, former dean of Washington University School of Business and Public Administration; Dr. Philip A. Shaffer, former dean of Washington University School of Medicine; and the Rev. James B. Macelwane, director of St. Louis University Institute of Technology.

334 "THREE WHO WOULD HAVE CARED MOST . . ." *Anat,* p. 318.

334 LOOK INTO ESTABLISHING A SCHOLARSHIP FUND HRC, FH/240/2, FH to Stern and Reubens, Sept. 18, 1953. No such fund was ever established, though in FH's final will and testament, she made Washington University a coexecutor of her literary estate with Brandeis University and established a chair in her name at each of the schools.

334 CAME TO TERMS WITH HER JEWISH HERITAGE HRC, FH/154/3, Israel, Sept. 1952. Also FH/183/4, NBC, Kendall Weisiger to FH, Dec. 22, 1953; and Merrill Mueller to FH, Dec. 31, 1953. Also WashSpc, FH Collection, FH to Lois Meier Toensfeldt, Sept. 21, 1952.

334 "GENERATIONS OF THE HUNTED . . ." *Anat,* p. 350.

335–336 "*ANATOMY OF ME*—JUST PUBLISHED . . ."/ FOUND HER NEW PUBLISHER'S EFFORT WANTING/ "I'VE NO WAY OF KNOWING . . ."/ MCCORMICK TOLD HIS COLLEAGUES LOC, Ken McCormick Papers, FH, *Anat* File, especially McCormick to Hardy Sargent, Nov. 12, 1958.

336 DOUGLAS SIRK'S REMAKE OF *IMITATION OF LIFE* For comparative studies of the two films, see Jeanine Basinger, *A Woman's View: How Hollywood Spoke to Women, 1930–1960* (New York: Knopf, 1993), pp. 202–207. Also Thomas Cripps, *Making Movies Black: The Hollywood Message from World War II to the Civil Rights Era* (New York: Oxford University Press, 1993), p. 270. Also Lucy Fischer, ed., *Imitation of Life* (New Brunswick, N.J.: Rutgers University Press, 1991).

336 AN APPARENT AFTERTHOUGHT *Anat,* p. 339. FH wrote: "My novel, *Imitation of Life,* was born of this consciousness and quickly made into the first of the 'race' pictures, and is being at this writing [*sic*]."

336 "SO MANY CRITICS PANNED IT . . ." HRC, FH/151/1, Ross Hunter to FH, May 22, 1959.

336 TOP-TEN ALL-TIME FAVORITE FILMS David Hinckley, "Rites of 'Passing' the Old Chestnut *Imitation of Life* Retains Its Pull on the Imaginations of Blacks and Whites Alike," NY *Daily News,* Dec. 5, 1995, p. 36.

336 "PERSONALLY, AT THE RISK . . ." HRC, FH/151/1, FH to Ross Hunter, June 28, 1959.

337 FANNIE TOLD LOUELLA PARSONS HRC, NY Journal-American Morgue, FH, Louella Parsons column, Nov. 21, 1959, 9:4.

337 HUNTER READ FANNIE'S LETTER OVER/ "WOMAN OF THE WORLD . . ." HRC, FH/235/1, Ross Hunter, Universal Studios, to FH, Nov. 16, 1959. Also, for a comparative discussion of all three films, see Basinger, *Woman's View,* pp. 202–203.

337 "WE HAVE ATTEMPTED TO DRAMATIZE . . ." HRC, FH/151/1, Ross Hunter to FH, undtd [1959–1960].

338 HALF A MILLION COPIES HRC, FH/140/3, Harper & Bros. remittance advice re: *Imitation of Life* Pocket Books ed., Feb. 2, 1960.

338 "OBSCURITY AND POVERTY" "Zora Hurston, 57, Writer, Is Dead," *NYT* [Associated Press], Feb. 4, 1960.

338 GRAVE LEFT FORLORNLY UNMARKED Zora Neale Hurston, *Hurston: Folklore, Memoirs, and Other Writings* (New York: Library of America, 1995), p. 980.

338 "LARGE GROUP OF US WHO FELT PUZZLEMENT . . ." FH, "Zora Neale Hurston: A Personality Sketch," *Library Gazette,* Yale University, 1961, pp. 19–20.

338 "A COMMON ANNOYANCE . . ." HRC, FH/237/3, Carl Van Vechten to FH, Feb. 5 and 17, 1960.

338 "FEEL NO OBLIGATION . . ." Yale, Za, Letter File, FH, FH to Donald Gallup, Mar. 8, [1960].

338 "ZORA HAD THE GIFT . . ." FH, "Zora Neale Hurston," pp. 17–18.

340 "SHE LIKES FOR ME TO DRIVE HER . . ." Zora Neale Hurston, *Dust Tracks on a Road* (New York: HarperPerennial, 1996), p. 195.

340 HOW STRANGE AND DEMEANING Recapping the known facts: FH met Zora Neale Hurston while judging the *Opportunity* magazine literary competition in the spring of 1925, then offered her a place to live that fall during Zora's first term at Barnard, perhaps in exchange for room and board or maybe even for financial help with her tuition and expenses. The arrangement did not work out, and after about two months Zora moved back uptown. The friendship continued, however, and in the years to come FH got Zora to make at least two long car trips with her, to upstate New York and Canada in 1931, and around Florida in 1934.

340 "YOU MAKE ALL THE GIRL'S FAULTS . . ." HRC, FH/237/3, Carl Van Vechten to FH, July 5, 1960.

CHAPTER THIRTY-SEVEN

PAGE

341 "FIRST LADY OF TELEVISION" HRC, NY Journal-American Morgue, FH, Jack O'Brien column, Nov. 22, 1958.

341 THE FANNIE HURST SHOWCASE was a program over WNYC, the public-broadcasting affiliate in New York, aired starting in Nov. 1958. A 1959 *Celebrity Register* bio quoted FH as saying that doing the show gave her "a guilty feeling, a belief that I shouldn't be doing this. So I started writing."

341 "HOW DO YOU DO, MR. MURROW . . ." CBS, *Person-to-Person,* segment of June 18, 1954, show, host and interviewer, Edward R. Murrow.

343 "AT THE TIME, *NIGHT BEAT* . . ." Int, Mike Wallace, Apr. 30, 1996.

343 "WE ENJOYED YOUR 'BATTLE' . . ." HRC, FH/162/1, Laceys to FH, Dec. 29, 1956.

343 "ONE OF THE GREAT NATURAL WONDERS . . ." "Powerhouse," *New Yorker,* Jan. 31, 1959, p. 22.

343 TELLING STORIES TO CROWDS OF CHILDREN *NYT,* Aug. 9, 1959, 76:3–4.

343 GONE TO BATTLE WITH . . . ROBERT MOSES HRC, NY Journal-American Morgue, FH, *NY Journal-American,* Apr. 7, 1956. Also *NYT,* May 27, 1956, 1:5.

344 DOUBLEDAY TO CONTINUE TO TAKE HER SERIOUSLY LOC, Ken McCormick Papers, FH, *Fool Be Still,* Sales Conference notes on *Fool Be Still,* Aug. 20, 1963.

344 "SHE HAD PRETTY WELL EXHAUSTED . . ." LOC, Ken McCormick Papers, FH, *Fool Be Still,* Personal note accompanying file, dated Feb. 28, 1989.

344 "BAUBLED AND BANGLED AUTHOR"/ "THE GUESTS ARE PROMISING STILL . . ." HRC, FH/197/7, *Pleased to Meet You,* Clippings, John Horn, *NY Herald Tribune,* Feb. 4 and Apr. 7, 1964.

344 CANCELED ANYWAY HRC, FH/197/7, *Pleased to Meet You,* Bud Meyers to FH, Apr. 8, 1964.

344 TESTIMONIAL DINNER HRC, NY Journal-American Morgue, FH, *NY Journal-American Weekly,* Mar. 31, 1958.

344 "THE FANNIE HURST DAYS" Jim Newton, "Fannie Hurst, Native of Hamilton, Dean of Women Writers, Is Dead," *Hamilton* (Ohio) *Journal News,* Feb. 24, 1968.

344–345 "MY REASON FOR ABSENTING MYSELF . . ."/ "WHICH REASSURES ME A BIT" Wash-Spc, FH Collection, Ser. 1, General Correspondence, FH to Lois Meier Toensfeldt, Apr. 27, 1967.

345 THE CALLA *Anat,* p. 170–171.

345 EACH OF THE SCHOOLS ACTUALLY RECEIVED Int with Nancy Pliske, General Counsel's Office, Washington University, who provided the figure of $979,000, Apr. 29, 1998.

345 PERRY KNOWLTON . . . REMEMBERED BEING TOLD Telephone int with Author, 1994.

345 CEMETERY RECORD New Mt. Sinai Cemetery, St. Louis, Mo. Record of Fannie Hurst conveyed by Mary Pool, cemetery office, Dec. 27, 1998.

346 "FANNIE HURST'S GREAT TALENT . . ." "Fannie Hurst, Popular Author of Romantic Stories, Dies at 78," *NYT,* Feb. 24, 1968, 1:3–4, 29:1–3.

346 "MR. MAPES . . ." Herbert R. Mayes, "Trade Winds," *Saturday Review,* Mar. 23, 1968, p. 19. Mayes edited "Candy Butcher" for *Pictorial Review.*

346 "BASICALLY A FAIRLY CORNY ARTIST . . ." "Fannie Hurst, Popular Author of Romantic Stories."

346 "EDITORS, MASSES OR CLASSES . . ." *Anat,* pp. 242, 208, 239, 318, 156, 328.

347 "UNABASHEDLY TO THE HUMAN HEART" *NYT,* Editorial page, Feb. 24, 1968, 28:1–2.

Index

462

472

Morgenthau, Henry, Jr., 255
Morgenthau, Henry, Sr., 239
Morris, Lloyd, 130–31
Moscow, 12, 13, 110–12, 170
Moses, Robert, 216–17, 344
Motion Picture Production Code
    Administration, 206, 301–2
motion pictures, 255–59
    censorship issues in, 205, 206, 301–2,
        303
    Fannie's comments on, 46, 74, 117,
        118–19, 152, 153–54, 257
    Fannie's original screenplays for, 165,
        171, 184–85, 237, 244–45
    Fannie's stories and novels produced
        for, xiv, xv–xvi, 51, 59–60, 74–75,
        78–79, 105, 117–19, 129, 131–32,
        133, 150–54, 165, 185, 186, 205–14,
        244, 252, 301–2, 324, 336–38
    silent era of, 46, 51, 59–60, 78–79,
        149, 150
    sound revolution in, 79, 149, 150,
        152
Munsey's, 17, 18
Muray, Nickolas, 116
Murphy, Edward F., 204
Murrow, Edward R., xvi, 328, 341–43
Museum of the City of New York, 345
Mussolini, Benito, 225, 232
"Muttsy" (Hurston), 158
My Life with the Eskimo (Stefansson), 85

Nash, Florence, 50
Nathan, Adele, 222
Nathan, George Jean, 18, 318
Nation, 45, 46, 49, 110, 146–47, 154
National Association for the
    Advancement of Colored People
    (NAACP), 190, 208
National Health Circle for Colored
    People, 104, 139, 188
National Public Housing Conference, 242
National Recovery Administration
    (NRA), 227–28
National Urban League, 121, 187, 316
National Woman's Party, 232
National Women's Painters Association,
    104
Nazimova, Alla, 118
NBC radio, 227, 306–7
NBC-TV, 327
Negro Digest, 316–17
New Deal, 182, 192
New Republic, 51, 120, 131
New Statesman, 147–48
New Story Magazine, 18
Newsweek, 311

"New Year's Adam and Eve, A" (Hurst),
    22
New York, N.Y.:
    Broadway theater, 17–18, 50–51, 53,
        79–80, 88–89, 104, 107, 140–42,
        307
    Carnegie Hall, 40, 65, 279, 328
    Central Park, 216–17, 226, 246, 298,
        326, 343–44
    Fannie's graduation trip to, 9, 12
    Fannie's move to, xv, 15–16
    Greenwich Village, 25, 29, 32, 40, 71
    Harlem, 73, 120, 187, 188, 207–8, 214,
        263, 310, 316–17
    hotels and restaurants in, 15, 29, 35,
        60, 103, 145, 178–79, 180, 216–17,
        223, 239, 298
    immigrant and working-class life in,
        xiii, 33, 35, 57, 59
    Lower East Side, 15, 33, 43, 57, 59,
        255
    political corruption in, 173, 175, 215
    Roaring Twenties in, 62, 71
    Swing Era in, 226
    Upper West Side, 15–18, 23–24, 40, 95
New York American, 76, 79, 82, 143, 178,
    314
New York Amsterdam News, 207, 208, 214
New York College of Music, 34
New York *Daily News*, xvi, 336
New Yorker, 35, 131, 147, 310, 343
New York Evening Journal, 35, 82, 151,
    228
New York Evening Post, 82, 93, 147
New York Graphic, 158
New York Herald, 88–89
New York Herald Tribune, 121, 129, 150,
    179, 193, 198, 206, 252, 311,
    344
    This Week Magazine of, 267, 268
New York Journal-American, 65–66,
    143–44, 296, 326
New York League of Business and
    Professional Women, 233
New York Post, 151, 227
New York Public Library, 72, 318
New York Suffrage Parade, 34–35
New York Sun, 80, 82, 140, 147, 161
New York Times, xv, 93, 144, 206, 255,
    302
    coverage of Fannie in, xvi, 63–65, 66,
        95, 110, 115, 132, 172, 234, 267,
        295, 300, 336, 346
    Fannie's published items in, 17, 145,
        164, 173
    national women's conference and
        symposia sponsored by, 298–99

474

476

Letter from Paul Revere Reynolds is housed in the Paul Revere Reynolds Papers, Rare Books and Manuscripts Library, Columbia University.

Letter from Benjamin Stern is housed in the Curtis Brown Papers, Rare Books and Manuscripts Library, Columbia University.

Some materials by Fannie Hurst are housed in the Fales Manuscript Collection, Fales Library, New York University.

Letter from Robert Hobart Davis is housed in the Robert H. Davis Papers, Manuscripts and Archives Division, The New York Public Library, Astor, Lenox and Tilden Foundation.

Letters by William Marion Reedy are housed in the William Marion Reedy Papers, Missouri Historical Society, St. Louis.

Grateful acknowledgment is made to the following for permission to use both published and unpublished materials:

J. William Dawson: Excerpts from letters written by Charles and Kathleen Norris to Fannie Hurst housed at the Bancroft Library. Used by permission.

Doubleday: Excerpts from letters from Ken McCormick to Fannie Hurst. Used by permission of Doubleday, a division of Random House, Inc.

The New York Times: Excerpts from book and film reviews published in *The New York Times* between 1912 and 1968 of Fannie Hurst–related works and excerpts from personal correspondence between Fannie Hurst and Arthur Hays Sulzberger. Copyright © 1912–1968 by The New York Times Company. Reprinted by permission.

Harold Ober Associates: Excerpts from private correspondence of Langston Hughes to Fannie Hurst housed in the Fannie Hurst Collection at the Harry Ransom Humanities Research Center of the University of Texas. Used by permission of Harold Ober Associates as agents for the Estate of Langston Hughes.

Penguin Putnam Inc.: Excerpt from "Re-Enter Miss Hurst, Followed by Mr. Tarkington," from *The Portable Dorothy Parker.* Copyright © 1928 and copyright renewed 1956 by Dorothy Parker. Used by permission of Viking Penguin, a division of Penguin Putnam Inc.

Peters Fraser & Dunlop: Excerpts from letters from Rebecca West to Fannie Hurst. Reprinted by permission of the Peters Fraser & Dunlop Group Ltd.

The Society of Authors: Unpublished postcard to W. Orton Tewson from Bernard Shaw, dated May 6, 1920. Reprinted by permission of The Society of Authors on behalf of the Bernard Shaw Estate.

St. Louis Post-Dispatch: Excerpts from material published in the *St. Louis Post-Dispatch.* Reprinted with permission of the *St. Louis Post-Dispatch.*

University of Illinois Press: Brief excerpt from page 60 of *Zora Neale Hurston: A Literary Biography,* by Robert Hemenway. Reprinted by permission.

Victoria Sanders Agency: Excerpts from letters and materials written by Zora Neale Hurston. Used by permission of Victoria Sanders Agency, Literary Agent for the Estate of Zora Neale Hurston.

Yale University Library: Excerpt from a letter from Edward Mandell House to Fannie Hurst. Letter is housed in the Edward Mandell House Papers, Manuscripts and Archives, Yale University Library.

About the Author

BROOKE KROEGER, the author of *Nellie Bly: Daredevil, Reporter, Feminist,* has been a reporter, editor, and foreign correspondent based in Chicago, Brussels, London, and Tel Aviv. She lives now in New York City and is a visiting associate professor of journalism at New York University.

28×4 DAYS

DATE DUE		
DEC 1 9 1999		
MAY 0 2 2000		
WITHDRAWN		

BIO .H944 K76 1999
Kroeger, Brooke, 1949-
Fannie

REDWOOD LIBRARY & ATHENAEUM
50 Bellevue Ave.
Newport, RI 02840-3292

VmT

GAYLORD M2